HONORING GOD AND THE CITY

HONORING GOD AND THE CITY

Music at the Venetian Confraternities, 1260–1807

Jonathan Glixon

OXFORD

UNIVERSITY PRESS

2003

OXFORD
UNIVERSITY PRESS

Oxford   New York
Auckland   Bangkok   Bogotá   Buenos Aires   Cape Town   Chennai
Dar es Salaam   Delhi   Hong Kong   Istanbul   Karachi   Kolkata
Kuala Lumpur   Madrid   Melbourne   Mexico City   Mumbai   Nairobi
São Paulo   Shanghai   Taipei   Tokyo   Toronto

Published by Oxford University Press, Inc.
198 Madison Avenue, New York, New York 10016

www.oup.com

Oxford is a registered trademark of Oxford University Press

Library of Congress Cataloging-in-Publication Data
Glixon, Jonathan Emmanuel.
Honoring god and the city: music at the Venetian
confraternities, 1260–1807 / Jonathan Glixon.
p.   cm.
Includes bibliographical references and index.
ISBN 0-19-513489-3
1. Music—Italy—Venice—History and criticism.
2. Confraternities—Italy—Venice—History.   I. Title.
ML290.8.V26 G55 2002
780' .945'31—dc21   2002001235

2 4 6 8 9 7 5 3 1

Printed in the United States of America
on acid-free paper

FOR BETH

PREFACE

Since its inception more than twenty-five years ago, this project has changed both shape and scope several times, both as the material took me in directions I had not expected to pursue, and as the growing mass and complexity of the documentation made it clear that my earlier approaches were simply not feasible. My doctoral dissertation (for Princeton University, under the direction of Lewis Lockwood) was limited to activities at just five of the largest confraternities in Venice, the *scuole grandi*, during one century in the Renaissance, and utilized a limited number and variety of documents (some 250 items from about fifty volumes in the Archivio di Stato of Venice). Return trips to the archives not only revealed how much I had missed even for the institutions and years covered in the dissertation, but also demonstrated that any picture I might try to draw with such limited chronological coverage and restricted to just those original institutions would be massively incomplete. I gradually worked both forward and backward in time, and even more hesitantly outward to other insitutions. The fragmentary state of the archives in some respects—and especially the uneven distribution of documents—eventually brought me to the realization that the only way to come close to understanding the role of music at the scuole grandi would be to study them from their origins in the thirteenth century to their ultimate suppression at the beginning of the nineteenth. It also became clear that I could not restrict my researches to the obvious sorts of documents, such as payment registers, but would need to examine, in effect, everything that survived regarding the activities of these confraternities. By the time this archival research was completed, I had transcribed over two thousand documents from hundreds of volumes. But even this would not be the end. The Venetian cultural-religious world extended, of course, well beyond the six scuole grandi. While an attempt to study everything in that world would clearly not have been practical (I have begun a new study of music for Venetian nuns, and others have been working on the *ospedali* and on the ducal *cappella* of San Marco), leaving the scuole grandi in isolation also would have been misleading.[1] The logical and inevitable conclusion I reached was that the reasonable context for the book was the entire world of confraternities in Venice, not only the famous ones I had already been studying, but also the several hundred less well-known ones called *scuole piccole*, whose remaining documents (which had, fortunately, never been as numerous as those of the scuole grandi) were scattered through dozens of archives in Venice. By the time I had completed this research, I had gathered, in all, over four thousand separate documents, and more than twenty years had passed.

How, then, to turn this mass of documentation into a book that would be both useful and readable? For a time, the working idea was a publication of transcriptions of all the documents, with an extended introduction. As the amount of documentation grew, however, this clearly became impractical, and was in many other ways unsatisfying. The ultimate result, the present book, represents, as do all such efforts, a compromise of sorts. It aims to provide, within a relatively modest scale, a comprehensive history of musical activities over more than five centuries at nearly four hundred institutions, with enough detail to make the history real and useful, but not so much as to make it unreadable. For much of the book, the approach has been to keep the camera angle wide, using details as illustrations and as support for the more general historical picture. At times, however, where it appeared that the potential reader might find details more valuable, I have tried to be a bit more complete, focusing more on particulars, especially regarding the period from about 1500 to 1650, when Venice in general, and the scuole in particular, were closest to the mainstream of European musical developments, employing musicians with international reputations. Whether this changing focus is successful will be, of course, up to the reader to decide. Rather than providing a bulky and ultimately hard to use documentary appendix, I have presented in the notes only the texts of documents actually quoted in the text. For the scholar or student interested in more detail, I plan to make the entire corpus of documents available in a fully searchable format on the internet.

COMPLETING A PROJECT OF THIS scope and duration has been possible, of course, only with the assistance of many institutions and individuals. I would first like to thank the following foundations and organizations for their generous financial support over the years, without which I could have accomplished nothing: the Mrs. Giles B. Whiting Foundation (for the dissertation fellowship that started all of this), the Renaissance Society of America, the Gladys Krieble Delmas Foundation (whose dedication to research in the Veneto has changed everything for American and British scholarship in that part of Italy) for three grants beginning in 1981, the American Philosophical Society, the American Council of Learned Societies, and the National Endowment for the Humanities. While some of the more recent grants involved research on a different project, they also provided me with the opportunity to complete some aspects of the ongoing project on the scuole. The University of Kentucky has also provided substantial support, through both the Research Committee and the Honors Program Summer Teaching and Research Grants.

In Venice, many archives and libraries have made their collections available to me, and I would like to thank them and the many people who oversee them and staff them for their assistance. Most important of all, of course, is the Archivio di Stato, whose extraordinary collections lie at the heart of my research. Many members of the staff of the Archive, under the direction for years of the beloved Dottoressa Maria Francesca Tiepolo, and now of Dottor Paolo Selmi, have assisted my work, but I would like to thank in particular the archivists Francesca Cavazzana Romanelli, Michela Dal Borgo, Alessandra Schiavon, Edoardo Giuffrida, and Claudia Salmini, and the staff members Roberto Greggio (now at the Archivio di Stato of Rovigo) and Renata Moressa, all of whom were not only generous with their time, experience, and expertise, but whose welcoming attitude made working at the Archive a wonderful experience. The Scuola Grande Arciconfraternita di San Rocco, and its Guardian Grande, Dottor Ermes Farina, were very gracious in allowing me to consult their archive. Much useful documentation for the scuole piccole is preserved in the Archivio Storico del Patriarcato di Venezia, under the direction of Monsignor Bruno Bertoli. The director of the indexing project, Dottoressa Francesca Cavazzana Romanelli, and staff members Manuela Barausse and Maria Giovanna Siet were especially helpful and accommodating. Particular thanks must go to the priests of a number of Venetian parishes, who allowed me to consult their archives despite the many demands on their time (some of those named have now moved on to other positions, but I list them as they were when I conducted my research): Monsignor Silvio Zardon of the parish of San Luca, Don Guido Scattolin at the Santissimo Salvatore, Monsignor Dottor Renato Volo (and his parishioner Signor Pratt Fongher) of San Giovanni in Bragora, Don Renzo Scarpa of San Geremia, Don Federico Niero (and his parishioner Niccolò Castellani) at San Marcuola, Padre Aldo Cornale at the Madonna dell'Orto, Monsignor Paolo Trevisan (and his parishioner Giorgio d'Alba) at San Felice, Don Cesare Maddalena at San Felice, Don Mario dal Tin (and the vicar of the church of the Santo Spirito, and a noted scholar in his own right, Don Gastone Vio) of Santa Maria del Rosario, Don Beniamino Pizziol of San Trovaso, Dottor Don Giuseppe della Puppa of San Silvestro, Don Alfredo Costa of San Cassiano, Don Ferruccio Gavagnin of San Pantalcone, Don Sergio Pennacchio of San Nicola da Tolentino, Don Giacomo Marchesan (and his parishioner Dottor Gianpaolo Lotter) of San Simeon Profeta, and Don Aldo Marangoni of San Giacomo dall'Orio. Finally, I would like to thank the following libraries and archives: Archivio delle Istituzioni di Ricovero e di Educazione (and its director Dottor Giuseppe Elero), the Biblioteca del Museo Correr (and in particular the now-retired "Moni"), and the Biblioteca Nazionale Marciana. Among U.S. institutions, I would like to thank in particular the staff of the Interlibrary Loan department of the University of Kentucky Library, who were extraordinarily efficient in tracking down and obtaining some rather esoteric items, and also the library of the Lexington Theological Seminary, Princeton University Library and Art Museum, and the Pierpont Morgan Library in New York.

Over the years, numerous individuals have offered support and encouragement for my project, and have freely and generously provided their time and expertise (sometimes during delightfully long coffee breaks near the Archivio di

Stato). Among them (and I apologize for any unintentional omissions) are Giulio Ongaro, whose knowledge of music at San Marco in the Renaissance (and his willingness to share it) is unparalleled, David Bryant (whose offer to publish my documents spurred my work, and who graciously allowed me to submit this manuscript instead to Oxford University Press when our concepts of the end result diverged), Rebecca Edwards, William Prizer (whose urgings to make my research more contextual finally sunk in), Richard MacKenney, Bob Davis, Guido Ruggiero, Stanley Chojnacki, the late Donald Queller, Noel O'Regan, Bonnie Blackburn, Giulio Cattin, Iain Fenlon, Tim Carter, and Blake Wilson. My colleagues at the University of Kentucky, Ron Pen, Lance Brunner, and Diana Hallman, and the director of the School of Music, Harry Clarke, have put up with my obsessions and frequent absences without complaint. Virginia Lacefield of the University of Kentucky Computing Services patiently assisted me in the preparation of the figures. I would like to acknowledge the contributions made by the editors of the various journals and books where earlier versions of some of this material have been published; their suggestions helped me to focus my ideas. I owe particular gratitude to the anonymous readers for Oxford University Press, whose attention and perceptions have made this book far better than it would otherwise have been, and to the copyeditor, Bonnie Blackburn, whose keen eye and sense of style saved me from many embarrassing mistakes and inconsistencies.

I would like to thank my parents, David and Helen Glixon, for their unquestioning support of my work for many decades. Finally, and most of all, I would like to thank my wife Beth. She has not only made the kinds of sacrifices that many spouses of scholars have made, without which I would have had to abandon this work years ago, but has made innumerable and invaluable professional contributions to this project. As an experienced and expert musicologist, she helped me over and over again to find the right direction for my research, and her extraordinary abilities and patience as an editor, which she generously lavished on this manuscript, sacrificing her own projects in the effort, enabled me to make this book what I had wanted it to be, but which I could not have done without her.

CONTENTS

A NOTE ON THE VENETIAN
MONETARY SYSTEM

For most usages, the basic Venetian monetary units were the *ducato* (ducat; abbreviated D.), the *lira* (£), and the *soldo* (s.). In the standard arrangement (employing what was called the *lira di piccolo*), used in nearly all the documents cited in this study, the relationships were as follows:

1 *lira* = 20 *soldi*

1 *ducat* = 6 *lire* and 4 *soldi*

Some sorts of accounting documents used another system, employing the *lira di grosso*. In this system, the relationships were as follows:

1 *soldo* = 12 *denari*

1 *lira* = 20 *soldi* or 10 *ducati*

1 *ducato* = 2 *soldi* or 24 *denari* (in this context usually referred to as *grossi*)

The ducato is equivalent in the two systems. The *lira di grosso* occurs only in the earliest of the documents of the scuole, such as the thirteenth- and fourteenth-century mariegole. Payments might be made either in ducats or in *lire di piccolo*, but the accounting was commonly done in *lire* and *soldi*, in the form, for example, £10 s. 4. When ducats were used as the basis for calculations, portions of ducats were expressed in *grossi*, but employing the abbreviation d. for *denari* (such as D. 20 d. 4).

The value of this currency is very difficult to express in modern terms, and for that reason the amounts discussed should be considered primarily in comparative terms. For a recent brief discussion of the prices of basic commodities in Venice between 1534 and 1769, see Sperling, *Convents and the Body Politic*, 242–43.

ABBREVIATIONS

ASP   Archivio Storico del Patriarcato di Venezia

ASR   Archivio della Scuola Grande Arciconfraternita di San Rocco

ASV   Archivio di Stato di Venezia

b.   busta

BC   Biblioteca del Museo Correr

BNM   Biblioteca Nazionale Marciana

CD   Consiglio dei Dieci

d.   denari

D.   ducats

IRE   Archivio delle Istituzioni per Ricovero e di Educazione

£   lire

m.v.   more veneto ("the Venetian way," the calendar according to which the
        year begins on 1 March)

PC   Provveditori di Comun

reg.   registro

s.   soldi

SPS   Scuole piccole e suffraggi

SSGE   Scuola Grande di San Giovanni Evangelista

SSM   Scuola Grande di San Marco

SSMC   Scuola Grande di Santa Maria della Carità

SSMM   Scuola Grande di Santa Maria della Misericordia

SSR   Scuola Grande di San Rocco

SST   Scuola Grande di San Teodoro

Note: In the transcriptions of original documents, abbreviations, except for those of monetary units in accounting documents, have been expanded silently, and punctuation and capitalization have been modified for clarity. Spelling has been left unaltered, but accents have been added as needed.

THE SCUOLE GRANDI

FOR THE HONOR OF GOD

The Origin and Nature of the Scuole Grandi

The Venetians have six fraternities or great schooles . . . and the Gentlemen and Citizens all give their names to one of them. . . . And in these schooles . . . they use to have exercises of religion. . . . These schooles give dowries yeerely to 1500. Virgins, and distribute among the poore much money, meale and clothes, for besides many gifts by last testaments daily given to those uses, each of the schooles hath some five or six thousand duckets in yeerely revenew, and they are governed like common wealthes. . . . and each of these hath his Church and Pallace, and precious monuments, and these are subject to the counsell of ten. —Fynes Moryson*

Like most visitors to the Most Serene Republic of Venice, the English traveler Fynes Moryson, who was there in 1594, was struck by the splendor, piety, and generosity of the great confraternities, or *scuole grandi*.[1] Lay religious institutions such as these were present in virtually every city of Europe, but rarely did they play such an important role in the religious, civic, and cultural lives of the people. Medieval in origin, the earliest founded in the thirteenth century, the scuole grandi operated continuously for over half a millennium, and were still active when Venice fell to Napoleon in 1797.

The Founding of the Scuole

The idea of the confraternity, that is, an organization of devout laymen, can be traced back to ancient times, and institutions of this sort seem to have been active in the Carolingian era. Spiritual leaders, usually clergymen, created these confraternities as outlets for the devotional and charitable energies of ordinary people that could not be accommodated within the confines of the parish or monastic churches that dominated medieval Christian life. They began to flourish in the twelfth and early thirteenth centuries, especially in much of Italy, under the influence of the mendicant orders of the Franciscans and Dominicans.[2] These confraternities encouraged devotion to the saints and, increasingly, the Virgin Mary, through corporate charity and, particularly in Tuscany, the singing of laude, vernacular songs of praise, from which latter activity came the term used to describe them, *laudesi*.[3] The first documented Venetian confraternity, organized to honor the newly transported relics of St. Stephen, appeared in 1110 at the Benedictine church of San Giorgio Maggiore.[4] Others followed in the thirteenth century, including one dedicated to the Virgin at St. Mark's (founded 1221), and one to the first patron saint of the city, St. Theodore, at San Salvatore, a house of Augustinian Regular Canons. From the beginning, these Venetian confraternities were referred to as *scuole*, not with the meaning of places for education, but rather, in a derivation from late Roman usage, a college or corporation of persons of the same profession, as a guild, the profession here being a common devotion.[5]

A second wave of new foundations, of a somewhat different character, arose in Italy in the middle of the thirteenth century in the wake of a widespread penitential movement.[6] Monks and friars had long used self-flagellation, in imitation of the suffering of Christ, as a form of personal penance, but the practice emerged into the public arena with penitential processions organized by Mendicants in the 1230s, in the face of increasing communal disorder and a generalized sense that sinfulness was on the rise. With no decrease in political instability, and the arrival in central Italy in 1259 of the latest outbreak of the plague, tensions and fear grew, spurred particularly, perhaps, by the prophecies of Joachim of Flora that the year 1260 would bring a cataclysm that would signal the end of an age.[7] In the spring of 1260 in Perugia, the hermit Rainero Fasani began to preach sermons advocating public displays of penance through self-flagellation, and the people of the city increasingly took up the call. By October, a large portion of the city's population was participating in these processions, to the distress of the local officials, and the movement began to spread rapidly through Italy, including Rome and Genoa. The northward progression passed through Imola and reached Bologna on 10 October, and Modena nine days later. On 10 November, the *disciplinati* or *battudi*, as they were known, arrived in the Veneto at Padua (about thirty miles from Venice), where the events were vividly described by an anonymous chronicler. The processions, which went on day and night, included "nobles as well as the low-born, old men and young, children of only five years." They walked through the city, two by two, "carrying a whip with which they continuously beat themselves on their shoulders until the blood began to flow, uttering groans and shrill lamentations."[8] A similar, if less explicit, description from Bologna says that the flagellants cried out "Mercy and peace" during the processions. Though the documentation is not clear, it seems that as the popular movement continued ever outward, the enthusiasm in each city for flagellation was channeled into newly formed confraternities, even if most appear not to have received official ecclesiastical charters for several years.

After Padua, the movement is recorded in Treviso (only twenty miles north of Venice), before spreading into German-speaking lands. There is no documentation of the usual sort of processions in Venice itself, which perhaps, in its zealous protection of public order, barred the disseminators of the practice from entering the city (as they would do a century and a half later with the movement of the Bianchi[9]). Nonetheless, just at the time that the forefront of the movement would have been closest to Venice, in December of 1260, a group of devout Venetians founded the earliest of the flagellant confraternities, the Scuola di Santa Maria della Carità. Within a few months (that is, no later than the end of February, when the Venetian year 1260 ended), a second, the Scuola di San Marco, came into existence, followed in early March by one dedicated to San Giovanni Evangelista.[10] These three *scuole dei battudi*, or flagellant confraternities, were the first of the great institutions that came to be known as the *scuole grandi*. Despite the lack of documentary evidence for flagellant processions in Venice before their founding, and the absence of any reference to Rainero in their statutes (which sometimes occurred in those from other cities), it must be assumed that the passage of the flagellants only a few miles from the city inspired their formation. Demonstrating a continuing demand for membership in such organizations, devout Venetians founded a fourth scuola dei battudi, dedicated to Santa Maria della Misericordia, in 1308. Of the several hundred confraternities eventually active in Venice, only these four (and one in Murano, Santa Maria dei Battudi) regularly practiced the discipline. By the time the fifth of the scuole grandi, San Rocco, was founded in 1480, actual flagellation seems to have disappeared almost entirely, and it was only a memory in 1552, when the Scuola di San Teodoro, which began as a devotional confraternity in 1258, joined the ranks of the scuole grandi. Confraternities in many cities of Italy, such as Florence, transformed the discipline of self-flagellation, which had been a mass outdoor expression of penance, into a private nighttime ritual performed by and for the brothers. The Venetian scuole dei battudi, however, retained the public, processional character of the discipline for more than two centuries.

The Statutes of the Scuole and Their Guiding Principles: Devotion, Charity, and Patriotism

One of the first actions of a newly formed confraternity was the drafting of its bylaws or constitution, modeled to a great extent on elements drawn from tradeguild charters and monastic constitutions. These rules, along with a list of the members of the scuola, were copied into a book known as a *mariegola* (or, in the medieval Venetian Latin form, *matricola*). This book, usually illuminated and beautifully written on fine parchment, bound in boards covered with red velvet or tooled leather, and bearing the symbol of the scuola, became one of its most treasured possessions.[11]

Each mariegola opened with a prologue, with material serving several different functions. Some of this is factual (or, at least, ostensibly so): the date of the foundation, the church in which the new confraternity met, and the dedication of the confraternity to a saint or to the Virgin Mary. More important are the guiding principles that make up the remainder of the prologue and sometimes the first several chapters. One element common to many (and familiar also in such bylaws for other, non-flagellant confraternities in Venice, and confraternities of all sorts elsewhere) is an assertion of the sin-filled and fragile nature of human life, as in the mariegola of San Giovanni Evangelista: "How fragile this present life is, and how fleeting is human fragility, is openly taught and demonstrated, such that miserable man is brought in haste to be tied by the bonds of diabolical subjection, and is always wrapped in sin . . ."[12]

The primary refuge from this fate, and perhaps the principal raison d'être for confraternities everywhere, is in communal devotion, as advocated by St. James:

> Therefore, inspired by Divine Grace, we thought and debated how, for the delectation of brotherhood and with the aid of prayer we might gain the health of our souls, remembering the [words] of the Blessed Saint James the Apostle, who said: Pray one for the other, so that you shall be saved, because the prayers of the just have great value.[13]

The growing attention to the concept of purgatory in this period increased the feeling of urgency regarding such prayer.

The prefaces also included an indication of the activity that has perhaps brought the most modern scholarly attention: good works, in particular charity toward those less fortunate. As the mariegola of the Scuola di San Marco explained, these are activities that not only help others, but, most important, aid the souls of those who perform them: "We must in Charity serve our neighbor with all our will . . . with perfect works that are in praise of God, and for the salvation of our souls."[14] The brothers of Santa Maria della Carità put it even more succinctly, quoting St. Peter (though confusing the passage with a similar one in James, whom they cite as the author): "charity covers the multitude of sins."[15] The Christian humility embodied in the carrying out of works such as charity was expressed in another form, of course, in that activity characteristic of these confraternies in particular, the discipline of self-flagellation that was the immediate cause of their creation. In the words of the mariegola of San Marco, "not seeking any other glory than that of the Cross of our Lord Jesus Christ, and in his example we must humble our bodies and our souls in carnal and spiritual discipline."[16]

The political and social turbulence of the times in which these confraternities came to be also is reflected in these prefaces. The call to fraternal order and peace, common in confraternities everywhere, finds its most detailed expression in the rules and regulations that follow the preface (see below) but can sometimes appear even here, as in the mariegola of the Scuola della Carità: "everyone should attend with peace and quiet, not speaking idle or vain words, and not rising up in pride one against another, and not clashing in anger, but solely speaking and saying things that pertain to the health of our souls."[17] The brothers identified themselves clearly as loyal subjects of the city of Venice and its doge, making it clear that these large new associations posed no political threat, but were, rather, dedicated to the good of the state: "we wish that everything we do from now on should be done for the honor and state of misser the doge, and of the city of Venice and of all the nation."[18]

Honor, a Fourth Guiding Principle?

The principles and practices outlined to this point are those that have usually been invoked by scholars to explain the development and later activities of confraternities. The expansion of ritual religion, in particular the care of the dying and dead, is a natural consequence of a dedication to mutual prayer. The ever increasing role of the scuole grandi as dispensers of charity, both internally, to brothers and their families, and externally, to the poor of the city as a whole, is, of course, one of their most important features. Processions both provided public displays of the penitential fervor of the brothers and, in the case of those commemorating civic occasions, offered concrete evidence of their patriotism. Some other prominent activities of the scuole, in particular their patronage of art and architecture, through the construction and decoration of their halls, and their support of splendid music, have been treated, to some extent, as distortions of their original purpose that only incidentally supported their basic goals. A closer examination of the histories of these institutions, however, shows that all of these seeming deviations from the true path can easily be accommodated within a principle that is expressed with great forcefulness in the mariegole of each of the scuole, though it has not been given equal prominence in the literature: honor.

The centrality of the idea of honor to the scuole is expressed clearly in the prologues to the mariegole, sometimes, as in that of San Giovanni Evangelista, at the very opening: "To the honor of the magnificent Lord Jesus Christ, and of the most glorious Virgin Mother, Madonna Holy Mary, and of the Most Blessed and most precious Apostle and Evangelist Saint John, chief and standardbearer of this blessed scuola."[19] While this invocation might be viewed as simply a sign of dedication to God and the saints, the concept of honor is broadened as the mariegola continues (here quoting again from that of San Giovanni Evangelista):

> It will be always our intention that what we do . . . should be to the honor of God, and of his sweet mother Madonna Holy Mary, and of the most merciful St. John, Apostle and Evangelist, chief and governor of this, our fraternity of discipline. And to the honor of the precious Evangelist St. Mark, patron and governor and defender of this blessed city, and we want that everything we do from now on to be done for the honor and prestige of misser the doge, and of the city of Venice, and of all the nation, and of every good Christian.[20]

San Marco's mariegola has a slightly varied list (and one very similar to that of the Misericordia). After the references to God, Mary, Sts. Peter, Paul, and John, and the "celestial court," it continues, "and in honor and reverence of the pope and his friars, and of all the Church of Rome, that is the faithful Christians, and in honor and reverence of misser the doge, and of all of his good council, and for the honor and prestige of the city of Venice."[21]

What did the drafters of these bylaws intend by their prominent references to honor? Aristotle wrote in the Nicomachean Ethics that "Honor is the prize of virtue, and the tribute that we pay to the good."[22] It was the recognition of a person's valor, good works, or other merits by individuals or the state. In the Judaeo-Christian tradition, the greatest honor was due to the possessor of supreme virtue, God, as in Psalm 66: "Sing forth the honour of his name: make his praise glorious." Honor was also something owed to one's parents, as in the Ten Commandments, or to whoever is devout and does good works: "But glory, honour, and peace, to every man that worketh good" (Romans 2:10). Honor was bestowed through praise, respect, obedience, or recognition, and perhaps by emulation.

From their origins, the scuole honored God and the saints through religious devotion and charitable good works. They honored the city of Venice by their presence at public ceremonies that displayed the power and unity of the city, and they honored the doge by doing him homage in processions and by obeying his (and his government's) commands. As originally conceived, therefore, honor as a guiding principle served to explain or justify all the scuola's activities. What makes this a particularly useful concept for understanding the later artistic and musical activities of the scuole is the way it changed and developed over the centuries that followed the founding of these institutions. The early and medieval Christian view saw honor as something owed to God by man, and granted to man by God, and that worldly honor should be avoided. Augustine, in *The City of God*, wrote that men should "avoid this desire of human honour, the glory of the righteous being wholly in God."[23] The scuole, then, in their early years, conceived of honor as something they gave to God, the saints, and the city, in recognition of their virtues, but did not seek for themselves.

In later centuries, however, honor was not shunned in the same way. Robert Ashley, in the first English book devoted to the subject of honor, wrote, in the late sixteenth century, "And to me yt seemes not only that there ys nothing amongst men more excellent than honour, but also that even god himself cannot geve or bestowe a greater or more excellent guyfte uppon man." Further, he asks, "For how can vertue stand yf you take away honour?"[24] Avoiding honor, in the Renaissance view, would be a form of pride, demonstrating that one is above what everybody else desires. Achieving honor through good works, further, is commendable because, as Erasmus wrote, "it may benefit a great many, and draw them to an imitation of itself."[25] With honor reconceived in this manner, the scuole could best honor God and the city by earning honor themselves, gaining the most recognition and praise for their activities, charitable, devotional, or artistic, as possible. With personal honor now valued, even the honor gained by the individuals who governed the scuole was legitimate. Thus, spending vast sums of money on halls and their decoration, or on singers and instrumentalists, was a legitimate way of following the guiding principles under which the scuole were established, rather than mere ostentation. As will be shown in the following chapters, whenever the leaders of a scuola wished to enhance the musical aspect of their activities, or preserve it from being diminished, they called upon the necessity of honor to justify their actions.

Not everyone, of course, recognized this revised idea of honor, or accepted it as a justification for additional expenditures. Some projects for such outlays were halted by internal opposition, and government authorities sometimes blocked those the scuole proposed. There was also a measure of popular opposition to the approach the scuole took, expressed best, perhaps, in Alessandro Caravia's scathing satirical poem of 1541:

> What's due to the poor is splashed out in vast oceans
> On building, but certainly not on devotions.

With sideshows in squares they make such commotions,
And every year brings a fresh influx of notions.
On trivial projects they've money to burn,
When their care and affection to Christ they should turn,
And for love of him use all their badly spent money
On clothes for the naked, on bread for the hungry.
. . .

Pride, envy and things which to others belong
Create in this world a great measure of wrong.
To the regions of darkness will go before long
Those unhappy souls in a criminal throng
Who in vices like these have been sinking their energy;
They've no love of God and no feelings of charity,
For, if God and if charity had any hold,
They wouldn't set store by pride, envy and gold.[26]

Housing the Scuola: Church and Hall

In most Italian cities, the clergy, usually of the mendicant orders, were the prime movers in the foundation of confraternities, and the newly formed institutions found their homes in or beside the churches of their sponsors. The Franciscan or Dominican friars assisted with the drafting of the bylaws (leading to remarkable consistency throughout Italy), and the relationship between a confraternity and its host in cities such as Bologna or Florence remained a close one. Friars provided direct spiritual and moral guidance to the confraternities in their roles as confessors, chaplains, or correctors, and played a prominent public role as deliverers of sermons at the religious observances of the confraternities.[27] The situation in Venice was very different. Laymen, not the clergy, were the founders of all of the scuole grandi, and of many, if not most, of the scuole piccole (see chapter 8). The Venetian confraternities, especially the scuole grandi, remained free of ecclesiastical control throughout their histories, being dependent, instead, on the state, as will be discussed below.

Since religion was, nonetheless, at the core of the scuola's activities, each scuola, at its founding, established a contractual relationship with a church, in which it could perform its religious services with the aid of the clergy and, at least at first, hold its meetings. The Scuola di San Marco was associated initially with the parish church of Santa Croce, and then, from 1437, with the great Dominican house of Santi Giovanni e Paolo (known usually as San Zanipolo) (see figure 1.1 for a map of Venice with the location of scuole and churches). Santa Maria della Carità (after initial ties with the parish church of San Leonardo and the oratorio of San Giacomo on the Giudecca) was linked with the church of the same name, a house of Augustinian Regular Canons, of the Lateran branch. San Giovanni Evangelista, after starting in association with the parish church of Sant'Apollinare (known as Sant'Aponal), obtained in 1307 property owned by the Badoer family that already housed a hospital and a private church, San Giovanni Evangelista; although the family always retained some rights, the scuola

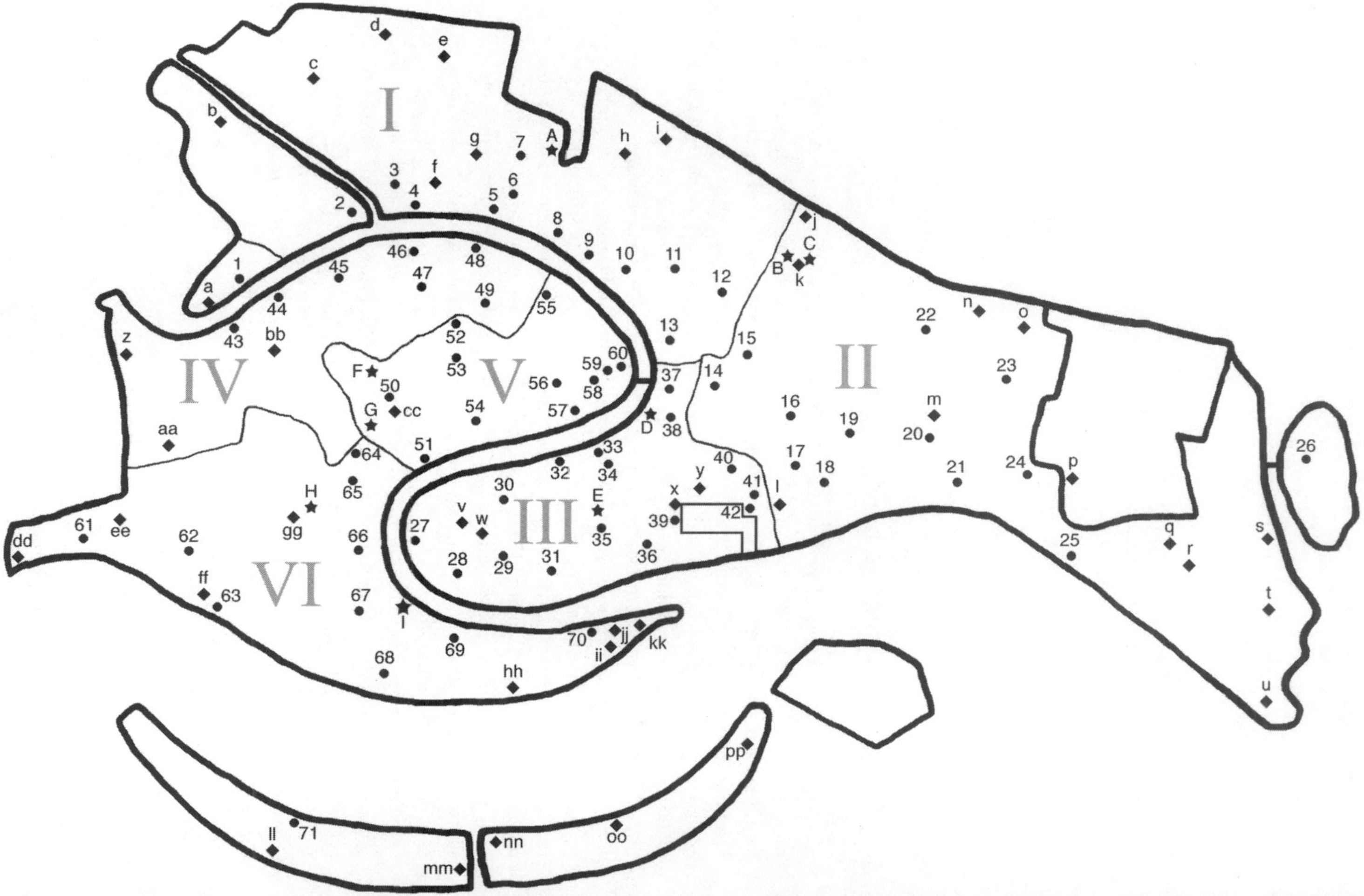

FIGURE 1.1. Map of Venice with locations of religious institutions

Legend

Parish Churches

I. Sestiere di Cannaregio
  1   Santa Lucia (also Augustinian nuns)
  2   San Geremia
  3   San Leonardo
  4   San Marcuola
  5   Santa Maria Maddalena
  6   Santa Fosca
  7   San Marziale
  8   San Felice
  9   Santa Sofia
 10   Santi Appostoli
 11   San Canciano
 12   Santa Maria Nuova
 13   San Giovanni Grisostomo

II. Sestiere di Castello
 14   San Lio
 15   Santa Marina
 16   Santa Maria Formosa
 17   San Giovanni Nuovo
 18   San Provolo
 19   San Severo
 20   Sant'Antonino
 21   San Giovanni in Bragora
 22   Santa Giustina (also Franciscan nuns)
 23   Santa Trinità
 24   San Martino
 25   San Biagio
 26   San Pietro di Castello (also cathedral)

III. Sestiere di San Marco
 27   San Samuele
 28   San Vitale
 29   San Maurizio
 30   Sant'Angelo
 31   Santa Maria Zobenigo
 32   San Benedetto
 33   San Luca
 34   San Paternian
 35   San Fantin
 36   San Moisè
 37   San Bartolomeo
 38   San Salvatore (also Augustinian regular canons)
 39   San Geminiano

 40   San Giuliano
 41   San Basso
 42   San Marco (also ducal chapel)

IV. Sestiere di Santa Croce
 43   Santa Croce
 44   San Simeon Piccolo
 45   San Simeon Grande
 46   San Giovanni Decolato
 47   San Giacomo dall'Orio
 48   San Stae
 49   Santa Maria Mater Domini

V. Sestiere di San Polo
 50   San Stin
 51   San Tomà
 52   San Boldo
 53   Sant'Agostin
 54   San Polo
 55   San Cassiano
 56   Sant'Aponal
 57   San Silvestro
 58   San Matteo
 59   San Giovanni Elimosinario
 60   San Giacomo di Rialto

VI. Sestiere di Dorsoduro
 61   San Nicolò dei Mendicoli
 62   San Raffaelle Arcangelo
 63   San Basegio
 64   San Pantalon
 65   Santa Margarita
 66   San Barnaba
 67   San Trovaso
 68   Sant'Agnese
 69   San Vio
 70   San Gregorio (also Benedictine abbey)
 71   Sant'Eufemia della Giudecca

Other Churches with Confraternities

 a   Corpus Domini (Dominican nuns)
 b   San Giobbe (Franciscan friars)
 c   San Girolamo (Augustinian nuns)
 d   Sant'Alvise (Augustinian nuns)
 e   Madonna dell'Orto (Umiliati)

(continued)

FIGURE 1.1.   Map of Venice with locations of religious institutions (continued)

Legend

Other Churches with Confraternities

f   Santa Maria dell'Anconetta (oratorio)
g   Santa Maria dei Servi (Servite monks)
h   Santa Caterina (Augustinian nuns)
i   I Gesuiti (Jesuits, formerly Crosecchieri)
j   San Lazzaro dei Mendicanti (hospital)
k   Santi Giovanni e Paolo (Dominican friars)
l   Santi Filippo e Giacomo (Primicerio of San Marco)
m   San Giovanni del Tempio (Knights of Saint John of Jerusalem)
n   San Francesco della Vigna (Franciscan friars)
o   Santa Maria della Celestia (Cistercian nuns)
p   Santa Maria dell'Arsenale (oratory)
q   San Francesco di Paola (Minimite monks)
r   San Domenico (Dominican friars)
s   Sant'Anna (Benedictine nuns)
t   San Giuseppe (Augustinian nuns)
u   Sant'Antonio di Castello (Augustinian regular canons)
v   Santi Rocco e Margarita (Augustinian nuns)
w   Santo Stefano (Augustinian hermits)
x   Santa Maria in Broglio (oratory)
y   San Gallo (oratory)
z   Sant'Andrea della Zirada (Augustinian nuns)
aa Santa Maria Maggiore (Franciscan nuns)
bb San Nicolò dei Tolentini (Theatine monks)
cc Santa Maria Gloriosa dei Frari (Franciscan friars)

dd Santa Marta (Augustinian nuns)
ee Santa Teresa (Carmelite nuns)
ff San Sebastiano (hermits of Saint Jerome)
gg Santa Maria dei Carmini (Carmelite friars)
hh Spirito Santo (Augustinian nuns)
ii Santa Maria dell'Umiltà (Teutonic knights, then Jesuits)
jj Santa Maria della Salute (votive temple)
kk La Trinità (Teutonic knights, then seminary)
ll Santi Cosma e Damiano (Benedictine nuns)
mm Sant'Angelo di Concordia (Carmelite friars)
nn San Giacomo della Giudecca (Servite friars)
oo Santa Croce della Giudecca (Benedictine nuns)
pp San Giovanni Battista della Giudecca (Camaldolite friars)

Scuole Grandi

A   Santa Maria della Misericordia (with priory)
B   San Marco
C   Santa Maria del Rosario (inside Santi Giovanni e Paolo)
D   San Teodoro
E   San Fantin
F   San Giovanni Evangelista (with church)
G   San Rocco (with church)
H   Santa Maria del Carmine
I   Santa Maria della Carità (with Augustinian regular canons)

eventually took over the operations of the church directly. They also maintained close links with the nearby Franciscan convent of Santa Maria Gloriosa (known as the Frari). Santa Maria della Misericordia (also known as Santa Maria della Valverde) was associated with the eponymous church, a priory under the control of the Moro family. San Rocco was created by the union of two smaller scuole, one at the parish church of San Giuliano, and the other at the Franciscan convent of the Frari, and established its own church near the Frari, with which it also maintained a loose tie. San Teodoro, which existed for three centuries as a scuola piccola in the church of San Salvatore (like the Carità, a house of Augustinian Regular Canons, from 1442 of the San Salvatore branch), maintained this relationship after its promotion.[28]

Unlike the great majority of scuole piccole, which continued to operate within their home churches, occupying an altar for religious services and meeting either in front of the altar or in the sacristy, the scuole grandi almost immediately began construction of separate halls for their meetings and for religious services other than masses (and later even these). These vast structures, built in rivalry with one another and also, to some extent, with the doge's palace, which was the meeting place for the nobility, are notable Venetian monuments. Of the oldest halls (called, like the institutions they housed, scuole), only one, the fourteenth-century Scuola Vecchia della Misericordia, retains anything like its medieval appearance, at least externally. The others were either remodelled or rebuilt entirely later, and all are masterpieces of Renaissance or baroque architecture (with later modifications), designed by such masters as Pietro Lombardo, Mauro Coducci, Bartolomeo Bon, Scarpagnino, Jacopo Sansovino, Baldassare Longhena, and Giacomo Massari.[29] They all have a fairly standard design, modified by the necessities of the site. The ground floor contains a large room, sparsely decorated, which was used, apparently, for ordering the processions. Also located on that floor, in some cases (as still at San Rocco) was the *cancelleria*, where the *cancelliere* kept his office for daily business, as well as places for storage of processional apparatus. A ceremonial double staircase leads to the *piano nobile*, which is dominated by the most splendid space in the building, the great hall, designed for meetings and celebrations. Also on the piano nobile was the *albergo*, the meeting room of the officers, where the *guardian grande* (see below for the administrative structure of the scuole) held court and where the serious business of the scuola was conducted. The albergo was dominated by the *banca*, the large bench behind which the guardian and his companions sat. The scuole employed some of the greatest artists of the Renaissance, including Jacopo, Gentile, and Giovanni Bellini, Palma Vecchio, Titian, Veronese, and Tintoretto, to decorate their great halls and alberghi.[30] Besides these, the scuole buildings contained several additional rooms, for the guardian da mattin, for the archive, etc. The Scuola di San Giovanni Evangelista had one exceptional addition: an extension of the building built to house the miraculous and precious relic of the True Cross that was the scuola's most valued possession, with walls covered with the famous late fifteenth-century series of paintings (completed between 1494 and 1510) by Gentile Bellini, Carpaccio, and others, now in the Accademia Gallery, depicting the miracles associated with the relic. Only the Scuola di San Rocco retains its complete original Renaissance decoration, the great cycle by Tintoretto. All the others have been in large part destroyed or dispersed, or at least removed to museums. San Giovanni Evangelista, after expanding its main hall, commissioned new works in the seventeenth and eighteenth centuries, still in place today.

The rules that followed the prologue of the mariegola were of several types, principally administrative (that is procedures for membership and the election and duties of officers), disciplinary (prescriptions for the moral behavior of the brothers with penalties for violations), and ceremonial (instructions for the religious observances of the scuola). These will be discussed briefly below.

Membership

Naturally, among the first rules that a newly founded confraternity needed to establish were criteria for membership.[31] The basic requirement for admission to one of the scuole grandi, at least in the early years, was very simple: the desire and ability to perform the discipline, that is, to participate in the flagellant processions. Prospective members had to be above a specified minimum age, usually 20, but sometimes as low as 15 or 16. The total membership was set at between 500 (Santa Maria della Misericordia) and 600 (San Marco), with new members to be chosen from those applicants who seemed suitable, although suitability is not clearly defined (preference is sometimes extended to sons of members). Chapter 5 of the mariegola of San Giovanni Evangelista states these requirements clearly:

> We also wish and ordain, that anyone who wishes to enter in this, our confraternity of discipline, may, by common consent of all our brothers, be received . . . , but only up to 550 persons. . . . No one may be accepted who is not able to perform the discipline and observe our rules, or is under the age of 20. And if, in the course of nature, some of our brothers should die, we wish that the first to be admitted [as replacements] should be those who appear most able.[32]

There were, of course, certain restrictions. Nobody could enter the scuola if he was currently a member of, or had ever been expelled from, another of the flagellant confraternities (membership in one of the scuole piccole, on the other hand, was no hindrance). A member's good reputation (*buona fama*) was of great importance, so that no candidate could be admitted if even one current member spoke against him. And, unlike confraternities in other Italian cities—and unlike many of the scuole piccole—membership was restricted to men (with the exception of special membership extended to nuns in convents whose churches housed a tomb belonging to the scuola).

Newly admitted members appeared at the scuola's altar, and swore on the mariegola to uphold all the rules contained therein. An entrance fee, or *benintrada*, usually about 15 *soldi di grosso*,[33] was assessed, and members were expected to make an annual charitable contribution at the time of the meal for the poor (see below) of about nine *soldi piccoli*. In addition, brothers were required to pay the *luminaria*, the cost of the candles that they were required to carry in processions, and also had to purchase the *cappa*, the white robe with the insignia of the scuola, which was worn at all functions. The cappa, which resembled a monastic habit (with the addition of an opening in the back for flagellation), served the same functions, both to identify the brother as a member of the group and to eliminate distinctions of wealth and class.

At least two of the scuole (the Carità and the Misericordia) required that members initially join a probationary group of sixty new brothers whose behavior was closely watched, and who were required to fast several times during the year-long trial period. Like the robes, this idea was also modeled on monastic practice, in this case the novitiate. At the end of the period these men could be admitted as regular members. If regular membership was not approved, the candidate was required to wait at least two years before trying again. The other scuole appear to have admitted successful applicants to full membership immediately.

The earliest mariegole made no mention of the social class of the members. The population of Venice was divided roughly into three classes. At the top were the nobles, or patricians, the oldest families in Venice, and the only ones allowed to participate in the deliberative and judicial bodies of the Venetian government.[34] Next were the *cittadini*, or citizens, the civil servants and professional class, the lawyers, doctors, notaries, and government secretaries.[35] Many of these families had been in Venice nearly as long as the patricians, and some were richer than a number of patrician families, but they remained outside of the governing class. These two groups were quite small, making up approximately 10 percent each of the total population. All the rest (excluding the clergy) were, technically, grouped into one class, the *popolani*. However, in practice, the class of *popolani* had several subdivisions: (1) the merchants and tradesmen, members of the various guilds of Venice, constituting a middle class; (2) the simple laborers; and (3) the poor.[36]

The earliest membership rules of the scuole grandi would seem to allow all Venetians to join, but, in practice, this was not the case. The original membership lists are made up almost entirely of *cittadini* and the upper stratum of the *popolani*, the guild members. There were also a few nobles, but the lower classes are almost entirely absent, probably because the admission fee was beyond their reach; more-over, they undoubtedly would not have met with the approval of the existing brothers. Unlike many of the scuole piccole, the scuole grandi did not have close ties with particular professions. The thirteenth-century mariegola of the Carità, for example, identifies over 150 occupations among 975 brothers (with another 500 named without profession; the 1,444 names represent the initial membership and their replacements over the first several decades of the scuola's history).[37] The membership of the scuole grandi, unlike many other confraternities, was also geographically diverse. While the membership lists reveal some bias toward those who lived nearest the scuola, brothers of each of the scuole came from nearly every parish of the city.

In the mid-thirteenth century, when the earliest scuole were founded, the line between patrician and *cittadino* was not absolute: some non-nobles still sat in the Great Council, the principal deliberative body of the government, and the membership in this council varied somewhat from year to year. In 1297, in one of the defining events of Venetian history, the system was changed (the so-called *serrata del Maggior Consiglio*), and membership in the Great Council, and thus, according to the Venetian constitution, in all other government bodies, was restricted to members of those families serving at that time or who had served within the past four years. From that point on, membership in the Great Council and the status of patrician, or noble, were one and the same. All others were placed permanently outside the governing class. The scuole quickly reacted (that is, within several decades) to this changed situation. First, although this is not said in so many words, they excluded nobles from regular membership, and prohibited them from holding office. On the other hand, each scuola now established a rule allowing a small number of patricians to be admitted with a special status, with the payment of an entrance fee significantly larger than that of regular members and a greater annual fee. They were exempt from leadership roles and from the discipline, but received all the benefits accorded regular members. The numbers of nobles that could be accepted varied from twelve (at the Carità) to fifty (at San Giovanni Evangelista and San Marco) and the minimum age from 30 (at San Giovanni Evangelista) to 50 (at San Marco). Candidates had to have good reputations (*bona fama*) and be approved by a majority of a group of thirty respected men of the scuola, including the officers. If accepted, a patrician paid a *benintrada* of 20 to 25 ducats and an annual charitable donation of 20 soldi. The exclusion of members of the governing class from positions of power in the scuole was very likely a major factor in allowing these institutions to continue to flourish, since, unlike the situation in Florence, they could not then be perceived as political threats.[38]

The reference to the election of patrician members by a small group of thirty to forty *boni homeni* (good, or respectable men) is another reflection of the changes in Venetian society. Just as the government was now restricted to members of the patrician class, the administration of the scuole was entrusted more and more to the *cittadini*. Although it would not become a restriction written into Venetian law until the fifteenth century, the trend was quite clear. The founding of a fourth scuola grande, Santa Maria della Misericordia, in 1308, just a decade after the closing of the Grand Council, might have come about as an outlet for the curtailed ambitions of these families of *cittadini*, who were no longer permitted to hold positions of power in the civic government.

The scuole made another change at the other end of the social spectrum. They dropped the probationary period for regular members, as only *cittadini* and the upper level of the *popolani* were considered for full admission. However, they maintained the group of sixty special members, beyond the statutory size limit of the scuola, those referred to as being in the *tollela*,[39] or as those in the *sessanta* ("sixty"), but changed the nature of its membership. Poor applicants, unable to pay the membership fee, the annual gift, or the cost of candles, could be admitted to this special group and receive all benefits of regular membership, such as medical care and funerals. In exchange, they were required to attend all functions of the scuola (technically, attendance was mandated of all brothers, but this was not enforced), perform the discipline at every procession—a practice that, in fact, was no longer required of regular brothers—and, as the system developed, carry the various torches, banners, canopies, and other paraphernalia required in the increasingly elaborate processions. The original intention was that these sixty poor brothers, often now referred to as *fadighenti*, or workers, could achieve regular membership after a year's service, but, in fact, as in Venetian society as a whole, this represented a separate class of members, permanently (with only rare exceptions) separated from the others. These poor brothers, in exchange for free membership and full benefits, performed all the difficult and unpleasant tasks that the middle-class regular brothers no longer wished to undertake.

Beyond the regular membership, patricians, and the sixty, the scuole also enrolled several groups of special brothers. Each scuola admitted either twenty-five or thirty priests beyond the regular membership limit to perform religious tasks for the brothers. Although they were required to say mass and lead observances at the regular celebrations of the scuole, their main job was to say frequent commemorative masses for the souls of deceased brothers. They received small charitable gifts for each mass, were exempt from *benintrada* and *luminaria*, and were barred from holding office, but they were entitled to full benefits. Also salaried and exempt were physicians, hired by the scuole to provide for the needs of ill brothers. Some of the earliest mariegole also list honorary ecclesiastical members, often non-Venetians, who, perhaps, assisted the scuola in some way, perhaps in the obtaining of indulgences. The list appended to the mariegola of Santa Maria della Carità, for example, includes the Patriarch of Grado, the Bishops of Budua, Parenzo, Cittanova, Ierapetra (in Crete), and Caorle, and a number of the *piovani*, or parish priests, of Venice.[40]

The Organization of the Scuole

The members of a scuola met as a body, the general chapter, three times each year: on the third Sunday in Lent, the second Sunday in August, and the Sunday before Christmas. To begin each of these meetings, in the procedures formulated in the earliest statutes, the mariegola was read aloud and a Mass of the Holy Spirit was said, to inspire the brothers. By the eighteenth century, things had gotten a bit more complicated, as outlined in a chart preserved in the archives of the Scuola di San Rocco (see the left side of table 1.1).

The principal business of these meetings was the admission of new brothers and the election of officers. Technically, all non-noble members were eligible to hold office, at least in the early years of the scuole, but in practice, and by law after 1409, the positions of authority were open only to *cittadini*. Before being eligible for election, a brother must have been in the scuola for at least one year for most of the offices, and two or three years, depending on the scuola, for the position of guardian grande. The scuole were also very careful to ensure that candidates were of good moral character, and conducted background checks to determine if any legal or financial problems barred them from holding office (see the right column of table 1.1). The scuole held most of their elections at the general chapter of Lent, but chose two of the *degani*, and some others, at the

TABLE 1.1.   Election procedures of the general chapter of the Scuola Grande di San Rocco in the eighteenth century

Procedures (in order of occurrence)	Basis of certification of candidates (items to check, in order of importance)
ringing of bells	mariegola
convocation of the chapter	government magistracies
verification of membership	previously approved regulations
quorum count	vetos of regulations
class of membership	revocation of regulations or vetos
brothers take their places	instructions from magistracies
campaigning for offices	check in lists of debtors
silence	check in lists of criminal convictions
oath	certification that not in list of ad-
nominations for offices	monitions
selection of candidates by lot	check list of banishments
balloting	check lists of pardons
verification of time since previous office	*assignamento*[a]
control of family ties to other officers	*collation*[a]
election of 12 "aggiunte" (former officers)	
election of reserve "aggiunte"	
election of commissari	
opportunity to refuse office	

Source: ASV, SSR II 456.

[a] The meaning of this term is unclear.

August meeting. In addition, the general chapter considered amendments to the mariegola, major expenditures, and other rules and regulations regarding the scuola and its members.

The chief official of the confraternity, to whom all the other members looked for guidance, was the guardian grande. The brothers chose him from among the most respectable senior members of the scuola, in most cases after he had served in several other lesser positions. After the priests celebrated Mass of the Holy Spirit, the candidates for guardian grande rose, each holding a lighted candle, and retired to a secure place while the voting took place. The winner, by simple majority, was expected to be "leader and corrector of all of us."[41] The guardian grande chaired the meetings, offered up motions to be voted on, placed names of new members before the membership, and was responsible for the financial affairs of the scuola. He also, during his one-year term, became the public symbol of the scuola. He acted for the scuola in all legal and governmental matters, and was at the center of all public processions and ceremonies. During his term of office he was identified, in all documents, by his title, and the rules required the other brothers to address him in respectful terms. While an ordinary *cittadino* was addressed as *clarissimo*, a guardian grande might be called, in the fifteenth through early seventeenth centuries, *dignissimo*, *eccelentissimo*, or *magnifico*. Also common in the later seventeenth and eighteenth centuries was the appellation *spettabile*. The guardian grande played a role within the scuola similar to that played by the doge

TABLE 1.2. The office of guardian grande of the Scuola Grande di San Rocco in the eighteenth century

Prerequisites	Responsibilities	Supervision	Authority
[not having] refused election	cash box	elections	rents
	accounts	silence in meetings	debts
[not having] renounced office	investment bank	campaigning	buildings
	rent collection	oath	lawsuits
confirmation [of eligibility]	expenditures	places [*luochi*]	documents
	keys	conventions with other institutions	church
appropriate interval since previous office	consigning belongings of the scuola to the next guardian	meetings	mansionari
[opportunity to] refuse		punishments	sacristy
vice guardian[a]	loans	hearings	hearings
			mint.[?]

Source: ASV, SSR II 456.

[a] The reference is unclear.

in the central government. Like the doge, and all other government officials, the brother elected as guardian or to any other office could not refuse. Also, as in the government, outgoing officers had to wait one year (two for the guardian grande), the *contumacia*, before running for another office. In addition, the guardian grande could never again hold a lesser office, as that would demean his stature. Both the requirements for holding the office and its extensive obligations are recorded in another chart from San Rocco, shown in table 1.2.

The guardian grande, like all other officers, received no salary for the position. The only concrete benefit, other than prestige and power, was that if he died in office, he usually received a more elaborate funeral than ordinary brothers. On the other hand, again like the situation among the patricians in the government, the position could prove very expensive to hold. Each guardian wanted to leave his mark on the scuola, to be remembered for his accomplishments. While some of this could be done through the normal procedures of the scuola, there were many limits, some of them governmental, on the amounts and types of expenditures the scuola could make. Therefore, if the guardian wished to have more elaborate processions or a more extravagant annual festa, or if he wished to add to the decoration of the scuola's hall (that is, if he wished in this way to add to his or the scuola's honor), he had to provide the money himself, sometimes with the assistance of the other officers. The guardians often spent very large sums of money, as they were competing not only with their predecessors, but with the guardians of the other scuole grandi. Recognizing this situation, a brother might sometimes (though rarely until the last days of the Republic) be allowed to refuse election to the rank of guardian grande on the grounds that he simply could not afford to uphold the prestige of the scuola as the position demanded.

According to the earliest mariegole, the guardian grande was assisted by only one other principal officer, the *scrivano*, elected at the August general chapter. His main duty was to "record the finances of the scuola, both the income and the

TABLE 1.3.   The office of vicario of the Scuola Grande
di San Rocco in the eighteenth century

Prerequisites	Reponsibilities
age	palms [for Palm Sunday procession]
residence	processions
oath	Maundy Thursday ceremonies
[no previous] refusals	robes of the brothers
vice guardian[a]	candles
	cash box
	furnishings of the scuola
	church
	ceremonies
	expenses
	choir

Source: ASV, SSR II 456.

[a]The reference is unclear.

expenses."[42] That is, he was the scuola's bookkeeper. He also, in practice, maintained the other records of the scuola: the lists of brothers, the records of chapter
meetings, amendments to the mariegola, and the like. The scrivano and guardian
grande were required to keep the funds of the scuola safe in a locked box, and
to balance the books and present the financial state of the scuola to the members
once or twice a year.

In the fourteenth century, the scuole created two additional offices to assist
the guardian grande with the ever-increasing activities of the organization. The
first of these, with no clearly specified duties, was the *vicario*, "who must gather
and lead the scuola when the guardian is not there."[43] The second, the *guardian
da mattin*, had, at least at the beginning, quite clearly defined duties: he was in
charge of processions, both the regular official ones and those held weekday
mornings (thus his title) by those brothers who wished to perform additional
penitential self-flagellation, "for the good and service of the souls of our brothers,
who because of their devotion like to go in the morning through the city, beating
themselves as is done on the ordained days."[44] In practice, as time went on, the
positions of guardian da mattin and vicario seem to have exchanged some of their
duties. While the guardian da mattin kept the surviving processional account book
of the Scuola di San Giovanni Evangelista,[45] similar books at the Scuola di San
Marco were the responsibility of the vicario.[46] It was one of these two men who
was in charge of the sixty probationary members who served in the processions.
An eighteenth-century version of the duties of the vicario at San Rocco is shown
in table 1.3. In any event, these were both positions of some responsibility, and
were usually stepping stones to the leadership of the scuola.

Young brothers of *cittadino* class who hoped to rise to an important office in
the scuola usually began with election as a *degano*. There were twelve *degani*, ten
(*degani di tutt'anno*) elected at the Lent general chapter, and two (*degani di*

mezz'anno) elected in August. The degani were responsible for gathering the brothers for the various functions of the scuola:

> And twelve degani, that is two for each *sestiere* [sixth of the city], each of whom must have the list of his portion of the membership, on which must be written the names of all of our brothers in that portion. And we wish that the said degani be required to announce to those brothers every ordained day, and every occasion.[47]

The guardian grande, scrivano, vicario, guardian da mattin, and degani made up the *banca* (named for the bench on which they sat at the meetings), the group responsible for the day-to-day running of the scuola. By the early fourteenth century, the banca was given permission to meet whenever it felt necessary to conduct the business of the scuola in lieu of the general chapter. This was usually done with the addition of a limited number of respected members. In 1330 the Scuola di San Giovanni Evangelista specified that thirty or forty "good and respected men" (*bonorum et consideratorum hominum*)[48] should be chosen to meet when the general chapter could not. With the creation of this group, made up in practice of all former office holders, the administrative structure of the scuola became nearly identical to that of the government. While historically the power remained with the membership, that is the general chapter (as, in theory, the people of Venice still had the right to refuse a doge), in reality the office-holding class made all decisions. This body, referred to usually simply as the chapter (parallel to the Great Council, which had all patrician males, that is, all potential office holders as members), elected the officers and had final say in changes to the mariegola. Matters were not even brought to this group, however, unless approved of by a smaller elected group, the guardian and banca (parallel to the Senate). At the top of the pyramid were the officers themselves (the doge and his counselors).[49]

By the sixteenth century, the scuole had made several modifications in this structure. They enlarged the banca itself, with the addition of a twelve-member *zonta*,[50] made up of former office holders (by this time degani usually held that position only once, but they could serve on the zonta while waiting their turn at high office). Additionally, they created several new offices. Most important among these were the two or three *sinici* (or *sindici*), responsible for assuring that all decisions made by the banca or the general chapter conformed to the mariegola and other existing regulations. Also in the inner circle were the *deffensori*, elected to defend the scuola in all legal matters, which proliferated as the scuole accumulated money and property. When necessary, the members elected additional officials or committees on an ad hoc basis, but these need not concern us here.

There were three remaining positions specified in the mariegole, but, unlike all the others, these were not held by *cittadini*. The chapter selected three *masseri* (sometimes called *nonzoli*) from among the poorer brothers, and paid them a salary, to "do all those things that the guardian or his fellow officers shall command them for the business of the scuola."[51] These men ran errands for the guardian, helped prepare the scuola for meetings, maintained the building of the scuola, acted as bodyguards for the officers, and helped the guardian maintain discipline.

Later in the history of the scuole, paid professionals took over some of the operations. The first of these, appearing in the late sixteenth and early seventeenth centuries, was the *quadernier*, or bookkeeper, who assumed the financial duties of the scrivano (an office that was no longer filled in some scuole, or became a position without duties), and kept accounts using the complicated, double-entry system employed in Venice for all business and government budgets. Later on, in the eighteenth century, several of the scuole turned over the day-to-day management of the scuola to another professional, the *cancelliere*, who was at the scuola every day along with assistants, to conduct business in the name of the guardian and banca. Although official decisions still had to be approved by the banca, they often simply rubber-stamped actions of the cancelleria.

An eighteenth-century diagram (see table 1.4) from the Scuola di San Rocco shows the complexity that was built into the administration of the scuole during their six-century history (once again, not unlike the situation in the government, whose Byzantine bureaucracy was world famous).

Rules and Regulations

Among the important duties of the officers, at least as forseen by the mariegola, was the maintenance of discipline and morality among the brothers. The rules of the various scuole were all quite consistent in their regulations, with forbidden actions and their punishments nearly identical in all. That the scuole would take on such an obligation is not surprising, given the origins of the movement that spurred their creation as an attack on the civic disorder and moral laxity that seemed rampant in thirteenth-century Italy.[52]

The scuole emphasized their role as forces for civic unity, as institutions that brought together all classes of Venetian society, by placing at the top of their lists of disciplinary rules a prohibition against treason or anything that might be against the interests of Venice: "First of all, we wish and order, that no one of our brothers dare or presume in any way or means, not even through others, promise, consent, or discuss any thing that would be against the honor and prestige of misser the doge and of the city of Venice."[53]

Most of the regulations, however, dealt with personal moral behavior. The scuole here demonstrated their dual nature as civic and religious organizations. They designed these regulations in part to help maintain peace and quiet, by focusing on behaviors that might not always be subject to civil punishment, but which threatened communal order. Beyond that, however, the scuole were interested in guiding their members away from sin, to help their quest for salvation, so that they could act as Christlike role models for the larger community. Some of the rules were painted with a broad brush: brothers were prohibited from committing any moral sin. If discovered they were to be admonished, given a penance, and have their name written in a special book. If the brother reformed, and did not repeat the sin during a probationary period of up to two years, his name would be removed from the book; if he repeated the sin, he would be

TABLE 1.4.   The organization of the Scuola Grande di San Rocco
in the eighteenth century

The scuola

---

general chapter
  banca e zonta
    banca
      guardian grande
      vicario, guardian da mattin, scrivano
      degani di mezz'anno and degani [di tutt'anno]
      masseri
    zonta
      sindici
      12 former officers
      outgoing guardian grande
      visitor (inspector)
      supervisors of the church, of lawsuits, of buildings, of debts, of the sacristy
    [others]
      12 in zonta
      reserve members
      commissari: Donà, Moro, Zucca, de Todaro, Vecchia, Soranzo, Perseo
  [other members]
    brothers
    captain, fadighenti
    6 heralds for the sestieri
    bagnadori
  employees
    scontro (maintain daily account book) and assistant
    quadernier (bookkeeper) and assistant
    rent collector and assistant
    attorney, notary

The church

---

  chaplain
  sacristan
  mansionari (mass priests), coristi (singing priests), organist
  acolytes
  messenger
  collectors of donations

Source: ASV, SSR II 456.

expelled. Interestingly, the public nature of the admonitions and penances comes at a time when, with the new requirement of annual confession (mandated by the Lateran Council in 1215), the official church itself relied less on public penance, and more on private atonement.[54] Perhaps the founders of the scuole believed that, in some respects, as with their very public penitential processions, bringing all this out into the open would be a more effective means of achieving their goals. Beyond the general prohibition against sin, the mariegole spelled out some individual sins or violations, with varying penalties: thieves, for example, were to be expelled on a first offence. Also grounds for immediate expulsion were blaspheming God or beating one's father or mother. Blaspheming a saint or one's parent resulted in an admonition, as did speaking ill of the scuola, of the guardian grande or banca, or of another brother. Discord between brothers was not tolerated: if they failed to make peace within eight days, they were admonished. The rules strictly prohibited dice playing: in addition to the tendency for such an activity to lead to more serious sin, participating in the same game as the Roman soldiers at the foot of Christ's cross was simply not considered appropriate. Adultery was not acceptable, but was clearly not considered to be as serious a violation as other mortal sins (or at least one that was harder to stop committing): the offender was given anywhere from eight (at the Misericordia and San Marco) to fifteen (at San Giovanni Evangelista) days to stop, before being officially admonished. The mariegole instructed the officers to punish certain other violations of scuola regulations by the awarding of points, which could accumulate to a level that would trigger the imposition of a more severe penalty. These minor offenses could include failure to attend required processions, failure to visit sick or dying brothers, arriving late at mass or meetings, or neglecting to pay required fees promptly.

The mariegole also required the brothers to perform certain individual acts of religious observance and charity, in addition to those ceremonies conducted by the assembled brothers, which will be discussed in the next chapter. Confraternities in many other European cities regulated individual religious observance in great detail. In Bologna, for example, as described by Nicholas Terpstra, brothers first entered a confraternity as novices, undertaking training in worship practices. A full brother followed "a regimen specifying the prayers and psalms to be used at waking and sleeping." The rules "specified appropriate times, places, and postures for prayer," and members "reviewed the sins of the day each evening . . . , devoted a prescribed time every week to prayer, meditation and fasting [and] each Saturday [said] all the hours of the Office of Our Lady."[55] At the Florentine *laudesi* companies, brothers made confession every evening after the lauda service, and took communion several times a year, at the confraternity, administered by the company's confessor.[56] Compared with these, the Venetian requirements were minimal. The mariegole contain no regulations at all regarding private prayer or meditation (except in connection with the dead; see below). They obligated brothers to make a confession only once a year (San Marco or the Misericordia), the minimum required by the 1215 decree of the Lateran Council, or twice (the Carità), and to take communion only on Christmas and Easter (feasts not otherwise in the calendars of the scuole). The brothers performed both of these sacraments at their parish churches, not at the scuole, since they never employed confessors. In individual religious matters, therefore, beyond the punishment of specific sins, the Venetian scuole limited themselves to reinforcing the guidelines of the official church and supporting the role of the parishes.

The scuole took very seriously their obligations to minister to the bodies of ill brothers. Not only did they hire doctors to attend to the ill, and pay for medicines when necessary, but they required members to visit their ailing brothers. In theory, the guardian could command any brother to make such visits, but this duty, like so many others, tended to be left to the poorer brothers. If a member away from Venice fell ill, any other brother who found himself in the same city was obligated to assist his less fortunate associate, even without instruction from the guardian.

The obligations of the scuola and its brothers increased with the death of a member, spurred on by the medieval belief that the prayers of the living could speed a soul's voyage through purgatory.[57] The basis for this practice lay in the idea of the treasury of grace, by which the grace accumulated by a person's good works and devotion that was in excess of that needed to pass through purgatory (the largest amount coming from the saints and Christ himself) could, through prayer or indulgences, be applied to those souls with a deficit. James's admonition to pray for one another, cited near the beginning of most of the mariegole (see above), was read in the Middle Ages in this light, and was, therefore, one of the principal reasons for which confraternities were created and flourished.

Upon notification that a brother of the scuola had died, the guardian grande dispatched the fadighenti known as *bagnadori* to wash the body and prepare it for the funeral, a task traditionally performed by the family.[58] In a development of the usual medieval practice, in which many people requested that they be buried in monastic habits, the bagnadori dressed the deceased in the *cappa* of his scuola. The funeral itself was, of course, the ritual centerpiece of the confraternal services for the dead (discussed in detail in chapter 2), but was by no means the only activity. All members were obligated, upon notification by the degani, to say prayers for the deceased. The standard requirement, in the early mariegole, was for each brother to say fifty Pater nosters and fifty Ave Marias, that is a total for the entire scuola of 25,000 or more of each prayer, a considerable spiritual benefit. Alternatively, a brother could pay a priest to say a commemorative mass, or pay 4 denari to the scuola to arrange a similar ceremony. If a brother died outside of Venice, any other members in that city were required to arrange for prayers and a funeral, with expenses to be reimbursed by the scuola, and to notify the scuola as soon as possible of the death. The guardian would then notify all members, and funeral masses would be said the following Sunday. As will be explained below, the scuole also commemorated all their dead at a mass each Monday, and again annually on the Day of the Dead. The wealthier brothers often left bequests to the scuole that provided for annual, monthly, weekly, or even daily commemorative masses.

The Finances of the Scuole

At the beginning, required payments by brothers formed the principal source of income for a scuola. These included the *benintrada*, or entrance fee, the *luminaria*, or fee for candles, funeral fees, and an annual charitable assessment. Of these three, only the *benintrada* provided freely dispensible funds.

The *luminaria* (which was, for example, 12 denari piccoli per year at the Carità in the thirteenth century), as might be expected, paid directly for the candles that the scuola distributed to the members; any amount paid by an individual member that might be beyond the actual cost of candles he received would go into a pool (*monte*) to provide candles for poor brothers and fadighenti, those who were assigned tasks in the procession and therefore received their candles free of charge. An important element in building up this pool, especially as the number of poor brothers grew, was the practice of collecting whatever wax remained unburned from the candles used in processions or other activities. This could then be recycled and thus save the scuola a considerable sum of money (the expense for candles was always one of the largest regular items in the budget). The scuole assessed each brother a small amount for the funeral of each of the members (2 denari at the Carità). This paid for the candles and other paraphernalia required for the funeral mass, as well as the fee charged by the priest, for transportation of the body, and for the services of the fadighenti who assisted.

In the original mariegole, the annual gift also had a specified use: the annual charitable meal. This earliest of the communal efforts of the scuole to perform good works took place in Lent (the third Sunday in Lent for the Misericordia, the fourth Sunday for San Giovanni Evangelista, Passion Sunday for the Carità, and Maundy Thursday for San Marco). This meal also had another function, as a re-creation of the traditional Christian communal meal, an occasion for conviviality in the name of Christian love.[59] The Carità, for example, assessed its members 3 soldi piccoli each (whether or not they came themselves) for a meal "of two dishes without fish, unless it be served wrapped in greens."[60] The ceremony began with a mass:

> And after the mass is said, each of the brothers should dine with peace and charity, without any murmuring, each speaking the truth and saying words for the edification of our souls. . . . And all of our brothers having eaten patiently, the leftovers shall be given to the poor and those who work in the trades.[61]

It was expected, and so specified at San Giovanni Evangelista, that one needy person would be fed for each member of the scuola, with the money paid by brothers who chose not to come, and also using the food not eaten by the brothers who did attend. In later years, the scuole abandoned this meal, but continued to assess the fee. The funds collected were now distributed to the poor, either in direct cash gifts, or in the form of wine or flour. While confraternities in most of Italy directed this charity almost exclusively to poor brothers and their families, the Venetian scuole grandi also consistently extended their generosity to non-members.[62]

The scuole designated any funds of the scuola not collected for specified purposes as *beni liberi*. They used these first for some statutory expenses, such as salaries for some employees, the annual payment to the church or monastery with which they were associated (for rent, religious services, etc.), and the cost of oil to keep lamps burning at the altars and tombs of the scuola. In addition, some expenditures could be classified as regular maintenance; although not specified in the mariegola, they were unavoidable: cleaning and maintenance of the scuola and its possessions, purchase and maintenance of apparatus for religious observances, purchase of blank books for the various records of the scuola, etc. The expenses were so numerous that with no additional funds the scuole would have been able to do little beyond the bare minimum. Fortunately, some other sources of money could be classed as *beni liberi*: the annual dues of noble brothers, the income from property or investments bequeathed directly to the scuola, and funds donated to the various collection boxes placed at the scuola and at its altar in the church and carried in processions.

With the funds accumulated from these various sources, the scuole could begin some of the works for which they became famous: the buildings with their elaborate decorations. However, the scale and richness they wished to achieve—because of both the desire to glorify God, the saints, and the city of Venice, and the need to guarantee corporate and personal honor, by matching the splendor of the other scuole, who were often viewed as competitors—was clearly beyond the capacities of the regular budget of the scuola.[63] Large, special expenditures, therefore, almost always necessitated raising funds from the membership. Naturally, the guardian and other officers contributed the largest amounts in these campaigns (registered in lists called *rodoli*), but all except for the poor brothers were expected to give what they could. Once again, as mentioned above, the element of competition played a role: the guardian wished that projects begun under his leadership be at least as splendid as those of his predecessors or contemporaries at other scuole, and, of course, be completed during his own term, if possible. Therefore, they usually raised large sums of money quite quickly, and the results are still visible today.

It is the funds classified as *beni liberi* that will be of primary concern to us here, as they were the ones available to the scuole for music. However, money derived from another source, bequests (in the form of property or interest-bearing investments of deceased members and other devout persons) eventually dominated the financial affairs of the confraternities. The scuole attracted such bequests for several reasons. On the spiritual level, beneficiaries received the prayers of the entire membership, and, in the case of charitable bequests, of all those who benefited. On the more practical side, the scuole promised a long-term stability not possible with secular executors. Many of these bequests were quite small, and provided only enough money for the funeral (that is, for a funeral more elaborate than the standard one provided free of charge by the scuola) and for a perpetual *mansionaria*, or commemorative mass, to be administered by the scuola. Others, however, were much larger. Some testaments delivered to the scuole (and this was particularly true at San Rocco) vast properties both in Venice and on the mainland. Already by the late fifteenth century, this type of income made up about 70 percent of the budgets of the scuole. In the seventeenth and eighteenth centuries, the figure was closer to 90 percent (see table 1.5, part A). These large

TABLE 1.5. Sample annual incomes and expenditures of the scuole grandi

Part A. Incomes (in ducats)

Income Source	SSM 1431 (SSM 243)	SSMM 1531 (SSMM 303)	SSGE 1601 (SSGE 435)	SSMC 1644 (SSMC 230)	SSMM 1674 (SSMM 305)	SSR 1793 (SSR 310)	SSGE 1797 (SSGE 402)
Carryover	**35** (2%)	—	**82** (1%)	**459** (6%)	**1180** (13%)	—	**1078** (4%)
Interest	**532** (35%)	**1050** (55%)	**3196** (35%)	**1100** (13%)	**1434** (16%)	**12847** (48%)	—
loans	—	—	—	100	—	4564	—
government bonds	532	1050	3196	100	1434	8283	—
Fees	**290** (19%)	**210** (11%)	**254** (3%)	**13** (<1%)	**46** (<1%)	—	**117** (<1%)
dues	74	—	—	13	40	—	—
luminaria	71	210	—	—	6	—	32
entrance fees	145	—	—	—	—	—	10
Gifts and debt repayments	**4** (<1%)	—	—	—	—	—	—
Charity	**645** (43%)	—	**20** (<1%)	**8** (<1%)	—	—	—
Value of robes returned	—	**20** (1%)	—	—	—	—	—
Rents	—	**640** (33%)	**5263** (57%)	**6630** (80%)	**6500** (71%)	**3975** (15%)	**20268** (86%)
scuola properties	—	310 (16%)	5236 (57%)	610 (7%)	—	3975 (13%)	937 (4%)
in Venice	—	—	2285	—	—	2832	937
other	—	—	2351	—	—	1152	—
commissaria properties	—	330 (17%)	27 (<1%)	6020 (73%)	—	(not included)	19331 (82%)
Deposits in scuola	—	—	—	—	—	**8283** (31%)	—
Funds deposited in scuola's bank	—	—	—	—	—	**1536** (8%)	—

28

	SSM 1431	SSMM 1531	SSGE 1601	SSMC 1644	SSMM 1674	SSR 1793	SSGE 1797
Sale of candles	—	—	—	—	—	—	2255 (10%)
Miscellaneous	—	—	300 (3%)	—	—	—	—
Total	1506	1920	9115	1399	9160	26642	23718

Part B. Expenditures (in ducats)

Expenditure	SSM 1431	SSMM 1531	SSGE 1601	SSMC 1644	SSMM 1674	SSR 1793	SSGE 1797
Salaries	93 (6%)	104 (5%)	732 (8%)	260 (2%)	80 (1%)	5228 (22%)	2053 (9%)
chaplains, etc.	—	24	250	5	80	1102	772
musicians	—	40	100	—	—	—	—
physicians	93	20	100	90	—	—	—
administrators/servants	—	20	282	105	—	4126	1281
Charity	1066 (68%)	437 (23%)	1636 (19%)	699 (7%)	250 (2.5%)	2771 (12%)	2719 (12%)
poor of the scuola	174	85	63	109	—	2271	93
dowries	330	160	971	590	—	—	2546
hospital	148	—	—	—	—	—	—
alms	169	180	425	—	—	—	—
medicines	—	22	100	—	—	—	—
to free prisoners/slaves	—	—	—	—	250	—	—
other	—	—	—	—	—	—	—
Commissarie (may include mansionarie, charity, etc.)	—	—	1023 (12%)	c.3000 (29%)	c.3500 (36%)	(not included)	11820 (51%)
Mansionarie	142 (9%)	105 (6%)	367 (4%)	—	—	1130 (5%)	—

(continued)

29

TABLE 1.5. Sample annual incomes and expenditures of the scuole grandi (continued)

Part B. Expenditures (in ducats) (continued)

Expenditure	SSM 1431	SSMM 1531	SSGE 1601	SSMC 1644	SSMM 1674	SSR 1793	SSGE 1797
Candles	64 (4%)	200 (11%)	997 (12%)	430 (4%)	290 (3%)	2221 (9%)	717 (3%)
Maintenance of property	—	—	494 (6%)	1550 (15%)	430 (4%)	—	1720 (7%)
Taxes and fees	—	160 (9%)	494 (6%)	659 (6%)	450 (5%)	1844 (8%)	743 (3%)
Taxes	—	160	494	626	450	553	567
Fees to Inquisitori	—	—	—	33	—	1291	176
Investments (some forced)	—	80 (4%)	680 (8%)	—	—	—	—
Galley oarsmen	—	210 (11%)	960 (11%)	2286 (22%)	—	—	—
Scuola expenses	27 (2%)	314 (17%)	517 (6%)	838 (8%)	1090 (11%)	5403 (22%)	1683 (7%)
cape	27	90	—	—	—	—	—
funerals	—	—	—	—	—	—	75
processions and festa	—	24	95	288	270	1354	899
decorations	—	—	—	—	600	—	210
other or miscellaneous	—	200	422	550	220	4049	499
Interest on loans	—	—	—	175 (2%)	900 (9%)	350 (1%)	82 (<1%)
Payments to depositors in scuola's bank	—	—	—	—	—	3737 (16%)	746 (3%)
Church (other than items listed above)	—	—	—	—	—	294 (1%)	154 (1%)

Other	—	50 (3%)	592 (7%)	502 (5%)	1000 (10%)	1011 (4%)	795 (3%)
To be carried over	164 (11%)	200 (11%)	48 (1%)	—	1817 (19%)	—	—
TOTAL	1556	1860	3540	10399	9807	23989	23232
Balance	50	60	575	(2189)	(647)	2653	486

Sources: SSM 1431: ASV, SSM 243 (Quaderno 1430–38); SSMM 1531: ASV, SSMM 303 (Quaderno 1531); ASV, SSGE 435 (Quaderno 1601–4); SSMC 1644: ASV, SSMC 230 (Quaderno 1644–59); SSMM 1674: ASV, SSMM 305 (Quaderno 1636–79); SSR 1793: ASV, SSR I 310 (Asse della scuola; this document does not include the accounts of the Commissarie); SSGE 1797: ASV, SSGE 402 (Bilanci).

NOTE: In some cases, because of errors or inaccuracies in the original accounts, the figures have been slightly adjusted.

bequests required an entirely new level of administration: the *commissario*. The scuole appointed or elected a member to supervise the affairs of each bequest, or *commissaria*, to keep separate account books and carry out the wishes of the donor. In most cases, the income consisted of the rent from the properties, which had to be collected by the scuola. Some of these funds, of course, had to be used to maintain the property, administer the estate, and pay real estate taxes. For the most part, however, the testament spelled out clearly the mandated expenditures. The scuola could not use these funds for its own purposes (except in rare cases in which the bequest indicated that the funds could be considered *beni liberi*), but had to spend them for specific charities, some limited to the poor brothers of the scuola and their families, and others open to the poor of Venice more generally. These charitable funds, which before long greatly exceeded those generated through regular activities, allowed the scuole to carry out this aspect of their basic principles on a scale that their founders probably could never have imagined.[64] The most common of these charities was the provision of dowries for poor women, either orphans or from poor families. Other bequests specified ordinary alms, flour or wine, housing for the poor, hospitals, or stipends to poor widows. Once again, this activity of the scuole mirrored the central government: one of the oldest and most respected magistracies was the Procuratia di San Marco. The nine procurators, in dignity second only to the doge, and, like the doge but unlike all others, elected for life, administered estates left to the state, especially those of the nobility, and those for which the deceased left no heirs or other instructions. It was this magistracy that funded the public housing, hospital, and welfare system.

While the funds of the commissarie were usually exclusively restricted to the purposes enumerated in the original bequest, and were never available to the scuola for its own purposes, they were occasionally diverted by government order. In times of war, the state imposed forced interest-paying loans on the nobility and, beginning in the late sixteenth century, on the scuole grandi. The sums involved became increasingly large, crippling the activities of the scuole at times; at one point in the eighteenth century, they reached the almost unbelievable sum of 1,000,000 ducats to be raised by the six scuole. Usually, however, the government paid off these loans, although often long after originally promised, and they usually paid the intended interest, so the scuole were not always badly off. In fact, the scuole became so expert at handling estates and other large sums of money that many people trusted them to act as bankers, pooling assets of numerous small investors to deposit in the state funds. In the eighteenth century this activity began to rival the administration of commissarie for the attention of the officers of the scuole. Except in rare cases, neither of these activities, however, had a direct impact on the musical efforts of the scuole, and need not occupy any more space here. It is worth noting, however, that the administration of the ever expanding financial affairs of the scuole in the late seventeenth and eighteenth centuries necessitated an entirely new class of budgetary expenditures: professional managers. As early as the sixteenth century the scuole had employed a professional accountant (*quadernier*) to organize their accounts and balance their books, but this part-time position represented not much more than 1 percent of the total budget (for example, 20 ducats at the Scuola della Misericordia in 1531, out of a total budget of 1,850 ducats,[65] or 150 ducats at the Scuola di San Giovanni Evangelista in 1601 out of a budget of 8,540 ducats[66]). At the Scuola di San Rocco, however, by the end of the eighteenth century, such expenditures amounted to over 20 percent of the budget (3,870 ducats out of a total of 18,359).[67] Certainly, such large increases reduced the ability of the scuole to spend money on such activities as music.

Administrative expenses were not the only new items that reduced the freely available funds of the scuole. Particularly damaging were mandatory payments to the government, many of which were, unlike the forced loans, levied on an annual basis. From the 1530s on, the Senate regularly required the scuole to provide oarsmen for the galleys of the Venetian navy. While they occasionally accomplished this by direct assignment of poor brothers, the most common method was to pay non-members to serve, with the additional promise, usually required by the state, that they would be granted free membership in the scuola upon completion of their service. This expenditure grew to approximately 10 to 20 percent of the total budget of each scuola.[68] Finally, the Magistrato sopra le scuole grandi (see below) assessed a growing amount, up to 7 percent by the late eighteenth century, in the form of fees for required services.

Table 1.5 shows representative budgets for several scuole. It should be noted that the number of complete account books surviving is relatively small, and that not all are arranged in a way that facilitates creating such summaries.

Government Supervision and Regulation of the Scuole

As explained earlier, the scuole grandi never came under the jurisdiction of either secular or monastic clergy. Not long after the scuole began, however, the government, in the form of the Council of Ten, started to concern itself with their activities. The government originally created the Council of Ten in 1310 to deal with internal rebellion, but it had expanded its powers (as it would continue to do for the remainder of the life of the Republic), and now considered all possible threats to the good order and well-being of Venice to be within its purview.[69] The scuole grandi came to its notice quite early for the disruption they caused in the early fourteenth century when rushing to arrive first at the Piazza San Marco for processions, especially, it seems, for the feast of Saint Mark. On 9 March 1312, the Council made the first of numerous attempts to control this problem, restricting the times they could meet or process.

By the middle of the century, the council, worried about the potential of the scuole as opportunities for individual nobles to gain greater influence, or as centers for conspiracies or rebellions of any sort, began to pay attention to their membership, requiring, in 1366, that the list of new members be brought to the council each March for its approval. In the early fifteenth century, the council addressed the social class of the members: in 1409 they eliminated all the old restrictions on the admission of nobles (limited numbers, restricted ages, and special fees); the numbers of nobles in each scuola, however, did not really change, nor did their role. That same year, the council put into law practices regarding the role of *cittadini* in the government of the scuole. They now required all the officers to be "cittadini originari per nation e non per privilegio," that is native-born members of that class.[70] A foreigner could be considered a *cittadino* after a specified number of years in the city exercizing a profession; his children could then qualify automatically, if born in the city. The rank of *cittadino originario* could be achieved only after three continuous generations of birth and residence in Venice. An exception was granted to those who had already been members of a scuola for twenty years. The strict limitation to *cittadini originari* seems not to have been enforced; many, if not most, of the officers were ordinary *cittadini*, that is lawyers, doctors, and notaries, rather than the government secretaries and notaries of the more exclusive class. The council instituted a restriction on this upper class in 1461, although never carefully enforced: so as not to be distracted from the duties of their important posts, no member of the Cancelleria Ducale, that is the highest level government secretaries, could serve as an officer. In 1484, the council prohibited any two persons related in any way from serving concurrently as officers.

Throughout the fifteenth and sixteenth centuries, the council continued to address problems concerned with disorders in processions, but these decrees, as well as others dealing with musicians, will be discussed later. At least once, in 1447, the council issued a decree to avoid a recurring public disturbance by the scuole. This stated that the scuole had adopted the practice of ringing bells for deceased brothers as long as three or four hours continuously. Now, in a time of plague, this continual ringing "is a great disturbance to severely ill persons living nearby, and also an annoyance to healthy ones,"[71] so they limited ringing to one half-hour per death.

In the sixteenth century, the council began the practice of overseeing the expenditures of the scuole. They were constantly concerned that the scuole were losing their original purpose as devotional and charitable institutions and becoming organizations for display and luxury. Just as they (and also another magistracy, the Provveditori alle Pompe) limited the display permitted the nobility, they now restricted the splendor of the scuole:

> The superfluous expenditures both for decoration and for meals made by the scuole grandi of our city have grown so much, that it has by now become an abomination, such that, if some provision is not made, a good part of the funds of the scuole, which should go for alms to the poor, will be consumed in such abuses. In addition, [because] the guardiani grandi and leaders of those scuole spend so much of their own money on pomp, in a short while one will not find anybody who wants to enter [those offices], not being able, nor wishing to compete in expenditures with their predecessors. Therefore, the motion is made that by the authority of this council, it is decreed, that from now on, in none of the five scuole is it permitted to make display or decoration or other ornament or construction, except for the backs along the benches, and the seats above them, and also it is not permitted, neither out of the scuola's funds nor out of their own [purses], to present a meal or dinner, either in the scuola or outside, under penalty of 50 ducats, to be dispensed to the poor of that scuola.[72]

Similar restrictions occurred several times during the century. Clearly, as stated above, the council did not entirely accept the justification that the acquisition of honor was a sufficient foundation for these expenditures.

Early in the sixteenth century, governmental bodies other than the Council of Ten had tried to extend their influence over the scuole, in part to raise money for military affairs, so in 1508, the council decreed that it had sole authority over the scuole, and that all decisions regarding them had to pass through their office before being executed. By the end of the century, the constant supervision they now felt necessary was becoming too burdensome for the entire council to deal with, and it was delegated to the powerful sub-group of the council, the heads (*capi*), three members selected for one-month terms, who were "on duty" nearly continuously during that term. By the early seventeenth century, the council decided that it had more important matters to deal with, and assigned the responsibility of dealing with the scuole, at first in 1623 for a two-year trial period, renewed once, and then in 1627 permanently, to a newly created body elected by the council (and later by the Senate): the Inquisitori e Revisori sopra le Scuole Grandi.

Although the Council of Ten retained ultimate authority over the scuole, it would step in only when absolutely necessary. The inquisitori existed solely to regulate these six confraternities, and they took the job very seriously. In 1644 the council clarified their authority, requiring that all decisions voted on by the scuole had to be approved by the inquisitori before they could take effect. Before long, the inquisitori also reviewed the financial records of the scuole, and continued to maintain a tight rein, frquently overruling or modifying decisions of the chapter, including elections of officers. They often issued decrees regarding expenditures, either as general policy for all scuole or on an individual basis, acting quickly to curtail any extravagances (often, as we shall see, regarding music, at least in part).

In at least one respect, the Inquisitors were of direct assistance to the scuole. It was often difficult for scuole to collect debts owed to them, either for dues or, more importantly, from rents on property they owned or managed. With the creation of the inquisitori, this was made easier: the officers needed only to appeal to the inquisitori for assistance, and an official messenger was sent, carrying the authority of the inquisitori and, by extension, of the feared Council of Ten, to the debtor. Payment usually followed within a very short interval.

The final government actions regarding the scuole were far worse than even the most restrictive decisions of the Council of Ten or the inquisitori. After the fall of the Republic to Napoleon in 1797, the new Democracy took direct control of the scuole. The government, especially after the French turned over Venice to Austria in late 1797, limited their freedoms, and often froze their officers in place: new laws prohibited the guardiani grandi, once proud leaders of ancient confraternities, from resigning their positions, and forced them to dismantle their institutions, delivering the silver and other possessions to the revolutionary government, and even turning over their halls to the army for use as barracks. The government, now back in the hands of the French, in the form of Napoleon's

Kingdom of Italy, seized their remaining assets on 25 April 1806.[73] Mercifully, perhaps, a decree of 26 May 1807 put the scuole out of their misery, and suppressed them definitively.[74] Only the Scuola di San Rocco, miraculously, and by somewhat questionable means (they declared themselves to be an educational and health-related institution) was allowed to continue in operation, although in greatly reduced circumstances.[75] The others, after nearly 550 years of continuous service to the community, both in terms of charitable works, spiritual edification, and artistic and musical splendor, simply ceased to exist.

The Archives of the Scuole

The scuole grandi maintained careful records of their activities throughout their history, in part because of the need to make decisions based on precedent. However, they sometimes preserved even papers of little value beyond the moment, probably simply out of habit. At the beginning, the various officers simply held the records that pertained to their particular responsibilities. Before long, however, they set aside a place in the scuola for the documents, first a cabinet, later a room. By the eighteenth century, the archives were so extensive that most of the scuole elected (or hired) an archivist to look after them.

Mariegole and Notatori

The heart of a scuola's archive in its primitive form was the mariegola, containing both constitution and membership list. The scrivano also maintained another book, containing a list of brothers who had been admonished for rules infractions, and some sort of register of financial matters; no examples of the latter two survive from the thirteenth or fourteenth centuries, so their format and contents are not well understood. The mariegola as originally designed was not long sufficient for the needs of the scuola. Although it contained sufficient room to add new regulations for at least a century, the section containing the membership list quickly needed replacement. The scuole then began new books containing only lists of brothers, also, confusingly, called mariegole, or sometimes *mare fratelli*, which were used until filled up, and then replaced. The lists, both in these supplements and in the original mariegole, sometimes had several special sections, other than that designed for regular members, including separate lists of nobles, priests, doctors, and, occasionally, musicians, when they were admitted as extra members. All of the lists included the name of the brother, an indication of his profession (often omitted), and the parish in which he resided. Some included the date of admission, but this became a consistent practice only later on. The name of a brother expelled for violations of regulations would be scraped off the vellum page. The scribes marked the names of deceased brothers with a cross, and occasionally indicated the date of death. The scuole sometimes maintained separate records of deaths and of officers. Several of these lists provide useful information regarding musicians. At times, the scuole inducted the hired singers and instrumentalists as regular brothers, so their names appear alongside all the others, usually bearing the designation, "per cantador," meaning that the person was admitted as a singer, not in the usual manner. There were also quite a few regular members whose professions, as indicated in the lists, were musical in nature: singers (*cantori*), instrumentalists (*sonadori*), wind players (*piffari*), organists (*organisti*), organ builders (*organari*), luthiers (*lauteri*), and the like.

By the fifteenth century, the original mariegola could no longer hold the newly enacted regulations, and a place was also needed to record decisions of the Council of Ten, which now began to issue decrees for the scuole. The solution was another parchment volume, sometimes known simply as such (*libro bergamena*), treated as a direct successor of the mariegola. At some point in the century, the scuole (or perhaps the Council of Ten, although no decree on this matter survives) decided that a record should be kept of each official meeting of the scuola, both of the general chapter and of smaller groups. The new book, usually referred to as a *notatorio* (sometimes also as *libro* or *registro di parti*), listed, for each meeting, the members attending, with officers listed first and so designated. When the scuole held elections, the scribes recorded all candidates and their votes, as well as motions proposed and the results of the balloting on those issues. Beginning in the sixteenth century, these books included lists of those granted various forms of charity, and also petitions for charity and any other matter that came before the officers. These books, varying greatly in format and period of time covered, continued to be used until the scuole were suppressed, and nearly complete series survive for each scuola; they form the single most important group of sources for documentation of musical activities. They provide not only the records of decisions to hire musicians, but also lists of their duties, problems with their performance or behavior, elections of individual singers and instrumentalists, and information on the construction and repair of organs.

By the seventeenth century, the number of notatori had grown so much that it had become difficult to locate the necessary precedents. Therefore, usually under the direction of the sindici, archivists prepared summaries and indexes. The summaries or compilations often contained every single decision, recopied and arranged by subject. Indexes could refer either to the original notatori or to the summaries. The scuole also kept separate books with copies of decrees by the Council of Ten and the inquisitori.

In the seventeenth and eighteenth centuries (and possibly earlier), the scribes did not record the events of the meetings directly into the notatorio, but wrote them first on loose sheets, to be recopied later. These loose sheets, the *atti diversi dei cancellieri*, survive from most scuole for the eighteenth century, and sometimes include supporting documentation not copied into the formal books. Also, during these last two centuries, all decisions had to be ratified by the inquisitori. The scribes made copies to be delivered to the inquisitori, to be returned with their approval (or disapproval). Packets of these *approvazioni* also survive, as do some of the books belonging to the inquisitori in which their secretaries copied decisions and approvals (at the expense, of course, of the scuole).

Account Books

Another vital type of documentation, less well preserved, is the account books of the scuole. It is not known what form they took in the earliest years, but they became quite standardized by the sixteenth century (this statement is based on only a few surviving examples; they are quite similar in format, however to the numerous, and nearly complete, series from the eighteenth century). The basic, and simplest, financial record was the *giornale cassier*, the book the *cassiere* of the scuola maintained, in which he recorded each expenditure and each deposit in the *cassa* as it occurred. This is probably also the way the scrivani kept the accounts in the fourteenth and fifteenth centuries. As amounts became greater and the variety of expenses grew, especially when the scuole began to deal with restricted funds, a simple journal was not sufficient. The solution was the *quaderno cassa*, employing the Venetian style of double-entry accounting. A bookkeeper copied entries from the *giornale* (or, in the eighteenth century, from a clean, verified copy known as the *scontro cassier*), into a section of the *quaderno* labelled *cassa*. Each entry now, however (and this was also done in the *giornale* itself), indicated not only the individual item of income or expense, but also to which fund, or budget line, it should be credited. The divisions included not only truly independent funds, that is the commissarie and capital investments, but also other specified items that the scuole wished to keep track of. These latter varied greatly with time and from scuola to scuola. Examples of such *voci* might be processions, candles, government fees, annual contractual payments to the church, musicians, rents, maintenance of houses, legal fees, "miscellaneous expenses" (*spese diversi*) and "extraordinary expenses." Restricted funds included alms, dowries, *mansionarie*, and the like.

Each division occupied a two-page spread. On the right side were the credits to the fund. These were sometimes direct income, such as rents, but could also be simply accounting transfers from the cassa. On the left side the bookkeeper listed the outlays, the debits to the account, transferred from the cassa section. Sometimes an additional layer was used: a first division into expenses for the scuola itself as distinct from the commissarie, and a second division into the various specific accounts. In all cases, the left and right hand sides of the page had to balance. In accounts with actual income (which, if it was rent, represented a transfer from a specific account for each tenant), the expenses had to be kept within the income. In accounts without actual income, money had to be transferred from the cassa as needed to balance the expenses already made. Therefore, each two-page spread contained, in theory, two entries for each item, on the debit side (almost always the left page) the payment itself, often in cash (*per contadi*), and on the credit side (normally on the right) the transfer of the same funds from the cassa. (In accounting terms, the transfer from the cassa, of course, had to precede the payment, as the money did not exist in the account until transferred; in reality, the payment was usually made first and the accounting transfer followed to balance the books.) In actuality, however, the accountants often indicated fund transfers into these accounts only at the end of the budget year, when balancing the books.

A single payment to a musician could be recorded numerous times in the archive: first, perhaps, in the form of a bill from the musician (these survive, and only partially, for San Rocco);[76] when the actual payment was made, it might have been written first on a slip of paper, and a receipt (either on another loose slip of paper or in a special book) signed by the musician (these survive only for San Rocco and San Giovanni Evangelista); next, or simultaneously, an entry was made in the *giornale;* this was later copied into the *scontro,* and then into the cassa section of the *quaderno;* then, if it was first classed simply as a *spesa di scuola* (not *commissaria*) it would be entered into that page; finally, it might appear under the specific rubric of singers, processions, or simply miscellaneous expenses; in some rare cases, each individual was given a separate *voce* in the *quaderno.*

Although this method seems complicated, the actual practices of the scuole were often even more involved. The above system represents the official and direct payments by the scuola's cassiere. There were, however, some separate accounts that appeared either lumped together in the official books or not at all. The guardian da mattin was responsible for processions, and was required to keep careful records (very few of which survive). The regulations allowed him a certain amount of money, and he had to pay all the fadighenti according to specifications. To this purpose, he maintained a type of *giornale cassa* of his own. In many cases, all that appears in the main books is a series of lump-sum payments, one for each procession, with no separation into actual payments to individuals or groups. The guardian grande bore the responsibility for the annual feast of each scuola (the situation is similar for certain large expenses such as for construction of the scuola or an altar and its decoration). If the scuola took on the expense, the situation was like that for processions, and a lump-sum would be the only record in the account books. Only for the Scuola di San Rocco do the accounts of the guardian grande survive, in the form of packets of loose papers labelled *cauzioni,* covering the period from 1600 on. For the first several decades, the situation is as described above: there are detailed records of expenses for the festa, but the accountants recorded only a grand total in the registers. Later on, the situation seems to be more like that at the other scuole: there are either no payments listed for the feast or only very small ones. Neither case represents reality. Instead, the guardian grande paid for the feast out of his own pocket, or with the assistance of his fellow officers. In the latter case, they divided up the expense in a *partidor* or *comparto,* in which each was responsible for a set fraction (usually expressed in carats, or twenty-fourths) of the total. With very rare exceptions, no records of such expenses survive in the archives of the scuole: the moneys, after all, were not the scuola's and there would be no reason to keep records of them (if private account books of any guardiani survived, they might fill in this important gap.)

Other Records Regarding the Scuola's Own Activities

In addition to their separate account books, the officials in charge of processions maintained several other kinds of records. One rare type (examples of which survive for San Giovanni Evangelista for the early fifteenth century and again in 1570, and for San Rocco from 1521) provides prescriptions for the processions and other ceremonies of the scuola, arranged in calendar order. These are invaluable for understanding musical activities, which sometimes occupy a prominent place in these books. Another form of information recorded for processions was lists of fadighenti, sometimes with the payment indicated (in cash or candles and bread), for each procession, or as they were elected annually. As singers and instrumentalists were often classified as fadighenti, these lists can provide the best indication of the musical personnel at the scuole. Lists of this type survive in scattered form for various scuole. Those scuole that had their own church (San Rocco, San Giovanni Evangelista, and the Misericordia) also kept service records for the singers employed there (sometimes these were entirely separate from those for processions).

Each scuola also kept a detailed inventory of its possessions, including paintings, silver ceremonial apparatus, processional paraphernalia (that is, candlesticks, banners, umbrellas, torches, etc.), relics, and books. On rare occasions, these provide some information directly useful for the present study, notably the presence of an organ in the scuola. Striking for their absence in these lists are books of music, with the exception of a few references to liturgical books. In fact, only one liturgical book from before the eighteenth century survives, a fourteenth-century gradual for selected feasts from the Scuola della Carità.[77] The San Rocco archive contains some eighteenth-century service books from its church along with the only examples of manuscripts of polyphonic music for a scuola to survive: two large books of simple three- and four-part masses and motets from the middle of the eighteenth century (see p. 177).

Records for the Commissarie and Investments of the Scuole

More than half of the surviving archive of each of the scuole comprises documents concerning the properties and funds managed by the scuole but not under their absolute control. The largest group of these are the commissarie: testamentary bequests of property and funds with specified purposes. The archives contain large numbers of original parchment testaments, some as old as the fourteenth century, and many more in copies. A portion of the documentation is concerned directly with the administration of these commissarie. There are detailed records of the property, including rents and maintenance, as well as of the distribution of the funds for the specified charitable purposes. Unlike the Florentines, Venetians did not request that commemorative musical services be performed, so the commissarie are of little value for the present subject; rather, they endowed *mansionarie*, the daily, weekly, monthly, or annual saying of mass by a paid priest at a specified altar. In many cases these are carefully documented.

Account books for the commissarie survive, as do voluminous records of the disputes between the scuole and other real or presumptive heirs. These *processi* represent both private resolutions of the problems and lengthy court cases, sometimes stretching over several generations. Much information on property and housing in Venice and in the surrounding territories can be found here. Of considerable interest to scholars in many disciplines are another portion of the records of the commissarie. Occasionally, a testament not only named the scuola as administrator of specific possessions, but made it the general executor of the estate. Non-income-producing assets of any value would be sold to benefit the estate, but the private papers of the deceased individual might end up in the scuola's archive. These have not been well studied, but one has long provided valuable information for another area of musicological research: the private papers of the seventeenth-century lawyer and opera impresario Marco Faustini in the archive of the Scuola di San Marco.[78] Treasures doubtless still lie hidden in other *buste* of the commissarie.

Another class of documents, of even less importance to this study, are records of the investments in government funds managed by the scuola. There are separate account books for these *capitali*, and numerous registers and packets of *instrumenti*, as the legal contracts for the investments were called. Also concerned with this aspect of the activities of the scuole are the *filze* (packets of loose papers, originally, and sometimes still, held together by a cord inserted through the middle) of *atti diversi*, which contain copies of the instrumenti and records of action taken by the scuola in their regard.

Later History of the Archives

With the suppression of the scuole in 1807, the government transferred their archives to the newly organized Archivio di Stato. Unfortunately, a substantial portion of each of them did not survive those turbulent times. Inventories of the archives made late in the eighteenth century, while the scuole were still active, include nearly complete series of filze, from the sixteenth century on, for the guardian grande and guardian da mattin, an almost uninterrupted run of account books, both giornali and quaderni, and numerous receipt books. None of those series of filze survives (for the different situation at San Rocco, see below), nor do the receipt books (except for a handful for San Giovanni Evangelista), and account books from before the eighteenth century number fewer than ten. Why these disappeared is not known: were they intentionally destroyed or thrown away to save space and effort, or were they forgotten because they were stored apart from the other documents of the scuole, or for some other reason? While the original archives of each scuola certainly numbered over one thousand items, the current *fondi* in the Archivio di Stato contain far fewer: San Giovanni Evangelista has just over 500 items, San Marco over 250, the Carità and the Misericordia each about 350, and San Teodoro (which, because of its late formation and relative poverty, probably had a much smaller archive to begin with) about 120.[79] A few additional items from these scuole, though dispersed at the time of the suppression of the scuole, survive outside the Archivio di Stato, with mariegole and membership lists for San Marco, San Teodoro, and the Carità now at the Biblioteca del Museo Correr.

The situation for the Scuola di San Rocco is very different. Unsupressed by the French, it alone preserved its archive in a much more complete fashion, and kept it, for a while, in its original home. During the nineteenth century, two major sections of the archive were transferred to the Archivio di Stato. The French moved the *prima consegna* in 1807, and the Italian government transferred the *seconda consegna* in 1885. These two contain over one thousand items, including, unlike the archives of the other scuole, filze of the guardian grande from 1599 to the early nineteenth century and a long run of receipt books. Here, in addition, are original copies of the earliest notatori of the scuola. Also included are quite a few documents concerning the administration of the church of San Rocco, over one hundred filze containing the certificates, or *grazie* of dowries awarded to poor young women, and numerous miscellaneous papers of varying value. Archivists inventoried both the *prima* and the *seconda consegna* in the late nineteenth century, but a revised index is now in progress. A third portion of the archive never left the scuola and remains there today. The Archivio di San Rocco includes the mariegola, a ceremonial, a complete run of notatori (the earliest two in late sixteenth-century copies made when the format was changed), numerous papers of various types, including some for commissarie (especially those that remained active into the nineteenth century), and more records of the church, including the two eighteenth-century choirbooks, as well as records of the nineteenth- and twentieth-century activities of the scuola.[80]

GATHERING TOGETHER

Ritual and Ceremony at the Scuole Grandi

Despite their various charitable, financial, and artistic activities, the scuole grandi were fundamentally religious organizations. They were originally founded to provide an opportunity for communal prayer and devotion, and these always remained at the core of their activities. Like all religious institutions, the Venetian confraternities established calendars of religious observances throughout the year and developed appropriate forms of ritual, often, as will be shown later, including music. Unlike secular and monastic churches, however, the scuole were not restricted to the official calendars and liturgies established in Rome or in other religious centers. Although their calendars, of course, were made up of officially approved feasts, unlike churches they had the freedom to celebrate only those that fit their individual needs. Furthermore, although formal liturgy certainly played a part in their observances, much of their ceremonial was participatory, and in the vernacular. Finally, and most interestingly, while processions played only a minor role in the ceremonials of secular and monastic churches, they formed the center of many of the rituals of the scuole grandi. These various ceremonies, all of them ostensibly opportunities to glorify and honor God and the saints, also served other purposes, either by design, such as the official processions that honored the city, or opportunistically, when individual officers (or groups of them) used them to bring honor to their scuola or even themselves.[1]

The Calendars of the Scuole

The original mariegola, or bylaws, of each scuola always included one or more chapters setting out the feasts on which the brothers were to gather for their communal devotions. The scuole modified these original calendars over the years, usually by adding new feasts, but sometimes by removing ones that had been celebrated for centuries.[2] Many of the events on the calendars were common to all of the scuole, including some of the most important feasts. Each scuola, however, also celebrated occasions not on the calendars of the others, for various reasons that will be discussed below. Further, an examination of those feasts omitted from the calendars reveals interesting aspects of the relationship between the scuole and local, parish-based religious life.

The feasts specified in the earliest mariegole numbered fewer than ten, including four Marian feasts, two from the Proper of the Time (Good Friday and Ascension), St. Mark's Day (as the patron of the city), and the Day of the Dead. In addition, the brothers were to gather once a month, on the first Sunday, which was declared their "ordained day." The relevant chapters, as in the following example from the thirteenth-century mariegola of the Scuola di Santa Maria della Carità, also establish the basic frameworks of the ceremonies, which the scuole gradually fleshed out over the following years:

> We also ordain and establish, that all the brothers of our confraternity and scuola who are in the city [at that time], unless they have a legitimate impediment, should always gather together on the days listed here in the church and place of the Blessed Virgin Santa Maria della Carità, with peace and humility, without any complaint. They must remove their worldly dress [and put on the robe of the confraternity], and with flagellation and peace they must go in procession in the city, carrying the cross and large candles.
>
> And these processions should be done the first Sunday of every month of the year, and on the four feasts of Holy Mary, that is her Purification, her Annunciation, her Ascension [*recte* Assumption], and her Nativity, and also on the feast of the Ascension of Christ, and on the feast of St. Mark the Evangelist with the [public] procession [in Piazza San Marco], and on Good Friday, and on the Day of the Dead after the feast of All Saints. On that Day of the Dead should be devoutly sung a mass for the souls of all our brothers who have passed from this life.
>
> And we desire that especially on these days, that is on the four feasts of Holy Mary and on the Ascension of Christ, and on the feast of St. Mark of the procession, and on the day of Good Friday, and on the Day of All Souls, each of our brothers should carry a lit candle in his hands throughout the entire procession.[3]

Almost immediately (perhaps from the beginning in some of the scuole), the scuole added a second feast of St. Mark, in June, to celebrate the rediscovery of the body of the saint in 1094 after the destruction of the basilica by fire. To the basic list, the Scuola di San Giovanni Evangelista added the feast of St. John the Evangelist, its patron, and Corpus Christi, while omitting, as did San Marco and the Misericordia, the feast of the Purification of the Virgin.

Most notable among the feasts excluded from the above list are Christmas and Easter. The absence, however, is quite easily explained. Although most of the spiritual obligations of the brothers were to be fulfilled communally, two, confession and communion, were treated differently, being almost always administered by parish priests. While the scuole did employ priests to say mass, they were not authorized to hear the two annual confessions (at times of their own choosing) the mariegole required of the brothers.[4] The mariegole also obligated the brothers to take communion twice annually, on Christmas and Easter, but the scuole deferred to the parishes on these important celebrations, and did not try to interfere with events traditionally celebrated with family and fellow parishoners.

The changes made to the calendars of the scuole during the fourteenth century reflect various aspects of the Venetian society of that time. The brothers of the scuole took very seriously their roles as citizens of the Venetian Republic. As discussed in chapter 1, the mariegole all expressed the brothers' devotion to the doge, and forbade any words or actions that might harm him or the state. One of the rare threats to the Venetian government, a rebellion by the Patrician Baiamonte Tiepolo and his followers, was thwarted on 15 June 1310, the feast of Sts. Vitus and Modestus. This minor religious recurrence quickly became an occasion for the state to celebrate its resilience, and the authorities decreed that there should be an annual procession, with the participation of the doge. In 1323, the scuole grandi added the day to their lists of ordained days, as in the decision by the Scuola della Misericordia, appended to its mariegola, "that the day of Saint Vitus should from now on be an ordained day just like the others, for the good health and preservation of our city of Venice."[5] The participation of the scuole added greatly to the splendor of the procession, ensuring the participation of an additional 2,000 robed marchers, carrying candles, with many of them flagellating themselves as a sign of devotion. After the defeat, on 16 April 1354, of the conspiracy of Marin Falier, the Senate declared that the feast of Saint Isidore would also be a day of celebration; the scuole grandi quickly added it to their calendars as well. This participation, at first perhaps a sign of the brothers' devotion to their city, soon became an obligation imposed on them by the state, expressly to ensure the splendor of the occasion and the participation of a large number of people from across the Venetian social spectrum. Since a major aspect of the myth of Venice was the support of the common people for the Patrician government, and since the two uprisings might be considered threats to that myth, the presence of a large number of *cittadini* and *popolani* joining together with the patricians of the government in celebration of the state was considered important enough to write into law.[6] The participation of the scuole added another element as well: whereas the governmental portion of the procession, centered on the doge, emphasized the secular power and dignity of the state (though the Primicerio and canons of St. Mark's participated, they were clearly part of the doge's retinue), the scuole served to project the image of ordinary Venetians as devoutly religious. When the government added new civic processions in later centuries, it always obligated the scuole to add them to their calendars as well.

The importance of trade and commerce to Venice and to its citizens resulted in another change to the calendars of the scuole. From the beginning, the scuole celebrated the feast of the Ascension with a procession. By the middle of the fourteenth century, however, that day had become the occasion for the principal trade fair of the city, the Sensa (the Venetian name for the feast). The requirement that the brothers participate in a procession on that day either must have had a negative effect on their business affairs, or, and this is even more likely, they were willing to suffer the penalties for missing a procession in order to attend to their businesses, resulting in poorly attended celebrations. In any event, by the late 1350s or early 1360s, the scuole began eliminating the occasion from the list of ordained days, "because of the business each of our brothers has, both with foreigners and for their guilds."[7] The Scuola di San Giovanni Evangelista, apparently unwilling to reduce the total number of processions, replaced the Ascension celebration with one on the feast of St. James (an important parish church nearby), on 25 July.

Two final fourteenth-century additions to the calendars of individual scuole were religious in nature. In 1369, the Scuola di San Giovanni Evangelista received its greatest treasure, a fragment of the Holy Cross, donated by Philippe de Mézières, a relic that would later show its power in several miracles, celebrated in the paintings of Gentile Bellini and Vittore Carpaccio now in the Accademia Gallery.[8] This Cross became the focus for the scuola's devotions, and a procession to the Venetian church of Santa Croce on the feast of the Holy Cross came naturally. Lastly, in 1385, the Scuola della Misericordia added the Purification of the Virgin, the only major Marian feast not previously celebrated by this Marian confraternity. Whether they included the feast out of real devotion, or so as not to be seen to be outdone in devotion by the Carità, the other Marian scuola grande, cannot be determined. By the early sixteenth century, then, the basic calendars were well established, with the scuole having most events in common, although with some individual variation (see appendix 1).

The number of events on the calendars of the scuole continued to increase during the succeeding centuries, primarily, but not exclusively, for the same reasons as the early additions. Several of the new occasions were civic processions: Santa Marina (17 July) in honor of the retaking of Padua in 1509 after the war of the League of Cambrai, Santa Giustina (7 October) to commemorate the 1571 naval victory over the Turks at Lepanto, the Redentore (in July) and Santa Maria della Salute (21 November) in thanksgiving for the lifting of the plagues of 1576 and 1631, respectively, and Sts. John and Paul (26 June) for the victory over the Turks at the Dardanelles in 1656. The scuole also established the practice of visiting their sister institutions on their annual feast days, so that St. Roch (16 August), St. John the Evangelist (27 November), and St. Theodore (10 November) were added to the existing Marian celebrations (already celebrated by all scuole) that served as the annual feste of the Misericordia and the Carità.

Some celebrations were limited to individual scuole, having been created for internal or local reasons. For example, the Scuola di San Giovanni Evangelista instituted processions in honor of miracles performed in the vicinity of two Venetian churches by its relic of the Holy Cross: San Lorenzo (10 August) and San Lio (19 April), and one to the church of San Martino to celebrate another of its relics, the leg of St. Martin. The Scuola di San Rocco added processions on the feast days of several churches with which it had connections: San Pantalon (27 July), as part of an unusual settlement of a property dispute, in which, as a sign of reconciliation, the scuola would visit the church on its feast day, and the chapter of the church would reciprocate on the feast of St. Roch; St. Francis (4 October), to the nearby Franciscan church of the Frari; and St. Thomas (21 December), the saint of San Rocco's parish church of San Tomà, among others.

One final class of celebrations was quite different: processions to the Cathedral of San Pietro di Castello on the Sundays of Lent. The cathedral and its bishop (who from 1453 held the title of Patriarch of Venice) had a different relationship with the city than in most other locales. The ducal basilica of San Marco, presided over by the *primicerio*, was the main church of the city and the site for all official religious state ceremonies, rather than the cathedral, which was located on the far eastern outskirts of the city. Because the government perceived him as a representative of Rome, and therefore a threat to the independence of the Republic, the bishop was kept at arm's length, even though he was always a Venetian patrician, and often, in effect if not officially, chosen by the Great Council. Consequently, he had a limited role in the official religious ceremonies of the city. As the religious leader, however, he apparently decided, in the early sixteenth century, to exercise some influence, and instituted a series of processions by the city's clergy to the cathedral on the Sundays of Lent, and "invited" (since he could not command them) the scuole grandi. They accepted, creating the only processions involving all the scuole with a destination other than the Piazza San Marco or one of the scuole themselves.

As the number of processions and other celebrations increased, the financial burden on the scuole grew proportionately. Eventually, the expenses became unbearable, and the scuole, either on their own, or at the direction of the Council of Ten or the Inquisitori sopra le Scuole Grandi, began to eliminate or combine events, or at least to make them less elaborate. In some cases, as will be shown, the principal economy became the elimination of musicians.

The preceding discussion has been concerned primarily with the religious celebrations of the scuole themselves. Two of them, San Giovanni Evangelista and San Rocco, also operated churches, and thus had much more extensive calendars, although the ceremonies conducted were often limited to a simple mass with organ accompaniment.

The scuole established particular rituals and ceremonies for the celebration of the varied events on their calendars. It is these rituals, including the role of music and musicians on these occasions, that will be the concern of the remainder of this chapter.

The Annual Festa

The most elaborate of all celebrations at the scuole were, ironically, those for which the least information has survived, the feast days of their patron saints: 25 March, the Annunciation of the Virgin, for the Carità; 25 April for San Marco; 15 August, the Assumption of the Virgin, for the Misericordia (changed in the late fifteenth century to 8 December, the Conception of the Virgin, to avoid conflict with the celebrations for the newly created Scuola di San Rocco); 16 August for San Rocco; 10 November for San Teodoro; and 27 December for San Giovanni Evangelista. At San Giovanni Evangelista there was a second annual celebration, 3 May, the feast of the Holy Cross, held in honor of the scuola's famous relic of the cross. These celebrations appear to have begun with a Vespers service on the vigil of the feast (Venetian practice called for the celebration of Vespers on the evening before many feasts without a vigil in the official Roman church calendar), a mass the morning of the feast itself, followed usually by a procession, and concluding with observance of second Vespers. Unlike the Florentine confraternities, among others, neither sermons nor sacred dramatic performances played a role on these occasions.[9]

As explained in chapter 1, the guardian da mattin or vicario was responsible for the ceremonies at all occasions except for the annual festa, and the extant books of ceremony all relate to that officer. In addition, the expenditures for most celebrations were from the scuola's funds, so that the account books record at least some information. The responsibilities and funding for the annual festa were quite different, most of the time. This celebration, alone, was the responsibility of the guardian grande, so that the books for the guardian da mattin or vicario make only passing reference to it. In addition, since the guardian often supplied the funds for the celebration, the scuola's account books record, most of the time, only a fraction of the true expenditures. It is likely, also, that the guardian grande exercised more latitude in organizing the celebration than that given the guardian di mattin or vicario for ordinary processions, as it represented, perhaps, the major event of his term of office, and an opportunity for him to demonstrate his wealth and power, as well as his devotion. A line in the otherwise highly detailed *Libro Vardian da Matin* of San Giovanni Evangelista, with prescriptions for all the events in the scuola's calendar (discussed further below), shows how different this one day was: "On the day of St. John on 27 December is made a solemn feast, and warning is made not to make a great feast since it is done with the funds of the scuola."[10] The limited contribution of the scuola itself came out of its ordinary funds, not out of those otherwise assigned to the guardian da mattin for processions, hence the warning regarding spending. In reality, the fiscal responsibility lay with the guardian grande.

The descriptions of the annual festa in the mariegole are minimal (as is the case, it must be said, for nearly all occasions in these early books). The mariegola of San Marco can serve as an example, describing only the usual procession with a mass:

> We also wish that on the feast of St. Mark in the month of April, all the brothers of this, our confraternity, must come with their robes to the procession, with lit candles in their hands, and they should have a mass to be said in that church under confession. And each time they go in procession in honor and revererence of misser St. Mark they should kneel before the door of that church, and each one should say three Our Fathers and three Hail Marys, so that the city of Venice, and all those who live there should and will have good health.[11]

A slightly more informative group of sources for these occasions are the agreements the scuole reached in their early years with the clergy of their host church. The late fourteenth-century compilation of rules and procedures for San Giovanni Evangelista includes in its description of the feasts of the year the following instructions for the Vespers on the vigil and mass and procession on the day of the feast:

Also, all the priests of the scuola should be made to gather on the day of St. Stephen, which is the vigil of misser St. John, patron of this blessed confraternity. The said priests, all honorably and magnificently dressed with their copes, should sing Vespers, with the organ playing, in reverence of the blessed evangelist our governor. Each of the said priests should always hold a lit large candle in his hand, and they should enter two by two in the manner of a choir, half to one side, and the other half to the other in front of the altar of the scuola of San Giovanni. After the Vespers are said, the guardian and his companions should provide a meal for the aforesaid priests.

Also, all the said priests and the brothers of our scuola should be gathered together on the other day, that is the day of misser St. John. All those priests, following the procedures described above, should sing the solemn mass. That mass having been said, the brothers should remove their street clothes [and put on their robes] and go in procession in this manner, that is, the said priests should go in front with the relics of the scuola under a parasol made of gold cloth or of silk. And on the said day the crystal cross should be carried. And after the said things have been done, each priest should be given his bread and his candle before leaving.[12]

One of the most interesting facets of the celebrations of the patron saints was the practice of all the scuole grandi assisting at each other's festivals. This mutual assistance insured the splendor of the occasion. This practice is spelled out clearly in the 1521 *Ceremoniale* of San Rocco, as in this entry for 25 March:

The day of the Madonna of March is the principal feast of the Scuola della Carità; our scuola is obligated to go and honor her because they come to us on our solemn feast. And the scuola should carry the crucifix, four golden large candles, and twelve golden double candles, all festooned, and the singers of song and instrumentalists, and it should go in the morning at the usual hour.[13]

On the feast of St. Mark, the scuole participated in two separate celebrations, the official procession in the Piazza, and the afternoon devotions at the Scuola di San Marco. The Scuola di San Rocco's contribution to the latter portion included music:

then [we] go to the Scuola di San Marco to honor them, and singing with our singers of song in the hall, and then sing in the albergo, the guardians greeting each other and rejoicing together. And then the guardian of San Marco shall give you a tied bundle of candles.[14]

The gift of candles was apparently standard for these occasions. The mariegola of the Misericordia indicates that on its feast, as a sign of respect (and probably also to guarantee a high level of splendor), the guardian should provide the officers of all the visiting scuole with elaborate gilded candles.[15]

Perhaps the best indication of the importance of the annual celebrations can be seen in the amount of money spent by the normally parsimonious scuole for those years in which they were funded as part of the normal budget. For example, the annual budget of the Misericordia for 1542 included 80 ducats for the procession on the feast of the Madonna. All the other processions, nearly twenty in total, were allowed a total of only 100 ducats, not including musicians, whose total annual salary for processions and masses was only 50 ducats.[16] Therefore, the average spent on most processions was less than 10 ducats, as opposed to 80 for the annual celebration. Contributions by the guardian grande and other officers very likely added to that amount. At San Rocco in the first half of the seventeenth century (as will be discussed in detail in chapter 6) the expenditure for music alone at the feast of St. Roch usually came to between 150 and 200 ducats (out of a total cost for the festa of about 250 to 300 ducats), significantly more than the combined annual salaries of the scuola's regularly employed singers, instrumentalists, and organist. Few annual musical events anywhere in the city (or outside) could have rivalled that splendor.

Processions

As mentioned above, authorities outside the scuole ordained two classes of processions in which all of the scuole were expected to participate regularly: the great civic processions, under the direction of the government, and the processions ordained by the Patriarch of Venice during Lent. In addition, each scuola held a number of processions alone or with just one or two other scuole, usually together with a neighboring church.

Personnel

These processions, details of which will be examined below, did not, of course, consist simply of a group of men walking down the street. They involved the wearing of specified costumes, the carrying and display of ceremonial and religious objects, always including candles, and sometimes including floats with depictions of people and events. The general membership of the scuole, however, had minimal responsibilty for such matters. They were obligated to wear the official robe, or *cappa* of the scuola, and to carry candles. The cappa, purchased by all except the group of *poveri fradelli* (the scuola provided theirs), was a long, white, hooded robe, bearing the insignia of the scuola. The earliest depictions[17] show the cappa with an opening in the back to allow for self-flagellation, but it is unclear whether the robe retained this opening as a symbol after the scuole discontinued actual flagellation. Though the evidence on this point is scanty, each scuola seems to have had its own type of candles, paid for by the annual *luminaria* assessed each brother (again, except for the poor brothers). Sanudo differentiates the scuole by the colors of their candles on at least one occasion, the procession for the alliance against the League of Cambrai on 15 October 1511. The brothers of the Misercordia carried green candles, those of the Carità red ones, and yellow for San Giovanni Evangelista. Instead of candles, the brothers of San Rocco carried green-gray torches. For San Marco, Sanudo failed to indicate the color of the candles.[18] He mentions candles elsewhere, but generally without reference to color. It may, however, have been a well-established tradition that was taken for granted in the documents. Because of the high cost of candles, the scuole (usually in the person of a designated *sachetiere*, who carried a sack for the purpose) collected the stubs and drippings to be melted down and reused.

The scuole assigned all the specific duties in the processions, the carrying of objects of various kinds, to *fadighenti*, selected from the *poveri fradelli*, or admitted specifically for the task, who in exchange for their labors received free admission, free candles, and some sort of charity, which could include alms, bread and wine, shoes, or even free lodging. These men were under the general supervision of the elected guardian da mattin, sometimes assisted by a senior fadighente, a sort of foreman, elected by the banca and paid a small salary, designated the *capitano*.

The types and numbers of fadighenti varied from scuola to scuola, and with time, including men to carry various sorts of objects to identify the scuola (banners, escutcheons, pennants), carriers of candles and torches of several types, men to carry relics and floats, along with canopies to protect them, and musicians. An examination of the practices at San Giovanni Evangelista, for which excellent documentation survives, can provide a fairly accurate picture. The 1570 *Libro Vardian da Matin* offers a list of these men divided into two sections.[19] The first (see table 2.1a) were those obligated to accompany the scuola at all processions and funerals. Even for those on this list whose particular functions were required only at funerals, attendance was mandatory at regular processions, but they simply marched as regular brothers. The second group (see table 2.1b) participated only in certain processions, when specifically called for by the guardian da mattin. The scuole gave each of the sixty-one individuals included in the two lists (that is, the statutory sixty poor brothers, described in chapter 1, plus the captain) one pair of white shoes each year, on the day on which the newly elected guardian da mattin took office. At other scuole and at other times, additional types of fadighenti can be found (see table 2.1c).

The records of several of the scuole indicate that fadighenti who remained brothers for many years changed jobs every few years, ascending a ladder of prestige (toward carrying the Cross or the *pennello*) as they gained seniority, and then to easier tasks, requiring less heavy lifting, as they approached retirement. When they were no longer able to perform any of the tasks, either because of advanced age or illness, or sometimes simply after many years of honorable service, fadighenti could retire and maintain their benefits, entering the ranks of the *giubilati*.

Annual Civic Processions

The most important of all processions in Venice were, of course, those ordained by the Signoria. While ostensibly religious in nature, many, in fact, as referred to above and in chapter 1, celebrated great political events of the Republic. Each also had its own particular route and procedures. The partcipants in these processions, the most important of the dogal *andate* (as the Venetians termed occasions on which the doge left the Palace in ceremonial fashion), included the doge and his retinue (with the *trombe d'argento* [ceremonial silver trumpets traditionally a gift in 1176 from Emperor Frederick I, Barbarossa], the *trombe e piffari*, and, often, the singers of the *cappella ducale*), the nobles of the city, the monastic and secular

TABLE 2.1.   *Fadighenti* of the scuole grandi

A. Fadighenti of the Scuola di San Giovanni Evangelista
required at all processions (from ASV, SSGE 16, section 7):

three pennant carriers [tre portadori del penelo]
four carriers of large candles [quatro de i zierii][a]
eight pallbearers [oto portadori da corpo]
four funeral singers [quatro cantadori vechi]
two to prepare the body [doi bagnadori]
one boatman [uno dalla barca]
one bell-ringer [uno dala canpanela]
two escutcheon carriers [doi scudelotti]
two reserve escutcheon carriers [doi scudelotti per respeto]
one foreman to lead the scuola [un capetanio guida la scuola]

B. Fadighenti of the Scuola di San Giovanni Evangelista
required at selected processions (from ASV, SSGE 16, section 7):

eight to carry the large float [oto porta el soler grando]
six to carry the large canopy [sei porta la onbrela granda]
four to carry the small float [quatro porta el soler picolo]
four to carry the small canopy [quatro porta la ombrela picola]
one to carry the large candle [uno dal cierio groso]
six candle bearers [sei candelieri][b]
five string players [cinque sonadori de lironi]

C. Other fadighenti regularly referred to in documents of the scuole[c]

three to six general assistants [masseri]
three to carry a monstrance with the consecrated host [portadori de Christo]
four to carry a relic of the Holy Cross or a processional crucifix [portadori de croce]
three to six to carry double candles [portadori di dopieri]
twelve to carry processional staves [portadori di aste]
four to twelve carriers of lanterns on poles [portadori di brazzaletti]
four torch bearers [portadori di torzi]

[a] At other scuole, and at other times at San Giovanni Evangelista, these are often specified as one or more of the following: ciri grossi, ciri d'argento, ciri d'oro, etc. These are the great candles with elaborate gilded holders that can be seen in Gentile Bellini's painting of the procession in Piazza San Marco.

[b] It is also possible that these were the men assigned to distribute the candles to the ordinary brothers, and to collect the stubs at the end of the procession.

[c] Note that the numbers indicated are only approximate; there was great variation over time and from scuola to scuola.

clergy (the latter particularly those in the nine congregations into which the principal priests were organized), and the scuole grandi. The Council of Ten regulated the participation of the confraternities, as discussed earlier, issuing numerous decrees concerning the order of appearance of the six scuole and their behavior.

Infomation about the activities of the scuole in the civic processions, outside of disciplinary procedures, is usually limited in the documents to lists of fadighenti and their fees. Three sources, however, do provide a bit more. The earliest, and least detailed, is a *ceremoniale* that forms part of a compilation prepared for San Giovanni Evangelista in 1355, and revised in the early fifteenth century.[20] A *Libro de ordeni* of 1521 in the Archivio di San Rocco, arranged by the calendar, describes the participants in each procession, with some of their activities, and, most importantly, for some of the processions, the order in which they marched.[21] Finally, the most detailed of all, the aforementioned 1570 *Libro Vardian da Matin* of San Giovanni Evangelista, describes not only the procedures, but also the routes taken by the scuola in each procession; most important from our point of view, it spells out carefully the role of music.[22]

The following discussion incorporates information from all three of the important sources mentioned above (and others, when available). For a complete listing, in calendar order, of the processions of the scuole, with brief discussions of their origins and routes, see appendix 1.[23]

ST. MARK (25 APRIL)

The celebration of the feast day of Venice's patron saint was, as one might expect, one of the more elaborate occasions in the calendar. San Rocco's ceremonial provides a detailed description of that scuola's participation, which included several floats (that is, platforms carried by the brothers in the manner of palanquins) with important relics, many candles of various types, ornamented with jewels and garlands of greenery, and musicians. Since this text provides the best picture of such an event, it is worth an extended quotation:

> On the day of St. Mark the Evangelist, [the scuola] goes to make an offering to the Most Illustrious Signoria in St. Mark's church. The two golden floats are carried, adorned with reliquaries, and on them are put St. Roch's finger and other things, adorned with candles and perfumes; and two canopies are carried, bearing the coats of arms of the five scuole grandi and of the Pope and of ambassadors of princes.
>
> Also, when leaving the scuola, twenty-four carriers of golden double candles are sent ahead, with three jewels for each candle and garlands.
>
> Also, behind those double candles are the four players of harps, viols, and lutes. Then, afterwards our glorious standard, that is the crucifix adorned with its outstanding and beautiful jewel, and with various ornaments, perfumes, and *oxelete* [bird-shaped censers?].
>
> Also, in front of that the monstrance of the host with two large candles, and two other golden candles all adorned with jewels and garlands.
>
> Also, the large candle carried on the night of Good Friday may be carried . . .
>
> Also are carried the small gilded double candles, and these are carried in

the hand; in all that is twenty double candles, divided in this way; and the double candles should be of wax weighing three pounds each, with their garlands:

In front of the first float are carried the aforesaid six double candles.

Behind the said float are carried six other double candles, which would be in front of the second float.

Behind the second float are carried the aforesaid eight double candles, which make, in all, twenty small double candles.

Also, after that come our singers of song, who sing as usual.

After them are our chaplain of our church with an accolyte, each with a candle in his hand.

After comes the guardian grande with all of his officers, each carrying the usual candle in his hand, and all the rest of the brothers.[24]

In addition to the usual circuit of the Piazza, where both Venetians and foreigners witnessed the spectacle, the ceremonial included a presentation before the doge in the Basilica, displaying the scuola's relics and offering a gift of candles to the doge, his retinue, and other dignitaries:

[The scuola] stops in the middle of the choir of St. Mark's with the Most Holy Cross, that is, the float is put on the floor, and is touched by our chaplain with the silver tassels, and [the relic?] brought to the Most Serene Prince for them to cross themselves, and similarly to the ambassadors, and one by one to all members of the Signoria; also are carried candles, to be distributed as [to the various dignitaries].[25]

Finally, the scuole went to the Scuola di San Marco for its annual festa, as described above. It should be noted (as will be discussed further in chapter 5), that the singers and players were near each other, but separated by at least three or four men, those designated to carry the monstrance and some candles. This practice has several implications for performance practice: they were probably too far apart to perform together while actually walking, given the softness of the stringed instruments in use (lute, harp, and vielle), but they were close enough to make possible their joining together whenever the procession stopped.

CORPUS CHRISTI

This celebration, though apparently purely religious in its origins, was used as yet another occasion to glorify the Most Serene Republic. It was the occasion for great display, including numerous floats and *tableaux vivants* mounted by the scuole. The funding for much of this elaborate pageantry came not from the scuola, but from the guardian grande and banca, some of whom apparently spent extraordinary sums of money attempting to outdo not only the guardians of the other scuole, but also their own predecessors. In the late sixteenth century the Council of Ten found it necessary to limit the amount of money a guardian could spend, as it became increasingly difficult for anyone to accept the post, knowing he had to produce a more elaborate and expensive display than his predecessor.

Among the essential elements of this procession provided by the scuole themselves was the display of silver vessels filled with flowers carried not only by brothers, but also by boys (perhaps young sons of members), who were dressed as angels, complete with wings:

Also there should be twenty-four angels dressed with our costumes, carrying in their hands various silver pieces with flowers and roses inside.

Also our brothers carry various kinds of silver in their hands; all of this silver is put in front of the guardian and his officers, and then the singers of song[26] go before the banca singing. The instrumentalists go in front of the monstrance. Then all the brothers with their candles in their hands follow behind the banca.[27]

Fadighenti carried the usual candles and banners, but the numbers were greater than at many other occasions. Those of San Giovanni Evangelista carried twenty-four "golden double candles adorned with garlands and jewels,"[28] and the men of San Rocco thirty-six.

The ceremonial of San Giovanni Evangelista makes only passing reference to the possibility of more elaborate apparatus peculiar to this occasion: "Sometimes some sort of representation is done with ancient figures drawn from the Holy Scripture, as desired by the guardian and his officers."[29] San Rocco's 1521 book is only a little more informative: "We make a beautiful apparatus with floats and people on foot according to the Old Testament, made entirely at the expense of the guardian and officers of the banca; because that is how it has always been done."[30] For more detailed information, we must turn to contemporary descriptions. Marin Sanudo's account of the Corpus Christi procession of 1515, for example, includes the following for the wealthiest of the scuole:

San Rocco, whose guardian is Ser Zuan Calbo, the great clothier, was very well ordered, with [boys dressed as] angels, silver, and many floats and *tableaux vivants* of the Old Testament; among the other floats were a globe with a *putto*, in another a ship with someone fishing in the sea [St. Peter?], and on another several nude *putti*. There were also the four Doctors of the Church on horseback: St. Jerome, St. Augustine, St. Ambrose, and St. Gregory. In sum, it was beautiful to see.[31]

Such depictions were the most famous aspect of the Corpus Christi procession, and the closest the Venetian scuole come to the renowned *sacre rappresentazioni* of Florence and elsewhere, but are never, outside of the brief references mentioned above, discussed in the documents of the scuole.

Following the circuit of the Piazza, on this occasion without entering the Basilica, the brothers were dismissed, and the guardian and banca of all the scuole went to the *canonica* of St. Mark's (beside the Basilica), where a room had been prepared for them (or perhaps one for each scuola). There, they removed their ceremonial robes, ate a meal, and waited until after Vespers, at which point a second procession began, with all the same participants, but this time "in secular dress" ("in veste mondane") to the church of Corpus Domini. This double procession was unique in the Venetian calendar.

THE OTHER PROCESSIONS

There were, by the end of the seventeenth century, eight other annual processions for which the Council of Ten ordered the participation of the scuole grandi (see appendix 1 for details): St. Isidore (16 April), Sts. Vitus and Modestus (15 June), the Invention of St. Mark (25 June), Sts. John and Paul (26 June), St. Marina (17

July), the Redeemer (third Sunday of July), St. Justina (7 October), and the Madonna della Salute (21 November). On these occasions, the scuole used the basic assortment of fadighenti, with occasional enrichments, such as additional candles, sometimes with garlands or jewels. The scuole went individually to the Piazza San Marco, where, after a circuit outside, along with the other participants, they passed through the basilica, stopping at an appropriate altar, and paying homage to the doge and Signoria, who were seated near the high altar. Then, all proceeded to the church dedicated to the saint of the day, if necessary crossing the Grand Canal, or the Canale della Giudecca by boat (for the Salute and the Redentore the crossing was made on a bridge of boats). In later years, this second portion of the day's events was often eliminated, at least as far as the scuole were concerned. Afterwards, the confraternities retraced their steps to their respective scuole for the brothers to remove their robes before returning home. Some of the scuole did participate, in a somewhat reduced fashion, in one other Dogal *andata*, on Easter Monday to the convent of San Zaccaria, though it was not legally mandated by the government.

Several important feasts did not inlcude the participation of the scuole. They did not join in the celebrations of the Sensa, the famous marriage of Venice to the sea, on the feast of the Ascension, nor did they go to St. Mark's for the official celebrations of the Marian feasts, though on some of these they held their own ceremonies or joined together at either the Carità or the Misericordia for their annual feasts. Also in this category were the *andate* of the doge to the churches of San Geminiano, San Giorgio Maggiore, Santo Stefano, San Giovanni di Rialto, San Giacomo di Rialto, and the Ognissanti, as well as celebrations at St. Mark's during the Christmas and Easter seasons. The official participation, therefore, was limited to those events with particular importance to the myth of Venice (commemorations of victories or the release from plague, and those dedicated to the city's patron saint), but not those more purely religious in nature, or related more directly to the doge as an individual figure. The scuole were omitted from the Sensa because, uniquely of all the *andate*, the procession was entirely aquatic, and the culminating ceremony took place at the exit from the lagoon into the Adriatic Sea; the logistics (and the expense) of the participation of the scuole in such an event were undoubtedly considered to be excessive.

Extraordinary Civic Processions

The *signoria* celebrated special events of many types with extraordinary processions, usually in the Piazza San Marco, with the participation of all those who usually marched in the most important regular processions. These special events ranged from solemn occasions such as state funerals to joyous celebrations of treaties and military victories and the welcoming of important visitors. An idea of the variety can be formed by examining the diaries of Marin Sanudo,[32] which describe, among others, the following processions in which the scuole participated: funerals of the ambassador of Milan (1497), Cardinal Zen (1501), Captain General Nicolò Pitiano (1510), and Captain General Bortolomeo Liviano (1515), as well as celebrations for the lifting of the papal interdict (1510), an alliance against the forces of the League of Cambrai (1511), the entry of the king of England into that alliance (1512), the signing of a peace treaty with France (1513), and the victory that ended the threat of the League (1515). The most elaborate of these was the procession in 1511 for the alliance against the League of Cambrai. Sanudo's description occupies seven long pages, detailing the participation of all the institutions of Venice, plus three pages listing all the patricians who participated. Holding a place of honor in the procession and in the description were the scuole grandi, who, as usual, led the procession, carrying adornments and floats far beyond the numbers employed even on Corpus Christi, many of which portrayed the members of the alliance and other symbols relating to the war.[33]

Such elaborate processions continued throughout the sixteenth century, with two of the most splendid occurring at the end of the period: one for the visit of some Japanese princes in 1585, and the other to celebrate the peace treaty between King Henry IV of France and King Philip II of Spain in 1598. Both are described in staggering detail in the updated versions of Francesco Sansovino's guide to the city of Venice and its customs.[34] Each of the scuole carried numerous floats, some to display their reliquaries and treasures, others depicting personages or events. Even the poorest of the scuole, San Teodoro, carried thirteen floats in the 1598 procession, while San Rocco carried over twenty, four of which portrayed the continents, and five of which depicted virtues.

In both of these processions, several floats carried musicians (apparently individuals and ensembles beyond those in the usual employ of the scuole, hired especially for the occasion), including four carried by San Rocco in 1585: one depicted "David, in royal dress, with a harp in his hand, which he played most sweetly";[35] another, in a series portraying the life of Christ, had "on a platform, the shepherds in their manger playing [instruments] for joy, and an angel above sang to them *Gloria in excelsis Deo*";[36] and, near the end,

> the Last Judgement, with Our Lord in a high place, and to his right he had flowers and roses, and to his left a very sharp sword; with these [on the right] he promised to the elect all contentment and happiness, and with those [on the left, he promised] to the damned every punishment and anguish. Below, one saw the dead issuing from their tombs, and one heard (without seeing) a great blaring of trumpets and drums, which brought great terror to those nearby. Afterwards followed a regal, played perfectly by a boy.[37]

The 1663 guide also described musical floats for the procession of 1598. One of those of the Scuola della Misericordia carried "a beautiful woman, costumed as Peace, accompanied on the same float by a marvelous and most noble consort of lutes, which played most excellently, and gave everybody pleasure."[38] One of San Teodoro's floats depicted "God, the Eternal Father, who was on the globe of the world, and at the feet of whom were five good musicians, who sang with beautiful melody, thanking His Divine Majesty for the peace granted to those two kings."[39] San Rocco carried a float with "a beautiful young man, richly dressed, who had one foot on the globe, and the other in the air, but he did not fall, playing most excellently a flared war trumpet; he signified Fame who went throughout the world."[40] Finally, following the six traditional scuole grandi, was the Scuola del

Santissimo Rosario, which had just been elevated to a rank approximating that of the other six, carrying, among others, a float "with four boys, who sang musically in praise of peace."[41]

Lenten Processions

Quite different from the civic processions were those held annually during Lent, organized not by the Signoria, but by the Patriarch. These Lenten processions had as their ultimate destination the cathedral of San Pietro di Castello, at the extreme eastern tip of Venice. The motivation for these processions is detailed in a document of San Rocco concerning the procession on *Domenica Lazzarea*, the fifth Sunday of Lent, in 1519:

> It seems that several years ago the Most Reverend monsignor patriarch at the time persuaded and beseeched all of the scuole to come after dinner on Lazarus Sunday to a procession that His Most Reverend Lordship made for all the parish priests of the city, and this was also done because of the many relics found in that church, and especially because of a piece of wood from the cross of our Savior, so that, for those reasons His Most Reverend Lordship does that procession for the praise and glory of Our Lord God.[42]

The first of these processions (in terms of the liturgical calendar) was the Sunday before Lent itself, Carnival Sunday, when "[the scuola] begins to go at night to Castello, leaving from the scuola at about 2 o'clock [in the morning], and visiting [churches on the way]."[43] In other words, the brothers did not go directly to San Pietro; in the case of San Giovanni Evangelista the procession stopped at the church of San Salvador, though it was the option of the guardian da mattin to extend the procession to other destinations, to make it more like those on the following Sundays.

The processions on the Sundays of Lent itself, including Palm Sunday, were considerably more complex, involving not one visit, but a series of them. The 1570 *Libro Vardian da mattin* for San Giovanni Evangelista describes the procedure in detail, including an important indication of the role of music, in particular the lauda. It should be noted that on these solemn occasions, the fadighenti carried fewer elaborate objects than on the festive processions in the Piazza, including only candles, torches, and lanterns. The route (see figure 2.1) was as follows:

> To San Salvador [Augustinian canons], a lauda is sung
> To Santo Sepulcro [Franciscan nuns], and a lauda is sung
> To San Giuseppe [Augustinian nuns], and a lauda is sung
> To the Hospital of Gesù Cristo, that is in the church, and a lauda is sung
> To Sant'Antonio [Augustinian canons], and a lauda is sung
> To Sant'Anna [Benedictine nuns], and a lauda is sung
> To San Pietro di Castello [the cathedral], and there, under confession a lauda is
>   sung, and then at our usual altar, with the pennant on the right side, at which
>   altar our chaplain says a mass
> Four yellow candles are brought for that altar, and twelve to put on the candlesticks
>   of the chapel, and on the return [the scuola] goes to the Madonna delle Vergini
>   [Augustinian nuns], and a lauda is sung

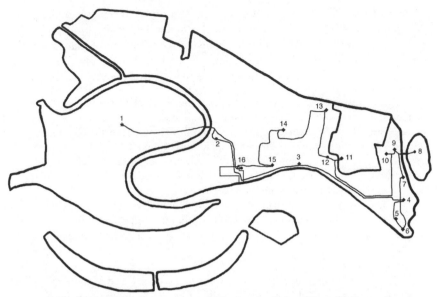

FIGURE 2.1. Routes of the processions of the Scuola di San Giovanni Evangelista for Palm Sunday and the Sundays of Lent

Legend: 1. Scuola Grande di San Giovanni Evangelista; 2. San Salvatore; 3. Santo Sepolcro; 4. San Giuseppe; 5. Ospedale di Gesù Cristo; 6. Sant'Antonio; 7. Sant'Anna; 8. San Pietro di Castello; 9. San Daniele; 10. Santa Maria delle Vergini (fourth Sunday in Lent only); 11. Santa Maria dell'Arsenale; 12. Ospedale di San Martino; 13. Santa Maria della Celestia; 14. San Lorenzo; 15. San Zaccaria; 16. San Marco

> To San Daniel [Augustinian nuns], and a lauda is sung
> To the Madonna of the Arsenal [a votive church], and a lauda is sung
> To the Hospital of San Martino, and a lauda is sung
> To Santa Maria della Celestia [Cistercian nuns], and a lauda is sung
> To San Lorenzo [Benedictine nuns], and a lauda is sung
> To San Zaccaria [Benedictine nuns], and a lauda is sung
> To San Marco, and at the altar of the Most Holy Sacrament, a lauda is sung, and
>   then return home.[44]

The documents do not explain the rationales behind the particular stops on this route, though devotion to particular saints, or the presence of noted shrines, particularly if an indulgence for visiting them could be obtained, would have been an attraction. Moreover, the scuola may also have been honoring locations where its dead were buried. On the other hand, the wide range of the procession could have been thought of as a way to bring the blessing of the patron saint of the scuola to people thoughout the city, or to demonstrate the city-wide role of the confraternity.[45] Although such descriptions (or prescriptions) do not survive for the other scuole, it can be assumed that they followed similar practices, although the specific routes probably varied. San Giovanni Evangelista omitted the procession on the third Sunday of Lent as on that day they held one of the regular meetings of the general chapter. On the fourth Sunday the scuola added some other ceremonies, including one stop on the return leg of the procession. The scuola had established relationships with several convents, principally involving exchanges of masses and commemorations for their deceased. This Sunday was the occasion for the scuola to commemorate the dead of the various convents:

> On the fourth Sunday of Lent [the scuola] goes at night to Castello with the procedures and visits as above, inquiring at the convents of the nuns who are our sisters if any of them died this year, and how many. If there were deaths, our funeral singers perform the ceremonies at the tombs as they do at funerals of our brothers, reminding everyone that they are obligated to say the Our Fathers as are said for our brothers at the place of their death; they are not told to say masses because that is not done for nuns.
>
> The old and new guardiani da mattin go together, the old one in front, and the new one behind. After the mass is said at [San Pietro di] Castello, [the scuola] goes to the church of Santa Maria delle Vergini, and our solemn singers sing a lauda.[46]

At San Rocco, the procession to Castello was preceded by one to the Frari, where the officers displayed to the friars their relic of the Holy Blood, returning to the scuola after a circuit of the *campo* of the Frari.[47]

On Palm Sunday, in addition to the procession, the scuole distributed palms to distinguished citizens of the city, including the patriarch, the doge, the grand chancellor, and the scuola's chaplain at the cathedral, as well as to the abbesses of five of the convents they visited (San Zaccaria, Sant'Anna, Santa Maria delle Vergine, Santa Maria della Celestia, and San Lorenzo). The brothers also carried palms for the guardiani da mattin of the other scuole, whom they expected to encounter as their varying routes to the cathedral crossed each other, creating an intricate sort of dance throughout the sestiere of Castello (San Giovanni Evangelista's route is reconstructed in figure 2.1): "when [the guardians] meet each other [they] shake hands and exchange the kiss of peace of Our Lord, saying 'May the peace of Our Lord be always with you,' and one gives the palm that he is holding in his hand to the other, and the other does the same."[48] Among all the brothers of the scuola, only the four singers received palms, perhaps in recognition of the extraordinary labors they were required to carry out during this season.

In addition to holding a ceremony similar to that at San Giovanni Evangelista (but described only summarily in its 1521 ceremonial) the Scuola di San Rocco conducted a service with polyphonic music in its church:

> On the said Palm Sunday a beautiful passion is sung in our church. Two platforms are built, one on each side of the main chapel, that is above the steps, covered with black cloth. On one are four singers, and on the other a priest, who sings [*biscanta*] the words [of the Evangelist]. These five receive three lire each. Then the six priests who respond in the mass receive ten soldi each.[49]

The climax of the Lenten processions came on the evening between Maundy Thursday and Good Friday. The fadighenti carried a number of items either used only on that day, or decorated in a manner unique to the occasion. The scuole participated in special ceremonies at San Marco (where they venerated a miraculous relic of the Blood of Christ) and conducted a series of visits, including to some churches not visited on other days. As with Palm Sunday and the Sundays of Lent, the procession was in the evening. The time of departure for the scuole was about one hour after sunset on Thursday, since no scuola was allowed in Piazza San Marco earlier in the day. The sixteenth-century documents of San Giovanni Evangelista and San Rocco depict an appropriately dark and somber affair. The fadighenti of San Giovanni Evangelista carried a number of items reserved for this occasion, including a black float with black parasol for the relic of the Holy Cross, and forty black lanterns, as well as some of the usual items specially covered in black for this procession: fifty double candles, the crucifix accompanied by twenty torches, and twenty lanterns on poles. The final item on the list in the ceremonial is of particular interest: "Flails for those who will come [to practice the discipline] for their devotion."[50] This is one of the clearest indications of the waning of the flagellant practice. No longer was the practice of the discipline the essential element of the activities of the scuole grandi, as it had been in earlier centuries. Even on Good Friday, only those who wished to do so performed the ancient penitential rite. In fact, this ceremonial book, although copied in 1570, preserves a late fifteenth-century text,[51] and this is the only sixteenth-century reference to the practice. Most likely, even that limited usage was extinct by the latter date.

The San Rocco procession was similar, but, as befits a wealthier confraternity, somewhat more elaborate (note that although this text refers to Maundy Thursday, the procession was held after dark, which, in Venetian practice, since the day begins after sundown, was already Friday; this probably explains why some other references to this procession, even in this same volume, designate it as Good Friday):

> On Maundy Thursday our relic of the miraculous thorn is carried on a beautiful float with the parasol newly made this year; it is carried in this manner, and first:
>
> The tabernacle with the thorn on the top of the float with eight silver candlesticks, with eight candles of four ounces each, and between each candlestick and the next should be a lit censer or other perfumes, and the tabernacle should be covered with a black veil.
>
> Also, four of our brothers who carry the parasol.
>
> Also, eight priests dressed in black copes with a double candle in the hand of each, that is eight double candles, four before and four after the float.
>
> Also, four priests dressed in black tunics who carry the float with the said thorn, that is in all twelve priests, and they have for their reward ten soldi each.
>
> Also, two accolytes with two thuribles, who go with incense in front of the said float.
>
> Also, two other accolytes who carry two incense boats in which are put storax [an aromatic resin].
>
> On the said Maundy Thursday our Crucifix is carried covered in black, and four large candles covered in black.
>
> Also, sixty double candles on poles are carried, because it was so determined this year by all of the scuole in agreement, and also because it is a beautiful thing to carry; afterwards are carried as many gilded lanterns as desired, but the sixty

double candles are sufficient; afterwards are carried by hand as many as are desired by the brothers.[52]

After making the usual circuit of the Piazza San Marco, the scuole entered the church. The two surviving descriptions of the ceremonies inside the Basilica have some common themes, but differ in their particulars. The brothers of San Giovanni Evangelista placed their crucifix and kneeled, witnessing the display of the relic of the Miraculous Blood owned by St. Mark's. At this ceremony, the *cantadori solenni* of the scuola sang a lauda. Then, at the altar of St. John, the brothers, again kneeling, presented the float with the relic of the Most Holy Cross while the singers sang another lauda. The guardian grande then removed the black covering from the relic, while the vicario uncovered the container with the sanctified Host; similarly, all the other objects were uncovered before the brothers left the church. The description of the rituals performed by San Rocco inside the Basilica is much briefer, and makes no mention of the Miraculous Blood: "And in the church they make their devotion and then sing, and then remove the covering from our glorious standard [and] uncover the crucifix. Then our guardian grande misser Bernardo de Marin kisses the feet of our crucifix asking for mercy."[53] The brothers, including some *batudi*, also brought an altar frontal to San Marco: "Remember that on Maundy Thursday the masseri send our altar frontal, on which are painted the Crucifix with kneeling batudi, to be carried to the church of San Marco, to be hung up over the door of the choir with its candles."[54]

The ceremonials of neither San Giovanni Evangelista nor San Rocco make reference to their procession to the cathedral of San Pietro di Castello itself on Maundy Thursday, although that is documented elsewhere (and perhaps taken for granted here), but both refer to several other visits.[55] The 1521 San Rocco book mentions going to the Hospital of Gesù Cristo for an indulgence, and to the nearby church of Sant'Antonio, both in the Castello district and not far from San Pietro. The list of visits made by the brothers of San Giovanni Evanglista is, as usual, more explicit, including San Zaccaria, Santo Sepolcro (an obligatory choice for this procession), the Pietà, the Hospitals of Sant'Antonio and Gesù Cristo, the church of Sant'Antonio, the Madonna of the Arsenal, and the Bridge of San Lio (figure 2.2).[56] As in the other descriptions in this book, the role of lauda singing is also explicit, with one required at each stop on the route. Missing from these processions were the *sacre rappresentazioni* standard for such Holy Week ceremonies in many other cities in Italy.[57]

In 1544, the scuole added to their calendars one more procession to Castello, on the Sunday after Corpus Christi, known as Domenica degli Angeli. By the middle of the seventeenth century, participation in the processions to Castello had fallen off, so to avoid scandal the Council of Ten approved their elimination, replacing them with masses in the churches of the individual scuole.[58]

Processions and Ceremonies of Individual Scuole

In addition to the civic and Lenten processions, official obligations shared by all of the scuole, the six confraternities performed numerous individual processions.

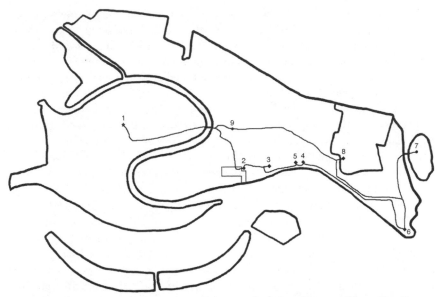

FIGURE 2.2. Route of the procession of the Scuola di San Giovanni Evangelista for Good Friday

Legend: 1. Scuola Grande di San Giovanni Evangelista; 2. San Marco; 3. San Zaccaria; 4. Santo Sepolcro; 5. Ospedale della Pietà; 6. Ospedale di Sant'Antonio; 7. San Pietro di Castello; 8. Santa Maria dell'Arsenale; 9. Bridge of San Lio

The reasons for these were quite diverse: honoring saints whose relics the scuola possessed, days associated with the founding of the scuola, celebrations of their host church or of churches in the neighborhood, and other occasions particular to the individual scuola. In some cases, more than one scuola participated because of some geographical or historical association. On one day of the year, the Day of the Dead (1 November), all the scuole held processions in honor of their deceased brothers, but with entirely independent routes and ceremonies. Finally, while many processions were permanent annual fixtures, others were one time only or had only a short lifetime. The recurring individual processions are listed, along with those already discussed, in appendix 1.

Most of the individual processions listed in appendix 1 entailed only very simple ceremony, with the fadighenti carrying a basic assortment of apparatus, and a route that consisted of a fairly straightforward walk around a nearby campo or directly to a church, returning to the scuola after a mass or Vespers. Some others, to be discussed below, had more complex ceremonies, or have particular historical or musical interest.

PROCESSIONS FOR SAN GIOVANNI EVANGELISTA'S
MIRACULOUS RELIC OF THE CROSS

The most famous possession of any of the scuole grandi was a relic of the True Cross donated to San Giovanni Evangelista by Philippe de Mézières in 1369.

Almost immediately, the relic began to work miracles, and it became an object of great devotion. In the fifteenth century, the scuola constructed an addition to its building for a special room to house the relic, and commissioned Gentile Bellini, Vittore Carpaccio, and others to paint a series of large canvasses depicting the miracles, as described in a pamphlet published around 1500, to decorate the room.[59] These paintings are still extant, but have hung for nearly two centuries in the Galleria dell'Accademia.[60] The ceremonial calendar of San Giovanni Evangelista included three important events connected with this relic: the feast of the Holy Cross (3 May) and processions to two locations associated with the miracles, San Lio (19 April) and San Lorenzo (10 August).

San Giovanni and the other scuole treated the feast of the Holy Cross very much like the annual feste. On this day, all the scuole came to San Giovanni for the celebrations, as they did for the feasts of the patron saints. The *Libro Vardian da Matin* states that in earlier times, until 1464, San Giovanni's procession had gone to the church of Santa Croce, but that was no longer the practice; it now went where the guardian grande and banca desired. They were perhaps given this flexibility because, unlike the majority of feast days, the ceremonies were not paid for by the scuola but "out of the pockets of the officers."[61] In spite of the presence of all of the scuole for the celebrations, only the brothers of San Rocco, the closest geographically, participated in the actual procession (which also included the thirty priests of San Giovanni) in return for San Giovanni's participation in theirs.[62] In the albergo of the scuola, the four chief officers (guardian grande, vicario, guardian da mattin, and scrivano) of the other scuole were each given painted candles. In addition, San Giovanni's guardian da mattin gave each of his direct counterparts four traditional half-yellow, half-white candles. In celebration of their most prized relic, the Scuola di San Giovanni Evangelista sponsored on this day some of the most elaborate music of the year. The *Libro Vardian da Matin* refers to the *cantadori solenni* and *sonadori* as usual, but indicates that they performed alongside the *cappella de San Marco*. Unfortunately, no further details are provided, as that would have been the purview of the guardian grande, not the guardian da mattin, for whom the book was prepared.

Observation of the feast of St. Leo began in 1474[63] in commemoration of a miracle associated with the precious relic. During a ceremony in the parish of San Lio in the early fifteenth century, the miraculous relic refused, according to the legend, to be carried across the bridge during the funeral of an unrighteous man. Only with the assistance of the parish priest could the procession continue (Giovanni Mansueti depicted the miracle in a canvas in the cycle painted for the scuola and now in the Galleria dell'Accademia). After singing a high mass in the church of San Giovanni Evangelista, the brothers, "with the miraculous cross on the large float with the large parasol,"[64] proceeded to the bridge of San Lio (now known as the Ponte di Sant'Antonio) where, stopping with the relic halfway across the bridge, the singers performed a lauda. Entering the church of San Lio, the brothers were to bring the relic to the choir "and the Reverend parish priest and other priests, and others nearby touch the silver tassels and make the sign of the cross,"[65] prior to returning directly to the scuola. In 1614, the scuola received permission to eliminate this procession, in order to save money. They would still celebrate the miracle, however, as they had always done, during the return procession from the church of San Lorenzo on that saint's day (see below).[66]

On the feast of St. Lawrence, the scuola commemorated the first miracle performed by their relic of the True Cross in 1369, while the brothers were crossing the bridge opposite the church dedicated to that saint. Dropped accidentally into the canal, the relic evaded all attempts at retrieval until, as depicted in Gentile Bellini's *tellero* now in the Galleria dell'Accademia, the guardian grande himself leapt into the water and brought it back to safety. On the anniversary of this event, after singing High Mass in their church, the scuola went in procession, carrying the relic on the large float with the golden canopy, to the Piazza San Marco and then to San Lorenzo, pausing on the bridge to sing a lauda. On their return journey to the scuola, the brothers stopped at the bridge of San Lio, the site of the miracle discussed earlier, and sang another lauda.

PROCESSIONS COMMEMORATING THE HISTORY OF THE SCUOLA DI SAN ROCCO

The crucial events in the history of the Scuola di San Rocco can be traced through celebrations marked on its calendar. They celebrated the last day of May with "a beautiful and solemn mass" (*una bella et sollemne messa*) sung at the altar of San Rocco to commemorate the date in 1478 on which the Council of Ten approved the creation of the scuola.[67] Shortly after that date, the scuola joined with another of the same name, and moved to the vicinity of the Frari, an event they recalled on the last day of September by singing a mass in the church of San Rocco. At the same time, the scuola reached an agreement with the nearby friars. In exchange for assistance in liturgical matters, the brothers of the scuola joined in the ceremonies of the Franciscan church of Santa Maria Gloriosa dei Frari on the feast day of the founder of the order, St. Francis (4 October). The brothers carried their relic of the Cross, accompanied by "the singers of song before the cross with our instrumentalists,"[68] as well as the usual candles and torches. They went first to the sacristy of the Frari, and then joined the friars in procession around the campo before reentering the church to the main altar and, finally, returning to the scuola.

On the feast of St. Andrew (30 November) in 1480 the scuola was elevated to the rank of scuola grande. From that point on the brothers could wear flagellants' robes as at the other four scuole grandi, and bury their dead in the same manner. In commemoration of this important event, the scuola had requested and been granted an indulgence (*perdon*) in their church, which commenced with the display of the body of St. Roch on the vigil of the feast, and climaxed with a procession by the brothers to the church of Sant'Andrea. Within a few years, a dispute erupted between the scuola and the Franciscan friars, from whom they had been renting the land on which their hall was built. Though the two institutions maintained their religious relationship, the scuola moved across the street on land they purchased from the chapter of the nearby parish church of San Pantalon. One element of the land transfer was the scuola's agreement to assist the church with the celebrations on the feast day of its patron saint, 27 July. The brothers went "in the morning at the usual hour to accompany their procession,"[69] carrying the usual assortment of torches and relics. They presented offerings of

bread and candles to the parish priests and six priests of the chapter before returning to the scuola.

MARIAN COMMEMORATIONS

In addition to the annual feste of the Carità (on the Annunciation, 25 March)
and the Misericordia (on the Assumption, 15 August, later changed to the Conception, 8 December), when all of the scuole attended, two others were the
occasion for special ceremonies. The feast of the Purification of the Virgin (2
February), known as the Madonna dele Candele (in English usually referred to
as Candlemas), was an occasion for elaborate ceremony, in which each of the
scuole donated candles, not only to their own members (including singers and
instrumentalists), but also to important members of the government. The largest
and most elaborate candles, of course, were given to the government officials and
officers of the scuola, while employees such as musicians received much smaller
tokens.

For reasons the writer of the *Libro Vardian da mattin* admits he could not
discover,[70] on the feast of the Nativity of the Virgin (8 September) the Scuola di
San Giovanni Evangelista, after a sung high mass in their church, went in procession to the Church of San Giobbe. They were met at the Fondamenta San
Giobbe by the brothers of the Scuola di San Giobbe (one of the *scuole piccole*),
who carried large candles and accompanied them into the church where certain
laude were sung, and a friar of the convent gave the benediction. Then the
guardian of the Scuola di San Giobbe handed to the guardian grande of San
Giovanni Evangelista a wooden image of the Virgin Mary.[71] This image, apparently the property of San Giovanni Evangelista, had been adorned previously by
the guardian da mattin with silk and jewels and brought in the morning to San
Giobbe. It would now be carried in the arms of the guardian grande back to San
Giovanni Evangelista after the conclusion of the ceremonies at San Giobbe. Beginning in 1421, the scuola introduced a small change in the ceremonies: in order
to compensate for dropping from its calendar the celebration of the Presentation
of the Virgin (21 September), the scuola went first to the church of the Frari,
instead of beginning with a mass at the church of San Giovanni Evangelista.

THE DAY OF THE DEAD

In Venetian tradition, as elsewhere, 2 November, the Day of the Dead, was the
occasion on which families commemorated deceased relatives. The scuole adapted
this practice for their own needs, including it in their calendars from their inception. The "relatives" in this case were the brothers of the scuola, whose souls
were the responsibility of the entire membership. The commemorations included
two principal components: a procession, in which only somber items were carried,
including (at both San Rocco and San Giovanni) twenty-four black torches, and
a ceremony at the church of the scuola. At San Giovanni Evangelista the procession appears to have come first, while at San Rocco the commemoration began
with the ceremony in the church.

The processions of the various scuole differed entirely in their routes, but
shared a common purpose: to visit one or more churches that housed tombs of

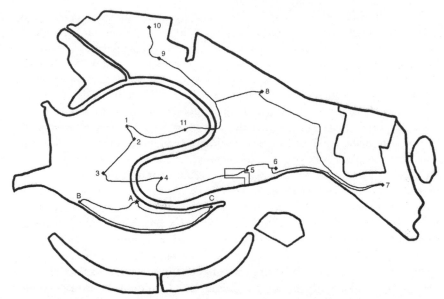

FIGURE 2.3. Routes of the processions of the Scuole di San Giovanni Evangelista and Santa Maria della Carità for the Day of the Dead

Legend: 1. Scuola Grande di San Giovanni Evangelista; 2. Santa Maria Gloriosa dei Frari; 3. Santa Maria dei Carmini; 4. Santo Stefano; 5. San Marco; 6. San Zaccaria; 7. San Domenico; 8. Santi Giovanni e Paolo; 9. Santa Maria dei Servi; 10. Madonna dell'Orto; 11. Sant'Aponal; A. Scuola Grande (and monastero) di Santa Maria della Carità; B. San Basegio; C. La Trinità

the scuola, or to other places of devotion appropriate for such an occasion. This was expressed simply, and in general terms, in the San Rocco ceremonial: "Then that night the scuola goes to the churches of the city according to our custom, praying to the great and eternal God for the souls of our departed brothers."[72] The San Giovanni Evangelista ceremonial of the late fourteenth century indicates something only a bit more extended than the prescription in its mariegola: a procession to San Marco. By the fifteenth and sixteenth centuries, the guardian da mattin had two options. One was not much more elaborate, involving a procession to San Marco and San Zaccaria, and then, on the return trip, stopping at Sant'Aponal, "where a funeral service is said under the portico of the church, where our tomb is, and where the guardian da mattin should commemorate all our deceased brothers."[73] The other option was a much more visible affair, a procession that must have taken many hours, demonstrating to a wide swath of the city the brothers' devotion, visiting eight widely separated churches with tombs of the brothers (see figure 2.3): the Frari, Santa Maria dei Carmini, Santo Stefano, San Domenico, Santi Giovanni e Paolo, Santa Maria dei Servi, the Madonna dell'Orto, and, as in the shorter procession, Sant'Aponal (San Marco and San Zaccaria are not mentioned, but probably were included as well).

In reaction, perhaps, to the extravagances of San Giovanni Evangelista (or perhaps of its own earlier, undocumented, practices), the procession of the Scuola della Carità, as prescribed in 1573, was quite limited in scope, not straying far from the scuola: "On the Day of the Dead the scuola should go as far as San Basegio, and go then on the *fondamenta* as far as the Trinità, and to the church of the Carità, where the memorials and prayers for our deceased brothers should conclude, without wandering elsewhere in the city."[74] (See figure 2.3.)

The ceremonies in the church of each scuola centered on a symbolic funeral for all the brothers deceased during the past year. At San Giovanni, the candles left over from the previous Maundy Thursday ceremonies adorned a catafalque on which was placed one of the scuola's burial cloaks. This, according to the late fourteenth-century ceremonial, was "as a symbol of and in memory of our deceased brothers."[75] The ceremony at San Rocco was somewhat more realistic (and a bit more gruesome): "A platform is erected in our church of San Rocco, and on it is put the catafalque with the embroidered funeral robe, and on that catafalque is placed someone dressed as if he were dead, and candles are placed around the platform, but these candles are not lit."[76] At San Giovanni, the commemoration for the dead concluded with a brief ceremony in the cemetery adjoining the scuola: "And after the mass for the dead is said, a procession is made around the cemetery with beating and the discipline for the souls of our brothers who have passed from this life to the next."[77]

On the Sunday following the Day of the Dead, the scuole celebrated funeral masses for their departed at their church, without a procession, but with the attendance of all the brothers, as explained in a decree of the Scuola di San Marco in 1515. The ceremony began with a funeral mass at the high altar in Santi Giovanni e Paolo, after which the brothers processed to the tombs of the scuola, "and the full Office of the Dead is said, with the presence of the guardian and officers and all the brothers; our priest-brothers are specifically obligated to come to that devotion, and with their surplices and stoles sing and pray for the souls of our deceased brothers."[78]

FRIDAYS IN LENT

At some point in the eighteenth century, not clearly documented, several of the scuole initiated the practice of displaying their most important relics at Compline on the Fridays of Lent (often referred to, regardless of the actual dates, as "li venerdì di marzo," or Fridays of March). The earliest reference is from the Scuola della Carità in 1724, when the officers decided to increase their expenditures for the occasion, which had been set the year before at 25 ducats, as they explained: "Because the said [ceremony] has gained the veneration, respect, and attendance of the devout, and the applause of the city, and thus deserved to be better supported and enhanced."[79]

At the Scuola di San Rocco, the relic displayed was that of a fragment of the Crown of Thorns, and the ceremony, held at the church of San Rocco two hours before sunset, attracted, according to the scuola's officers, a great number of the devout of the city. The *mansionari di coro*, the priests hired by the scuola to satisfy the musical needs of the church, were required to perform the Compline ceremony, concluding with the hymn *Vexilla regis.*[80] The Scuola di San Giovanni Evangelista transferred its ceremony in 1760 from the scuola itself to the church, where they exhibited their relic of the Holy Cross at the high altar. The *coristi* of the church, accompanied by the chaplain and sacristan, sang "hymns of praise to the Lord with the sound of the organ, and also the psalm *Miserere* with the benediction, accompanying [the relic] processionally to the scuola, to be replaced in the container on its altar."[81]

OTHER ANNUAL OBSERVANCES

Two other annual ceremonies in the calendar of the Scuola di San Giovanni Evangelista are worthy of note. The scuola possessed a relic of a leg of St. Martin, which they honored on that saint's day, 11 November, beginning in 1441, with a mass in their church followed by a procession, in which fadighenti carried the relic on a float, accompanied by candle bearers and torchbearers with the singers and instrumentalists, to the church of San Martino. The commemoration on the feast of St. Catherine of Alexandria (25 November) was one of the rare occasions on which the members of the banca of San Giovanni Evangelista participated in a ceremony without the remainder of the brothers. On both the vigil and the feast of St. Catherine, following the testamentary wishes of a deceased brother, Francesco Belli, the officers of San Giovanni Evangelista went to the relatively distant church of Santi Giovanni e Paolo, where they heard Vespers and High Mass at the altar of Santa Caterina, which had been decorated with "our candles and double candles and chair backs."[82] According to the agreement between the scuola and the Dominican friars of Santi Giovanni e Paolo, in return for annual payment by the scuola of 2 ducats, the friars were required to perform the Vespers and mass "in song and with organ."[83]

The celebration of the anniversaries of the deaths of members, paid for by testamentary bequests, was rare in Venice, though at similar institutions elsewhere this was an important aspect of the ceremonial calendars. To be more precise, the usual Venetian practice comprised only spoken or chanted masses to be celebrated by endowed mansionari. Only very rarely was more required. The most notable of the exceptions was the anniversary for Doge Antonio Priuli, listed in the *tariffe* of annual ceremonies at San Rocco alongside the civic processions and other major events, and requiring nearly as much pomp and circumstance.

Monthly and Weekly Ceremonies

In addition to the annual events on the liturgical calendar described above, the scuole grandi also performed a number of monthly and weekly observances. Naturally, those scuole that controlled a church (San Giovanni Evangelista and San Rocco) bore heavier responsibilities in this area than the others. Completely unknown in Venice, however, was anything resembling the frequency of the ferial services of the Florentine *laudesi* companies, in which the members met every week night at compline for lauda singing.[84]

The First Sunday of the Month

From the beginning, each scuola had reserved the first Sunday of each month for an elaborate mass attended by the entire membership, to be celebrated either in its church or jointly with the church or monastery that served its spiritual needs. The scuole celebrated separately, restricting the ceremonies to the church, the scuola itself, and the immediate neighborhood. Several of the scuole specified that the primary function of this ceremony was the salvation of the souls of its deceased brothers, and both San Marco and the Misericordia required the priests, following the mass, to say prayers at the scuola's tomb. The mass itself was usually said in the host church (except, apparently, at San Giovanni Evangelista, where it was said in the scuola itself, as the church was quite small) by the priests of that church, as part of the basic agreement between the two institutions. At San Rocco, which had an agreement with the convent of the Frari, but also had its own church with its own priests, a jurisdictional dispute arose, which was settled in 1539 by an arrangement in which the duties were shared, alternating month by month, with those not presiding in a given month assisting the others.[85]

At the Carità in 1544, the guardian grande, "to satisfy our patrician brothers and other devout brothers of our scuola," put through a resolution to "have sung a beautiful and solemn high mass" in the scuola instead of in the church, hoping to increase devotion (and, therefore, income).[86] By the next year, however, it was evident that this change was a failure. The officers realized that in order to maintain their rights to the high altar in the church of the Carità, run by Augustinian canons, they had to continue to say mass there on the first Sunday of the month, in addition to the elaborate ceremony in the scuola. This created extra expense, was difficult for the scuola's priests, who had to participate in both ceremonies, and ended up reducing attendance, so that they decided to revert to the old custom of saying the mass only in the church.[87] The problem of double duty for priests also obtained at San Giovanni Evangelista, where the priests on the first Sunday of the month performed both the regular weekly mass in the church and the principal one in the scuola. They were, however, admonished to use "diligence in singing the mass in the church as early as possible so that they might also serve in the scuola."[88] None of the documents for the scuole makes any mention of a sermon at these services, but it seems likely that one was delivered, especially when the mass was celebrated by a member of a preaching order such as the Dominicans of Santi Giovanni e Paolo.

Preceding (and sometimes following) the mass was a procession from the scuola to the church where the mass was said, in which the brothers carried the usual sorts of apparatus, including the scuola's relic of the Holy Cross (that is, at those scuole that possessed such a relic: San Giovanni Evangelista, San Marco, San Teodoro, and the Carità) or some other important holy object. Since San Giovanni Evangelista held the mass in the scuola, and its church was an adjoining building, they specified a procession in the nearby Campo San Stin, the site of their parish church, with various sorts of candles and the instrumentalists.[89]

In the early sixteenth century, under the leadership of the guardian grande Vettor Ziliol, the ceremonies for the special Sunday service at the Scuola di San

Marco became particularly lavish. A 1515 document describes a procession around the Campo of Santi Giovanni e Paolo with the assistance of the friars of the Dominican convent. The float carrying the relic of the Cross was protected by a parasol, illumined by candles, and accompanied by the singing of the scuola's *cantadori*. A sung high mass in the church was followed by a procession returning to the scuola. Ziliol's contribution was to mandate the inclusion of instruments, to add to the splendor, "both for the health of the souls of our brothers, as well as for honor of our scuola. This [is done] because our [scuola] is exalted above all the others as it is the most beautiful, and is under the protection of misser St. Mark."[90]

Ordinary Sundays

Only the two scuole that operated their own churches, San Giovanni Evangelista and San Rocco, maintained observances on ordinary Sundays. At San Giovanni Evangelista, the *mansionari* (according to a regulation of 1591), were obligated to sing (that is, chant) both a High Mass and Vespers each week. At San Rocco, through the first third of the eighteenth century, only the Vespers service involved any music, with the *coristi* and organist (his obligation was first listed in 1568) participating. The mass was only spoken. In 1741, the officers of San Rocco instituted a change, because Vespers "is usually performed at an inconvenient time, and without any attendance by devout people."[91] From that date, the celebration of Vespers was to be eliminated, and replaced with a sung high mass.

It appears that, in addition to the mass, the Scuola di San Giovanni Evangelista celebrated even ordinary Sundays with a small procession. The mariegola of 1307 specified that this was to be led by the guardian da mattin. By 1570, it appears to have been considerably downgraded, with a minimal number of participants led not by one of the two officers normally in charge of such ceremonies, the guardian da mattin or the guardian grande, but by one of the rather lowly employees known as *masseri*. The brothers were to go "at least as far as San Rocco," that is, about a five-minute walk.[92] Whether or not such a procession actually was performed regularly is open to question, as it is never again mentioned even in the detailed accounts that exist for some periods.

Other Weekly Ceremonies

Each scuola, in its mariegola, designated one day each week for the remembrance of the dead: "Every Monday throughout the year should be said and sung a mass for the souls of all of our brothers who have passed or will pass from this life."[93] The guardian grande and his officers were obligated to attend this commemoration, but the ordinary brothers were exempt. This day of remembrance occurred on Monday at all of the scuole with the exception of San Rocco, which selected Wednesday.

In addition to the weekly commemorative mass, San Rocco also held observances on Fridays. There is some inconsistency in the records, however, concerning the exact liturgical event. A 1531 regulation of the duties of the mansionari specifies "a sung mass at the altar of the Sacrament,"[94] but the 1568 listing of the duties of the organist indicates that he should play at Compline.[95] As other documents make no mention of any service at all on Friday, it may be that neither mass nor Compline was regularly performed.

Funerals and Other Services for the Dead

No benefit was more important to members of a scuola than the spiritual and physical assistance rendered after death. Certainly the fact that the family would be spared at least some of the expense of a funeral was important, but even more vital were the participation and prayers of the brothers, whose spiritual exertions helped speed the deceased's soul on its journey to heaven. Without membership in a confraternity, the deceased's family bore the primary responsibility for this spiritual task, through the performance of a funeral and its related prayers, and through regular prayer in the days and years following. Since the number of prayers influenced the duration of the trip through purgatory, according to the belief at the time, the power of the family to assist was limited, and the possibility that the family might eventually become extinct was a real peril. With confraternity membership, prayers by numerous brothers (over five hundred in the case of the scuole grandi) represented a significant benefit; moreover, there was the added assurance that the prayers would continue for the forseeable future, as these institutions seemed, at the time, to be perpetual. The financial and legal authority of a scuola was also a considerable guarantee that testamentary bequests for commemorative prayers would be carried out faithfully.[96]

The first of the death benefits obtained through membership in a scuola grande, chronologically and in terms of visibility, was the right to an elaborate funeral (as already mentioned in chapter 1). The regular members were required to provide for partial funding for such ceremonies in their wills, but the scuole provided funerals for the poor members free of charge, *amore dei*. The funeral rituals of the scuole, though simpler than those for public ceremonies, were quite involved. The brothers (as described in San Giovanni's 1570 manual for the guardian da mattin[97]) went to the home of the deceased to collect the body, which had already been prepared by the *bagnadori* of the scuola (see above, chapter 1). In the home, with the guardian da mattin standing and all the others kneeling, the *cantadori vecchi* said (or sang) three times "Jesus Christ have mercy," to which the assembled brothers responded with the same words.[98] The brothers then carried the body to its place of burial. San Giovanni Evangelista's ceremonial makes no reference to the music sung during the procession, though the cantadori vecchi were listed as participants. The mariegola of the Carità, otherwise quite lacking in detail in such matters, cites an Italian prayer or lauda to the Virgin to be sung by the brothers: "Our Lady Holy Mary, receive this sinner, and pray to Jesus Christ that he be pardoned."[99] At some point in this ceremony, probably either during the procession or at the burial, in the early years at least, the attendant brothers practiced the discipline.[100]

At the place of burial, the brothers repeated the ceremony that had been conducted at the house of the deceased, and the cantadori vecchi sang "their song."[101] This was probably either some portion of the Office for the Dead or an appropriate lauda. The guardian da mattin then spoke the following words: "Dear brothers, we turn to Our Lord God to draw to himself the soul of this, our brother, and I remind you that we are [each] obligated to say fifty Our Fathers and fifty Hail Marys, and we [the scuola] will have said the fifty masses, so that the eternal God may bring his soul to eternal life."[102] The brothers responded "Amen," and the ceremony was concluded.

There were occasions, not surprising given the mercantile character of Venice, that brothers of a scuola died outside of Venice. In most cases, the deceased was buried where he died, unless the family made a special request to the scuola, which could then make arrangements to return the body to Venice, where the usual funeral could be conducted. When this was not done, the scuole replaced the above ritual with a ceremony on the Sunday following receipt of the news of the death. The mariegola description for the Scuola di San Marco is typical:

> all the brothers of this confraternity must come the first Sunday after it becomes known, with their robes, and have said a mass in the church of Santi Giovanni e Paolo, and they should flagellate themselves as if the body were present. And similarly, they must do all the other things, that is masses and prayers, as are done when [the deceased] is here.[103]

While the mariegole never distinguished between the funerals of regular members and those of poor brothers, in practice there were indeed differences. Tables 2.2a and 2.2b show the fadighenti required for funerals at San Giovanni in 1570, both those performed *amore dei*, and those for which the deceased had paid (other scuole had very similar specifications). The differences in cost and splendor are quite clear. Note that the cost disparity is caused not only by the presence of more fadighenti at the funerals done *con spese*, but also because the standard payment to many of them was greater than for those *amore dei*. That is, they earned less for the funerals of poor brothers, making the occasion part of their own charitable effort.

Another clear difference in the two types of funerals appears in the total attendance figures listed in the 1570 document. Though all the mariegole required every brother to attend every funeral, by the sixteenth century, if not earlier, the obligation was only imposed on the poor or probationary brothers, those in the group of sixty, later the fadighenti or other recipients of monthly alms or rent-free houses. Though some other brothers undoubtedly attended out of a sense of devotion or friendship with the deceased or his family, the number in most processions was quite small. At most of those funerals performed *amore dei*, no more than thirty to fifty brothers attended (including the fadighenti), and the highest figure for the year was ninety-eight. The funerals of the wealthier members were quite a different matter, even though some of them were not in fact regular brothers, but rather were members of the Venetian patriciate who had joined the scuola specifically for the funeral benefits. These included members of the Pisani, Loredan, Marcello, Badoer, Contarini, Pesaro, and Vendramin families. The great importance of these men was certainly one reason for the higher

TABLE 2.2.   Fadighenti for funerals

A. *Fadighenti (and others) of the Scuola di San Giovanni Evangelista required for funerals* con spese *(paid for by the estate of the deceased), with their payments*

Chaplain of the scuola and assistant	£1 s. 4
three banner carriers	£2 s. 8
four candle bearers	£3—
two to prepare the corpse	£4—
eight to carry the corpse	£5 s. 12
four funeral singers	£2 s. 8
four escutcheon carriers	£—s. 8
a boat to carry the casket	£—s. 10
a bell-ringer	£—s. 6
the Captain to lead the procession	£—s. 4
three *masseri*	£1 s. 4
to carry the wax back to the scuola	£—s. 6
for fifty masses	£2 s. 10
Total	£23 s. 17

B. *Fadighenti (and others) of the Scuola di San Giovanni Evangelista required for funerals done* amore dei *(paid for by the scuola), with their payments*

for the Chapter of the parish where the brother died	£3—
two to prepare the corpse	£1 s. 12
eight to carry the corpse	£ 1 s. 4
the sacristan to open the tomb	£—s. 8
a boat to carry the casket	£—s. 8
a bell-ringer	£—s. 2
[four] funeral singers	£1—
for fifty masses	£2 s. 10
Total	£10 s. 4

Source: ASV, SSGE 16, section 9.

attendance, but even more significant was the fact that at many of these funerals every participant received alms, ranging from 4 to 20 soldi each. Those funerals at the expense of the deceased at which no alms were provided averaged seventy to eighty participants, while the eight in 1570 with alms provided—with one exception (the deceased had stipulated a simple funeral with limited atten-dance)—had a minimum of more than 100 brothers in attendance. Two had more than 200, two others had more than 300, and one, that of Piero Loredan, doge of Venice, had the astonishing total of 740. Since the official membership of the scuola was only 500, all the *fradelli nobeli*, the priests that were nominal members (so as to represent the scuola in commemorative masses in churches around the city), and many others with some kind of claim to membership must have been included.

In later years, the scuole developed distinctions in their *tariffe* beyond those between funerals *con spese* and *amore dei*, depending on the rank of the deceased, both within the scuola and in Venetian political life in general. In the new tariffa of the Misericordia approved in 1787, for example, the classifications were the following: (1) the doge, the patriarch, ambassadors, or other "conspicuous personages"; (2) the current guardian grande; (3) a former guardian grande; (4) a patron, that is, a male patrician, or the chaplain; (5) a current or former captain, *masser*, or *esattore* (collector of rents on the scuola's property); and (6) fadighenti and other simple brothers.[104] For each of these classifications, the tariffa required different numbers of fadighenti.

The number of funerals a scuola performed could, of course, be very large, especially in plague years. Even in normal times, though, the demand could be great; during one week in 1516, for instance, the Scuola di San Marco performed six funerals, two of them paid, the other four *amore dei*.[105] Altogether there were, for example, forty funerals at San Marco in 1497, eighty-nine in 1527, thirty-six in 1531, and sixty-eight in 1560.[106] The extant guardian da mattin's register of the Scuola di San Giovanni Evangelista, which provides the most complete documentation available, records eighty-four funerals in 1570, fifty-three of them *amore dei* and thirty-one *con spese*.[107] Brothers of the scuola who died during 1570 had resided in all parts of the city, though the greatest number were from the three sestieri on the same side of the Grand Canal as the scuola. Fifty-four of the burials took place in the scuola's own cemetery, but the remaining thirty-five were scattered among twenty-three other churches. In many cases, the place of death and the place of burial were quite distant, providing for an extended funeral procession. In addition, the relative locations of place of death and place of burial often necessitated the further expense of a boat to ferry the participants accross the Grand Canal.

The efforts by a scuola on behalf of its deceased brothers did not end with the funeral. As soon as possible after the death, each brother was required to say a specified number (usually fifty) Our Fathers and Hail Marys, and the scuola paid its mansionari to say fifty votive masses. Every Monday, the scuole commemorated all those who had died the previous week, and on 2 November, the Day of the Dead, they honored all those of the previous year (see above for both of these). For many brothers, those would probably be the final occasions on which they were commemorated by name. Wealthy brothers, especially patricians and those who had served as guardian grande, frequently made additional provisions in their wills. The most common was for the celebration of weekly or monthly votive masses, but sometimes they even requested daily masses. Also usual was the provision for an *anniversario*, the celebration of a high mass, usually with deacon and subdeacon and the attendance by at least the officers, annually on the date of the deceased's death.[108] These were usually funded by a bequest of either property or investment capital, and were administered by the scuola as *mansionarie*, which sometimes formed part of a larger *commissaria* that also administered charitable bequests of the deceased. Mansionari celebrated commemorative masses at whichever church and altar the will designated. It was extremely rare for the will to request anything other than a simple spoken mass (see pp. 237–38 for the two exceptions I have found). Polyphonic commemorations such as confraternities in the Low Countries commonly performed were almost unheard of, and wills never requested lauda services, such as those usual at the Florentine *laudesi* companies and elsewhere.[109]

THE CEREMONIES OF THE scuole grandi were certainly their most visible activities, and might have done even more than their charitable works or splendid halls in establishing their fame and reputation among the Venetian people. These numerous and varied occasions placed the brothers of the scuole in the public eye (and ear) with great frequency. As the following chapters will show, they took very seriously the role of music, both vocal and instrumental, in these events.

SINGING FOR THE SOULS
OF OUR BROTHERS

Musical Beginnings to the Middle of the Fifteenth Century

The scuole did not, of course, perform the various ceremonies described in chapter 2 silently, nor were they merely spoken. From their origins, the Venetian scuole grandi considered music to be an essential part of their common devotions, whether in church, at funerals, or in processions. The musical aspect of these events involved not only voices, but, beginning in the fourteenth century, instruments as well.

Liturgical Chant

The Venetian confraternities, like nearly all medieval religious institutions, employed liturgical chant in their observances. To carry out this function, the scuole, as explained in chapter 1, both established relationships with nearby churches, whose priests could assist them, and hired their own clergy. The mariegole of several confraternities indicate the occasions on which the priests were obligated to serve, and provide some information about how many priests were involved.

In the earliest, thirteenth-century mariegole, many of the descriptions of religious ceremonies are rather vague, with specifications that the masses on even the most important occasions be "said" or "celebrated." Although singing is not explicitly called for, it is almost certain that sung high masses were the practice at solemn events. The 1260 mariegola of Santa Maria della Carità does use the verb "cantare," but gives no indication of who, precisely, was to do the singing.[1] One of the two references to singing, for the weekly Monday mass, seems to specify that only part of the mass should be sung (or it may be, alternatively, acknowledging some terminological ambiguity): "that the guardian and his companions should be conscientious, and see that always on every Monday throughout the year be said and sung a mass for the souls of all of our brothers who have passed or will pass from this life."[2] The other reference, describing the memorial services on the Day of the Dead, is more precise about the singing, but equally vague as to whether the singers would be the priests of the church of the Carità or those employed by the scuola (since this involved a procession, however, and not just a ceremony held in the church, the latter is more likely).[3]

By the fourteenth century, the picture becomes a bit clearer. Several of the scuole seem to have relied primarily on the priests of their host church for their liturgical (and musical) needs. The 1308 mariegola of the Misericordia calls for one of the priests of the nearby abbey to come to the scuola on the first Sunday of the month. The priest was to celebrate the mass itself and then afterwards sing at the tombs of the brothers.[4] At the end of the century, the situation at the Misericordia appears to have changed, at least temporarily. From 1390 to 1400, the scuola paid Servite friars from the nearby monastery of Santa Maria dei Servi, with which, however, the scuola had no statutory agreement, for services on the first Sunday of the month (the ordained day) and on the feast of the Assumption. The scuola paid them 1 ducat per occasion "to sing in the choir [of the church] at the mass" and to play the organ.[5] This arrangement with the Servites might indicate that the small Abbey of the Misericordia was not able to supply an adequate number of clerical singers for important occasions.

The Scuola di San Giovanni Evangelista operated its own church, and therefore employed the priests it needed directly. On at least two occasions, the feast of St. Stephen, that is the vigil of St. John the Evangelist, and the feast of the patron saint itself, all of the priests (perhaps as many as twenty-five), according to a late fourteenth-century ceremonial, sang the solemn mass.[6] The scuola gave each priest, for this service, some bread and wine. On the Day of the Dead, according to the same document, six of the priests sang a requiem mass at the scuola.[7] The scuola required only a single celebrant at the ceremony preceding the procession for the feast of the Madonna of Candles:

> First the candles should be blessed on the day of Our Lady Holy Mary, which comes on the second day of February, and when the said candles have been blessed, the priest at the altar, singing *Lumen ad revelationem gencium*, should be given one of the large candles that the officers hold at the masses.[8]

The 1365 "Antefenario" of the Scuola della Carità

The ceremonial's rare reference to a specific verse[9] raises the question of the particular texts and chants the scuole employed in their ceremonies.[10] Fortunately, one of the chant books for a scuola survives, an illuminated manuscript dated 1365,[11] compiled for the Scuola di Santa Maria della Carità, containing mass propers for the major feasts of the year and several sets of mass ordinaries.[12] This large-format book, which preserves its original binding, originally comprised ninety-six parchment folios. At some later date, probably in the late fourteenth or early fifteenth century, a scribe added music on the last three original folios and on seven folios of a newly added quinternion. Two final mass ordinary movements were entered after that.

According to the inscription on the verso of the first opening, the guardian grande Francesco Spirito and his fellow officers commissioned the manuscript for the scuola, and it was completed in 1365:

> This antiphoner was made using the funds of the scuola and confraternity of the precious Virgin Mother Holy Mary of Charity, for the good and salvation of our souls, and of those of all our brothers, living and dead. So that all the blessings that for this purpose will be sung and said, we are joined together for the good and salvation of our souls.[13]

The reference to this book, which can best be described as a selective gradual/kyriale, as an "antiphoner" is not surprising, as it was a fairly common Venetian practice to refer to any large book of chant by that term.

On the second folio, decorated with an illumination of St. Francis (the patron saint of the guardian grande who commissioned the book) bearing the insignia of the scuola (a cross inscribed inside a double circle), follow the names of the guardian and thirteen officers, and then an inscription giving the name and origin of the scribe of the manuscript, Giustino son of Gherardo of Forlì, who was, according to the art historian Mirella Levi d'Ancona, one of the more important illuminators working in Venice during this period.[14] The first folio of the manuscript proper is decorated at the bottom with a painting of fifteen brothers of the scuola, wearing their full processional regalia, carrying flails, candles, a crucifix, and the *gonfalon*, or painted banner, of the scuola, and kneeling before a tabernacle containing the Madonna and Child, over which is the Lion of St. Mark. The opening text describes the contents of the book: "In this book are contained Introits, Graduals, Alleluias, Offertories, and [Communions] for the mass of the Blessed Virgin Mary for the entire year, with Kyries, Glorias, and Credos, and everything necessary for those, with notes."[15]

There are several unusual aspects to this collection. First is the choice of feasts included. The four specific Marian feasts (Purification, Annunciation, Assumption, and Nativity) as well as the opening mass for all other Marian occasions, are to be expected in a book for a Marian confraternity. Also not too surprising, although they are not among the days listed in the mariegola as important feasts, are those for the Circumcision, Epiphany, and All Saints. Three of the masses can be connected with the meetings of the general chapter of the scuola: the Mass of the Holy Spirit was standard for all such meetings, and two of the three meetings were held the week before Christmas (the mass for the fourth Sunday of Advent seems appropriate) and in Lent (the mass for the Sunday *in medio quadragesimae*); the third meeting was held on the last Sunday of August. Among those feasts present, the most curious is that for Sts. Phillip and James, a feast not referred to in any documents of the scuola. Mysterious absences include several feasts celebrated from the earliest days of the scuola: the Ascension and, most importantly of all, St. Mark's Day. This may, perhaps, indicate that on those occasions, clergy other than those of the scuola itself celebrated the masses, or that the brothers attended mass elsewhere, perhaps at the Basilica of San Marco; the absence of Ascension may also indicate that, as discussed in chapter 2, the scuola had already droppped the feast from its calendar. One of the sets of propers has lost its rubric and some of its music, and the remaining chants correspond to no identifiable mass (in either the San Marco or the Roman traditions; see below). Of the feasts for which at least some of the texts are used, those for St. Nicholas, St. Silvester, and St. Leonard, the last seems most likely. Though it does not appear in the early calendars of the scuola, the parish church dedicated to St. Leonard was the site of the first gatherings of the brothers in the year of the scuola's founding, and the feast is among those listed as an obligation for the singers of the confraternity in the late fifteenth century.[16]

Another intriguing aspect of the book is its liturgy, because of the coexistence in Venice of at least two liturgies, the standard Roman one and the rite of San Marco, usually referred to as the *patriarchino*, the original liturgy of the city.[17] The Venetian rite (which Giulio Cattin has demonstrated does not, as has long been assumed, derive from that of Aquileia[18]) was universal in the secular churches of the city in its early years, while the monastic establishments, it must be assumed, followed their orders' versions of the Roman liturgy. By the thirteenth century, the Roman rite had begun to spread among the parish churches, despite diligent efforts to contain it by the various bishops that continued through the first part of the fifteenth century.[19] In 1456, Maffeo Giovanni Contarini, the second patriarch of Venice, in an about-face, obtained a new papal constitution for his cathedral (San Pietro di Castello) that called for the Roman rite to be employed there. The secular churches that had retained the old practices followed in short order, with the exception of San Marco, which retained the *patriarchino* until the fall of the Venetian Republic in 1797.

The Carità chant book is one of the best witnesses to the complexity and fluidity of interactions between the two liturgical camps. The chants selected for the feasts do not correspond entirely with Roman usage, but neither do they fully match the San Marco practice. This ambiguity might have arisen because of the peculiar nature (in terms of its place within the Venetian religious landscape) of the scuola. It was, as we have seen, an independent secular institution carrying out religious functions. Not a parish church, and therefore not under the immediate control of the bishop, it was responsible, instead, to civic authorities, unconcerned with details of liturgy. Though the Augustinian canons of its host church, Santa Maria della Carità, conducted most of its religious services, the scuola had no obligation to follow their liturgy, although one would expect that their traditions and practices would have had a considerable influence. The members of the scuola, as expressed in their mariegola, clearly felt a strong tie to the Republic and its doge, and might therefore have wished to show their loyalty by retaining, at least in part, the liturgy that was particular to the city and practiced in its purest form at the doge's private church, and the city's symbol, San Marco. The resulting liturgy, however, is neither Roman nor Venetian, but occupies a rather strange middle ground.

The Roman and Venetian rites are not, of course, completely independent, sharing the same liturgy for many feasts, among them three that are included in the Carità manuscript: the Purification of the Virgin, Epiphany, and the fourth Sunday in Lent. The masses for the fourth Sunday of Advent and the Holy Spirit follow the Roman rite, except for the use of a Venetian Introit verse. In several cases, notably the Marian votive mass (which, paradoxically, also shows some tendencies in the other direction) and those for the Annunciation, All Saints, and Sts. Phillip and James, the Carità chant book shows very clear leanings toward the Venetian liturgy, employing some of its characteristic texts. On the other hand, some masses in the scuola's book diverge from those of San Marco to follow the Roman liturgy. A detailed analysis of the liturgy of the Carità gradual, therefore, reveals a strange conglomeration of Roman and Venetian elements, resulting in a liturgy that corresponds completely in almost none of the masses with either of the two traditions (except those shared by both). Unfortunately, the near total absence of other Venetian sources of this period from outside of the Basilica of San Marco makes it impossible to determine whether this source represents the lone survival of a mixed liturgy common to many churches in Venice or a unique testament to the peculiar situation of a lay confraternity.

The survival of a missal of the same period belonging to the Scuola della Carità (dated three years before the gradual and now in the Biblioteca comunale of Treviso)[20] unfortunately answers few of these questions. The first opening of the missal bears an inscription almost identical to that of the Carità gradual, with one (other than the date and the description of the contents) crucial difference: "This missal was bought and adorned as it is with the money and goods of the worthy men of the scuola and confraternity of the precious Virgin Mother Holy Mary of Charity, for the good and salvation of our souls, and of those of all our brothers, living and dead."[21] The phrase "bought and adorned" provides the key to the question why this missal does not solve any of the mysteries of the gradual. Unlike the gradual, which was made to order, the Treviso manuscript is, essentially, a standard Roman missal that the officers of the scuola purchased and had decorated. The calendar (which lacks, for example, the typically Venetian second feast of St. Mark on 25 June and the feast of St. Isidore) and the texts of the masses it shares with the Carità gradual, follow, almost entirely, the Roman rite, and not the Venetian one.[22] The scuola added the opening bifolium, which, in addition to the inscription transcribed above carries the names of the officers and a miniature that can be attributed, according to Levi d'Ancona, to the same Giustino who illuminated the Carità gradual.[23] Patterns of use indicate that the scuola's priests did indeed employ the manuscript. While much of the book seems to have been handled very little, some pages show the grease stains and candle wax spatters that result from repeated use. The masses on these pages are just those one would expect to have been celebrated regularly, based on the calendar of the scuola: the fourth Sunday in Lent, Palm Sunday, the Assumption of the Virgin, Corpus Christi, and All Saints, as well as the votive masses for the Virgin and the Holy Spirit (five of these seven are also found in the Carità gradual).[24] Apparently, neither the priests nor the brothers of the scuola were bothered by the discrepancies between the liturgies in their two books, the pure Roman one of the missal, and the mixed one of the gradual.

The music of the propers in the Carità gradual shares some of the same hybrid nature as the liturgy. Cattin has shown how the chants in the San Marco gradual contain numerous small differences (and a few major ones) from the readings not only in the Roman tradition, but also in other northern Italian sources. The Carità book has readings that, somewhat like the texts, at times are close to the Venetian tradition, and elsewhere more like the Roman, but occasionally are independent of either.[25]

The mass ordinaries that end the manuscript are, for the most part, standard chants, but the Credos have some noteworthy aspects. The one in the first mass is not among the standard Gregorian melodies, but appears to have been in use at San Marco.[26] In addition, it displays some evidence of rhythmic notation. The Credo in the second mass, with the melody of Gregorian Credo 4, is an excellent example of *cantus fractus*, employing quite clear mensural notation. The presence of such notation seems to indicate that the singers who used this manuscript had at least some musical training beyond the basic instruction in traditional chant singing. The final Credo, in the section added by a second scribe, is the standard melody, once again employing some simple metrical notation.

Organs and Organists

If the size of expenditures indicates importance, then organs and organists should be considered the major musical concerns of the scuole for the first 200 years of their histories. The earliest significant musical payments we can document at the scuole were for the building of organs, and organists were the first truly professional musicians on their payrolls. To some extent this arose because one of the scuole, San Giovanni Evangelista, operated its own church, and another, the Misericordia, shared that responsibility with the monks of its host church. The Scuola di San Marco, on the other hand, until the middle of the fifteenth century, merely occupied space in the church of Santa Croce, yet it was responsible for the organ. Only the Carità, which relied on a major monastery for its religious services (as would San Marco from the mid-fifteenth century on), had no need (in the early years) to build an organ, although the scuola later played a major role in building a new one for the monastery, and, for a few years in the sixteenth century, hired its own organist.

Remarkably, in all of Venice, only the ducal basilica of San Marco preserves records for the hiring of organists earlier than at one of the scuole, and that scuola's organ was built three years before the first documented one at San Marco (although, since the basilica already had organists, it must have owned an instrument).[27] The Scuola della Misericordia began construction of its organ, located in the church of Santa Maria della Misericordia, sometime in 1371, making its first payment, of about 25 ducats, for construction of the organ loft, in August.[28] By the end of the year, Ser Jacomello delli organi (the same master who, three years later, would build an organ for the Basilica di San Marco[29]) completed the instrument itself, and the scuola paid him 50 gold ducats for his labors. The scuola also gave Jacomello about 30 ducats for additional work on the loft, and apparently enrolled him as a brother, presumably in exchange for a more reasonable price. They also paid 3 ducats to a stonecutter for brackets under the organ loft, and to other craftsmen for the construction and painting of the case.

The work on the organ was completed around the beginning of March 1372, and the scuola immediately proceeded to hire its first organist, pre Andreas, a priest at the parish church of San Silvestro, at an annual salary of 5 gold ducats. What pre Andrea's duties might have been can only be surmised, as no documentation is extant. It seems most likely that his principal task was to introduce and accompany the chanting of the priests hired by the scuola for its ceremonies. Whether he or another organist was separately paid for services for the monks of the Misericordia cannot be determined. His duties must not, however, have been too onerous, for he continued to serve at the scuola through 1377, even after having been hired, in 1375, as organist at St. Mark's.

The assignment of an annual salary continued to be the method for a little over a decade, but in 1386 the scuola made a switch to separate payments of 24 soldi (8 *denari di grosso*) for each service, which appear to have been limited to the ordained days, the first Sunday of each month. By 1390, the system changed again: the scuola did not hire the organist separately, but as one of a group of friars from the nearby monastery of Santa Maria dei Servi, to whom they paid 1 ducat "to sing in the choir [of the church] at the mass and to play the organ"[30] on each ordained day, and, at least in 1399, again on the day of the Assumption, the annual feast of the scuola. In the early fifteenth century the scuola returned definitively to the payment of a regular salary, stabilized now at 6 ducats annually. The individuals who held the post of organist during the first half century at the Misericordia were all clerics, both secular and monastic.[31] Not until about 1424 did the scuola hire a layman, mistro Giacompi dell'organo, followed in 1429 by another, mistro Bernardin, who served until at least 1439.

The organ itself required considerable attention from the scuola during these years. The first repairs, totaling 3 ducats, were made in December 1372, less than a year after the completion of the instrument. In 1374 a major repair came to 24 gold ducats, nearly half the original cost, a sum that was matched barely seven years later. Smaller payments, for minor repairs and tuning, continued through about 1394, at which point there is some evidence (from later documents) that the organ had become unusable because of its steady deterioration. At this point the scuola turned to a friar at the Servi who was one of the principal musical figures in Italy, the composer and organ builder fra Andrea di Fiorenza (d. c.1415). They paid him 8 ducats in 1399 to restore the instrument, which then remained stable for about a quarter of a century. Whether the connection to a composer such as fra Andrea indicates any particular musical awareness on the part of the officers of the scuola cannot be determined. Certainly the monastery of Santa Maria degli Servi was, at this time, quite active musically, but it was also the closest major church to the scuola, and a logical place to turn for both priests and musicians.

By 1427, however, the old organ was apparently beyond repair, and the scuola hired Thomaxo Inzegner (who would in 1444 also make an instrument for the great Benedictine monastery of San Giorgio Maggiore[32]) to build a new instrument just like the one he had recently completed for San Salvatore (a convent of Augustinian regular canons), only bigger (by two keys at each end) and better (using a higher quality leather for the bellows). Thomaxo agreed, in a signed contract written in his own hand, to provide all the materials and labor for the new instrument in exchange for 70 gold ducats and the old organ. The parties settled the contract on 8 July 1427, the scuola made a down payment on 29 July, and paid him the remainder, upon the completion of his work, on 13 March 1428.[33]

The Scuola di San Giovanni Evangelista also expended considerable money and effort to obtain an adequate organ. The scuola's earliest surviving inventory, dated 1400, lists "one large organ in the church on the choir loft"[34] which, by 1420, needed major repairs (significant enough for the matter to be brought to the chapter for approval).[35] These repairs, as at the Misericordia, apparently did not appreciably improve the instrument, as by the end of the decade the scuola decided to build a new one.[36] It is also possible that the existing organ was still in working order, but that the scuola wished to match the splendor of the new instrument at the Misericordia.

In any event, work on the organ was completed by March of 1430, as indicated by the inventory of that date.[37] The newly elected guardian grande and his officers, however, expressed their dissatisfaction, saying that the instrument "is not of that goodness and perfection which it should be," and they refused to accept it, choosing instead, with permission of the chapter, to build a new one that would be "of honor to our scuola"[38] (this is, perhaps, the first time at one of the scuole that something musical was defined in such terms). Work was under way by March of 1431,[39] and finished shortly afterwards. A final upheaval (for this period, at any rate) occurred a decade later. In the course of major reconstruction of the church, begun in 1441, the architect reoriented the interior spaces, moving the entrance from the side facing the cemetery to the courtyard facing the scuola. As a consequence, the scuola moved the organ to the position it still occupies today, at a cost, including repairs performed by maistro Marcho d'organi, of about 30 ducats.[40]

Though, as mentioned earlier, the Scuola di San Marco did not have its own church, it did own, in the early fifteenth century, an organ in the church of Santa Croce, where its chapel was located.[41] From at least 1431 (the earliest surviving accounts), the scuola paid an organist £16 a year to play on the ordained days. The two organists for the years documented, 1431–39 (fra Antonio and fra Stefano d'Arezzo) both came from Santa Maria dei Servi, the same monastery that had supplied the Misericordia with organists for many years.[42] In 1437, San Marco moved its official seat to a location beside the Dominican monastery of Santi Giovanni e Paolo. Part of the agreement with its new hosts to provide a chapel and religious services included the obligation of the friars "to have its organ played solemnly" whenever the scuola celebrated mass on its ordained days or other occasions.[43] In exchange for this service, the scuola made an annual payment to the monastery of 2 ducats, a considerable savings over their previous situation; in addition, they no longer were obligated to maintain the instrument, an expense that, as we have seen, could be quite burdensome. Settled in its new situation, the scuola terminated its earlier agreement with Santa Croce in 1444. In exchange for release from its perpetual obligation to pay 4 ducats annually to that church, the scuola agreed to give them its organ.[44] One additional reference to an organ occurs in the early fifteenth-century records of the Scuola di San Marco, but to an instrument of a rather different sort. In 1433, as part of the same procession honoring a Milan–Venice peace treaty for which the scuola had hired several instrumentalists (see p. 87), they also rented, for 6 lire, a small organ, probably, like the harpists and lutenist, for performance on one of their floats. The perils inherent in such a situation are evident by the scuola's need to pay an extra £5 s. 8, nearly the price of the rental, to repair several of the organ's pipes, damaged during the celebrations.[45]

Singing Brothers

The scuole grandi frequently enacted at least one type of ceremony in the early years that required singing, but with performers other than priests: the funerals of deceased brothers. As described in chapter 2, a funeral, to be attended by the brothers, was one of the principal benefits of membership in a scuola. While priests sang commemorative masses for deceased brothers each Monday and on the Day of the Dead, the funeral itself was, in part, a communal, non-liturgical event. The early fourteenth-century mariegola of the Scuola di San Giovanni Evangelista describes the ceremony in chapter 3: "and all the brothers should go with that body to bury it, with beating and discipline as they do in procession, singing for his soul, as far as the place in which he is to be buried."[46] All the brothers of the scuola, therefore, were to sing and practice self-flagellation.

The thirteenth-century mariegola of the Scuola della Carità is more specific (in chapter 18): "that each brother of this confraternity is obligated to go to bury our brothers who shall pass from this life, and go in peace and quiet in procession, with discipline and beating, singing this verse: 'Madona senta maria, receve sto pecatore, fa vui prego a leson Christo ke li debia perdonare' (Our Lady Holy Mary, receive this sinner, and pray to Jesus Christ that he might be pardoned)."[47] The brothers, then, sang not a liturgical text, but an Italian one, possibly a lauda, although one so far unidentified in that repertory.

Unlike the Florentine *laudesi* companies, where communal singing was the common practice,[48] the Venetian scuole apparently required it only for funerals. It is, however, possible that the brothers also sang laude in this manner during other processions, at least through the beginning of the fifteenth century. Although such lauda singing appears to have been quite common throughout Italy, no mention is made of music of any kind in these Venetian processions before 1400. Shortly after that date, as will be discussed below, the first references to music involve a small number of fadighenti described as *cantadori*. Most probably, these musically skilled brothers were selected from among the membership to sing in place of the entire group, either because not enough brothers were capable of singing even the simple laude that were in use, or out of a desire sing more complex music (perhaps polyphony?) beyond the capabilities of any large group of untrained laymen.[49]

The membership lists of the scuole for the thirteenth and fourteenth centuries contain numerous brothers identified as singers (*cantadori* or *chantadori*), but, in most cases, it is impossible to say whether they served the scuola in that capacity or were simply being identified by their profession, common practice for most members. The first indications of the use of individual brothers as singers come at San Giovanni Evangelista in several documents dating from the third decade of the fifteenth century. The prescriptions in the 1422 ceremonial for the Day of the Dead seem to indicate that a select group of musically capable brothers had taken over the task of funeral singing previously performed by the membership as a whole: "[the brothers] go to our tombs, and there kneel with beating and discipline, making our singers sing as they would if one of our brothers died."[50] The same book again refers to a group of cantadori (a later addition specifies six), among those brothers to whom the guardian grande traditionally gave a gift, in this case 1 ducat each, at the completion of his one-year term in March.[51] Finally, a document concerned with the distribution of houses owned by the scuola to poor brothers identifies one of the recipients, Fantin Piater, as "our singer."[52]

It seems clear that these singers were not, in the true sense of the word, professionals, though they did receive remuneration in the form of charity (certainly rent-free housing, perhaps also alms) and an annual "gift." They were, rather, no more than fadighenti, whose task, instead of carrying candles or banners or preparing the body of a deceased brother for burial, was to sing. Just as fadighenti had begun, by the fifteenth century, to take over from the membership as a whole what had been the universal requirement of self-flagellation in processions (see pp. 16–17), they now relieved the other brothers of the task of singing at funerals. This change might perhaps be seen as an early sign of a switch in the conception of the role of music from an essential and integral part of religious devotion to an ornament, something to observe, not to do, and as something that could bring honor to the scuola. While these cantadori undoubtedly had to demonstrate some musical competence (and there is nothing to rule out their having been quite talented or even trained), they were poor brothers first, and singers only secondarily.

The Scuola di San Giovanni Evangelista was certainly not alone in designating some brothers as cantadori. Records for this period are extremely fragmentary, but the one surviving early fifteenth-century account book from the Scuola di San Marco includes annual gifts (regalie) to singers. Each April from 1431 to 1438 (the span covered by the book) the vicario paid approximately 4 ducats to the singers, probably four in number; this undoubtedly corresponds to the annual gift by the outgoing guardian grande that was the custom at San Giovanni Evangelista. The vicario paid a fifth singer, Biagio de Jachomo Negro, perhaps retired (the 1438 entry says that he "had been a singer" ["fo chantador vechio"]), approximately 1 ducat each December.[53]

Singing at a more "professional" level seems also to have made its appearance at about this time, although probably not with great frequency. The occasions, not surprising considering later events (see chapter 6), were the annual festivities for the patron saint of the scuola. The Scuola di San Marco made a payment on 25 April 1438 (the feast of St. Mark) of £3 s. 15 to the singers of the doge's cappella, "since the meal had not been arranged."[54] The implications of this are several: most important, that the practice of employing the best singers in the city on at least one occasion a year was a continuing one. That it appears in the account book only on this single occasion can be explained by the usual method of remuneration—not a cash payment, which, as in this case, would have to be registered separately, but through the offering of a free meal, the costs of which, little more than half a ducat, would normally be included among the general festal expenses. Whether the doge's singers performed during the procession, at Mass or Vespers, or at some other event, cannot be determined, nor whether the practice spread beyond this particular scuola, whose sharing of its patron saint with the city itself might well have led to a more elaborate celebration than elsewhere.

Instrumentalists

Traces of instruments and their players (other than organs, for which see above) can be found only rarely at the scuole grandi before the fifteenth century. As with singers, a number of instrumentalists were members, even as early as the thirteenth century, but there is no evidence that they served in a musical capacity. The indication *trombador* or *sonador* alongside the name of a member, like the earliest references to cantadori, probably should be taken simply as the man's profession. It is tempting to think that at least some of these men were among the *trombe e piffari* of the doge, the shawm and sackbut ensemble that accompanied the doge, along with the ceremonial silver trumpets, when he participated in processions, although, unlike the later situation in several of the scuole piccole, none are so designated. An early fifteenth-century payment by the Scuola di San Marco to two *tronbeti* might indicate that, at least occasionally, trumpeters were hired to announce some special event (what that event might have been in this case is unknown).[55]

On the one occasion before the late fifteenth century for which instrumentalists can be documented in actual performance, the evidence is that these were men specially hired for the event, and not in regular use. In May of 1433, as part of the celebrations ordered by the government to celebrate the peace treaty between Venice and the duke of Milan, the Scuola di San Marco (probably along with the other scuole grandi), participated in a procession. The first payment listed, out of a total of £160 s. 4 (which included floats, wreaths of roses, and elaborate candles), was £8 for four harpists and one lutenist[56] (for more on the additional expenditure for an organ, see above). While these men might have performed alongside the regular (or supplementary) singers, as was the practice at the end of the century, the splendor of the procession makes another possibility likely: the harpists and lutenist might have been used to add an aural element to the visual allegories on the floats that celebrated the great event. Such music was often noted by observers on similar occasions in the next century, and seems to have been one of the highlights of these spectacles (see chapter 4).

DURING THE FIRST TWO centuries of their existence, the four scuole grandi developed fairly simple and compartmentalized musical establishments, which varied little from scuola to scuola. Priests, either hired by the scuole or provided by agreement with their host church, supplied music, in the form of liturgical chant, for their major religious ceremonies, particularly the first Sunday of each month and their annual feast day. Either the scuola or the host church hired an organist to accompany the priests, playing an instrument that might belong to either institution. On at least some occasions, the scuole made the annual feast more elaborate by hiring outside singers. For the weekly commemorative masses and on other lesser occasions, one or more priests, without organ, served. At funeral processions, a group of poor brothers, the *cantadori*, sang prayers in the vernacular. In these early years, music apparently played primarily a functional role, intended for an audience made up of the brothers themselves, although even this represented a change from the original, participatory role of devotional music. Only small hints of further changes in the picture occur, such as San Giovanni Evangelista's decision, in 1431, to build a new organ that would bring honor to the scuola. This kind of alteration, from music as a necessary function for private, internal consumption to something that could enhance the public image of the scuola, would have profound consequences in the centuries to come.

SINGING PRAISES TO THE LORD

The Early Use of Professional Musicians, 1445–1500

Beginnings: Petitions to the Council of Ten

The date 20 July 1446 marked a fundamental change in the history of musical activities at the scuole grandi, one that signaled their entry into the Renaissance musical mainstream. In a petition submitted to the Council of Ten, and granted that same day, the officers of the Scuola di San Giovanni Evangelista recognized both the importance of music and the impossibility of maintaining adequate ensembles if they were to continue to rely on the poor brothers of the confraternity:

> Respected and most excellent council of magnificent lords, the Council of Ten. The guardian and his companions, officers of the Scuola of San Giovanni Evangelista, humbly request, that since the said scuola has the greatest need for singers, who accompany the said [scuola] and sing in processions for the dead and other of its usual solemnities, as is clear and known to Your Lordships, owing to the small number of singers at the said scuola as well as to the great age of those that are here at present, that if singers are not permitted to be received [into the scuola to be apprenticed] under those here at present, to learn from them their customs and manner of singing, in a brief time the said scuola will have no singers at the said processions, funerals, and ordained days, as well as other solemnities of the said scuola. And so that such a disturbance to the honor of God and of his glorious Apostle and Evangelist Saint John should not occur, [we ask] that the aforesaid respected Lordships concede to the said scuola that the guardian of the said scuola, at present and in the future, may allow up to six men who are not members of the said scuola to wear the robes of the said scuola, and accompany the said scuola as singers whenever the said scuola will go out in its robes, so that the said [men] may, at the appropriate time, be received into the said scuola so that it will not lack for singers.[1]

From this petition we learn the functions for which singers were needed at the scuola—ordained days, funeral processions, and other solemnities—and the inability of the scuola to maintain adequate numbers so that these ceremonies could be performed, in words similar to those in its mariegola, "for the honor of God and . . . Saint John the Evangelist." The petition also makes it clear that the singers had to be properly trained in the musical traditions of the scuola, a task that only the existing singers could accomplish. This most likely indicates that the scuola's singers performed music that was more complex than the monophonic laude that must have been the norm in earlier periods, when ordinary brothers did the singing. In addition, the scuola officials did not expect this problem of acquiring sufficient numbers of singers to solve itself: they requested the use of up to six singers, dressed in the *cappa* of the scuola, but not members, that is, men whom they selected for their singing ability. Recognizing, perhaps, the possible objection to making this a permanent situation, the drafters of the petition indicated that any singers so selected would be admitted as members as soon as there were vacancies. The motion granting the petition, significantly, made this a one-time exception to the rules limiting the number of brothers, making no mention of the future.[2]

The timing of this petition is suggestive, since in recent years the Church had begun paying increased attention to the state of liturgical music. Pope Eugenius IV (in secular life the Venetian patrician Gabriele Condulmer) issued a series of bulls between 1435 and 1442 (including several for the Venetian cities of Treviso, Padua, and Verona) concerning cathedral singing schools, perhaps based on the model established by the Venetian Senate for St. Mark's a few decades earlier.[3] Unfortunately, no documentation of any kind concerning the ducal cappella survives from the 1440s, but it is likely that this was a period of advancement there as well. The possibility exists that San Giovanni Evangelista's real goal was upgrading the music in its processions in emulation of the doge's chapel, rather than simply maintaining its traditional singing.

The Council of Ten, which had granted the petition of San Giovanni Evangelista with a little reluctance (as evidenced by the close vote of eight in favor, five opposed, and one abstention), had no such problems with a similar one submitted by the Scuola di San Marco the following November. This request was opposed by only one vote, with fourteen in favor.[4] Once these precedents had been established (something of great importance in the Venetian political and legal system), similar requests in future years met with little resistance. The third scuola to request permission to admit non-member singers to their processions was Santa Maria della Carità. They specified their need in their petition of November 1447: "since because of the plague they do not have singers."[5] The Scuola di San Giovanni Evangelista was back again in February 1447/48 with a new request, citing, this time, two important funerals that had lacked singers owing either to death or their transfer out of the city.[6] The Misericordia finally joined the other scuole with a petition that arrived later the same month (February 1447/48), specifying that they needed singers when the scuola went in procession carrying the Cross, and San Marco was back with another request in early March.[7]

The situation must have stabilized somewhat after that date, as no new petitions arrived for more than four years. In addition, while the earlier petitions had all requested the addition of six singers, those in 1452 expressed a need for only one or two. One 2 June 1452, the officers of the Scuola della Carità, in an effort to hire more suitable singers, asked for two more.[8] The request from San Giovanni Evangelista that arrived three weeks later signals yet another development. In this, the officers express eloquently their reasons for wanting music in their processions: "Wherever we go in the city, in processions and otherwise, carrying the magnificent and exalted Holy Cross, we glorify the name of the Lord in song, singing pleasantly and sweetly, praising both God and the glorious Cross of our Lord Jesus Christ."[9] They also name the individual singer, Antonio Polegrino, clearly one selected for his ability, whom they wished to admit. The Council of Ten, in granting the petition, reiterated that their accession to the request did not imply permission to increase the total number of brothers, and that the scuole had to use these singers to fill the first vacancies. Music had by now clearly moved from being merely an adjunct to religious and ceremonial ritual to being an important tool, in and of itself, for achieving the goals of the confraternity.

After 1452, either the scuole were able to maintain adequate numbers of singers from their membership, perhaps by filling regular vacancies with singers, or the Council of Ten had become less strict about requiring petitions for the use of non-member singers. In any event, the number of such petitions to the council drops off drastically. After eight in a period of six years, there were none for nearly eight years, and only two in the entire decade of the 1460s, two in the 1470s, and one in 1480. If the practice of selecting brothers for their musical ability and training was apparently no longer extraordinary, there must have been specific reasons, not revealed by the extant records, for these few requests. While San Giovanni Evangelista's 1452 petition had been eloquent in its expression of the reasons singers were needed, one submitted by the officers of the Scuola di San Marco in 1460 (and repeated almost verbatim in 1463 by the Scuola della Carità), is almost humorous in its expression of frustration at the situation in which they found themselves:

> It is most devoutly requested by the guardian and companions of the scuola grande of San Marco: Because their singers have become so old, that it is with great difficulty that they are able to bury the dead and go to processions and to devotions in the city, since they are ill, and it is not suitable that they go through the city silently as if dead, instead of going singing praises to the Lord, as is the custom.[10]

Elena Quaranta has argued that these petitions to the Council of Ten do not, in fact, represent any real change in the musical situation at the scuole, and that the men selected were no more (or less) professional than their undocumented predecessors.[11] She suggests that the only reason for these petitions is that the council had recently (with a decree of 9 March 1446) cracked down on abuses of the regulations regarding the size limits of the scuole.[12] She is undoubtedly correct that this was the immediate motivation for the submission of the petitions, but the urgency of the requests indicates an attitude toward music not evident earlier: when the Council of Ten had issued a similar decree eight years earlier, the scuole apparently felt no need to request exceptions for singers.[13]

While these men may not have been professionals in the strictest sense of the word—those whose livelihood depends primarily on exercizing their craft—they were clearly selected for membership in the scuole because they possessed a skill and training not found among the numerous brothers already present. They would, therefore, reap a financial reward for singing, and must be considered, in at least a limited sense, professionals. Given the absence of earlier documentation, it is, of course, impossible to determine whether the scuole had been selecting men on the basis of musical skill before this period, granting them membership in exchange for their services. As will be demonstrated below, however, there is no doubt that within a very few years the documents of the scuole clearly indicate that the officers were concerned with the quality and ability of their singers. These petitions, therefore, may not mark the moment at which attitudes and practices changed, but certainly provide evidence that such changes were under way.

Early Difficulties: Attendance Problems
of the Singers at the Scuola di San Marco

The difficulties that originally led the scuole to petition the Council of Ten did not end with the last of the requests of the 1460s; a series of annual registers of the Scuola di San Marco (thirteen survive for the period 1448–1500) maintained by the vicario (the officer at that scuola charged with supervision of the fadighenti and the organization of processions, excluding the one for the annual festa, which was the responsibility of the guardian grande), contain revealing information on the development of the vocal ensemble at this scuola.[14] An element of each of these registers is an alphabetical list of the fadighenti, with an accounting of their service. Although a number of these, including the earliest, dated 1448, do not indicate the duties of the men involved, it is possible, in part based on later records, to identify at least some of those assigned to the task of singer, or *cantadore;* it is unclear, however, whether any of these were among the six men admitted two years earlier with permission of the Council of Ten. Very few of the men are indicated as being professional singers; they were instead practitioners of a wide variety of trades, such as goldsmith, shoemaker, seller of pots and pans, stonemason, or bargeman.

For each man listed (as with all the other fadighenti), the vicario kept a record of attendance, marking the book for each appearance in the four categories of service required: ordained days (the first Sunday of each month and some other occasions), ordinary Sundays, funerals, and processions. It becomes immediately apparent that attendance at these events was not what it was supposed to be. Determining the exact number of events in each category is not possible, but some indication can be obtained by looking at the maximum number attended by one of the fadighenti. For example, for ordained days, which must have numbered at least twelve (one per month), only two of the five singers (Polo di Michiel and Tomado de Nicollò) managed excellent attendance, twelve each, in 1448. Zuane de Nicollò appeared only nine times, Andrea de Jacomo six, and Andrea da Monte only two. Andrea da Monte, however, apparently fell into a different category from the others (perhaps he was one of those admitted specially by the Council); next to his name is the annotation "in pien," meaning that he was transferred from the ranks of fadighenti to full membership. Although his name appears in lists of singers through 1482, he is never again listed among the fadighenti.

The attendance situation for ordinary Sundays was even worse than for ordained days. Of the forty Sundays under consideration in 1448 (subtracting the twelve first Sundays), no singer managed more than the twenty-three served by Polo de Michiel; two others were there only sixteen times, and one only fourteen (da Monte was listed for only five Sundays, but, as mentioned above, this is probably not an accurate reflection of his service). Similar numbers can be found for funerals and processions. While there may have been other singers in this year than those who have been identified, it is clear that on most occasions the majority of singers were absent, and there might even have been more than a few events in which, as the petitions to the Council seem to indicate, there were none there at all. The presence of only one or two singers at some occasions was certainly not compatible with the scuola's desire to raise the level of music at its ceremonies.

The officers of the Scuola di San Marco did not look only to the Council of Ten for assistance in guaranteeing sufficient numbers; they apparently tried some internal solutions as well, such as designating a larger number of singers. The vicario's register for 1452[15] includes in the alphabetical listing four of the five names found in 1448 (excluding Andrea da Monte), and adds two more, both designated as *cantadore*. This book also includes a separate listing of fadighenti (and, perhaps, others) by assignment. The heading *cantadori* appears twice, once with eight names, and a second time with two. The attendance records in the alphabetical section offer much the same picture of spotty service as in the 1448 book. The listing by assignment, however, also includes an attendance record, whose relationship with the alphabetical listing is unclear (there appears to be no precise correlation between the two sets of figures), but it does indicate that additional singers did participate. It is unlikely that the scuola expected that all eight singers would attend regularly; the officers probably hoped that with a larger pool, an adequate number would show up. This continued to be the practice in 1469 (the extant books for intervening years do not designate singers), when the alphabetical listing, with most of the singers now identified, included twelve names, and in 1475, when seventeen are so identified.[16] Even more remarkable is a separate list of singers that appeared in the 1475 book: it contains twenty-three names. While some of these men apparently made a real effort to participate (Piero de Nichollò, a native of the Friuli living in the parish of San Luca, for example, served on eighty occasions), others showed up only a handful of times, or not at all. For some of the latter, the reasons for the extended absences are clear: one was in Flanders, another in Puglia, and a third was on a galley in the Mediterranean. Another, who apparently had no valid excuse, was expelled from the scuola at the end of the year, having attended only once in twelve months.

Division of Labor: Cantadori di Corpi
and Cantadori de Laude

As the scuole continued to seek to raise the level of their music-making, it became increasingly evident that the ordinary fadighenti, in comparison with new members selected specifically for their singing ability, could not keep up. Always reluctant to abandon tradition, the scuole, beginning with San Marco, began to separate the singers into two groups, the longstanding body of poor brothers on the one hand, and the new, more professional singers on the other. The way the scuola's musical requirements had developed made this division, in fact, a quite natural and useful one. Singers were needed most frequently for funerals, occasions that offered little opportunity for display, and were, by their very nature, essentially identical from one to the next. The small processions around the square in front of the scuola held on normal Sundays were also similar in their requirements. These two kinds of occasions, then, were most suitable for the traditional fadighenti ensemble, which could satisfy the scuola's needs by learning and performing just a few simple selections, which would be repeated as needed. On the more public and festive events, the extended processions on the first Sunday of each month and the occasions, civic and otherwise, on which the scuola left its neighborhood, the officers desired more variety of music, that is, works suitable for the occasion, and a level of sophistication that would bring honor to the scuola. This more complex task was best suited to professional musicians. In addition, while the scuola did not possess the financial means to pay for professional singers for the dozens of funerals and ordinary Sundays each year, hiring them for the far less frequent but more elaborate occasions was entirely feasible. This division of the singers into two distinct groups was made explicit for the first time in a list in the vicario's book for 1478 (although, as will be shown below, the division was already in effect a few years earlier). The traditional group of fadighenti is headed "the singers who sing for funerals and on the street," while the others are labeled "the singers who perform, that is laude and in processions."[17] In simpler terms these were known at the Scuola di San Marco, respectively, as the *cantadori di corpi* and the *cantadori de laude*. Interestingly, at some of the other scuole grandi the historical development of the two ensembles became part of their nomenclature, with the traditional fadighenti referred to as *cantadori vecchi* (old singers) and the newly hired professionals as *cantadori nuovi* (new singers).

The formation of two groups of specialized singers perhaps inevitably created new problems. While pulling out the best of the singers to form the cantadori de laude meant that they could aspire to more sophisticated music, it also required them to learn a new repertory. The same was true for the older group: without the best musicians, who undoubtedly were the leaders, the cantadori di corpi needed additional training. The chapter of the Scuola di San Marco addressed both situations in the 1470s, beginning with the cantadori de laude in 1474, with the selection of one of their number to teach the new arrivals: "It being necessary for our scuola to have singers of laude, for the honor of the processions and other solemnities performed by our scuola . . . Batista de Felipo . . . [should] teach our apprentice singers."[18] By 1476, the situation with the thinned ranks of the cantadori di corpi had become quite desperate, so, as with the cantadori de laude, the officers selected the best of the group to instruct the others, for an additional payment (in fact, doubling his wages), and admonished the new "students" that they had better shape up:

> It is known to all the diligence Andrea da Monte has had in coming to the scuola to sing at funerals, such that one could almost say that there are no other singers than him who sing at funerals at present. For that reason, the other singers are admonished that they must learn to sing.[19]

Determining exactly how many singers made up the two ensembles at the Scuola di San Marco, particularly the cantadori de laudi, and who they were, is not always a simple task, despite what appears to be sufficient documentation. Part of the difficulty comes from the mixing of fadighenti with professional singers who might also be admitted as brothers, but not classed among the fadighenti. Adding to the confusion is the persistence in the lists of fadighenti of some men, identified as singers, who are not listed in either of the ensembles; they were, perhaps, men who no longer possessed sufficient ability for the more professional status now expected (either because their voices had deteriorated with age or because their modest talents could not keep up with the increasing complexity of the music), but who were allowed to stay on as a gesture of courtesy. For a variety of reasons, therefore, lists such as those in the vicario's books for 1482 and 1484, which both include an ensemble of cantadori de laude with only two names (the same two, Alvise de Antonio and Marco de Polo),[20] should not be considered an accurate reflection of the real state of affairs.

In 1483, between the two lists cited (both of which appear in books maintained by the vicario, the officer in charge of fadighenti) the guardian grande and members of the banca reached a new agreement (which also expresses with vigor the importance of music to the scuola) with the singer who had first been hired nine years earlier to teach the cantadori de laude, Batista de Felipo. This pact obligated him to select three additional singers who he would train, to serve with him as the scuola's ensemble:

> It is noted that for the honor of this our blessed scuola, it is required to provide for those things necessary on a daily basis, and that are necessary for its needs, and most of all singers of laude, of which there is a great lack in our blessed scuola. Therefore . . . Ser Batista should have alongside him, as his singing company, three other apprentices, whom the said Ser Batista is suited to direct and teach.[21]

Although Batista had been with the scuola for many years, and was clearly a cantadore de laudi, he had not been included in the listing of the previous year, probably because he was not a fadighente, and thus not under the supervision of the vicario.

In the event, the agreement with Batista lasted no more than a year, as in 1484 payments were made to another man, pre Michiel, the first singer of the scuola to hold clerical orders (and therefore ineligible for regular membership), to teach five apprentices.[22] The members of this new ensemble (at least this seems to be the case) appear as the first six names in a listing of singers of the scuola in a new mariegola created at about this time.[23] This list (which would be updated for more than forty years) is notable for several reasons. Separate from the list of regular brothers (which includes both fadighenti and full brothers), it is one of several special lists (others include priests and nobles) of those whose membership or participation in the activities and benefits of the scuola was limited in some way. That this ensemble was, in fact, truly professional, and of the highest level, is revealed by two of the other names, Alberto and Girardo, both from the ducal cappella at St. Mark's. The former can be identified as the Alberto Francese who became the first maestro of the cappella in 1485; Girardo is evidently one of his singers.[24] This list does not include any of the members of the much more stable ensemble of cantadori di corpi, who were included instead along with all the other brothers in this mariegola's basic alphabetical listing.

In fact, it may be that this listing represents yet another division of responsibilities among the singers of the Scuola di San Marco, beyond those of cantadori di corpi and cantadori de laude. Unfortunately, the documents themselves are somewhat contradictory, or, at the least, inconsistent, and there may even have been some confusion among those keeping the records. The records contain two sets of names associated with the term "cantadori de laudi": first, the traditional group, listed (if not always completely) in the books of the vicario, and second, the newer one, made up of pre Michiel and his associates. The original intent might have been to raise the level of the single ensemble of cantadori de laudi by adding higher level professionals. In the event, however, these professionals might have been too busy with their official duties at the ducal cappella, or elsewhere, to attend to all of the functions of the scuola, so were used, probably along with the ensemble of brothers, only on the more important solemnities, leaving the more ordinary ones to the traditional ensemble. Unfortunately for the historian, the records do not always make clear the distinctions between the two groups.

A series of documents of the 1490s from the Scuola di San Marco illustrates this confusing situation, while at the same time revealing the way the scuola moved ever closer to the center of sacred music in Venice, the ducal cappella (despite having to spend enormous sums to rebuild the scuola, which had burned in 1485). In 1492, the officers approved the following resolution, which bears the rubric "Of the singers of laude" ("Di cantadori di laude"):

> Our scuola used to have eight singers of polyphony to honor the Masses and Vespers of the feasts and other solemnities of this our scuola; of those eight, only four are found at present. Because among the other ornaments at such solemnities such singers are much to be commended . . . maestro Piero de Fossis, messer pre Marco Bussati, messer pre Antonio Schatoler, and messer pre Nicolò Balanzer [have] offered to supplement the said eight.[25]

Piero de Fossis was, of course, the maestro di cappella at the ducal basilica, and the other three were his colleagues there.[26] Although the marginal rubric refers to cantadori de laudi, the document itself refers instead to "singers of polyphony" ("chantadori de chanto figurado"). In addition, no reference is made to the chief obligation of the cantadori de laude, that is processions; Piero de Fossis and his companions were, rather, to serve at masses and Vespers. Finally, despite their prestige, these men were to divide among all eight of them an annual payment of only 1 ducat (as well as bread and a candle at each occasion), an indication, in part, that the number of events at which they would serve must have been limited. Most likely they also were entitled to some benefits of brotherhood in the scuola.

The more traditional ensemble of cantadori de laude appears in a resolution of the following year (this time, the rubric is the simple "Regarding our singers" ["Per nostri cantadori"]):

> Because among the other things that are most necessary to this our scuola are the singers of laude, without whom it is hard to do honor to our scuola, it is also necessary to have persons who, at every need, both in feasts and in processions, and in every other solemnity and festivity, can and must serve, not only tenors but also sopranos and contras.[27]

This time, the obligation to serve at processions, and at other events in which the brothers wore the cappa of the scuola, is clear. Three of the men listed were already brothers of the scuola. The payment they were to receive was considerably greater than that offered to the prestigious singers of St. Mark's. Instead of only 15½ soldi each (1 ducat per year divided among eight singers), plus the bread and candle, these new cantadori de laude (along with those already serving) would divide 1 ducat but also be paid 12 soldi each for each occasion, which probably numbered at least twenty (twelve ordained days plus processions of various types) annually. This greater payment stemmed not from an estimation of their talent, but because they had more extensive duties. Piero de Fossis and his companions had offered to serve on a few prestigious occasions for a token payment in exchange for the honor of appearing with the scuola. Perhaps the most significant aspect of this last document, however, is the listing of voice ranges, leaving no doubt that even the regular ensemble of cantadori de laude sang polyphonically, probably in three parts.

In 1494, the scuola offered two of the singers mentioned in the 1493 agreement, Zuane Polo and Chabriel, a new form of payment: instead of 12 soldi per occasion, they would be paid a monthly fee of 40 soldi, with a deduction of 8 soldi for any occasion they missed.[28] Forty soldi is, in fact, the standard stipend of any poor brother fadighente—in other words, these men, although cantadori de laude, had gone back to the status occupied by singers at the scuola before professionalization began. The situation is not clarified by the payments recorded in the vicario's register for 1494–95.[29] Entries include some that would be expected, in particular, monthly payments to cantadori de laude and di corpi, and annual gifts of 1 ducat to each ensemble on Corpus Christi and the feast of St. Mark. The vicario made no payment to a third ensemble of the scuola, the one that had been led by Piero de Fossis, but a payment of 3 ducats on Corpus Christi "to the singers of St. Mark's" ("ai chantadori de San Marco"), as well as a similar one for the procession of St. Mark in June, suggests that the scuola had decided to employ those elite singers only as needed. Over the next half century, the scuola would rethink this practice several times, achieving different solutions, each maintained for varying numbers of years. At the end of the fifteenth century, in any event, the Scuola di San Marco seems to have settled on just two permanent ensembles, cantadori de laude and cantadori di corpi. The last of the vicario's registers for the fifteenth century preserves a listing of singers in what was, at least for the time being, the definitive form: five members in each group, all brothers of the scuola.[30]

More restricted documentation makes it impossible to trace in similar detail the employment of singers at the other scuole grandi; no service or attendance records survive, and financial documents are scarce. It appears, however, that no scuola except San Marco even toyed with the idea of a third fixed ensemble, though they do all seem also to have divided their singers into two ensembles, referred to, however, as cantadori vecchi for funerals, and cantadori nuovi for processions and the like. By the date of the earliest relevant document at Santa Maria della Carità, 1492, the system had already been in effect, although not perhaps working smoothly. There were six cantadori nuovi, who "should sing laude and other devotions every time the banner of the Holy Cross shall go out with our brothers, both for processions [to the Piazza San Marco] and to other places,"[31] and six cantadori vecchi, who "should sing according to their custom at the funerals for our brothers."[32] Both ensembles had rather poor records of attendance and behavior, so the guardian grande proposed a reform in the payment method and the institution of a system of penalties for absences. Replacements would first be sought "among our brothers [if there are] those who know how to perform that office," and only if none could be found would outsiders be considered.[33]

By the following year, the situation at the Carità had not improved, at least for the cantadori nuovi. As the guardian complained, despite numerous admonitions,

> the said [singers], or the greater part of them, have decided not to observe anything they promised, rather they have totally interrupted that order and promise they made, such that when they come, the tenors will come but the sopranos will be absent, and when those two [parts] are there, the contras will be absent, such that their songs are never in order, with great confusion and distress to this blessed scuola.[34]

The chapter voted to fire the existing ensemble and replace it with a new one made up entirely of non-brothers. Pre Antonio Papale, who directed the new group, was obligated to provide "four other good and able voices, that is two sopranos, and two tenors, and a contra."[35] The scuola would not pay them by the occasion, as in the past, but, perhaps as a sign of respect (hoping the gesture would be reciprocated), offered them an annual salary, and one that represented considerably more money than under the old system. The agreement listed about thirty occasions each year at which the singers would serve, including the first Sunday of the month (at Mass and Vespers), processions in Lent, feasts of the Virgin, and all the usual processions. At the old rate of 10 soldi per occasion (and sometimes less), this would have brought each singer about 2½ ducats in all for the year; now each would receive 8 ducats. By May of 1496, the scuola found it necessary once again to hire a new ensemble, using the same system. This time, the officers reached an agreement with an individual, the layman Nicholò Chamelin, from Flanders, who would be responsible for providing a complete ensemble of five voices, presumably with the same distribution of voices as previously: two sopranos, two tenors, and a contra.[36]

The importance attached to the hiring of singers can be seen also at the Scuola di San Rocco. In 1488, after drawing up and refining their statutes as a newly created scuola grande, the first act the officers undertook, registered as the first item in their original notatorio, was the decision to hire singers, three of whom they stole away from other scuole through the generous offer of a salary of 6 ducats each plus equal shares of gifts totaling 7 ducats.[37] This practice of luring singers from one scuola to another would be a continuing source of problems at the scuole in future years. In fact, within a year, two of the three stolen singers rejoined, at least temporarily, the Scuola della Misericordia, forcing San Rocco to hire replacements.

Disciplinary Problems with Singers

Poor attendance and "jumping ship" were only two of the many problems the scuole encountered with their singers. As might be expected, musicians were not always willing to live within the rather strict rules established by these devout confraternities, even when the scuole made real efforts to keep them happy and show them respect by rewarding good service with increases in pay, or through the establishment of new, more secure methods of payment.[38]

Not satisfied with what they received in compensation for funerals, some of the fadighenti at the Scuola della Misericordia, including the cantadori di corpi, adopted some rather unpleasant behavior in 1490, following the funeral of the wealthy nobleman, and brother of the scuola, Andrea Zorzi. "Forgetting their fear and love of God and of his mother the glorious Virgin Mary . . . [they] acted so that [the body] could not be removed until first they were given that payment they desired, using ignominious and injurious words," and attempted to extort additional reward from the mourners.[39] As was usual in such cases, the officers decided to admonish the offenders, spell out the policy clearly, and warn them that the next time they would be fined all or a portion of their monthly alms; if the offense were repeated, they would be expelled from the scuola. In this case, the warning had to be repeated in 1494, when, after a similar offense, all were pardoned "in observance of the title of this glorious scuola, which is named for the Mother of Mercy."[40] In 1486, the Scuola di San Marco had lamented the same sort of situation, in which cantadori di corpi and others had used "many strange customs" ("molti strani chostumi") at funerals of poor brothers, those done *amore Dei*, at no cost to the family, for which the fadighenti were required to perform their duties without remuneration. The officers of San Marco reminded the fadighenti that they should behave responsibly, and that "since the scuola will not receive from those people anything at all on those occasions, the said singers should have patience."[41]

Individual singers also might behave badly or dishonestly in search of greater remuneration. In 1490, the singer Domenego dale Nape, who had earlier gotten into trouble with the Scuola della Misericordia for leaving to serve San Rocco in 1488, resorted to rather extreme behavior to exact additional payment from the officers at the feast of Corpus Christi. He first refused to come, citing illness. The officers doubted his claims, but not wanting to go without singers, secretly sent him a bribe of 1 ducat. He promptly came to the scuola, and joined the procession as far as St. Mark's, where "he then pretended to have a nosebleed, and he got secretly into a boat, which was tied up at the quay of the [doge's] Palace, and he went for pleasure to Mazorbo . . . leaving the scuola to go with distress and shame in the piazza."[42] It was decided that the extra ducat would be withheld from his next payment, and that a similar fine would be levied if he ever misbehaved again.

The scuole had enshrined in their mariegole the requirement that all brothers use polite language and be respectful toward their superiors, so the behavior of one of the Carità's singers in 1490 certainly distressed the scuola's officers. According to their complaint, the incorrigible Sebastian, "presumptuously, showing little reverence to the guardian, and turning his back on him, and with little fear either of God or of the rules of our scuola, and with many angry and insulting words, demonstrated more iniquity than charity."[43] The officers warned him that further episodes of this sort would result in his being expelled from the scuola. Five years later, however, Sebastian had returned to his old ways; he had "used injurious and inappropriate words against all the officers of the albergo."[44] This time the scuola simply expelled him.

At the Misericordia, disiplinary problems, which manifested themselves as early as 1447, resulted from the worldly behavior of the singers, sometimes exacerbated by the scuola's charitable offerings of food and drink. As the officers lamented,

> there is [with these singers] no devotion and no virtue, but only dishonesty; they come to the scuola and sing in order to practice dishonest and abominable things that they do and have done daily, with great distress and shame to all of this blessed confraternity, and against the spiritual and virtuous practices all of us must observe.[45]

The chapter had a simple solution: it forbade all the officers to offer food or drink to singers either at the scuola itself or in their own homes (or even in homes of others). Unfortunately, this rule was not always heeded, leading, on a Sunday in 1464, to a rather dramatic recurrence of the earlier problems. The singers locked themselves inside the scuola, along with some friends, and "stayed there partying until after supper." When the officers and brothers returned later for a funeral, they were unable to get in until the guardian grande himself arrived, and then "the said singers began to use injurious and dishonest words against our masseri, insulting and menacing them." The singers, the account concludes, "did not have any reverence toward the guardian and his companions, such that it was a dishonest thing."[46] The solution this time, and perhaps it was successful, as the documents record no further problems, was to forbid anyone to bring food and drink into the scuola except under certain limited circumstances.

The Question of Repertory

When the cantadori were not absent, or misbehaving, or drunk, what did they sing in the fifteenth century? Unfortunately, the documents are not at all precise, but the evidence does permit some tentative conclusions. Part of the problem is the general absence of musical sources, or even of good documentation from any institution in Venice during this period. While we know the makeup of the cappella ducale from the 1480s on, there are no identifiable composers of sacred music until the next century, and no surviving musical sources. Given the presence of northerners, and the exchanges of personnel with other, better understood chapels in Italy, it is probable that the repertory at St. Mark's centered around the same sort of polyphony sung at such places as Rome, Milan, or Ferrara.[47] It is likely, therefore, that when members of the cappella sang for the scuole, they, at least sometimes, sang their usual sort of music, that is motets or, when appropriate, even masses.

At the other end of the spectrum, the non-professional cantadori di corpi would not have had the ability to sing such complex music. Their standard funeral service might well have been monophonic, since there are no references to voice ranges for this ensemble, and they seem to have managed well enough (though at the displeasure of the officers of the scuole), with only one or two members present. On the other hand, the repetitive nature of their service might have allowed eventually for the mastery of some simple polyphony.

The most interesting ensemble, in many ways, was that of the cantadori de laude. This was, from its origins, an ensemble of trained singers, almost certainly capable throughout its history of singing polyphony. In the last two decades of the century, the documents occasionally designate the members of the ensemble by voice part: soprano, contra (whether this is a high or low contratenor is not indicated), and tenor. The context seems to imply three-part singing as the norm (a 1493 report discussed above bemoans the frequent absence of one of the three parts, with deplorable musical results), but with an ensemble of five (designated as two sopranos, two tenors, and a contra) or six, four-part singing would have been possible. The ensemble's very name, and the descriptions of its duties, make it clear that central to its repertory must have been the lauda, sung, most probably, not while the procession was in motion, but during stops at churches.

But what sort of lauda? Not one source of laude, either poetic or musical, can be linked to any one of the scuole. There is also no indication in any of the inventories of the scuole that they ever possessed a laudario, with or without music. Though Venice was one of the important centers of lauda composition in the fifteenth century, the extant manuscripts and printed books, and the repertory they contain, originated in other circles. The greatest Venetian associated with the lauda was undoubtedly the patrician poet Leonardo Giustinian (c.1383–1446), brother of Venice's first patriarch, Lorenzo.[48] Giustinian's laude circulated in manuscript, and from the 1470s in printed form, and were known throughout much of Italy. There is nothing, however, to link either Giustinian or his laude with the scuole grandi. Further, the two important extant fifteenth-century Venetian musical lauda sources both have monastic associations. Venice, Biblioteca nazionale marciana, MS ital. IX, 145 (7554), a Franciscan source from about 1430–40, with later additions (probably from Venice, but possibly from one of the mainland cities of the Veneto), has two repertories of laude. The earlier, though more sophisticated, portion of the source has nine laude *a 2* and two *a 3*, in a style reminiscent of Dufay's simpler liturgical works. The second section contains two monophonic laude and ten in primitive, note-against-note two-voice polyphony.[49] The Cape Town manuscript (Cape Town, South African Public Library, MS Grey 3.b.12), dating from about 1500, has Venetian or Veneto Benedictine connections, and a repertory of both early two-voice laude and later fifteenth-century three- and four-voice works.[50] Certainly the cantadori de laude of the scuole grandi would have been capable of singing any of this music, since none of it is particularly complex. It is also possible, on the other hand, that they had begun to sing Latin motets, while the non-musical scribes continued to use the traditional designation *lauda* in the documents. Based on the existing evidence, any of these alternatives would have been possible.

Instrumentalists: Piffari and Strings

Nearly forty years after the scuole grandi had begun to employ singers on a regular basis they added a new layer to their musical practice with the similar hiring of instrumentalists. There is little evidence for the use of instrumentalists in the middle third of the fifteenth century, but it must be assumed that the scuole hired them when needed for special occasions, as they had earlier (see chapter 3). The situation at San Rocco in 1478 was an unusual one: though not yet a scuola grande, its annual festa had already become a day of great devotion because of the importance of the patron saint as a protector against the plague. In that year (or perhaps a few years earlier) the scuola enrolled as members the six "trombe e piffari" of the doge, in exchange for their services on the feast day.[51]

Instrumentalists appear at the other scuole grandi in the next decade. The earliest reference is somewhat confusing. The fadighente Alvise Zelato, who had been listed in the Scuola di San Marco's vicario's registers of 1475 and 1478 as a singer,[52] appeared in the mariegola dated 1470–82 with the annotation "sonador."[53] No other name in the book is so identified, and Zelato disappears after that date. It might be no more than a slip of the pen, or the first sign of an evolving situation. He may also have been an instrumentalist by profession, but employed by the scuola as a singer. Another document from San Marco in 1482 is equally anomalous: in a listing of expenses for funerals appears an entry for 3 ducats for sonadori, who were to be paid £16 s. 10 for regular funerals, and £12 s. 16 for those for poor brothers.[54] This practice seems unlikely, for as a rule, rarely broken in three hundred years of documents, the scuole grandi performed funerals with singers only, and no instrumentalists. As this same listing omits any payment to cantadori, perhaps the scribe was simply confused, and knew only that the ceremony required musicians of some sort. The other alternative is that this was in effect an experiment, one that was quickly abandoned.

The first unequivocal documentation of a decision to employ instrumentalists on a salaried basis comes from San Giovanni Evangelista, also in 1482. Entered on the day of the scuola's annual festa, the notation may reflect that the officers' original intention to hire the individual, a lutenist named maestro Nicolò, only for the occasion. In the end they decided to make the arrangement more permanent.[55] The agreed-upon salary of 5 ducats is quite respectable, considering that no singer at the scuole during this period received more than 8. This contract does not indicate who would join Nicolò in playing for the scuola, nor whether any companions would also be salaried, but it is likely that, as at the other scuole in following years, this was to be an ensemble of lute, harp, and a bowed string instrument referred to variously as *lira* or *viola*.[56] In 1486, the Scuola di San Marco followed suit, and hired two sonadori (their instruments are not specified, nor is their salary) to play at "all of our processions and solemnities that might occur."[57]

The account book for the vicario of the Scuola di San Marco for 1494 and 1495 seems to indicate that this scuola had, perhaps, abandoned the use of salaried players, and paid them by the occasion, in particular for the processions for Corpus Christi and St. Mark. For two of the three occasions for which payments are listed, one or two members of the company are mentioned by name: for Corpus Christi 1494 it was maestro Zentil dal'arpa, who along with his companions received about 2 ducats, and for St. Mark 1495, "Ser Batistian da lautto e Ser Zulian dal'arpa e compagni," who were paid just over 1 ducat (the Corpus Christi payment was larger because there were two processions on that day).[58]

By 1497, at least at San Marco, the custom of hiring instrumentalists had solidified: the vicario's book, which contains, as discussed above, clear listings of the two vocal ensembles, also records an ensemble of two lutes, harp, and three *viole,* that is, six musicians.[59] On two occasions, however, payments to instrumentalists appear elsewhere in the book to a group of four. Whether this dimished number resulted from poor attendance, or rather represented the desired number of performers (with two others kept in reserve for emergencies) is unclear, but some evidence from other scuole seems to indicate the latter as more likely. At the Scuola della Misericordia in 1496, the officers clearly had the intention of hiring an ensemble of three players (lute, harp, and *viola*), and were reluctant to pay a fourth player, a German lutenist named Magnio (perhaps a member of the Tieffenbrucker family?), who had also been called, apparently as a result of miscommunication (in the event, he misbehaved so badly, speaking disrespectfully to the guardian grande, that he was expelled).[60]

This same sort of ensemble of three players, one each of lute, harp, and *viola*, appears in a different sort of document from the Scuola di San Giovanni Evangelista from about the same date: the painting by Gentile Bellini (now in the Accademia Gallery) depicting a miracle performed by the scuola's relic of the Holy Cross during the Corpus Christi procession of 1444, but showing the piazza and members of the scuola as they were at the date of the painting, 1496.[61] There, at the left edge, leading the heart of the procession, are the expected three instrumentalists and a vocal ensemble of five members.[62] In this painting, the two ensembles appear to be performing together; this practice is difficult to document, but will be discussed further in the next chapter.

In addition to paying its instrumentalists an annual salary, or a fee for individual occasions, the Scuola di San Marco offered them a special benefit: strings, a constant supply of which was needed by players of that era.[63] The vicario's account book for 1497 records two such payments, both apparently considered unusual. In June, for an extraordinary procession to San Segondo, he paid Ruzier dal'arpa 2 lire for strings. That September, he gave Sabastian dal lauto a slightly smaller sum (£1 s. 6) for strings for an unspecified, but again perhaps extraordinary procession, but only after approval by the guardian grande and all the members of the banca.[64] Before two years had passed, the sonadori had demanded this added benefit repeatedly, so the officers decided, at least temporarily, to make the practice more regular, offering them 10 soldi each for every procession for strings "out of kindness and not obligation."[65]

Organs and Organists

For those scuole that maintained their own church, and sometimes for the others, the organ remained, as in their early years, an important, and occasionally expensive, part of their musical concerns. The records for this period are incomplete, so that it is not possible to document the situation at all of the scuole, but some significant indications do remain.

The earliest known organist at the Scuola di San Giovanni Evangelista, which had moved and renovated its organ in the early 1440s (see chapter 3), was one Vettor Turian, apparently hired in September of 1453 at an annual salary of 3 ducats. In 1457, perhaps as an alternative to granting him a raise, the scuola admitted him among its provisional members, and he entered the ranks of regular brothers the following year.[66] He signed receipts for his salary annually through 1460, always in August or September, and then once more, in March 1462 for 5 ducats;[67] most likely he terminated his employment at that time, for reasons not recorded, and this final payment was for one full year and the additional months up to the date of his departure. The documents make no mention any replacement for Turian, nor indeed for any other organist at this scuola prior to the sixteenth century.

The records of the Scuola della Misericordia, which had documented the employment of organists from the 1370s through 1439 (see chapter 3), are silent for the following thirty years. This may, of course, result from missing documents, but might also reflect a crisis of some sort. Perhaps as a result of a financial shortfall, the officers in 1468 were willing, rather than hire an organist in the usual manner, to accept the offer of a poor brother named Polo Zazo, who asked to be granted a room in the scuola's hospice in exchange for serving as organist and scribe.[68] The following year, however, the scuola returned to its traditional practice of employing professional organists, usually clerics, and hired pre Puzo da Perosa for 5 ducats a year (perhaps Polo Zazo, if he had not died in the interval, remained as scribe, after the termination of his musical duties). Pre Puzo contin-ued in his post through at least 1479, the date of the last document before another gap extending through the end of the century.[69] Probably the biggest event during his tenure, although the surviving records are quite terse, was the rebuilding of the organ in 1477, exactly fifty years after the completion of Tomaxo Inzegner's instrument, itself a replacement made fifty-five years after the construction of the scuola's first instrument (see chapter 3).[70]

One other scuola, Santa Maria della Carità, participated in the building of an organ during this period. In 1481, the canons of Santa Maria della Carità, the host church for the scuola, decided that their organ needed to be replaced. They reached an agreement with the scuola in which the costs would be divided almost equally. The canons would contribute 30 ducats in cash, and the scuola would offer its old and probably unusable organ that had been in the church, which was sold for 28 ducats. The scuola insisted on maintaining its rights to use the new organ for its services, and to hire an organist as needed; moreover, in public recognition of their contribution, the insignia of the scuola would remain forever visible on the exterior of the organ.[71]

THE SECOND HALF OF the fifteenth century represented an awakening of sorts for the scuole, as they adapted their long-standing traditions to make room for a new role for music, ever more valued during the Renaissance. The occasions for music remained the same as always, but the music itself was more up-to-date. The new polyphonic styles required a level of musical sophistication that could not be reliably found among the poor brothers of the scuole, who had traditionally done the singing, so the scuole turned, not without some initial difficulties, to professionals, and also began to hire trained instrumentalists. The patterns of music-making established during this period, including two or three ensembles of singers, differentiated by their duties, and one of stringed instruments, would remain essentially unchanged for over a century.

THE BEST IN THE CITY

Salaried Musicians, 1500–1650

No little honor to our scuola of misser San Rocco . . . results from having most excellent and diligent musicians who come on the principal feasts and are ready to sing the divine offices.[1]

In statements such as this, from a resolution of 1578, the officers of the scuole made it clear that the role of music at their institutions was no longer limited to the traditional one of honoring God and the saints, the souls of their dead brothers, and the city of Venice, but had expanded to include bringing honor to the scuola, to the officers as a body, and even to the guardian grande as an individual. In the Renaissance, the mixture of sacred and civic, one of the peculiar characteristics of the medieval scuole, now stood alongside the more purely secular, the personal and corporate ambitions of the Venetian citizens who directed and financed them. These merchants and civil servants discovered what the secular rulers of the Italian city-states had already recognized: the commissioning of sacred music, like the building of churches or the purchase of religious paintings, could, at the same time, bring honor to God and to the patron. This was, indeed, the period during which the scuole grandi made their greatest impact on the Venetian artistic scene. In the first half of the sixteenth century, San Giovanni Evangelista and San Marco completed the building (or renovation) of their halls, the Misericordia began the building of a new one, and San Rocco raised the most magnificent of all such structures. These years also brought Titian's *Presentation of the Virgin* for the albergo of the Carità, and the first appearance of Tintoretto, with the beginning of a cycle of paintings for San Marco. The second half of the century was dominated by Tintoretto, who completed work for San Marco and produced the monumental cycles that fill the three principal rooms of the Scuola di San Rocco. While the Misericordia's project to build a new hall ground to a halt because of the lack of funds, the brothers of the Scuola di San Teodoro, newly made a scuola grande, were able to complete all but the façade of theirs. These projects were, of course, designed to glorify the respective patron saints of the scuole, but also served to place the cittadino-led scuole in the mainstream of the patrician-dominated Venetian artistic culture. The same artists and architects who built and decorated the great private palaces and public buildings of Renaissance Venice brought increased honor to the scuole and their leaders. The developments in musical activities at the scuole grandi in the sixteenth and seventeenth centuries similarly reflect these sometimes conflicting goals as well as the counterbalancing forces of economics and the ever-present, watchful eye of the patrician authorities in the government.

The patterns established in the late fifteenth century, as discussed in the previous chapter, provided the foundations upon which the scuole brought their musical activities to their most elaborate and renowned level. In many respects, this rise occurred in tandem with developments at the city's musical hub, St. Mark's; this was, after all the period during which Venice, with such towering figures as Adrian Willaert, Andrea and Giovanni Gabrieli, and Claudio Monteverdi, became arguably the most important musical center in Italy. The least amount of change can be seen in the cantadori vecchi, the ensemble of brothers who sang at funerals. On the other hand, the cantadori nuovi, the trained processional singers, became the subject of intense competition among the scuole, each striving for the highest quality it could afford. Some of the scuole also expended effort on upgrading their instrumentalists and organists, and all, to some degree, tried to make the annual celebrations of their patron saints occasions for more and more elaborate music, rivaling the splendor of events at St. Mark's.[2]

Cantadori Nuovi/Cantadori Solenni

The musicians who bore the greatest responsibility both for carrying out a scuola's mandate to honor God and the city and for bringing secular honor to the scuola itself were those who sang in the public processions. This ensemble (as discussed in the previous chapter), the latest to be created, was known variously as cantadori nuovi (in contrast to the cantadori vecchi, the original group, now relegated to singing primarily for funerals) or cantadori solenni (and only occasionally in this period as cantadori de laude). It was created, as has been shown, in the 1470s, when the poor brothers of the scuola who had served as singers were no longer able to satisfy the increasing musical demands for the occasions in which the scuola appeared in public. Unlike the original singers, who received charity as compensation (singing was their obligation to the scuola as poor brothers), the cantadori nuovi had always been professionals, hired for their skill and paid either a salary or a fee for each procession, and then often admitted as brothers.

The duties of the cantadori nuovi fell into several categories, common to all six scuole: they sang at public processions, at processions to Castello during Lent, at annual visits to the other scuole, and on the first Sunday of each month. Most important, perhaps, were the public processions, both ordinary and extraordinary (that is, for special occasions, as demanded by the government) throughout the year. They were both civic and religious occasions, and, moreover, were witnessed by the largest number of people. Most of these, as described in chapter 2, were centered at the Piazza San Marco, but some went also to other churches. The scuole grandi were central participants, following one another in designated order, and appearing with their entire membership (at least according to statute and official decree) wearing the *cappa* of the scuola, and carrying candles and other ceremonial objects. The Lenten processions, held on Sunday evenings and the night between Maundy Thursday and Good Friday, to the Cathedral of San Pietro di Castello (later that for Maundy Thursday went no farther than the Piazza San Marco) were similar in many respects, except that the scuole travelled individually, and therefore were not in direct competition with each other. The annual visits each scuola grande made to the other five (usually in the sixteenth century also to the Scuola dei Mercanti, even though it was not a scuola grande) also included individual processions, though they are described less precisely in the surviving ceremonials than the others.

Exactly what the cantadori nuovi sang at these processions is unclear. The only documentary references are in the 1571 ceremonial of San Giovanni Evangelista (recording, however, the practices of the late fifteenth century), which describes the singers as performing laude each time the procession stopped at a church.[3] No mention is made of whether they also sang while walking, nor whether they sang along with the instrumentalists. The evidence of Gentile Bellini's painting for the same scuola of a procession in the Piazza is difficult to interpret (see chapter 4): the singers and instrumentalists are next to each other, and appear to be singing and playing in the midst of the procession. However, Bellini might have chosen to show them performing their characteristic duties, even if they would not normally have done so at the precise point in the procession depicted.[4] San Rocco's 1521 ceremonial book[5] carefully indicates the location within the procession of singers and instrumentalists (usually, it should be noted, not together), but makes no mention of their activities. Whether they continued to sing laude in the sixteenth and seventeenth centuries is also unclear, but it seems likely that the repertory would have been more varied, and more sophisticated, as indicated by the employment, as will be discussed below, of the singers of the cappella of St. Mark's, who were certainly capable of singing more than simple laude. It should also be noted that by the sixteenth century the scuole almost never used the older term cantadori de laude, which clearly described the function of the ensemble at its time of origin. Another city of the Veneto, Treviso, provides a suggestion of what the repertory might have been like; the singers employed there by the principal confraternities sang works from the standard printed motet repertory (albeit tailored for local needs and preferences).[6] Unfortunately, in Venice, since the music itself was apparently supplied by the singers, not by the scuole (there are no payments for purchase or copying of music in the surviving account books, nor do such items appear in the inventories of the possessions of the scuole, nor in their extant archives), no clear answer is possible. It is most likely that the singers performed the same sort of music they sang in their regular cappella jobs—motets and similar works. At the Lenten processions, the repertory probably included penitential psalms, motets, and laude. For the annual visits to the other scuole, they probably sang motets or laude in praise of the patron saint of the celebrating scuola. The increase in the size of the standard ensemble from four to five around the middle of the sixteenth century also points toward motets as the focus of their repertory: while the increase in number of voices during the sixteenth century is one of the characteristics of the motet, no evidence suggests a tradition of laude for more than four voices.[7]

The obligations of the cantadori nuovi on the first Sunday of each month differed from those at the various kinds of public processions. Though each scuola did sometimes perform a short procession around a nearby square, the focus of the celebration was a mass in the scuola's church or in whichever nearby monastic church it maintained an altar, or sometimes in the hall of the scuola itself, which often contained a sanctified altar. Precisely what the cantadori sang is not clear. At San Marco in 1544, for example, the newly elected singers were instructed that they were required "to sing . . . the high mass."[8] This might seem to indicate, especially since this was a quintet of singers from the cappella ducale, that they would sing a polyphonic mass ordinary (such, perhaps, as those published by their maestro di cappella, Willaert). A document from San Giovanni Evangelista from 1597, however, apparently describes a somewhat different practice: the scuola needed singers because their church did not have sufficient priests to "say high mass and respond [in the] mass."[9] In this case, they might have served as a liturgical choir, singing the responses in chant, and alternating, perhaps in *falsobordone*, with the celebrant. The only other indication of their duties is found in the reappointment of singers at San Marco in 1550: no mention is made of singing at mass, but rather they were required to "sing the requiem for the dead over the tombs of the scuola," in the other ceremonial activity of the first Sunday of the month.[10] As with the processions, the evidence simply is not sufficient to reach more definite conclusions about the repertory.

Occasionally, agreements with cantadori nuovi listed different requirements from those indicated above. At the Scuola della Misericordia, for example, none of the documents before 1612 makes any reference to service on the first Sunday of the month. On the other hand, the singers were regularly required to perform not only at the Maundy Thursday procession, as at the other scuole, but also to sing the mass and Passion in the church.[11] San Rocco's singers also sang masses beyond those on the first Sunday of the month: a 1517 listing included masses for several feasts of the Madonna and at Vespers on the vigils of the Assumption and the feast of St. Roch.[12] A 1553 list added masses for the installation of the new banca and new guardian da mattin.[13] Similarly, at San Giovanni Evangelista in 1609, the cantadori sang at Vespers on the vigils of the scuola's two main feasts (St. John and the Holy Cross), and also at the benediction of the oil on Palm Sunday and the benediction of the candles on the feast of the Purification (the latter known familiarly as the Madonna of the Candles).[14]

The reasons the scuole thought it important to have musicians in their processions, when they were most clearly on public view, were quite complex. Certainly, the original view, as expressed by San Giovanni Evangelista in its 1446 petition to the Council of Ten, that singers were needed to preserve "the honor of God and of his glorious Apostle and Evangelist St. John,"[15] still persisted in the sixteenth and seventeenth centuries. One of its clearest expressions was that by San Marco in 1542, that keeping singers was "to honor the Lord God."[16] Similarly eloquent were the officers of San Rocco in 1526: "the scuola, for fear of glorious

God and of St. Roch, cannot do without having four singers."[17] Similarly, if more narrowly, San Giovanni Evangelista needed singers "for the honor of the Holy Cross,"[18] that is for their famous relic of the True Cross, and San Marco, in 1526, "to honor the divine worship."[19] Sometimes hiring singers was simply "necessary,"[20] or "most important,"[21] or even "a praiseworthy, honorable, and necessary thing."[22] At times, the reasons were not religious but civic, in line with their other major focus: the Council of Ten decided in 1553 to again allow the scuole to hire musicians, after the practice had been banned shortly before (see below), "for the honor of this city."[23] The view of the Misericordia in 1591 was perhaps similar: singers were necessary "for the honor of the processions."[24]

All of these approaches were quite consonant with the founding purposes of the scuole, but a new attitude also emerged alongside the traditional ones, especially in the latter half of the sixteenth century, that having music was not only good for the honor of God and the city, but also for the honor of the individual scuole. In 1591, the Misericordia needed singers for the "honor of our scuola,"[25] as did San Giovanni Evangelista in 1597.[26] At San Rocco, singers were necessary "for the honor and decorum of this our scuola" in 1578,[27] or, in 1631, for the "honor and grandeur of our scuola,"[28] or because "the nobility of this most dignified scuola requires it."[29] This desire for corporate honor was not purely an abstract one: each scuola, at least in part, compared itself with the others. When, in 1610, the Misericordia found itself in a procession without singers, the officers said that this situation could not be tolerated "so that the scuola would not in the future lose that reputation it has always conserved with the other scuole and before the entire city."[30] San Marco's lament in 1590 was in the same vein: they had looked bad "in the processions in respect to the other scuole grandi, which, beyond the ancient and usual ornament [of singers] have advanced further, so that it was a miserable thing to see the scuola of our protector [St. Mark] go by in this manner."[31] This purely secular desire to maintain the image of the scuola extended even to the individuals who governed a scuola, as expressed by San Marco in 1501, that singers were necessary "for the honor and reputation of this banca and fraternity."[32] Not having singers, on the other hand, would bring "shame."[33] These men realized that by hiring musicians they could satisfy several needs at once: they could honor God and Venice, and at the same time increase the reputation and prestige of their scuola, and of themselves.

At times, the scuole seemed content merely to have singers, regardless of their quality. In other words, shame, or lack of honor, was brought about simply by the absence of singers in processions. More often, however, and increasingly so during this period, the officers were clearly concerned with the ability of their salaried musicians. They manifested this concern more often when disappointed. For example, in 1524, the Scuola di San Rocco had, according to the banca, "many times suffered shame because [our] singers are not excellent."[34] The Misericordia's situation in 1540 was even worse. They found it necessary to fire their singers for reasons eloquently expressed in a motion put to the chapter:

> There is no money of our scuola that is spent with less result and more shame
> and bother to the officers than is the payment made to the *cantadori nuovi*, who,

for their ill manner of singing, without any harmony or sweetness of voice, are held in general contempt and displeasure by all.[35]

They also, it turned out, often failed even to show up at processions, all of which was something "certainly shameful to those in charge." The Scuola di San Marco, on the other hand, was very pleased with the singers who had served in 1551, since, as described in a motion to rehire them, they had helped the scuola to maintain its high status among the five scuole then active:

> It being an honest thing to provide for the honor of our fraternity, as has always been done by our respected predecessors, who have always, with all diligence, striven that our scuola would be the most honored in the city in all things, and because employing cantori solenni, most of all those who have usually served the scuola in past years, who are in effect the best in this land, is a thing of great honor.[36]

San Teodoro, which, as the youngest and poorest of the scuole grandi, had no hope of outclassing the others, was happy to find, in 1570, "four singers who are adequate and the equal of [those of] the other scuole."[37]

The scuole had several methods for finding appropriate singers, with an aim of not only maintaining the quality they had achieved, but, whenever possible, raising the level even higher, so as not to be outdone by their competitors. These procedures were both direct (that is, selecting candidates based on hearing them sing) and indirect (hiring singers from the major cappelle of the city, those of the major Dominican, Franciscan, and Augustinian monasteries and the ducal chapel of St. Mark's, relying on the ability of those institutions to choose able musicians). The auditioning process ranged from casual to quite formal, though in the majority of the cases the documents say nothing about the procedures employed. At times (as in modern academia) the officers only considered as a candidate someone who had been serving as a substitute.[38] When the Misericordia needed a new ensemble in 1540, the officers first received reliable opinions about a candidate group ("having had excellent reports") and then verified them by audition ("and had experience of their sufficiency").[39]

The scuole might hold formal auditions for individual singers or for entire ensembles. When in 1552, as a newly chartered scuola grande, San Teodoro needed to hire its first ensemble of singers, they "saw and heard many musicians" before deciding on two friars from the Dominican monastery of Santi Giovanni e Paolo, who would be responsible for finding two other singers "who are good and sufficient in that art."[40] Some officers announced auditions in a very public manner, using the places designated by the city for all official announcements, Piazza San Marco and the Rialto. Heralds made such a proclamation on behalf of San Giovanni Evangelista in 1610: "By order of the magnicent guardian grande of the Scuola of San Giovanni Evangelista de Battudi of Venice, be it known that any singer who wishes to audition as a *cantor solenne* of the said scuola, should appear this coming 3 April after supper, when his magnificence wants to hold the election."[41] When the Scuola di San Marco needed to replace a tenor in 1544, it limited the announcement to the institution where the outgoing man had served: "his magnificence intends to put before all the singers of the said monastery of Santi Giovanni e Paolo, that whoever wishes to be considered provide notice today."[42] In this case, as in the few that survive involving the selection of a single singer, only two candidates appeared, fra Perin Relievo and fra Hippolito Ciera. In the usual manner of Venetian elections, every elector (unless he had a family relationship with the candidate) had to vote either yes or no for each man. This time, fra Perin received seventeen votes in favor and five against, and fra Hippolito only twelve in favor and nine against; Perin was hired.

The details of auditions are not at all clear, but we can get at least a vague idea from one held at San Rocco in 1524, when the entire ensemble needed to be replaced. "Because it is a thing of some importance," the motion reads, "in recent days several companies of singers sang in our church, and were listened to by the [guardian grande] and banca together several times."[43] The twenty-five members of the banca and zonta, gathered together in the albergo in the name of the Holy Ghost and St. Roch, voted on three ensembles. Interestingly, these were not three entirely different ensembles, but several arrangements of a small number of singers, nearly all from the nearby Franciscan convent of the Frari:

soprano:	Andrea Salamon	el Furlan di fra menori	Andrea Salamon
alto:	fra Zuan Antonio	fra Zuan Antonio	fra Zuan Antonio
tenor:	fra Zuan Michiel	pre . . .	fra Zuan Michiel
bass:	fra Sarafin	fra Sarafin	pre Paulin
votes:	16–9	14–11	7–18

Note that the most and least favored groups differed only in their bass singer. Were the officers concerned perhaps with the blend of the four voices? Unfortunately, the document provides neither the reasons for the choice, nor information about what these ensembles sang at their audition.

One last method the scuole used occasionally was to rely on the efforts, or good fortune, of the others, that is, they lured good singers away from one scuola to serve another. That had been the method San Rocco used as a newly created scuola grande in 1488 to select its first ensemble of singers, and the practice seems to have continued into the sixteenth century. While the phenomenon is not often discussed in the documents, it can sometimes be traced in the rosters of the ensembles—a singer resigns from one scuola and is shortly afterwards hired at another. For San Marco in 1525, this had apparently become a regular problem that needed to be addressed. The officers had always attempted to employ good singers, and therefore, "because we had some good singers and virtuous individuals, the other scuole, not observing the love that one scuola owes to another, lured them away from our service to go to theirs, with the promise of a greater salary."[44] The solution, in this case, was to offer the singers membership in the scuola free of charge, in addition to their regular salary.

The singers selected as cantadori nuovi through audition and other procedures were quite diverse in their stature in the Venetian musical world. Though the earliest ones certainly were professionals, they do not appear to have been singers of real prestige, with a few exceptions. During the sixteenth century, this would change, as the scuole increasingly hired singers from the most prestigious musical establishments in the city, the major monasteries and St. Mark's itself. While the ducal cappella was certainly the most famous and highest quality ensemble in the city, other Venetian institutions also maintained a regularly salaried polyphonic choir. Three major monastic houses employed such an ensemble in the sixteenth and seventeenth centuries, with a maestro di cappella (though not all with the same continuity as St. Mark's): the Dominicans of Santi Giovanni e Paolo, the Franciscans of Santa Maria Gloriosa dei Frari (referred to simply as I Frari), and the Augustinian hermits of Santo Stefano.[45] There were also numerous freelance secular singers and priests, and individual singers from other monasteries; most likely, however, few of them achieved the level of quality or skill of those in the cappelle. The scuole grandi drew on all of these sources for their cantadori nuovi, with their choices depending on several factors, notably cost (since those from the cappelle, especially St. Mark's, demanded higher pay), convenience (the busy schedule of the ducal chapel could create conflicts, on the one hand, while on the other, some of the monasteries were adjacent to some scuole), and, as indicated above, the desire to maintain or increase their reputation for musical excellence.

Of course, views on the importance of singers, the methods used to hire them, and the balance between expense and prestige varied constantly, not only from scuola to scuola, where different traditions were maintained, but also with the annual succession of guardians, who held personal views on all of these issues, which they sometimes succeeded in imposing on their scuole, even in the face of precedent. All of these factors created histories of the cantadori nuovi at the six scuole grandi, to be examined below, that differed considerably one from another in many respects.

San Giovanni Evangelista

Though the Scuola di San Giovanni Evangelista was the first, in 1447, to request permission to hire singers (see above, chapter 4), its commitment to maintaining an ensemble often waivered, which made singers a ready target for the regular budget cuts that occurred in the sixteenth and seventeenth centuries. As with most of the scuole, the documentation for the cantadori nuovi has many gaps, but the trends, and many of the details, are clear. The first documentation of singers, referred to, as was the practice at this scuola, as cantadori solenni (solemn singers), after the fifteenth-century petitions to the Council of Ten is, in fact, a 1537 record of their firing to save money.[46] The scuola notified the men (at least two of whom, pre Alexandro Zatta and pre Zefiro, were members of the ducal chapel) that they were fired, since the scuola, burdened with the expense of sending men to the galleys (see below), "no longer wanted the expense of singers."[47] At some point before 1561, the scuola had again employed a prestigious ensemble from the cappella, but, as the officers explained in 1561, they had "experienced the inconveniences that arise in waiting for singers obligated to the church of San Marco." Clearly, the scuola still wanted singers at its processions, so the officers made an offer of 50 ducats a year (the statutory maximum; see p. 153) for a period of five years to a company of singers from the Frari, "which is near our scuola, and convenient, so that they conveniently can and have offered to serve us."[48] For some unknown reason, the friars rejected the offer, and the scuola apparently turned, once again, to an ensemble made up, at least in part, of singers from St. Mark's, who, in a by now predictable pattern, they fired in 1563 to save money.[49] Just as predictably, shortly after the chapter made the decision to stop offering salaries to singers, a new guardian grande, without bothering to get permission from the chapter, resumed the practice, usually without problems. Therefore, though they never passed a motion to rehire singers, the scuola gave them a bonus for the feast of St. John the Evangelist in 1569.[50] In 1573, as part of a comprehensive budget-cutting exercise, the chapter, in language they certainly believed would be clear to those who followed, made the decision never again to salary singers, which had cost the scuola 50 ducats annually, but to allow the guardians only to hire them as needed, spending no more than 25 ducats a year.[51]

Within two years, however, San Giovanni Evangelista had resumed paying salaries to cantadori solenni,[52] and for the next twenty years (perhaps the longest uninterrupted stretch for this scuola) maintained a prestigious ensemble of four singers, many of them from St. Mark's (including Giovanni Croce, Paulo Veraldo, and fra Girolamo Carmelitano), paying them 10 ducats each annually. This practice came to an end, again, in 1594, after the government imposed on them a galley tax of 4,000 ducats, and the chapter declared that "from now on, it is forbidden, under any pretext, method, mode, or form that one can imagine, to elect or retain cantori solenni," except that the guardians might, from time to time, hire "extraordinary singers," as at the Misericordia and the Carità, at a total annual expenditure of no more than 20 ducats.[53] Within three years, the scuola realized the necessity of keeping singers "to honor our most Holy Cross," and hired padre Augustin Fasuol, from the ducal cappella, and four others, for about 27 ducats a year ($£14$ each month).[54] Another brief golden age ensued, with choirs made up almost exclusively of singers from St Mark's, culminating, in a manner of speaking, with the decision in 1609, for the first time in the scuola's history, to define in detail the duties of the singers and their conditions of election and payment.[55] The scuola would pay the four-man ensemble 50 ducats a year for fifteen processions, the first Sunday of each month, the visits to the other scuole, and several other occasions in the scuola; they would also give them candles for the feasts of St. John and the Purification. An officer would record attendance, and after a third unexcused absence, a singer would be replaced.

In order to save money, in 1614 the scuola once again reduced salaries, this time by 20 ducats,[56] and decided in 1622 to reballot all salaried employees, including singers, every two years, so that those derelict in their duties could be identified and replaced.[57] The reduced salary had a clear effect on the quality of the singers: as best as can be determined, the ensembles were now made up of priests from local parish churches, rather than singers from the ducal cappella. The leader of the ensemble in 1631, one pre Bernardo from San Stin, requested, in light of the difficult times (the city had just suffered a devastating plague), that he and his four companions receive a raise from 20 ducats a year to 25.[58] The chapter failed, in three attempts, to approve the request, but was willing to offer an

increase of 4 ducats instead. The last documented singer of San Giovanni Evangelista, pre Iseppo Alberti, agreed to the same terms for his company in 1633.[59]
A budget cut imposed by the Council of Ten in 1639 resulted in further reductions, to about 16 ducats,[60] and the scuola suspended the salary entirely, at least
temporarily, in 1643.[61] With the War of Crete, in 1647, the financial burdens on
the scuola were so great, that, despite being allowed by the Council of Ten to
pay 22 ducats for singers and instrumentalists, the scuola decided to fire pre Iseppo
and his companions.[62] San Giovanni Evangelista apparently never again salaried
an ensemble of singers, assigning their duties instead to the priests of the scuola's
church.

Santa Maria della Carità

While the Scuola della Carità was not significantly richer than San Giovanni
Evangelista, its budget seemed to fluctuate less, or, at the least, the officers seemed
to manage to preserve their activities with fewer disruptions through most of the
sixteenth century. After some controversies in the late fifteenth century, the scuola
established a practice that endured through 1588, with only one significant modification. For the first half of the century, the scuola paid the four singers in the
ensemble of cantadori nuovi, most of them not members of any of the major
cappelle, 11 ducats each. From the late 1550s, the singers, now primarily drawn
from the cappella ducale, received a salary of 12½ ducats each, for the statutory
maximum of 50 ducats. As might be expected, problems arose from time to time.
Apparently, the guardian grande had had the discretion to hire the singers he
pleased for the term of his office, but in 1534, while the mass for the feast of the
Annunciation was in progress, one of the singers, pre Francesco from the church
of San Zuan de Furlani, persuaded the banca, presumably by threatening to desert
the service, to confirm him at the existing salary not only for the current year,
but for as long as he wished to serve.[63] When the new guardian took office a
short time later, he was distressed to realize that his prerogative had been usurped:
if he wished to hire singers of his choice, he would have to do so in addition to
pre Francesco. At his instigation, the chapter passed a resolution, which had already been approved by the Council of Ten, that declared pre Francesco's contract
null and void, and reestablished the authority of the guardian grande to hire
whomever he wished.[64]

What could have been the most serious threat to music at the scuole grandi
began as a salary dispute between cantadori nuovi and the Scuola della Carità in
1553. The singers had been serving at 11 ducats each, but, emboldened after the
formation of a new singers's company (see p. 152), they came to the guardian
Vicenzo Quartari and demanded a raise to 16. While Quartari was angered by
this request, he, along with his fellow officers, agreed to a raise to 13, covering
the increase out of their own pockets. The singers were, however, not satisfied,
and turned instead to the Scuola della Misericordia, which offered them what
they asked. Since they had broken their contract with the Carità, the guardian
sued them before the Avogadori di Comun, who ordered the singers to return,
and to serve as they had earlier agreed. While still in court, Quartari was suddenly

inspired by the Holy Spirit, "and knew truthfully before God and catholic and pious people, that it would be better to spend these 70 or 80 ducats to assist many of our poor, or to provide dowries to many poor girls, rather than spend this money on those singers, for worldly pomp and self-aggrandizement."[65] He told the singers right then and there that they were fired, and then submitted a proposal to his banca (and then to the chapter) to forbid permanently the guardians or officers of the Carità from hiring singers with an annual salary. When, as was the standard practice, the decision was sent to the Council of Ten for ratification, they extended the ban to all the scuole. Only after several months of controversy (treated in more detail below), did the council rescind that draconian measure.

After again being permitted to hire singers, the Scuola della Carità displayed a clear desire for the best musicians possible (clearly, the earlier controversy had been the result more of a personal crusade by the serving guardian than of a widespread feeling within the scuola). In 1558, they were very pleased with their ensemble of four singers from St. Mark's (Luca Gualtiero, Perissone Cambio, Giovan Zelst, and Gerardo Molin), who had served "solicitously and most sufficiently, with the satisfaction and honor of our scuola and the entire city," and they declared that "one could not expect more from such men." To reward them, to ensure their continued service, and to avoid the constant disruptions caused by new singers every year, they were "assumed, approved, and confirmed" as cantadori nuovi "forever," and admitted as brothers into the scuola, receiving all the benefits of membership, as long as they continued to carry out their duties.[66] When, in the late 1560s, Cambio and Molin died, the scuola looked only to St. Mark's for replacements. Before 1568, however, they had found no "appropriate voices," and had left the permanent positions unfilled. Finally, "having been hired in the cappella di San Marco two singers, one, Joseph Bressan, who sings contralto, and the other, Antonio de Ribera, a Spaniard, who sings soprano, who are exellent singers," the scuola was satisfied, and offered the two men positions as singers and brothers, on the same conditions as their predecessors.[67] The scuola confirmed its attachment to these fine singers in 1580, when the aged Luca Gualtiero petitioned to be allowed to keep his membership and salary, even though he was too feeble to serve as singer. Both banca and chapter approved this almost unprecedented request (unheard of for this scuola) by overwhelming margins.[68]

The Carità's long tradition of employing fine singers was broken in 1588 when, in order to compensate for a law that mandated the scuola to pay a galley tax of 50 ducats every month, the banca approved a resolution banning the paying of salaries to singers. As at San Giovanni Evangelista, in future singers were only to be hired for processions and festivals as needed.[69] This new method appears to have been followed for the remainder of the sixteenth century and through the middle of the seventeenth. There is, unfortunately, no record of the names of the singers hired during this period, but the surviving accounts, beginning in 1644, show payments totaling about 20 ducats a year.[70] Then, in 1647, in the same decree that forced San Giovanni Evangelista to abandon its practice of hiring singers, the Council of Ten ordered the expenses for musicians at the Carità to be cut in half.[71] When the singers refused to continue to serve for the reduced amount, the first reaction of the banca was to fire them and hold new elections, but the syndic overturned the decision, and the parties apparently reached some sort of accommodation.[72] The scuola continued to pay singers in the 1650s at the rate of only about 10 ducats annually.[73] While the Carità held on to its tradition of employing singers for its processions at least a few years longer than San Giovanni Evangelista (they appear to be, in fact, the only one of the six scuola to employ singers on a continuing basis through as late as 1660), the heights reached in the mid-sixteenth century were not approached again.

Santa Maria della Misericordia

The Scuola della Misericordia, for much of the sixteenth century in better financial shape than San Giovanni Evangelista and the Carità, was also able to maintain an ensemble of cantadori nuovi with fewer interruptions. This scuola also drew upon a wider variety of sources for its singers, relying less, until near the end of the century, on the cappella ducale. In addition, the officers seem to have experimented a bit more with methods of payment, switching between yearly salary and fees for service rendered.

The system the Misericordia had used in the fifteenth century of paying singers by the occasion continued into the beginning of the sixteenth century. In 1505, the banca reached an agreement with one Jacomo Tais, whose company had served the scuola the previous Lent, that would pay them 10 ducats for their earlier services, and a little over a ducat for each procession during the year, with a 2-ducat payment for the heavier duties on Corpus Christi.[74] A decade later, the guardian grande, desiring to maintain a tradition of hiring "good and perfect singers," reached a different sort of agreement with an ensemble to be supplied by pre Zuanne Antonio Negro, maestro di cappella at the cathedral of San Pietro di Castello: the scuola would pay the four-member choir a flat salary of 16 ducats for the year.[75] By the 1520s, such singers cost considerably more: the ensemble hired in 1521 agreed to a salary of 40 ducats (with one of the men, pre Alvise dela Vilote, receiving an extra 3 ducats annually to sing the Gospel on the first Sunday of each month).[76]

The Misericordia began to use individual singers from St. Mark's beginning in 1528, when pre Alvise di Bortolomeo joined the ensemble.[77] Though he apparently did not stay long, the scuola always employed at least one cappella singer through 1543 (following which there is a considerable gap in the records). During most of this period, the ensemble found some degree of stability, with three of the four men serving for nearly ten years. The scuola hired pre Francesco Zefiro, of the ducal cappella, as a replacement in 1540, and later that year the guardian grande also began to pay two additional cappella singers, pre Alexandro Zatta and pre Zorzi Carpenelo, that is, an ensemble of six.[78] Despite these prestigious singers, however, the scuola was not well served. In September, the officers lamented that there was no expense of the scuola that brought less fruit than for these singers, who had shamed the scuola both by singing badly ("without any harmony or sweetness of voice")[79] and, at times, by failing entirely to show up. The scuola, of course, fired them, and some officers expressed the opinion that it might be better to pay them only by the occasion, to ensure their service. The new guardian (who took office on 8 December), however, preferred to retain the salary system, and hired a distinguished quartet on the same terms as the previous ones. The ensemble included two singers from the cappella ducale (Zorzi Carpanello, again, and fra Sigismondo, also at the monastery of Santi Giovanni e Paolo), one from the Frari (fra Antonin), and a well-known freelancer, Mateo dala Viola (better known as an instrumentalist).[80] Within a year, however, the scuola replaced this group with one that included two singers previously fired (Francesco Zefiro and Alexandro Zatta), along with a different pre Alexandro and a singer from the Augustinian house of Santo Stefano, at an increased salary of 48 ducats.[81] Some years later, the scuola apparently flirted briefly with an even higher salary for the singers: in 1553, when their request for a salary of 16 ducats was rejected by the officers of the Carità, that scuola's singers persuaded the Misericordia to take them on at that unusually high rate. This situation, however, was very short-lived, as the guardian of the Carità, as discussed above, successfully sued the singers before the Avogadori di Comun, and forced them to return to their posts (before firing them and precipitating a crisis).[82]

For much of the second half of the sixteenth century, the Misericordia seemed to prefer to employ monastics as cantadori nuovi. A document of 1574, though it mentions no names, does praise the service of the "reverend padri singers," and decrees that they can only be removed by vote of the banca and zonta.[83] A decade later, the officers were less pleased with an ensemble led by fra Sigismondo of Santi Giovanni e Paolo, and fired the singers, replacing them with a quartet of unnamed Augustinian friars from Santo Stefano, replaced in its turn, within two years, by four Dominicans from Santi Giovanni e Paolo.[84] This last ensemble apparently served satisfactorily, but the finances of the scuola then took a turn for the worse. Already burdened by the expense of attempting to complete their new hall (designed by Sansovino), the new galley tax of 1588 forced them to eliminate most salaried employees, including singers.[85] The officers attempted to replace the salaried ensemble with singers hired for the occasion, but with poor results. The scuola needed to have singers, so as not to be shamed by the other scuole, but freelance singers demanded money in excess of what annual salaries would have cost. As a result, in 1592 the scuola resumed its old system, and elected four singers from Santi Giovanni e Paolo, at least three of whom (the fourth is un-named) had been members of the ensemble released several years before.[86] This time, despite its previous good record, the ensemble failed to fulfil its duties, and the scuola fired them in 1593.[87] The next ensemble whose singers are named, newly elected in 1595 at a salary of 48 ducats, consisted primarily of singers from the ducal cappella, including Nicolò da Vandali, Lucio Mora, and fra Agostino.[88]

Now, having at last joined the other scuole in using the prestigious singers of the cappella ducale, the Misericordia suffered the same problems as had the other scuole with these busy and much desired men. By 1605, three of the four singers hired ten years earlier, although still employed by the scuola, no longer served personally, but rather sent replacements from the cappella: fra Agostino, the bass, had sent pre Baldissera Soto; pre Piero di Rinaldi, the tenor, had gone to Rome, and his replacement, pre Vicenzo Spontini, often deserted the scuola in processions; and Lucio Mora, the alto, had left to serve the Scuola di San Teodoro, sending Francesco Canigliano as his substitute.[89] A new ensemble chosen in 1605 featured two of those substitutes, along with another singer fom St. Mark's. The scuola's bad luck continued, and five years later they fired all these men for bad service, and hired a new quartet, all clerics, and only two from the ducal cappella, at the slightly lower salary of 40 ducats.[90] The downhill slide continued in 1612, when an ensemble of priests from the cathedral and parish churches began serving, for the same salary, but with the addition of a gift of 1 ducat each on the scuola's feast.[91] Then, just three years later, the scuola's galley-tax bill of over 10,000 ducats forced it to eliminate salaried singers and limit total expenses for the year, for singers hired for the occasion, to 10 ducats.[92] In practice, the officers treated this as a salary, paying it to the singers in two annual portions of 5 ducats each, through the plague of 1631.[93] For most of the 1630s and 1640s, the scuola paid the ensemble—whose members only once included a singer of the ducal cappella—by the occasion, and, though the chapter never approved such a raise, gave them as much as 30 ducats in some years.[94] As with other scuole, however, the financial impact of the War of Crete, in 1648, spelled the end of the tradition of employing cantadori nuovi—from then on the scuola could hire singers only for Maundy Thursday and Corpus Christi, and even then relied on choirs of priests.[95]

San Teodoro

As the youngest and poorest of the six scuole grandi, San Teodoro was often forced to seek ways of economizing while still maintaining the decorum and honor expected of its status. As mentioned above, among the first actions of the new scuola in 1552 was to audition and hire an ensemble of cantori solenni. They selected an ensemble of four Dominican friars from Santi Giovanni e Paolo, and offered a salary of 32 ducats, somewhat lower than those at the other scuole, which paid, at this period, 40 to 50 ducats.[96] This arrangement lasted little more than five months, and was then terminated, at the instigation of the scuola, but with the consent of the friars.[97] For the next several years, San Teodoro attempted to get by through the expedient of paying their cantadori vecchi (see below) something extra for additional services. This cost the scuola about 20 ducats annually for processions, and 12 to 15 ducats for Sundays. As a result, they not only spent more than necessary, but were "served as we are, and as everybody well knows," that is, poorly, and with little honor to the scuola. The chapter then decided in 1560 to salary five singers at a cost not to exceed 36 to 40 ducats.[98] They hired five singers unconnected with any of the major cappelle in the city, spending more than they had hoped, with costs eventually rising within a few years to 48 ducats. A few years after that, in 1568, the scuola felt it necessary, once again, to reduce costs; as a new ensemble had offered its services, they dismissed the old one, and signed a new sort of agreement.[99] This time, the four singers, including several foreigners, perhaps of higher quality than the previous ensemble, were willing to accept a lower salary, 32 ducats, in exchange for free admission to the scuola, with all the attendant benefits. This strategem was to remain the only avenue open to San Teodoro to secure acceptable singers.

After two members of the ensemble resigned to leave the city in late 1569, the chapter instructed the guardian grande to find new singers, which he accomplished the following spring, but at an increased cost of 40 ducats a year, 10 ducats below the statutory maximum paid by the other five scuole, plus the usual membership.[100] For the remainder of the century, the documents are silent on the subject of singers at San Teodoro, except for including some of them in the membership roles (perhaps others are also listed, but as they are not identified as singers, and as their names do not appear elsewhere, they cannot be identified).[101] Similar listings in the early seventeenth century contain, for the first time at this scuola, the names of two singers from St. Mark's, Lucio Mora (who had earlier served at the Misericordia) and Paulo Veraldo (previously at San Giovanni Evangelista). By 1611, when the scuola's budget situation had worsened, the singers received a salary of 36 ducats (four men at 9 ducats each).[102] This respectable sum was only possible because it did not come from the scuola's own funds, but rather from the *partidor*, private money of the officers, assessed according to their rank. Two years later, the deepening fiscal crisis obliged the scuola to seek a further reduction in the payments, so they negotiated a new agreement.[103] For a few years after this, singers' names still appear in the membership registers, and as late as 1628 the accounts still list an annual salary of 24 ducats for singers,[104] but by the time of the drastic cuts imposed at other scuole in 1647 and 1648 because of the War of Crete, San Teodoro lacked entirely the means to allocate any of their limited funds for singers.

San Marco

The Scuola di San Marco took very seriously its status as the only one of the six scuole grandi under the protection of Venice's patron saint. The officers tried to ensure that the scuola maintained the prestige of having the most beautiful hall, the most elaborate processions, and the best music. In the late fifteenth century and for much of the sixteenth they were able to achieve this goal, but their financial base was not strong, and by the early seventeenth century they finally had to yield primacy to others. As part of their efforts to offer the best music in the public processions, the Scuola di San Marco alone maintained, for nearly all of the first half of the sixteenth century, three separate vocal ensembles, and they were also the first to turn consistently to the cappella ducale for singers.

At the beginning of the sixteenth century, San Marco's cantadori de laude, as they referred to them, numbered only two (out of the five listed in 1497), both of them registered in the scuola as poor brothers, which they had been since the mid-1470s. The scuola gave them alms or housing of about 4 ducats annually, instead of salaries. These two singers alone could not meet the needs of the scuola, particularly as sometimes only one would show up to sing, bringing dishonor to the scuola, especially since the other scuole "had more than the basic number" ("hano de superflui"). Therefore, the scuola added a third singer, one Cosmo

Colona, a barber who was also a lutenist.[105] Shortly afterwards, the officers apparently made an attempt to upgrade the status of these musicians. The scuola hired another singer, pre Zanantonio, and began paying all of the singers a salary, which they then raised by 2 ducats each, to 12 ducats, in 1509.[106] Despite the raise, later that year the officers needed to admonish the ensemble to do a better job.[107] Pre Zanantonio, as their leader, begged for forgiveness, and the scuola allowed them to continue. By 1513, however, Zanantonio was gone, and, to save money, the scuola removed the salaries of the remaining three singers, and assigned to them, once again, monthly alms or houses, whichever would be available, this time at about 6 ducats annually.[108] As a result of the low remuneration, the singers, along with other fadighenti, constantly bombarded the officers with requests for additional offerings of bread and candles on major feast days, a practice that they banned in 1517, and tried to avoid having to buy their own *cappe*, which the chapter forced them to do beginning in 1519.[109] Despite the low wages, these men remained loyal to the scuola for extraordinarily long periods (though perhaps they were not skilled enough to seek other employment). Cosmo Colona, hired in 1501, served until his death in 1541; Polo di Zorzi, with the scuola by 1509, remained as a singer until 1552 (singing also with the cantadori di corpi); and Lorenzo de Alvise served from 1509 until he left the city in 1528.

A few years before his death, Cosmo Colona had become too ill to continue, and the guardian grande agreed to an offer by a friar from the nearby monastery of Santi Giovanni e Paolo, fra Tomaso Contarini, to fill his place without payment, on the condition that he would be appointed to the regular position upon Colona's death, which he was, in 1542.[110] Shortly before that date, the guardian had filled another vacancy with another friar of Santi Giovanni e Paolo, fra Dionisio, who was to bring along with him a soprano to fill out the ensemble.[111] When fra Thomaso left the scuola in 1544, the suola replaced him with yet another friar, fra Perin Relievo (whose opponent in the election, fra Hippolito Ciera, was not only a fellow Dominican friar, but the son of the guardian grande).[112]

Beginning as early as 1492, the Scuola di San Marco had decided to supplement its cantadori de laude, all of whom were brothers of the scuola, with high-quality external singers. As discussed in chapter 4, in that year the scuola accepted the offer of Pietro de Fossis, maestro di cappella at the basilica of San Marco, to sing at the scuola on feast days along with three companions, also from the cappella. The documents make no further mention of this practice for several decades, but it seems to have continued, at least intermittently, or resumed after some interruption, some years before 1525. In March of that year, the guardian grande proposed making permanent what had been an informal habit of paying additional singers 8 ducats each per year to sing in the processions and at the masses on the first Sunday of each month. This was necessary, he said, because, without a formal agreement, the other scuole (who were willing to offer them some stability) regularly snatched up the better singers. The new ensemble of four singers included two from the cappella ducale and one from the Augustinian house of Santo Stefano.[113] With this document also begins a significant confusion in the records—both ensembles, the traditional one made up of brothers receiving alms, and the new, salaried one, are referred to as cantadori de laude. Less than two years later, another guardian grande deemed the additional expense superfluous. Why, he added, pay external singers a salary of 8 ducats a year, when the regular ensemble of cantadori de laude was perfectly acceptable for ordinary Sundays, and could be cheaply supplemented, as needed, for more important occasions? He demonstrated that the savings could be as much as 16 ducats a year (to which he also added a savings of 4 ducats by eliminating some wind players; see below).[114]

By early in the next decade, while the practice continued of hiring, for the occasion, what were now sometimes called cantori solenni, the regular cantadori de laude were becoming old and less able to perform as desired. Since they were still brothers, however, the scuola could not really fire them, so the guardian grande serving in 1533 decided once again to hire an ensemble of four external singers for the major feasts, at a salary of 12 ducats each for three of them (including Domenego Stringer from the cappella), and 8 for fra Dionisio of Santi Giovanni e Paolo, who was also a member of the regular cantadori de laude.[115] The chapter ratified this contract with the condition that the hiring would be done at the pleasure of each year's guardian grande, to be approved by the banca and zonta. This rehiring and approval followed regularly through 1543, in which year the guardian grande selected three new singers alongside fra Dionisio, presumably with the same arrangement as before.[116] The following year, shortly after taking office, the new guardian grande decided to make a further change, and institutionalized even further this ensemble of cantori solenni as one entirely independent of the cantadori de laude. As part of this change, the singers were now among the best in the city, including four from the cappella ducale (pre Arcangelo di Piisimi delle Marche, Daniel Grisonio, pre Fabritio da Bologna, and Piero da Salò), along with pre Domenego da San Stin, who would later be one of only two non-cappella musicians in the singers' company founded in 1552 (see below).[117] The scuola was to pay these distinguished singers 12 ducats each per year, and would also give them the annual gifts presented to fadighenti. As a result, their names appear in the surviving lists of luminaria for the period (the confusion generated by the proliferation of ensembles is clear in this list—in the first year, the scribe abandoned any attempt to separate the ensembles, and simply listed all the singers together).[118] Despite the official separation between the cantadori de laude and the new cantori solenni, fra Dionisio apparently continued to sing in both, was rewarded by substantial gifts (5 ducats each) in 1545 and 1546, and became a formal member of the more prestigious group for several years after fra Arcangelo departed in 1548.[119] As Dionisio's skills began to fade, the scuola added another singer from St. Mark's, Francesco Greco (Francesco Londariti) in 1551, though he remained only one year.[120] That same year marked the end of the traditional ensemble of cantadori de laude, which no longer served the needs of the scuola; its members joined together with the cantadori di corpi, and the scribes listed the resulting ensemble as "cantadori da corpo et laude" from 1551 through 1561, after which all references to laude cease.

Following the debacle of the singers' company (see below), the chapter reconfirmed, in 1554, the same ensemble at the now statutory limit of 50 ducats (12½ each).[121] As a reward for their excellent service, and for bringing honor to the scuola, the chapter voted to accept these men, who were considered by the scuola as "the best in the city," as brothers in the same category as priests (that is, eligible for benefits as long as they served, but not eligible to run for office or to receive alms). In following years, the scuola replaced a few departed singers, usually with others from the ducal cappella (including Galeazo da Pesaro and Julio Bonagiunta around 1563[122]), but otherwise things seemed to proceed without incident. The documents list few names in the 1570s, but the ensemble seems to have begun to include more friars from Santi Giovanni e Paolo (two are listed in 1577, and two more, when they were fired for unexcused absences, in 1584), and from the Frari (fra Angelo da Bologna in 1586).[123]

This long run of distinguished singers was interrupted in 1587 when, after the imposition of a galley tax, the chapter decided to eliminate the salaried positions and hire men as needed for the occasion.[124] This experiment only lasted three years, since (as had happened at other scuole) it ended up costing more money, and often left San Marco to go in procession disgracefully without any singers. In a rare unanimous vote, 102 to 0, the general chapter decided to allow the guardian to hire salaried singers again.[125] As before, the Scuola di San Marco began to employ well-respected musicians, including, between 1597 and 1602, two singers from the cappella ducale (fra Agustin di Frari and Nicolò di Vandali) and two from Santi Giovanni e Paolo (fra Costanzo Gabrieli and fra Michiel Press).[126] The poor financial state of the scuola began to have an effect on the hiring of cantori solenni, however. In 1603 the chapter set the maximum salary for the ensemble at 40 ducats, and in 1609 enacted a prohibition against hiring singers (or instrumentalists) on a salaried basis.[127] The guardians continued, apparently, to hire singers as needed, but in 1639 the chapter eliminated even this option.[128] Though the Council of Ten, the following year, decreed that such a ban was detrimental to the "charity and decorum" of the scuola, professional singers never again appear in any of the records of this now much diminished confraternity.[129]

San Rocco

Though San Rocco was, in the sixteenth and seventeenth centuries, the richest and most successful of the scuole grandi, its experience with professional singers was not much different from the others. Because of the scuola's great prestige and deep pockets, the roster of singers employed here relied more consistently on the elite cappelle, especially St. Mark's, than the others. Though this certainly brought musical benefits to San Rocco, it sometimes also suffered the consequences when these mobile and much-in-demand men deserted the scuola's processions to accept better offers. Further, with a more solid financial foundation, the scuola was able to maintain singers when bad times or government intervention forced the others to eliminate those salaries, but, as we shall see, even San Rocco eventually succumbed.

The continuing attention of San Rocco to quality is evident as early as 1506, when it was willing to grant a significant raise (from 3 to 7 ducats to each of four singers), because it was important and an honor to employ singers "of such quality as these," and also because the singers claimed to provide more service than singers at other scuole, who were already paid comparable amounts.[130] When the singers (and instrumentalists) employed in 1516 proved unsatisfactory, the banca decided (rashly, it turned out) to simply eliminate the expense entirely, claiming reasons of economy, and arguing that the scuola could make better use of the money.[131] Barely four months later, however, they explained that the real reason had also involved quality: for the salary they offered, the officers felt that they "could have the best singers in the land."[132] Instead, they had been forced to hire additional singers in processions to make up for the defects of the ensemble. Rethinking their earlier decision, the banca now hired a new quartet, including one singer from the ducal cappella and two from the Benedictine priory of San Gregorio, at an increased salary of 32 ducats annually.

Problems arose again by 1524: three of their four singers had gone to serve elsewhere (precisely where is not indicated), and the remaining member of the ensemble, fra Zuan Michiel, had filled the gaps on his own, often bringing singers who were not, according to the banca, "excellent."[133] The scuola held auditions (as described on p. 112), and hired a new ensemble, made up of two singers from St. Mark's (fra Zuan Michiel and Andrea Salamon) and two Franciscans from the Frari, institutions that supplied almost all of San Rocco's singers for the next century. In the following year the chapter overturned the election, since only the banca, and not, as the regulations specified, the entire chapter, had made the choice.[134] For several months, San Rocco got by with no singers, but in May of 1526 the officers rehired the original ensemble, since going in processions without singers did not show the proper respect to "God and St. Roch."[135] A rather long period of relative tranquility ensued. For more than a century, despite sometimes difficult changes in personnel, San Rocco employed singers continuously (except for the brief interruption the Council of Ten mandated of all scuole in 1553). Several times, the scuola was even willing, in order not to lose good musicians, to allow its singers to take a leave of absence: in 1526 Andrea Salamon took a four-month galley trip (probably for private business reasons), and in 1530 fra Zuan Michiel left temporarily to take up a benefice, and was then readmitted.[136] Still pleased with the service of the singers, the scuola granted them a raise to 44 ducats (from 36) in 1535.[137] After the controversy surrounding the singers' company in 1553 (see below), San Rocco hired an ensemble entirely from the ducal cappella: pre Francesco Zeffiro (who had previously served the scuola), Don Anzolo Piissimi, Piero Gaietano, and Bernardo Salandi.[138] Some of these men continued to serve the scuola for many years. Don Anzolo finally became infirm and unable to serve in 1570 (to be replaced by another Anzolo, this time from the Frari), and pre Francesco Zeffiro, claiming to have served for fifty-nine years (though not listing the interruptions, sometimes of several years), requested, and was granted, a pension in 1573, and the scuola replaced him with another singer from the ducal cappella, Don Galeazzo.[139] By 1577, the scuola replaced the two remaining singers hired in 1553 with Baldassare Donato and Nicoletto da Castello.[140] The new ensemble, especially in comparison with its predecessor, was remarkably short-lived. Within just a few months, all but fra Anzolo had quit, and he, somewhat indisposed, and without his company, was fired.[141] Soon after, the scuola hired the singers who had served as substitutes during the absences of the regular members: Stefano Lippomano, Cesare Camerino, and two Spaniards, Antonio di Ribera and Piero Valenzuola, all from the cappella ducale.[142]

The members of this quartet, and some of those who followed, also proved to be less than reliable, perhaps because they were well enough known to be offered more money to sing elsewhere. In 1578, Antonio Ribera inappropriately deserted the scuola on its own feast day, and was fired along with Cesare da Camerino, who had been out of the city for several months.[143] In their place, the scuola hired two friars from the Frari, fra Anzoletto and fra Fabricio, the latter also a singer at St. Mark's.[144] The following year a third member of the quartet, Piero Valenzuola, also left town, to be replaced by the Roman Cesare Pinto.[145] In the mid-1580s, San Rocco hired such prized singers as a Frenchman from the cappella ducale, Guilelmo Fort, to replace fra Anzoletto, and fra Agustin Milanese, of the Frari and St. Mark's, for the position held by the recently fired fra Fabritio.[146]

Following over a decade of unbroken service, the singers requested in 1602 a favor that the scuola had apparently granted in the past to singers with many years at San Rocco: that they be made brothers of the scuola. The chapter, in the hopes of ensuring loyalty, granted the request,[147] apparently with good results, for the situation seems to have remained quite stable, with the usual replacements for deaths and departures, for nearly three decades. In the face of the great plague of 1631, however, during which the government banned most public processions and the scuola's resources were strained, the chapter thought it advisable to suspend the singers' salaries.[148] After barely six months, however, the insult to the "honor and greatness" of the scuola was too great to bear, and the banca and then general chapter almost unanimously approved rehiring the singers.[149] Several years later, for the first time in its history, the Scuola di San Rocco was not able to sustain the expenses of singers (and other musicians and employees) in the face of a galley tax, and in 1639 again suspended their salaries.[150] Two years after that, perhaps perceiving that the financial situation had improved, the singers (including three from St. Mark's) petitioned the banca to be rehired, at a slightly lower salary, since having singers "was called for by the nobility of this most dignified scuola."[151] The chapter accepted this offer, with strict instructions that the singers were to carry out their duties faithfully. By the late 1640s, the finances of the scuola had improved sufficiently that there was no need for them to fire the singers, as all the others had done, in the face of the heavy burdens imposed upon them to support the War of Crete in 1647 and 1648. This good fortune, however, would last only another decade. After another round of galley taxes, and perhaps seeing that they were practically alone at this point in retaining a salaried ensemble, San Rocco definitively eliminated singers in 1657.[152]

BY THE MIDDLE OF THE seventeenth century, therefore, the vocal ensembles known as cantadori nuovi or cantori solenni, created in the late fifteenth century to bring honor to the scuole and their processions, had disappeared for good.

Even the desire for honor could not stand up to the financial realities of a changing world. The scuole, as will be discussed in chapter 7, would need to seek elsewhere for the musical enrichment of their ceremonies.

Cantadori Vecchi/Cantadori di Morti

The original singers of the scuole, those poor brothers known usually as cantadori vecchi or cantadori de morti, did not receive the same attention in the sixteenth century as the more prestigious cantori solenni. The officers never considered this ensemble to be an important source of honor to the scuola, nor toward helping the scuola honor God or Venice. Rather, the music these men sang was considered a necessary component of the funerals with which the scuola honored the memory of each of its departed brothers. Their absence or misbehavior might well bring shame on the scuola, but their presence usually went unnoticed.

The primary tasks of the cantadori vecchi, as in previous centuries, comprised participating in funeral processions from the houses of the deceased to the places of burial, and singing at the funerals themselves. The traditional ceremonies, as prescribed in the mariegola, and discussed earlier, continued to be practiced in the sixteenth century, and it is likely that the music remained similar as well. Certainly, the cantadori vecchi were capable of singing polyphony, but their repertory was probably limited to simple settings of the same texts that they had previously sung monophonically. The documents do not, however, describe this music, nor do they mention what these men sang when they fulfilled that other portion of their obligations, the participation, like all fadighenti, in every public procession of the scuola. Since the scuole each had their ensembles of professional cantori solenni to sing sophisticated polyphony for such processions, the older group probably had a more limited role, perhaps singing traditional laude, or simply walking among the other fadighenti.

Unlike the cantori solenni, the cantadori de morti were not outside professionals, but poor brothers of the scuola, performing a required service in exchange for charity. The scuole filled openings either with existing brothers who possessed the necessary abilities, or with outsiders who qualified for such membership and were then accepted into the scuola according to the usual procedures. These men tended to keep their positions for the remainder of their adult lives, or at least for as long as they were able to sing, once again unlike the cantori solenni, who often departed after a brief period of service to follow other opportunities. Usually service of these singers was terminated only after long periods, and when such action could no longer be avoided. At the Carità in 1508, for example, three places were open, because one longtime singer had died, another was aged, infirm, and now totally deaf, and the third had lost his voice as a result of a syphilis infection.[153] As poor brothers of the scuola, however, according to the standard practice, the cantadori vecchi were entitled to continue to receive alms even if unable to carry out their duties. Rather than being an exceptional act for particularly meritorious service, as such pensioning had been for cantori solenni, this was the expected end of a career for cantadori vecchi (as with other fadighenti).

One unusual exception to the rule that singers in this ensemble were limited to poor laymen occurred at San Marco in the 1550s. When that scuola decided to enhance its musical establishment not by upgrading the cantadori de laude, as the others had done, but by employing a new ensemble, the cantori solenni, as discussed above, the two original groups eventually merged, with the new title of "cantadori di corpi e laude." As part of this process, a friar from Santi Giovanni e Paolo, fra Dionisio, who had sung with both the cantadori de laude and the cantori solenni, joined the poor brothers of the cantadori di corpi, where he remained for the rest of his professional career at the scuola. By the early 1560s, the ensemble regained the title that most appropriately described its duties, cantadori di corpi.[154]

Cantadori vecchi almost never received salaries, being paid instead with one or both of two methods: fees for each service performed and monthly alms (or, at times, free housing). The alms were usually 20 to 40 soldi per month, or 2 to 4 ducats a year. The singers received different amounts for funerals depending on who paid the expenses. For those of financially solvent brothers, for which expenses were paid either out of the estate of the deceased or by his family, the funerals "di spese," cantadori vecchi received anywhere from 6 (at San Teodoro in 1552 or the Carità in 1508) to 15 soldi (at the Misericordia in 1565), but 10 or 12 was standard.[155] The scuola itself paid for the funerals of poor brothers, designating them as being done "amore Dei" (see above, chapter 2). The singers received substantially less, usually half the amount, for these, but sometimes nothing at all (the Carità in 1508 and San Teodoro in 1552).[156] It is difficult to estimate the annual income from such services, given the incomplete state of the records, but some indication can be gathered from the guardian da mattin's 1570 register for San Giovanni Evanglista.[157] In that year, the scuola performed eighty-four funerals, fifty-three of them "amore Dei" and thirty-one "di spese," bringing to the singers about 5 ducats each. Payments for regular, non-funeral processions varied greatly. Sometimes the cantadori vecchi were required to attend with no remuneration, other times for a fee similar to that for funerals, and occasionally for considerably more, especially at the Misericordia, where, in 1556, for a limited number of processions, the singers received 31 soldi, or one quarter of a ducat, each.[158] The total cash payments to these men, therefore, probably came to somewhere around 10 ducats annually, for something in excess of one hundred services. In addition, most received candles free once a year, and a pair of shoes, but, on the other hand, were required, like all brothers, to provide their own *cappa*.

While many of the singers apparently had other employment (including as furrier, tailor, shoemaker, linen dealer, and dealer in silk scraps), they all were low enough on the financial ladder to be eligible for charity from the scuole. It is not surprising, therefore, that they were often dissatisfied with their payment. When such singers performed acceptably, the scuole seemed ready to increase alms and fees, especially since, as they were poor brothers, most of the money could be drawn from the charity accounts, and not from the operating funds of the scuola, and the amounts concerned were usually quite small, at least from the viewpoint of the scuole, if not the singers themselves. Not surprisingly, however, these singers sometimes resorted to unwelcome strategies to increase their income, and disputes were not uncommon. The most usual stratagem, of course, was simply not to show up if a better opportunity arose. The Misericordia, fed up at being left without sufficient singers at funerals, began, in the 1560s, to employ reserve singers (*cantadori di rispetto*), who received half pay unless the regulars failed to appear, in which event the scuola would pay them the full amount. After a regular singer failed three times, the reserve singer would get his post, and the full wages.[159]

One subterfuge singers and other fadighenti occasionally employed involved, after having managed to extract some extra alms from a guardian, the claim in future years that they were entitled to that money as part of their traditional payment. Future guardians did not always catch on immediately, but when they did, they issued severe admonitions, and had regulations passed that banned similar practice in the future.[160] In another illegal strategem, as carried out at San Marco in 1504, "some of [the singers] came [when required] and others not, but nonetheless divided the payment among both those who came and those who did not."[161] At times, singers claimed that the scuola was responsible for providing them with the cappa, and some even managed to get through several years without having to make this expenditure. The singers and other fadighenti of San Giovanni Evangelista recognized another opportunity to get additional money: they used "very bad and shameful corruption," preying on new brothers, who did not yet know fully the rules and practices of the scuola. "When somebody is accepted as our brother at the altar of the Most Holy Cross," the complaint reads, "before he can step outside the scuola, he is so set upon by many of our bad brothers that, either out of goodness, or for shame, he is forced to give them much money, not without disturbance and to our great anger."[162] In all of these cases, the scuole either dismissed the offending singers summarily, or warned them that they would be fired if they repeated their actions.

Three singers at San Rocco in 1544 showed up at a funeral as required, but balked at singing what they interpreted as being beyond their duties: "to sing at the elevation of Our Lord Jesus Christ and also after the mass [to sing] the laude and prayers." Three of the four singers walked out of the church, refusing to sing unless paid four "marcelli" (that is, 2 lire). The scuola, of course, promptly fired them.[163] Three times in the first half of the sixteenth century, the Carità was forced to deal with disputes among the singers themselves. When two singers in 1533 argued about who was entitled to serve and receive alms, the scuola decided in favor of the one who had served longer, but designated the other man to be his substitute, and to succeed him after his death.[164] At the same time, a different arrangement was worked out between two further singers: one, Francesco Brisighella, would henceforth sing in the church, and the other, Francesco de Tomaso, at the burial, but both would receive reduced alms, and be fired immediately if the "scandal or fighting" recurred.[165] In 1542, after the death of one of the singers, the scuola chose two men to fill his place, each to serve two months at a time, in alternation. Both men, therefore, could receive some financial support from the scuola. In this particular case, the scuola also required one of them to teach the other "the tenor and soprano [parts], so that [he] can learn what he does not know."[166] Given that the same limited repertory was repeated at each funeral, it is likely that the ability to read music was not a requirement for this job; the training of a new singer by one who was more experienced might well have been the standard. The reference to "tenors and sopranos" might imply that this was two-part music, probably note-against-note counterpoint similar to that found in laude of the fifteenth century.[167]

Since the scuole paid the cantadori vecchi out of the charity accounts of the scuole (unlike the cantori solenni, whose salaries came from the scuola's operating funds), their employment was not threatened in the same way by galley taxes and other financial emergencies. The evolving circumstances of the scuole did, however, result in similar outcomes: by the middle of the seventeenth century, only one scuola continued to employ cantadori vecchi. The scuola with the shortest lived tradition was San Teodoro, which hired both types of singers in 1552, the year of its charter as a scuola grande.[168] After a dispute with the cantori solenni later that year, San Teodoro decided to pay the cantadori vecchi an additional salary to take over those tasks as well as their own.[169] When the officers realized, in 1560, that the musical results of this arrangement were not satisfactory, they hired a new ensemble of cantori solenni, and fired the cantadori vecchi, not only in regard to their added duties, but entirely.[170] To fill the gap, the scuola's chaplain began hiring four priests to sing at funerals, a situation that the chapter made permanent in 1583, when the scuola offered the priests a salary of 8 ducats each.[171] Three more scuole eliminated this ensemble in the early years of the seventeenth century. San Marco was the first, in 1602, firing them without recording an explanation in the notatorio, followed by the Carità in 1617.[172] In 1615, San Rocco had been looking to cut out expenditures that "brought neither advantage nor any ornament" to the scuola, "as is that for the cantori da corpo, whose singing, in the present day, has become ridiculous."[173] Since only two of the singers remained, the scuola pensioned them off without appointing replacements. These three scuole, along with San Giovanni Evangelista—which never seems to have taken any concrete action—assigned to clerics (either the regular coristi of their church or hired chaplains), the tasks previously carried out by the cantadori vecchi. Only the Misericordia continued to use secular singers, a practice maintained there through nearly all of the eighteenth century (see chapter 6).

Instrumentalists

Though instrumentalists never functioned, according to the documents, to honor God, and only rarely to bring honor to the city, they became essential elements in the public ceremonial activities of the six scuole grandi. The scuole were loath, even in times of financial distress, to do without instrumental ensembles, and were even willing, at times, to pay them salaries in excess of those paid to the prestigious cantori solenni. Indeed, instrumentalists would remain the only one of the processional ensembles established in the fifteenth century to survive the turmoil of the late sixteenth and early seventeenth centuries at most or all of the scuole.

Piffari

While the employment of an ensemble of wind instrument players, usually referred to as *trombe e piffari*, can be documented as early as the fourteenth century
at a number of scuole piccole (see chapter 8), such a practice seems rarer at the
scuole grandi, at least according to the surviving documentation, until the beginning of the sixteenth century. Before its transformation into a scuola grande in
1552, San Teodoro used such instruments in the manner most common at its
fellow scuole piccole: to help in announcing its annual festa. In 1537, the chapter
allotted the gastaldo 18 lire to send two floats, one with an angel and the other
with the dragon slain by their patron saint, to Rialto and St. Mark's on the eve
of their feast, accompanied by trombe and piffari.[174]

In the early sixteenth century, two of the scuole grandi, San Marco and San
Rocco, began to use (or, at least, to document the use of) wind instruments, but
in a way quite different from that most usual for the scuole piccole; they served
not merely as heralds, but, as far as can be determined, as integral parts of their
public ceremonies. The earliest reference, at San Marco in 1502, indicates that
the players were obligated to serve on the vigil and feast of the patron saint and
on that of St. Agnes, the day on which the scuola distributed dowries to poor
girls.[175] The five men, mostly of non-Venetian origin (four of them indicate Man-
tua, Padua, Arezzo, and Córdoba as their native cities), were, it seems, brothers
of the scuola, perhaps admitted for this purpose, since the scuola did not pay them
a fee, but simply gave them their luminaria (candles on the feast of the Purification) free of charge, as was the practice also with fadighenti. Their duties expanded beginning in 1515, during the term of the guardian grande Vettor Ziliol,
who began a practice that the notatorio describes as "most devout and most
welcomed by God, and equally honorific for our city, and in particular for our
scuola."[176] On the first Sunday of each month (the scuola's ordained day), the
celebrations were to be enhanced. The practice had been for the brothers to
process from the scuola around the adjoining square to the church of Santi Giovanni e Paolo, carrying their relic of the Holy Cross, and accompanied by the
friars of the church and many noblemen. Once there, the cantori solenni, who
had sung during the procession, would sing a solemn mass, and then the procession would be repeated back to the scuola. Ziliol and his fellow officers wished
to "multiply the aforesaid devotions, both for the health of the souls of our
brothers and for the honor of the scuola, because it is exalted above the others
because it is the most beautiful and under the protection of St. Mark."[177] This
they did by adding an ensemble of four "trombetti e piffari" (including one,
Bernardin de Bortolamio, who was a member of the doge's piffaro ensemble),
who would play during both processions and "also at all of the mass."[178] There
is, unfortunately, no indication whatsoever of what they actually played, nor
whether they did so along with the singers or separately. In recompense for their
labors, the scuola would pay them 4 ducats annually. Though this amount seems
quite modest, it was one of those expenditures (along with extra singers) the
scuola eliminated as "superfluous and of little value" in 1526.[179]

At San Rocco, piffari can be documented as early as 1521, when they were listed in the ceremonial book of that year as playing for every ordained day of the scuola (that is, the first Sunday of the month) without payment, but, presumably as brothers, receiving their luminaria free of charge.[180] At some point between then and 1542, the scuola began to pay the piffari a salary, a change that apparently resulted in some disorder; perhaps the players, no longer brothers, and thus without ties of loyalty to the scuola, failed to attend as required. In any event, the officers in that year fired the existing ensemble and reached an agreement with one Paulo Padoan and three companions,[181] who were obligated to play, as at San Marco, on the first Sunday of the month and also on the feast of St. Roch, for a remuneration of 8 lire for the Sunday services and 3 ducats for the festa, and were also, to guarantee their loyalty, made brothers of the scuola, without having to pay for their luminaria. In addition, they were to play at the ceremony in which the general chapter installed the new banca, without further payment. The total cost for all this was 16 ducats a year, an amount that the succeeding guardian, in 1543, thought the scuola could very well do without, especially since it was an expense not borne by any of the other four scuole.[182] Trombe and piffari thereupon disappear from the records of the scuole. One question remains (given that no evidence at all survives regarding the repertory for these instrumentalists): what instruments did they play? The usual meaning of the phrase "trombe e piffari," at least in the Venetian context, is taken to be trombones and shawms, the latter sometimes replaced with cornetti. While these instruments were undoubtedly part of the arsenal of the players employed at San Marco and San Rocco, documents at both scuole indicate that they were expected to play others as well. The 1542 San Rocco agreement required the musicians "to perform on all the sorts of instruments they play."[183] San Marco in 1515 required its instrumentalists to play "both trombe and piffari [that is trombones and shawms] as well as flutes [that is, recorders] and cornetti."[184] These men therefore, could play whatever sort of wind instruments the scuole needed or desired.

Stringed Instruments

While at least two of the scuole used wind instruments for the first Sunday of the month and a few other occasions, the standard instrumental ensemble for the public processions to the Piazza and elsewhere comprised only strings. As discussed in the previous chapter, most of the scuole had begun using players of lute, harp, and *viola* sometime in the late fifteenth century, and this practice persisted through the first two or three decades of the sixteenth century. The scuole continued to replace individual players for failure to appear or for refusing to play for the agreed-upon wages, and some of the replacements agreed to free membership in lieu of wages. The ensemble at San Rocco, which had seen its wages reduced, from 32 soldi each per month to 18, successfully argued in 1521 to be returned to the original amount.[185]

The string ensemble of the scuole underwent a dramatic and sudden modernization in the years around 1530. Instead of a mixed ensemble of plucked and bowed instruments that preserved a medieval sound, the scuole all now began to hire a homogeneous ensemble of bowed strings. Despite some terminological confusion, it is clear, as Rodolfo Baroncini has convincingly demonstrated, that the new quintet (later sextet) was a violin band.[186] The earliest documentary indication of this change is found in the records of the Scuola della Misericordia, where a new regulation of expenditures made on 8 January 1530 [m.v.] refers to "the [four] new players, who play *lironi* or *violoni*."[187] The ensemble listed less than a month later as having served the previous year with no pay, however, had eight players, including three from Bergamo and one Brescian, the areas of northern Italy where the new violin band seems to have originated.[188] One member, Antonio de Bortolomeo da Verona, had earlier formed part of the mixed ensemble of the Scuola di San Marco, as a player of the "violeta."[189] By 1534, the Misericordia's ensemble was back to four players, including two of the eight from 1530.[190] The scuola confirmed their wages at the earlier figure of 3 lire for the ensemble for each time they played. Additionally, they were listed as brothers of the scuola eligible to receive their luminaria gratis.

San Rocco followed suit in 1533, when it decided to replace the "old players" and elect "players of violoni."[191] Baroncini suggests that an earlier document from San Rocco, dated 1531, might represent the actual point of change, but the decision then was to exchange "our players of harp, lute, and viola," who had served badly, with the ensemble that had done a good job for the scuola at the recent procession for Corpus Christi.[192] While it is possible the three instruments were named so as to distinguish them from a different new ensemble, it seems just as likely, especially given that there is no indication that the new one would have a different makeup, that the nomenclature was used to avoid confusion with the players of piffari, which were also employed by this scuola. A few years later, San Giovanni Evangelista also made the switch, reaching an agreement with four "sonadori de viola e lironi," at a salary of 15 lire each per year.[193] Documents marking the switch in ensembles are lacking for San Marco and the Carità, but they had certainly followed the others by 1541.

The terminological confusion evident in the earliest documents continued for years. The most common term for the instruments was *lironi*, but *lire*, *viole*, and *violoni* also appear regularly, as does, especially later in the century, *violini*. The ensemble is clearly a band of string instruments all of one family, differentiated into ranges. That eliminates, as Baroncini argues, all possibilities except for the violin family and the viola da gamba family. The latter is unlikely, given the processional nature of the duties of the ensemble, and the former is made more likely by the identification of many of the earliest players in these ensembles as from those areas where violin playing flourished in the first half of the century. In the latter part of the century, the evidence is even clearer, with more consistent terminology and more identifiable players.

While some of the earliest ensembles (those of the Misericordia and San Giovanni Evangelista from the 1530s and 1540s) comprised four players, six was the most common for the sixteenth century (San Rocco and San Marco throughout, San Teodoro from 1553 through at least 1566, San Giovanni Evangelista around 1560, and the Carità in the 1540s). Ensembles of five players were employed at the Carità in 1541 and after 1577, at San Giovanni Evangelista after 1570, and at all but San Rocco (which held steady at six) through most of the early seventeenth century. Several of the documents link the individual members of the ensembles with instruments of specific ranges. The earliest to include a complete ensemble is from the Carità in 1541, listing players of *soran* [soprano], contra altro, tenor, bassetto, and basso.[194] The instruments in this ensemble are evenly distributed from high to low, as are the six-part ensembles listed in a series of documents from San Marco in the 1550s and 1560s. Two listings from 1558 are similar, both including soprano, falsetto (in one of the two this also bears the name contra-soprano), alto, tenor, basson, and basso (or, in the second listing, bassetto).[195] The document for 1561 lists two sopranos, contra alto, tenor, basso, and basson, that for 1562 includes soprano, viollin, contra alto, tenor, bason, and bassetto, and the last of this group, that of 1563, two sopranos, contra alto, tenor, basso, and basson.[196] The one early seventeenth-century ensemble listing, from the Misericordia in 1619, is similarly evenly distributed, with, perhaps, a slight shift in the upward direction: soprano, falsetto, contr'alto, tenor, and basso.[197]

Most of the evidence tends to indicate that the instrumental ensemble performed on its own, not together with the singers in processions. Of evidence from the scuole themselves, the only item indicating the contrary (as discussed above) is Gentile Bellini's painting of a procession of the Scuola di San Giovanni Evangelista, which appears to show both ensembles performing together.[198] Supporting the separation are items of several kinds. The two surviving ceremonial books of the period provide complementary evidence. The 1521 San Rocco book says nothing about what was played or when, but is very careful to indicate the order of the processions, and the singers and instrumentalists are nearly always separated by large numbers of other brothers.[199] On the other hand, the 1570 guardian da mattin's book for San Giovanni Evangelista is vague on placement of personnel within the processions, but does include instructions as to when during these events laude should be performed.[200] In every case, the instruction refers specifically to the singers, with no mention of instrumentalists. The most important document of all in this matter is also the only one that gives an indication of what they might have played. The officers of the Scuola di San Rocco decided in 1550 that they could no longer tolerate the sort of music their instrumentalists had been performing from the time of the ensemble's creation (whether that refers to the first time violins were hired in 1533 or when the most recent ensemble contract was drawn up, in 1547, is unclear). The players had gone in processions "playing many canzoni and other works more lascivious than devout, something that is neither pleasing to Our Lord God, nor an honest thing." From now on (and they were, in fact, offered 1 ducat as an enticement to change), they were to play "motets and laude in honor of Our Lord God, our protector St. Roch, and other saints, and not otherwise." If they ever again played "canzoni or amorous things" they would be fired.[201] It seems clear that this ensemble had played without the singers (or they also would have been admonished), and that their repertory consisted primarily of arrangements of vocal works. In this case they had been playing secular music, but would now be required to play, more appropriately, sacred pieces.

The general obligation of the instrumentalists was to play in processions, but the extent of this service varied considerably. At most scuole, the ensemble probably began with a fairly limited list of duties, such as that at San Giovanni Evangelista in 1537, which included processions on ten feasts each year (four civic processions to San Marco plus the double procession for Corpus Christi, visits to the four other scuole, and those to San Lorenzo and San Giobbe that were particular to this scuola). Appended at the end of the list was the phrase "and all the other feasts on which the scuola goes out."[202] Since the scuola paid this particular ensemble an annual salary (see below on this issue), the officers could and probably did call on them for extra work at no additional cost. By 1574, the list at the Carità had reached twenty-four days, including visits to additional scuole, more civic processions, the processions to San Pietro di Castello in Lent, several occasions particular to this scuola, and the three days on which the general chapter of the scuola met. As with San Giovanni Evangelista, these salaried players might be called on for additional processions as they occurred.[203] Such growth, whether planned or not, became extreme at San Rocco just a few years later. In 1577, the players petitioned for a raise, since, they claimed, their salaries were lower than those at other scuole (they received 10 ducats each annually, and said some of the others got 14, a figure, however, that seems considerably higher than those recorded in the surviving documents), but "they do not do half the processions that we do, because we do twice as many as they do."[204] While their salary claims might not be verifiable, those regarding workload are close to the truth. The list attached to the petition includes forty-one days, including all those processions to Piazza San Marco and to the other scuole, a wide range of processions performed only by San Rocco, and the first Sunday of each month. Sometimes, the players added, there were even more. The officers of the scuola, aware of both the truth of the claims and the exaggerations, agreed to a minimal raise, to 12 ducats each annually.

An annual salary was not, in fact, the usual method of paying instrumentalists at most scuole until the latter half of the sixteenth century. Five of the six (San Rocco was the lone exception) paid them by the occasion for several decades. The amounts they allocated were sometimes quite small, as low as 10 soldi for each player per procession at the Carità in 1524 or 12 at San Giovanni Evangelista in 1541—about the same, that is, as the cantadori vecchi.[205] Also, like the cantadori vecchi, and unlike the cantori sollenni, the scuole almost always admitted instrumentalists to the scuola as brothers without payment of the luminaria. Over time, the players requested, and were granted, significant increases, so that most were receiving 20 soldi, or 1 lira, each, by the middle of the century. With an average of twenty processions annually, these payments added up to a yearly wage of a little more than 3 ducats, certainly not enough to live on; on the other hand, most undoubtedly continued to play as freelance musicians at weddings and other secular festivities in the city, or at annual feast days at parish or monastic churches or scuole piccole.[206] At San Rocco, an annual salary was the practice as early as 1521, but the net results to the players were not significantly different, at first. Until 1547, they earned 3 ducats each, raised to 4½ in that year.[207] San Rocco's desire to keep its players happy is made clear in that same document. The scuola required the ensemble, without exception, to play in regular processions, including those on the first Sunday of each month, always bringing those instruments they used in secular weddings and festivities.[208] In addition, the scuola asked that they play at the masses on those Sundays (something never before required), but, knowing that these instrumentalists derived most of their income from freelance work, they offered them some flexibility. The instrumentalists were obligated to perform at those masses only "if they did not have to play in some wedding."[209]

A major change occurred in the second half of the century: one by one, all of the scuole switched to paying the players an annual salary, probably in imitation of San Rocco, which not only had been following that system for years, but had recently increased the amount, to 8 ducats around 1550 and then to 10 in 1561.[210] The first to follow suit was San Teodoro, in 1566, after little more than a decade as a scuola grande, and trying its best to make up for the lack of historical tradition by spending lavishly and employing the best men possible.[211] In this case, they reached an agreement with the famous ensemble led by the Paganini family and paid them the same high salary as the players of San Rocco, 10 ducats each.[212] The banca recognized that the scuola's budget did not allow for such an extravagant expenditure, and mandated that half the amount should be paid out of the *partidor*, the additional funds collected from the officers to pay extraordinary expenses. Even this arrangement proved beyond their capabilities, and in 1568 the players refused to serve for a lower figure.[213] The scuola quickly reached an agreement with another (unnamed) ensemble for much less, 6 ducats each, an amount maintained for the remainder of the century.[214]

The Scuola della Carità was the next to change its system, in 1574.[215] In this case, they made the switch to remove the tensions caused by the earlier system. On occasions for which the scuola went in procession to two different churches on the same day, not an uncommon occurrence (for instance, in February of that year a procession to San Leonardo that stopped at San Teodoro on the return leg), the players often demanded double payment, while the scuola insisted on the usual amount. The scuola, unable to tolerate the disobedience of the players, fired them, believing that the problem could be solved by offering an annual salary, as with the singers. The sum agreed upon was 6 ducats each annually, plus the usual free admission to the scuola. Shortly afterwards, the city was struck by the plague, and the Carità lost four of its six violinists. The new ensemble hired to replace them, in 1577, was not only "able and very much appropriate," but noted for its "valor and fame," and the scuola offered them a salary to match their reputation, 14 ducats each.[216] In addition, and most unusually, the scuola agreed to provide their cappe as well. This salary, the highest yet paid to any instrumentalists, did not go unnoticed. The players of San Rocco, in a petition referred to above, pointed out that, while they had far more duties, they were paid less than those at other scuole (though they used the plural, it was only the Carità that paid this much), and demanded a raise to 20 ducats each. The scuola agreed to an increase of 2 ducats, from 10 to 12, which apparently satisfied the players, perhaps because of the added reputation they gained by playing for what was then the most prestigious scuola. A few years later, the San Rocco players received an added benefit—up until that time, they, along with the cantadori da corpi, had been admitted as brothers, but were listed in a separate booklet, not in the regular mariegola. They were, therefore, barred from receiving certain benefits, a situation that the chapter rectified in 1581, when it decided to enter them, in the future, in the main mariegola.[217] In a concession, perhaps, to more conservative members of the chapter, the officers agreed that when the scuola needed replacements, the officers would search first among the brothers of the scuola, only going outside when necessary.

The years 1582 and 1583 saw yet more changes to the situation of the violinists at the scuole, when two of the remaining ones, San Marco and San Giovanni Evangelista, made the switch to annual salaries. The players at San Marco issued an ultimatum in July of 1582, as the guardian reported: "they have let us know that they no longer wish to serve the scuola if they are not given salaries on an annual basis, as do the other scuole."[218] Reaching an agreement took over a year, but the players finally agreed to 8 ducats each on 5 December of 1583.[219] Word of the agreement spread quite fast. On 17 December, the players of San Giovanni Evangelista, still paid on a per-service basis, described themselves in a petition as "afflicted" and extracted a promise to be paid an annual salary, fixed at the respectable amount of 12 ducats.[220] This then spurred changes at the Carità, which had been accustomed, as the instrumentalists stated in a petition of 21 December, "to have in its service the best players that can be found."[221] The new group, which included Giovanni Giacomo Busti of Brescia, who had, they said, been "lifted" from San Rocco, first requested the usual admission as brothers, and also the customary annual gift of candles and shoes, and then proceeded to the matter of salary:

> your lordships know that first our thought was to ask for 20 ducats a year for each, that in another draft was reduced to 18. But to show that we desire to serve you, and also so that the loving kindness your magnificences show us would increase, we are resolved to serve you at the rate of 16 ducats each per year.[222]

The officers accepted the concession, and agreed to pay the highest salary a scuola had ever offered to instrumentalists (even San Rocco never paid this much, peaking at 15 ducats around 1600). Not surprisingly, a scuola that paid high salaries could attract the best players, such as the Paganini at the Carità and members of the Bonfante family at San Rocco; in order to keep them, however, high fees had to be maintained. The case of San Rocco shows that players would desert even a prestigious post, if the money were better elsewhere.

Not until 1591 did the last of the scuole, the Misericordia, fall in line. The officers had long sought to maintain the honor of their processions, but still paid musicians of all sorts less than the other scuole (and insisted on paying them by the occasion), with, predictably, poor results. Finally, "because it is necessary to do what the other scuole usually do," they decided to pay the musicians "in their fashion," that is, to hire and salary them annually.[223] The general chapter only grudgingly agreed, by a vote of 68 to 51, and settled upon the rather small salary of 6 ducats for each player, a figure that was adjusted upwards, to near what the other scuole paid (48 ducats for the five players, or about 9½ each), some three years later.[224]

As it had with the cantori solenni, the government's imposition of taxes to pay for galley oarsmen had significant impacts on the employment of instrumentalists by the scuole. The financial burden forced San Marco, the Carità, and the Misericordia to fire players in 1587 or 1588, and San Giovanni Evangelista to do the same in 1594.[225] The documents do not always record the rehiring of the ensembles, but this seems to have happened, probably with some small reduction in payments, within a few years. At San Marco, the officers apparently decided to try again to hire players (and singers) by the occasion, but the result "was completely contrary to the intention" of the change. They now had "to spend much more than was done in proportion to similar occasions," and often ended up going in procession without musicians at all. As a result, the general chapter accepted unanimously the banca's decision to resume paying salaries.[226]

The relationships between scuole and instrumentalists varied considerably. On the one hand, San Rocco, which paid the players competitive fixed salaries, excited considerable feelings of loyalty. Some players remained in service for extraordinarily long periods, and were consequently rewarded with pensions after they were no longer able to perform their duties. The earliest record of such a benefit dates from 1566, when the scuola granted Jacomo Bressano, who had reached the age of 80 and was affected with gout so that he could no longer leave his house, and had sunk into poverty, his request to continue to receive 5 ducats a year, half his current salary.[227] Another Jacomo, probably Jacomo de Francesco Coron, declared in 1589 that he had served the scuola for over fifty years (the earliest extant record, however, is from 1547), during which time he had lost companions three and four times over, and had "always worked to find companions from among the best in the land for the honor and service of this most religious scuola." Now 80 and feeble, he asked to be released from his duties but still receive his full salary.[228] The scuola acknowledged his devotion, and the chapter gave the request unanimous approval. The scuola granted similar pensions to Bortolamio Bonfante in 1592, at age 70 after more than thirty years' service, in 1601 to Zamaria dai Violini after twenty-seven years, and in 1610 to Pasqualin de Floris, at age 82 and decrepit, after more than thirty years.[229]

On the other hand, the scuole that paid by the occasion, paid less, or frequently eliminated ensembles in order to save money, suffered as a result. Certainly most of these disputes concerned money, but some had other complicating factors, and could even degenerate into violence. The most extreme case occurred at San Teodoro in 1566. The players came to the albergo of the scuola and demanded haughtily, showing little "respect to the place," that they each be given a pair of shoes, which they claimed they were owed for their services (such gifts were, in fact, fairly common to various categories of fadighenti). The guardian replied that the records would be examined, and that if indeed they were owed the shoes, the scuola would not shirk its obligations. One of the officers then checked in the books and found no record of such a practice. One of the players (according to some witnesses it was Piero Piater, leader of the ensemble), then angrily, with no respect at all, shouted "You are lying through your teeth! It's pitiful that you would try that way to deprive us of what is ours!" At the same time, he reached into his cloak, as if to grab his knife (though several witnesses admitted that they had no idea whether or not he was, in fact, armed). The guardian grande scolded him for such insolence, and ordered that the Council of Ten be notified, but that only made the players even angrier, and they continued to menace the officers, "saying many injurious and dishonest words." The son of the guardian grande then forced the musicians downstairs and out of the scuola, at which point they then threatened him: "When we find you outside the scuola, we'll cut you, you sad liar!" One of them later came back and apologized, but the guardian considered this insufficient, and fired all of them.[230] No record of any action by the legal authorities survives. It was following this unfortunate incident that San Teodoro decided to hire future ensembles on a salaried basis.

After 1600, the situation remained essentially the same. At most of the scuole, financial problems caused occasional firings of the instrumental ensemble; as with the singers they were often rehired at slightly (or even drastically) lower wages. The Carità persuaded the players in 1635 (it is unclear how long this lasted) to serve without pay at all, but simply for free membership in the scuola.[231] Even the financially secure San Rocco fired its ensemble twice: once suspending their salaries during the plague of 1630/31, when the government had banned most public processions, and again, after the imposition of a galley tax in 1639.[232] Unlike the situation with the vocal ensembles, however, the scuole continued to employ instrumentalists. Though the evidence is not entirely clear, it seems that nearly all of them paid instrumentalists well into the second half of the century. The scuole could not, as they had done with the singers, replace the players with priests, and were unwilling to let this traditional, and much appreciated, processional ornament disappear.

Organs and Organists

The organ was indispensable for most religious ceremonies in sixteenth- and seventeenth-century Italy. The scuole grandi, therefore, needed to make arrangements to ensure that they had both an instrument and a player available to them. The way they accomplished this differed greatly between, on the one hand, the two that owned their own church (San Rocco and San Giovanni Evangelista), and, on the other hand, those which relied on a nearby monastic church (San Marco, San Teodoro, and the Carità). The Misericordia's situation was unlike the others: while it did not own its own church, the organ in the adjacent priory church it used for its services belonged to the scuola. Two of those scuole without their own church, San Marco (after it moved next to Santi Giovanni e Paolo in the fifteenth century), and San Teodoro (at San Salvadore), had no direct involvement in the employment of the organist. Rather, the churches, under the agreements signed by the scuole and their hosts, bore the responsibility for providing both instrument and player for all the needs of the scuole. The Carità had a similar agreement with the eponymous monastery, but in this case the responsibilities were shared. San Rocco, San Giovanni Evangelista, and the Misericordia, in contrast, bore full responsibility both for building and maintaining their organs and for the employment of the organist.

Before 1481 (as discussed in chapter 4) the Scuola della Carità owned its own organ in the church of the Carità, which it sold in that year to pay part of the costs of a new organ being built by the Augustinian regular canons.[233] In exchange, the scuola retained the rights to use the organ and to decorate it with its insignia. The scuola would also contribute an appropriate share to the salary of the organist, though it is unclear whether the canons made the hiring decisions unilaterally or with the participation of the scuola. The scuola became involved in the repair of the organ several times in the sixteenth century. In 1525, the canons of the Carità came to the officers of the scuola and explained that they had spent 30 ducats to repair the instrument. They requested that the scuola pay not the usual one-fifth of the expenditure, 6 ducats, that being the proportion of the original contruction expenses they had borne, but rather 10, since, they asserted, the monastery had many times spent "a good sum of money in repairing the said organ without having had any assistance from our scuola."[234] Not wishing to risk losing their rights to the organ, but at the same time not wanting to spend too much money and perhaps set another precedent, the scuola agreed to a compromise of 8 ducats. Over the next few decades, the organ deteriorated to the point that it could no longer be used. As the guardian explained in 1557, his predecessors, rather than spend 10 ducats for repairs, had chosen to neglect what many considered "the best and most perfect [organ] to be found in this city"; they opted instead to rent organs when the need arose.[235] However, at a cost of 7 or 8 ducats annually, the rentals had not saved any money at all. Now, for an expense of only 8 ducats, the organ could be put aright, "in such a way that for many many years the scuola will be freed from that expense."[236] That hope was not fulfilled, unfortunately: only six years later, in 1563, the canons asked the scuola for 5 ducats toward repairs.[237] After this, the documents remain silent on the subject.

There is no evidence that the Scuola della Carità participated in the selection of the organist, but the monastery did sometimes officially notify it of new appointments. At times the scuola paid its portion of the salary directly to the performer, even though this should technically have come out of the annual payment to the monastery. A 1532 agreement with a new organist, maestro Bernardo (replacing one Alvise de Jacomo, who had been selected in 1530), is the only documentary indication of the player's duties.[238] Bernardo (assisted by his son Marco) agreed to play for the canons on all feast days, vigils of major feasts, and every Saturday, for 20 ducats (and also, if asked, to teach one of the canons). For an additional 8 ducats, paid by the scuola, he would play at a mass on the first Sunday of each month and on the vigil and day of its annual festa. After this point, documents regarding organists for the scuola della Carità are quite sparse: one note specifies that a certain "maestro Minin" began serving at the monastery in 1545, and there are payments to misser Josef for 1565 and 1566.[239] After that, for about a century, the scuola seems to have reverted to the statutory system, in which they merely paid the required sum to the canons, and left everything up to them.

While the Misericordia was responsible for its organ and organist (the salary for the latter being shared with the priory of the Misericordia), documentation for this is quite patchy for the sixteenth and seventeenth centuries. The instrument built in 1477 (see chapter 4) was undoubtedly still in use in 1528 when the prior of the Misericordia repaired it, and demanded that, as usual, the expenses be borne by the scuola.[240] In 1552, the scuola undertook a more significant rebuilding of the organ, at the hands of Massimian Furlan, at a cost of about 25 ducats.[241] No further records regarding the instrument survive. Most of the players whose names are recorded are not known to have served elsewhere, and the documents are somewhat inconclusive regarding their tenures in the post.[242] The two earliest documented, in 1539 and 1552 (pre Domenego Negro and pre Camillo, respectively) are the only clerics in the list. Two of those who followed, Michiel da Monte, listed in 1571, and Andrea Romanin, who is first listed in 1572 and still served in 1580, later appear in the records of other important institutions: da Monte was hired at the Augustinian friary of Santo Stefano in 1592 (though he only served a year),[243] and Romanin was briefly at the Basilica di San Marco in 1600. Nothing is recorded of the duties of these men, but their annual salary, divided evenly by scuola and priory, was 20 ducats.

It is much easier to trace the histories of organs and their players at the two scuole that bore full responsibility in this matter, San Rocco and San Giovanni Evangelista. Both recorded their activities in considerable detail (though not all the records survive), documenting the sometimes great expenses involved and the frequent employment problems that recurred during the sixteenth and early seventeenth centuries. Nothing is known of the organ in San Rocco's old church before 1556, when it was "in total ruin," and needed to be replaced with one that would be "beautiful and good."[244] To get the process started, the chapter elected three brothers as supervisors (two of whom they replaced the following year), but little seems to have been accomplished for a full decade, perhaps while they were raising funds (the financial details of this construction project are not extant). In 1567, the banca of the scuola approved the removal of the existing organ loft over the main door of the church, so that the new instrument (whose maker is not named) could be installed there,[245] and by the following March, the organ, whose "quality and beauty" were evident, was complete.[246] A year later, after the standard period during which the builder retained responsibility for maintenance, the scuola hired Vicenzo Colombo, the best known organ builder of the day, and very likely the man who had constructed the instrument, to serve as salaried tuner, at 3 ducats annually (increased to 4 in 1572).[247] By the early seventeenth century, the instrument's condition had deteriorated. The bellows had been patched numerous times, but such repairs were no longer possible, so the chapter allocated 25 ducats to rebuild them.[248] The instrument again required major repairs in 1620, including the replacement of one of the large pipes, at the cost of another 20 ducats.[249] The scuola expended little on the organ over the next twenty years, so that by 1645 regular tuning and maintenance no longer sufficed. The instrument was "in a very bad state" and could not "be used in the divine functions because it is broken and out of order due to age, and because nothing at all has been done to it for more than about forty years." So that things would not get worse, and realizing the "most urgent need," the scuola asked the opinions of "trained and expert" men, who judged that necessary repairs would cost about 30 ducats, an expenditure the banca unanimously approved.[250]

The story at San Giovanni Evangelista was somewhat more complicated, because there were two instruments involved, one in the church itself and a second one in the scuola. The instrument in the church was built in 1440 (see chapter 4), but there is no extant documentation regarding the construction of the instrument in the scuola, which was undoubtedly somewhat smaller. The one in the church was in quite poor condition by 1550, and very out of tune, a situation that the officers decided to remedy, "being a just and honest thing to provide for the praise of the Lord God."[251] By 1559, that instrument and the one in the scuola needed tuning again. While the church instrument was apparently repaired successfully, it was discovered that "the organ of this magnficent scuola is in such disrepair that there is no way to tune it that would enable it to be used as needed." Some remedy was therefore needed, the officers said, "to provide for the honor of the majesty of God and of the said scuola."[252] A motion was approved to replace the instrument with "a new one that would be perfect," for which purchase the banca allocated approximately 50 ducats.[253] Even combined with the value of the materials from the old organ, this sum represents far less than the 300–500 ducats a church organ might cost. It is likely, then, that the instrument in the scuola was a small, one-manual instrument.

Over the following decades, repairs and tunings of the two organs were a regular expenditure for San Giovanni Evangelista: 15 ducats in 1567, 10 ducats in 1577, 16 (paid to the well-known builder Vicenzo Colonna) in 1580, and 9 in 1583.[254] By the mid-1590s, however, neither instrument was playable. The general chapter authorized the spending of 200 ducats out of the church operational accounts in 1594 to rebuild an altar in the church and the organ, whose pipes "were being consumed by rust, to our most notable shame and damage" (the allocation between the two projects was not specified).[255] A few months later, work on the altar had been completed, but the organ, the rebuilding of which by fra Iseppo San Mattia had, perhaps, become essentially the construction of a new instrument, was still imperfect, so the chapter authorized another 100 or so ducats of expenditure.[256] Six months later, in November 1595, the project needed yet more money, this time 50 ducats, and in March 1596 the scuola authorized spending a final 85 ducats.[257] This sort of cost overrun was extremely common in such projects (see below, chapters 9 and 10 for similar incidents at some scuole piccole); an original allocation of something under 100 ducats ballooned to more than 300. After some repairs in 1600 (a few pipes apparently needed to be replaced),[258] the organ remained functional with only normal tuning, for which the scuola salaried a specialist at 2 ducats annually, through the middle of the century. Not until 1647, however, did the scuola complete the decoration of the instrument, with the painting of the portals by Pietro Vecchia, for the sum of 40 ducats.[259]

Though by 1596 the organ in the scuola had reached the same unusable state as that in the church, the officers made no efforts to repair it. Rather, for a period of about fifteen years, the scuola obligated the organist to provide a portable one for those services that required it.[260] Finally, in 1612, in an effort to return dignity to the scuola and greater honor to the monthly mass in the scuola, the guardian proposed that 50–60 ducats be spent to rebuild the instrument or purchase a new one.[261] In a rare example of rebellion by the members of the general chapter, they defeated the proposal by a 31 to 26 plurality (with ten abstentions), so that use of a portable organ continued as the normal practice.

The men employed as organists at San Giovanni Evangelista were, like those at the Misericordia, not musicians of particular renown, though many did also serve at the nearby monastery of the Frari, certainly an important post. In the earliest years of the sixteenth century, the scuola's practice was to hire two different players for the two organs. In an effort to save money, the scuola decided in 1526 to release pre Ettor, who had played the organ in the scuola, and give a raise, to 10 ducats annually, to the organist in the church, fra Marcantonio Zucchato, from the Frari, to take over those duties as well.[262] The next year, however, fra Marcantonio was temporarily unable to serve, because of an outbreak of the plague in his monastery, so that the scuola recalled pre Ettor.[263] However, instead of taking over all of fra Marcantonio's duties, he resumed his old post in the scuola, at 6 ducats annually, and an unnamed brother of fra Marcantonio took over in the church, for the same amount. By 1533, the scuola reunited the jobs once again, in the person of fra Jacomo of the Frari (perhaps the unnamed brother referred to earlier), to whom the scuola granted a raise from 10 ducats annually to 12, an amount that would remain stable for more than a century.[264] It is not clear how long fra Jacomo served after this date, but his successor, once again, was fra Marcantonio, who, upon promotion within the Frari in 1535, resigned from the scuola, which replaced him with a secular performer, Vicenzo Crivello.[265] There is a gap in the records until the 1550s, when a succession of otherwise unknown men took up the post: Domenego Brisighella (from before 1558 to 1566), fra Andrea of the Frari (beginning in 1566), Antonio Marchesini (or Marchesani, from San Salvador, from 1573 to 1577), and pre Nicolò Rampazetto from 1577 until the church was closed for rebuilding (to be followed by the reconstruction of the organ) around 1590. By the time the new organ was finished, in 1596, pre Nicolò had been appointed piovano of San Stin, and was no longer able to hold the post of organist.[266]

On 6 September 1596, the organist pre Francesco Sponga[267] approached the officers of the scuola and asked to rent one of their houses, which was available at a rate of 25 ducats a year.[268] He offered to pay 12 ducats and also to provide his services as organist for Vespers and masses for all feasts in the church (and also weekdays if requested) and at mass the first Sunday of each month, the feast of the Holy Cross, and the feast of St. John the Evangelist in the scuola, for the latter services bringing his own organ (since, as mentioned above, the permanent organ no longer functioned). The scuola accepted his offer (without mentioning that it represented, in effect, a salary of 13 ducats, that is 1 more than the usual), but in 1597 and again in 1598 problems arose.[269] The difficulty seems to be that the house Sponga rented from the scuola was in poor shape, and he refused to pay the rent. The scuola fired him, and, following his humble petition, rehired him, but he then complained again. The house, he explained, was so old and decrepit that it leaked at all the joints when it rained, and on the open market could bring no more than 20 ducats in rent. Since he was paying 12, that left him a salary of only 8 ducats as organist, which was further reduced because of the expense of bringing his organ to the scuola, which he estimated at 4 ducats annually. He complained that the net salary of 4 ducats was less than that of any altar boy the scuola employed, most of whom made two or three times as much. He still wished to serve the scuola, Sponga asserted, but asked that the scuola give him the house rent-free, a benefit that with all his expenses, he suggested, would not even be a tiny amount more than had been paid to previous organists in salary. These arguments swayed the banca, and they unanimously accepted the proposal. Sponga continued to serve until 1606, when the scuola elected him chaplain (a post he held until his death in 1641), and he resigned as organist.[270]

To fill the now open position, once again at a regular salary of 12 ducats, the scuola, following what was becoming the standard Venetian procedure for such situations, made a public announcement of auditions to be held on 5 February.[271] Two candidates presented themselves, Zuane Picchi, organist at the Frari, and Giacomo Rondenin, who identified himself as a student of Gabrieli.[272] In a close vote, the latter won the post, but he did not serve for long. In the summer of 1608 the officers admonished him for not bringing an organ to the scuola when needed, and the following April, Rondenin's father brought word to the scuola that Giacomo had voluntarily renounced the post.[273] At the audition that followed several months later, in November, once again two candidates presented themselves: Gabriel Sponza, probably the nephew of the earlier organist, and Zuanne Battista Rizzo dal violin.[274] The documents do not indicate the winner of the contest, but the successful candidate did not last long, as the scuola held another audition the following April.[275] Unfortunately, the documents this time do not even mention the names of the candidates, but it is possible that the post went to fra Michele Stella, of the Frari, who was there no later than 1612, and remained until 1620, when the scuola replaced him with Antonio Misserini, whose name last appears in 1615.[276] From that point until the death of the chaplain Francesco Sponga in 1641, the documents name no organists, as the scuola paid the fee to the chaplain, who himself arranged for the organist (or even performed himself when needed); at his death the scuola identified Sponga as "capo [director of the church] e organista." At any event, the last person San Giovanni Evangelista hired as organist during this period was Don Francesco Giusto (perhaps a relative of the Paolo Giusto who was at St. Mark's from 1588 until about 1624), the only candidate at an audition held in 1643.[277]

San Rocco, as the richest scuola during this period, eventually offered the highest salary for its organist (along with the heaviest duties) and therefore attracted the most distinguished roster of performers. The extant documents also provide the most complete indications of the duties of a scuola organist. The earliest recorded holders of this position, in the 1530s and 1540s, were, however, no more distinguished than those of the other scuole, and received comparable salaries. Domenego Busati Finestrer replaced maestro Biagio in 1539 at a salary of 6 ducats annually.[278] The duties of the newly elected organist were spelled out quite clearly: to play every Friday of the year at Compline, the first Sunday of each month at Mass, for Mass and Vespers on the feast days of Christmas, Easter, Ascension, and Pentecost, similarly on the Marian feasts of the Nativity, Annunciation, and Visitation, the day of the Holy Cross, and on the days dedicated to Sts. Apollonia, Lawrence, and Sebastian, as well as at all votive masses, the vigil and feast of St. Roch, and any other time Mass or Vespers was sung in the church. For such extensive obligations, the salary appears quite low, and it was perhaps for that reason that Busati left barely a year later, to be replaced by one Marco Serafin, at an increased rate of 10 ducats, similar to the amount earned by organists of other scuole.[279] In addition, beginning in 1543, the chapter granted Serafin his annual luminaria free of charge.[280] Upon his death in 1549, the scuola replaced him with Angelo Lupini, at the same salary.[281] Beginning sometime before 1568, the position was held by another otherwise unknown musician, pre Nicolò di Fausti.[282]

That the scuola did not hold this last player (or perhaps his predecessors) in high regard is demonstrated by the action the chapter took in March 1568 after the completion of the scuola's new organ.[283] With an organ of discernible "quality and beauty," they said, it was now necessary that they find a "valentuomo" to play it, somebody who would be "expert and sufficient." Pre Nicolò, who at the time still held the post (he would be paid through June), was clearly not the sort of player the officers had in mind. In order to attract someone appropriate, the guardian grande proposed offering a salary of 24 ducats, twice that of any other scuola. The banca did not immediately accept this proposal: they voted against it twice by margins of 13 to 11, but after making a minor change in the procedures for the election of the organist, the motion passed 18 to 6. The man they selected was Vincenzo Bell'haver, whose career would later conclude at the Basilica of San Marco, where he was first organist from 1586 until his death a year later.[284] The obligations the scuola imposed on the new organist were proportional to the increased salary, and comprised nearly 150 services annually: to play at Mass and Vespers on thirteen feasts, Vespers only on another thirteen, and Mass only at one more; at Vespers every Sunday and Mass also on the first Sunday of the month (except during Lent and Advent); and at Compline every Friday. After ten years of service on these terms, Bell'haver requested that the scuola grant him a raise, as had been done for "priests, violinists, singers, and others."[285] He asked for 12 additional ducats, but the chapter approved a raise of 6, for a total of 30, which he continued to receive until 1584, when he left Venice to serve in Padua briefly before winning the competition for first organist at St. Mark's. His successor, at the original salary of 24 ducats, was none other than Giovanni Gabrieli, who had recently been elected second organist at St. Mark's, and was one of the most sought-after musicians in Venice.[286] As late as 1602, Gabrieli still earned the same salary from San Rocco, and (as had Bell'haver) he held both posts simultaneously (and at San Rocco uneventfully) until his death in 1612.

At that point, what had been a long succession of smooth transitions in the post of organist at San Rocco descended into near chaos. Three candidates presented themselves at the auditions held on 28 August 1612: Zuanne Picchi (organist of the Frari), Zambattista Rizzo, and Zambattista Grillo.[287] The latter (who would later serve at St. Mark's) won the audition, but Picchi contested the results; he hired lawyers, and brought a case before the Chiefs of the Council of Ten, claiming that the scuola had conducted the election "with many disorders." After hearing also from Grillo and his lawyers, the Capi decided on 13 September to cancel the election results and order the scuola to hold new auditions.[288] When that was done, in March, only Rizzo and Grillo appeared, and the scuola again chose the latter.[289] The following year, still obviously smarting from what they perceived as unjust accusations, and angered that after winning his legal battle, Picchi chose not to even enter the second audition, the officers took up the issue again.[290] Picchi had been heard saying that he did not really want the job, and that it was sufficient that he had made trouble for the scuola. He had now continued with this "evil spirit," and tried to persuade a newly elected guardian da mattin to hire him, against the will of the banca. Upon failing in this attempt, this officer, clearly an ally of Picchi's, refused his own election, again disrupting the orderly procedures of the scuola. The guardian grande now proposed a motion that Picchi should be permanently banned from any service at the scuola, as regular organist or substitute. The chapter overwhelmingly approved the motion, but the scuola's syndic prevented the regulation from taking effect, as it violated San Rocco's bylaws.

It would seem that this should be the end of the story, but Picchi resurfaced after Grillo's death in 1623. The document recording the new election is somewhat confused at this point:

> The post of organist being vacant because of the death of the late Giovanni Battista Grillo, and the usual proclamations being made, according to the custom, nobody appeared [for the audition] but Don Zuanne Priuli, organist. Therefore, the motion is made . . . that Don Zuanne Pichi should be elected our organist.[291]

While it is possible that the scribe made an error, substituting Picchi's name for Priuli's (Priuli had been third organist at San Marco a decade earlier), Pichi did return at some point before 1635, and continued to serve the scuola as organist until just before his death in 1643.[292] Perhaps the earlier incidents had arisen because of some personal differences between Picchi and the officers at the time, and he could now (with new officers in power) be considered purely on his merits. At any event, at the 1643 audition, two men presented themselves, Francesco Giusto, who had been elected organist at San Giovanni Evangelista a little more than a month earlier, and Jacomo Arigoni. San Rocco elected the former, undoubtedly to the disappointment of the officers of San Giovanni Evangelista.[293] Giusto held the post for fourteen years, and was well liked enough to be granted membership in the scuola, free of charge, in 1649.[294]

It is worth noting that, unlike the case with singers or instrumentalists, the scuole never fired their organists as part of government-ordered cost-cutting. They clearly saw them as essential to their religious ceremonies and not as dispensible ornaments.

Singing Priests

The organists of the scuole certainly played alongside their professional singers on the major religious occasions of the church calendar, but, as in all churches, it was priests or other clerics who performed the sung portions of ordinary religious services. As explained in chapter 3, the majority of the scuole grandi relied on

monks or friars from their host churches for this service, but several also employed
their own. For the most part, these hired priests were those normally occupied
with performing the numerous *mansionarie* administered by the scuole, but their
obligations included coming to the scuola or church on designated days. The two
scuole with their own churches, San Giovanni Evangelista and San Rocco, relied,
as with organists, entirely on their own employees.

The arrangements with host churches and the obligations of the hired priests
of the scuole were long established and rarely changed, so such matters rarely
appear in the extant documentation except in case of controversy. Since the system
seems to have run smoothly at both San Teodoro and the Misericordia, their
archives for the sixteenth and seventeenth centuries are practically silent on the
subject. Through the early seventeenth century, San Marco and the Dominican
convent of Santi Giovanni e Paolo operated under an agreement dating back to
1437, under which, in addition to an annual payment of 50 ducats for rights to
the high altar, the scuola paid 70 ducats annually for the friars of the convent
to say the necessary masses (and also 2 ducats for the organist and 3 for an annual
"piatanza" or meal).[295] This agreement, however, did not cover all eventualities.
The mass and office of the dead to be performed on the Sunday after the Day
of the Dead were the obligation of the scuola's own priests (that is, the assembled
mansionari). The scuola's chief priest, their chaplain, appears (though the documents are not clear) to have celebrated masses with both groups—the friars and
the scuola's own priests. He certainly led the priests whenever they participated,
and a document of 1573 says that "the Reverend chaplain and the six priests of
Santi Giovanni e Paolo" sang the mass at a dowry distribution at the scuola.[296]
In the early seventeenth century, as San Marco's finances began to falter, they
were no longer able to afford to pay Santi Giovanni e Paolo as they had done
for nearly two centuries, so the parties reached a new agreement, under which
the scuola was no longer obligated to pay the 70 ducats for masses. Henceforth,
they would rely as much as possible on their own priests, paying the friars only
as needed.

While at San Marco the friars of the host church appear to have done the
bulk of the liturgical singing, at the Carità, at least until 1629, the balance seems
to have been somewhat different. The agreement between monastery and scuola
called for the participation of a choir from the monastery on the first Sunday of
the month, eight feasts of the Virgin, the Day of the Dead, Palm Sunday, and a
mass in memory of Cardinal Bessarion (who had donated to the scuola its precious
relic of the Holy Cross), but the total payment by the scuola was only about 7
ducats, one-tenth of that paid by San Marco to Santi Giovanni e Paolo.[297] Despite
the statutory payment for the first Sunday of the month, witnesses from both
sides in a 1534 dispute over rights to the high altar agreed that on those days "the
scuola has mass sung by its chaplains."[298] On four other instances, the three single
occasions listed in the agreement above and Easter vigil mass, the friars sang.
Regarding the Marian feasts, the friars admitted only that the scuola had provided
the choir for the Annunciation, their annual feast, while for the others, especially
the Assumption, "the friars do the feast, and decorate the church, and sing the
offices." It is not clear from the documents how the latter issue was resolved. In

1544, the scuola did enact a change in its procedures that involved the priestly choir: so as not to be seen as doing less than the other four scuole grande, and to please the noble brothers, the guardian proposed, "for the honor and decorum of our scuola," that on the first Sunday of each month, a "beautiful and solemn high mass should be sung in the hall of our scuola."[299] The next year, however, the new guardian condemned the excess ambition of his predecessor, and instituted proceedings to revert to the usual method, because the results had been the opposite of what had been intended.[300] In order to preserve the scuola's rights to the high altar of the church of the Carità, he explained, the scuola's priests, immediately following the new mass in the scuola, had to sing another in the church. The inevitable outcome was "great inconvenience to the priests and [financial] damage to our scuola." It is clear, therefore, that the scuola did not pay the priests who made up the choir on an annual salaried basis, but by the occasion.

The chaplains of San Giovanni Evangelista and San Rocco, who were required to provide all the liturgical singing (since these scuole operated their own churches), had duties considerably more extensive than at the other four scuole. The 1591 codification of these obligations at San Giovanni Evangelista shows that the duties were indeed onerous: to sing "the canonical hours, High Mass, and Vespers all the Sundays of the year and all the other festal days" in the church; a mass in the scuola as well as a procession on the first Sunday of the month; a mass for the dead every Monday and on the vigil and Day of the Dead; masses and offices at churches throughout the city, according to tradition; and at all processions and funerals, Sunday nights during Lent, and other occasions observed by the scuola.[301] Since these men also served as mansionari for the scuola, theirs was essentially a full-time job. The scuola included a few additional requirements and specifications in a revision of the regulations in 1610: (1) in addition to Sundays and feast days, the capo and chaplains were required to say mass three times a week; (2) on feast days, the High Mass should be sung an hour after Terce, and the Vespers as soon as the bells of the nearby Frari signaled the end of their Vespers observance; and (3) they were also required to sing the masses on Christmas Eve and Christmas Day. Above all, the rules specified that High Masses, Vespers, and the offices of Holy Week "must be sung, and not read, and they should be done with devotion and edification."[302]

While no indication suggests that San Giovanni Evangelista selected its chaplains based on their singing abilities, a document of 1558 shows that the scuola expected musical skill, if not training, and intended that they would sing more than simple chant. In December of that year, the scuola decided to pay an additional six ducats annually to one of their mansionari, pre Francesco de Domenico Luppi, who was not otherwise required to serve in the choir, "so that our church would be supplied with skilled priests, and that on feast days they can sing in polyphony."[303] The heading in the margin for this entry in the notatorio is even more explicit: "Motion to pay a salary of 6 ducats a year to teach polyphony." Unfortunately, the documents make no further mention of this practice, nor of successors to pre Francesco, so it is impossible to know what kind of polyphony would have been heard at these occasions, whether composed or simply falsobordone.

Through much of the sixteenth century, San Rocco formed its choir entirely from its regular mansionari, those priests hired to say commemorative masses paid for by testamentary bequests to the scuola. The scuola, according to a 1543 regulation, required all eight mansionari to serve in the choir as follows: to sing Mass and Vespers on Easter, Christmas, Pentecost, Epiphany, feasts of the Virgin, the Holy Cross, St. Sebastian, St. Apollonia, and other feasts generally celebrated in the city; to sing votive masses as required, Compline services every Friday, and funeral masses and offices every Tuesday; to sing mass, funeral office, Vespers and Matins on the Day of the Dead; to serve at funeral masses and offices when held in the church of San Rocco; and to sing at the Feast of St. Roch, the first Sunday of every month, Palm Sunday, Good Friday, Corpus Christi, St. Mark, the annual visits to the other scuole, and on the day the new officers take up their posts.[304] In compensation for their labors, the scuola paid these priests 8 soldi for each mass, 4 soldi for each funeral, monthly alms, a candle for the Purification, a palm on Palm Sunday, and the luminaria on the feast of St. Roch. On the other hand, the officers fined the priests 8 soldi (double that on major feasts) if they arrived after the first psalm at Vespers or Compline, or after the Kyrie at masses, or without the proper attire. No mention is made here, or elsewhere, of whether they sang chant or polyphony.

By 1577, it was clear that simply relying on the regular mansionari to serve as the choir, paying them small fees in exchange, would no longer work, as the guardian grande explained:

> Our church needs for the solemnities of the Divine Offices, which are continuously performed in reverence of our Lord God and the glorious St. Roch our protector, and for the dignity and honor of that sacred temple, five mansionari, who along with our chaplain would take care of the choir, and without which they [the Divine Offices] cannot be done.[305]

To guarantee this service, the scuola assigned five of the current mansionari to this duty, at the annual salary of 36 ducats each (ironically, this was considerably more than any of the musicians—professional or otherwise—in the scuola's employ). Though a few adjustments in procedures were occasionally required, this system worked well for over a century. Beginning in the 1640s, the notatorio of the scuola records the elections for new mansionari di coro, but there is no indication during this period (as there would be a century later) that musical ability or voice range were criteria for selection, and none of the priests hired appears elsewhere as a singer.

DURING THIS "GOLDEN AGE" OF music at the scuole grandi, they situated themselves as close to the center of the Venetian musical world as they were able, employing salaried singers and instrumentalists of the highest quality, and at correspondingly high cost. In their quest for honor, both directed outward toward God and the saints, and inward toward themselves and their confraternities, the cittadini in charge of the scuole did their best to keep up with the musical establishment sponsored by the nobility, the ducal chapel of St. Mark's.

SO SUPER-EXCELLENT

Music for the Annual Festa, 1500–1650

Since all of the scuole ostensibly participated as equals at civic processions, each of them presumably drew equal attention from the onlookers.
The officers of each scuola were concerned, above all, to maintain the
scuola's honor by ensuring that, among other things, they appeared with musicians
at least as numerous and as good as those at the other scuole. At the annual feast
of the patron saint of each scuola (usually referred to as "nostra festa"), however,
all eyes were on the host institution. The other scuole came to visit, and, because
participants could almost always receive the benefit of an indulgence, Venetians
and foreigners of all sorts, sometimes even including ambassadors and the doge,
came to the religious services. For St. Roch, St. John the Evangelist, and St.
Theodore, the celebration at the scuola was the only substantial one in the city
held that day. For the others, the multiplicity of major events on the day itself
necessitated more complicated planning. Many churches organized celebrations
for the Annunciation and Conception of the Virgin (the feste of the Carità and
Misericordia), but these were usually in the morning, as was the official commemoration of the feast of St. Mark in the Piazza and Basilica. In the afternoon,
then, attention shifted to the respective scuole. This was the one event at which
the scuole, and in particular the guardian grande and other officers, could best
demonstrate their wealth and prestige. In order to accomplish this, the scuole
often expended great sums of money.

The celebrations, as referred to in chapter 2, included several elements, which
took place either in the scuola's hall or in the associated church (or both): Vespers
on the vigil of the feast,[1] Mass and Vespers on the day itself, and often a procession
in the vicinity of the scuola. The scuola elaborately decorated both hall and
church: they displayed relics and their most elaborate liturgical apparatus, installed
luxurious cloth hangings, exhibited paintings and silver objects normally kept out
of public view (this became an especially important feature at San Rocco, where
wealthy patrons added to the display with their own possessions),[2] and completed

the visual picture with flowers and greenery. All the priests associated with the scuola participated in the sung Vespers and solemn High Mass, and, of most concern here, the scuole and their officers usually added significantly to the regular complement of salaried musicians.

All of this, of course, cost a great deal of money, especially as each new guardian (along with his officers) wanted to be sure not only to look good in comparison with the other scuole, but also, and perhaps equally important, in comparison with his predecessors in the same position. This striving for personal honor and glory, beyond that which would come to the scuola itself, led to cycles of rapidly increasing expenditures, and disputes between the guardians and membership over the source of the funds. Allocations by the scuole were often not sufficient for the desires of the guardians, who only sometimes successfully persuaded the chapter to authorize greater expenditures from the often scanty coffers of the scuola. Other times, the scuola made the decision to place all or most of the financial burden on the shoulders (or, rather, pockets) of the individual guardian, sometimes with the assistance of the other officers. The great burden that might then be faced by a potential guardian grande, however, sometimes led to hesitancy to accept the office, so that other solutions had to be found. One of the results of placing all or most of that burden on individual officers is that for most of the scuole few records survive with details of the musical participation at these occasions. What is extant, however, is sufficient to demonstrate that these were at times truly extraordinary events, that must have, in many ways, been among the most anticipated annual events in the city.

The earliest documentation for added expenditures for the annual festa comes from San Marco, which in the early sixteenth century was probably the most prestigious and well-off of the scuole. As the guardian explained in 1517 (on the day before the festa): "always at the times of our festa of misser St. Mark, our scuola has disputes with the singers who are hired for that festa, and every time it is necessary to draw up new agreements."[3] To alleviate the difficulties, the guardian came to an agreement with Piero de Fossis, maestro di cappella at the ducal basilica, along with eleven of his singers. They would "every year at the vigil of St. Mark come to our scuola and in our hall sing Vespers with the usual solemnity, and then the day of the festa in the morning come to sing the Mass and then after dinner the Vespers."[4] Presumably, the morning mass would be early enough so that they could return to the Basilica for their official duties there, to return to the scuola for Vespers after the completion of the mass and the procession in the Piazza. In addition, the singers agreed to come back the following morning to sing a requiem for the souls of departed brothers. In exchange for all of this, the scuola admitted Piero and his singers as brothers, paid them 2 ducats (for the entire ensemble), and gave them a loaf of bread and a candle. This arrangement certainly ensured the highest quality singing for the day, but there is no indication that it lasted beyond the first year.

Just two years later, expenditures for the festa became too much for the scuola to handle out of its own accounts, so the guardian proposed, on the day of the feast itself, that from then on, "to save the money of the scuola," it should be done at the expense of the banca, with the guardian himself being responsible for twice what each of the others would owe.[5] Once again, no documents extant attest to the duration of this agreement: a note entered into the notatorio in 1530 lists expenditures for the festa, but makes no reference to whether or not the officers contributed additional funds. On that occasion, the scuola paid pre Antonio about 5 ducats as "leader of the singers for two Vespers and mass of the dead," about 3½ ducats to instrumentalists, and another ducat for an organist, for a total expenditure for music of about 10 ducats. Other festal expenses included 15 ducats for decorations, 3 for festoons, and about 14 for a meal, for a grand total of just under 50 ducats.[6]

The celebration at the Misericordia for the feast of the Conception just a few years later, in 1535, was a bit more elaborate.[7] Adriano Willaert, maestro di cappella at the ducal basilica, in the only such documented occasion, directed the singers, for a fee of just over 15 ducats. The instrumental company "of San Beneto" and Zuan "maestro del corneto" also played, for a combined fee of a little more than 6 ducats, and almost 3 ducats went for the organist and bellows pumper. The amount for music came to about 24 ducats, out of a total of just over 70.

Singers' Companies and Government Regulations

The practice of hiring the maestro di cappella of St. Mark's as director of music for the annual festa does not appear to have been standard. Rather, the scuole would negotiate with one of several smaller companies of singers (and probably of instrumentalists as well) that included members of the ducal cappella as well as others. While this process undoubtedly was cumbersome, it had the benefit, for the scuole, of keeping the costs lower through competition. This was not, of course, looked upon as favorably by the singers, especially those of the cappella, who would have expected to get the lion's share of the jobs at scuole grandi and scuole piccole, as well as at parish church celebrations, and also to command the highest wages. In February of 1553, therefore, to solve this problem and to avoid disputes among colleagues, fifteen of the adult singers of the cappella ducale (with the notable exception of Willaert, the maestro di cappella) joined together, along with two from outside the cappella.[8] They explained their reasons in the preamble to the new agreement:

> The singers named herein, having united and come together in the name of the Most Holy Trinity, for the preservation of the peace and the increase of their earnings, in order to perform amicably all of the feasts that are assigned to them, and to put together all of the earnings accruing therefrom to be divided among all in equal portions, as among good brothers, and in order to avoid all the disagreements that could easily arise and cause dissension and discord among them, and establish one all-inclusive company, which will last as long as the lives of the members.[9]

The agreement established rules for the maintenance of the company and discipline of its members, and fixed severe penalties for those members who sang with musicians from outside the company. Two members of the company were to be elected to negotiate with scuole and others regarding the selection of musicians for feste (though other members who heard of opportunities were expected to jump in when needed), and to communicate the arrangements with the rest. The clear intent suggested by the document was that, on most occasions, the sponsors of the festa would want two choirs, totaling eight to ten voices, so that if two such jobs came up on the same day, the seventeen singers in the company would be sufficient. One paragraph in the agreement listed the members of the four choirs (one of five voices, the others of four) into which the company could be divided on those admittedly rare occasions when sponsors demanded single choirs. Since the officers of the scuole grandi and other organizations wanted the best singers, this company would have effectively eliminated the competition and caused costs to rise.

Reaction to this new company was not long in coming. Several of the singers were cantadori nuovi at the Carità, and showed a copy of their new agreement to the guardian grande when they made a request for a raise in their regular salary. On 26 March, the irate guardian of the Carità offered a motion to the chapter that began by rehearsing the history of singers at the scuola, from the hiring of cantadori vecchi, to the addition of cantadori nuovi by certain past guardians "for pride and vainglory," to the constant demands for increased salaries that diverted the scuola's scant funds originally destined for the poor, to the present moment, when

> these same singers, not satisfied with having brought our scuola to such a pass, nay, their hearts filled with avidity, have created a reprehensible compact and sect, with bylaws drawn up by a notary public, with several abominable and nefarious chapters that redound to the greatest harm of all churches and catholic and holy places, and especially to the extreme harm of the scuole grandi and of their poor.[10]

Despite this outburst, the guardian and banca (as mentioned in chapter 5) agreed to meet some of the singers' demands out of their own pockets, but when they broke their agreement with the Carità and went to serve the Misericordia, for 16 ducats, the guardian of the Carità brought them to court. The Avogadori di Comun ordered that the singers return to the Carità, and at their previous salary, but the guardian, inspired by the Holy Spirit, decided to fire the singers altogether and return the money to the scuola for charitable purposes. As was customary in such major changes in practice, the scuola brought the decision to the Council of Ten, which not only reaffirmed it, but extended it to the other scuole grandi as well, making it a total ban on the employment of singers.[11]

The distressed singers, deprived of a major source of income, made a humble request to the council, explaining the reasons for the company and its benefits to the scuole, and promising that if they could be rehired by the scuole they would never again request raises.[12] The guardians of the other five scuole joined the singers in their protests to the council, and made an impassioned plea to be allowed to hire musicians again:

Our holy fathers having, with the greatest prudence and utmost consideration, introduced sounds and music into the Holy Church, following the precept of the Prophet David, who in the Psalms sings, "Psallite Domino in cithara, et voce psalmi, in tubis ductilibus, et voce tube cornee," and "Laudate Dominum in tympano et choro, in cordis et organo," because, in truth, we cannot praise our Lord God in enough ways that we should not [search for more]. Besides, by this means the people are moved to come to the holy churches and other sacred places, where they are prompted to devotion and not given occasion for idleness, which tends to be the root of all evil. And since music, because of its excellent effects, has continued in use in all the cities of the faithful and in this, your city, which has always been the most observant of the divine cult above all others: we, the guardians of the scuole grandi . . . are certain that it was not the intention of this Illustrious Council to prohibit totally the use of music in the scuole.

They wished, they explained, to resume having musicians "both for the honor of this most happy city, where all of the world gathers, and for the good of the scuole, whose means are increased by the number of people that come to them because of the music and other ceremonies."[13]

The claims of neither history nor of practicality nor honor, however, swayed the council, and several motions offered between April and August to overturn the original ban failed to win the necessary two-thirds majority.[14] On 22 April, however, a different motion did pass: to disband the singers' company.[15] The singers now turned to their regular employers at the ducal cappella, the Procuratori di San Marco, and explained that without income from service at the scuole, they would require increases in their salaries at the cappella ducale.[16] The powerful Procuratori took up their cause, and wrote to the Council in favor of overturning the ban, both to save themselves money, and because "it seems to us that the grandeur of those scuole ought to be accompanied by those singers, as has always been the custom, those scuole being quite able to save their money by avoiding other expenses in which they indulge unnecessarily."[17] This argument finally persuaded the Council of Ten, and on 14 August they voted to allow the scuole to hire musicians again, but with an annual limit on expenditures of 50 ducats.[18] With a slight reduction in costs, therefore, the situation returned to what it had been before—regular salaried singers for most of the year, and open competition for special musicians for the annual festa.

Little documentation survives regarding the festa for several decades following this episode, but documents from three of the scuole indicate that they were still expending substantial funds. At the Misericordia in 1569, the official allocation for the occasion was 75 ducats.[19] A 1571 record from San Giovanni Evangelista put the usual cost for all aspects of the festa at 50 ducats, a sum reduced two years afterwards to 36, and it is likely that music represented about half the amount.[20] On the other hand, at the Carità, an account book entry for 1566 lists expenditures of more than that for music alone: 26 ducats to "Josef Zerlin maestro di capella a San Marco," that is Zarlino, with his company of singers, about 20 ducats for wind players, a little over a ducat for a violin band, and 4 ducats for two organists.[21] While on this occasion the scuola hired the maestro di cappella himself, probably with a single company from St. Mark's, the old problems caused by competition had not disappeared, and antagonism between two competing companies of singers became so acrimonious that in 1579 the doge himself intervened, advising "each and every above-mentioned church singer of any church whatever . . . [that] out of two, only one society should be made," in other words, reconstituting, in altered form, the company of 1553.[22] No records regarding such a company survive, however, and competition continued unabated.

Despite all the references to competition among companies, only one record from this period refers to an audition for a specific annual festa. On 13 October 1585, the officers of San Teodoro met "to determine the things of the festa," and held two auditions, one of singers and one of instrumentalists.[23] The two competing companies of singers were both led by senior singers (and future maestri) of the ducal cappella, Zuane Croce (il Chioggiotto) and Baldassare Donati. The officers appreciated both groups, but Donati's choir received nine positive votes and five negatives, while approval for Croce, the winner, was almost unanimous, with thirteen in favor and only one opposed. The competition for instrumental ensembles was not as close: the company of the Fidelli received a split vote of 7 to 7, but that of Giovanni da Udene, maestro dei concerti at St. Mark's, got eleven favorable votes and only three negatives. Two years later, the process at San Teodoro did not work as smoothly. There was apparently some misunderstanding, with one unnamed company of musicians believing they had an unwritten agreement to serve, while the banca voted for another. The Council of Ten decided that the banca "may elect those who please them most."[24]

As might be expected, problems continued, and finally in 1588 the Chiefs of the Council of Ten stepped in with an entirely new and reasonable solution, as set out in a resolution of 11 April:

> understanding with what difficulty and preoccupation the guardians . . . of the scuole grandi must obtain the services of the singers and instrumentalists for their solemnities, both because of the competition that exists among these musicians, and because of the character of the fees requested by them, from which arises, on every occasion, much noise and disorder . . . the Most Excellent Lords . . . decree, declare, and determine that Baldassare Donato with his company should serve in the solemnities of the scuole of the Misericordia, of San Marco, and of San Giovanni, and pre Zuanne [Croce], called Il Chiozoto, with his company, should serve at the scuole of the Carità, of San Rocco, and of San Teodoro.[25]

On 22 April, the Capi did the same for instrumentalists, this time using three companies: "that of Girolamo da Udene should serve at the scuole of San Marco and the Carità, that of the Favretti at the scuole of San Giovanni and San Teodoro, and that of the Bassani at the scuole of the Misericordia and San Rocco."[26] One year later, the Capi had to modify this second decree because of the poor health of Girolamo da Udene. It had become too difficult for him to serve both at the basilica, as maestro dei concerti, and at the scuola on 25 April, the feast of St. Mark, so they reassigned him to San Giovanni Evangelista, and had the Favretti serve at San Marco.[27]

The final step in this process came the following year. The scuole had evidently not been satisfied with the limitations placed on them in the earlier decrees, and had hired more than one of the companies at their feste. The Capi thought this expenditure excessive, and decreed, therefore, in April 1589, that each scuola could hire no more than one group of singers and one of instrumentalists, that is those already assigned to them.[28]

Feste at San Giovanni Evangelista and the Carità

From the 1580s until the middle of the following century, the paths of the scuole apparently diverged considerably. Nothing is known about activities at the Misericordia, San Marco, or San Teodoro (presumably, the guardians made all the arrangements, leaving behind no documentary trail in the archives of their scuole), but the Carità and San Giovanni Evangelista predictably struggled with finding solutions for the problem of paying for an acceptable festa in times of financial hardship, while well-off San Rocco's celebrations became ever more elaborate and expensive.

The usual system for celebrating the annual festa at San Giovanni Evangelista, according to the guardian da mattin's ceremonial of 1570, was for much of the expense to be paid from the accounts of the scuola—the guardian da mattin was, therefore, advised "not to make a grand celebration."[29] The amount the scuola made available for the festa in that period was 50 ducats, an amount increased by half for the year 1571, since the ambassador of the King of Spain would be joining them to adore the scuola's relic of the Holy Cross in celebration of the victory over the Turks at Lepanto.[30] A 1573 document noting a reduction in the statutory allotment to 36 ducats also reveals that the masseri traditionally covered some of the expenses for the festa: they decorated the hall and the altar, and built the platform for the musicians.[31] When the scuola underwent major budget cuts in 1594, the chapter reaffirmed the 36-ducat limit, with the specification that no more than 25 ducats of that could be spent for singers and instrumentalists. In addition, the regulation forbade the officers from augmenting that amount out of their own pockets, since this only encouraged "the excess of greedy demands by the musicians, and the bothersome urgings to hire more than one company [of musicians] and many organs."[32] It is unclear whether this had been happening at San Giovanni itself, or if the officers had observed the practice at other scuole where the guardians did spend their own money. Not all the guardians, apparently, heeded the admonitions against increased spending, according to a decision of 1598. These men, violating the rules "for their personal desires," had forced the scuola to spend more than it could afford.[33] The amount allocated by the scuola would be returned to the earlier figure of 50 ducats, but any attempt to spend more would result, according to the decree, in the removal from the scuola of any officers involved.

While the scuola continued to limit expenditures to 50 ducats for the feast of St. John in the seventeenth century, the officers found another way to enhance their contributions to the honor of the scuola (and, not incidentally, their own personal honor). Unlike the other five scuole, San Giovanni Evangelista had always celebrated two annual feasts: that of its patron saint on 26 December, and the day of the Holy Cross, in commemoration of the famous relic of the cross they owned. While historically, the celebrations of the patron saint would be the most important, the restrictions on expenditures for that occasion caused the officers to turn more of their attention to the other. A 1621 decree, designed principally to shift the administrative responsibilities for both feste from the guardian grande (burdened by many onerous duties) to the vicario (who had little to do), also revealed that while the expenses for St. John the Evangelist were still limited to the 50 ducats the scuola provided, the celebrations for the Holy Cross would be paid for out of the pockets of the officers, with no limit specified.[34] When, a few years later, some groups of officers failed to celebrate the feast in the usual fashion, the general chapter passed, by a large majority, a decree mandating that the tradition be followed:

> In the past several years a pernicious abuse has been introduced into our scuola, by which it has neglected to revere the holy relic on the day of the Most Holy Cross with that honor of music which always before had been the custom to do, without interruption, so that the city might come with that veneration that it has always held. And this happened because the four chief officers and the degani failed to make the usual collection (*rodolo*), the proceeds of which are used for that solemnity. Therefore, to demonstrate the most devout religion, and the greatness of our scuola, and also to placate those who mutter, scandalized, that the celebration is not performed . . . the guardian grande is obligated to form the *rodolo* on the day he accepts his office.[35]

The officers were to donate the amount they thought appropriate for music for the Mass on the day, and for Vespers the evening before. If the guardian grande failed to create the *rodolo*, he would be obligated to pay for the necessary music himself.

The situation at the Carità was similar in many ways to that at San Giovanni Evangelista. In 1600, the chapter confirmed a statutory limit of 25 ducats for music at their festa, noting that some of the past guardians, "in order to please the singers and instrumentalists, had hired two, three, or four companies, with great expense to the scuola," which could not afford such extravagance.[36] With the scuola's contribution limited, guardians who wanted to celebrate the festa with greater solemnity began to spend "great sums of money out of their own pockets." While this practice certainly created a fine impression, it set a dangerous precedent: "on many occasions, various men who would be most suitable to govern our scuola abandon the opportunity to be elected in order to avoid the inconvenience of the expense." Moreover, when the guardians spent all the scuola's allocation on music and decorations, they apparently neglected to hire enough priests to make the Mass and Vespers sufficiently solemn, "which resulted in much murmuring by all the nobility and citizens who come on that day."[37] In order to relieve the pressure on guardians to spend their own money, therefore, the scuola's expenditures were raised to 60 ducats. While this increase was probably sufficient to cover the expenses of the festa celebrated in a manner pleasing to the guardians, it was clear, after a few years, that it was more than the fragile budget of the scuola could support, so in December 1624 a committee appointed to review the accounts of the scuola ordered it cut. The scuola would henceforth be obligated only to pay for the priests and choir for the High Mass, "hoping that in praise of God and of the Most Holy Mother that [future guardians] would be content to spend their own [money]" for music on the day of the festa.[38] The decree resulted in a quite unsatisfactory celebration only four days later, for the guardian's personal finances proved no stronger than those of the scuola. While resuming the expenditure of 60 ducats was out of the question, the chapter did agree to allocate 30 "in honor of the Blessed Virgin our protector, and for the reputation of our scuola."[39]

The Festa di San Rocco

San Rocco suffered through none of the tight budgets that caused such problems at other scuole, and the annual celebrations for the feast of St. Roch were therefore celebrated with a considerably greater degree of splendor. The documents, unfortunately, do not make clear the procedure for dividing the expenses between the accounts of the scuola and those of the guardian grande himself. No reference is made to this issue in the notatori, and standard account books for the period are not extant. However, uniquely among the scuole grandi, there survives an almost complete series of files of original bills and receipts for all the financial activities undertaken by the guardian grande, beginning around 1600.[40] Listings of the expenses for music at the festa, sometimes quite detailed, are found among the hundreds of loose sheets of paper in each of the annual files. These apparently represent what the guardian spent, but with no indication of whether, or how much, the scuola reimbursed him (not until the eighteenth century did the scuola fix upon a sum of 160 ducats for this purpose). This remarkable set of documents depicts a series of extraordinarily extravagant celebrations, costing hundreds of ducats for music alone for only two days of activities each year. Perhaps the best way to gain an understanding of these events is to quote in its entirety a contemporary description by the English traveler Thomas Coryat, who visited Venice in 1608:

> This feast consisted principally of Musicke, which was both vocall and instrumentall, so good, so delectable, so rare, so admirable, so super excellent, that it did even ravish and stupifie all those strangers that never heard the like. But how others were affected with it I know not; for mine owne part I can say this, that I was for the time even rapt up with St. Paul into the third heaven. Sometimes there sung sixteene or twenty men together, having their master or moderator to keepe them in order; and when they sung, the instrumentall musitians played also. Sometimes sixteene played together upon their instruments, ten Sagbuts, foure Cornets, and two Violdegambaes of an extraordinary greatnesse; sometimes ten, six Sagbuts and foure Cornets; sometimes two, a Cornet and a treble violl. Of those treble viols I heard three severall there, whereof each was so good, especially one that I observed above the rest, that I never heard the like before. Those that played upon the treble viols, sung and played together, and sometimes

two singular fellowes played together upon Theorboes, to which they sang also, who yeelded admirable sweet musicke, but so still that they could scarce be heard but by those that were very neare them. These two Theorbists concluded that nights musicke, which continued three whole howers at the least. For they be-ganne about five of the clocke, and ended not before eight. Also it continued as long in the morning: at every time that every severall musicke played, the Organs, whereof there are seven faire paire in that room, standing al in a rowe together, plaied with them. Of the singers there were three or foure so excellent that I thinke few or none in Christendome do excell them, especially one, who had such a peerlesse and (as I may in a manner say) such a supernaturall voice for the sweetnesse that I thinke there was never a better singer in all the world, insomuch that he did not onely give the most pleasant contentment that could be imagined, to all the hearers, but also did as it were astonish and amaze them. I alwaies thought that he was a Eunuch, which if he had beene, it had taken away some part of my admiration, because they do most commonly sing passing wel; but he was not, therefore it was much more admirable.[41]

The pay slips for 1608 confirm Coryat's seemingly extravagant claims. San Rocco employed the two companies of singers associated with the ducal cappella, under the direction of pre Bortolo Morosini. Zuanne Bassani supplied two companies of wind players (Coryat's "sagbuts" and "cornets"), presumably, based on details from preceding years, his own and that known as the Favretti, and Niccolò dalla Casa (referred to here as Niccolò da Udene) provided a third. Each of these leaders supplemented his band with a violin ("treble viol"), and the scuola hired one violone player (perhaps the second mentioned by Coryat was included among the members of one of the ensembles). There were, indeed, seven organs, as Coryat described: five with players provided by Giovanni Gabrieli, the regular organist of the scuola, and two others played by the organist of Santi Giovanni e Paolo and by Giambattista Grillo. Also included on the pay slip are substantial amounts for four vocal soloists: Don Vido Rovetta da Piove, Bartolomeo Barbarino, known as il Pesarino, Giulio da Padoa, and Mattia Fernando, called il Spagnol. These were certainly those "three or four so excellent" singers Coryat refers to, and two of them may also be the ones who played theorbos and sang (there is no separate payment for theorbists, but many such solo singers accompanied themselves regularly). The total cost of all of this, for the two days of music, was over 220 ducats (note that the scuola spent less than 150 ducats throughout the remainder of the year for singers, instrumentalists, and organist). Perhaps most remarkable of all is that this was not an extraordinary celebration for the feast of San Rocco, but its usual fare: the scuola spent between 140 and 350 ducats almost every year between 1595 and 1634 (the participation of musicians in all these celebrations is charted in appendix 3).

While different musicians performed from year to year during this period, several components remained nearly constant: two companies of singers, two companies of instrumentalists, and several organs. The singers were presumably the members of the cappella ducale (numbering about two dozen men), who usually divided themselves into two companies to be able to serve in more than one location on a given occasion (as with the singers' company discussed earlier), but were here present together, along with some others not part of the cappella. For most years, the documents provide no details of the makeup of these choirs, but the few clear references as well as the consistent participation of either the maestro di cappella of San Marco or another senior musician as director (see below) make this the most likely situation. It is difficult to know precisely the size of these ensembles, but the documents provide some hints. In 1624, San Rocco employed only one company, but then added other singers "in place of a company" ("in cambio di compagnia"). Though there are a few ambiguities in the document, the additional singers seem to have numbered sixteen: five so-pranos, three altos, five tenors, and three basses. In 1628, the guardian again paid only one company, this time designated as having fifteen singers. From 1595 (the earliest dated pay sheet) through 1609, the cost for the two companies was 60 ducats, an amount that then dropped to 50 in most years from 1610 through 1620. The corresponding cost for a single company was 25 ducats in 1624 and 1627, or, in 1628, for the one designated as having fifteen members, almost 30 (180 lire).

In addition to the choirs, San Rocco also hired solo singers, sometimes quite prestigious ones, both local and foreign (often from Padua), paying sometimes quite remarkable fees. In 1608, for example, the year of Coryat's description, while the local singer Fernando received about 3 ducats, and the Paduan Giulio about 5, the more famous Barbarino earned 10, and Don Vido over 11. In most years the scuola hired at least four and sometimes as many as eight of these soloists in addition to the choirs, at a cost of 20–50 ducats. For years in which they used only one choir, the number of singers, and the corresponding costs, could be much higher. In 1627, for example, the twenty-one soloists, many of whom also played theorbo, presumably to accompany themselves, received over 87 ducats, and the scuola paid the nineteen singers hired in 1624 the remarkable sum of nearly 130 ducats. Rounding out the vocal forces were occasional low-paid "ex-traordinary" singers, perhaps used to supplement the choirs, and the singers of the scuola itself, who received the statutory 14 lire for a day's work. It is possible, in light of the large numbers of prestigious singers present, that these men did not even perform, but received their payment simply because it was required by the rules of the scuola.

The scuola also drew the core of the instrumental component of these cel-ebrations from the ducal chapel. San Rocco hired two, and sometimes three (in 1608, 1614, and 1619), companies of wind players. In the earliest years, from 1595 through 1609, Zuanne Bassani's name is always mentioned as the head of one or both companies, often paired with the company of the Favretti. In 1609, Bassani's two companies were joined by that of Niccolò da Udene (note that these three companies are the same ones assigned to the scuole by the Council of Ten nearly twenty years earlier, as discussed above). Bonfante appears as leader of one or both companies in 1614, 1617, and 1624, but for most of the later years in this series, the companies are unnamed. To each company of wind players was appended a violinist, and a violone player (often Ventura or, later, his son, Zamaria de Ventura). From 1595 through 1608, each company cost 20 ducats, an amount that dropped to 15 in 1609, in a situation analogous to that of the singers, but, unlike the singers, returning to the original level in 1618 and sub-sequent years. The added violinists cost 2–3 ducats each, and the violone player about 3. In some years, unspecified "aggionti" were added to the ensemble, as were additional violinists or violonists, or players of plucked instruments, usually lutes (as many as four in 1604), harp, theorbo (usually one or two, but five in 1619), or cittern. Only once, in 1620, was a keyboard instrument other than organ included: a spinet. These supplemental instrumentalists usually received something on the order of 1½ ducats (about 10 lire) each. The pay list for 1615 offers a different sort of information on the instrumentalists: instead of hiring and paying two or three companies, the guardian paid forty-seven individual (but unnamed) players. Except for the two cittern players, who earned 7 lire each, and the violone player, who received the most, about 2 ducats, the players re-ceived a uniform payment of just over 1½ ducats each (£9 s. 14). For organizing the instrumental forces, one of the heads of the companies, always Bassani in the early years, or later sometimes Bonfante, could expect a gift ("donativo") of be-tween 3 and 5 ducats (though this gift was not always recorded on the pay slip, it must have been paid regularly).

Another characteristic feature of the annual musical celebration of St. Roch, as pointed out by Coryat, was the presence of multiple organs, arranged for by the scuola's salaried organist. In most years, there were three to five instruments, each with its own player, but on a few occasions at the beginning of the century the scuola paid for six (1602, 1603, and 1605) and twice, in 1604 and 1608, for seven. Through about 1620, the standard fee paid to each outside organist was a little more than 3 ducats, for which sum the player was apparently obligated to also provide his own instrument. A separate expenditure of 2–3 more ducats was usually recorded for the rental of a large organ. In later years, the scuola apparently desired more than one large instrument, and therefore paid 5 ducats to two or three of the players to provide those instead of the usual small ones. The scuola's salaried organist (men such as Giovanni Gabrieli, Giovanni Priuli, Zambattista Grillo, Paolo Giusto, and Giovanni Picchi) also received a payment, usually la-beled as a gift or courtesy, of 10 ducats. In his final four years (1608–11), Gabrieli's gift approached 15 ducats, an amount equivalent to more than 60 percent of his annual salary. A series of small payments for repairs make it clear that the scuola took on the responsibility of ensuring that the rented organs were returned in the same condition as when they arrived.

Directing all of these musicians was a maestro, usually one of the most dis-tinguished musicians in the city, often the maestro di cappella of St. Mark's. These included Zuanne Croce (head of the singers' company and, from 1603 to 1609, maestro di cappella; 1595, 1598, 1600, 1602, and 1606), pre Bortolo Morosini (vice maestro di cappella; 1603–5, 1608–10), pre Gasparo Locadello (maestro di coro at St. Mark's; 1612 and 1614), Alessandro Grandi (vice maestro; 1624), Zuanne Rovetta (vice maestro; 1628 and 1630), and Claudio Monteverdi (maes-tro di cappella; 1623 and 1627).[42] The usual "gift" for the maestro's services was about 10 ducats, but the figure was less stable than for other similar payments, and was sometimes included in the lump sum paid to the maestro for contracting the other musicians. The pay slips include a few other items of some interest, most notably additional fees for rehearsals, and reimbursements for travel. The latter usually was limited to trips from nearby Padua, but some musicians came from as far as Modena or Ferrara. Finally, the scuola sometimes made substantial payments to the maestro di cappella of the Frari, who perhaps supplied singers from the nearby friary, or to the priests of nearby churches, who probably did the liturgical singing for Mass or Vespers.

The records, as usual for such sorts of documents, include no indications of what sort of music all these men actually performed at these extraordinary occasions. Coryat describes in general terms a wide variety of works, including pieces for one or two choirs, for various instrumental ensembles, and for solo voices with theorbo accompaniment. With the names of musicians provided by the documents, at least one specific work can almost certainly be identified: the three exceptional violinists, accompanied by Gabrieli at the organ, would have played his *Sonata a tre* published in the 1615 *Canzoni et sonate*.[43] Another identifiable work for the festa of San Rocco is Monteverdi's solo motet *O beate viae*, but it is not possible to pinpoint its first performance, as it was published in an anthology of 1620,[44] while the composer's first documented presence at San Rocco is not until 1623. It is, of course, likely that the work was revived both that year and in 1627. It is entirely possible that many of the other works by Gabrieli and Monteverdi, as well as those by Grandi and Rovetta, which have always been described by scholars as having been composed for St. Mark's, were performed at, or even written for, San Rocco. The forces present at the festa were sufficient to perform even the largest of Gabrieli's grand motets. Similarly, some of the extant music by composer/performers like Barbarino was also very likely heard in the scuola.[45]

For at least thirty years, then, the celebrations on 15 and 16 August must have been among the most notable events on the Venetian musical calendar, with nearly all of the city's best known musicians (numbering close to one hundred), as well as notable foreigners, coming together at the Scuola di San Rocco. Each successive guardian grande, from 1595, if not earlier, through 1634, endeavored to match, or sometimes outdo, his predecessors. While there are a few gaps in the records (pay slips are missing for 1596–97, 1599, 1601, 1607, 1622, and 1632–33), all but one of the documented years show similar extravagance. For some reason, the guardian grande in 1625 decided to break the pattern, spending a meager 23 ducats total, less than one-tenth of the usual (though it may be that this is the amount the guardian expected to be reimbursed for by the scuola, and the remainder was entered only in his personal account book). The high level of expenditures for the occasion occurred even through the various financial crises of the early seventeenth century, including the plague years of 1630 and 1631 (undoubtedly, St. Roch's status as patron saint of plague sufferers made this celebration an important tradition to continue even when much public ceremony had been suspended). The cessation of documentation in 1634 does not seem to indicate that the festa had been scaled back, but rather that, for at least some time following, the guardian grande no longer included the payment in his accounting to the scuola, perhaps covering it entirely out of his private funds. It is possible, of course, that at some point the scuola reduced the extravaganza that was the festa di San Rocco, but for as long as it lasted, it can be seen as the zenith of musical activities at the Venetian scuole.

ONLY A FEW APPEAR,
AND OFTEN NONE

The Scuole in Decline, 1650–1807

Historians generally acknowledge that by the second half of the seventeenth century Venice was in decline. It was no longer the great power, either militarily or economically, that it had been earlier, and it was increasingly famous instead as a place of entertainment and leisure. Especially in the later eighteenth century the city began to be viewed by the rest of Europe as a decadent symbol of the past, a society that had outlived its usefulness. Napoleon's arrival, then, in 1797, only hastened what was the inevitable end. While the common views certainly hold much truth, it is also important to recognize that the Venetians themselves were still proud of their city and its traditions, and made great efforts to maintain their public and religious institutions. The brothers of the scuole grandi participated actively in these efforts. Several of these confraternities struggled with greatly depleted resources, coupled with increasing demands for their charitable services, and could therefore no longer match the splendor that had been common in the sixteenth century; others, however, retained a sound financial footing, and all continued to fund at least some music, endeavoring to preserve a measure of their traditional honor. The changes they introduced were of several types. All continued to employ instrumentalists for processions, but, for the most part, at considerably lower wages than earlier, with a consequent reduction in quality. On the other hand, the scuole eliminated almost entirely salaried secular singers from their processions. Nonetheless, the scuole, especially those which managed their own churches (San Giovanni Evangelista and San Rocco), devoted substantial resources to choirs of priestly singers and organists. It was inevitably the officers who compensated for the deficiencies in the official budgets, through both mandated and voluntary contributions. Through these various strategies, most of the scuole preserved at least some of their traditions until the Republic fell to Napoleon, when the occupying governments imposed severe limitations on these ancient institutions for a decade, before finally suppressing them in 1807.

Continuity of Tradition: Instrumental Ensembles

Of the various types of ensembles that the scuole grandi had employed in the fifteenth and sixteenth centuries, only one, the ensemble of bowed string players, continued to be employed at all of the scuole throughout all (or nearly all, in one case) of the eighteenth century. As discussed in the previous chapter, despite considerable financial hardships in the 1630s and 1640s, all of the scuole managed, with only a few interruptions, to maintain the tradition of accompanying their public processions with instrumental music. They had, unfortunately, been forced to cut wages drastically, from a high of 10–15 ducats for each of four to six men, down to about 3 or 4 each, in order to be able to afford to continue the practice. The result, not surprisingly, was some dissension in the ranks, as well as considerable difficulty in attracting and retaining high-quality players.

Some of this instability remained into the 1650s and beyond. The guardian grande of the Misericordia explained the situation, and reiterated some of the factors that had led the scuole to attempt to continue this (and other) traditions:

> The scuole grandi of this city all enter into competition to venerate our religion and embellish the city, and among all, ours has never, by the grace of God, been inferior, except that in the present time we have gone out [in processions] without instrumentalists, with, it is believed, some decline in reputation, [for they] are seen and heard in all the others.[1]

The solution, of course, was to guarantee sufficient funds, in this case 15 ducats, to hire players. An intolerable scandal had arisen at the Carità as well, when the officers abandoned their long-term efforts to ensure that the scuola would appear in processions "with all the luster and great pomp that is deemed possible."[2] Instead, they had gone before the doge in the Piazza without instrumentalists. In this case, the chapter judged that the failure was primarily owing to the players themselves, who they promptly fired and then replaced.

At four of the scuole, San Teodoro, San Marco, the Carità, and the Misericordia, the situation stabilized during the third quarter of the seventeenth century, and remained essentially unchanged for the duration of the eighteenth century. In these four scuole, an ensemble of five string players served in twelve to fifteen annual processions (except the Misericordia, which had six until 1784, and then four from 1787). The scuole paid them either a fixed salary or a per-procession fee, as established in *tariffe*, often printed for permanent reference by the officers. Such fees varied somewhat from scuola to scuola, over time, and depending on the importance of the occasion, ranging from 5 to 15 lire for the ensemble. Whether by fee or in the form of a salary, the amount a scuola paid to each player over a year's time was nearly always in the range of 3–5 ducats, or about the same figure to which they had declined after the major budget cuts of the 1630s and 1640s. For San Teodoro, even these small wages were beyond the capability of the scuola's finances, so in 1690 the chapter passed a regulation that required the officers to cover the expense themselves.[3] The original decision did not specify how the *partidor* would be arranged, but a new tariffa of 1703 established a system under which different officers would be responsible for the expenses, including instrumentalists, for different processions.[4] Under this plan, the vicario paid the costs of eight of the thirteen annual occasions, and the guardian da mattin of three (St. Mark, Domenica degli Angeli, and Santa Maria della Salute). The scrivan and the two degani di mezz'anno bore the responsibility for St. Theodore (at least for the procession, while the festa itself fell to the guardian grande), and the ten degani di tutt'anno covered the feast of the Redeemer. Two later tariffe, of 1727 and 1787, implemented some reassignments, but the system itself proved successful and remained essentially intact.[5]

In addition to paying the instrumentalists' wages, the scuole usually granted them free membership for the period of their employment. The scuole covered the expense for robes for the players (which could be up to 50 ducats for six robes), something they did for few other members. Fortunately, these robes (which had to be in good condition to preserve the decorum of the processions) were quite durable, and lasted several decades.

San Marco, San Teodoro, and the Carità (as well as the remaining two, to be discussed below) seem to have maintained their instrumental ensembles through the fall of the Republic in 1797. At the Misericordia, however, despite having as late as 1749 declared that this was a "service considered necessary for so many centuries,"[6] change became inevitable in the 1780s. First, in 1784, as a result of unspecified disorders and budgetary problems, they reduced the ensemble from six players to four, that is two violins, viola, and violoncello (though a fifth individual was retained on the rolls temporarily).[7] Three years later, in 1787, the scuola apparently disbanded the ensemble (though no such decision is recorded), since the names of the players disappear from the attendance records.[8] Certainly by 1799, two years after the fall of Venice, the processions of the Misericordia lacked instruments, as a new tariffa issued in that year omits them from the lists of required attendees.[9]

San Giovanni Evangelista proceeded somewhat differently in the matter of instrumentalists than the four confraternities just discussed. In 1662, the scuola hired an ensemble of five men at an annual salary of 16 ducats, or just over 3 ducats each, about what the other scuole paid.[10] When problems arose in 1670, however, the officers decided that, in light of the dignity brought to the scuola by having good players, they should hire a new ensemble at more than twice the salary per player.[11] The new group, with only four players (led by one Paolo Masuro, called Napoli, a member of the Venetian instrumentalists' guild,[12] along with two of his brothers and a fourth man), earned 27 ducats annually, or nearly 7 ducats each, along with free membership. The same ensemble was still serving San Giovanni in 1687 when the Council of Ten ordered a temporary reduction in the expenditure to 10 ducats, an amount restored to 27 within the year.[13] The quartet, however, now wanted 40 ducats or threatened to quit. The officers proposed to the chapter a raise to 32 ducats, but when this was rejected, in November of 1688, the players indeed resigned.[14] Six months later, it had become clear that no adequate players could be found for the lower salary, and since the matter was one of "great urgency, necessity, and need," the banca granted the increase to 32 ducats, and rehired the ensemble.[15] Since four other scuole had been able to find players willing to serve for half the amount, San Giovanni Evangelista clearly refused to accept poor-quality players. The concern for quality was manifested again nearly a century later (at a time when the scuola's finances were in particularly good shape and they had undertaken, unusually for this period, a major reconstruction of their scuola) when the ensemble requested an additional payment of 1 lira each for each procession in 1768. Before granting the request, the chapter mandated that the one vacant position in the quartet, and any future spots, be filled by players "of greater ability and skill in playing the instruments," to be demonstrated through auditions.[16] The scuola paid the increase, amounting to more than 2 ducats each per year, to almost 10½, in 1771 to an ensemble headed by Pietro Dragonetti (who had begun serving at least two years earlier), father of the famous bass virtuoso.[17] San Giovanni's players continued to receive this amount until 1796, stopping only with Napoleon's arrival in Venice.

As in previous centuries, the story of instrumentalists at San Rocco during this period differs, for the most part, from all the others in that it was characterized by extraordinary stability. Players served for long periods at high salaries, were granted pensions, and were replaced through orderly processes. The solid financial foundations of the scuola enabled the officers to pay higher salaries than at the other scuole, remaining at 12 ducats each until 1770, and then increasing slightly, following a petition by the players, to 14, for the rest of the century. The high salary was undoubtedly the principal reason for the longevity in service of many of the instrumentalists. At least three players during this period, Iseppo Tonini, Antonio Ziffra, and Francesco Coppia, served for more than thirty years, and one, Costantino Berini, for at least forty-five. In many cases, men remained on the payroll as active musicians until their deaths, and at least four times, beginning in 1756, long-term instrumentalists petitioned for and were granted pensions, that is, they continued to receive their salaries and benefits without the obligation to play in the twenty or so annual events requiring instrumentalists.

When the occasion arose to select replacements, San Rocco almost always relied on the practice of holding auditions. The guardian grande, upon authorization by the banca, commissioned a *commandador*, or herald, to announce, "in the usual and customary places," that is, Rialto and Piazza San Marco, that an audition would be held at a specified date in the future, usually about a week later. On that day, a herald repeated the announcement from the door of the albergo of the scuola, and those interested made themselves known to the cancelliere. Then, one by one, they were admitted to the presence of the guardian and his companions, informed of the conditions of employment, and required to demonstrate their abilities, after which, before the next candidate was admitted, the officers voted. The scuola then offered the candidate with the greatest percentage of positive votes the position. Unfortunately, though the announcement and election process is set out quite clearly in the documents, the actual audition is not described. While occasionally only one candidate would audition for each opening, sometimes the competition was quite intense, with as many as five appearing for a single position. Through about 1760, the entire banca, as many as thirty men, voted on the candidates, but later on, as part as a process of administrative streamlining, only the five to seven officers of the cancelleria participated. Occasionally, the officers selected a new player without benefit of an audition, but rather on the basis of information regarding the "ability and sufficiency" of a single candidate. On at least one occasion, the officers seem to have taken into consideration some factors beyond the ability of the player. In the period between the announcement, on 23 November 1754, of a vacancy for a violist, and the date set for the election, 1 December, one of the candidates, Francesco Coppia, appeared before the officers. He begged them to vote for him, claiming not only to be "a man of ability and with the knowledge to play his part well," but burdened also with the weight of a family to support.[18] He asked that the scuola grant him this charity, in return for which he would serve faithfully and pray incessantly for the health of each of the officers. On the appointed day, five candidates, including Coppia, auditioned, and he was the only one to receive a majority of positive votes. He did, in fact, serve faithfully, becoming head of the ensemble, and was still playing nearly forty years later, in 1791 (the actual date of his death or retirement is not documented, but the scuola hired a new violist in 1794).[19]

San Rocco had few difficulties with its players, except for absenteeism, which at times became a significant problem. On 10 July 1674, the guardian noted that on days of processions "not only does one not see all of the players, but rather only a few appear, and often none."[20] From then on, absentees were to have penalties subtracted from their salaries. This remedy seems not to have worked very well, since in July of 1677, the notatorio contains a remark that five of the six elected instrumentalists had ceased to serve personally, but were instead sending substitutes.[21] In the following September, the scuola fired the entire company, and a few months later held new elections.[22] Seven candidates auditioned for the six posts, and all received a substantial majority of positive votes. The lowest total, 21 to 5, was that received by Andrea Ganassetto, who had apparently performed well as a temporary player in recent months, so that rather than deny him a post, the officers decided to hire all seven, with the stipulation that the first to depart, for whatever reason, would not be replaced.[23] When, for the procession to San Pantalon in July of 1755, the two violinists failed to appear, the result was "a grave disturbance" with "scandal among the people and lamentations by the reverend members of the chapter [of San Pantalon]."[24] The officers voted to dismiss the two immediately, and ban them forever from serving the scuola. The following week, the two men, with the support of the piovano of San Pantalon himself, petitioned for mercy, and were allowed to return to service (one, Antonio Zifra, remained for an additional thirty years, so that the pardon was apparently well deserved).[25] In an effort to ensure the continued obedience of their employees, the officers decided, in the eighteenth century, to adopt a procedure begun earlier for the choir of priests (see below), and periodically vote to confirm the players currently serving. On the four documented occasions they conducted this exercise, the banca confirmed all six players.[26]

Only once in the late seventeenth or eighteenth centuries was the existence of San Rocco's instrumental ensemble threatened. In 1657, the Council of Ten ordered budget cuts that would have eliminated the players,[27] but any effect was temporary, as the scuola held a regular replacement audition less than six months later.[28] Even with the fall of the Republic in 1797, when the other scuole eliminated such musicians, San Rocco persisted. Though the instrumentalists were removed from the now limited number of officially salaried "ministri" of the scuola, they continued to be paid their regular 14-ducat salaries through the beginning of the next century.

It is difficult to determine much about the quality of the instrumentalists that these four scuole employed. For San Marco and San Teodoro, names are entirely absent from the records for this period. Of the few names in the documents of the Carità, only one, Piero Recaldin, serving in 1656, also played for the ducal cappella, but several others were members of the instrumentalists' guild.[29] The situation for San Giovanni Evangelista is similar. The documents for the latter part of the eighteenth century at the Misericordia are the most complete of all, including attendance records from 1747 through the end of the century.[30] None of the men listed for this entire period ever served at the Basilica of San Marco, according to extant records (guild records are missing for this period, however). At San Rocco, as might be expected, the players were of a somewhat higher caliber. Though only in 1677 did players associated with the Basilica of San Marco (Francesco and Antonio Donaducci, Iseppo Caorlin, and Michele Locatello, the last of whom only later, in 1689, entered the cappella) serve San Rocco, nearly all of those employed there between 1675 and 1730 (the period for which records survive) were members of the guild.

There was surprisingly little movement of players from one scuola to another during this period. Only two successful moves are, in fact, documented: Ettore Giacomazzi was at the Carità in 1656 before being hired by San Rocco two years later, and Francesco Popolan served briefly at the Misericordia from 1761 to 1763 before an even briefer stint at San Rocco. On the other hand, six men employed at other scuole auditioned unsuccessfully at San Rocco, demonstrating once again the superior quality demanded at that wealthy institution.

Secular Singers at the Misericordia—A Last Remnant

By the middle of the seventeenth century, as explained in the previous chapter, the scuole grandi had eliminated nearly all their ensembles of secular singers, the cantadori vecchi, nuovi, and solenni. Only at the Misericordia did the tradition continue of maintaining an ensemble of singing fadighenti for funerals, the cantadori de corpi. Though documents are missing for most of the second half of the seventeenth century, an ensemble of four men can be traced from about 1695 through the end of the eighteenth century. The ensemble was composed of poor brothers of the scuola, who, like all fadighenti, received the benefits of membership without payment, but rather in exchange for work, in this case, singing at funerals. The extant documents enable us to learn several interesting aspects of the roles these men played throughout their years at the scuola. While some were indeed inducted into the scuola as singers, presumably upon demonstration of some ability, others began in other tasks. Zuanne Battista Chiton, for example, entered the scuola in 1726, at the age of 40, and was assigned to carry a processional staff (*asta*). Not until 1752, that is after twenty-six years' service, and now aged 66, did he become a member of the vocal ensemble.[31] Others carried the escutcheon or pennant before becoming singers. In other words, singing was just one among several tasks that a fadighente could fulfill. It is unclear whether this was a coveted post, awarded usually to those with long service, or simply one into which the scuola could push those who had become incapable of carrying out the more strenuous physical tasks of carrying heavy objects through the city in processions. Because these men were not professionals, with the option of moving to another scuola for better pay, they tended to remain in service for many years, usually until their deaths or until they became too infirm to participate even as singers. Many appear in the records as singers for more than twenty years, a few for more than thirty, and one, Zuanne Battista Roncato, for forty-seven.

These cantadori de corpi did not earn very much money, as their fees for each funeral were quite small. According to a tariffa of 1773, the four men had previously earned a total of £1 s. 10 for each funeral, a sum then increased to £1 s. 12.[32] With about twenty funerals annually (plus the annual commemoration of all the scuola's deceased on the Day of the Dead), each man thus received only a little over 1 ducat in fees, plus about the same again in gifts on Maundy Thursday, Christmas, St. Zacchary, and St. Isidore. The scuola nearly doubled the per-funeral amount in 1784, to £2 s. 8, yielding the singers almost 2 ducats each annually, but then reduced it to £2 only three years later, in 1787, at which time the annual gifts were also reduced, to about ½ ducat a year.[33] At this time, though the effect would have been small, the scuola offered the singers slightly higher fees for the rare funerals of high officers of the scuola who died while in office (£3 instead of £2 per occasion). There was one final increase in fees, in 1799, to £3 for regular funerals and £5 for special ones.[34]

A rare series of attendance records for funerals in the second half of the eighteenth century reveals curious information about attendance by the singers.[35] In many years, it was more common for at least one singer to be absent than for all to be present. In 1747, for example, of the twenty-three funerals (one of the larger number recorded), only ten saw the participation of all four singers. On seven occasions three attended, and on six others only two. Similar figures continued to be the norm for many years (with, rarely, only one showing up). The situation improved somewhat in the 1760s and 1770s, but in the mid-1780s (strangely enough, immediately on the heels of the most substantial pay increase they ever received) the singers' attendance declined precipitously—in 1786, for example, only one of the nineteen funerals saw all four singers in attendance. In that year, the scuola performed two funerals without any singers at all. For some reason, the situation turned around completely in 1788. From then through the end of the series of documents in 1793, the attendance records of all the singers were perfect. While it might seem that this attendance information is of little value, it does make it clear (not surprisingly in any case, given that these were not professional singers) that whatever music the cantadori di morti were singing was probably monophonic or simple harmonizations of monophonic melodies that could work, if perhaps less effectively, with one or more parts missing.

Priestly Singers for Church and Procession:
Coristi and Mansionari di Coro

Perhaps nothing better illustrates the fundamental changes in the attitudes of the scuole toward music, ceremony, and religion than the switch, beginning in the middle of the seventeenth century, from the use of ensembles of secular singers to priestly choirs. The highly paid (though often difficult to manage) secular singers not only provided sophisticated and up-to-date music for the processions of the scuole, but also brought them honor, both through the quality of the music, and because many of them were the same men who sang for the doge at the Basilica di San Marco. A combination of factors, including financial difficulties and, perhaps, some sort of counter-reformation sense that such singers were inappropriate for religious ceremonies performed for pious institutions (since the scuole were private, civic organizations, they were not under the control of ecclesiastical authorities, so this would not have been the result of any direct command), led to the abandonment of secular ensembles by about 1650. In their place, the scuole employed choirs of priests, men with far less musical skill than their predecessors, and, at least until the middle of the eighteenth century, no musical prestige at all. In part this was a money-saving change for some of the scuole, but it also signals a change in attitude. Whereas they had earlier viewed their processions not only as religious ceremonies but also, and perhaps primarily, as vehicles to bring honor to the city, the scuola, and its officers, these events now came to be valued more as traditional signs of devotion. Even San Rocco, whose wealth remained impressive, opted to make this change. The documents from this period rarely speak of honor, as had the earlier ones, but more often of necessity and decorum. The scuole were now willing to sacrifice the quality and splendor of the music to create a simpler, more devout, more decorous image of themselves.

San Marco, San Teodoro, and the Misericordia

Two of the scuole, San Teodoro and the Misericordia, used even priestly choirs only once a year, at the Maundy Thursday procession, and a third, San Marco, employed them only a bit more, on Maundy Thursday and a few additional occasions during Lent. None of these scuole ever employed such choirs on a salaried basis, but simply hired them for the occasion.

The tariffa for San Teodoro of 1691 indicates that 20 lire (about 3 ducats) should be spent for a choir of "eight priestly singers," that is 50 soldi each.[36] The scuola increased its expenditure in 1703 by enlarging the choir to sixteen, and paying each priest half again as much, for a total of almost 8 ducats, a rather substantial sum for such a poor scuola.[37] By 1727, a reduction to twelve singers and less than 6 ducats was necessary.[38] The chapter eliminated entirely all such expenditures by the scuola in 1787, when it issued a new tariffa that indicated that for the Maundy Thursday procession, whether or not to hire a choir, and how large it would be, was up to the guardian, since he bore all the costs.[39] The final reference in this scuola's archives to such a choir is in a document from Lent of 1797, which indicates that in the upcoming procession (without reference to the source of funds) a "turba di religiosi" would be used, but without the "coretto," most likely an ensemble of soloists.[40]

At the Misericordia, the situation was much the same, even though, as finances were not as tenuous, more funds would have been available, presumably for a choir that was either larger or of higher quality. Since all of the scuole grandi, and undoubtedly other institutions as well, performed ceremonies on Maundy Thursday, competition for the more able singing priests was certainly a factor. In contrast to San Teodoro's maximum expenditure of less than 8 ducats, the Misericordia allocated, according to its 1746 revised tariffa, 20 ducats for the choir.[41] This was by far the costliest part of the procession, which also included the chaplain and mansionari of the scuola, two priests to accompany the relic of a fragment of the Crown of Thorns, and two to accompany the monstrance, in all about thirty non-singing priests earning a total of almost 14 ducats. A revised tariffa of 1780 reduced the expenditure for the choir to 15 ducats, where it remained until after the arrival of the French, when a 1799 budget cut left only 12 ducats for the Maundy Thursday choir, still half again as much as at San Teodoro.[42] The 1787 tariffa included references to the hiring of smaller ensembles of eight singing priests for several non-processional occasions: the Octave of the Day of the Dead (at 2 lire each) and three endowed commemorative services (at 1 lira per singer on each occasion).

Things were handled a bit differently at San Marco, where the scuola allocated the guardian grande a fixed sum, 180 ducats (for most of the years, beginning in the 1750s, for which documentation survives), for all the expenses for Lent.[43] These expenses included 60 ducats for palms (usually, apparently in the form of medallions bearing representations of palms) for the members of the banca, 20 ducats for images presented to the doge and grand chancellor, also on Palm Sunday, and 50 ducats for the choir for the Fridays in Lent, Lazarus Sunday, and Maundy Thursday. The scuola made no change in this allocation until 1800, when by order of the new government, they cut Lenten expenditures by two-thirds, to under 60 ducats, with the guardian grande given permission to pay for anything additional out of his own pocket.[44] In 1801, the only subsequent year with documented expenditures, the scuola eliminated the choir except for Maundy Thursday, but still spent 100 lire (about 16 ducats) on other expenses for that occasion.[45] Beyond the Lenten observances, only a few other isolated references to the choir appear in the records, with the exception of the annual festa, which will be discussed below.

The Carità

The Scuola della Carità adopted a two-tiered practice. In addition to ad hoc choirs hired by the guardian grande for individual occasions, as at the three scuole discussed above, this scuola also employed a salaried, or at least regularly employed, choir for more frequent services, primarily processions. The guardian grande, like his counterparts at the Misericordia, San Marco, and San Teodoro, hired a priestly choir annually for the Maundy Thursday procession, in this case with his own funds. He was also responsible for similar choirs for Corpus Christi and the third Friday of March. On this latter day, the scuola displayed its relic of Christ's robe ("sacra porpora"). A 1761 note explains that six singers participated in the ceremony when the relic was removed from the church and brought to the altar of the scuola.[46] The sung mass at the scuola was ornamented with music under the direction of a maestro, who directed an organist, violoncello or bass, and nine singers (it is not clear whether these are from the priestly choir or are secular musicians). The day concluded, after dinner, with a procession, possibly to return the relic to the church. A "maestro o direttor" received £12 to lead a choir of twenty-four, divided into a "coretto" of four and a "pien coro" of twenty. According to a tariffa of 1766, the guardian di mattin bore the responsibility for a choir for Domenica degli Angeli,[47] but in a 1784 revision this latter duty was taken over by the scuola itself, which allocated 12 ducats for a choir of ten priests.[48] Similarly, in 1783, the scuola decided to lighten the burden on the guardian grande by allocating him 60 ducats for all expenses, including choirs, for the occasions for which he was responsible.[49]

The origins of the Carità's salaried choir are not documented, but the ensemble is first referred to, in rather vague terms, in 1698.[50] The officers questioned the value of this stable choir when they discovered in 1724 that they did not have sufficient funds for expositions of their relics on the Fridays in Lent. While the total amount available for this "pious work" was only 25 ducats, less than the 40 that doing it properly would require, it was noted that the scuola paid salaries of 24 ducats annually for the priestly choir, an expenditure that was "useless and non-functional." The problem was, as the guardian explained, that they really had no duties at all, since when it needed singers, the scuola "selected and paid [them] . . . according to their function."[51] In other words, though the scuola had a salaried choir, the guardians chose to hire outsiders anyway. The chapter approved the proposal to eliminate the salary in October 1724, but it seems clear that the choir was not, in fact, disbanded. Rather, though the documents are not explicit about this, it seems that under a new system, the scuola would engage a small choir of four for processions, paying them small fees on each occasion. The scuola saved, in this manner, a great deal of money, but also, presumably, was spared the bother of finding a choir for regular processions and other functions. However, there were evidently some difficulties with the new procedures. In 1729, the choir failed entirely in its obligations during Lent, in order to "transport themselves to more genial [i.e., higher paying] functions in other churches."[52] Fortunately for the historian, the document describes the services the singers had failed to fulfill: singing the *Veni creator spiritus* and Litany of the Virgin at the meeting of the chapter on the third Monday of Lent, the *Miserere* and Litany at the exposition on the last Friday of March, and unspecified items at the scuola's festa of the Annunciation. The absence of singers scandalized the large numbers of devout citizens who attended, since the priests had irreverently abandoned the service and diminished the honor that was owed to the holy relics. The chapter permanenetly banned those seven clerics involved from serving the scuola as singers. In later years, the stable choir no longer had any duties on such important occasions, when it was replaced with singers hired by the guardian, but it was relegated instead to service at lesser processions.

Beginning in 1748, the scuola decided to engage on a stable basis only a chief singer ("capo cantori"), who was obligated to find three other priests to sing with him at processions.[53] The wages paid to the choir for these reduced duties were, in fact, quite small, but so, then, were the duties. In the tariffa of 1766, the scuola assigned the four-man choir fees of £3 s. 4 for processions on six simple feasts, and £4 for each of five occasions designated as doubles, for a total of £39 s. 4, or barely 1½ ducats each annually.[54] Their obligations, however, were few: to sing a *versetto*, or hymn, while passing the high altar of the Basilica of San Marco. The scuola increased these fees slightly in 1784 to £4 s. 16 and £5 respectively.[55]

The history of the choir of the Carità came to an end with a series of developments in 1795. Zorzi Maria dall'Aqua, the guardian grande, commissioned the scuola's chaplain to undertake two tasks on September 20 of that year.[56] He was to determine first whether the priests in the scuola's employ, including the choir, carried out their duties and "conducted exemplary lives," and second, whether the duties of the singers could be taken over by the regular mansionari, that is those priests charged with saying mass and conducting other services for the scuola. The chaplain reported that all the priests were indeed carrying out their duties as required, either personally or through appropriate substitutes. All but one also behaved as befitted priests. The exception was Don Giulio Artusi, a priest of San Samuele, who had been elected by the scuola as a corista only one week earlier. Artusi, it seems, "was dedicated to assisting public theatrical performances . . . in particular as regards correct pronunciation, the precise pantomimic gestures, and the correct movements of the actors," and therefore did not enjoy the sort of reputation a priest should have.[57] Moreover, there had been some unspecified scandal surrounding his participation in the opening of the summer theatrical season in Udine. In addition, because of his secular occupations, he rarely celebrated mass, and too often sent substitutes to the scuola. He was, therefore, dismissed. The chaplain also reported that the minimal duties of the singers—to sing during processions only one or two verses of the appropriate hymn in front of the Signoria in San Marco—could be performed not only equally well, but "better still, and with greater decency and punctuality," by the regular mansionari.[58] On 28 September 1795, therefore, the Scuola della Carità finally disbanded its last remaining musical ensemble.[59]

San Giovanni Evangelista

As we have seen earlier, San Giovanni Evangelista and San Rocco operated under very different situations than the other four scuole—they were responsible not only for public processions and for ceremonies in the scuola itself, like the others, but for the entire liturgical calendars of the churches they ran. They had always, therefore, employed a substantial body of priests, both to celebrate mass and other ceremonies, and to serve as the responding choir for those occasions that required a sung mass or office. Before the middle of the seventeenth century, the responsibilities for singing in processions, on the one hand, and responding in church ceremonies, on the other, were carried out by different bodies: the ensemble of secular cantadori and the priestly choir, respectively. With the elimination of the secular singers, who had also participated in major occasions in the church, however, the priestly choirs had to expand their duties; they eventually came to serve not solely as liturgical bodies carrying out a necessary service, but as musical ensembles responsible for maintaining the honor and decorum of the scuole. This process of transformation took quite a long time, nearly a century, in fact, to complete.

At San Giovanni Evangelista, the first indication that musical skill, rather than just piety and good habits, was a criterion for election as a corista, comes in 1760, when Don Antonio Dolcetta, a proposed replacement for one of the six members of the ensemble, was certified by his piovano as having served his church "with all his great natural ability for singing."[60] Later that same year, the scuola made major revisions in the procedures for the church and its singers, and published a booklet of "obligations and rules," including regulations for the five regular members of the choir and their maestro.[61] Before the chapter could appoint a candidate to the choir, he was required to audition, singing at sight his part along with the rest of the choir and the organ. He was also obligated to present a certification (such as that done earlier for Dolcetta) that he was skilled in such singing. The choir had considerable obligations, all to be performed following the instructions of the maestro, singing the parts assigned to them without question. They were required (1) to participate in Mass and Vespers at each required feast (*festa di precetto*), singing prayers and psalms; (2) to join with the larger choir selected by the guardian grande at the ceremonies for Palm Sunday in the scuola and at the processions on Maundy Thursday and St. Lawrence's Day; (3) to sing the appropriate hymn and the *Miserere* in the procession from scuola to church on the Fridays of Lent and the feast of the Holy Cross; (4) to join in all the ceremonies of Holy Week; (5) to attend all the public processions of the scuola; 6) to participate in the processions in Campo San Stin on the first Sunday of each month and Lazarus Sunday, and to the Frari for the exposition of the Holy Blood; and (7) to sing the *Veni creator spiritus* and Te Deum on the day the scuola elected new officers. For these duties the scuola paid each of the priests 12 ducats a year.

In addition to leading his colleagues in all the above duties, the maestro di coro, in exchange for a salary of 28 ducats (plus small fees for each procession), had some special musical obligations. He was required, first of all, to compose ("estendere sopra la parte") a mass, vespers, and all prayers necessary for the functioning of the church. Further, each year on Easter he was obligated to compose a new mass and vespers, providing the remainder of the choir with all the necessary copies, without additional charge to the scuola. The first man the scuola selected for this position, in 1760, was Don Giacomo Carli, a priest at San Pantalon and a "maestro di musica professore."[62] After his appointment, the scuola selected an entirely new choir, with Carli certifying each successful candidate as "capable and suitable for chant and polyphony."[63] Carli served until his death in 1767, when the scuola replaced him with one of the coristi, Francesco Groggia.[64] He was replaced within two years, by Biagio Caratelli, who remained in the post until the the fall of the Republic.[65] If these men carried out their duties faithfully each year, they would have composed, before the suppression of the ensemble in 1800, forty masses, forty vespers services, and numerous smaller works, none of which, unfortunately, has come to light.

San Giovanni's choir was remarkably stable; there seem to have been no real controversies, such as were common elsewhere. The only change of any kind occurred in 1768 when, after two unsuccessful attempts, the chapter approved a motion to grant the members of the choir the rights and privileges of membership in the scuola.[66] The salaries set out in the 1760 foundation also remained unchanged. As indicated in those regulations, the guardian grande bore separate responsibility for hiring the choirs for masses on Palm Sunday and the feast of the Holy Cross and processions on San Lorenzo and, as at all other scuole, Maundy Thursday, for which the scuola allotted him, according to a tariffa of 1755, 50 ducats.[67] He had the option of using members of the salaried choir, but was not obligated to do so.

San Rocco

The Scuola di San Rocco had established a choir of five priests in the sixteenth century to assist its chaplain with liturgical duties in its church. There is no indication for two centuries that musical ability of any kind was a criterion for employment, nor that the priests were required to sing anything other than simple chant. On major feast days, the secular singers of the scuola, or outside musicians hired by the guardian grande, provided whatever polyphony was needed. For nearly a century after San Rocco ceased employing a salaried ensemble of cantadori, however, the documents reflect no change in the makeup or singing duties of the choir. Through the 1660s, there are payment records to external musicians for the semi-annual expositions of the Holy Sacrament, and, of course, for the annual festa, but nothing for the other feast days or processions. It is unclear whether the *mansionari di coro*, as they were called at San Rocco, began to fill a more important musical role, or whether the officers paid for some outside musicians out of their own pockets. The lists of duties of the choir in the 1650s and 1660s are of little help in deciding this matter.[68] The five priests were required to (1) sing Vespers every Sunday and all feast days; (2) sing Compline every Friday; 3) assist in the choir for the Day of the Dead and the feast of St. Roch; (4) participate in the celebrations for Expositions of the Holy Sacrament; (5) sing Mass and the Passion on Palm Sunday; (6) join in the processions to San Pietro di Castello on evenings in Holy Week; (7) accompany all funeral processions; and (8) participate in all public processions and visits to the other scuole grandi. For these extensive (if perhaps not always musical) duties, the scuola paid them salaries, in 1653, of 10 ducats each, raised to 12 in 1666.[69] In addition, like the fadighenti of the scuola, they were entitled to small fees, ranging from 12 soldi to 1 lira, for each procession and funeral. The mansionari petitioned for a raise to 16 ducats in 1698, but the motion to grant this did not achieve sufficient votes (the yes votes were sixteen out of twenty-six, but regulations required a five-sixths majority).[70] Again in 1708, they asked for a raise, but motions to increase their salaries by 4, 3, 6, and again 4 ducats each never achieved the necessary support.[71] In addition to salaries, San Rocco sometimes granted choir members with long service paid retirement if they were no longer physically able to perform their duties because of age, as did other scuole.[72]

The chapter approved in 1741 the only significant change in the duties of the choir.[73] The officers noted on 13 July, that despite their constant efforts to ensure that their church was "officiated with the true order appropriate to the sanctity of the place" with the intention of "increasing the devotion and concourse of the faithful," they discovered "with an inner sense of sadness" that the church "remained today almost entirely abandoned."[74] They decided that those services performed with the choir (festal Vespers and Friday Compline), took place at a time the potential congregants found inconvenient. Therefore, the scuola made the decision to eliminate those services, and instead replace the low masses traditionally done on Sundays and feasts with sung masses, with the participation of the choir. Vespers would henceforth be performed only on the feast of St. Roch, and Compline only on the Fridays in Lent, when the scuola displayed to the public its relic of a piece of the Crown of Thorns. At the end of those Compline services, the choir was required to sing the hymn *Vexilla regis*. Finally, it remained responsible, in addition to processions and funerals, for Vespers and office of the dead on All Saints. Further reguations in 1754 divided the sung masses into two classifications: on the eleven principal feasts of the year the mass was to be performed "a cappella in organo," that is in accompanied polyphony, while on ordinary Sundays and lesser feasts it would be done in "canto fermo," or plainchant.[75]

By the time of the 1754 regulation, clearly, the choir was capable of singing more than just chant. The elevation of the musical capabilities of the choir was brought about through a rather complicated series of decisions by the officers of the scuola, not all of which had the desired effect. The situation first came to a head in 1729 when, during the renovation of the church, the organ had to be removed. Those in charge wanted to ensure that "the divine praises should be decently sung," but realized that without the organ, a five-person choir was insufficient to intone the psalms adequately, so that an additional three coristi were to be chosen, one of them to be the now unemployed organist, Santo Pesenti.[76] There are two possible musical explanations for this change. Possibly, the practice had been for the psalms to be done alternatim, with the choir (probably singing falsobordone) alternating with either organ alone or organ with a soloist; without the organ, a second four-man choir would be required for the responses. On the other hand, however, additional choir members might simply have provided a more solid support for single-choir singing in the absence of the organ.

The size of the choir remained at eight for only a few years, slipping down to seven, without explanation in the documents, around 1732.[77] Then, in 1738, the scuola failed to confirm two of the members in the biannual reballoting, and, perhaps in expectation that the organ would be rebuilt shortly, did not replace them.[78] When, in 1741, the scuola, as described above, decided to replace the Vespers and Compline services with sung masses, the chapter also decided to enlarge the choir once again, by selecting from among the regular mansionari of the church the four with "the greatest ability" as singers, to serve, in addition to their usual liturgical duties, as "sotto coristi" at half the usual 12-ducat salary.[79] Just three years later it became clear that this new system had one major flaw: "since the vice corista was chosen from among the mansionari of the church [who had been chosen for their qualities as priests], it might never be the case that one could select someone with a good voice, nor somebody learned in singing, reducing the dignity of the holy services."[80] For the first time, the officers clearly recognized the need for trained singers in this choir, and mandated that future vacancies would be filled only through auditions. None of the nine priests selected by the old system had been adequate to the task, though the scuola, as usual, felt it could not fire them as long as they continued to attend functions; the officers, however, now selected three additional musically trained "sotto coristi sopranumerarii," to be paid the same 6 ducats as the four other sotto coristi.[81]

When, in 1749, the original four sotto coristi complained about the difference in salary, despite the identical obligations, the chapter approved raising theirs to match the regular coristi.[82] Strangely enough, though the sotto coristi cited the lack of musical ability of the original coristi as a reason they deserved a raise, the scuola did not apply new amount to the three truly able sotto coristi sopranumerarii. The scuola partially rectified this injustice two years later, when these men saw their salaries increased to 10 ducats each.[83] Also in 1751, the scuola added a fourth trained member, so that the four capable singers could cover the musical needs of the choir at the now well-attended sacred functions in the church.[84] It seems clear that after this development the original coristi and sotto coristi satisfied their obligations by singing plainchant, while the new group of four, along with any of the others who might be capable, would sing any needed polyphony.

Still unsatisfied with the results, the officers undertook one final major reform in 1754. The choir had been reduced to eleven by vacancies, but of these, six were deemed "entirely untrained in singing."[85] It was clear that the two replacements needed to be skilled performers, but reforms had to be made before this could be accomplished in the proper manner, to make the choir complete and "perfect." First, the scuola unified the different categories of choir members, so that all would now be classified as coristi, and all would receive a raise to 16 ducats. Second, since the scuola only needed eight trained singers, the size of the choir would be reduced gradually from thirteen by attrition, replacing only those musically trained until the entire choir would be capable of singing polyphony. In the meantime, the scuola gave the bulk of the assignments for celebrating mass to those unable to sing, so as to even out the workload. Third, and perhaps most importantly, the scuola would hire a capo or maestro di coro, who would direct the choir, select and audition appropriate singers for replacements (with final approval by the banca), and monitor the attendance of all the coristi. The officers selected as the new maestro a man of "probity, knowledge, and singing ability," Don Giovanni Battista Tosini, from the church of San Pantalon, to whom they offered a salary of 40 ducats.[86]

The reforms needed one additional refinement in 1766. The replacements of skilled singers were not taking place in an orderly manner, in part because the officers had not been paying attention to the distribution of voice parts. The six capable singers currently serving were two tenors, two contraltos, and two basses, leaving to be filled, for the balance desired, two bass positions.[87] From that point on, all audition announcements carefully indicated the part desired. In the event, the size of the choir never dropped down to eight, but only to eleven, plus the maestro, with the non-singers gradually replaced by singers. In the final extant listing, from May of 1796, one of the original untrained coristi was still employed, and the other members consisted of two contraltos (including Don Carlo Bellato, the maestro since Tosini's death in 1791), five tenors (apparently, though not usually specified, divided into first and second tenors), and four basses.[88]

As the various reforms took effect, and created a choir capable of singing polyphony, the officers of the scuola needed to provide them with music. In 1754, therefore, they authorized an expenditure of £132 for "a chant book that would satisfy our needs."[89] The resulting book, with music almost certainly by the new maestro di coro Giambattista Tosini (to whom the scuola paid the fee), and copied by Matteo Zener (one of the coristi), remains today in the archive of the scuola.[90] It contains five masses and eight Credos in a style that combines sections for solo voice (probably with improvised organ accompaniment) alternating with falsobordone, music certainly within the capabilities of a choir of priests. It also includes two masses for two voices and several motets. Twenty years later, in 1775, the church again needed new music:

> It was recognized as indispensible the need to provide for our church new choir books, for use in the masses and vespers that are frequently solemnized there. The old book was reformed, and in the same manner a second volume was added, containing twelve new masses, all written with Roman letters in score, which renders the choir sufficiently furnished for the recurrences of the various functions throughout the year, in addition to all the feasts that are solemnized with a sung mass.[91]

The scribe Zener added two masses and a credo to the first book. The second volume, also in the scuola's archive, contains, in fact, only five (not twelve) masses, but also ten motets, all composed by maestro di coro Tosini, and copied again by Zener.[92] The cost for all this work, including the binding of both volumes in matching leather, was a bit over 75 ducats. As at San Giovanni Evangelista, the maestro di coro of San Rocco was evidently expected to provide music for his choir, but unlike his counterpart, he was paid for this service in addition to his regular salary.

At San Rocco, there were two annual occasions for which entirely different rules obtained: the feast of St. Roch (which will be discussed below) and the Maundy Thursday procession. As at the other scuole, providing a choir (which might include the members of the scuola's regular choir, though it need not) for the evening procession to Piazza San Marco became one of the important responsibilities of the guardian grande. The evidence is not entirely clear whether the funds allocated by the scuola for this purpose were usually supplemented by private funds of the officers, though this did happen at least once. The only seventeenth-century record of music for this occasion is an expenditure in 1676 of £136 s. 8 for a choir of eight.[93] As in all subsequent documented cases, the scuola paid the regular choir its usual processional fee, without any indication of whether they sang with the special choir, on their own, or not at all. The one document that describes the makeup of the special choir is a pay list, unfortunately undated, but probably from sometime in the first two decades of the eighteenth century, recording musical expenditures for the Maundy Thursday procession, the Passion on Palm Sunday, and the feast of St. Roch (on the latter, see below).[94] For the procession, the guardian grande paid sixteen singers, eleven of them specifically designated as clerics, and the majority of them members of the cappella ducale, and a maestro. None of the members of the scuola's choir is listed. As best as can be determined, there were four sopranos, three altos, three tenors, and six basses. The first man on the list, signor Raffellini, clearly a soloist, earned one doppia (£37 s. 10), and all the others received 15 or 17 lire. The fee for the maestro was 66 lire; altogether the cost for the choir was about 55 ducats. The Passion performance on Palm Sunday would be paid for by a *partidor* of the officers if done in chant, but entirely by the guardian grande if done "in musica," that is polyphonically, as it was on this occasion.[95] The guardian paid the same soloist as for the procession, here called Signor Raffaele, 22 lire to sing the role of Christ. The *turba* was made up of seven men (two sopranos, two altos, a tenor, and two basses), all but one of whom also sang in the Maundy Thursday procession, and each earning about half of Raffaele's fee. They were joined by players of violoncello and bass. As in the procession, the unnamed maestro received a fee of 66 lire, and the total cost of this performance came to just under 30 ducats.

After this, the eighteenth-century documents recording payments for Maundy Thursday survive almost exclusively for the years from 1740 to 1754, and refer usually to two choirs, sometimes supplemented by a "corretto."[96] In several years, a maestro, who received the payment and apparently organized the choir, is named. In 1747 the scuola paid two maestri, each presumably having provided one of the choirs. Interestingly, these were the future maestri di coro of San Giovanni Evangelista, Don Giacomo Carli, and of San Rocco, Don Giambattista Tosini.[97] The fee in most years was about 40 ducats, but the account for 1749 indicates that the officers, in the form of a partidor, contributed an additional 67 ducats.[98] The accounts after 1754 list no expenditure for the choir beyond the usual small fee to the scuola's coristi, but an undated document from the early 1770s indicates a payment of about 70 ducats for the occasion, "at the expense of the guardian grande."[99] In the mid-1780s, however, another undated document explains that the guardian grande was entitled to reimbursements for the music for Maundy Thursday and Palm Sunday in the amount of 180 ducats, more than the 133 he actually spent.[100]

Several problems occurred during the eighteenth century involving this procession. It seems surprising, but it took until 1749 for the officers to realize that it was rather inconvenient for a choir to process after sunset.[101] Since the priests were not members of the scuola, they had not automatically been given candles to carry, so, despite the the great expense for candles and torches for the regular brothers, the singers were "totally in the dark," and often obstructed from the light of other candles or torches by the crowds watching the procession.[102] In addition, of course, they were unable to see their music. The chapter authorized, for the decorum of the scuola, the assignment of thirty-six brothers, each with a torch, to walk alongside the choir, half on each side.

The practice of hiring an outside maestro for Maundy Thursday did not sit well with the scuola's own maestro di coro, Tosini, who, in 1763, petitioned the chapter to assign him this responsibility on a stable basis, leaving, on the other hand, the St. Roch celebrations entirely in the hands of the guardian grande.[103] The cancelleria thought this a reasonable request, but both the banca and the general chapter rejected it. Tosini resubmitted his request six years later, and, though the cancelleria again approved it, it was similarly rejected by the larger bodies.[104] It seems likely that, in both cases, the sitting guardian grande was willing to yield this prerogative, and could sway his closest associates, but that future holders of the office sitting in the larger bodies felt it wise to retain the option of selecting an outsider who could bring them and the scuola honor.

With the fall of the republic in 1797, San Rocco's choir was removed from the ranks of salaried employees of the scuola, though the members were allowed to continue participating in processions for which they would collect the traditional small fees.[105] In 1800, however, without recording the reason, the scuola gave the choir a special payment of 100 ducats for their services, and when San Rocco, alone among the scuole, was reconstituted in the early years of the century, it reestablished the choir at its old salary.[106]

Organs and Organists

By the middle of the seventeenth century, only the two scuole grandi with their own churches, San Rocco and San Giovanni Evangelista, still employed organists. The other four relied entirely on their host churches for this service. The Carità, in dire financial straits, and having eliminated most musical activities beyond their annual feast, even went so far as to discontinue, in 1674, paying the portion of their annual fee of 8 ducats to the monastery of the Carità that went toward the salary of the organist.[107] In 1690, the monastery petitioned the scuola for repayment of the accumulated deficit, arguing that while the scuola might not currently be using the organ, they needed to pay the arrears if they wished to maintain the right to do so at any time in the future.[108] After considerable debate, the question seems never to have been settled definitively, but as all documented musical events after this period seem to have taken place in the hall of the scuola, which had its own consecrated altar, it seems likely that the officers stood their ground and did not resume payments to the monastery. San Giovanni Evangelista and San Rocco, with their own churches, did not have this option, since organ music was an essential component of all their church services. Both of them built and maintained organs, often at great expense, and both salaried organists, who performed along with their priestly choirs.

San Giovanni Evangelista

The job of organist at San Giovanni Evangelista appears not to have been a very desirable one, most probably because of the relatively low salary of 12 ducats a year, not raised until 1760. In no recorded case (though there are some gaps) was there any competition for the post. Either one candidate only appeared for the announced auditions, or the guardian hired a temporary replacement without audition who the chapter then approved as permanent. Even in 1760, when the scuola more than doubled the salary, to 25 ducats, only one man, Don Domenico Levis, appeared.[109] Levis, the only organist of this scuola known to have served at other institutions as well, held the post for much longer than any of his eighteenth-century predecessors, thirty-five years.[110] His duties, included in the same printed booklet with regulations for the choir,[111] included playing at every sung Mass and Vespers at the church, and in particular at the midnight mass on Christmas and the dawn mass on the feast of St. John the Evangelist. To assist him, the scuola employed a salaried bellows pumper.

The instrument in use at San Giovanni Evangelista in the mid-seventeenth century seems to have been the one built in 1559, and then restored several times in the intervening century (see chapter 5). By 1681, it was in such a state that "the honor of God and of the cult of the Holy Church" required a major repair, completed by Carlo di Beni, organ repairer at the Basilica of San Marco, for a fee of 50 ducats.[112] Perhaps because of the age of the instrument, it soon fell into disrepair, so that the officers could lament in 1688 that "we find that for some time the organ in our church has been broken."[113] Once again, the work cost 50 ducats, but this time the officers decided to reinstate the position of salaried tuner and repairman, in the hope that regular maintenance would reduce the necessity for major repairs. This effort was to some degree successful, with significant work not needed before 1723, but again in 1724, 1729, and 1733 (this last operation made necessary by the ravages of mice, who had damaged nearly half the pipes and the bellows).[114] After the 1729 repair, the scuola hired both Antonio Giorgio and Felice Beni as tuners/repairmen, at the rather high rate of more than 12 ducats.[115] By the late 1750s, however, it must have become clear that the 200-year-old organ could no longer serve the needs of the scuola; for a new instrument, the scuola turned to one of the most important builders in the city, Giovanni Battista Piaggia, for a fee of about 400 ducats.[116] The instrument was completed in 1760 (and still remains in the church today), and the scuola hired Piaggia as the tuner, a position he held until his death in 1771, when he was succeeded by his disciple Francesco Merlini.[117] It is probably the completion of this important new instrument that spurred the 1760 increase in salary to the organist and the arrival of a more distinguished player, Levis, than in the recent past.

San Rocco

As befits its status as the richest and most prestigious of the scuole grandi, San Rocco, for the most part, employed distinguished players. When the previous organist, Don Francesco Giusti, left the city in 1657, the announcement of the vacancy, at the respectable salary of 24 ducats (twice that at San Giovanni Evangelista) attracted three candidates, with the post going to the well-known composer and performer Gasparo Sartorio.[118] His replacement, in 1680, following an election with one other candidate, was the teacher and maestro Ludovico Fuga, who served the scuola for forty years, until his death.[119] In 1692, Fuga sought a raise in salary, claiming that his duties had increased significantly.[120] Whereas before, he claimed, organists at San Rocco had been obligated to play on feast days and Fridays in Lent, he was now required to play as well at Compline every Friday. He found sympathetic ears (and a solid financial situation) and the scuola granted him a substantial increase, to 36 ducats annually. As Fuga approached the end of his life, he became too feeble to attend to his duties, and a certain Don Santo Pesenti began to take his place, though without payment from the scuola (possibly, Fuga turned over at least some of his wages, though that is not at all clear). After five years, in 1719, Pesenti requested, and was granted, the title of substitute organist, with the understanding he would take over upon Fuga's death.[121] That followed not too long afterwards, in 1721, but Pesenti served only six years before the rebuilding of the church forced the dismantling of the organ and the suspension of his salary.[122] He was allowed to join the choir, with the provision that he would get his post back when the organ itself was returned to service; the banca, however, dismissed Pesenti from the choir in 1738. When the scuola reinstated the organ position in 1743, he requested that the earlier agreement be implemented.[123] The banca first denied this request, but then allowed him to return temporarily and ordered an internal investigation after Pesenti took his case to the inquisitori. The scuola's church supervisors found that, indeed, Pesenti had a legitimate claim, but discovered other significant problems, pertaining, evidently, to the organist's keyboard technique.[124] The builder of the new instrument, Pietro Nacchini (see below), who had also been hired to maintain it, declared that he would resign if Pesenti continued as organist, since his playing was causing damage. To ensure that Nacchini's objections were not based on personal bias, the Procurators invited a distinguished organist (who remained unnamed in the documents) to examine the instrument. He declared, in no uncertain terms, "that the said organ was constructed perfectly by the artisan, but that whoever had been playing it had made it go out of tune, with the danger of greater damage if he continues to play it, since an organ so recently built and rarely played could not be out of tune unless whoever was employed to play it had no more than a mediocre ability."[125] Faced with that evidence, the scuola confirmed its prior decision, and announced a new competition. They also, however, decided to reward Pesenti for his earlier unpaid service, and offered him a generous one-time payment of 40 ducats.[126]

A few months after his election, the scuola gave the new organist, Don Antonio Pasinetti, the responsibility, in exchange for a raise of 6 ducats, of maintaining the organ at his own expense.[127] It was during Pasinetti's tenure, in 1754, that a major reform of the choir was completed (see above), with the result that the scuola required the now more musically able ensemble to sing polyphonic masses on major holidays, for which they also received a raise. Pesenti complained that this resulted in more work for him as well, and that he also deserved an increase, which the chapter duly granted, raising his salary to the quite impressive sum of 45 ducats (plus the 6 for maintaining the instrument).[128] Within another two decades, the financial situation of San Rocco began to worsen, however, so the officers looked for ways to save money. Though they would not change the salary of the incumbent organist, Pasinetti, they declared that his successor would be hired at the considerably lower figure of 30 ducats, which was reasonable, since, though several sung masses had been added to the duties, the twice weekly services of Sunday Vespers and Friday Compline had been replaced by a once weekly mass, except for Lent.[129]

After Pasinetti's death in 1784, the scuola held the audition as usual, and, for the first time, recorded the official evaluation of the performances of the candidates. The maestro of the choir, Giovanni Battista Tosini, reported:

> I heard first the reverend Don Giacomo Segato, who, in my judgment, succeeded most ably, both in the precision of his technique and in the graciousness of his playing. I then heard the reverend Antonio Nitor, a man truly of great ability, and his playing seemed to me quite straightforward and spirited, but, more often than I would like, the ear desired to hear that note that his technique quite often swallowed up.[130]

Based on that judgment, the officers elected Segato, from the nearby church of San Pantalon. Segato's tenure lasted until just before Napoleon's invasion of the city, and his temporary replacement Giovanni Battista Pasinetti (probably a relative of the earlier organist) served only five months before the revolutionary government's mandated budget reductions resulted in the elimination of the position.[131] However, as with the choir, discussed above, an organist (unnamed in the documents) was rehired the following year, and continued to be employed into the nineteenth century.[132]

As is always the case, building and maintaining a fine church organ was a time-consuming and expensive process. In the century and a half from 1650 to 1800, San Rocco's organ required nearly twenty separate interventions (including one entirely new organ and several major overhauls) at a cost of over 1,000 ducats (not including at least 500 ducats more for work on the organ case). In 1650, the original sixteenth-century organ was still in use, kept in service with a series of interventions, notably one in 1681 by Carlo di Beni (costing 70 ducats) and another in 1690 by Antonio Giorgio.[133] Following the latter, the scuola hired a regular tuner (the post held from 1713 to 1727 by Giorgio), at 4 ducats annually,[134] and managed to keep the instrument functioning until 1726, when it was dismantled for the rebuilding of the church.[135] The scuola apparently originally intended to rebuild the organ, carefully storing the pieces in a room above their chaplain's house. By the time the church construction neared completion, however, the officers decided to build a new instrument suitable for the splendid new sanctuary. In 1739 the scuola hired the architect Michiel Domenico Magni to make designs for the case,[136] and in 1742 signed a contract with Pietro Nacchini, the most prolific and best known of Venice's organ builders, for a new instrument, at a cost of 525 ducats, to be reduced to 480 by turning over to the builder the pieces of the dismantled old organ.[137] The contract called for an instrument of twelve registers (about average in size), made of fine materials, and Nacchini completed the work, after some delay caused by continued construction on the church, in August 1744.[138]

The new instrument turned out to be unsatisfactory, in the long run, in part owing to continuing work on the façade of the church (since the organ was above the main door, this work directly affected the instrument). After a major cleaning and tuning by the late Nacchini's disciple Francesco Dacii,[139] another important builder, Gaetano Callido, began a series of significant repairs and reconstructions in 1757.[140] In that year, he completely dismantled, cleaned, and repaired the instrument (for 30 ducats), a process repeated in 1762, at which time he entirely rebuilt the windchamber (for 60 ducats).[141] When the scuola rebuilt the façade of the church once again in 1767, Callido removed the organ to the scuola, and an instrument rented from Domenico Levis, organist at San Giovanni Evangelista, was used in the interim.[142] When, in the following year, Callido returned San Rocco's organ to the church, he not only fixed much that had been in disrepair, but replaced entirely the forty-eight pipes of two registers, the *voce umana* and the *cornetto*, at a cost of 90 ducats.[143] Callido returned one more time, in 1774, for a general tuning and cleaning.[144]

The final major work on the instrument was conducted in 1789 by another important builder, Francesco Merlini.[145] In addition to a total cleaning and repair job (including replacing stop pulls and parts of the keyboard), Merlini added "il piano ed il forte," that is, a form of swell box, at the request of the organist. Merlini estimated the cost at 100 ducats, but eventually agreed to do the work for 50.

The Festa and Other Annual Occasions

With the elimination of almost all of the salaried musical ensembles at the scuole, and the decrease in quality and prestige of those that remained, the musical portions of most of their ceremonies could contribute little to the honor of either the scuole or their individual officers. There were still opportunities available, however, when the guardian could, as discussed above (see the discussion of the Maundy Thursday procession), hire well-known external musicians who could bring attention to the scuola. Unfortunately for the musicologist, the financial responsibility, in most cases, would also have belonged to the individual officer, so the archives of the scuola would contain no record, but enough remains to provide some clues as to what might have been normal practice.

Expositions

The rise in the seventeenth century of the practice of expositions, of either the Holy Sacrament or of relics, provided a new occasion for a guardian to hire musicians. These events, often lasting two or three days, included three elements: (1) a ceremony with a procession when the venerated object was put on display;

(2) continuous prayers, sometimes with music, usually motets, throughout the period of public viewing; (3) and a mass or other service when the object was returned to its sanctuary. Expositions of the Sacrament became regular by 1700, in churches throughout the city (see below, chapter 10), but can be documented among the scuole grandi only at San Rocco. Even there, records survive for only two years, but it is likely that such events continued with private funding, and probably also occurred also at San Giovanni Evangelista, with its own church. On each of the four occasions documented, in April and August of 1662 and 1663, the scuola spent about 20–25 ducats for motets on two days and a procession, hiring three to six singers, two instrumentalists (two violins or violin and cornetto), and an organist.[146] That bringing attention to the scuola was important to the officers is made clear by the names listed, including some of the best known church and operatic singers in Venice at the time: Antonio Formenti, Antonio Divido, Sebastiano Cioni, Pietro Veralli, Gabriele Battistini, and fra Pietro dei Carmini. It is likely that these men sang solo and perhaps duo motets of the type widely published during this period.[147]

The closest parallels to this practice at another scuola were the expositions of relics in Lent at the Carità, documented in the second half of the eighteenth century. On most Fridays in Lent the scuola performed a relatively simple ceremony, including a mass and some sort of music, with a total cost, for the entire season, of 40 ducats.[148] The scuola spent more than three times that amount, however, for the single exposition of the Sacra Porpora on the third Friday of March, for sung masses and a procession. One pay sheet details the number of musicians involved: the scuola hired nine singers, violoncello or violone, organist and a maestro for the sung mass, and a coretto of four singers, a choir of twenty, and a maestro for the procession. The fees for the musical portion of this event came to about 40 ducats, all paid by the scuola.[149] In 1765 the celebration attracted the attention of the Venetian chronicler Pietro Gradenigo, who, if he noticed the scuole at all, usually described events at the wealthier San Rocco. He noted on 15 March: "At the Scuola Grande della Carità they display the Robe of Our Lord with a mass in music, and with a plenary indulgence obtained through the famous Cardinal Bessarion."[150]

The Annual Festa

By far the most important single annual event for a scuola, from the musical point of view (and in most others ways as well) was its annual festa. As shown in the previous chapter, these occasions, in the sixteenth and early seventeenth centuries, stood out as some of the musical highlights of the Venetian calendar. While the documentary evidence is far more spotty for the later seventeenth and eighteenth centuries, there is no doubt that all of the scuole (or, in some cases, the individual officers) continued to direct considerable attention and finances toward these occasions, and that music remained an important aspect. For the poorer scuole, bringing off these events in a respectable manner was often quite difficult, since the individual officers also tended to be less prosperous than elsewhere, as made clear by the Misericordia in 1708:

One cannot deny that the principal solemnity of our scuola, customarily celebrated on the day of the Conception of the Blessed Virgin . . . is done with
somewhat less splendor than is usually observed at most of the scuole grandi,
which happens because of the great expense needed to decorate the albergo and
the two great halls upstairs and downstairs, so that sometimes singing the mass
in music, as was always done by our predecessors, is omitted.[151]

The situation was complicated, as the resolution pointed out, by the vast size of
the scuola's building, comparable only to that of San Rocco. The chapter decided
that the guardian grande would now take full responsibility for decorating the
albergo, the vicario for the main hall upstairs, the degani di mezz'anno for the
ground-floor hall, and the cancelliere for the church. The 25 ducats previously
budgeted by the scuola for those expenses could now be devoted instead to music,
though that is a rather small sum that could not pay for much in the way of
musical splendor.

San Giovanni Evangelista employed a similar division of expenditures for the
festa, with, beginning in 1646, a contribution from the scuola's budget of 50
ducats.[152] Sometime before 1739 the scuola suspended that allocation. As a consequence, the burden on the vicario, who apparently bore the responsibility for
music at the festa, became so great that the chapter decided to restore 30 ducats
of the scuola's contribution.[153] By 1760, the financial situation of San Giovanni
Evangelista had apparently improved considerably, since the officers requested permission from the inquisitori to implement a new tariffa that included nearly 200
ducats of contributions by the scuola toward the annual festa.[154] Of that amount,
about 92 ducats was designated for music at Mass and Vespers, including ten
singers and an orchestra of ten violins, three violas, violoncello, two violoni, two
oboes, two trumpets, and timpani, under the direction of a maestro. Though this
was only about half the amount spent at San Rocco in that period (see below)
the event must still have been quite splendid.

Little is known about the festa at San Rocco in the second half of the sev-
enteenth century. The only documentation shows a payment of 14 ducats to fra
Pietro di Carmeni (a singer in the ducal cappella) for motets in 1658, and "the
usual" 25 ducats to Giovanni da Pesaro in 1676, to be paid out of the partidor.[155]
Presumably, the officers paid for most of the expenses out of their own pockets.
In the first half of the eighteenth century, documented expenditures increased to
almost 50 ducats. The same undated pay sheet with information on the Maundy
Thursday procession and Palm Sunday Passion discussed earlier (see above) con-
tains a list of musicians paid for the performances on the feast of San Rocco.[156]
Included are ten singers, nearly all from the basilica (and headed once again by
Raffaelle, the lead singer in the Holy Week music discussed above), Antonio
Pollarolo as organist (he was later vice maestro and then maestro at San Marco),
and an orchestra of six violins, three violas, violoncello, violone, trumpet, and
oboe, again principally members of the cappella ducale. Slight increases in the
expenditures are documented in 1736 (when the maestro was Maccari), and again
in 1738, in which year a foreign singer, probably a castrato, named Giovannino,
sang motets.[157]

A major spur to increased splendor at the festa was the Vatican's approval, in 1748, of a proper liturgy for the feast of St. Roch; the scuola decided to perform, in addition to Vespers on the vigil of the feast and sung mass, also second Vespers, and to generally upgrade the festivities, with the budgeting of 70 ducats for the purpose.[158] This amount would be added to the 50 ducats that were to be spent through a partidor specifically for music on the morning of the feast. Later that year, after the festa—with the recognition that there were also considerable expenses for building the platform for the musicians (see below)—the chapter decided to add another 50 ducats for the music, plus 10 more to satisfy the scuola's salaried choir, who demanded extra pay for the added duties. Before the 1750 celebration, however, the officers realized that the day's mass had not been elevated to the level of the other services. They felt that this deficiency would be all too noticeable to the large number of people, including foreigners, who attended:

> we believe it rather inappropriate and indecent, that on the morning of such a solemn day, the mass is not sung in the same manner, when on every other feast day it is usual for this church to sing it with three celebrants, and when there is no scuola, or church, or suffragio, or confraternity however poor, that does not solemnize the day of its saint with a sung mass in the church or scuola in which is erected an altar dedicated to that saint.[159]

The scuola allocated additional funds, amounting to 200 ducats (including a motet sung during the private low mass held for the doge when he came to venerate the saint's relics), an amount they readjusted shortly to 160, where it stayed for the remainder of the century.[160]

While this amount was still a bit less than the scuola had spent in the early seventeenth century, there is no doubt that the resulting celebrations, directed by the most important maestri in the city, were quite magnificent. Among these, as recorded by the diarist Gradenigo, were Baldassare Galuppi in 1759, Bonaventura Furlanetto (maestro at the Pietà and later St. Mark's) in 1771 and 1772, and Ferdinando Bertoni (then organist, and later maestro at St. Mark's) in 1773, described thus:

> This morning the doge, with a numerous group of senators, went to the church of San Rocco . . . and there heard a private mass, but one accompanied by musical motets and harmonic symphonies. [Later] they began . . . the High Mass, and on a magnificent platform one saw the leading singers and instrumentalists, under the virtuous direction of the above-mentioned Signor Maestro Bertoni, applauded by a great crowd of people.[161]

Another of Gradenigo's remarks is worth noting: in addition to music, an attraction of the celebrations was an exhibit of notable paintings,[162] which included, in 1771, a portrait by Alessandro Longhi of that year's maestro, Furlanetto, that depicted him at a small table in the act of composing. While nearly all of the music for these occasions has disappeared, three such works can, at present, be identified. A mass for the festa by Andrea Lucchesi, dating from before 1772 (though apparently not in its original arrangement) is in the archive of the Seminario Patriarcale in Venice.[163] Two others survive in the collection built up at St. Mark's in the nineteenth century (there may be many more, but most bear no designation of function). One of these is a setting by Bertoni of the psalm *Laudate pueri*, first performed in 1795, with an ensemble including soprano, alto, and tenor soloists, an SATB choir (for which thirteen parts survive), strings, two oboes, two horns, two trumpets, and continuo.[164] From the following year there is a *Gloria* by Furlanetto for two soprano and two alto soloists, choir (with twenty-four extant parts), and orchestra of strings, pairs of flutes, oboes, horns, and trumpets, and continuo.[165]

Platforms for the Musicians

One of the notable elements of the annual celebrations at the scuole was the construction of impressive platforms for the musicians, splendidly decorated and with elaborate architectural features, as alluded to in Gradenigo's description of the 1773 event at San Rocco. Given the limited space available for musicians in the churches used by these scuole, such platforms were, as explained in a 1748 document for San Rocco, "necessary to build for the effect of the music."[166] In that case, the officers determined that 50 ducats would be an appropriate annual expenditure for such structures. Sometimes, the size of these platforms caused problems in the restricted spaces available. The church of San Giovanni Evangelista was so small, in fact, that after the construction of the three platforms required, there was little room left for the brothers to squeeze in. Therefore, in 1785, the scuola requested of the inquisitori, and was granted, permission to move the event to the much larger hall of the scuola, across the small courtyard.[167] The Carità had long held its celebrations in its hall, for which they had apparently constructed a platform that could be disassembled and then reused. When the scuola rebuilt the façade of the scuola (finished in 1756 to a design by Massari), and then, in 1766, completed a new grand stairway to the main hall and the floor of that hall, the old platform no longer served, so the officers paid 20 ducats for a temporary one, a practice they apprently observed for several years.[168] They lamented in 1774, however, that the construction of the platforms each year damaged its splendid new inlaid floor.[169] The officers proposed instead to build a permanent pair of platforms (which could be dismantled after the festa, and reassembled the next year) whose architecture would be harmonious with the hall. For an expense of 800 ducats, not only could damage to the floor be contained, but future competition among guardians to build ever more elaborate platforms could be avoided. The inquisitors, however, were not persuaded, since, they explained, in many years there might not even be music, since the individual guardian grande determined what money would be spent. The magistracy went further, and declared that in the future, even when a guardian decided to put on elaborate music, he could not build platforms without express permission from their office.[170]

Not surprisingly, it was San Rocco, rather than the Carità, that actually went ahead with a permanent platform, and in grand style. As the officers argued in their petition to the Inquisitors,

impartial reflection reveals how much more decorous the festivity of the glorious
St. Roch would be, on the occasion of the music with which it is solemnized
with such pomp in the church dedicated to the glory of that saint, and in reverent
recognition of the special honor that it receives by the visit on that day of the
Most Serene Prince, if there would be a permanent construction of a choir gallery
of good form and fine architecture, with inlay and gilding, which the harmony
of the place requires, rather than the useless annual expenditure of having it built
by the decorator.[171]

This scuola, with its solid financial situation, received a favorable hearing, and
proceeded with construction, finally completed in about ten months at the
astounding cost of 4,850 ducats (that is, more than six times what the Carità
proposed), to which was added another 80 ducats to alter a space in the scuola
to store it between festivals; and another 70 ducats would then be required each
year for assembly and disassembly. This vast and splendid structure, which spanned
the entire entrance wall of the church around the organ, and curved around the
corners toward the nave, a total of 14 meters long and 7 high, was installed in
the church as late as 1927, and still survives.[172]

Music at the Three New Scuole Grandi

In the late seventeenth century the Council of Ten, after a gap of more than one
hundred years, created a new scuola grande, a process they performed twice more
nearly a century later. From the middle of the fifteenth century, there had been
at the parish church of San Fantin a confraternity, dedicated to Santa Maria della
Consolazione, whose mission was to accompany condemned criminals to the
gallows. This scuola joined with another, at the nearby church of Sant'Angelo,
under the protection of St. Jerome, and continued to grow in wealth and prominence. In 1689, the Council of Ten declared the confraternity, often known
simply as the Scuola di San Fantin, where the combined institutions had built a
magnificent hall, a scuola grande, so that it filled the same civic and political role
as its six predecessors, participating, for example, in all the official processions in
Piazza San Marco.[173] As discussed above, however, by this time the scuole had
greatly reduced their music-making at such occasions, and San Fantin seems not
to have had salaried musicians of any sort. Rather, all its efforts in this area were
directed toward just three annual occasions. From at least 1705 (the date of the
earliest documentation), the officers contributed annually to a partidor to supplement the scuola's own expenditures for the annual festa of St. Jerome, Palm
Sunday, and the Maundy Thursday/Good Friday procession.[174] The scuola's contribution came to about 100 ducats, and the officers, led by the guardian grande's
gift of 60 ducats, added more than 200. The largest portion of this substantial
sum of over 300 ducats went for elaborate gifts distributed to distinguished Venetians on Palm Sunday: in 1706, for example, the officers spent 180 ducats on
pictures of St. Jerome with cherubims, in tortoise-shell frames inlaid with mother-
of-pearl and decorated with real flowers and silver leaves, and another 100 on
silk palm leaves. There was, therefore, little left for other expenses such as music,

but they did allocate amounts between 10 and 30 ducats on Palm Sunday for a choir of priests to sing the Passion, as well as similar amounts for the same sort of choir to sing two Vespers and a Mass on the feast of St. Jerome and to sing in the Holy Week procession.

The scuola had long-term arrangements, from before its elevation to the status of scuola grande, to celebrate the annual feasts of its two patrons at the parish churches in which the original scuole piccole had been founded. In 1795, however, the priests of San Fantin complained that they had been treated unfairly, since the scuola provided the music in Sant'Angelo for the feast of St. Jerome, but did not do the same for the feast of the Annunciation at San Fantin.[175] The scuola clearly had no intention of making this occasion as elaborate as their annual festa, but did agree to pay the chapter of San Fantin the small sum of £22, the same as had been designated for music in their fifteenth-century agreement with Sant'Angelo (but which, of course, represented only a small portion of what the scuola actually spent on its festa). Later that same year, the officers of the scuola noticed that though they, like several of the older scuole grandi, possessed a relic of the Holy Cross, they did not honor this precious object with celebrations on the feasts of the Invention or Exaltation of the Holy Cross (on 14 September and 3 May, respectively). The chapter approved an annual expenditure for each occasion of about 15 ducats, of which about 7 were to be paid to a maestro for vocal music, including the singing of the hymn *Vexilla regis*.[176] In a revised budget imposed by the Austrian governors of the city in 1798, expenditures for these two late additions to the scuola's calendar were eliminated, and those for the three traditional occasions were cut by more than half.[177]

In 1765 and 1767 the Council of Ten raised two more confraternities to the rank of scuola grande. The Scuola di Santa Maria del Rosario was founded in 1575 by the Dominican friars of Santi Giovanni e Paolo in honor of the great Venetian (or, rather, Christian) victory over the Turks at Lepanto, which occurred on the day dedicated to that celebration. Little documentation for music at the Scuola del Rosario survives. From as early as the 1630s, the officers, through payments to a rodolo, bore full financial responsibility for music for the festa.[178] That this practice continued even after the scuola's promotion to the rank of scuola grande can be confirmed by the complete absence of expenditures for music in the otherwise detailed tariffa for the festa issued in 1788.[179] The scuola's willingness to contribute 100 ducats to the friars of Santi Giovanni e Paolo in 1790 for the construction of a new organ demonstrates that religious celebrations in the church, with at the least organ-accompanied chant, must have been a regular practice, but further details have not come to light.

The last of the scuole grandi, Santa Maria del Carmine, was founded by the Carmelite friars in 1593 as a confraternity for women, but by the time it received the more exalted rank it included both sexes, and was run primarily by men. From the beginning, the friars performed the scuola's religious services, including sung masses,[180] but there were also occasions on which the scuola paid for music separately. In October 1686, for example, the scuola spent about 27 ducats for singers and string players for an exposition of the Holy Sacrament. After becoming a scuola grande, beginning no later than 1789, the Scuola del Carmine paid an annual salary to an organist of five ducats, raised to ten in 1791. For the major event of the year, however, their annual festa on 16 July, music was apparently the responsibility of the officers, through the usual mechanism of a rodolo. Unfortunately, there are no extant documents for this before 1800, but for the last few years before being suppressed, the amount paid to a maestro di musica was substantial, usually more than 70 ducats,[181] comparable to the amount spent by the better-off of the original six scuole grandi. Confirmation of this practice (or perhaps of a slightly different one, in which the guardian grande funded the event entirely on his own) for earlier decades comes from two passages in the *Notatori* of Pietro Gradenigo. The first dates from 1765, two years before the scuola was recognized by the Council of Ten as a scuola grande, perhaps as part of a campaign for promotion: "the merchant Francesco Piccardi, guardian of the rich scuola [del Carmine] undertook to spend his money generously, so that the platform and the music and the decorations would be superlative, to the immeasurable pleasure of the audience."[182] The celebration in 1772, according to Gradenigo, seems on a par with the most splendid anywhere in the city:

> In the main chapel [of the church of the Carmini] were erected two platforms, one in front of the other, quite elegantly designed, upon which the music was directed by the Reverend Francesco Polazzo, all at the expense of the rich guardian Bianchi, one of the holders of the tobacco tax concession.[183]

Special Events

The only rivals to the annual feste in terms of musical splendor were the occasional special celebrations occasioned by important political events or visits to the city by eminent personages. One class of events, discussed also in chapter 3, were extraordinary processions ordered by the government, requiring the participation of all the scuole grandi. Such a procession took place in July 1758 in celebration of the election of the Venetian patrician Carlo Rezzonico as Pope Clement XIII.[184] In this case, San Rocco (the only scuola for which documentation survives) simply paid its choir and instrumentalists a fee proportional to what they would normally earn for a regular procession, with the singers getting a little extra to sing a Te Deum. A much more elaborate celebration was that held by San Rocco in April 1763 to celebrate the election of one of the scuola's patrician protectors, Alvise Mocenigo, as doge.[185] As described in an official commemorative announcement (and confirmed in Gradenigo's diaries), the celebration in the church included a specially built platform for the musicians under the organ for the performance of a solemnly sung High Mass, followed by a Te Deum, the latter further enlivened by the firing of 200 or more mortars outside. The music, under the direction of an unnamed maestro, cost about 50 ducats.[186]

When Mocenigo died fifteen years later, in 1778, the funeral performed by the scuola was even more elaborate (and better documented).[187] Altogether, the scuola spent almost 1,700 ducats, of which 135 were for music. The listing of singers includes twenty-three names, all from the ducal cappella except for the five members of the scuola's choir. In addition, the scuola hired an orchestra of twelve violins, four violas, two violoncellos, three violoni, two bassoons, two oboes, and four horns. Besides the sung mass the ceremony included the performance of a concerto for violin (perhaps as an interlude or during the offertory). All of this was performed under the direction of Ferdinando Bertoni, at the time first organist at St. Mark's (his fee, probably also for composition of the music, came to more than one-quarter of the total). Of similar magnificence was the celebration in 1782 for the visit to the scuola by the pope.[188] This event must have featured the performance of a specially composed cantata, or something similar, since one of the payments is to a poet. The ensemble employed was similar in size to that for the doge's funeral: a choir of twelve, fourteen strings, trumpets and timpani, horns, flutes, oboes, and organ, all, including the large fee for the maestro, for about 125 ducats.

The Scuola di San Marco made relatively modest expenditures, under 10 ducats, for a choir for two special occasions in the last decade of the eighteenth century: for the evacuation in January 1798 of the French soldiers from the scuola, which they had used as a barracks for several months after taking over the city, and in 1800 for a Te Deum for the election of Pope Pius VII.[189] On a much different scale was the funeral, in 1789, of the penultimate doge of Venice, Polo Renier, performed, by ancient tradition (that is, for doges who were not members of another scuola grande), by the Scuola di San Marco.[190] The fee paid to the maestro di coro for that ceremony, with funds coming from the doge's son and other patricians, was the extraordinary sum of 148 ducats.

One of the last major musical events documented at the scuole grandi is the only one at San Giovanni Evangelista during this period for which information survives. At the order of the Patriarch, that scuola (and possibly the others as well) performed a solemn Te Deum for the departure of the French conquerors.[191] A maestro named Cervelini received just over 90 ducats for this occasion. Ironically, the arrival of the Austrians, to whom Napoleon had ceded Venice, resulted for the scuole not in a revival—which must have been the hope, given the scale of the celebrations—but in a rapid and fatal decline, with their assets seized and operations restricted. It took the return of the French in 1805 to put an end to their story, but when the new government suppressed them in 1807, little remained for them to eliminate.

THE SCUOLE PICCOLE

PROCESSION, VESPERS, SONGS, AND ORGAN

The Scuole Piccole and Music to 1600

While the six (and later nine) scuole grandi were without a doubt the most important confraternities in Venice, they were by no means the only ones. Scattered throughout the city, in every parish and nearly every monastic church, were several hundred less influential, and usually smaller, confraternities, known as the *scuole piccole*.

The Nature of the Scuole Piccole

The term *scuola piccola*, signifying only in part their size, but more importantly their individual significance in the cultural and political fabric of Venice, was applied to most confraternities (either lay or religious) other than the six flagellant scuole grandi. In the period between the founding of the earliest confraternities in the thirteenth century and the fall of Venice at the end of the eighteenth, approximately 450 scuole piccole came into being, with more than 200 active at times in the sixteenth and seventeenth centuries. Because these scuole had a tendency to fade out (sometimes to be refounded), to combine, to change their dedication, to split into two, or to send out offshoots, it is nearly impossible to arrive at a clear account of how many were active at any one time.[1] These confraternities were not all identical in purpose, organization, or function, but fell into several fairly distinct types, not all of which were present at all times; as might be expected, some showed greater interest in music than others.

The largest group of scuole piccole can be described by the general term "devotional confraternities." Members of such organizations gathered together in their devotion to a patron saint or to the Virgin, centered in a parish or monastic church at an altar that was built and maintained by the confraternity.[2] Members were required to pay an entrance fee and dues and to attend regular meetings and religious ceremonies. The benefits to members were primarily spiritual, most im-

portantly after death: the scuola provided a burial (with the members in attendance), a funeral mass, and anniversary commemorations (usually endowed in the
deceased's will). Such masses (as many of them as could be afforded) were considered essential for the salvation of the soul, since they helped speed the deceased's
journey through purgatory, and (as with the scuole grandi; see chapter 1) were
the primary raison d'être for these scuole.[3] While many such confraternities match
the appellation "piccola," with memberships of fewer than fifty, a number had
more than a hundred brothers, and some were actually larger than the legal limits
for the scuole grandi (set by the Council of Ten at 500 to 600).[4] The Scuola di
Sant'Orsola, for example, not only had its own meeting hall outside (though
adjacent to) a church, usually a characteristic of the scuole grandi, but numbered,
at times, more than 800 brothers and sisters.[5] The Scuola di San Gregorio had a
statutory limit of 500.[6] The members of devotional confraternities belonged
mostly to the middle classes, ranging from workmen to such professionals as lawyers and notaries, but some of them also included the poor and, occasionally,
nobles. Members of a given scuola could come from any part of the city, though
the majority probably resided near the church that housed the scuola's altar. Unlike
the scuole grandi, many of the scuole piccole also admitted women, who could
not only receive the spiritual and communal benefits of membership, but could
also sometimes participate in the direction of the scuola. Though women
could not aspire to hold the main statutory offices of a scuola, they acted within
a separate, parallel administrative structure run for and by women.[7]

There were two significant subgroups of devotional confraternities: national
scuole and those tied to a particular trade. Foreigners residing in Venice (both
Italian, such as Florentines, and non-Italian, such as Albanians) often formed their
own confraternities, which served the same functions as those already mentioned,
but also helped the members retain some of their native traditions. Similarly,
groups of men who practiced the same trade sometimes were the founders of
scuole, and while some gradually evolved to a more general membership, others
retained their close knit natures.[8]

Beginning in the early sixteenth century, scuole of another sort, though bearing many similarities to the devotional confraternities, were founded in response
to a movement to increase devotion to the Holy Sacrament. Known as Scuole
del Santissimo Sacramento or Scuole del Venerabile, these were strictly parish-
based.[9] They held their services at (and maintained) an altar dedicated to the
Sacrament in the parish church,[10] and were open to all residents, men and women,
rich and poor, of the parish. They not only provided the functions of a devotional
confraternity, but also assisted with poor relief in the community (though this was
increasingly the responsibility of the parish-based *fraterne dei poveri*, run for the
poor of the parish by those more fortunate, also founded in the sixteenth century).
In addition, each scuola worked closely with its parish priest (and chapter in
collegiate churches) and gradually took on responsibilities within the church.
These responsibilities often included running catechism classes, maintaining the
church structure and its furnishings, including the organ, and sometimes employing the church organist.[11] By the late sixteenth century, every parish in the city
had its own Scuola del Santissimo Sacramento.

Another type of scuola began to appear in the seventeenth century, often as an outgrowth of a devotional confraternity: the *sovvegno*.[12] Though the sovvegno held occasional religious ceremonies (especially on its annual festa), its principal function was to serve as a sort of medical insurance cooperative. Members (usually limited to sixty at a time), paid, in addition to a membership fee, monthly dues. The sovvegno employed a pharmacist and/or physician to minister to the members, and provided daily financial assistance to ailing members if their illnesses lasted longer than a certain minimum duration. Like modern medical insurance plans, there were restrictions on the age of members, and waiting periods before coverage could begin, and they excluded certain ailments (including venereal disease and injuries resulting from fights). While most sovvegni (like all the other scuole piccole) included only laymen as members, a number of them comprised only secular priests, especially those who made their living saying endowed masses for deceased Venetians: because their income depended on being able to say mass, when ill they risked starvation without some sort of assistance.

Another category of single-function scuole, especially widespread in the late seventeenth and eighteenth centuries, was the *suffragi di morti*, which existed exclusively to minister to the dying and the dead. Certain members, exempt from paying dues, were assigned to attend at another's deathbed and to accompany the corpse to burial. The suffragio also hired priests to say funeral masses and administered annual commemorative services. Most dues-paying members, however, neither performed duties for the suffragio nor attended functions for deceased members: they joined simply to ensure that prayers were said and masses sung for them at their deaths.

Finally, a number of scuole had unique functions. One of them, the Fraterna Prigioni, was devoted to assisting poor prisoners, including paying their fines to liberate them. Similarly, the Scuola della Trinità e Riscatto degli Schiavi at Santa Maria Formosa raised money to free Venetians enslaved by pirates, while San Fantin (which in the eighteenth century was elevated to the rank of scuola grande) provided spiritual comfort to prisoners sentenced to death: accompanying them to the scaffold, providing burial, and performing funeral services.[13] The Fraterna Grande di Sant'Antonino established a pharmacy to provide medical assistance to the shamefaced poor (that is, poor from respectable, even patrician, families), and also established an Oratorio and schools for instruction in Christian Doctrine.[14]

While in many ways the scuole piccole resembled the scuole grandi, they also differed considerably. These confraternities did not have the same official role in the public processions, and therefore were not considered responsible for upholding and projecting the honor of the Republic. While scuole piccole did go in procession on important religious feasts, these were limited in number, and usually restricted to the immediate vicinity of their home church, with the exception of the Maundy Thursday/Good Friday processions, which were more extensive. And while the administrative structure of these scuole was similar to that of the scuole grandi, with a leader—called variously gastaldo, guardiano, or rettore—several minor officers, and a council, election to one of these posts did not carry the same sort of prestige. Finally, because so many scuole piccole flourished in the city, and an individual was free to join more than one, membership carried less status than in a scuola grande. While the scuole grandi gradually expanded their charitable efforts beyond their membership, the scuole piccole remained, with few exceptions, focused on their own brothers and sisters. Because of their prestige and large membership, the scuole grandi, as has been discussed, ammassed huge fortunes, which, along with the combined wealth of the members, allowed them to act as important patrons of art and music. The fortunes, and therefore the patronage, of the scuole piccole, were much more limited, though some of them, at certain periods of their histories, did possess sufficient funds to make significant impacts in the cultural sphere.

The Earliest Signs of Music at the Scuole Piccole: Piffari

As with the scuole grandi, among the first actions necessary for the founding of a scuola piccola was the drafting of a set of bylaws, known as a mariegola, and the conclusion of an agreement with a host church.[15] It is in these two documents that the earliest indications of music at the scuole piccole can be found.[16] As with the scuole grandi, these smaller confraternities established a calendar of religious occasions to be celebrated by the members. However, while the calendars of the scuole grandi were quite extensive, including occasions for frequent public processions as well as regular services in the church or scuola itself, those of the scuole piccole were usually limited to the commemoration of the feast day of the patron saint, but sometimes included a few other major feasts, one Sunday a month, or, rarely, a smaller weekly function, either a Sunday mass or, in later years, a Friday Compline service.

Many of the earliest mariegole (those from the thirteenth through early fifteenth centuries) make no reference to music whatsoever. Several, however, indicate the employment of wind players, usually referred to as *piffari* or *trombe e piffari*, that is, ensembles of shawms and sackbuts, for the annual festa.[17] An early fifteenth-century regulation from the mariegola of the Scuola della Beata Vergine Assunta in the church of San Stae contains many of the usual elements, but also calls for a drummer, and indicates one of the most common strategies for funding the festa, contributions from the members or officers:

> we are all gathered and congregated here together to make the feast of Holy Mary of Grace, which comes in the middle of August, in the church of Sant'Eustachio; and to increase and multiply the scuola we each contribute 10 soldi from our own purses. With this money we begin, and there should be hired two trumpets, two piffari, and one drummer to honor the said festa, and with the rest of the money we start to make a meal [for the brothers].[18]

At the Scuola di San Giovanni Battista in San Giovanni Decolato, the wind players were not paid outsiders, but, rather, brothers of the scuola, who were exempted from many of the obligations of membership, but were, according to a 1340 agreement, obligated to come and play "according to the practice of the scuola" on the feasts of both St. John the Evangelist (27 December) and St. John the Baptist (24 June).[19] By 1373 the possibility of entering a scuola free of charge and receiving all benefits in exchange for playing on only two days a year had apparently attracted too many instrumentalists, and the officers of San Giovanni Battista determined to reduce the number to eight through attrition (helped by dismissing any player who missed two occasions). Any additional players would have to fulfill all the obligations of regular membership.[20]

Piffari and *tromboni* appear frequently in the early membership lists of the scuole piccole, but in only two cases is their role as performers made specific (in other cases they might have been ordinary brothers with no musical duties): at the Scuola di San Martino, where the fourteenth-century mariegola includes a separate listing, with four names, of the "Sonadori dela Scuola di Sen Martin" (with two additional men listed as having entered in 1398),[21] and at the Scuola di Sant'Anna di Castello (also in the late fourteenth or early fifteenth century), where a group of five men is listed with the indication that they "must play at the feasts of St. Anne." [22] The performers at one scuola may have stood out among the others: at the Scuola di Santa Maria dei Mercanti, the six players who joined the scuola in about 1506 were the "trombe e piffari" of the doge, probably the best in the city, and the forerunners of the famous instrumentalists of St. Mark's.[23]

In some cases, the host church supplied the piffari, especially when scuola and church shared the same annual feast day. The scuola was apparently usually responsible for all or a portion of the fee paid to the musicians. In a 1528 agreement between the Scuola della Beata Vergine Assunta and the convent of Santa Maria della Celestia, the scuola was obligated to pay 9 lire to the nuns for the feast of the Assumption.[24] Similarly, according to the 1443 convention between the Scuola di San Pietro Martire and its host church of Santi Giovanni e Paolo, repeated in the scuola's mariegola of the following year, the gastaldo of the scuola paid the friars to supply the instrumentalists, using the general funds of the scuola.[25] When, in the sixteenth century, the musical element of these joint church/scuola feste became more complex, with the addition of singers, in many cases the scuola continued to pay for instrumentalists, while the church took on the cost of the singers. In the 1580 mariegola of the Scuola del'Angelo Raffaele in Sant'Angelo, this was the basic framework, with a further clarification that only half of the money for instrumentalists would come from the general fund of the scuola, and the remainder was to be paid by the officers. If the gastaldo failed to collect money from the other officers, the entire cost of the instrumentalists would fall to him.[26]

The exact role of these wind players is not clear. Some mariegole, such as the early fifteenth-century one from the Scuola di San Francesco at the Frari, seem to indicate that they performed at the religious ceremonies themselves. The trombe e piffari there were required to perform on the feast of the Purification, "at the Vespers and at the Mass."[27] Almost identical wording can be found in the 1510 mariegola of the Scuola di San Giuseppe in San Silvestro.[28] Even clearer is a passage from the mid-fifteenth-century mariegola of the Scuola di Santa Maria e San Gallo at San Maurizio. The piffari, admitted free of charge to the scuola, were required "to honor God as do the other scuole on the days of their feste," to "play the vigil of St. Gall and that of St. Maurice at Vespers, and the following morning at dawn, and when the gastaldo and his companions will rise to make their offering, and when the body and blood of Christ will be raised up."²⁹ At the Scuola dei Milanesi at the Frari, however, the players seem instead to have been used to lead the procession held by the brothers on the feast day of St. Ambrose. The brothers were to gather outside the scuola, all carrying candles, and then begin the procession "with four trombones[?] and with trumpets and drums with two shawms."³⁰ The attention-grabbing loud instruments were similarly employed at the Scuola di Sant'Orsola: an early sixteenth-century account book includes a payment of a little more than a ducat to six "ttrombetti [sic] ett pifari," named as maestro Zuane and companions from the Fontego.³¹ They were to play not only at the scuola on the feast, but also on the vigil, when they accompanied a float in the shape of the ship St. Ursula used on her journey, carrying two Dominican novices from the friary of Santi Giovanni e Paolo. In 1533, the Scuola di Sant'Antonio at the Frari instituted a similar practice for the vigil of their feast: "Also that on the vigil of St. Anthony [the scuola] must send a small adorned float with a boy on it dressed as an angel [accompanied by] piffari to St. Mark's and to the Rialto."³²

For one scuola, the piffari served to make a more personal announcement. An ancient custom found the doge and his retinue visiting the church of Santa Maria Formosa once each year; in return, the Scuola della Beata Vergine della Purificazione of that church presented him with a gift. From at least the beginning of the seventeenth century (earlier records are missing) the scuola made an annual payment for instrumentalists, presumably accompanying brothers of the scuola, to carry the gift to the doge, for which service they were paid 2 ducats.³³

Music in Church and Procession

The Annual Festa

The agreements the scuole piccole negotiated with their host churches also provide some of the earliest clear evidence that music beyond the use of piffari played a role in their religious ceremonies. In 1507, for example, the officers of the Scuola del Venerabile Sacramento in San Geremia made an agreement with the parish priest that obligated the chapter of the church to provide "procession, vespers, songs, and organ" for the scuola's festa (on the feast of St. Joseph), and also singers and organist for the High Mass on the third Sunday of each month. For all the services combined, the scuola paid the church 1½ ducats.³⁴ Though polyphony is not specified in this case, a similar agreement between the Scuola di Sant'Orsola and the Dominican friars of Santi Giovanni e Paolo in 1501 indicates that the monastery was required to provide "singers and discanters" ("cantadori e biscantadori").³⁵

Frequently, however, the music provided by the host church was not sufficient for the scuole, and they augmented it through their own expenditures. In at least one case, considerable controversy resulted: the Scuola dei Mercanti wanted to provide its own singers, but the convent of the Frari insisted that it had exclusive rights to provide singers in its church. The friars insisted that the scuola would have to pay the convent for such services if they wanted to enhance their festa. In 1543, this dispute apparently grew so heated that the Friars actually removed the scuola's altarpiece from the altar, and transferred it to the sacristy.[36] Because the officers felt that this and other demands would limit the scuola's freedom, making it a slave to the convent,[37] they resolved to withhold any payment or charity to the convent, except for the insignificant rent of 25 lire specified in the original 1408 agreement.

The practice of the scuole hiring their own musicians during this period, as described in the previous document, actually appears quite rarely in their archives. As so often happens, the surviving documents frequently reflect a practice only by its curtailment or outright ban. Numerous examples, often in the mariegole of confraternities newly created in the sixteenth or early seventeenth centuries, or in revisions of older rules, document severe limitations on expenditures for music at the annual festa. Typical of the regulations is that from the 1514 mariegola of the Scuola della Beata Vergine in San Basilio: "[the officers] may not spend more than 6 lire of the funds of the scuola to celebrate our feast of the Visitation of the Madonna in July for singers, instrumentalists, decorations, or other expenses."[38] Any additional expenditures were to be made from the personal funds of the individual officers. How often the officers decided to pay for an elaborate celebration out of their own pockets is, unfortunately, impossible to document, but 6 or 8 lire for music and decorations was a rather paltry sum. The fact that it was necessary to limit expenses indicates that the desire for elaborate celebrations existed; these rules were not intended to turn the annual feasts into dull and somber affairs, of course, but rather simply to lighten the burden on the limited budgets of the scuole and transfer it to the often quite deep pockets of the officers.

Vincenzo Quartari, the guardian of the Scuola dei Mercanti, brought a particular vehemence in favor of the idea of cost-cutting in the motion he proposed to his council in 1552:

> A damaging and reprehensible corruption has been introduced into our scuola regarding the expenses made to celebrate and solemnize our feast on the day of the Nativity of Our Lady, which, if a remedy is not quickly provided, will get worse from year to year, such that, over time, one will easily find that the guardians, without fear of God, but rather filled with [desire for] worldly pomp, will think it legitimate to spend 100 ducats, which will be damaging to our scuola and to our poor brothers.[39]

He proposed, and the chapter approved, a limitation on all festa expenses to 25 ducats. If a guardian exceeded this figure, the entire amount would be billed to him personally. It is clear that at the scuole piccole, as at the scuole grandi, some elected officers attempted to use their one-year term as an occasion for increasing personal honor, even at the risk of damaging the confraternity.

If all the scuole had succeeded in transferring the expenditures to the individual officers, we would probably have remained ignorant about the details of music at these institutions, as private accounts documenting such activities would be unlikely to survive (to date, none has turned up). Fortunately, some confraternities continued to fund music, at least in part, with their own money, and the extant account books and other documents paint a rich and detailed picture of varied musical celebrations, often employing the best singers and players of the city. While these well-documented examples are rare for the sixteenth century, that is due in part to the poor survival rate of the archives for this period. In the eighteenth century, when the number of extant account books is quite large, significant expenditures for music can be documented at dozens of scuole. It is therefore quite likely that musical activities such as those to be discussed below were fairly common in the Renaissance.

The archive of the Scuola del Venerabile Sacramento in the church of San Giuliano contains an account book whose first entries date from 1502.[40] In that year the scuola was granted a new indulgence for its annual festival on Corpus Christi, and for the first year's celebrations the officers turned to the most prestigious musicians available. They hired singers from the cappella ducale, along with some others, for a little more than 1 ducat, and a group of wind players at about the same cost.[41] The scuola made similar payments yearly, usually in simplified form with no specific indication of who they hired, but occasionally with the addition of intriguing details about personnel or practices. In 1507, the payment was to "singers who psalmized,"[42] in 1509 the singers accompanied a monstrance with the Holy Sacrament,[43] and in several years it was specified that the payments covered Mass, Vespers, and a procession. The 1508 celebration was particularly lavish, with the scuola paying 3 ducats to the cappella of Santo Stefano, the largest Augustinian friary in the city, for two Vespers (that is, one on the vigil and one on the day) and a High Mass with its procession.[44] Normally, there were payments to only one group of instrumentalists, presumably wind players, but in 1515 a second, smaller payment was made to "those who played in back with harp, lute, and *violeta*."[45] Probably, the usual wind players led the procession, and the string ensemble, identical in makeup to the standard ensemble of the time at the scuole grandi, walked near the end.

Several changes in practice are documented at this scuola beginning in the 1530s. In 1535, the scuola increased the usual payment of 1 or 2 ducats for singers to 3,[46] and in 1536 to 4, when the record specifies that there were eight singers in two choirs for the celebration.[47] In that latter year, for the first time, appears a payment of less than half a ducat for an organist. In 1538 the entry identifies the singers for Corpus Christi as those from the Dominican house of Santi Giovanni e Paolo, but also lists payments for a second occasion, the feast of the Madonna (undated, but probably the Assumption in August), this time to singers of St. Mark's.[48] As so often happens in such account books, the entries at a certain point become less specific, and after 1540 all expenditures for the annual festa are lumped together. One special occasion, however, is documented in more detail: in 1566, for the jubilee proclaimed by Pope Pius V for the defense of Christendom against the Turks, the scuola paid four singers of the cappella ducale 2½ ducats to sing the litanies at three processions.[49] One further change occurred around 1582: while music is never specified after this date for the Corpus Christi celebration, regular entries begin, and continue through the seventeenth century, of payments of 3 to 4 ducats for singers for a ceremony on Good Friday, specified later as an evening procession.

As discussed above, the Scuola di Sant'Orsola and the friars of Santi Giovanni e Paolo reached an agreement in 1501 according to which the friars were responsible for providing singers for the festa. In 1509 the two parties reaffirmed the agreement, but with the specification that on the day of the feast the scuola would pay the organist and the friars should take care of the rest of the music.[50] By 1516 at the latest, however, the scuola began spending its own money to hire outside singers as well as an organist. In that year—the starting date for the earliest surviving account book of the scuola—there were several notable expenditures for the two Vespers and Mass, including 1 ducat to the organist pre Ettor, who was accompanied by a boy who sang, and nearly 2 ducats to fra Vizenzo (a singer of Santi Giovanni e Paolo) and some other singers who sang polyphony ("chantto figurao").[51] Though the agreement between scuola and convent, still in effect, called for the convent to arrange for the singers, the scuola had taken over that task, but for some reason still used singers from the convent. Evidently, the scuola did not own an organ, as pre Ettor supplied his own (however, the scuola was obligated to spend 7 soldi for unspecified repairs to the organ). The same musicians served in 1517. In 1518, the third and last year for which detailed expenditures survive, the payments were to fra Battista for the singers, Zuan Maria dal Cornetto for the piffari, and the usual pre Ettor.[52]

In 1519, the scuola apparently changed its procedures, though clear documentation is lacking until 1521. The situation reverted to that which was more traditional among the scuole piccole: the singers and instrumentalists were no longer paid by the scuola, but by the officers, out of their own pockets.[53] In October 1525 the scuola made yet another modification: it apparently acquired its own organ (probably as a gift, as no expenditure is listed), and began employing a salaried organist, Andrea Vicentino, who, for an annual salary of 2½ ducats, was required to play on ordained Sundays and the annual festa, and to keep the instrument tuned.[54] Vicentino's employment can be documented at Sant'Orsola through 1543. The organ itself caused some internal dissension a few years later. The practice had apparently arisen of lending the instrument, which must have been small enough to be portable, to others (perhaps other scuole) for celebrations, resulting in damage both to the finances of the scuola (which could have rented it out for a fee) and to the organ itself. In 1546, the officers decided to end that practice and ordered that a wooden case for the organ be built so that it could never again leave the scuola.[55]

In 1557, the council of the Scuola della Santissima Trinità at the church of the Trinità did what so many other scuole had done: it limited expenditures for music and decorations for its feast, setting the total outlay of the scuola's funds at 8 ducats per year.[56] Fortunately for posterity, the surviving account book of the scuola, beginning in 1577,[57] treats the festal expenditures in an unusual way. Apparently, the officers hired and paid whatever musicians they preferred, charging only the legislated 8 ducats to the scuola; the entries in the account book list all of the musicians in most years, but do not indicate (except rarely) how much they were actually paid, recording only the standard 8 ducats that were the responsibility of the scuola. The remainder came from the pockets of the gastaldo and other officers. The two instances in which the actual total is recorded indicate that this figure could be quite substantial: in 1585 the total expenditure was more than 24 ducats and in 1590 more than 15. In 1599 the gastaldo recorded in the official account book the regular 8 ducats, but inserted the annotation that his personal account book listed payments of many more ducats "which are my responsibility."[58]

As shown in table 8.1, in the eight years in the sixteenth century for which the account book provides names, the Scuola della Trinità hired some of the most renowned musicians in Venice, such as Baldassare Donati, Giovanni Croce, and Giovanni Gabrieli. Included are organists, maestri dei concerti, and maestri di cappella from St. Mark's, and some well-known freelancers: the same men sought out by the scuole grandi for their feste. In the early seventeenth century, the scuola occasionally picked up more (or perhaps all) of the expenses, up to 20 ducats. While names are rarely listed, the 1615 payment was to the maestro di cappella of the Frari, and that of 1620 to pre Piero Soardi as cashier of the singers' company from St. Mark's, who provided, in addition to singers and players, two organs, maestro di cappella, and *falsetti*, the last presumably soloists, either actual falsettists or castrati.[59]

At one other scuola, the musical expenses matched those for the Scuola della Trinità, for at least one year. In a book dedicated primarily to expenditures for earlier years, the guardian of the Scuola di San Mattia, the confraternity of Venice's German community, housed in the church of San Bartolomeo, recorded the festal expenditures for the day of their patron saint in 1594. Out of a total cost of about 42 ducats, almost 18 were for singers and instrumentalists, to which was added the cost of four torches to provide light for the musicians to read their scores.[60]

Holy Week and Beyond

For at least some of the scuole piccole, religious music-making extended beyond the annual festa, particularly to Holy Week. As with the annual festa, funding arrangements for such events varied, and could become a source of tension. The successful agreement between the Scuola della Passion and the Frari, concluded in 1579, obligated the scuola to pay 12 ducats a year to the convent. In exchange, the maestro di cappella, with all his singers, would sing the Passion on Palm Sunday and Good Friday, and Mass on Palm Sunday, at the high altar of the church.[61] On the other hand, the Scuola del Santissimo Sacramento in Santa Maria Zobenigo and the parish priest (*piovano*) had apparently come into dispute over who would pay for the musicians for their joint Holy Week observances, but worked out a compromise in about 1590, according to which the gastaldo would give 2 ducats to the piovano to help defray the cost of singers for the three days of Lamentations and the procession on Good Friday. Beyond the 2 ducats, the piovano was free to spend as much as he wished.[62]

The Scuola del Santissimo Sacramento in San Giacomo dall'Orio apparently had a similar arrangement with its parish church, paying the piovano almost 4

TABLE 8.1.   Musicians for the festa of the Scuola della Trinità in the sixteenth century

Year	Singers	Winds	Strings	Organist
1577	fra n.n. of I Frari	Geronimo da Udene[a]	Zuane dal violin 2 n.n. dal violon	2 n.n.
1578	Zan Francesco Spin	Paulo Laudis[b]	Michiel Bonfante[c]	Vicenzo Bell'haver[d]
1583	Baldissera Donati[e]	Geronimo da Udene	—	Vicenzo Bell'haver
1588	Giovanni Croce[f]	Francesco Laudis[g]	Michiel Bonfante	Antonio Romanin[h]
1589	Giovanni Croce	Geronimo da Udene	Giacomo dal Violin[i] n.n. dal Violon	Paulo Giusti[j]
1590	Giovanni Croce	I Favretti[k]	n.n. dal Violin n.n. dal Violon	Giovanni Gabrieli[l]
1593	Giovanni Croce	Pasqualin Savioni[m]	—	—
1597	Giovanni Croce	I Favretti	n.n. violin	2 n.n.

[a]"Jeronimo da udene": he was *maestro dei concerti* at San Marco from 1568 to 1601. He also was employed with his company at the Scuola Grande di San Teodoro in 1585 and at the Scuola Grande di San Rocco in 1608.

[b]"Paulo Greco": a *piffaro del doge* and player at San Marco from the late 1570s. He joined with another *piffaro del doge*, Paolo Vergelli, nicknamed Favretto, to form a company of players known as the Favretti. This group was continued by his sons Francesco and Marco (Ongaro, pers. comm.). The Favretti provided music for the annual festa at the Scuola Grande di San Rocco in 1595, 1598, 1600, and 1603.

[c]"Michiel dal violin": Michiel Bonfante worked as a substitute violinist at San Marco from 1584, and regularly from 1588 until at least 1598 (Ongaro, pers. comm.).

[d]"Vicenzo organista": Bell'haver was organist at the church of the Crosecchieri until 1568, when he was hired by the Scuola Grande di San Rocco, where he served until 1584. In 1586–87 he was an organist for the cappella di San Marco.

[e]Donati served in the cappella of San Marco from at least 1546 (Ongaro, pers. comm.). In 1568 he was appointed vice maestro di cappella, and served as maestro from 1590 to 1603. He also served at the Scuola Grande di San Rocco in 1577 and was unsuccessful in a competition to provide the music for the annual festa at the Scuola Grande di San Teodoro in 1585.

[f]"Il Chiozoto": Giovanni Croce, from Chioggia, was already employed at the cappella of San Marco in 1586 (Ongaro, pers. comm.), and served as vice maestro di cappella in the 1590s. He was appointed maestro in 1603 and held that post until 1609. He served as maestro for the annual feste at the Scuola Grande di San Teodoro in 1585 and at the Scuola Grande di San Rocco in 1595, 1598, 1600, 1602, and 1606.

[g]"Misser Francesco Laudis fiol de Misser Paulo Greco"; see above, note b.

[h]Antonio Romanin served as organist at the Scuola Grande di Santa Maria della Misericordia from 1572 until sometime after 1580. He also auditioned unsuccessfully for a post at San Marco (Ongaro, pers. comm.).

[i]"Jacomo dal violin": this man is found in the records of the cappella of San Marco with several variant forms of his name: Giacomo dal violin, Giacomo casseler, Jacometto bressan dal violin, and Giacomo Rovetta or Roeta. Roeta was elected *piffaro del doge* in 1605, and was still serving in 1612 (Ongaro, pers. comm.).

[j]"Paulo organista": Giusti (also known as Zusti) auditioned unsuccessfully for the post of organist at San Marco in 1586 (Ongaro, pers. comm.). In 1588 he was hired for the third organ, and in 1591 as first organist, where he served until about 1624 (Selfridge-Field, *Venetian Instrumental Music*, 294–96). Giusti also played for the annual festa of the Scuola Grande di San Rocco in 1623.

[k]See note b above for Paulo Laudis.

[l]"Il Gabrieli": Giovanni Gabrieli served as organist at San Marco from 1574 until his death in 1612. He was also organist at the Scuola Grande di San Rocco from 1585 until his death.

[m]Savioni was associated with the cappella of San Marco from at least 1580. He was a *piffaro del doge* from before 1612 until his death in 1617 (Ongaro, pers. comm.).

ducats in 1568 for singers for the Passion on Good Friday. In 1572, however, the scuola paid the musicians directly, but at the lesser rate of only 16 lire for all of Holy Week. This latter practice held for at least the rest of the decade, with payments varying between 12 and 18 lire annually.[63] In 1577, following the great outbreak of the plague, this scuola joined the procession to the Scuola Grande di San Rocco, whose patron was the protector of plague victims, on which day they also performed Mass and Vespers. The musical expenditures were substantial, totaling 17 ducats: almost 7 for instrumentalists, 8 for singers, and about 2 for an additional violinist and an organist.[64]

No evidence suggests that any of the Venetian scuole piccole, unlike the scuole grandi, established salaried choirs during this period. However, one of the confraternities in Murano, the Scuola di San Giovanni Battista dei Battuti, apparently did employ such a group in the sixteenth century. While this institution was in some ways similar to the scuole grandi, in that it was in origin a flagellant confraternity, it operated, in general, on the scale of the larger scuole piccole (and was, like the scuole piccole, also under the supervision of the Provveditori di Comun). The four singers submitted a petition (undated) to the guardian and banca of the scuola in an attempt to solve some disputes that had arisen, apparently because they were paid not a fixed salary, but rather by the occasion. They now proposed, for the annual salary of 4 ducats each (plus candles), to sing whenever needed, including at what had evidently been the source of most of the difficulties, funerals of deceased brothers. No record survives in the scanty archive of the scuola regarding the officers' reaction to the petition, nor is there any other mention of music in the documents before the eighteenth century.[65]

It is almost certain that, as with the scuole grandi, the actual music for any polyphony at the scuole piccole would have been provided by the singers themselves, and would, therefore, have been their standard repertory. Similarly, the priests who served the scuole probably used their own books, or those of the host church, for liturgical chants. At least one of the better-off scuole, however, like the scuole grandi, commissioned its own liturgical manuscript, probably containing all the necessary chants for its services.[66] The Scuola dello Spirito Santo, which became, in the seventeenth and eighteenth centuries, an active musical center (see chapters 9 and 10), showed as early as 1503 that it paid particular attention to its liturgical music:

> We also wish and ordain that Don Desiderio, a monk at San Gregorio, make an antiphoner in good vellum, with the following conditions: the said Don Desiderio obligates himself not to spend more than 2 ducats in good-quality vellum, and if he spends more, he spends his own, and for his writing and illuminating in blue and cinnabar, 3 ducats, except the initials, which should be decorated with brush [and paint]. It is intended that he should put into the book as much as is necessary for our scuola.[67]

Organs and Organists

The single most important instrument for most of the scuole piccole was always that quintessential sacred instrument, the organ. In some cases, the only references to music in the extant archives of a scuola concern the building or repair of an organ or the employment of an organist. While sometimes the organ under consideration was the property of the scuola itself, at others it belonged to the parish church that housed the scuola. That the organ and its contribution to the religious ceremonies was seen as important is evident as early as the first third of the fifteenth century. The agreement between the Scuola di San Giuliano e San Carlo and its host church of San Giuliano makes it clear that the scuola wanted to be absolutely sure the organ and its music would form a part of its ceremonies:

> at masses on ordained days [the parish priest] must have the organ played at his expense; in the event that he does not have it played, we may hire a maestro to play, giving him the 16 soldi. If the organ is broken in such a way that it cannot be played, we may hire a maestro with his own organ, giving him the 20 soldi, subtracting the 16 or 20 soldi that are paid [from our annual payment to the church].[68]

The building of an organ was a time-consuming and expensive job, rarely taken on by a scuola on its own. In one case, however, this did occur during the period under discussion. In 1626 the chapter of the Scuola di Santa Marta, in the church of the same name, decided to build an organ, and received an estimate from a builder, including the instrument and its case, of 150 ducats.[69] In order to guarantee that the money not be spent unwisely, the scuola elected four brothers to supervise the operation, with instructions that no money should actually be paid until the builder completed the entire job, and that it all be done "for the glory of His Divine Majesty, and of the Most Blessed Virgin Mary, and of Madonna Saint Martha, and of misser Saint Nicholas our protector."[70]

In most cases, however, scuole shared the expenses of an organ, either with other scuole housed in their church, or with the church itself. In 1575 the parish confraternity of San Marziale, known as the Convicinato, played a major role in building a new organ for the church. The priests had approached the scuola with the idea of building an organ, having received an estimate of 100 ducats, offering to pay 60 and asking the scuola for 40, which, combined with the sale of the old organ (which would yield another 40), was expected to be sufficient (perhaps the price already included the old organ). When a new estimate showed that the total cost would actually be 220 ducats, the church asked the scuola for additional funds; in exchange, the church officials ceded authority to deal with the organ builders to the scuola, turning over all money to them.[71] As at Santa Marta, the scuola did not make any actual payments until the builder finished his work. In June 1578, they paid 100 ducats to Hieremia Fianatta, a carpenter from Feltre, for the case. Not until over a year later, in August of 1579, was the instrument itself finished, and the Convicinato paid 100 ducats to the organ master Vicenzo Collona for his labors.[72] The work, and expenditures, however, were not really completed, for the scuola spent 20 additional ducats on the case only five years later (completing, apparently, the original 220-ducat estimate).[73] Nonetheless, more work remained to be done; within a few years another scuola in the church, the Scuola del Santissimo Sacramento, noted that though the rest of the church had finally been brought to perfection, the organ was still imperfect. They offered to contribute 40 ducats, and in 1602, with the gilding taken care of, the organ was at last complete.[74]

The Scuola della Beata Vergine dell'Anconetta ran into a rather unusual problem regarding its organ. Sometime in the early 1580s, the old instrument must have become unusable, since in 1585 the chapter approved a motion to sell the organ pipes.[75] Three years later, in September of 1588, the scuola decided to buy a small organ that had belonged to a priest of San Marcuola, one pre Alessandro Girardini, who agreed to accept payments over a period of time.[76] The scuola made expenditures totaling 30 ducats in 1589 and 1590 (though this might not represent the entire price).[77] Two months after purchasing the organ, the scuola hired an organist, pre Francesco Cassini, to play Saturday evenings and feast days for 4 ducats a year.[78] The problems began shortly afterwards. Sometime following the acquisition of the organ, the guardian of the scuola, Bortolo de Francesco, paid, out of his own pocket, for the construction of a case for the instrument. As a deliberation from November 1589 explains, however, the newly built case, for some unexplained reason, did not fit the organ, "since the case was large and the organ small."[79] In order not to waste the money that had already been spent on the case, the officers decided to build a new instrument that would fit better, which they thought they could do for about 40 ducats. The officers appointed two brothers to negotiate the best contract possible, covering as much of the fee as they could by selling the organ they had bought from pre Alessandro as well as the pipes from their old organ. It appears, in fact, that the procedure was nearly complete by this time, as they recorded the first payment for the new organ, of a little more than 11 ducats, in April 1589, to a builder named Ser Aleandro.[80] The scuola made additional payments through the end of October, for a combined sum of 40 ducats, as planned. There is no record of whether the scuola sold the organetto and old pipes to raise the money, or kept them for some other use. In 1602, the scuola made one final expenditure for this project: the gilding of the instrument was one of a series of embellishments made to the church, which also included work on the high altar, the painting of two altarpieces, and building cabinets in the albergo, all for a sum of 100 ducats.[81]

Once an organ was built, of course, it was necessary to hire an organist. While the church itself often arranged for this, and exacted an annual fee from each scuola housed there, sometimes a scuola took a more active role, as, for example, at the church of San Nicolò dei Mendicoli. In 1581, the parish priest approached the chapter of the Scuola del Santissimo Sacramento, and explained that "since the organ in the said church is so good and beautiful, it is also necessary to find an excellent man to play it, and not a bungler who would break it."[82] He proposed that the scuola offer 3 ducats annually, to be matched by the other three confraternities housed in the church. Combined with the 8 ducats the priest would supply, this would make a reasonable salary of 20 ducats, with which it would be possible to hire "an excellent man who will play [the organ]."[83] The scuola agreed, with two conditions: that the other three scuole must also participate (which they did), and that they would only contribute if the organist was chosen with the presence and consent of their gastaldo.[84] In this case, so as not to place an undue burden on the scuola's budget, the officers agreed to pay the 3 ducats out of their own pockets.[85]

Laude at the Scuola dei Fiorentini

Though the documentation for musicians at the scuole piccole is quite rich, references to the actual music are rare, and relate directly to liturgical function rather than to the music itself: Mass, Vespers, procession, litany. Noticable by its rarity is the genre most commonly associated with Italian confraternities, the lauda. Those sixteenth-century documents that do call for the singing of laude concern a scuola that differed in one very important way from all the others.

This unusual institution (housed in the Franciscan church of the Frari) is, not surprisingly, the scuola of the Florentines, whose native confraternities were renowned for their lauda singing.[86] Their 1555 mariegola names among the officers to be elected two of great importance that are not found in any other Venetian scuola: the *ceremonieri*, who bore the responsibility for religious observances of the scuola:

> [They] give order to who leads the office, to who says the lessons, the antiphons, the hymns, the versets, and all the other things required, according to the occasion. They must take care to assign the sermon, the verses of the Passion, the chapter, the prayers, the lauda, and, in sum, all that would be judged necessary for the consolation of the brothers. It is their duty, in the psalmody of the office, to order that part of the choir that should sit to do so, and that those whose turn it is should rise.[87]

Services, it is clear, were not run by a priest of the church or a hired chaplain, which was standard for other Venetian scuole, but by elected lay officers, so that Florentine practices could be maintained.

Another chapter of the mariegola listed the *tornate,* or days on which the members should gather for the Divine Office: every Sunday, feasts of the Apostles, Annunciation and Assumption of the Madonna, Christmas, St. John the Baptist, second and third ferie of Easter, All Saints, St. Joseph (the anniversary of the founding of the scuola), three days of Holy Week, and Fridays in Lent. On these occasions, the brothers celebrated a Marian Matins with laude, hymns, a verset, and prayers, except during Lent, when penitential psalms and litanies at Vespers replaced the Matins.[88] In the case of a testamentary bequest, the Marian Matins could be replaced with the Matins and laude for the dead. Perhaps the most unusual practice, as compared with that of the other Venetian confraternities, is that, in general, all this singing was to be done by the brothers themselves, who were required to enter the choir in order according to their age, "[and] there, without noise or murmuring, follow the order of the office, [singing] neither high nor low, but in concord with the tone of the others."[89] Exceptions to this practice were made only for the three tornate of Holy Week, for which the scuola elected three special officers, the *festaioli*. They provided modest and devout decorations for the scuola, and were also permitted, "if they wish, for their consolation, [to] arrange for outside musicians."[90]

BY THE END OF the sixteenth century, then, the numerous scuole piccole had made a significant impact on the musical life of the city. Many provided substantial musical accompaniments to their annual feste, scattered throughout the city and distributed over the entire calendar, and some also offered music during Holy Week or other occasions. Several had also begun what was to be one of their most important and lasting musical contributions, the construction of organs in Venetian parish churches.

AN HONORABLE AND
NECESSARY WORK

Music at the Scuole Piccole in the Seventeenth Century

In many respects, musical developments at the scuole piccole in the seventeenth century paralleled those at the scuole grandi. They expended their greatest efforts on the annual festa, and when funds were available, the officers preferred to hire well-known maestri, especially those with connections to the doge's cappella at San Marco. In addition to the annual festa, many of the scuole piccole, like the more prestigious institutions, began to direct some attention to the musical enhancement of other religious recurrences, such as expositions of the Holy Sacrament. The scuole dedicated to the Holy Sacrament, connected with parish churches, continued to be deeply involved (as were the two scuole grandi with their own churches) in the construction and maintenance of organs.

Elaborate Music for the Annual Festivity

In the early seventeenth century, the officers at some of the scuole piccole began to increase the splendor of their music, in search of personal or corporate honor, sometimes to an extraordinary extent. However, with the modest and sometimes shaky financial means of such institutions, sustaining these efforts was not always easy.[1] At the Scuola della Beata Vergine Assunta in San Geremia, for example, new regulations of 1626 attempted to alleviate the burden on the guardian and his companions, who were saddled with the expenses for the annual ceremonies on the feast of the Assumption, which, according to the decree, had risen to "hundreds of ducats," as each newly elected group of officers wished to match or exceed its predecessors. Their creative solution, rather than to try to reduce the expenditures, was to increase the number of officers from three to six, thus reducing the individual responsibilities.[2] This scuola had also begun, in 1604, the practice of providing a "musical Compline" every Sunday, and employed salaried

singers and instrumentalists for that purpose, a very rare practice at a scuola piccola, and one that clearly could not be sustained.[3] In the same 1626 decree referred
to above, they fired one singer, Zuanne Arzignan (a member of the ducal cappella),[4] who had been receiving an annual salary of 20 ducats, and replaced him
with two priests of the parish church of San Geremia who had sung at the Compline services for twelve years without pay, and were now officially hired at 8
ducats each (that is, two singers in place of one, and at a savings of 4 ducats
annually). The officers also decided to reduce the size of the instrumental ensemble: "among the number of instrumentalists, everybody judges that the trombone
is superfluous"; therefore they eliminated that position, along with its 20-ducat
salary.[5]

The importance of music to some of the scuole piccole is also demonstrated
by the events surrounding the founding in 1636 of the small and quite poor
Scuola di San Domenico di Suriano in the church of San Domenico di Castello,
organized by former residents of the Calabrian town of Suriano (the site of an
important Dominican convent) now living in Venice. Despite their very limited
financial resources, the opening ceremonies were accompanied not only by trumpets and drums, for which the brothers spent a little more than 5 ducats, but also
by music directed by one of the more prominent musicians in the city, Francesco
Cavalli. Though the amount the scuola could afford, about 16 ducats, could not
have provided much splendor, the prestige (and presumably high quality) offered
by Cavalli must have attracted considerable public attention to this new institution. Thirty years later, at the time of its founding, in 1666, the Scuola del Nome
di Gesù at the Frari was in the fortunate position of having one of the most
respected musicians in Venice as a member, and presumably received his services
for the opening ceremonies free of charge (with perhaps a discount for the services
of the other musicians). The scuola was proud enough of this event to enter a
description of it in its mariegola:

> the day of the first of May last year [the scuola] solemnized its foundation, and
> began with elegant decorations in the church and on the aforesaid altar, accom-
> panied again by celebrated music, both at the Mass and at Vespers, performed
> by the virtue of the Excellent and Reverend Don Natale Monferrato, one of
> the first to join and be enrolled in the same confraternity.[6]

In 1639, perhaps in reaction to the sort of events described above, the Venetian
government attempted for the first time to regulate music at the scuole piccole,
and issued an extraordinary decree to be copied into the mariegola of every
confraternity. By this, the government, at the recommendation of the ecclesiastical
authorities, tried to reform the music at the scuole piccole (something never done
in a similar manner for the scuole grandi), which had begun to function more as
entertainment than as an aid to devotion. The decree addresses a number of issues,
including the dress of the performers, the use of instruments not traditionally
associated with the church, and even the origin of the texts chosen and how they
were set to music. The government officials in charge of the scuole, the Provveditori di Comun, began with a general statement of principles, and an assessment of the problem:

The most illustrious Lords . . . [the] Provveditori di Comun, have learned from the exposition made by the Patriarchal Court of this city how, with the zeal of Christian religion, they have tried to return the music ordinarily performed at solemn festivals to that decorous and devout practice that well corresponds to public piety. The abuses have reached such heights that not only the clothes of the musicians, but also the musical instruments and the words that are sung seem designed more for the pleasure of the listeners than for the devotion for which such solemnities were piously instituted.

Their first order was that the scuole should eliminate unsuitable instruments from their celebrations:

[Therefore,] the Illustrious Lords, supporting the religious request of the said Patriarchal Court, have ordained that, in future, the guardiani, gastaldi, and any other sort of leader of the scuole subject to our magistracy are obligated in the musical solemnities to forbid the use of instruments other than those normally employed in churches, abstaining in particular from the use of warlike instruments, such as trumpets, drums, and the like, [which are] better suited for use in armies than in the house of God.

Second, the Provveditori insisted that the musicians wear choir robes, and not elaborate secular dress. Third, and perhaps most importantly, they issued fairly detailed instructions dealing with the texts. The Provveditori were concerned both with the souces of the words (with few exceptions the texts were to be biblical), and with the way they were set to music:

Finally, [they are obligated] to ensure that in this music the words [not] be transposed, nor may newly written words, not found in holy books, be sung, except that at the offertory, at the elevation, and after the Agnus Dei, and similarly at Vespers between the psalms they may sing motets with pious and devout texts, which are taken from holy books or from ecclesiastical authors. In this regard, [officers] who do not have sufficient knowledge can and must receive instruction from the reverend piovani and priests of the churches or other learned persons, under penalty for each infraction of 25 ducats.[7]

The results of this decree are uncertain, but extravagant music continued unabated, at least for a few years, as illustrated by events at the Scuola di Santa Caterina di Siena at Santa Maria Zobenigo. At this scuola, which had earlier in the century usually allocated 5 ducats for music at its festa, and only once, in 1630, spent as much as 30 ducats,[8] the years 1641 and 1642 saw music as elaborate as that at far wealthier confraternities (and more expensive than at several of the scuole grandi).[9] In the first of those two years the officers divided an expenditure of 48 ducats for the festa. In 1642, they hired Natale Monferrato (soon to become vice maestro di cappella and later maestro at St. Mark's), who had earlier that year provided music for the ceremony at which the outgoing guardian turned over authority to the newly elected one, and paid him 100 ducats for music at two Vespers and Mass. It should be noted that this is also an illustration of the new method for providing music for the celebrations of the scuole that obtained in the seventeenth century: instead of hiring individual performers or separate companies of instrumentalists and singers, as had been the practice earlier, the scuole now hired a maestro, who bore full responsibility for providing all the necessary performers, as well as the music itself, perhaps even composing new works for the occasion. The sudden rise in expenditures on music for this two-year period at the Scuola di Santa Caterina also demonstrates the central role of the tastes and ambitions of the individual elected officers of the scuole.

The changing musical preferences of the officers of the Scuola di San Nicolò at the church of San Nicolò dei Mendicoli, and of their parish priest, led to considerable variation in the celebrations of the annual feast of their patron saint in the early seventeenth century (though they never ascended to the heights of the Scuola di Santa Caterina). The long-standing agreement between church and confraternity called for the piovano to pay for the singers, and the scuola for the instrumentalists (with the priests making all the arrangements), for which purpose the officers each were assessed 2 lire a year. In 1606, the gastaldo Zamaria Piteri and his vicar proposed that they themselves would hire seven or eight additional singers, to perform alongside those hired by the priest. The scuola's chapter easily approved the proposal, with the condition that the extra musicians be paid for entirely out of the pockets of the officers.[10] In 1607 and 1608 (and presumably the two following years, for which there is no documentation), church and con-fraternity maintained the basic agreement. In 1611, however, the gastaldo, Zuanne Ferrari, desired more splendor, and made a proposal to combine the usual allo-cations from scuola and church, and supplement that with additional contributions from the officers, to hire the company of pre Bortolo Morosini, vice maestro of the cappella ducale.[11] The situation then reverted back to the norm for over a decade, with the exception of 1623. That marked the first patronal feast of a new piovano, and he wished to perform a more than usually elaborate celebration ("far festa granda"), at his own expense. Nonetheless, he asked the officers of the scuola if they still wished to participate, and they decided not only to offer their usual 2 lire each, but to more than double their contribution, to a total of 10 ducats.[12] The new priest must certainly have been pleased, and his parishioners impressed, by the extraordinary music on the parish's most important day.

Music for Pentecost at the Scuola dello Spirito Santo

The continuing importance of music for some of these institutions can perhaps be best illustrated by examining the history of one particularly active confraternity. The Scuola dello Spirito Santo and the convent of the same name had operated, since 1492, under an agreement by which the scuola provided the music and decorations for their common celebration of the three days of Pentecost but, in the late sixteenth century, a series of disputes erupted. In a declaration to the Provveditori di Comun, the government body that supervised the scuole piccole, the nuns of the Spirito Santo complained that

> one time several years ago they [the scuola] wanted to sing the great mass . . .
> but it was done with such little solemnity and music, that the result was rather

derision than devotion. Even though a down payment had been made, and the church all prepared, and the best musicians of the city, both singers and instrumentalists, as was the custom, were ready, to spite us the guardian of that year decided not to let them do the usual music, but rather remain silent; the next two days, however, having slept on it, he put on the music in the church as had been usual in other years.[13]

In 1619, the nuns stated, the scuola had failed entirely in its obligation to provide the music for Pentecost.[14]

As a result of these disputes, the Provveditori required in 1637 that the scuola deposit 30 ducats with them before Pentecost to guarantee that the music would take place.[15] Though he made the deposit as required, the guardian seemingly wanted nothing further to do with the business, and after Pentecost the Provveditori had to turn over the money to the maestro who had been engaged to arrange for the music: Francesco Cavalli.[16] This was not, however, Cavalli's full payment for what was clearly an elaborate three days of music. Not until the following March did he receive the remaining 100 ducats of his fee. The documents show, however, that even then he was not paid by the scuola as he should have been, but by the abbess.[17] The same problem recurred in 1638, and the maestro for that year, Giovanni Rovetta, was once again paid by the abbess, this time not until August of 1640.[18] It is clear that though the guardian of the moment felt differently, music was an essential (and expensive) aspect of the celebrations of both scuola and monastery.

The expenditure, borne in great part by the rector (as the elected leader was commonly called at the Spirito Santo, especially after the middle of the century), could at times be a real burden. The scuola decided in 1682 to reelect the outgoing rector, a practice usually forbidden, so that he could have the opportunity to recoup some of his personal funds expended during the two years of his term for music and decorations for the Pentecost festivities.[19] In 1690, in an attempt to control the burden, which was discouraging brothers from running for office, the scuola established a new system, specifying not only the total obligation of the officers for the festal expenditures, but how that should be divided: of the 150-ducat sum, the rector would contribute 50, the vicario 25, the cancelliere 11, and the members of the council 1 each; the remaining 31 ducats came from the scuola's treasury.[20]

The next year, 1691, the council voted to reform the method for hiring their maestro di cappella.[21] Noting that good results had been seen when such skilled maestri as Giovanni Battista Facin and Giovanni da Pesaro (both singers in the ducal cappella)[22] had been hired, they decided to establish a five-year term (instead of the more usual one-time-only appointment), in an effort to attract the best person. They also established the duties and obligations of the future maestro: (1) to provide Mass and Vespers on the three days of Pentecost, with the masses to include motets and sonatas; (2) on the first day, to hire the best singers and instrumentalists from the cappella ducale, specifically twelve singers and an orchestra of eighteen (see table 9.1); and 3) on the second and third days employ "one-eighth fewer singers and one-third fewer instrumentalists than on the first day."[23]

TABLE 9.1.   Musical ensembles at the Scuola dello Spirito Santo

Personnel	1691ᵃ		1695		1695—Lotti's Proposal	
Singers (total)	12	reduced by 1/8	12	8	12	5
soprano	3		3	2	—	—
altos	3		3	2	—	—
tenors	3		3	2	—	—
basses	3		3	2	—	—
Instrumentalists	18	reduced by 1/3	13	7	15	9
organs	3		3	1	3	1
violone	1		1	0	1	1
viols	2		0	1	0	0
violins	4		3	2	4	2
violas	4		3	2	4	2
cornetti	2		1	(1)	0	0
theorbo	1		1	0	1	1
trumpet	1		1	(1)	1	1
violoncello	—		(—	—	1	1)
Total Expenditure	90 ducats		100 ducats		100 ducats	

Source: ASV, SP 670.

ᵃ The first figure in each column is for the feast of Pentecost itself; the second figure is for the two following days.

This new system apparently failed to work smoothly over the next few years, as a decree of 1695 refers to "maestri" (in the plural, meaning that they were not serving full, five-year terms) having, despite all diligence, found it impossible to hire the required musicians at the specified fee of 90 ducats.[24] The brothers voted to increase the amount to 100 ducats, and to reduce the required forces, as can be seen in column two of table 9.1. At the same time, the officers expressed their support for the maestro who had served for the past few years, the young Antonio Lotti (appointed in 1689 a singer in the cappella ducale at San Marco, and in 1692 its second organist). Ten days after his election to a five-year term, Lotti presented a petition to the council, thanking them for their confidence, and pledging loyalty to the confraternity. He also indicated, however, that he needed to make some changes in the legislated specifications for music at the feast (see also table 9.1, third column): "having observed the distribution of the voices and instruments, it is necessary on the first day, [in order] to create a good sound, to increase the number of instruments, and to regulate also the voices on the following days so as not to exceed the decreed expenditure."[25] The changes proposed by Lotti are notable in several ways. For the feast of Pentecost itself, the vocal ensemble was apparently to be left unchanged, but Lotti suggested that the orchestra should be enlarged, and changed, to provide better balance. Restoring the number of violins and violas (*violette*) to four each (the numbers before the most recent reductions), was only the beginning. More interesting are the moderni-zations. The old-fashioned *viole*, that is, probably, viole da gamba, were replaced by a violoncello (*violoncino*), and the by-now essentially obsolete cornetto was eliminated.[26] The alterations for the second and third days were also significant. While the earlier practice had been to preserve the choral nature of the vocal ensemble, maintaining a balance among the four parts, but simply reducing the numbers from three to two each, Lotti proposed a more radical change, dropping the number to five, perhaps emphasizing soloistic possibilities. The instrumental ensemble was, as with the feast of Pentecost, enriched, particularly as regards continuo instruments. The earlier specification called for an ensemble of seven, including only two continuo players, that is, an organist and a viola da gamba player. The new nine-part ensemble replaced the viola da gamba with violoncello, as in the large ensemble, but also retained the violone and theorbo. As for the first day, Lotti proposed eliminating the cornetto. Unfortunately, it has not yet been possible to establish whether any of Lotti's surviving works might correspond to his specifications, though large-scale settings of psalms appropriate for Vespers at Pentecost do appear among his surviving works.[27]

At the conclusion of Lotti's five-year term, the scuola, because of increasing financial obligations, was forced to reduce the expenditures for music from 100 ducats to 80, "with the employment of those voices and instruments that can be managed proportionate to the [reduced] expense."[28] Lotti, by now established at San Marco not only as an organist (he would in 1704 become first organist and later maestro di cappella) but as a composer, was reelected, but this time—whether at his insistence or the scuola's is unknown—for a period of only three years, at which point the documents cease to record details of musical practices.

Disputes Between the Frari and its Scuole

Disputes between a scuola and its host church over music, such as the one be-tween the monastery and scuola of the Spirito Santo, discussed above, were not all that unusual. An interesting series of such disagreements occurred in the sev-enteenth century between the Franciscan convent of Santa Maria Gloriosa dei Frari (usually known simply as the Frari) and several of the scuole piccole who possessed altars in its church. We have already seen how in the middle of the sixteenth century the convent came into conflict with the Scuola dei Mercanti when the latter wanted to hire its own musicians for the festa, instead of the cappella of the convent (see pp. 200–201). A similar dispute arose in 1606 with the Scuola della Concezione, which turned to the Council of Ten for assistance. On 29 November, the Capi (or chiefs) of the Council issued an order requiring the friars to cease interfering and allow the scuola to select whichever musicians it pleased.[29] In December, however, both sides made declarations to the Capi. The Frari insisted that the order should be revoked, because their own maestro di cappella had the right to direct all music in the church, especially since the convent and scuola were tied together by an official agreement. The guardian of the scuola declared, however, that since the musicians were paid for out of the private funds of the officers (and not the regulated accounts of the scuola), the maestro di cappella had no right to interfere. The Capi reaffirmed their earlier decision, and did so again three years later after another appeal by the convent.[30] Some fifty years later, when the issue reemerged in 1667, the guardian apparently thought that since the scuola provided its own musicians, he need not make the annual payment for singers contained in the agreement with the Frari; the Avogadori di Comun disagreed, and required that the payment be made as usual.[31]

The problems between the Frari and its scuole were not over yet, however. In 1675, the convent had yet another similar dispute, but this time with the Scuola di Sant'Antonio. Once again, since the officers used their own funds, the court declared that they were not obligated to use the musicians of the convent (though, presumably, like the Concezione, they had to continue to pay the small fee contained in their original agreement), but could employ the maestro of their choice.[32] Fortunately for the budget of the Frari, not all the scuole it housed tried to avoid using its musicians: for most of the century, the Scuola di San Francesco maintained its obligation to pay the convent 1 ducat a year for instrumentalists for its festa, and, from 1668, 5 ducats to the maestro di cappella for singers.[33]

Music Beyond the Annual Festa: Compline, Processions, and Expositions of the Sacrament

One of the most notable developments in the seventeenth century was the expansion of music at the scuole piccole to include recurring occasions other than the annual festa (special-event celebrations, of course, had long been opportunities for music). A number of the confraternities initiated annual, monthly, or even weekly religious observances, some with quite elaborate music (beyond, that is, the quite common use of the organ on Sundays).

When the Scuola della Beata Vergine Annonciata in San Cassiano was founded in 1615, its mariegola required the celebration of Compline every Saturday or Sunday, "with songs and sounds in music, as we are able," to be paid for with the money deposited in the alms box at their altar.[34] A similar practice (and this would continue as well in the eighteenth century) can be documented in more detail at the Scuola della Beata Vergine dell'Anconetta. A mid-century account book includes a list, dated 1665, of the annual expenses of the scuola, divided into payments made from the scuola's own funds and those made by the guardian and officers. The first category included 12 ducats for musicians to sing every Tuesday and 8 ducats to the organist (one Pre Paulo Baldi) to play on the same day (he was also paid 12 ducats annually for other services and 3 to tune the organ). Payments made by the officers included the substantial sum of 36 ducats a year for the singing of Compline.[35] It is unclear whether the Compline service and the Tuesday ceremony were one and the same, or whether there were two different weekly events. The situation is rendered even more complicated by an expense record for 1669/70. The first of two semiannual payments to musicians was "for Complines" ("per compiete"), while the second, for approximately the same amount, specified "officiating of the Complines and Saturdays."[36] Were Saturdays a third occasion, or had Tuesdays simply been replaced? Unfortunately, there is no better documentation to clear up the issue.[37]

In its 1638 agreement with the monastery of the Spirito Santo, the Scuola della Beata Vergine della Salute created a different sort of weekly ceremony. It stipulated that the chaplain of the monastery was obligated to intone the litany on Saturdays, but that "if we want to have music, we must find it ourselves, and pay the musicians out of our own funds."[38] This is, apparently, what they decided to do, at least by 1650, in which year they hired Don Giulio Gasparoni as organist at an annual salary of 8 ducats, with the obligation "also to sing the litany of the Blessed Virgin every Saturday of the year."[39] When the scuola replaced Gasparoni as organist in 1666, it was with the well-known musician Giovanni da Pesaro. His annual salary was to be much higher, 50 ducats, but this included, in addition to playing the organ every Saturday and singing the litany, the obligation to direct two solemn masses annually, on the day of the Madonna della Salute (21 November) and the third Sunday of July (the feast of the Redentore), each with "four of the best voices and two instruments."[40] Within two years, however, recognizing that its finances were stretched to the limit, the scuola decided to eliminate the additional elaborate masses, and renegotiated the agreement with Giovanni da Pesaro for a salary of 12 ducats and the requirement to play the organ and "intone the litanies with one voice every Saturday of the year."[41]

The Scuola di Sant'Anna (at the nunnery of the same name) is one of two confraternities for which we can document monthly musical ceremonies in the seventeenth century. They established regulations in 1631 for a procession to be held the second Sunday of each month, in which the brothers, each carrying a candle, went along the *fondamente* (streets bordering canals) of the district of Castello with an image of St. Anne, four torches, and four singers accompanying their chaplain, all paid for out of funds deposited in an alms box carried around the city; if the collection proved insufficient, donations from the members filled the gap. The scuola's funds were not to be used, even for this rather simple function, which probably involved only the singing of chant.[42]

In 1692, the Scuola del Nome di Maria in Sant'Antonio di Castello (associated with the four chief guilds of the nearby Arsenal) decided on a much more elaborate monthly musical event, to accompany what would become, in the eighteenth century, the occasion for some of the most elaborate music-making at religious institutions throughout the city, the exposition of the Holy Sacrament:

> It is moved, that at the expositions that are done annually on the fourth Sunday of each month, a concert of music should be performed, with motets and *sinfonia*, and at the end should be sung the litany with the *Tantum ergo*. For the aforesaid music, about 30 ducats should be spent, and a contract with a music master should be agreed to regarding both the expenditure and the personnel that should come to sing and play, so that the people should be more greatly edified, and inspired to devotion.[43]

An indication of the importance this ceremony held for them can be seen by the contrast with their requirements for their annual festa, in an agreement with the monks of Sant'Antonio only three years earlier. The music for the festa was to consist of "a mass with the organ in chant," at the cost of only 1½ ducats.[44]

Six months after the decision to increase the level of music at the exposition, the scuola signed a contract with Oratio Molinari, who agreed, for 30 ducats annually, to come to Sant'Antonio the fourth Sunday of each month, after supper, "and bring with him also five musicians, that is an organist, two voices, [and] two violins (or a viola in place of one of the violins), who must sing and play motets from the beginning of the exposition through to the end, finishing with the litanies and *Tantum ergo*."[45] This, then, was not merely a liturgical event performed in polyphony, but a sacred concert of vocal and instrumental music, one designed quite specifically not for the brothers of the scuola, but for *il popolo*.

Beginning during the seventeenth century, the patriarch (with support from the government) began to organize a regular series of expositions of the Holy Sacrament, involving all the parish and nuns' churches in the city (each church performed the service two or three times per year), such that during every day of the year there would be at least one church performing the devotion. The exposition was performed using the ceremony of the Forty Hours Devotion, which involved an opening mass, continuous prayers for forty hours, and a concluding mass of reposition. This practice involved the scuole because in many of the parish churches, it was, as discussed above, the Scuola del Santissimo Sacramento that took responsibility for providing music whenever necessity demanded it (see appendix 2 for the expositions performed by these scuole as scheduled for 1699). The authorities did not specify how much music was to be employed at the expositions, but it was intended that at least the initial presentation of the Host and its reposition would be accompanied decorously. Some of the scuole appear to have done only the minimum required. For example, the Scuola del Santissimo Sacramento in San Canciano spent only 2 ducats for music at the first of the expositions in 1620, and barely more than 1 ducat at the third.[46] At the other extreme was the Scuola del Santissimo Sacramento at the church of San Geremia. In 1660, they hired Pre Giovanni Battista Faccini, a singer in the cappella of San Marco, to provided the music, paying him a total of 50 ducats. The following year, they again hired Faccini, and his payment, including this time music also for a procession during Holy Week, was more than 122 ducats. In 1663, the last year for which payment records exist, the expositions alone cost just over 70 ducats, and were entrusted to the well-known composer and organist Giovanni Battista Volpe (known as Rovettino).[47]

The Scuola del Santissimo Sacramento at San Geremia was not alone in its hiring of musicians for ceremonies during Holy Week. A procession on Good Friday evening, in fact, would become in the eighteenth century an important occasion for music (see also chapters 5 and 7 for similar processions at the scuole grandi), and the practice can be documented at some scuole from the early seventeenth century, primarily at Scuole del Santissimo Sacramento. The obligation of one confraternity in this regard was set out in a series of reminders to the guardian of the Scuola del Santissimo Sacramento in San Luca in 1675, to whom the brothers had allocated 10 ducats for both the priestly choir of the church and singers from outside, for the procession and ceremonies in the church.[48] No detailed records survive from San Luca regarding how this money was spent, but the situation at another Scuola del Santissimo Sacramento, at San Felice, was typical. This scuola, from as early as 1602, spent approximately 4 ducats annually on singers, often identified as priests, for the procession.[49] From the 1660s on, the scuola often made payments to a maestro di cappella (although the cost only rarely exceeded what it had been previously), notably, in 1678, to Gasparo Sartorio, a respected organist and composer. For several years in the 1680s, the scuola made payments not directly to the musicians, but to the sacristan of the church, who then made the arrangements.[50]

The Scuola del Santissimo Sacramento in San Giacomo dal'Orio did not provide music for a procession on Good Friday (perhaps the church retained that responsibility for itself), but did so instead for Corpus Christi (which was the natural celebration for scuole of the Holy Sacrament). Though the amount of money they spent in the seventeenth century was never great, usually 5 ducats, the scuola did make a practice of hiring respectable maestri, including the opera composers Zuanne Varischini in 1688[51] and Marc'Antonio Ziani in 1699, and the organist Alvise Tavelli (from the Basilica of San Marco) in 1698.[52]

Unlike similar confraternities in other cities, especially Florence, the Venetian scuole rarely appeared as beneficiaries of testamentary bequests calling for the performance of music.[53] An exception occurred in 1681, when the Scuola del Santissimo Sacramento in San Moisè was named in the will of a man named Zuanne Bonci. He instructed that 20 ducats be paid to the scuola each year so that an anniversary could be performed, "sung in music with instruments and organ."[54] From that point on, the scuola hired a maestro annually for the occasion, including, in the seventeenth century, Giacomo Spada and Antonino Biffi, both of them organists at St. Mark's.

Laude at the Fraterna Grande di Sant'Antonino

One confraternity is worthy of special attention, as it is the only one in the seventeenth century at which the singing of laude can be documented.[55] These references occur in the records of the Fraterna Grande di Sant'Antonino, a confraternity originally established by a group of wealthy Venetians to supply medicine to the so-called shamefaced poor (*poveri vergognosi*), respectable Venetians, including patricians, who had fallen on hard times. Unlike all the other Venetian confraternities, which bestowed their spiritual and charitable benefits primarily on their own poor brothers, Sant'Antonino's efforts were all directed outwards. In 1611 the brothers founded an oratorio, dedicated to Santa Maria dell'Umiltà, and established rules for celebration of the divine office there: "When a good number of brothers are gathered, the Reverend Father, if he is present, or the custodian will begin the Matins, which is recited in two choirs, but clearly, distinctly, and devoutly, and with voices rather low than high, and thus also will be sung the laude."[56]

All services, both masses and offices, were to be celebrated only in chant:

> At the altar of the oratorio, Holy Mass may be celebrated the first Sunday of each month and at the Assumption and Annunciation of the Glorious Virgin,

but mass may be said only by an approved priest; at no time are admitted in the oratorio concerto, song, or music, but both the divine office and the mass are celebrated with low voice.[57]

Revised rules of 1640 explain that instruments or other elaborate music were disallowed, in particular for the exposition of the Holy Sacrament, "so as not to distract from the mood of the devotion."[58]

Laude and other congregational singing also played a role in another venture of the Fraterna Grande, their Scuola Maggiore, which organized instruction in Christian doctrine. Each month the students displayed their knowledge of the catechism by a series of debates and sermons, the *disputa generale*. The confraternity regulations spell out the procedures in careful detail: after the prior arrives, "immediately everybody kneels and sings *Benedicta*."[59] Next, four students debate and prizes are awarded, followed by the singing of two laude by the students, divided into two groups, "for an interlude, and to relieve the tedium."[60] After two students conduct a discussion on an issue of doctrine, another lauda is sung, followed by a sermon by an advanced student, benediction by the prior, and another lauda. Then follow a group discussion, a lauda, and a series of concluding activities. At the end, while processing out of the hall, and before returning home, the students again sing a lauda.[61] In a 1639 revision of the rules, music provided by outside performers would be permitted, but limited to a few singers accompanied by the organ, and paid for by the scuola (that is, no officer could spend great sums to enhance his own prestige).[62]

There is only one indication that singing by members of a scuola piccola was not limited exclusively to the two lauda-singing confraternities discussed so far, the Scuola dei Fiorentini in the sixteenth century (see above, chapter 8) and Sant'Antonino. A 1671 decision by the council of the Scuola del Santissimo Crocefisso Centurato in Santa Croce seems to indicate the survival of a tradition going back to the earliest days of the Venetian scuole, though not otherwise documented after the fifteenth century: communal singing at the funerals of deceased members. At this scuola piccola, the officers apparently wanted either to maintain or to revive such a practice, and allowed the admission of six singers to the confraternity, with full benefits but without any expense, if they would teach the brothers to sing the *Miserere* at funerals.[63]

Organs and Organists

Not surprisingly, the construction and maintenance of organs and the employment of organists continued in the seventeenth century to occupy a considerable proportion of the time and money of some of the scuole piccole, especially the Scuole del Santissimo Sacramento. While in the eighteenth century, as will be shown below, these scuole often assumed complete responsibility for such matters, many in the seventeenth century merely assisted the parish priest and his chapter. For example, when it was decided, in 1609, to construct what may have been the first permanent organ in the parish church of San Mauritio, the Scuola del Santissimo Sacramento felt itself too impoverished to contribute more than 20 ducats. The officers would attempt to raise this amount by circulating a *rodolo*, or pledge list, among the brothers, but were prepared to dip into their alms box if necessary. They would pay the money either directly to the piovano or to the organ builder himself, Messer Vicenzo dalli Organi.[64]

At times, the original estimate for the cost of organ construction proved to be quite inaccurate, not without serious consequences to the budget of the sponsoring scuola. In 1607, when the church of Santa Croce decided to build an organ, the Scuola del Santissimo Sacramento offered to contribute 30 ducats "one time only."[65] Soon after, however, the brothers contributed another 25 "for one time only" to finish paying the carpenter and for the pipes. The payments, each one intended to be the last, continued: in 1614 to assist with the doors of the case, and in 1616 25 ducats for additional work. In 1626, the decoration of the organ began, and the scuola took up a collection for the 320 ducats needed. All but 50 were raised that way, and the remainder taken "for one time only" from the scuola's own funds. The next year, finally, the organ was completed with another 20 ducats spent on three paintings.[66] An original "one-time-only" payment of 30 ducats became, over twenty years, a total outlay of 420 ducats!

Even when the original cost estimate proved accurate, a scuola might find it difficult to come up with the money. In about 1618, the Scuola del Santissimo Sacramento in San Trovaso signed a contract with the organ builder Francesco Sandrioli to fabricate an organ for their church for a fee of 400 ducats.[67] By May of 1619, Sandrioli had completed most of the work, but had been paid so far only half his fee. He offered to install the pipes (presumably completed and waiting in his workshop) if he were paid 100 ducats immediately, and then 50 ducats in each of the two following years. The scuola did not have the funds in the budget, but, on instructions from the Provveditori di Comun, took 50 from the alms box, and agreed to collect another 50 in part from contributions by the brothers (in the form of a rodolo), and the rest by going around the city asking for alms, all because "this is such an honorable and necessary work, to honor and give praise to our Lord God and to His Glorious Virgin Mother Mary, our advocate."[68] They were willing, in other words, to jeopardize their charitable works in order to complete the instrument. Three years later, the funds still had not been found. The 50 ducats from the alms box had been put aside, but not paid, as the attempts to raise the remaining 50 (of the first 100 owed) had fallen 10 ducats short. Now, the guardian called a special meeting of the chapter to authorize taking another 60 ducats from the alms box immediately, and 30 more as soon as possible.[69] With this, a total of 180 out of the 200 needed, the scuola hoped to finish the job— perhaps the organ builder had agreed to discount the remainder of his fee (not an unheard-of practice) to get the matter over with.

Organs have always been notoriously expensive instruments to maintain, and can quickly become unusable if neglected, as several of the scuole discovered. They were, however, considered both necessary in a practical sense and vital for the honor of the churches and the confraternities they housed, so that the scuole were often willing to part with considerable sums (when they were able) to ensure a functioning instrument. The Scuola del Santissimo Sacramento in Santa Ternita, in 1636, examining the state of their church, determined that there was nothing as much in need of attention as the organ, "being in terrible state and most extreme need . . . such that it cannot be played."[70] So that the situation would not deteriorate further, they hired the organ tuner Nicolò, who examined the instrument and determined that it could be brought back to working order for 50 ducats, which they agreed to spend.

Sometimes it was the church that came to the scuola, employing the same sort of pitiable terms seen above to describe the state of the organ. This was the case when the convent of the Frari turned to the Scuola di San Francesco in 1626 for assistance with its instrument "which is found in a state of such destruction that it can no longer be played." Since the scuola needed the organ for its own festivities, the convent asserted, "it should make this donation happily and abundantly."[71] Despite the impassioned plea of the friars, the scuola agreed to part only with the rather paltry sum of 15 ducats.

Perhaps they were wise not to get further involved with the maintenance of the organ. The experience of the Scuola del Santissimo Sacramento in San Barnaba shows what might happen. Though they already paid 2 ducats a year to one Nicolò Lupini (perhaps the same man who had worked on the Santa Ternita instrument)[72] to maintain their organ, it was, in 1643, "in a bad state and in need of being repaired."[73] The scuola agreed with the piovano that, as long as it was guaranteed use of the organ, the right to place symbols of its participation on the case, and the power to elect the organist, it would pay for the needed repairs. The amount agreed to, and paid to Lupini, was 70 ducats. Less than three years later, in July 1646, the scuola was forced to pay another 40 ducats.[74] Over the next few years, it continued to salary an organ repairman, at about 2 ducats a year, and to make several small repairs, including one costing 10 ducats in 1655 and another of 15 in 1667. In 1672, the organ needed another substantial repair, this time for 30 ducats, but the officers were able to persuade the other two scuole in the church to begin annual contributions of 1 ducat each annually for maintenance and tuning, and 2 each toward the salary of the organist. Though the annual tuning and repair costs had risen to 3 ducats, this was insufficient to avoid yet another major (40 ducats) repair in 1689, after which, of course, the annual 3-ducat fee continued. Over the course of fewer than sixty years, then, the scuola had spent on the order of 250 ducats simply for tuning and maintenance of the organ (and the saga, it must be noted, continued into the next century, with nearly 75 ducats of repairs required in 1701).[75]

One of the more unusual incidents concerning an organ began in 1664 and involved the abbey and parish church of San Gregorio and its Scuola del Santissimo Sacramento. The organ in the church had been unusable for many years, as it was in quite poor shape. The brothers of the scuola came to Monsignor Erasmo Segreti, a resident of Venice who was the agent of Cardinal Flavio Chigi, the possessor of the abbey, and asked that the organ be turned over to them free of charge. They offered, in exchange, to repair and maintain it and to hire an organist, all at their own expense. Segreti agreed, imposing several conditions, contained in a notary document dated 17 April. He required that all repairs and renovations be completed within three years, and that the scuola should also rebuild the case in the "modern" style, leaving the old one in the event that the church should want to make use of it. The scuola was also to maintain the organ and, with the approval of the vicar, hire an organist who would play for both scuola and church, whenever requested by either party. Finally, the rebuilt organ should bear both the symbol of the scuola and of Cardinal Chigi. If these conditions were not met, the organ, and any work done on it, would revert to the possession of the abbey.[76] At the end of the three-year period, however, the conditions either had not been met or had been violated. Not only was the organ not repaired, but it had been removed from the church. On 27 May 1667 Segreti ordered the scuola either to restore the organ to its proper location or to supply a new one of equal size in its place.[77] Unfortunately, no further documentation has come to light regarding the conclusion of the dispute.

In most cases, the employment of the organist himself was not a matter of controversy. He was hired either by the church or the Scuola del Santissimo Sacramento with the salary sometimes divided, and often with small contributions from other scuole in the church. Problems sometimes arose, however. In 1614, the Scuola di Santa Croce in San Nicolò became dissatisfied with the arrangement, in which, though obligated to contribute 3 ducats a year toward the organist's salary, "we do not know who is playing [the organ], neither do we participate in the election of the said player."[78] The result was often that the organists did not show up for the scuola's services. The council decided that in future, the organist would be required to pay back to the scuola 3 lire for each time he missed, and that if the scuola was not allowed to participate in the election of any future organist, it would discontinue contributions entirely.

Sometimes a dispute between church and scuola could become so heated that government officials had to step in. In 1670 the Capi of the Council of Ten, to settle a disagreement at Santa Maria Mater Domini, instructed the brothers of the Suffragio del Santissimo Croce to use the organist hired by the church, unless he was unsatisfactory, in which case they could choose another, at their own expense.[79] A situation at San Cassiano became even more difficult, and eventually resulted in the Council of Ten getting directly involved in the selection of the organist. When, in 1672, it became necessary to choose a new organist, the church chapter and the banca of the Scuola del Santissimo Sacramento held separate elections and chose different players, each claiming the right to do so. The officers of the scuola requested, on 11 January, that the Capi of the Council of Ten either annul the chapter's election entirely, leaving the scuola's choice in place, in which event they would agree to pay his entire salary, or order a new election, to be held under the auspices of the scuola but with the participation of the chapter (in which joint meeting, of course, the scuola would have the majority). The chapter countered that they had the right to elect the organist, and cited a 1587 decision in which the Capi had annulled an election made by the scuola.[80] On 16 January the Capi called together both sides, annulled both elections, and declared that they themselves would choose the new player, someone other than the two musicians involved in the earlier actions. They brought in as an advisor the most prominent organist of the city, Giovanni Battista Volpe (known as Rovettino), to select four suitable candidates. Volpe offered the names of Nicola Galia,

Gasparo Sartorio (already organist at San Rocco), Giacomo Rubbi, and Antonio Zamberlli, and the Capi unanimously selected Galia as organist at San Cassiano for life.[81]

Perhaps the most heated controversies involved neither the construction and maintenance of the organ, nor the hiring of the organist, but the fundamental matter of ownership and control of the instrument. In other words, when a scuola built a new organ for its church, to whom did the completed instrument belong? The practical side of the issue regarded the question of who would hold the keys to the organ and whether scuola or church needed a license from the other to use the instrument. The most difficult and longest lasting controversy of this type involved the church of the Angelo Raffaele and its Scuola del Santissimo Sacramento. The early history is unclear, but it appears that around 1661 the piovano had refused to allow the scuola to use the organ for one or more of its observances, as it had always done in the past. The officers petitioned the Capi of the Council of Ten, who issued a decree on 30 August that the piovano "must not interfere in any matter pertaining to the Venerated Scuola del Santissimo Sacramento in that church," particularly regarding the use of the organ for ordinary Sundays and expositions of the Holy Sacrament.[82] The piovano apparently protested that his rights had been infringed upon, so, in May 1662, the Capi issued a new order. The scuola was, indeed, required to request a license from the piovano, but that license would be granted without question, and must "serve forever in the future, so that never again must either the current guardian, or those in the future, nor any other officer or anybody else in the scuola have any obligation to request anything at all in the above matter."[83] The required "permanent" license was issued two days later. This should have ended the matter, and things seemed to work smoothly for almost two decades. Apparently both scuola and church hired their own organists, but with no interference between the two.

The situation, however, took a turn for the worse around 1680. Beginning in 1677, the scuola undertook to build a splendid new organ, raising the immense sum of 1,200 ducats from its own coffers and from the private funds of its members and other pious donors. Of this, 800 ducats were paid to the builder Carlo di Beni, and the remainder spent for the case and other accessories.[84] When the instrument was completed, the scuola apparently turned over the key to the piovano, as was the custom, but the latter then interfered with the scuola's use of the organ, as he had done twenty years earlier. Once again, the case went to the Council of Ten, and on 9 April 1680, the Capi issued a decree that the piovano not only must cease interfering, but must return the key to the guardian of the scuola.[85] This order, which contradicted the one of 1662, opened the floodgates. Both sides amassed documentation to present to the Council. The scuola offered copies of receipts demonstrating their long use of the organ and the great expense they had gone to in the building of the new instrument. They also offered the precedent of a similar dispute between the monastic and parish church of Santa Croce and its Scuola del Santissimo Sacramento in 1666. In that case, the initial decision of the Provveditori sopra Monasteri, the government body in charge of monasteries and convents, ordered that the key of the organ should be held by the abbess, but when both sides presented their evidence, the fact that the scuola

had built and maintained the organ weighed heavily, and the decision was re-
versed, with the key returning to the guardian of the scuola.[86]

The church of the Angelo Raffaele presented not only the earlier decisions
of the Capi of the Council of Ten, which, though guaranteeing the scuola's rights
of use, also established the church's ownership, but also some more recent materials. Most decisive were the attestations they had gathered regarding the situation at the other parish churches of the city. They collected the signatures of
priests (usually, but not always the piovano) of forty-seven of the sixty parish
churches in the city, and two in Murano. Every one of these swore that they
themselves kept the keys to the organ. Thirty-eight also claimed full responsibility
for the organist. Six indicated that they kept the keys and elected the organist
even though the scuola paid part of the costs, and three others (plus one in
Murano), said that they kept the keys in spite of the fact that the organ belonged
to their Scuola del Santissimo Sacramento.[87] The council seems not to have been
concerned with the particulars of the remaining churches. Before the council
could issue a revised ruling, however, the two parties came to an agreement,
reestablishing, in effect, the earlier situation: though the organ might belong to
the scuola, the keys were to be kept by the piovano who would never interfere
with the scuola's use of the instrument; both scuola and church were free to hire
organists.[88] The agreement apparently, at least in the short run, went beyond that.
Before the end of the month, the scuola held an election for a new organist, who
would be obligated, for an annual salary of 25 ducats (as compared with the earlier
salary from the scuola of 10 ducats), to play at every occasion in the church,
whether the responsibility of piovano or scuola. The two candidates were the
former organist of the church (and one of its priests), pre Gasparo Fogliarol, and
the former replacement organist of the scuola, pre Gasparo Gaspardini. On the
second ballot, by a very close vote, Gaspardini won.[89] Peace was restored.

The Musicians' Scuola: The Sovvegno di Santa Cecilia

Dwarfing all the other annual confraternal celebrations in the city as regards the
number of famous musicians involved were the ceremonies for the feast of Saint
Cecilia in the church of San Martino, performed by the members of the Sovvegno
di Santa Cecilia, a confraternity that served the city's musicians, especially those
employed by the ducal cappella. This institution came about through the efforts
of Giovanni Domenico Partenio, vice maestro di cappella at St. Mark's from 1685
to 1691, who was also a titled priest in the parish church of San Martino, which
possessed an altar dedicated to St. Cecilia, the patron saint of musicians. In 1685,
wishing to increase the devotion this saint, Partenio prevailed upon the ducal
maestro di cappella, Giovanni Legrenzi, to compose and direct music for that
year's festivities, and many of the best musicians of the city, particularly those in
the cappella, consented to perform. Partenio himself agreed to take care of all the
expenses, including building the platform for the musicians, decorating the
church, and renting organs.[90] The event was a great success, and was repeated in
the two following years. Partenio and the others realized that the best way to

perpetuate the practice would be to found a confraternity, so in November 1687 nearly 100 of the city's musicians gathered together and elected Partenio and two others to make the necessary arrangements.[91]

It took nearly two years, but by November of 1689 the proposed constitution was completed and, with the approval of all the musicians, was submitted to the Council of Ten. The Council sought the opinion of the Provveditori di Comun, who made several recommendations, and the new Sovvegno di Santa Cecilia and its constitution were finally approved in September of 1690. Though this new institution was in some ways an ordinary trade-related scuola piccola, its difference from all the others was clear from the beginning. The opening of the first chapter of the scuola's constitution, exceptionally, deals not with the organization of the confraternity, but with the annual festa and its music, which was, in fact, the chief activity of the scuola:

> How and when the feast of Saint Cecilia should be solemnized:
>   The motion is made that the solemnity of Saint Cecilia must be sanctified with all the brothers singing the mass and vespers on 22 November at the usual hour in the church of San Martino; all of them should be used according to their abilities and in conformity with the need of the maestro or vice maestro, one of whom must organize the music, that is the maestro when he can, or if he is unable, the vice maestro.[92]

The following day, a funeral mass, again with all the musicians participating free of charge, was sung in memory of deceased members. In the event that neither the maestro or vice maestro were available (or if neither was a member of the sovvegno), the elected prior would select, by lot, from among those members who were composers.

The constitution makes it clear that only certain types of musicians were welcome to join the sovvegno, whose membership was limited to 100 brothers. The Provveditori di Comun had recommended to the Council of Ten that singers and instrumentalists could only be admitted after certification by the maestro di cappella (or vice maestro) of St. Mark's, but the final regulations are even more specific. Eligible for consideration were only those able to sing or play "all'improviso."[93] The significance of the phrase is not what a modern reader might expect, however: these are to be musicians who can read, or better, sight-read, music, as opposed to instrumentalists, particularly those who play for dances, who play "per prattica," that is, by rote. This was, therefore, to be a confraternity for the elite musicians of the city.

Further chapters of the constitution lay out the kinds of obligations and benefits that were usual for any sovvegno. Members were required to pay an entrance fee and monthly dues, and to pray and arrange for masses whenever a brother died. In exchange, in addition to the spiritual benefits deriving from funeral masses, they were eligible for financial support should they be ill, amounting to 2 ducats a week for up to three months, or longer with special approval. The requirement to participate in funerals apparently was the cause of some initial controversy, since the standard Venetian practice excluded instruments from such occasions:

even though this requirement might not appear just, since singers are obligated to sing for the death of instrumentalists, while instrumentalists are not obligated to play (since that is not the custom), it is nonetheless established that their mere presence, in clerical dress, is enough. And if there are among them any who know how and are able to sing, then they are urged to do so, but if they do not know how, or are not able, they are obligated to accompany the voices of the choir of singers with their hearts and with a continual silence, so as not to disturb the others and not produce a cacophony in the harmony of the music.[94]

The sovvegno salaried only one employee, a *bidello*, among whose tasks was "to assist in gathering up the papers [i.e. the music] for the maestro or whoever is the director of the music."[95]

This then, was not, like all the others discussed above, a confraternity that hired musicians for its religious observances, but a professional musicians' organization, whose chief function was to organize its members to celebrate the feast day of its patron saint.[96]

WITH JUBILANT VOICES

The Final Century of Music at the Scuole Piccole, 1700–1807

Though the eighteenth century is usually seen as a period of decline for the Venetian Republic, musical activities at the scuole piccole seem to have flourished. It is possible that an exaggerated impression results simply from the copious documentation that has survived, but it seems more likely that these years can be considered a golden age. Not only is there extensive evidence for elaborate music at the annual feste of many scuole, but similar activities can be documented for other regular occasions at many others. Some scuole began in the eighteenth century to employ regularly salaried musicians for the first time, including choirs of priests. And, as always, organ building and maintenance occupied the time and money of officers and members of a number of confraternities. On the other hand, this final blaze of musical glory might also be viewed as yet another symptom of the decadence of the Republic, emphasizing brilliant show over substance.

The Annual Festa and Freelance Maestri

For most of the scuole piccole, the musical focus in the eighteenth century remained on the celebrations of the annual festa. Few, if any, bypassed this opportunity for display, though the amount they spent, of course, varied substantially. Detailed documentation is lacking for most of the nearly 300 confraternities active during this period, but what survives is sufficient to indicate the wide variety of practices, which ranged from minimal enhancement by an organist or a pair of trumpeters to elaborate, multi-event celebrations lasting several days and involving dozens of singers and instrumentalists (see appendix 2).

Most of the scuole took advantage of a phenomenon that became widespread in Venice during this period (though its origins go back to at least the sixteenth century): the profession of freelance *maestro di musica*. In the eighteenth century there were dozens of men, many of them clerics, who—though often holding some sort of regular job, either as a singer or organist for a major monastic church or as a priest attached to a parish church—greatly enhanced their incomes by hiring themselves out to smaller institutions. Not only scuole piccole, but also nunneries and, as was discussed earlier, some of the scuole grandi, turned in this direction.[1] Instead of employing salaried musicians, therefore, the scuole piccole usually contracted for one occasion at a time with one of these maestri, who, for an established fee, would supply all the necessary performers, as well as the music they would perform.

The men documented to have been employed by the scuole piccole in the role of maestro di musica range from otherwise unknown priests appearing only once or twice to well-known professional musicians such as Baldassare Galuppi and Ferdinando Bertoni of St. Mark's (for a scuola located in the Basilica itself)[2] and Antonio Polarolo (who served at the Scuola della Beata Vergine del Gonfalon in San Bernardo, Murano, in 1723, 1726, and 1730).[3] The most often used of these maestri, however, all clerics, held minor musical posts at best, but clearly had widespread reputations in this particular area. For example, Don Giovanni Battista Scomparin was employed on at least twelve occasions at four different scuole from 1758 to 1785 (and also three times at the convent of San Daniele).[4] It should be noted that perhaps the majority of references to maestri in scuola account books omit the name of the person employed, referring to him only by title, making complete documentation of the careers of these men impossible. Don Pietro Scarpari, a tenor in the cappella ducale at San Marco and second priest at the parish church of San Bartolomeo, served at the Beata Vergine del Gonfalon seven years in the 1730s and every year but one from 1733 to 1746 at the Scuola del Santissimo Sacramento at San Moisè (though not for the festa, but for another annual occasion).[5] All this time, in fact from 1724 to 1756, he also served regularly for the convent of Sant'Andrea della Zirada.[6] Perhaps the most widely used maestro was Don Francesco Menegatti, who between 1764 and 1792 can be documented more than fifty times at thirteen different scuole piccole (inlcuding twenty years at the Scuola di San Gaetano in San Fantin).[7]

While some scuole relied for extended periods of time on a single maestro, who probably had become familiar with their needs, others switched constantly. This latter practice is well documented at the Scuola della Beata Vergine del Gonfalon in San Bernardo, Murano.[8] In the eighty-four years from 1719 to 1802 covered in the scuola's final account book, maestri are named for fifty (for seventeen there is no reference to expenditures for music, and for seventeen others payments are to an unnamed maestro). During these years, the scuola hired fifteen different maestri, only three of whom appeared five or more times (Giacomo Maccari five times, Pietro Scarpari six times, and, most frequently of all, Antonio Gasparini, nineteen times between 1753 and 1780); seven were used only once. We cannot know whether this frequent change was caused by the varied preferences of the guardiano, by the lack of ability of some of the maestri (which might explain why they were used once and never rehired), or simply because of competition: as a Marian confraternity, its feast day coincided with those of numerous scuole and convents throughout the city.

As mentioned above, the standard practice was for the scuola to pay the maestro for all (or nearly all) of the musical expenses for the festa. The maestro then provided, with those funds, the music and musicians for the required ceremonies. The minimum would have been a single sung mass on the day of the feast, but other ceremonies were often added, most commonly expositions of the Holy Sacrament, Vespers on the feast day, and Vespers (and even a mass) on the vigil. The fee paid to the maestro varied greatly, depending on the number of ceremonies and size of the musical forces required. In most cases, accounts record only the total fee, but occasionally they provide a little more information. In August 1766, for example, the Scuola della Beata Vergine della Cintura in San Giuseppe di Castello paid Giovanni Battista Scomparin about 13 ducats, for a "sung mass in the morning with a motet, and after dinner the Exposition with psalms and sonatas, and the reposition with the litany." Scomparin was to supply four singers, three violins, two "trombe da caccia" (probably horns), violone, and organist.[9] The approximate cost per musician of just over 1 ducat (clearly some would actually have been paid much more than others) seems to hold for a considerably more elaborate occasion: in 1719, the Scuola della Beata Vergine del Golfalone in Murano paid an unnamed maestro 24 ducats for twenty-four musicians (including eight singers) for Mass only on the day of the Visitation, its annual festa.[10] The year before, however, the cost for twenty-two musicians (with the same size vocal ensemble) was 35 ducats for both Mass and Vespers; the scuola also spent about two ducats for two trumpets (perhaps these were included among the twenty-four musicians the following year, as no separate payment was listed), and a bit more than 6 ducats for a choir of priests.[11]

These accounts enable us to imagine the splendor of those other occasions documented only by a total fee without specific reference to the number of performers. At the Scuola del Gonfalon in Murano, the amounts in other years remained consistently over 30 ducats, climbing once, in 1750, to almost 60.[12] While the Scuola della Beata Vergine del Rosario in San Domenico usually spent between 25 and 30 ducats for music on its festa, the amount rose to almost 50 in 1746 and 1749, and to 67 (paid to maestro Francesco Antoniacci) in 1747.[13] The Scuola dello Spirito Santo spent nearly the same amount (65 in 1748),[14] and the Scuola di San Giuseppe, which regularly after 1774 spent over 65 ducats, reached the extraordinary sum of 96 ducats (including almost 5 to brass and drums for an outside "concerto") in 1791.[15] Such high expenditures continued, in rare cases, even after the fall of the Republic: the Scuola di San Giuseppe continued to spend over 65 ducats each year from 1798 to 1802 and almost 50 in 1803, before dropping to about 32 for the last three years of its existence. On these occasions, the performers must have numbered in the dozens.

The Scuola del Corpus Domini, which had sponsored elaborate musical celebrations in the sixteenth century (see chapter 8), resumed the practice in the eighteenth, but in a manner different from that of most other scuole: the members elected a regularly salaried maestro for annual celebrations of the octave of Pentecost, their annual festa. It is not certain when this practice began, but a petition by the maestro in 1768, Giorgio Petrodusio, a member of the coro (not the cappella) of San Marco, states that he had served in the position for sixteen years.[16]

He had been responsible during that period for providing music for three functions, that is two Vespers and a Mass, for a total fee of 80 ducats. For this fee, he was obligated to provide a specified number of musicians (not listed here), which, he said, had become insufficient. He asked, and was granted, 20 ducats additional (for a total of 100), but in turn was required to add to the original specifications an oboe, a trumpet, a violone, and a violin, and also to guarantee that the singers be the best available.[17] Petrodusio continued to serve as maestro until his death in 1791, when the scuola held an election to choose a successor. The officers made an official announcement and two maestri presented themselves for the 21 April election, Don Biasio Caratelli (maestro di coro at San Giovanni Evangelista) and Francesco Gardi, with Caratelli victorious.[18] He continued in the same manner as Petrodusio, with the exception that from 1793 on the scuola paid him an additional 15 or 16 ducats to hire the choir of priests that had previously been the responsibility of the nuns of Corpus Domini, who had become too few and too poor to fulfill their obligation. Moreover, his duties, for the remarkable sum of over 110 ducats, now apparently also included a second Mass, on the Sunday in the Octave of Pentecost.[19]

For all of the scuole discussed so far, musical elaboration of their annual feste was one among many activities, a public display of the devotion that they expressed in other, more personal and practical ways throughout the year. For the Scuola di San Giuliano in the parish church of the same name, however, such musical display was the sole reason for its creation, as the organizers explained a few years after its founding: in 1747 twenty-eight priests gathered together and agreed to each contribute 10 soldi every month and, "for the honor of God and the greater ornament of the church of San Giuliano," to perform on the feast of that saint solemn Mass and Vespers and a musical celebration.[20] In 1749, the clerics were joined by secular members of the parish, and the combined membership revised the rules to provide for a funeral for each member, something typical of all other scuole. Each year, the scuola elected one or two presidents, a priest and an optional lay brother, to supervise the music for the festa. The presidents were allotted a substantial budget of 40 ducats for the musicians, to be paid to the maestro they selected, 12 ducats for the platform to hold the performers, and another 6 ducats for illumination.[21]

The officers appended to the 1749 resolutions a list of the musicians hired for that year, to serve as a guide to future presidents. It includes eight singers (plus one outside soloist) and nineteen instrumentalists (eight violins, pairs of violas, violoncellos, violoni, oboes, and trumpets, and an organ), many of them members of the cappella ducale. In 1751, "to bring to perfection the musical orchestra on the day of our solemnity," the scuola decided to include two more violas, at an additional cost of 2 ducats.[22] The brothers added another 10 ducats in 1753, though they required no specific enlargement of the musical forces; perhaps costs had simply risen.[23]

The 1750s and 1760s brought new problems to the scuola, however. The plans suffered a temporary setback in the mid-1750s, while the church was under repair. Since a full-scale celebration could not be carried out, the officers allotted only 14 ducats of the total budget of 64 to music; the remainder they designated to assist with the work on the building.[24] A different problem arose a few years later when, in 1763, the regular organ of the church had become so derelict that it could no longer be used. The presidents were constrained not only to provide two portable organs, but also to increase the number of instrumentalists to compensate for the missing organ. To assist them in this effort, the scuola increased the presidents' budget, until such time as the organ would again become usable, to the extraordinary sum of 100 ducats.[25] By the end of the decade, the musical costs began to seem extravagant, as many of the founders of the scuola had died, and either were not replaced or were succeeded by others with less interest in such display. The budget was consequently reduced to 50 ducats (though the presidents were no longer obligated to illuminate the altar), a sum which, though still respectable, substantially scaled back what must have been, for about two decades, one of the more notable musical events of the Venetian calendar.

Beyond the Festa: Other Regular Celebrations

As discussed in the previous chapter, the scuole piccole began in the seventeenth century to expand their musical efforts beyond their annual feste. This tendency continued in the eighteenth century (though, as mentioned above, some of this continued expansion may once again reflect the more completely preserved archives for this period). The most notable area of growth, not surprising for institutions that served as expressions of popular piety, was into areas that had traditionally remained informal and outside of organized religious settings: the *novena* of Christmas, the *triduo* of the Purification, the *triduo* of August, and the *ottavario* of the Dead, in November. Equally important were the solemn commemorations of the Passion during Lent, and, in particular, Holy Week. The practice of celebrating monthly Masses or weekly Compline services also continued in some confraternities.

The Novena di Natale

The *novena di Natale* was a traditional paraliturgical preparation for Christmas, beginning, as the name suggests, nine days before the feast; it served for individuals as did the Advent season for the formal church. In some cases, the musical portion of the novena was minimal. At the Scuola dell'Anconeta in 1726, for example, of the more than 30 ducats spent by the officers for the nine days, only 5, a little over one-half ducat per day, was for music (just over 16, on the other hand, were for candles).[26] This small expenditure, naturally, did not allow for anything elaborate. Instead, those attending the services heard only three priests singing with the organ. The records do not specify what the ceremony consisted of nor what music these priests sang; most likely they performed an organ-accompanied version of the traditional novena prayers or motets.

Several Marian confraternities, however, attached more importance to the novena, as demonstrated by considerably greater expenditures. The Scuola della Beata Vergine Assunta in Santa Maria in Broglio devoted more than 100 ducats to the nine days and Christmas itself, one-third of which covered expenses for music.[27] The Scuola del Rosario in San Paternian coupled the morning novena service with an afternoon exposition of the Holy Sacrament on each of the nine days, and, in 1783, hired Don Francesco Menegatti, the well-known maestro di coro, to provide music.[28] Though 10 ducats over nine days for two services each day is a rather small sum, the indication that Menegatti was obligated to provide the novena and litanies in music, with the organ, seems to imply something more than simple accompanied chant. Another Scuola del Rosario, in Santi Filippo e Giacomo, also regularly hired a maestro for the occasion, spending between 13 and 20 ducats each year for a choir and an organist.[29] Predictably, the men selected (for those few years in which names are recorded) also made the rounds of the various scuole on their respective feast days.

Tridui

The *triduo*, a traditional three-day observance, could occur several times during the year, most commonly in February, around the feast of the Purification, and on the first three days of August. Music can only be documented at one scuola piccola for the triduo of the Purification: the Scuola del Rosario in Santi Filippo e Giacomo (which also celebrated the novena in music). Beginning in 1741, it regularly hired a choir, often specified after 1743 as being made up of four singers, and an organist.[30] As with the novena, the exact nature of the ceremony and the obligations of the musicians are unclear, but one can assume the performance of settings of traditional Marian prayers, as well, perhaps, as a motet.

The triduo of August was a much more solemn affair, devoted primarily to remembrance of the dead. At the Scuola degli Agonizanti in San Raffaele (whose particular charitable activity was praying at the bedsides of those near death), the music was limited to organ accompanying priests, with a correspondingly small expenditure of only about 10 lire. Unusually, in 1776, the scuola also paid a certain Don Giuseppe Gritti to play the "liron" for the three days. It is unclear what specific instrument was meant at this point in the late eighteenth century, but it was probably some sort of bass that could join with the organ to accompany chant.[31]

The commemorations at the Scuola di San Pietro in San Simeon Profeta were considerably more involved. In a printed tariffa of 1781, the scuola budgeted a sum of about 32 ducats for a sung mass, the office of the dead, and the exposition of the Sacrament on each of the three days.[32] In a receipt signed in 1783, Don Biagio Caratelli, the designated "regular maestro of the company," accepted payment as "director of our music in the organ loft" for the three days.[33] The particularly lavish musical element in this observance for these years might be attributed to the fact that Caratelli, a well-respected maestro, was an officer of the scuola, serving as prior that year. As late as 1805, this scuola still observed the triduo, though with reduced expenditures, and a ceremony limited to "decorously" singing the *Miserere* at the exposition. This musical aspect, however, was clearly still of considerable importance, with a budget of about 18 ducats.[34]

The Ottavario di Morte

As might be expected, the most important commemorations for the deceased were linked to the annual Day of the Dead, 2 November. At a number of scuole piccole, especially those whose particular focus concerned the dead or dying, the events extended beyond the normal single day into an *ottavario*, the popular version of the true liturgical octave. The ceremonies centered around a daily exposition of the Holy Sacrament, accompanied by a sung *Miserere* (and sometimes the *Tantum ergo)*.[35] In addition, the Sunday within the ottavario featured a sung mass in the morning, and a procession (the destinations are not specified) in the afternoon. On the final evening at the suffragio in San Salvatore, after the concluding benediction of the Holy Sacrament, the choir sang the *De profundis*.[36]

In general, the musical expenses for the ottavario di morte were limited to a choir of priests, usually from the scuola's host church, and an organist. Several scuole, however, as on other occasions, hired a maestro to supply the choir, spending, consequently, appreciably more money. At the lower end of the spectrum were practices such as that at the Scuola degli Agonizzanti at San Raffaele, where the cost for the choir of priests for the entire eight days in 1767 was only a little over 1 ducat, with another ducat for the organist.[37] The Suffragio di Morti in San Geremia divided the responsibilities among several groups. In 1791 they entrusted the daily singing of the *Miserere* to the priests of San Geremia, for a fee of 12 ducats;[38] for the Sunday sung Mass and procession, however, the scuola's regular maestro di coro, Don Bortolomeo Riccoboni, hired a considerable number of additional singers, at a cost of 20 ducats, while both Riccoboni and the organist performed at all these occasions as part of their regularly assigned duties. The Suffragio di Morti in San Salvatore, on the other hand, hired a maestro specifically for the occasion, requiring him to bring a choir of sixteen singers (reduced in 1737 to twelve), and, for the final day only, perhaps for the singing of the *De profundis*, a violone player, all for an expenditure of nearly 28 ducats.[39] While these scuole drew the funds for this music from their regular accounts, two others, Santa Croce in San Pietro di Castello and San Gaetano in San Fantin, both of which regularly hired a maestro for amounts ranging from 5 to 20 ducats, made the expenditures out of the private funds of individual officers, who accepted this burden upon election to their posts.[40]

Lent and Holy Week

Of the extra occasions celebrated by the scuole that had origins in the official liturgical calendar (including feasts of saints other than the patron saint), by far the most important were the observances during Lent, and in particular Holy Week. Several scuole hired clerical singers for sung masses on Fridays in Lent, or for Mass in Holy Week, and the Suffragio di Morti in Santi Filippo e Giacomo annually offered expositions of the Holy Sacrament with singers and organ on eleven occasions during the period.[41] The central observance for the confraternities, however (once again, particularly those with a concern for the dead or dying), was a procession on Good Friday.[42] Though this is described in different ways in the records of the various scuole, a resolution passed by the chapter of the Scuola del Nome di Dio in San Domenico about 1775 (reinstating the procession after a period during which the practice had been discontinued), contains what may be the most complete account. The brothers, accompanied by a choir (at a cost of about 16 ducats), would go to four places: the church of San Sepolcro, the Cathedral of San Pietro di Castello, the Basilica di San Marco, and the local parish church.[43] Indeed, the visit to San Marco seems to have been standard for most scuole, while at least one other (the Agonizzanti in San Martino) refers to unspecified monasteries.[44]

The scuole that partipated in this type of procession (each took its own route) usually employed more clerical singers on this day than on any other occasion, with the possible exception of their annual festa. At both the Suffragio di Morti in San Salvatore and the Scuola di San Gaetano in San Fantin the coro included sixteen priests, directed by one of the freelance maestri discussed above, at a cost of between 17 and 25 ducats.[45] The Suffragio di Morti in San Geremia does not specify the number of singers in its records, but does refer, in 1753, to both *coro* and *coretto* (see above, p. 171); with an expenditure of 32 ducats, this probably indicates the standard choir of sixteen with the addition of a smaller ensemble of four or eight singers.[46] On an even grander scale, the Scuola dello Spirito Santo, as will be discussed below in further detail, employed two choirs of twelve (and later eighteen) voices each, and sometimes, in addition, a coretto. Whether this indicates some sort of antiphonal or *cori spezzati* style of performance, or just a division of duties, cannot be determined; similarly, the nature of the music sung for any of the scuole remains obscure.

Other Occasions

As has been discussed in previous chapters, the performance of weekly or monthly liturgical ceremonies with music was standard at the scuole grandi. Although the expenses involved in maintaining that kind of practice were beyond the capabilities of most of the scuole piccole, they can be documented at two of them in the eighteenth century, though on a smaller scale, of course, than at the larger confraternities. The regularly contracted maestro at the Scuola di San Pietro in San Simeon Profeta was paid the small sum of about 5 ducats, over the period of a year, for having played the organ at the scuola's regular function on the fourth Sunday of each month.[47] The Scuola del'Anconetta in the middle of the century paid 10 ducats to its organist, and another 5 for a priest to sing at Compline services on Tuesdays and Fridays throughout the year.[48] Clearly, the music in these cases could neither have been extended nor complex, and was, perhaps, nothing more than accompanied chant.

The practice of hiring musicians to enrich the performance of annual commemorative masses for benefactors of a scuola expanded somewhat beyond its minimal appearance in the seventeenth century. The oldest documented tradition, beginning in 1681, was the anniversary for Zuanne Bonci performed by the Scuola del Santissimo Sacramento in San Moisè according to specifications in his will (as discussed in the previous chapter). In the eighteenth century, the maestri hired to organize that commemorative service, to be performed with singers and instrumentalists in the organ loft, included most of the well-known freelance maestri, among them Benedetto Vinacesi and Francesco Menegatti.[49] Several other scuole paid small sums to their regular organist or priestly singers for similar occasions. The most ambitious of all came as a result of the will of Orazio Prandi Bisancio, a canon of San Marco, who left money (amounting to 5 ducats a year) so that the annual commemoration of his death performed by the Scuola di San Giuseppe in San Silvestro would be enhanced by the appearance of the singers of the ducal chapel.[50]

Salaried Clerical Singers: The Coristi

In musical terms, one of the characteristic differences between the scuole grandi and the scuole piccole was the reliance of the former group on regularly salaried musicians, while the latter usually employed freelance singers and instrumentalists as the need arose. This was, of course, a consequence of the vast differences between the two classes of institution in terms of the number of annual occasions on which music was required: dozens at the scuole grandi and often only one at a scuola piccola. As has just been shown, however, a few of the scuole piccole expanded their liturgical activities, especially in the eighteenth century: indeed, they bridged the gap, and joined the scuole grandi in the practice of hiring salaried musicians. Like the scuole grandi, who had switched from employing secular singers to priests in the eighteenth century, these few scuole piccole relied on clerical *coristi*.

It is not possible, unfortunately, to document precisely when these scuole began to hire coristi. The records (when they exist) are vague in the early years of the century about whether certain salaried priests are *mansionari*, that is priests hired to say masses funded by bequests to the scuola or by the scuola itself, or what were sometimes called *mansionari di coro*, that is, singers. It seems probable that the scuole began to use their regularly salaried mansionari when a choir was needed, and only gradually, probably around 1730, began to select them as much for their abilities as singers as for their moral probity, the chief standard for hiring a regular mansionario.

The earliest clear references to the priestly choir as singers occur in the same year, 1730, from the Suffragi di Morti at Santi Filippo e Giacomo and at San Salvatore, both as a consequence of problems that had developed, but both also implying that the mansionari had already been thought of as singers. At Santi Filippo e Giacomo, the officers realized that the priests they had been hiring simply were not up to the job, so they decided to ensure the quality of those they employed by selecting them only from among the group of thirty-three priests who were members of the recently founded Scuola di San Gregorio, in the same church, under the direction of a maestro with whose abilities they were already familiar.[51] The members of the Scuola di San Gregorio were described in their mariegola of 1725 (the scuola had actually been founded two years earlier in the church of San Geminiano before transferring to Santi Filippo e Giacomo)

as "priests cultivating the chant according to the use of the papal chapel" (documents in Italian refer to them as "reverendi sacerdoti cantori").[52] They further
characterized themselves and their goals as follows: "we are keen to train our
voices according to the standard of the art and the rule, so that they may bring
about that harmony which sweetly keeps the faithful in the church and entices
them to hear the divine offices."[53] Prospective members had to be recommended
by existing ones, and the officers had to determine their qualifications: "test
whether he has full knowledge of how to sing according to the use of the
chapel."[54] The Suffragio di Morti, therefore, could be quite certain they had hired
capable singers.

The officers of the suffragio regularly reconfirmed the coristi and maestro,
according to regulations, until 1750, by which time the situation had again deteriorated. They fired their existing choir, which had apparently failed both in
terms of quality and attendance, and decided to hire reputable priests to take its
place. The implication of the decision is that concerted music was no longer
considered worth the bother, and would be replaced with liturgical chant.[55]

The Suffragio di Morti in San Salvatore, the other scuola piccola whose
employment of a fixed *coro* can also be documented from 1730, proceeded somewhat differently. It had long employed a group of twelve mansionari, whose duties
included participation in the various ceremonies described above. Many of the
mansionari, however, had apparently been at the scuola, some as brothers as well,
for many years, having been hired when singing ability was not a significant factor
in their employment. In any event, when in 1730 it became necessary to replace
five aging mansionari, the documents record, for the first time, the voice parts of
the candidates to replace them: two contraltos, a tenor, and a bass.[56] In the following two years, the officers regularly reconfirmed the mansionari, but without
mention of voice parts. In January of 1733/34, however, the scuola apparently
began to take more seriously the musical qualifications of the mansionari, and
fired seven of the existing members of the coro because of their deficiencies.[57]
The replacements were three tenors, two basses, and two contraltos; two of the
remaining members of the previous choir were elected as *capo* and *sottocapo*. From
that point on, all confirmations and all elections of new members refer to their
voice parts, and with the designation *mansionari cantori* rather than mansionari.

It was not long before the officers realized that they needed to impose even
tighter regulations to ensure the correct and decorous performance of religious
functions, so in 1737 they fired all the existing singers and drew up some new
rules. First of all, the twelve members of the new choir (and all future replacements) were to be selected (by an officer assigned that duty) on the basis of singing
ability, with the requirement also that they become members of the suffragio,
either as members of the *deposito grande*, that is full members if qualified, or of
the *deposito piccolo*, the poor brothers.[58] As a confraternity devoted particularly to
the burial of the dead, funeral services were, of course, the principal obligation
of the coro. At every funeral, the choir was to accompany the body to the burial
site, and there sing the *Miserere;* upon returning processionally to San Salvatore,
they would sing the *De profundis* at the scuola's altar. As discussed above, the
suffragio performed solemn processions on the Day of the Dead and Good Friday,

for which a choir was required. Since, however, many of the priestly singers would have been obligated to serve at their home churches on those important days, they were permitted to send qualified replacements in their stead. The officers would also select from among the members of the coro one to serve as capo, and another as his replacement if needed. The newly elected *mansionari cantori* were to receive all the benefits of membership, but were relieved of all regular membership expenses except for the purchase of the cappa. Chief among these benefits, of course, was a funeral along with the offering, if they were members of the deposito grande, of 312 masses in their memory. Those in the deposito piccolo received burial but only two masses. Mansionari in the deposito grande received no payment for their services (that is, no payment before death), but those in the deposito piccolo received 20 soldi for each funeral. There were, as might be expected, penalties for failing to serve. Mansionari in the deposito grande were fined about one-third of a ducat for each absence, while those in the deposito piccolo had their payments withheld; for both, an accumulation of five absences was punished by expulsion.

The scuola considered a choir of twelve sufficient for funerals, but not for the ceremonies on Good Friday and the Ottavario della Morte, for which it required sixteen voices. Since the officers did not wish to support four voices during the entire year, these were to be hired as needed, with the advice of the capo. The scuola was to pay all sixteen singers at these ceremonies, whether or not members of the deposito grande, according to a fixed tariffa: about 18 ducats for Good Friday and almost 27 for the ottavario, with the capo (also referred to here as the maestro) receiving an additional fee for each event. In order that no mansionario could claim ignorance of the regulations, they were to be printed, and a copy given to each upon his election.

Over the following twenty years, the officers reconfirmed the members of the coro, replaced them following deaths or resignations, and sometimes even offered them retirement after many years of service. Among the members, at least two, Alvise Giorda and Antonio Moro, appear in the archives of other scuole as freelance maestri.[59] In 1753, in order to further encourage the coristi to do their jobs with the proper devotion to the suffragio, the officers decided to provide them with cappe at the expense of the confraternity.[60] That things had run smoothly for twenty years was somewhat remarkable, but eventually the situation deteriorated (a sequence seen frequently, as disussed earlier, at the scuole grandi). The mansionari cantori had begun to accumulate more frequent absences, and sometimes events took a decided turn for the worse, even resulting in unspecified scandals.[61] The officers decided therefore, on 3 October 1758, to fire them all, except for the two who were members of the deposito grande (clearly, over the years, more and more newly elected members had opted for a regular payment while alive rather than the extra masses after death). The officers were to hire a new choir made up of priests who would be selected for musical ability, quality of voice, and docile demeanor. Since it would have been impossible in the brief time before the Ottavario della Morte to find such a group willing to serve permanently, the guardian grande was given permission to select a temporary choir for that function only. By early December, however, the new permanent choir had been selected, with four each of tenors, contraltos, and basses (including four new members of the deposito grande), and everyone seemed pleased with the results.[62] The guidelines of 1737 were revised slightly, but essentially the duties of the choir remained unchanged, and the records through the 1780s (after which point no documents for the suffragio survive) indicate that the choir continued to operate smoothly.

The Scuola dello Spirito Santo, whose elaborate annual musical celebrations at Pentecost were discussed in the previous chapter, also employed, in the eighteenth century, a choir of priests, and followed a model almost identical to that of the suffragio at San Salvatore. Indeed, the first set of regulations, dated 1747, differs little from those of the suffragio of ten years earlier. The nine choir members were to participate in every funeral, singing the *Miserere* at the grave site. Further, on the Day of the Dead and each day of its ottavario, they were to assist at the High Mass and recite the office of the dead, and participate at the High Mass and reposition of the Sacrament on the feasts of the Holy Cross, the Redeemer, and Santa Maria della Salute, and on Fridays in March. For these services, they would each earn an annual salary of 20 ducats.[63] Within the year, however, the original guidelines proved inadequate, and in May 1748 the scuola decided to enlarge the choir to twelve members and name Don Alessandro Moro as capo, since he had been so successful as a director and in finding needed replacements.[64] At the same time, the chapter revised the rules for the procession on Good Friday. There were to be two choirs, each of twelve voices (one of which would be the regular choir, and the other hired for the occasion), to each of which, in jubilee years, would be added two able sopranos. The two choirs were to divide a payment of 20 ducats, with funds to be supplied by the officers out of their own pockets. In the event that the guardian in any year felt unable to provide two choirs, the scuola's regular coro was to be hired, at the reduced cost of 12 ducats (more than half the normal cost, presumably because the burden could no longer be shared between two choirs).

In 1755, the scuola's finances (or, at least, those of its officers) were apparently in good shape, as the officers decided to increase the number of singers at the Good Friday procession, and broaden the special duties of the regular choir, now under the direction of Francesco Manetti, who had been unanimously recommended by the choir to succeed Moro on his death in 1752.[65] The scuola increased the size of the choirs for Good Friday from twelve singers each to eighteen, at an added cost of about 14 ducats, increased the supplemental payment for the special mass on the Day of the Dead (leaving unchanged a similar payment for Pentecost), and added a third special mass, on the day the newly elected officers replaced those from the previous year.[66] The archives do not indicate how long the scuola was able to maintain such an elaborate and expensive system, but in 1758 the officers decided that the addition of a coretto beyond the two normal choirs was a luxury that they could eliminate (it is possible that what was actually meant was the second, freelance choir, but it is unclear why, with its size identical to the other, it would be called a coretto).[67] The scuola's coro was still active in 1778, when a new capo, Don Alvise Giorda, was chosen. Notably, he was still serving as maestro di coro at the Suffragio di Morti at San Salvatore at the time, a post he only resigned from in the following year, claiming that he was too busy to attend to his duties properly.[68]

Conflicts between the various jobs of the priests who served in the cori of the scuole are the reason for the only document that reveals the employment of a coro at yet another scuola piccola, the Scuola della Beata Vergine Assunta in Santa Maria in Broglio. In an undated decision of about 1782, the officers of the scuola decided to fire eight members of the choir (which included twelve coristi plus the capelano and sagrestano, who were required to join with them). Three were let go for simple incompetence, while the other five, though capable, were absent too often as a result of their service as titled priests at parish churches.[69] The new regulation banned entirely the hiring of titled priests, and reduced the total number of coristi to nine, which the officers felt would be sufficient, as long as they were competent singers and well behaved.[70]

Holy Year Pilgimages to Rome

As we have seen from the outset, the principal goal of most of the Venetian confraternities was to aid the souls of their departed brothers and sisters. They arranged for often elaborate funerals with numerous masses and performed regular commemorative masses for individuals and for all their deceased together. They also went in procession to churches where papal indulgences offered relief for souls in purgatory, and tried to obtain such indulgences for themselves. When, especially in the eighteenth century, the pope declared jubilee years with special indulgences for those who made the pilgrimage to Rome, it was an opportunity that some of the scuole could not resist. For two of these scuole, the Suffragio di Morti in San Salvador and the Scuola di San Gaetano in San Fantin, who were among those discussed above with expanded musical participation in their activities, the provision of a coro of clerical singers for the pilgrimage was considered essential, despite the elevated cost and difficult logistics associated with such a venture. The two scuole took quite different approaches to finding suitable singers.

The officers of the suffragio in San Salvador, recognizing the difficulties of transporting a choir to Rome, decided before the jubilee year of 1700 to try to arrange for a choir of Roman singers to meet them there upon their arrival. In January of 1699/1700 they wrote a letter to Abbate Valerio Rota in Rome[71] with a request for assistance, explaining the prohibitive expense of bringing a choir from Venice. They wondered whether he could find for them an appropriate choir of eight or ten, made up of sopranos, altos, tenors, and basses. After several anxious reminders from the scuola, Rota finally, on 30 January, provided them with the good news: he had arranged for a choir of musically trained priests, just as they had asked. The absence of any further exchanges on this issue lead to the conclusion that all went as planned.

The Scuola di San Gaetano took a rather different approach for their pilgimage in 1725, one that was more complicated and, undoubtedly, more expensive.[72] Instead of contracting for a choir to meet them in Rome, they arranged with a Venetian priest to put together a choir of eight to travel from Venice to Rome to assist the brothers there. For the trip itself, the scuola arranged for a boat to take the singers from Venice to Pesaro, from which point they would make their way to Rome either on foot or on horseback. The guardian paid for the boat to Pesaro, and the scuola gave the singers 20 ducats each to cover the remainder of the expenses of the round trip, including food, lodging, travel from Pesaro to Rome, and the entire return to Venice. Once in Rome, the singers were to receive a daily fee of 5 lire to cover their services (which, unfortunately, are not described) and food and lodging. The scuola hoped to receive room and board for themselves and their singers from its affiliated confraternity in Rome, the Santissima Annunziata, but the singers were not to ask for additional payment even if the hoped-for arrangement did not materialize. The singers were obligated to serve the Venetian scuola in all its liturgical and musical needs for the entire stay, and were forbidden from offering their services to any other church or confraternity until their duties with San Gaetano were completed, and were not under any circumstances to assist any other Venetian scuole who might also be in Rome for the jubilee. The eight priests all signed the agreement, and, it seems, went to Rome as planned. The maestro, Mattio Rubelli, received in April and May the payment for the voyage and the sixteen days in Rome (plus one additional beyond those planned), as well as an extra fee for a last-minute replacement for one of the original eight singers who had fallen ill. In all, the scuola paid just over 280 ducats for the services of its choir.

The 1725 trip must have been a success for San Gaetano, since, when planning for another pilgrimage for the 1750 holy year, they decided to follow the same course, though using their regular maestro di coro instead of hiring one especially for the event.[73] The singers asked for an increase in payment over the previous time, demanding 30 ducats for the voyage (instead of 20) and a payment of 5 Roman paoli a day instead of the five Venetian lire offered in 1725.[74] The scuola agreed, but with the stipulation that the singers would provide their own boat for travel between Venice and Pesaro. Restrictions on the activities of the singers in Rome similar to those in 1725 were included in the agreement, as was the insistence that they not ask for additional payment in the event that the scuola could not arrange lodging in Rome with the Confraternity of the Santissima Trinità. In the hope of obtaining that lodging, the singers were made brothers of San Gaetano, which also meant that they could partake of all the spiritual benefits accruing to the pilgrims as well.

Though maestro Conagin provided names of likely coristi, the scuola insisted on open auditions (to ensure the suitability and capability of the candidates) for a choir of two sopranos, three tenors, and three basses. Once again, the singers all signed agreements, and the scuola established a budget for the entire operation of 250 ducats, which would include, in addition to the eight Venetian priests, two sopranos (perhaps castrati) to be hired in Rome. The cost of the entire trip, including candles, chaplain, banner, and gifts for their hosts and others in Rome, but not including the travel expenses of the brothers, who would have to sustain that cost themselves, was 1,730 ducats.

This time, however, unlike in 1725, things did not go as planned, as we learn from a document of early April, when the majority of the singers decided, almost at the last minute, that they did not wish to make the trip. Given the restrictions of time, the scuola decided to proceed as had the suffragio in San Salvador in 1700, and hire a choir of twelve of the "most able and most distinguished" persons in Rome.[75] Apparently, since they did not have to spend money to send the singers all the way from Venice, the officers decided they could afford a larger and more capable group of singers, which would, in the end, bring them more honor and less aggravation.

Organs and Organists

As far as organs and organists were concerned, the eighteenth century was no different for the scuole piccole than earlier centuries: for many, especially Scuole del Santissimo Sacramento, this instrument and its players represented their principal musical activity. They continued to be involved in (and often direct and fund) the construction, repair, and maintenance of organs, and the hiring of organists. The archives of the scuole, in fact, are rich sources for contracts for the building of new organs, including some by the most important makers of the period, and can add much to our understanding of the history of this instrument in eighteenth-century Venice.

The variety of ways the scuole handled the tremendous expense of building a new organ provides some insight into the importance these projects had for the confraternities and their host churches. Some of these methods were already in use in earlier centuries, while at least one is new to the eighteenth, and comes as a result of some of the liturgical changes discussed above. One of the traditional methods can be seen in the series of restorations and rebuildings undertaken at the church of San Marziale, with the significant participation of the Convicinato, which occupied the place in this church that the Scuole del Santissimo Sacramento did in others. In 1706, with construction nearly completed, the piovano (the chief priest of the parish), speaking on behalf of the chapter of the church, approached the Convicinato council, and, reminding them both of the importance of an organ to the church, and of their past generosity in such matters, appealed for a donation of 200 ducats (the same amount the scuola had given three years before, probably for the commencement of the work), which the scuola agreed to pay, in two annual installments.[76]

When the piovano approached them again in 1748 for funds for an urgently needed repair of the organ, the officers agreed, with the condition that the payment of the 20 ducats only be made upon completion of the work (to be undertaken by Francesco Capelli), and after it had been judged acceptable by experts.[77] The effects of this repair were short-lived, and by 1760 the situation had gone too far downhill to be ignored, since, as the piovano explained to the Convicinato, the organ was now entirely useless for any sacred function.[78] The task of assessing the necessary repairs was undertaken by the well-known builder Niccolò Moscatelli, who had recently built or restored organs at San Moisè, San Canciano, and Sant'Alvise.[79] He came to the conclusion that a major rebuilding, at a cost of 350 ducats, was the only solution. The chapter of the church demonstrated its commitment to the project by offering 100 ducats, which had originally been designated for some new liturgical apparatus, but which they would divert for this most pressing need. The Convicinato agreed to pay the remaining 250 ducats from its apparently healthy accounts.

The 350-ducat price set by Moscatelli had been a reduction agreed upon, as the piovano explained, after lengthy negotiations. The builder, however, whether in the hope of getting more money, or because he really believed it was necessary, did more in the reconstruction than had been called for in the agreement, and added two new ranks, eight-foot and sixteen-foot *tromboncini*, to make the organ "harmonious and perfect."[80] Having done this, he then, in 1762, appealed for a donation, which the Convicinato granted in the amount of 30 ducats. Two years later, after he explained that the actual cost of the new ranks was 60 ducats, the scuola offered him another 10, particularly since he had agreed with the piovano at the time of the construction of the organ to maintain it without cost.[81] The 10-ducat gift quickly became an annual retainer for tuning and maintenance.[82]

Moscatelli undoubtedly expected to be selected in the event of any further restorations or repairs, but when, in 1787, the banca designated one of officers to spend the 50 ducats deemed necessary for a major renovation, he chose some-one else, Gerolamo Amadio, who, at an actual cost of 60 ducats, 10 more than originally planned, brought the organ back to what the officer in charge of the operation called in 1789 "a state of perfection."[83] It turned out, however, as expressed in a presentation ten years later, that this assessment was not quite accurate. Examinations of the instrument, first by Moscatelli, and then by two other builders, Francesco Merlini and Giulio Martinelli, determined that Amadio had not only left the organ in worse state than before he worked on it, but had omitted several ranks altogether when he reassembled it. The end result, of course, was an additional expense, and the rehiring of Moscatelli, who also resumed his steady job as repairman, apparently until the suppression of the scuola in 1806.

The practice of sharing the expense of a new organ between the church itself and a scuola was a common one. In addition to San Marziale and its Convicinato, similar scenarios played out at the monastic churches of Santi Giovanni e Paolo and San Giacomo della Giudecca. At Santi Giovanni e Paolo in 1790, when the Dominican friars wished to rebuild their organ, they turned to the Scuola del Rosario (which had, in fact, recently been named a scuola grande), which contributed 100 ducats toward the expense.[84] The Scuola di San Giacomo di Galizia, hosted by the Servite brothers of San Giacomo della Giudecca, shared one-third of the 450-ducat cost of a new organ in 1788.[85] Though the Scuola del Rosario had been able to pay its share immediately, in one lump sum, the much smaller and poorer Scuola di San Giacomo first thought of paying 25 ducats in each of six annual payments, but even that proved too great a burden, and settled on the sum of 10 ducats for fifteen years.

Similarly, the Suffragio di Morti in the church of Santi Filippo e Giacomo agreed in 1725 to aid the chapter of its church, which had been forced to take out a mortgage on some of its property to cover the 600-ducat cost of a new organ, in the amount of 10 ducats annually for ten years, with the provision that the organist of the church supply also the needs of the suffragio for expositions of the Holy Sacrament, the Day of the Dead, the feasts of St. James and St. Anne, and services in Lent, all at no additional expense.[86] After the ten years had expired, the suffragio agreed to an annual expenditure of 2 ducats to cover their share of the maintenance of the organ and, as before, the services of the organist for their needs.[87] When, in 1791, Francesco Merlini assessed the costs for repairing the then badly deteriorated organ at 35 ducats, the suffragio felt capable of supporting nearly half the expense.[88]

In a number of cases, the host church contributed nothing to the construction of its new organ, leaving it entirely up to its Scuola del Santissimo Sacramento. At San Barnaba, where in the previous century the scuola had agreed to maintain the organ as long as it had the right to place its symbols on it and to use it when necessary, a major renovation became inevitable in 1701, because the instrument was broken, and unusable for sacred functions, and thus "indecorous for the church and scuola."[89] The banca contracted with Antonio Giorgio of Uderzo for the job, and covered the cost, 74 ducats, with contributions from the officers of the scuola and other residents of the parish; at the completion of the work, the scuola proudly compiled a list of contributors who had made the project possible.[90] Similarly, the Scuola di San Giovanni Battista dei Battuti in Murano, which operated its own church, was unable in 1759 to cover the 825-ducat cost for a new organ and case out of its regular funds. Each officer was asked to contribute 50 ducats to the project, with the promise (whether or not it was fulfilled is unclear) that the "loans" would be repaid as funds became available.[91]

When the church of San Barnaba underwent major renovations in 1736, the Scuola del Santissimo Sacramento took charge of the dismantled organ, keeping the pipes in the albergo, and entrusting the bellows and other materials to the organist.[92] The brothers elected two officers to decide what to do with the material, and an examination showed that they could not be used in the new organ that would be built, both because of the damage that would result from long storage, and because they were of poor quality to begin with. The officers decided, therefore, to sell them, but with no success, as an entry in an inventory of the scuola's belongings in 1775 shows that the pieces (valued at about 6 ducats as firewood) remained in storage.[93] In 1739, realizing that the church would not be finished for quite a while, the officers decided, with the aid of a small contribution from two other scuole located there, Sant'Anna and Sant'Apollonia, to purchase a small organ for only 50 ducats.[94] When the church was finally completed decades later, in 1772, the scuola decided to build an organ worthy of their rebuilt home and hired Francesco Merlini. The magnificent new instrument, at a cost of 650 ducats, was to be housed in an equally splendid case, costing another 250 ducats. The scuola, surprisingly, was able to cover the entire 900-ducats expenditure out of its own funds, without the help of Sant'Anna and Sant'Apollonia.[95]

Such expenditures, however, were not usually possible for Scuole del Santissimo Sacramento, especially since several new obligations had been imposed upon them during the eighteenth century. One of the most burdensome, in terms of finances, was the system of continual expositions of the Holy Sacrament *per carta*. The patriarch (supported by the Provveditori di Comun and Provveditori sopra Monasteri) issued an annual schedule for these expositions, printed (on paper, thus the designation) and posted in every church, that guaranteed that on every day of the year, at least one parish or nunnery church would be open for that purpose, and would be suitably prepared and with appropriate music. This meant usually two three-day periods each year for each church. While the nunnery churches were required to undertake the task directly, at the parish churches the obligation was shifted to the Scuole del Santissimo Sacramento, with predictable consequences for their budgets (appendix 2 includes the assignments of expositions to the Scuole del Santissimo Sacramento for 1698, as an example). The problem, and its solution, can be seen in a petition submitted by the Scuola del Santissimo Sacramento in San Simeon Profeta to the Provveditori di Comun in 1745 (a similar one was presented simultaneously by the chapter of the church to the patriarch). They pointed out the disastrous state of the organ, caused in part by the rebuilding of the façade of the church, and the urgent necessity of building a new one. This, however, was well beyond their capabilities to pay for, so they asked that the scuola be relieved of the obligation of one of the annual expositions for ten years. This would save at least 80 ducats a year, sufficient to build a new organ, "a work so necessary, in order to decorate the holy functions, to the greater glory of God, and so that the church might exclaim with jubilant voices, *Laudate eum in cori et organo*."[96] The Provveditori granted the petition, as seems to have been the norm. Similar petitions were made by the Scuola del Santissimo Sacramento in San Cassiano in 1742 (where two annual expositions were both suspended for ten years), at Santa Maria Maddalena in 1745 (one exposition for ten years), at San Polo in 1757 (one exposition for ten years), and at San Simeon Profeta again in 1792 (one exposition for ten years).[97]

The building and maintenance of a church organ was, of course, only the beginning, as clearly expressed in a petition to the Scuola del Santissimo Sacramento in San Moisè from the chapter of the church in 1753:

> Just as the organ was built by a distinguished maker with the union of many registers, it required a distinguished player, who knows how to manage it well, and since a distinguished maestro had been found, who can always shine to the pleasure of the parish and the entire city, so does he merit an appropriate salary, which would not be far from the merit of the musician.[98]

In this case, the handsome salary of the new organist was to be contributed by three sources, 30 ducats from the chapter, 20 ducats from the scuola, and an unspecified amount from the *fabrica*, the council of laymen that managed the physical properties of the church. The scuola agreed to make this contribution for a period of five years, a term regularly renewed in future years.

The importance, and consequent monetary value, a scuola placed on the playing of the organ could vary considerably over time. The Scuola del Santissimo Sacramento at San Barnaba which, as shown above, devoted considerable effort, and hundreds of ducats, to the building of the organ in their church, paid their organist Domenico Martinelli for the period 1746 to 1759 only the small sum of 2 ducats annually.[99] When he then asked for an increase, the scuola, citing his excellent service, agreed to raise the salary to the still meager sum of 5 ducats, rather than the 6 he had requested. Perhaps the low salary was in part related to the situation of the instrument—the permanent organ had been dismantled during the reconstruction of the church, and Martinelli would have been playing a smaller instrument, perhaps even a portable one. In any event, after completing the new organ in 1773 to everybody's great satisfaction, at a cost of 900 ducats, the scuola apparently reconsidered its position: now it needed to find a player equal to the instrument. The officers felt that the salary they could afford, 40 ducats (comprising 30 from their funds and 10 more from the chapter and other scuole) was not sufficient to hold a formal election (even though it was eight times what they had previously been paying). They had, however, identified someone who would do the job well, the maestro di musica Don Giorgio Petrodusio, known as Il Zorzetto, and hired him.[100]

Six years later, in 1779, the guardian and his companions finally felt that the budget was in good enough shape that they could add 5 ducats to the 40 they were paying, and hold a formal election, according to the regulations established by the Provveditori di Comun. On 28 November, the announcement of the competition was made at the door of the church, and two candidates submitted their names, the incumbent, Petrodusio, and Stefano Fedeli. After each had played, the officers and chapter retired behind closed doors and voted, giving the nod to Petrodusio by a substantial margin.[101] Upon Petrodusio's death in 1790, the scuola elected Antonio Lucadelli, a priest at the church of San Geremia, but replaced him in 1792 with Pietro Fedeli, perhaps the son or nephew of the unsuccessful candidate in the 1779 election.[102] Fedeli served until the suppression of the scuola in 1807.

The salaries and obligations of the organists of the various scuole provide a clear indication of the wide divergences in the amount of music they sponsored. For many, the organist apparently played only on the major feast and perhaps once a month at the regular commemorative mass, for which limited services the scuola spent only 2 or 3 ducats. At the opposite end of the scale was a scuola such as the Santissimo Sacramento at San Tomà, which had taken on all the responsibilities of music for its church. The mariegola recorded the duties and emoluments of their organist as newly codified in 1784. The organist was to be paid an annual salary of about 44 ducats, just about what the San Barnaba organist received. This consisted of 30 ducats from the Scuola del Santissimo Sacramento, 6 from the chapter, plus additional small amounts adding up to almost 8 ducats.[103] In exchange for this considerable salary, the new organist had a long list of obligations, carefully set out in the mariegola.[104] These consisted for the most part of the High Mass or Vespers (or both) every Sunday and on numerous feasts, and several expositions of the Santissimo Sacramento. In addition to the fifty-two Sundays of the year, the list included sixty-two feasts; altogether, he had to play over two hundred services (including ninety-six masses, ninety Vespers, twenty expositions, and one Matins). It is difficult to know how elaborate or sophisticated this music was, but there is no doubting that there was a great deal of it.

UNLIKE THE SCUOLE GRANDI, whose decline in the eighteenth century can be tracked with some consistency, the scuole piccole seemed unaffected, in terms of their sponsorship of music, until almost the moment of their suppression. Indeed, about thirty confraternities (the Scuole del Santissimo Sacramento in the consolidated parishes that resulted from the Napoleonic reforms) were allowed to continue operating after the suppression of the rest, and throughout the nineteenth century. They worked with the parish priests as representatives of the local people, and continued, in many cases, to play a major role in the musical activities of their churches.

11

CONCLUSIONS

The traditional approach to studying a city's musical history—with its focus on major institutions such as the cathedral, the court chapel, and the opera house, and on the music that posterity has considered the most important—does not, in truth, provide a complete and accurate picture. It is limited, by its very nature, to just a few of the many active institutions, to the patronage of a small elite, to only a portion of the working musicians, and to a small percentage of the geographical and social spectrum of a city. In Venice, this type of approach has resulted in a history with only three or four significant features: sacred music at the ducal basilica of San Marco in the sixteenth and seventeenth centuries, with such composers as Adrian Willaert, Andrea and Giovanni Gabrieli, and Claudio Monteverdi (along with the production of madrigals and the like by the same men); the world of opera in the seventeenth century, especially the activities of Monteverdi, Francesco Cavalli, and Antonio Cesti (and an international cast of star singers); and, finally, the curious phenomenon of the female musicians at the *ospedali*, and in particular the music of Antonio Vivaldi. This picture certainly places Venice in the forefront of European musical developments, as one of the great cultural centers for three centuries. It is an attractive, even exciting picture, but it is a misleading one that omits the vast majority of performers, patrons, and listeners in a city that did not, in fact, have just a few musical centers, but was, in many respects, permeated by music performed by local musicians, with local patronage, and for a wide and varied audience. While the major institutions will inevitably remain at the center of the picture, it is only through widening the frame to include such sponsors of music as the confraternities (and also nunneries, monasteries, parish churches, guilds, and the like) that the real image can begin to come into focus. An important step in this process was taken by Elena Quaranta, in her recent book *Oltre San Marco*. This study is notable for its breadth, for the first time taking into consideration parish and monastic churches as well as confraternities, but it is limited in its scope, being restricted to the Renaissance, and to certain types of documentation.

The sequence of musical styles in the traditional view of Venetian sacred music is a fairly simple and straightforward one: from the *a cappella* Renaissance style of Willaert, to the multiple-choir concerted motets of the Gabrielis, to the large- and small-scale sacred *concerti* of Monteverdi and his successors, to the High Baroque choral works and motets of Vivaldi. Certainly, a portion of the music at the confraternities followed this same sequence, as their leaders strove to emulate, above all, St. Mark's. In the sixteenth century in particular, the scuole grandi did their best to engage singers from the ducal cappella, who undoubtedly performed the same sort of music as they did in their principal jobs. Even when the scuole could not sustain this sort of musical activity throughout the year, the annual feste (of scuole piccole as well as scuole grandi) continued right through the fall of the Republic at the end of the eighteenth century to include music by the most important composers in the city, and therefore in the latest styles, rivaling (or even surpassing) in splendor their more famous counterparts. But the picture was, in actuality, far more complicated than that. Alongside the "mainstream" styles, the scuole sponsored several other sorts of music absent from the usual view.

Throughout their histories the scuole accompanied their religious celebrations with chant, a constant that is far too often neglected in musical histories of the periods after the arrival of polyphony. The confraternities entered into agreements with churches, both secular and monastic, to provide chant, and some, especially the scuole grandi, employed their own priests, sometimes even paying for the copying of manuscripts containing the required chants. Through the fourteenth century, the brothers of some of the scuole provided yet another sort of music, singing as a group in processions and at funerals, a task that was then taken over by selected brothers and, in part, by paid professionals. This music, including laude (unfortunately none associated with the scuole survives), continued to be used even after the scuole began to employ more expert singers. In addition, and unlike many other sorts of religious institutions, the scuole grande included instrumental music both in their processions and in their church services (though, once again, little can be discerned about the music itself). Around 1500, then, at a Venetian scuola grande, one might encounter some five different sorts of music: chant sung by priests (accompanied by or alternating with organ), simply harmonized music sung by poor brothers at funerals (cantadori di morti), polyphonic laude sung by semi-professionals (cantadori de laude), an instrumental ensemble of bowed and plucked strings (shortly to be supplanted by a violin band), and sophisticated motets and masses performed by singers from the ducal chapel (cantadori solenni).

Practices at the confraternities changed in the later seventeenth and eighteenth centuries, in large part for financial reasons, but perhaps also in the spirit of the Counter-Reformation. While the annual festa still included elaborate and up-to-date Baroque-style music, the scuole eliminated some of the other layers—in particular salaried professional singers and instrumentalists—and replaced them with choirs of priests. These men, performing *a cappella* during processions and accompanied in church by the organ, sang a sort of music quite different from that of composers like Lotti or Vivaldi: simple three- or four-part polyphony and falsobordone. It is this kind of music, in fact, that seems to have dominated the Venetian musical scene in the Baroque, while the more elaborate styles were reserved for special occasions and used on a regular basis at only a few extraordinary institutions.

Naturally, such a wide variety of musical styles called for an equally wide variety of performers. The documents of the scuole are filled with names of musicians far different from those who performed at St. Mark's or in the opera theaters (though some of them appear as well). Venice was home to hundreds of singers and instrumentalists, and dozens of organists, who never held a performing post that paid a living wage, but instead had to piece together adequate incomes from jobs at the scuole and elsewhere. There were also hundreds of priests who could not have survived solely on the payments they received for saying masses, and instead filled the ranks of choirs at the scuole, both in salaried positions and for single occasions throughout the year. Even for the high-level musicians of St. Mark's, the scuole were essential. This latter point is attested to by the eagerness of these men to serve at the scuole even for relatively small fees, and by their desperation when their attempts in 1552 to solidify their incomes by forming a company to monopolize the best jobs resulted in a ban on salaried musicians at the scuole. Even the Procuratori di San Marco, the employers of the cappella singers, recognized during that incident that the wages from the scuole were essential, and that they would have to increase salaries if those opportunities disappeared.

While salaried positions at the scuole certainly provided a steady income for a corps of singers and instrumentalists, the real gold mine for Venetian musicians was the series of annual feste and, later, expositions of the Holy Sacrament. In 1620, Claudio Monteverdi, deflecting an offer of employment from Duke Ferdinando Gonzaga, explained to Alessandro Striggio that he could easily add half again to his salary from St. Mark's by accepting jobs from the scuole for music at their feste.[1] Would Monteverdi, or any other famous composer, have remained in Venice so long without such opportunities? Appendix 2, which lists (to the extent possible with surviving archival documents) the feste, processions, expositions, and similar occasions at all the scuole, shows how extensive these opportunities really were: by the eighteenth century, there were, potentially, over 1,000 occasions each year at the scuole for which music of some kind was employed. While the elite musicians undoubtedly got the most prized jobs, there were many poorer scuole that could only afford second- or third-rank performers, and on the most important feasts, when many scuole celebrated simultaneously (see, for example, the feast of the Assumption, 15 August), it is likely that every available singer or instrumentalist found work. Add to this the feste of parish churches and nunneries (and the celebrations of events involving individual nuns), and Venice could support a roster of professional musicians many times the size of the ducal cappella of San Marco.[2]

An important aspect of the myth of Venice, so carefully cultivated over the centuries, was that all classes of society had important roles to play, not only the patricians who ran the government, but also the citizens and even the merchants and other *popolani*. In the traditional picture of Venetian musical history, however, it is almost exclusively the patricians who appear as patrons: St. Mark's, the state church, was the chapel of the doge, the *ospedali* were governed by committees of noblemen, palaces of the upper class were the sites for private music-making, and the opera houses were supported above all by members of the patrician class (though non-patricians ran some of the theaters and made up a portion of the audience). As the present study has demonstrated, however, that picture is far from complete. With very rare exceptions, the Venetian confraternities were run by non-patricians: citizens for the scuole grandi, and citizens, merchants, and even ordinary popolani for the scuole piccole, and it was these men (and very occasionally women) who desired, organized, and paid for the hundreds of musical events sponsored by the scuole annually. Members of a scuola, no matter what their social or economic status, could rightfully claim to be patrons of music and the arts.

The confraternities probably made their greatest impact in the expansion of the audience for music, both socially and geographically. The standard history has described just a few institutions, most of them centrally located, with audiences primarily made up of patricians, foreigners, and wealthy citizens. The scuole, however, as illustrated in appendix 2, sponsored music on approximately three hundred days each year, in more than one hundred churches (on some days in several dozen simultaneously), throughout every district of the city, with processions in nearly every public space, bringing music not only to the brothers and sisters of the confraternities, but to practically the entire population. Through their desire to honor God and their city, the scuole, through their sponsorship of music, made at least part of the myth of Venice a reality.

APPENDIX 1

Processions and Ceremonies of the Scuole Grandi

Listed below are the days of the Venetian church calendar celebrated by the scuole with processions or other religious ceremonies. In parentheses following the name of each feast are its Italian designation, the date celebrated, and any alternate Venetian designations. In square brackets following that are indications of which of the scuole grandi included the feast on their calendars (note that no complete calendar for San Teodoro survives). No attempt is made here to list the scuole piccole that also celebrated these occasions. Excluded from this listing are ordinary religious recurrences celebrated in the churches owned by the scuole of San Giovanni Evangelista and San Rocco, and those *andate* of the doge performed without the participation of the scuole. Occasions for which no description is provided were performed by the individual scuole either in their own church or in the church dedicated to the saint of that day. It is important to be aware that these feasts entered and left the calendars of the scuole at various times, and were not all celebrated throughout their histories. In some cases, in fact, a feast appears only once in the documents, and may have been celebrated for only a brief period, perhaps even only once.[1]

Saint Sebastian (San Sebastiano; 20 January) [SSR]
   A procession by the Scuola di San Rocco to the church of San Sebastiano, for
   reasons not specified in the documents.
Purification of the Virgin (Candlemas, 2 February; Madonna dele Candele)
      [SSGE, SSMC, SSMM, SSR]
   At each of the scuole it was the practice to distribute candles to fadighenti,
   patrician patrons, and distinguished members of Venetian society.
Sundays in Lent (Domeniche di quaresima) and Palm Sunday (Domenica delle
      olive) [all]
   The scuole and clergy of Venice were invited by the patriarch to visit the
   cathedral of San Pietro di Castello on each of the Sundays of Lent to partake

255

of indulgences connected with important relics preserved there. Each of the scuole processed separately, using a route of its own choosing.

Maundy Thursday/Good Friday (Giovedì Santo, known also as Zuoba Santo; Venerdì Santo) [all]

Processions of each of the scuole on the evening between Maundy Thursday and Good Friday. Originally, these separate processions included both the cathedral of San Pietro di Castello and the Basilica di San Marco, but from the seventeenth century they went only to the basilica to venerate a miraculous relic of the Blood of Christ.

Easter Monday, to San Zaccaria [all]

The official *andata* of the doge to the great indulgence at San Zaccaria to commemorate an agreement under which the City obtained land from the Benedictine nuns to expand Piazza San Marco. The scuole went to San Zaccaria individually to benefit from the indulgence.

Annunciation of the Virgin (25 March) [all]

The annual festa of the Scuola di Santa Maria della Carità. All the other scuole visited the host for its celebrations.

Saint Isidore (Sant'Isidoro, 16 April, known also as San Sidro) [all]

This procession commemorated the defeat on this date in 1354 of the conspiracy headed by doge Marin Falier, who had attempted to wrest power from the Senate and Council. The celebrations consisted primarily of a procession around the Piazza San Marco and through the basilica, with a stop at the altar of St. Isidore.

Saint Leo (San Lio; 19 April) [SSGE]

A celebration (beginning in 1474) by San Giovanni Evangelista in commemoration of a miracle associated with their precious relic of the Cross. During a ceremony in the parish of San Lio in the early fifteenth century, the miraculous relic refused, according to the legend, to be carried by an unrighteous man. The scuola went in procession to the bridge and church of San Lio. After 1614, the scuola commemorated the event on 10 August along with its procession to San Lorenzo.

Saint Mark (San Marco; 25 April) [all]

In the morning, the scuole joined the official procession in Piazza San Marco to honor the patron saint of the city. This was also the annual festa of the Scuola di San Marco. In the afternoon, all the other scuole visited the host for its celebrations.

Invention of the Holy Cross (Santissma Croce; 3 May) [all]

In honor of the precious relic of the Holy Cross owned by the Scuola di San Giovanni Evangelista (donated by Philippe de Mézières in 1369), all the other scuole attended celebrations there.

Last Day of May [SSR]

Celebrated by the Scuola of San Rocco at the high altar of their church to commemorate the date in 1478 on which the Council of Ten approved the creation of the scuola.

Corpus Christi [all]

Originally a purely religious occasion, this became one of the great civic processions of the year, in which scuole and city demonstrated their splendor and riches in a procession around the Piazza San Marco.

Domenica degli Angeli (the Sunday after Corpus Christi) [all]
Similar to the processions for the Sundays in Lent, to the cathedral of San Pietro di Castello; added in 1544.

Saint Anthony of Padua (Sant'Antonio di Padova; 13 June) [SSMM, SSR]
With the rise of the cult of St. Anthony, this festival, with a procession to Piazza San Marco, was added to the calendars of several scuole in the seventeenth and eighteenth centuries.

Saints Vitus and Modestus (Santi Vito e Modesto, 15 June; also known as San Vido) [all]
Like San Sidro, this feast also celebrated the defeat of a conspiracy: in 1310 the rich merchant Baiamonte Tiepolo and his followers attempted to overthrow the government, but doge Pietro Gradenigo, on the feast of Sts. Vitus and Modestus, quelled the uprising. The procession started at the Piazza San Marco and moved to the parish church of San Vido, crossing the Grand Canal on a bridge of boats, before returning home.

Ascension Sunday (La Sensa) [all; only until the fourteenth century]
In the early years of the scuole, this day was celebrated with a procession, but as it developed into the major annual trade fare of the city it was removed as a required celebration.

Saint John the Baptist (24 June) [SSGE]
Celebrated by the Scuola di San Giovanni Evangelista in its church apparently because of this saint shared his name with the scuola's patron.

Invention of Saint Mark (25 June; also known as San Marco de Zugno or San Marco de l'aqua ruosa) [all]
This celebrates the rediscovery, in 1094, of the body of St. Mark during the dedication of the newly rebuilt basilica. The body of the Evangelist, which had been hidden to prevent its theft (the Venetians themselves had stolen the body from Alexandria), was believed lost in the fire that destroyed the earlier wooden church. After three days of fasting and prayer, a stone fell from a hollow pillar that had been saved from the old church, revealing the body of the saint. This incident is depicted in a twelfth-century mosaic in the south transept of the basilica. The procedures were almost identical to those for San Sidro, with the omission of the pause at the altar of Saint Isidore.

Saints John and Paul (Santi Giovanni e Paolo, 26 June, also known as San Zanipolo) [all]
Instituted by command of the Senate in 1656 in honor of the Venetian victory of the Dardanelles, in the War of Crete, on this date. The doge and his retinue, along with the scuole, went in procession to Piazza San Marco and to the church of Santi Giovanni e Paolo.

Holy Trinity (Santissima Trinità, 13 July) [SSGE, SSMC, SSR]
Standard liturgical celebration in the church.

Santa Marina (17 July) [all]
This celebration was instituted in the early sixteenth century to commemorate the retaking of the city of Padua from the forces of the league of Cambrai on

this day in 1509. The procession began, as usual, at San Marco, and then proceeded to the church of Santa Marina, not far from the Rialto Bridge, where the participants attended the *pardon*, or indulgence, granted to that church.

Saint Mary Magdalen (La Maddalena, 22 July) [SSR]
 The reasons for this procession to the church of Santa Maria Maddalena are not provided in the extant documents of the scuola.

Saint Christine (Santa Cristina, 24 July) [SSMM]
 This was one of the traditional celebrations of the abbey of Santa Maria della Misericordia.

Saint James (San Giacomo, 25 July) [SSGE, SSMC, SSR]
 The documents do not explain why these scuole celebrated this occasion.

Saint Pantaleone (San Pantalon, 26 July) [SSR]
 The Scuola di San Rocco joined the priests of the parish church on this day to commemorate the day on which they signed an agreement for the scuola to purchase the land from the church on which they built their scuola.

Redeemer (Redentore, third Sunday of July) [all]
 This celebration was ordained in 1576 to honor a vow made by the city for release from a great plague. The participants crossed the Canale della Giudecca on a bridge of boats to the church of the Redentore, built as part of the vow, and, after a mass celebrated by the patriarch, returned by the same route to the piazza.

Saint Martha (Santa Marta, 29 July) [SSM]
 This procession is listed only in a tariffa of 1687, and no explanation is provided.

Saint Lawrence (San Lorenzo, 10 August) [SSGE]
 The scuola di San Giovanni Evangelista commemorated (with a procession to the church of San Lorenzo) a miracle performed by their relic of the True Cross in 1369, while the brothers were crossing the bridge opposite the church dedicated to that saint. Dropped accidentally into the canal, the relic evaded all attempts to recapture it until the guardian grande himself leapt into the water and brought it back to safety.

Assumption of the Virgin (15 August) [all]
 The annual festa of the Scuola della Misericordia until the late fifteenth century (moved to the Conception, 8 December, to avoid conflicts with the festa of San Rocco). All the other scuole visited the host for its celebrations.

Saint Roch (San Rocco, 16 August) [all]
 The annual festa of the Scuola di San Rocco. All the other scuole visited the host for its celebrations.

Nativity of the Virgin (8 September) [all]
 Most of the scuole celebrated this feast in their church, without a procession, though there were times, especially in the sixteenth century, when the scuole grandi visited the Scuola di Santa Maria dei Mercanti, at the Madonna del Orto on its feast day. San Rocco, on the other hand, went in procession to the church of San Giobbe, carrying, on its return, a costumed figure of the Virgin.

Exaltation of the Holy Cross (14 September) [SSGE]
 In honor of its miraculous relic of the Holy Cross the scuola offered a sung mass in either the scuola or the church.

Saint Michael Archangel (29 September; San Michele) [SSMC]
The reasons for this celebration are not provided in the documents.
Last Day of September [SSR]
Celebrated by San Rocco with a mass in their church to commemorate the
date in 1480 when two scuole piccole dedicated to the saint joined forces and
moved to the vicinity of I Frari.
Holy Rosary (Santissimo Rosario) [SSMC]
This procession is first listed in a tariffa of 1784, and is probably the visit to
the Scuola di Santa Maria del Rosario (at Santi Giovanni e Paolo), which had
been declared a scuola grande in 1765.
Saint Francis of Assisi (San Francesco, 4 October) [SSR]
Celebrated by the Scuola di San Rocco along with the Friars of Santa Maria
Gloriosa dei Frari as part of the agreement by which the Franciscans assisted
the scuola in liturgical matters. The brothers brought their cross to the sacristy
of the church and then joined the friars in their procession around the church
before the mass at the high altar.
Saint Justina (Santa Giustina, 7 October) [all]
Like the celebrations for Santa Marina, this was also instituted to commemorate
a victory, in this case the famous 1571 defeat of the Turks at Lepanto by the
combined Christian fleets. The doge and his retinue went to the church of
Santa Giustina by boat, and upon their return placed themselves in the choir
of San Marco where they reviewed the scuole and other participants, who
passed through the basilica after their usual procession around the piazza.
Archangel Raphael (Angelo Raffaele, 24 October) [SSR]
The reasons for this procession to the churches of the Angelo Raffaele and
Santa Maria Maggiore are not provided in the documents.
All Saints (Ognisanti, 1 November) [SSGE, SSM, SSMC, SSMM]
Standard liturgical celebration in the church. San Rocco also went in procession
to the church of the Ognisanti.
Day of the Dead (Giorno dei Morti; 2 November) [all]
Each of the scuole went individually in procession around the city, visiting
churches housing tombs of their brothers. The ceremonies concluded with a
commemorative funeral mass at the church.
Sunday in Octave of the Day of the Dead [SSM, SSMM]
These scuole repeated the commemorative mass of the Day of the Dead in the
church
Saint Leonard (San Leonardo, 6 November; also known as San Lunardo) [SSMC]
The annual festa of the original host church of this scuola.
Saint Theodore (San Teodoro, 10 November; also known as San Todaro) [all]
The annual festa of the Scuola di San Teodoro. All the other scuole visited the
host for its celebrations.
Saint Martin (San Martino; 11 November) [SSGE]
The Scuola di San Giovanni Evangelista owned a relic of the leg of Saint
Martin, which it carried in procession to the church dedicated to that saint.
Santa Maria della Salute (21 November) [all]
This was another procession, like the Redeemer, instituted as part of a vow

for the lifting of a plague, this time in 1630. Again, a bridge of boats was employed, but here to cross the Grand Canal to the votive church of the Madonna della Salute.

Saint Catherine of Alexandria (Santa Catterina; 25 November) [SSGE]
Celebrated by the officers of the Scuola di San Giovanni Evangelista at the altar of St. Catherine in the church of Santi Giovanni e Paolo following instructions in the will of a wealthy brother.

Saint Andrew (San Andrea, 30 November) [SSR]
On this day in 1480 the scuola was elevated to the rank of scuola grande. In commemoration of this important event, the scuola had requested and been granted an indulgence (*pardon*) in their church, which commenced with the display of the body of St. Roch on the vigil of the feast, and climaxed with a procession by the brothers to the church of Sant'Andrea.

Conception of the Virgin (8 December) [all]
The annual festa of the Scuola di Santa Maria della Misericordia after the late fifteenth century. All the other scuole visited the host for its celebrations.

Saint Thomas (San Tommaso, 21 December; also known as San Tomà) [SSR]
The Scuola di San Rocco went in procession to the church of its parish on this day.

Saint John the Evangelist (San Giovanni Evangelista, 27 December; also known as San Zuane Evangelista) [all]
The annual festa of the Scuola di San Giovanni Evangelista. All the other scuole visited the host for its celebrations.

APPENDIX 2

A Calendar of Religious Occasions Celebrated by the Scuole

The following table is intended to offer an idea of the overall contribution of the scuole grandi and scuole piccole to the Venetian musical scene. It includes the annual feste and other regular ceremonial occasions for each scuola (with the scuole grandi in bold), as observed around 1700, the period for which documentation is most complete. No attempt is made to distinguish those occasions with elaborate music from more ordinary occasions, in part since this was often the responsibility of the annually elected guardian or officers, whose tastes and means varied. Some scuole celebrated the vigil of their festa with a musical Vespers, and some also with a mass (often a requiem) the day afterward, neither of which is indicated in the following list. Most scuole designated one Sunday each month as a *dì ordinado*, on which the priests of their church sang mass for the souls of the brothers, usually with organ. Finally, most scuole ordered funeral masses to be said once each week, and, in a much more solemn manner (perhaps with music) in the week following the Day of the Dead (2 November). Because of the fragmentry state of the documentation for some scuole, this calendar cannot be complete.

In addition to the feste called for in the regulations of the individual scuole, the parish-based Scuole del Santissimo Sacramento (and also the Scuola del Santissimo Crocefisso in San Marcuola and the Scuola dell'Anime del Purgatorio) were required to perform regular expositions of the Holy Sacrament in their churches, according to a schedule devised by the patriarch (the so-called "esposizioni per carta") to ensure that on every day of the year, the faithful could find at least one church, either parish or monastic (churches of nuns, but not friars or monks, were included in the schedule), in which to adore the Sacrament. This schedule changed frequently (probably every year) to accommodate the movable feasts and also requests by individual churches or scuole to suspend the celebration for a period of time in order to redirect the funds that would have been spent for masses, decorations, and music. Included in the chart below are the days assigned to each parish church and its Scuola del Santissimo Sacramento (in italics to distinguish them from the fixed feasts) for the year 1698[1] (see p. 220 for more on this practice).

January

	Occasion	Scuola	Location
1	Circumcision	Nome di Dio	San Domenico
		Nome di Dio	Santi Giovanni e Paolo
2			
3			
4	*Exposition*	*Santissimo Sacramento*	*Santa Lucia*
5	*Exposition*	*Santissimo Sacramento*	*Santa Lucia*
6	Epiphany (Blessing of the Water)	Santissimo Sacramento	San Felice
		Santissimo Sacramento	San Geremia
	Exposition	*Santissimo Sacramento*	*San Marziale*
7	*Exposition*	*Santissimo Sacramento*	*San Marziale*
8	St. Lorenzo Giustinian	San Lorenzo Giustinian	Santa Sofia
	Exposition	*Santissimo Sacramento*	*San Severo*
9	St. Julian	San Giuliano	San Giuliano
	Exposition	*Santissimo Sacramento*	*San Severo*
10	*Exposition*	*Santissimo Sacramento*	*San Pietro di Castello*
11	*Exposition*	*Santissimo Sacramento*	*San Pietro di Castello*
12	*Exposition*	*Crocefisso*	*San Marcuola*
13	*Exposition*	*Crocefisso*	*San Marcuola*
14	Most Holy Name of Jesus	Nome di Gesù	San Francesco della Vigna
		Santissimo Nome di Gesù	Santa Maria Gloriosa dei Frari
	St. Felix	San Felice	San Felice
15			
16	*Exposition*	*Santissimo Sacramento*	*San Cassiano*
17	St. Anthony Abbot	Sant'Antonio Abbate	San Giacomo di Rialto
		Sant'Antonio Abbate	San Polo
	Exposition	*Santissimo Sacramento*	*San Cassiano*
18	Translation of St. Lucy	Santa Lucia	Santa Lucia
19			
20	St. Sebastian	**San Rocco**	San Sebastiano
		San Sebastiano	San Giacomo dal'Orio
		San Sebastiano	San Sebastiano
	Exposition	***San Giovanni Evangelista***	*San Giovanni Evangelista*
21	*Exposition*	***San Giovanni Evangelista***	*San Giovanni Evangelista*
22	St. Vincent Martyr	Santi Alessandro e Vincenzo	San Silvestro
23	St. John the Almsgiver	San Giovanni Elimosinario	San Giovanni in Bragora
24	*Exposition*	*Santissimo Sacramento*	*Sant'Eufemia*
25	*Exposition*	*Santissimo Sacramento*	*Sant'Eufemia*
26	*Exposition*	*Santissimo Sacramento*	*Santa Maria Nuova*
27	*Exposition*	*Santissimo Sacramento*	*Santa Maria Nuova*
28	*Exposition*	*Santissimo Sacramento*	*Santa Marina*
29	*Exposition*	*Santissimo Sacramento*	*Santa Marina*
30			

January

	Occasion	Scuola	Location
31 —	Sunday before St. Anthony Abbot	Suffragio di Morti	San Matteo

February

	Occasion	Scuola	Location
1	*Exposition*	*Santissimo Sacramento*	*Sant'Angelo*
2	Purification of the Virgin	**all scuole grandi (except San Marco?)**	at each scuola
		San Giobbe	San Giobbe
		Madonna	San Marziale
		B.V.[2]	Angelo Raffaele
		B.V. dei Mascoli	San Marco
		B.V. della Purificazione	San Giovanni Nuovo
		B.V. della Purificazione	Santa Maria Formosa
		B.V. della Purificatione	San Samuele
		B.V. del Rosario (with triduo)	Santi Filippo e Giacomo
		B.V. di Pietà	San Giobbe
		B.V. e San Mattio	Sant'Angelo
	Exposition	*Santissimo Sacramento*	*Sant'Angelo*
3	*Exposition*	*Santissimo Sacramento*	*Santa Maria Formosa*
4	*Exposition*	*Santissimo Sacramento*	*Santa Maria Formosa*
5	*Exposition*	*Santissimo Sacramento*	*San Biagio*
6	St. Dorothy	Santa Dorotea	San Simeon Piccolo
	Exposition	*Santissimo Sacramento*	*San Biagio*
7	*Exposition*	*Santissimo Sacramento*	*San Polo*
8	*Exposition*	*Santissimo Sacramento*	*San Polo*
9	St. Apollonia	Sant'Apollonia	San Barnaba
	Exposition	*Santissimo Crocefisso*	*San Marcuola*
10	*Exposition*	*Santissimo Crocefisso*	*San Marcuola*
11	*Exposition*	*Santissimo Sacramento*	*Santa Fosca*
12	*Exposition*	*Santissimo Sacramento*	*Santa Fosca*
13			
14	St. Valentine	San Valentino	San Samuele
		San Valentino	San Simeon Grande
15	*Exposition*	*Santissimo Sacramento*	*San Mattio*
16	*Exposition*	*Santissimo Sacramento*	*San Mattio*
17			
18			
19	*Exposition*	**San Rocco**	*San Rocco*
20	*Exposition*	**San Rocco**	*San Rocco*
21			

(continued)

February

	Occasion	Scuola	Location
22			
23			
24	St. Mathias	San Mattia	San Bortolomeo
25	*Exposition*	*Santissimo Sacramento*	*San Geminiano*
26	*Exposition*	*Santissimo Sacramento*	*San Geminiano*
27			
28			
—	First Sunday in Lent	**all scuole grandi**	procession to San Pietro di Castello and other churches in that district
—	First Monday in Lent	San Cristoforo ai Gesuiti	I Crosechieri
—	Second Sunday in Lent	**all scuole grandi**	procession to San Pietro di Castello and other churches in that district
—	Third Sunday in Lent	**all scuole grandi**	procession to San Pietro di Castello and other churches in that district
—	Fourth Sunday in Lent	**all scuole grandi**	procession to San Pietro di Castello and other churches in that district
—	Fifth Sunday in Lent (Lazarus Sunday)	B.V.M. di Pietà	San Silvestro
—	Lent (days not specified)	Suffragio di Morti	Santi Filippo e Giacomo
—	Palm Sunday	**all scuole grandi**	procession to San Pietro di Castello and other churches in that district
		Santa Maria della Consolazione e San Girolamo	San Fantin and procession
		Passion	Santa Maria Gloriosa dei Frari
—	Monday in Holy Week	Santissimo Crocefisso	San Giovanni in Bragora
—	Maundy Thursday/ Good Friday	**all scuole grandi**	procession in Piazza San Marco (earlier also to San Pietro di Castello)
		Agonizzanti	San Martino[3]
		Passion	Santa Maria Gloriosa dei Frari
		Santissimo Crocefisso	San Giovanni Nuovo
		Santissimo Sacramento	San Felice
		Santissimo Sacramento	San Geremia
		Santissimo Sacramento	San Giovanni Grisostomo
		Santissimo Sacramento	San Luca
		Santissimo Sacramento	San Stae
		Santissimo Sacramento	Santa Giustina
		Santissimo Sacramento	Santa Marina
		Santissimo Sacramento	Sant'Eufemia
		Suffragio dei Morti in San Geremia	San Marco
		Suffragio di Morti	San Salvatore (with procession)

February

	Occasion	Scuola	Location
—	Easter Monday	**all scuole grandi**	San Zaccaria
—	Second Sunday after Easter	B.V. Annonciata	San Cassiano

March

	Occasion	Scuola	Location
1			
2			
3			
4			
5	*Exposition*	*Santissimo Sacramento*	*San Felice*
6	*Exposition*	*Santissimo Sacramento*	*San Felice*
7	St. Thomas Aquinas	San Pietro Martire	Santi Giovanni e Paolo
	Exposition	*Santissimo Sacramento*	*San Fantin*
8	*Exposition*	*Santissimo Sacramento*	*San Fantin*
9	*Exposition*	*Santissimo Crocefisso*	*San Marcuola*
10	*Exposition*	*Santissimo Crocefisso*	*San Marcuola*
11	*Exposition*	*Santissimo Sacramento*	*San Stae*
12	St. Gregory	San Gregorio	San Gregorio
		San Gregorio	Santi Filippo e Giacomo
	Exposition	*Santissimo Sacramento*	*San Stae*
13	*Exposition*	*Santissimo Sacramento*	*San Gregorio*
14	*Exposition*	*Santissimo Sacramento*	*San Gregorio*
15	*Exposition*	*Santissimo Sacramento*	*San Bortolomeo*
		Santissimo Sacramento	*Santa Giustina*
16	*Exposition*	*Santissimo Sacramento*	*San Bortolomeo*
		Santissimo Sacramento	*Santa Giustina*
17	*Exposition*	*Santissimo Sacramento*	*San Bortolomeo*
18	*Exposition*	*Santissimo Sacramento*	*San Bortolomeo*
19	St. Joseph	Buona Morte	Sant'Antonin
		San Giuseppe	San Felice
		San Giuseppe	San Giuseppe
		San Giuseppe	San Silvestro
		San Giuseppe	San Stin
		San Giuseppe	Santa Fosca
20			
21	*Exposition*	*Santissimo Sacramento*	*Santa Sofia*
22	*Exposition*	*Santissimo Sacramento*	*Santa Sofia*
23	*Exposition*	*Santissimo Sacramento*	*San Luca*
24	Vigil of the Annunciation	**Santa Maria della Carità**	Santa Maria della Carità
	Exposition	*Santissimo Sacramento*	*San Luca*
25	Annunciation of the Virgin	**all scuole grandi**	Santa Maria della Carità (church and scuola)
		B.V.	San Salvatore
		B.V.	San Simeon Grande

(continued)

March

	Occasion	Scuola	Location
		B.V. Annunciata	San Giacomo dall'Orio
		B.V. Annunciata	Santa Margarita
		B.V. Annunciata	Santa Maria dei Servi
		B.V. Annunciata	Santa Maria Mater Domini
		B.V. Annunciata	Sant'Aponal
		B.V. Annunciata de' Zotti	Sant'Angelo
		B.V. del Parto	San Leonardo
		B.V. delle Gratie	San Paternian
		Concezione della B.V.	San Francesco della Vigna
		San Giobbe	San Giobbe
	Exposition	*Santissimo Sacramento*	*San Luca*
26			
27			
28			
29			
30			
31			
—	Third Friday in March	San Gaetano	San Fantin
—	Sunday after Annunciation	Annunciazione B.M.V.	San Giovanni in Bragora

April

	Occasion	Scuola	Location
1			
2	St. Francis of Paola	B.V. Assunta	Santa Maria in Broglio
		San Francesco di Paola	San Felice
		San Francesco di Paola	San Simeon Piccolo
		San Francesco di Paola	San Trovaso
		San Francesco di Paola	Santa Sofia
3			
4			
5	St. Vincent Ferrer	San Vincenzo Ferrer	Santa Maria Zobenigo
		San Vincenzo Ferrer	Santi Giovanni e Paolo
		San Vincenzo Ferrer	Sant'Agostin
	Exposition	*Santissimo Sacramento*	*San Marcuola*
6	*Exposition*	*Santissimo Sacramento*	*San Marcuola*
7	*Exposition*	*Santissimo Sacramento*	*San Provolo*
8	*Exposition*	*Santissimo Sacramento*	*San Provolo*
9	*Exposition*	*Santissimo Sacramento*	*San Giuliano*
10	*Exposition*	*Santissimo Sacramento*	*San Giuliano*
11	*Exposition*	*Santissimo Sacramento*	*Angelo Raffaele*
12	*Exposition*	*Santissimo Sacramento*	*Angelo Raffaele*
13	*Exposition*	*Santissimo Crocefisso*	*San Marcuola*
14	*Exposition*	*Santissimo Crocefisso*	*San Marcuola*
15	*Exposition*	*Santissimo Sacramento*	*Santi Apostoli*
16	St. Isidore	**all scuole grandi**	San Marco

April

	Occasion	Scuola	Location
	Exposition	*Santissimo Sacramento*	*Santi Apostoli*
17	*Exposition*	*Santissimo Sacramento*	*San Giovanni Grisostomo*
18	*Exposition*	*Santissimo Sacramento*	*San Giovanni Grisostomo*
19	St. Leo	**San Giovanni Evangelista**	procession to San Lio (suspended after 1614)
	St. Triphon	Santi Giorgio e Trifone	San Giovanni del Tempio
	Exposition	*Santissimo Sacramento*	*San Vidal*
20	St. Agnes	Sant'Agnese	San Barnaba
	Exposition	*Santissimo Sacramento*	*San Vidal*
21	*Exposition*	*Santissimo Sacramento*	*San Barnaba*
22	*Exposition*	*Santissimo Sacramento*	*San Barnaba*
23	St. George	Santi Giorgio e Trifon	San Giovanni del Tempio
	Exposition	*Santissimo Sacramento*	*Sant'Agostin*
24	Vigil of St. Mark	**San Marco**	Scuola Grande di San Marco
	Exposition	*Santissimo Sacramento*	*Sant'Agostin*
25	St. Mark	**all scuole grandi**	morning: Piazza San Marco afternoon: Scuola Grande di San Marco
	Exposition	*Santissimo Sacramento*	*San Silvestro*
26	*Exposition*	*Santissimo Sacramento*	*San Silvestro*
27	St. Liberale	San Liberal	Santa Maria Maddalena
	Exposition	*Santissimo Sacramento*	*Sant'Aponal*
28	*Exposition*	*Santissimo Sacramento*	*Sant'Aponal*
29	St. Peter Martyr	San Pietro Martire	Santi Giovanni e Paolo
	Exposition	*Santissimo Sacramento*	*San Pantalon*
30	St. Catherine of Siena	Santa Catterina di Siena	Santa Maria Zobenigo
	Exposition	*Santissimo Sacramento*	*San Pantalon*

May

	Occasion	Scuola	Location
1	Twelve Apostles	XII Apostoli	Santi Apostoli
2			
3	Holy Cross	**all scuole grandi**	San Giovanni Evangelista
		Buona Morte	Sant'Antonin
		San Mattia	San Bortolomeo
		Santa Croce	San Moisè
		Santa Croce (with ottavario)	San Pietro di Castello
		Santa Croce	Santa Croce
		Santissima Croce	Sant'Angelo
		Santissima Croce	San Nicolò dei Mendicoli

(continued)

May

	Occasion	Scuola	Location
		Santissima Croce	San Salvatore
		Santissima Croce	Santa Maria Mater Domini
		Santissima Croce	Sant'Aponal
		Santissimo Crocefisso	Angelo Raffaele
		Santissimo Crocefisso	San Giovanni Nuovo
		Santissimo Crocefisso	San Marcuola
		Santissimo Crocefisso	Santa Maria Maggiore
	Exposition	*Santissimo Sacramento*	*San Samuele*
4	St. Gothard	San Gottardo	Sant'Aponal
	Exposition	*Santissimo Sacramento*	*San Samuele*
5	*Exposition*	*Santissimo Sacramento*	*Santa Croce*
6	*Exposition*	*Santissimo Sacramento*	*Santa Croce*
7			
8			
9	*Exposition*	*Santissimo Sacramento*	*Sant'Agnese*
10	*Exposition*	*Santissimo Sacramento*	*Sant'Agnese*
11	*Exposition*	*Santissimo Crocefisso*	*San Marcuola*
12	*Exposition*	*Santissimo Crocefisso*	*San Marcuola*
13			
14			
15			
16			
17	St. Pascal Baylon	San Pasquale Baylon	San Francesco della Vigna
	Exposition	*Santissimo Sacramento*	*San Mauritio*
18	*Exposition*	*Santissimo Sacramento*	*San Mauritio*
19			
20	St. Eustace	Sant'Eustachio	San Stae
	St. Bernardino of Siena	San Bernardino	San Giobbe
21			
22			
23			
24			
25	*Exposition*	*Santissimo Sacramento*	*San Benetto*
26	St. Phillip Neri	San Filippo Neri	San Canciano
		San Filippo Neri	San Gregorio
		San Filippo Neri	San Martino
	Exposition	*Santissimo Sacramento*	*San Benetto*
27	*Exposition*	*Santissimo Sacramento*	*San Salvatore*
28	*Exposition*	*Santissimo Sacramento*	*San Salvatore*
29	St. Maximus	Santissimo Sacramento e San Massimo	San Canciano
30			
31	—	**San Rocco**	San Rocco
—	Second Sunday in May	Santa Catterina di Siena	Santa Maria dei Servi
—	Third Sunday in May	Madonna	San Felice
—	Fourth Sunday in May	San Valentin	San Samuele
—	Second Sunday after Holy Cross	Santissimo Crocefisso	Sant'Andrea della Zirada

May

Occasion	Scuola	Location
— Pentecost	Spirito Santo	Spirito Santo
— 2nd Festa of Pentecost	Santissimo Crocefisso	San Giacomo della Giudecca
	Spirito Santo	Spirito Santo
— 3rd Festa of Pentecost	Spirito Santo	Spirito Santo
— Corpus Christi	**all scuole grandi**	Piazza San Marco and in the afternoon to Corpus Domini
	Corpus Domini	Corpus Domini
	Santissimo Sacramento[4]	Angelo Raffaele
	Santissimo Sacramento	Sant'Angelo
	Santissimo Sacramento	San Basilio
	Santissimo Sacramento	San Benetto
	Santissimo Sacramento	San Geremia
	Santissimo Sacramento	San Giacomo dal'Orio
	Santissimo Sacramento	San Luca
	Santissimo Sacramento	San Maurizio
	Santissimo Sacramento	San Nicolò dei Mendicoli
	Santissimo Sacramento	San Pietro di Castello
	Santissimo Sacramento	San Simeon Grande
	Santissimo Sacramento	Santa Maria Formosa
	Santissimo Sacramento	Santa Maria Zobenigo
	Santissimo Sacramento	Santa Trinità
	Santissimo Sacramento	Santi Apostoli
weekdays within Octave of Corpus Domini	Corpus Domini	Corpus Domini
— Domenica degli Angeli (Octave of Corpus Christi)	**all scuole grandi**	San Pietro di Castello
	Corpus Domini	Corpus Domini
	Santissimo Sacramento	San Basso
	Santissimo Sacramento	San Cassiano
	Santissimo Sacramento	San Giminiano
	Santissimo Sacramento	San Giovanni Decollato
	Santissimo Sacramento	San Giuliano
	Santissimo Sacramento	San Martino
	Santissimo Sacramento	San Silvestro
	Santissimo Sacramento	San Simeon Piccolo
	Santissimo Sacramento	San Tomà
	Santissimo Sacramento	Santa Lucia
	Santissimo Sacramento	Santa Margarita
	Santissimo Sacramento	Santa Maria Mater Domini
— Sacred Heart of Jesus (Friday after the Octave of Corpus Christi)	Sagro Cuor di Gesù	San Canciano
	Sagro Cuor di Gesù	San Fantin
— Second Sunday after Corpus Christi	Santissimo Sacramento	San Bortolomeo
	Santissimo Sacramento	San Leonardo
	Santissimo Sacramento	Sant'Aponal

(continued)

May

	Occasion	Scuola	Location
—	Ascension	**all scuole grandi**	Piazza San Marco (suspended after 14th century)
		B.V. Assunta	Santa Maria in Broglio

June

	Occasion	Scuola	Location
1			
2	St. Erasmus	Sant'Erasmo	San Barnaba
3			
4			
5	*Exposition*	*Santissimo Sacramento*	*San Simeon Grande*
6	*Exposition*	*Santissimo Sacramento*	*San Simeon Grande*
7	*Exposition*	*Santissimo Crocefisso*	*San Marcuola*
8	*Exposition*	*Santissimo Crocefisso*	*San Marcuola*
9	*Exposition*	*Santissimo Sacramento*	*San Giacomo dall'Orio*
10	*Exposition*	*Santissimo Sacramento*	*San Giacomo dall'Orio*
11	*Exposition*	*Santissimo Sacramento*	*San Lio*
12	*Exposition*	*Santissimo Sacramento*	*San Lio*
13	St. Anthony of Padua	**all scuole grandi**	Santa Maria della Salute and San Vio
		B.V. Assunta	Santa Maria in Broglio
		B.V. del Rosario	Sant'Antonin
		Sant'Antonio	Madonna dell'Orto
		Sant'Antonio	Sant'Angelo
		Sant'Antonio	San Cassiano
		Sant'Antonio	San Giovanni Grisostomo
		Sant'Antonio	San Vio
		Sant'Antonio (with Novena)	Santa Maria Gloriosa dei Frari
		Sant'Antonio di Padova	San Benedetto
		Sant'Antonio di Padova	San Nicolò dei Mendicoli
		Sant'Antonio di Padova	San Severo
		Sant'Antonio di Padova	Santa Maria Maddalena
		Sant'Antonio di Padova	Sant'Eufemia dela Giudecca
		Santi Antonio e Gaetano	San Giovanni Decollato
	Exposition	*Santissimo Sacramento*	*San Nicolò dei Mendicoli*
14	*Exposition*	*Santissimo Sacramento*	*San Nicolò dei Mendicoli*
15	Sts. Vitus and Modestus	**all scuole grandi**	San Marco and San Vio
		Santissimo Sacramento	San Moisè
		Santissimo Sacramento	Sant'Agnese
	Exposition	*Santissimo Sacramento*	*San Trovaso*
16	*Exposition*	*Santissimo Sacramento*	*San Trovaso*
17	*Exposition*	*Santissimo Sacramento*	*San Vio*

June

	Occasion	Scuola	Location
18	*Exposition*	*Santissimo Sacramento*	*San Vio*
19			
20			
21	*Exposition*	*Santissimo Sacramento*	*San Giovanni in Bragora*
22	*Exposition*	*Santissimo Sacramento*	*San Giovanni in Bragora*
23	*Exposition*	*Santissimo Sacramento*	*San Bortolomeo*
24	St. John the Baptist	**San Giovanni Evangelista**	San Giovanni Evangelista
		Fiorentini	Santa Maria Gloriosa dei Frari
		Milanesi	Santa Maria Gloriosa dei Frari
		San Giovanni Battista	San Giovanni Battista della Giudecca
		San Giovanni Battista	San Giovanni del Tempio
		San Giovanni Battista	San Marcuola
		Santissimo Sacramento	San Giovanni in Bragora
	Exposition	*Santissimo Sacramento*	*San Bortolomeo*
25	Invention of St. Mark	**all scuole grandi**	San Marco
	Exposition	*Santissimo Sacramento*	*San Bortolomeo*
26	Sts. John and Paul	**all scuole grandi**	San Marco and Santi Giovanni e Paolo
	Exposition	*Santissimo Sacramento*	*San Bortolomeo*
27	*Exposition*	*Santissimo Sacramento*	*San Tomà*
28	*Exposition*	*Santissimo Sacramento*	*San Tomà*
29	Sts. Peter and Paul	San Pietro	San Simeon Grande
		San Polo	San Polo
	Exposition	*Santissimo Sacramento*	*San Giovanni Nuovo*
30	*Exposition*	*Santissimo Sacramento*	*San Giovanni Nuovo*
—	First Sunday in June	B.V. de Sette Dolori	San Stin
—	First Sunday of the Month after Corpus Christi	Santissimo Sacramento	San Stae

July

	Occasion	Scuola	Location
1	St. Gall	Santa Maria e San Gallo	San Maurizio
	Exposition	*Santissimo Sacramento*	*San Pietro di Castello*
2	Visitation of the Virgin	B.V.	San Basilio
		B.V. di Pietà	San Giovanni Elimosinario
		B.V. e Santa Maria Elisabetta	San Severo
		Santa Maria Elisabetta	Santa Maria Maddalena
		Santa Maria Elisabetta e B.V. di Loreto	San Cassiano

(continued)

July

	Occasion	Scuola	Location
		Santissimo Sacramento e B.V.	Santa Maria Nova
		Visitatione della B.V.	San Nicolò dei Mendicoli
	Exposition	*Santissimo Sacramento*	*San Pietro di Castello*
3	Holy Trinity	**San Giovanni Evangelista**	San Giovanni Evangelista
		Santa Maria della Carità	Santa Maria della Carità
		San Rocco	San Rocco
		B.V. della Concezione	San Matteo
		Santissima Trinità	San Vitale
		Santissima Trinità	Santa Trinità
	Exposition	*San Giovanni Evangelista*	*San Giovanni Evangelista*
4	*Exposition*	*San Giovanni Evangelista*	*San Giovanni Evangelista*
5			
6			
7	*Exposition*	*Santissimo Sacramento*	*Santa Maria Mater Domini*
8	*Exposition*	*Santissimo Sacramento*	*Santa Maria Mater Domini*
9	*Exposition*	*Santissimo Sacramento*	*San Marziale*
10	*Exposition*	*Santissimo Sacramento*	*San Marziale*
11	*Exposition*	*Santissimo Sacramento*	*San Paternian*
12	Sts. Ermagora and Fortunatus	Santi Pio, Ermagora, e Fortunato	San Marcuola
	Exposition	*Santissimo Sacramento*	*San Paternian*
13	*Exposition*	*Santissimo Crocefisso*	*San Marcuola*
14	*Exposition*	*Santissimo Crocefisso*	*San Marcuola*
15	*Exposition*	*Santissimo Sacramento*	*San Geremia*
16	Blessed Virgin of Mt. Carmel	B.V. del Carmine	San Pietro di Castello
		B.V. del Carmine	Sant'Aponal
		B.V. delle Grazie	Santa Marina
		Buona Morte	Sant'Antonin
		Santissimo Abito della B.V. del Carmine	Santa Maria del Carmine
	Exposition	*Santissimo Sacramento*	*San Geremia*
17	St. Marina	**all scuole grandi**	Piazza San Marco, Santa Marina
		Santa Marina	Santa Marina
	Exposition	*Santissimo Sacramento*	*San Basilio*
18	*Exposition*	*Santissimo Sacramento*	*San Basilio*
19			
20	St. Margaret	Santi Rocco e Margarita	Santi Rocco e Margarita
21	Transit of St. Joseph	San Giuseppe degli Agonizanti	San Basilio
		Transito di San Giuseppe	San Provolo
	Exposition	*Santissimo Sacramento*	*San Leonardo*
22	St. Mary Magdalen	**San Rocco**	San Rocco
	Exposition	*Santissimo Sacramento*	*San Leonardo*
23	*Exposition*	*Santissimo Sacramento*	*Santa Maria Zobenigo*
24	St. Christine	**Santa Maria della Misericordia**	Santa Maria della Misericordia
	Exposition	*Santissimo Sacramento*	*Santa Maria Zobenigo*

July

	Occasion	Scuola	Location
25	St. James	**San Giovanni Evangelista**	San Giacomo dall'Orio?
		Santa Maria della Carità	San Giacomo dall'Orio?
		San Rocco	San Giacomo dall'Orio?
		San Giacomo	San Giacomo dall'Orio
		San Giacomo di Galizia	San Giacomo della Giudecca
		Santissima Croce e San Giacomo	San Fantin
		Suffragio di Morti	Santi Filippo e Giacomo
	St. Christopher	San Cristoforo	I Gesuiti
		San Cristoforo	Sant'Agostin
26	St. Anne	Sant'Anna	San Giovanni Grisostomo
		Sant'Anna (with Novena)	San Paternian
		Sant'Anna	Sant'Alvise
		Sant'Anna	Sant'Anna di Castello
		Suffragio di Morti	Santi Filippo e Giacomo
26	St. Pantaleone	**San Rocco**	San Pantalon
27	*Exposition*	*Santissimo Sacramento*	*Sant'Eufemia*
28	*Exposition*	*Santissimo Sacramento*	*Sant'Eufemia*
29	St. Martha	**San Marco**	Santa Marta
		Santa Marta	Santa Marta
30			
31			
—	Holy Redeemer	**all scuole grandi**	San Marco and the Redentore
		Buona Morte	San Giminiano
		Santissimo Crocefisso	San Gregorio
		Santissimo Redentore	San Severo
—	Third Sunday of July	B. V. del Carmine	Sant'Angelo di Concordia della Giudecca

August

	Occasion	Scuola	Location
1	Triduo of August	Agonizanti	Angelo Raffaele
		San Pietro Apostolo	San Simeon Grande
2	Triduo of August	Agonizanti	Angelo Raffaele
		San Pietro Apostolo	San Simeon Grande
	Exposition	*Santissimo Sacramento*	*Sant'Angelo*
3	Triduo of August	Agonizanti	Angelo Raffaele
		San Pietro Apostolo	San Simeon Grande
	Exposition	*Santissimo Sacramento*	*Sant'Angelo*
4	St. Dominic	San Domenico	Santi Giovanni e Paolo
5	Blessed Virgin of the Snow	B.V. della Neve	San Girolamo
		B.V. della Neve	San Luca

(continued)

August

	Occasion	Scuola	Location
		B.V. di Pietà	San Giovanni in Bragora
	St. Oswald	B.V. e Sant'Osvaldo	San Silvestro
		Sant'Osvaldo	San Basilio
		Sant'Osvaldo	Santa Sofia
6	*Exposition*	*Santissimo Sacramento*	*San Polo*
7	St. Gaetano	San Gaetano	San Fantin
		San Gaetano	Santa Maria Maddalena
		Santi Antonio e Gaetano	San Giovanni Decollato
	St. Albert	Sant'Alberto	Santa Maria del Carmine
	Exposition	*Santissimo Sacramento*	*San Polo*
8	*Exposition*	*Santissimo Sacramento*	*San Fantin*
9	*Exposition*	*Santissimo Sacramento*	*San Fantin*
10	St. Lawrence	**San Giovanni Evangelista**	San Lorenzo (after 1614 also to San Lio)
		San Lorenzo	San Barnaba
	Exposition	*Santissimo Crocefisso*	*San Marcuola*
11	*Exposition*	*Santissimo Crocefisso*	*San Marcuola*
12			
13			
14			
15	Assumption of the Virgin	**all scuole grandi**	Santa Maria della Misericordia (until late 15th century)
		B.V.	San Polo
		B.V.	Santa Maria della Celestia
		B.V. Assunta	San Geremia
		B.V. Assunta	San Giacomo dall'Orio
		B.V. Assunta	San Giacomo di Rialto
		B.V. Assunta	San Stae
		B.V. Assunta	Santa Maria della Celestia
		B.V. Assunta	Santa Maria Maggiore
		B.V. Assunta	Santa Sofia
		B.V. da Lonigo	San Giobbe
		B.V. degl'Angeli	Angelo Raffaele
		B.V. degl'Angeli	Santa Trinità
		B.V. del Terremoto	San Bortolomeo
		B.V. della Cintura	San Giuseppe di Castello
		B.V. della Cintura	Santo Stefano
		B.V. della Natività	Santi Apostoli
		B.V. di Pietà	San Canciano
		San Giobbe	San Giobbe
		Santa Maria del Carmine	Santa Maria del Carmine
	Vigil of St. Roch	**San Rocco**	San Rocco
16	St. Roch	**all scuole grandi**	San Rocco
		San Rocco	San Canciano
		San Rocco	San Giuliano
		Santi Rocco e Margarita	Santi Rocco e Margarita
		Santissimo Crocefisso	San Giovanni Nuovo
17			
18	*Exposition*	**San Rocco**	*San Rocco*

August

	Occasion	Scuola	Location
19	St. Louis of Toulouse	Sant'Alvise	Sant'Alvise
	Exposition	**San Rocco**	*San Rocco*
20	*Exposition*	*Santissimo Sacramento*	*San Canciano*
21	*Exposition*	*Santissimo Sacramento*	*San Canciano*
22	*Exposition*	*Santissimo Sacramento*	*Santa Maria Maddalena*
23	*Exposition*	*Santissimo Sacramento*	*Santa Maria Maddalena*
24			
25			
26	St. Alexander[5]	Santi Alessandro e Vincenzo	San Silvestro
	Exposition	*Santissimo Sacramento*	*San Giovanni Decollato*
27	*Exposition*	*Santissimo Sacramento*	*San Giovanni Decollato*
28			
29	Decollation of St. John the Baptist	Fiorentini	Santa Maria Gloriosa dei Frari
		San Giovanni Battista	San Giovanni Decollato
30			
31	?	B.V. del Rosario	San Paternian
—	First Sunday of August	San Cristoforo	Gesuiti
—	Third Sunday in August	B.V. Assunta	San Stin
—	Sunday after Blessed Virgin of the Snow	Suffragio di Morti	San Giovanni in Bragora
—	Sunday after St. Louis	B.V. della Pietà	Sant'Alvise
—	sometime in August	B.V.	Santa Fosca

September

	Occasion	Scuola	Location
1	*Exposition*	*Santissimo Sacramento*	*San Moisè*
2	*Exposition*	*Santissimo Sacramento*	*San Moisè*
3	*Exposition*	*Santissimo Sacramento*	*San Geminiano*
4	*Exposition*	*Santissimo Sacramento*	*San Geminiano*
5	*Exposition*	*Santissimo Sacramento*	*Santa Maria Formosa*
6	St. Magnus	San Magno	San Geremia
	Exposition	*Santissimo Sacramento*	*Santa Maria Formosa*
7	Vigil of the Nativity	Anconetta	Santa Maria del Anconetta
8	Nativity of the Virgin	**San Rocco**	San Giobbe
		all other scuole grandi	Scuola di Santa Maria dei Mercanti at the Madonna del Orto
		Anconetta	Chiesa dell'Anconetta
		B.V. dei Ciecchi	San Moisè
		B.V. del Parto	San Gregorio
		B.V. del Parto	Santa Maria Mater Domini

(continued)

September

	Occasion	Scuola	Location
		B.V. della Natività	San Barnaba
		B.V. della Natività	San Benetto
		B.V. della Natività	San Giovanni Decolato
		B.V. della Natività	San Maurizio
		B.V. della Natività	San Trovaso
		B.V. della Natività	Santi Apostoli
		B.V. della Natività	Sant'Agnese
		B.V. della Natività	Sant'Aponal
		B.V. della Pace	Santa Croce
		B.V. delle Grazie	Santa Marina
		San Francesco	Santa Maria Gloriosa dei Frari
		San Giobbe	San Giobbe
		Sant'Anna	Sant'Anna
9			
10	St. Nicholas of Tolentino	San Nicolò di Tolentino	Santo Stefano
11			
12			
13	*Exposition*	*Santissimo Crocefisso*	*San Marcuola*
14	Exaltation of the Holy Cross	**San Giovanni Evangelista**	San Giovanni Evangelista
		Santissima Croce	Santa Maria Mater Domini
		Santissimo Crocefisso	San Giovanni Nuovo
		Santissimo Crocefisso	San Tomà
		Volto Santo	Santa Maria dei Servi
	Exposition	*Santissimo Crocefisso*	*San Marcuola*
15	St. Nicetas	San Nicolò	San Nicolò dei Mendicoli
16			
17	*Exposition*	*Santissimo Sacramento*	*San Matteo*
18	*Exposition*	*Santissimo Sacramento*	*San Matteo*
19	*Exposition*	*Santissimo Sacramento*	*Santi Apostoli*
20	*Exposition*	*Santissimo Sacramento*	*Santi Apostoli*
21			
22	St. Maurice	Santi Gallo e Maurizio	San Maurizio
23	*Exposition*	*Santissimo Sacramento*	*Sant'Aponal*
24	*Exposition*	*Santissimo Sacramento*	*Sant'Aponal*
25			
26			
27	Sts. Cosmas and Damian	Santi Cosma e Damiano	San Giovanni Nuovo
		Santi Cosma e Damiano	Santi Cosma e Damiano
	Exposition	*Santissimo Sacramento*	*San Giuliano*
28	*Exposition*	*Santissimo Sacramento*	*San Giuliano*
29	St. Michael	**Santa Maria della Carità**	Santa Maria della Carità
		San Michiel Arcangelo	Madonna dell'Orto
30	St. Jerome	San Girolamo	San Girolamo
	last day of September	**San Rocco**	San Rocco
—	First Sunday in September	Santissimo Sacramento	San Marcuola
—	Second Sunday in September	B.V. delle Grazie	Santa Marina

September

	Occasion	Scuola	Location
	Blessed Claire of Montefalco (third Sunday in September)	Beata Chiara	Santo Stefano
—	in month of September	B.V. delle Grazie	San Marcuola
—	Sunday in the Octave of the Nativity of the Blessed Virgin	B.V. delle Grazie	San Trovaso

October

	Occasion	Scuola	Location
1			
2			
3	*Exposition*	*Santissimo Sacramento*	*San Bortolomeo*
4	St. Francis	**San Rocco**	Santa Maria Gloriosa dei Frari
		San Francesco	Santa Maria Gloriosa dei Frari
		San Pasquale Baylon	San Francesco della Vigna
	Exposition	*Santissimo Sacramento*	*San Bortolomeo*
5	*Exposition*	*Santissimo Sacramento*	*San Bortolomeo*
6	*Exposition*	*Santissimo Sacramento*	*San Bortolomeo*
7	St. Justina	**all scuole grandi**	San Marco
	Exposition	*Santissimo Sacramento*	*San Bortolomeo*
8	*Exposition*	*Santissimo Sacramento*	*Santa Giustina*
9	*Exposition*	*Santissimo Sacramento*	*Santa Giustina*
10	*Exposition*	*Santissimo Sacramento*	*Santa Trinità*
11	*Exposition*	*Santissimo Sacramento*	*Santa Trinità*
12	*Exposition*	*Santissimo Crocefisso*	*San Marcuola*
13	*Exposition*	*Santissimo Crocefisso*	*San Marcuola*
14	*Exposition*	*Santissimo Sacramento*	*Angelo Raffaele*
15	*Exposition*	*Santissimo Sacramento*	*Angelo Raffaele*
16	*Exposition*	*Santissimo Sacramento*	*Sant'Antonin*
17	*Exposition*	*Santissimo Sacramento*	*Sant'Antonin*
18	*Exposition*	*Santissimo Sacramento*	*San Cassiano*
19	St. Peter of Alcantarà	San Pietro d'Alcantarà	Santa Maria Maddalena
	Exposition	*Santissimo Sacramento*	*San Cassiano*
20	*Exposition*	*Santissimo Sacramento*	*San Luca*
21	St. Ursula	Sant'Orsola	Santi Giovanni e Paolo
	Exposition	*Santissimo Sacramento*	*San Luca*
22	*Exposition*	*Santissimo Sacramento*	*San Boldo*
23	*Exposition*	*Santissimo Sacramento*	*San Boldo*
24	Archangel Raphael	**San Rocco**	Angelo Raffaele?
		Angelo Raffaele	Angelo Raffaele
		Suffragio di Morti	Angelo Raffaele

(continued)

October

	Occasion	Scuola	Location
	Exposition	*Santissimo Sacramento*	*San Giovanni Grisostomo*
25	*Exposition*	*Santissimo Sacramento*	*San Giovanni Grisostomo*
26	*Exposition*	*Santissimo Sacramento*	*San Simeon Piccolo*
27	*Exposition*	*Santissimo Sacramento*	*San Simeon Piccolo*
28	*Exposition*	*Santissimo Sacramento*	*San Trovaso*
29	*Exposition*	*Santissimo Sacramento*	*San Trovaso*
30	*Exposition*	*Santissimo Sacramento*	*San Vidal*
31	*Exposition*	*Santissimo Sacramento*	*San Vidal*
—	Most Holy Rosary	**Santa Maria della Carità**	Santa Maria della Carità
		Santa Maria della Misericordia	Santa Maria della Misericordia
		Santa Maria del Rosario	Santi Giovanni e Paolo
		B.V. Adorante il suo Divin Parto	Spirito Santo
		B.V. Assunta	Santa Maria in Broglio
		B.V. del Rosario	Angelo Raffaele
		B.V. del Rosario	San Domenico
		B.V. del Rosario	San Matteo
		B.V. del Rosario	San Niccolo dei Mendicoli
		B.V. del Rosario	San Paternian
		B.V. del Rosario	San Simeon Grande
		B.V. del Rosario	Santa Maria dell'Umiltà
		B.V. del Rosario	Santa Maria Zobenigo
		B.V. del Rosario	Santi Filippo e Giacomo
		B.V. del Rosario	Sant'Angelo
		B.V. del Rosario	Sant'Antonin
—	Fourth Sunday in October	Angelo Custode	Santi Apostoli

November

	Occasion	Scuola	Location
1	All Saints	**all scuole grandi?**	at each scuola
2	Day of the Dead	**all scuole grandi**	procession to churches throughout the city
		Santa Maria della Morte	San Basso
		Santa Veneranda	Corpus Domini
		Suffragio di Morti	Santa Trinità
		Suffragio di Morti	Santi Filippo e Giacomo
	in Octave of the Dead	San Giuseppe	Corpus Domini
	Sunday in the Octave	**San Marco**	San Marco
		Santa Maria della Misericordia	Santa Maria della Misericordia
		Sovvegno della Trinità	San Leonardo
		Suffragio di Morti	San Geremia
	Ottavario della Morte	Agonizanti	Angelo San Raffaele
		Suffragio di Morti	San Salvatore

November

	Occasion	Scuola	Location
		Suffragio di Morti	Santi Filippo e Giacomo
3	*Exposition*	*Santissimo Sacramento*	*San Barnaba*
4	St. Charles Borromeo	Milanesi	Santa Maria Gloriosa dei Frari
		San Carlo	San Leonardo
	Exposition	*Santissimo Sacramento*	*San Barnaba*
5	St. Elizabeth	B.V.	San Giuliano
		Santa Maria Elisabetta	San Tomà
6	St. Leonard	**Santa Maria della Carità**	?
		San Leonardo	San Leonardo
		San Leonardo	San Salvatore
7	*Exposition*	*Santissimo Sacramento*	*Santa Marina*
8	*Exposition*	*Santissimo Sacramento*	*Santa Marina*
9	Vigil of St. Theodore	**San Teodoro**	San Teodoro
	Exposition	*Santissimo Sacramento*	*San Martino*
10	St. Theodore	**all scuole grandi**	San Teodoro
	Exposition	*Santissimo Sacramento*	*San Martino*
11	St. Martin	**San Giovanni Evangelista**	San Martino
		Agonizzanti	San Martino
		San Martino	San Martino
	Exposition	*Santissimo Sacramento*	*San Salvatore*
12	*Exposition*	*Santissimo Sacramento*	*San Salvatore*
13			
14			
15	*Exposition*	*Santissimo Sacramento*	*Santa Margarita*
16	*Exposition*	*Santissimo Sacramento*	*Santa Margarita*
17	*Exposition*	*Santissimo Sacramento*	*San Stin*
18	*Exposition*	*Santissimo Sacramento*	*San Stin*
19			
20			
21	Presentation of the Virgin (Santa Maria della Salute)	**all scuole grandi**	San Marco and Santa Maria della Salute
		B.V.	San Polo
		B.V. della Morte	San Basso
		B.V. della Presentazione	San Boldo
		B.V. della Presentazione	San Geremia
		B.V. della Salute	Spirito Santo
		San Giobbe	San Giobbe
		Suffragio di Morti	San Vio
	Exposition	*Santissimo Sacramento*	*San Gregorio*
22	St. Cecilia	Santa Cecilia	San Martino
	Exposition	*Santissimo Sacramento*	*San Gregorio*
23			
24			
25	St. Catherine of Alexandria	**San Giovanni Evangelista**	Santi Giovanni e Paolo
		Santa Catterina	San Giminiano
		Santa Catterina	San Stae
	Exposition	*Santissimo Sacramento*	*San Felice*

(continued)

November

	Occasion	Scuola	Location
26	St. Alipius	Sant'Alipio	San Basilio
	St. Bellinus	San Bellino	San Gregorio
	Exposition	*Santissimo Sacramento*	*San Felice*
27			
28			
29	*Exposition*	*Santissimo Sacramento*	*San Basso*
30	St. Andrew	**San Rocco**	San Rocco and Sant'Andrea
		Sant'Andrea	Sant'Andrea
	Exposition	*Santissimo Sacramento*	*San Basso*
—	Third Sunday in November	Buona Morte	San Silvestro

December

	Occasion	Scuola	Location
1	*Exposition*	*Santissimo Sacramento*	*San Giacomo dall'Orio*
2	*Exposition*	*Santissimo Sacramento*	*San Giacomo dall'Orio*
3	St. Francis Xavier	Buona Morte	Sant'Antonin
4	St. Barbara	Santa Barbara	Santa Maria Formosa
5			
6	St. Nicholas	San Nicolò dei Marineri	Sant'Antonio di Castello
		San Nicolò	San Nicolò dei Mendicoli
		San Nicolò	San Salvatore
		San Nicolò	Santa Maria dei Carmine
7	St. Ambrose	Milanesi	Santa Maria Gloriosa dei Frari
	Vigil of the Conception	**Santa Maria della Misericordia**	Santa Maria della Misericordia
	Exposition	*Santissimo Sacramento*	*San Provolo*
8	Conception of the Virgin	**all scuole grandi**	Santa Maria della Misericordia
		B.V. della Concezione	San Giacomo dall'Orio
		B.V. della Concezione	San Moisè
		B.V. della Concezione	Santa Maria Gloriosa dei Frari
	Exposition	*Santissimo Sacramento*	*San Provolo*
9	*Exposition*	*Santissimo Sacramento*	*San Simeon Grande*
10	Blessed Virgin of Loreto	B.V. dell'Umiltà e di Loreto	San Lio
	Exposition	*Santissimo Sacramento*	*San Simeon Grande*
11	*Exposition*	*Santissimo Sacramento*	*San Tomà*
12	*Exposition*	*Santissimo Sacramento*	*San Tomà*
13	*Exposition*	*Santissimo Crocefisso*	*San Marcuola*
14	*Exposition*	*Santissimo Crocefisso*	*San Marcuola*
15	*Exposition*	*Santissimo Sacramento*	*San Lio*
16	*Exposition*	*Santissimo Sacramento*	*San Lio*
17	*Exposition*	*Santissimo Sacramento*	*Santa Lucia ("per l'Espettation del Parto")*

December

	Occasion	Scuola	Location
18	Expectation of the Birth	B.V. dell'Espettazion del Parto	Santa Lucia
	Exposition	*Santissimo Sacramento*	*Santa Lucia*
19	*Exposition*	*Santissimo Sacramento*	*Santa Lucia*
20	*Exposition*	*Santissimo Sacramento*	*Santa Lucia*
21	St. Thomas	**San Rocco**	San Tomà
	Exposition	*Santissimo Sacramento*	*Santa Lucia*
22	*Exposition*	*Santissimo Sacramento*	*Santa Lucia*
23	*Exposition*	*Santissimo Sacramento*	*Santa Lucia*
24	*Exposition*	*Santissimo Sacramento*	*Santa Lucia*
25	*Exposition*	*Santissimo Sacramento*	*San Bortolomeo*
26	St. Stephen	Santo Stefano	Santo Stefano
	Vigil of St. John Evangelist	**San Giovanni Evangelista**	San Giovanni Evangelista
	Exposition	*Santissimo Sacramento*	*San Bortolomeo*
27	St. John the Evangelist	**all scuole grandi**	San Giovanni Evangelista
		San Giovanni Battista	San Giovanni Decolato
	Exposition	*Santissimo Sacramento*	*San Bortolomeo*
28	*Exposition*	*Santissimo Sacramento*	*San Bortolomeo*
29			
30	St. Liberale	B.V. di Sette Dolori e San Liberal	San Paternian
31			
—	Novena of Christmas	Anconetta	Chiesa dell'Anconetta
		B.V. Assunta	Santa Maria in Broglio
		B.V. dell'Espettazion del Parto	Santa Lucia
		B.V. del Rosario	San Paternian
		B.V. del Rosario	Santi Filippo e Giacomo
—	Last Wednesday of Novena	Santa Maria del Carmine	Santa Maria del Carmine

Other Regular Occasions

Compline every Saturday	*B.V. Annonciata in San Cassiano*
Compline every Sunday	B.V. Assonta in San Geremia
First Sunday of each month	*Exposition at Anime del Purgatorio in Sant'Angelo*
Second Sunday of each month	*Exposition at Anime del Purgatorio in San Martino*
Third Sunday of each month	*Exposition at Anime del Purgatorio in Santa Lucia*
	Exposition at B.V. e Riscatto dei Schiavi in Santa Maria Formosa
Fourth Sunday of each month	*Exposition at Anime del Purgatorio in San Samuel*
	Nome di Maria (Maestranze dell'Arsenale) in Sant'Antonio di Castello
Fifth Sunday of each month	*Exposition at Anime del Purgatorio in San Giacomo dall'Orio*

APPENDIX 3

Musicians for the Festa of San Rocco, 1595–1634

Year	Maestro	Choirs	Instrumentalists	Organs	Solo Singers and Other Performers	Cost
1595	Giovanni Croce	2 companies of singers; cantori of the scuola	Bassani and Favretti companies with violins and violoni	Giovanni Gabrieli and others	—	£840 D.135
1598	Giovanni Croce	singers; cantori of the scuola	Bassani and Favretti companies with 2 violins and 2 violoni	Giovanni Gabrieli and 3 others	—	£856 s. 8 D.138
1600	Giovanni Croce	2 companies of singers; cantori of the scuola	Bassani and Favretti companies; Venturin and another violone; 4 additional players; Priuli on the lute; harp	Giovanni Gabrieli and 3 others	—	£864 D.139
1602	Giovanni Croce	singers; cantori of the scuola	Bassano directing 2 companies of players; 2 violins, violas, violone, lutes, harp	Giovanni Gabrieli for 6 organs	falsettist	£1252 s. 15 D.202
1603	pre Bortolo Morosini	2 companies of singers; cantori of the scuola	Bassani and Favretti companies, 4 violins, violone	Giovanni Gabrieli for 6 organs	boys	£1014 s. 15 D.164
1604	pre Bortolo Morosini	singers; cantori of the scuola	Giovanni Bassano for 2 companies of players, each with 2 violins; 4 other violins, 4 lutes, violone	Giovanni Gabrieli for 7 organs	singers from Padua: don Vido Rovetta da Piove, pre Terentio, pre Benedeto, pre Giachomo, pre Zamaria, pre Otavio, Bortolamio; bass from Poland	£1381 s. 12 D.223
1605	pre Bortolo Morosini	2 companies of singers; cantori of the scuola	Giovanni Bassano for 2 companies, each with a violin; Ventura dal violin	Giovanni Gabrieli for 6 organs	additional singers	£1021 D.165
1606	Giovanni Croce	Steffano Rinieri for 2 companies of singers; cantori of the scuola	Giovanni Bassano for 2 companies, each with a violin; 2 additional violins, Ventura dal violon, 2 lutes	Giovanni Gabrieli for 4 organs	2 additional falsettists, fra Agustin of the Frari	£1017 s. 9 D.164

Year		Singers	Players	Organs/Composers	Names	Cost
1608	pre Bortolo Morosini	pre Bortolo Morosini for 2 companies of singers; cantori of the scuola	Giovanni Bassano for 2 companies, each with a violin; company of Nicolò da Udine with a violin; violone	Giovanni Gabrieli for 5 organs; Orindo, organist at SS. Giovanni e Paolo; Giovanni Battista Grillo	Don Vido Rovetta da Piove, Bartolomeo Barbarino (il Pesarino), Giulio da Padoa, Mattia Fernando (il Spagnol)	£1376 D.222
1609	pre Bortolo Morosini	2 companies of singers; cantori of the scuola	Giovanni Bassano for 2 companies with 6 additional players; 4 violins	Giovanni Gabrieli, 5 organs, Giovanni Priuli	Don Vido Rovetta da Piove, Bartolomeo Barbarino, Visentino, piovan de San Stin	£1268 s. 4 D.205
1610	pre Bortolo Morosini	singers; cantori of the scuola	players, violone	Giovanni Gabrieli and 4 organists	Don Vido Rovetta da Piove, Mattia Fernando, Bartolomeo Barbarino	£901 s. 12 D.145
1611	?	singers, cantori of the scuola	players, violone	Giovanni Gabrieli and 4 organs	Don Vido Rovetta da Piove, Bartolomeo Barbarino, 2 boys, pre Bortolo [Morosini?], Piovan de San Stin	£909 s. 12 D.147
1612	pre Gasparo Locadello	2 companies of singers; cantori of the scuola	wind players with two additonal players (violins?); violin, violone	Giovanni Priuli for 4 organists	Bartolomeo Barbarino, Alesandro falsettist from Grace	£899 s. 12 D.145
1613	Giovanni Priuli	singers	wind players, violin, viola; Francesco Bonfante	Giovanni Battista Grillo for 3 organs	Bartolomeo Barbarino, Don Vido Rovetta da Piove, soprano and Don Greco, Grighetto, Michel Angelo, pre Gasparo Locadello	£958 s. 16 D.155
1614	pre Gasparo Locadello	singers	3 companies of players, cittern, 2 lironi, Giovanni Bassano, Francesco Bonfante	Giovanni Battista Grillo for 5 organs	Don Vido Rovetta da Piove, Don Antonio da Treviso, Bartolomeo Barbarino, Don Geronimo, Don Giovanni Battista, Piovan de San Geremia	£1303 s. 4 D.210
1615	?	2 companies of singers; cantori of the scuola	44 players, trumpets, 2 citterns, violone	Giovanni Battista Grillo and 3 organists	—	£870 s. 16 D.140
1616	?	choir of San Marco, cantori of the scuola	2 companies of players with 3 additional players, theorbo, guitar, Zamaria de Ventura dal violin	3 organs	maestro di capella of the Frari, Don Vido Rovetta da Piove, Bartolomeo Barbarino, Calzeta falsettist, pre Ricardini of the Frari	£1050 s. 4 D.169

(continued)

Year	Maestro	Choirs	Instrumentalists	Organs	Solo Singers and Other Performers	Cost
1617	Gabriele Susper	singers	Bonfante with 2 companies of players	Giovanni Battista Grillo; organist of the Frari; Gabriele Susper; Battista organista	additional bass, Bartolomeo Barbarino, Don Vido Rovetta da Piove, falsettist of Abbate Morosini, contralto of the bishop of Padua, Calzetta, 2 boys of Cavalli	£1115 D.180
1618	?	the comapies of singers of Stefano Ferarese and Battista Coradin	players, 2 lironi, 3 theorbos	Giovanni Battista Grillo with 3 large organs and 2 small organs	Don Vido Rovetta da Piove, Don Giovanni Battista Cattaben, Bartolomeo Barbarino, boy from Ca' Grimani, 2 Greghetti, 2 basses, Gottardo Menegotto, Ferrarese, Roman, signor Ferdinando	£1501 D.242
1619	?	2 companies of singers; cantori of the scuola	3 companies of players, 2 lironi, 5 theorbos, lute	5 large organs, Giovanni Battista Grillo	Don Vido Rovetta da Piove, Bartolomeo Barbarino, priest from the Madonna dell'Orto, boys from Ca' Grimani, Gottardo Menegotto, Ferrarese, Buranello, Lucio Mora, Alessandro	£1592 D.257
1620	?	singers	players, lironi, theorbos, spinets	Giovanni Battista Grillo for 5 organs	Don Vido Rovetta da Piove, padre Zocolante, Bartolomeo Barbarino, bass from Padua, maestro di Cappella [of the Frari], il Veronese, Capello e Lazzarini, 2 singers	£2203 s. 16 D.355
1621	?	—	—			£2046 s. 2 D.330
1623	Claudio Monteverdi	—	—	Paolo Giusto, Gabriele Susper		£713 D.115
1624	Alessandro Grandi	1 company of singers; cantori of the scuola	2 companies of players, 4 theorbos, 2 lironi, harp, Bonfante	Giovanni Picchi, Carlo Filago, 4 other organists	3 basses (Gandello, Don Francesco, Dominico), 5 tenors (Gottardo Menegotto, Don Vicenzo, Don Giovanni Battista Giove, Don Giovanni Battista from the Carità, Don Giacomo from the Misericordia), 3 contraltos (Badoer, fra Pietro del Carmine, il Greco), Don Francesco da Mantova, Alvise Grani, Bartolomeo Barbarino, 5 sopranos (padre Zoccolante, Don Vido Rovetta da Piove, Grimani, friar from Santo Steffano, boy from the Misericordia)	£1782 s. 8 D.287

Year	maestro	choir/singers	players	organist	other singers	cost
1625	?	cantori of the scuola	2 players	organist	pre Piero, li Rossi, friar from Santo Stefano	£144 D.23
1626	padre Finetti	singers; cantori of the scuola	players	Giovanni Picchi, 2 organs	Felicino, il Mantovano, Menegeto	£1170 D.189
1627	Claudio Monteverdi	choir of San Marco; cantori of the scuola	2 companies of players directed by Rosso and Giacomazzo, 2 lironi	Pighetti [Picchi?], 4 organists	Don Vido Rovetta da Piove, friar from Santo Stefano, Jacometto, Don Domenico (with theorbo), Don Giovanni Battista (with theorbo), il Greghetto (with theorbo), Don Giacometto Battin, Don Vicenzo (with theorbo), Gottardo Menegotto, Felice (with theorbo), Giovanni Battista Giove, Franesco Cavalli, pre Angelo di Carmini, Buranello (with theorbo), Don Giacomo bass, Nardo bass, padre Benedo, padre Bolognese bass, padrino da Padova, Girardo and Magnetto (with theorbos), a young foreigner	£1391 s. 5 D.224
1628	Giovanni Rovetta	company of 15 singers; cantori of the scuola	2 companies of players, 4 theorbos and other instruments, 2 violins	Giovanni Picchi, 4 other organs	other singers	£1493 s. 12 D.241
1629	maestro di cappella of the Frari	—	—	—	—	£1371 s. 16 D.221
1630	Giovanni Rovetta	—	—	—	—	£1730 D.279
1631	?	—	—	—	—	£1054 D.170
1634	?	—	—	—	—	£1768 s. 12 D.285

Source: ASV, SSR II, 155–171.

NOTES

Preface

1. Elena Quaranta has attempted just such a broad study in her important new book *Oltre San Marco*, but her approach, though invaluable, is also somewhat problematic. On the positive side, she deals with the entire breadth of religious institutions in Venice (other than the cappella ducale), including parish and monastic churches and the scuole grandi and scuole piccole. She has, however, limited her study in two ways, one for practical reasons (the temporal restriction to the Renaissance), and the other methodological. Much of her data is derived from a few series of documents that have the virtue of including all institutions of a certain class at one point in time, or at one point in their histories (such as tax declarations for parish and monastic churches or the statute books of confraternities). The commonalities evidenced by this type of documentation are what she intends to highlight, with substantiation of their validity achieved through a more in-depth study of a few sample institutions (this method has been advanced, as well, by David Bryant). Outside the scope of this method are many of the aspects I find the most interesting, and that are the focus of the present study: wide variations among similar, contemporary institutions, brought about by their particular circumstances and histories, and changes over time, both within single institutions and throughout entire classes of institutions. Such variations can only be discovered through the rather messier process of studying all extant relevant documentation.

Chapter 1

1. Moryson, *Itinerary*, 1:184–85. This passage, like others in his description of Venice, is freely derived from Sansovino, *Venetia città nobilissima*, originally published in Venice in 1581.

2. The pathbreaking early studies of confraternities are Meersseman, *Ordo fraternitatis* and Monti, *Le confraternite medievali*. For a more recent study placing the origins of confraternities within the context of widespread corporative leanings in Europe, see Greci, "Economia, religiosità, politica." The modern literature on confraternities is vast and growing. There is an excellent bibliography of works appearing between 1971 and 1991 in

Elizari Huarte, "Gremios, confradias y solidaridades." Each issue of the journal *Confraternitas*, the bulletin of the Society for Confraternity Studies, includes a listing of recent publications in the field, and the Society maintains a comprehensive listing on its website (http://citd.scar.utoronto.ca/CRRS/Confraternitas/collect.htm).

3. See D'Accone, "Le compagnie dei laudesi" and Wilson, *Music and Merchants.*

4. Meerssemann, *Ordo fraternitatis,* 1:90–94 and Monti, *Le confraternite medievali,* 1: 73–75.

5. Charlton T. Lewis and Charles Short, *A Latin Dictionary* (*The Perseus Project,* http://www.perseus.tufts.edu, July 2001), s.v. "schola," definition I.B.2.b.

6. On this movement, see Meersseman, *Ordo fraternitatis,* 2:451, and Monti, *Le confraternite medievali,* 1:199–202.

7. See Daniel, *Joachim of Flora* and Reeves, *Influence of Prophecy.*

8. Henderson, "The Flagellant Movement"; the quoted passages are on p. 150.

9. Bornstein, *Bianchi of 1399.*

10. For a recent discussion of the origin of the scuole see De Sandre Gasparini, "La pietà laicale" (esp. 944–53).

11. The term is said to be a corruption of the Italian phrase "madre regola," or mother rule. The most important surviving early mariegole are the following: for the Scuola Grande di San Giovanni Evangelista, ASV, SSGE 7 (a Latin mariegola of 1261), 3 (an Italian version of 1307), and 41 (a late fourteenth-century copy of the 1307 Italian mariegola); for the Scuola Grande di San Marco, ASV, SSM 216 (a seventeenth-century copy of a fourteenth-century Italian version); for the Scuola Grande di Santa Maria della Carità ASV, SSMC 233 (the original 1260 Latin version) and 233bis (a thirteenth-century Italian version); and for the Scuola Grande di Santa Maria della Misericordia, ASV, SSMM 3 (the 1308 Latin original), busta A no. 1 (the 1308 Italian original), and busta A no. 3 (a fourteenth-century Italian version). The insignia of the scuole, found wherever the scuola was present, from its own documents and processional apparatus to houses it owned for rental income, were as follows: Santa Maria della Carità, a Greek cross inscribed within two concentric circles; San Marco, the letters SM or the Lion of St. Mark; Santa Maria della Misericordia, the letters SMV (for Santa Maria della Valverde, its alternative name) or the Madonna of Mercy (a standing Mary with brothers protected by her broad cloak); San Giovanni Evangelista, a bishop's crozier; San Rocco, the letters SR and an elongated cross; and San Teodoro, the letters ST or an image of St. Theodore killing a dragon.

12. ASV, SSGE 41, ch. II: "Quanto la presente vita sia fievele, e caduca in stesa la humana fragilitade apertamente ne amaistra e demostra, ch'el misera huomo continuamente si porto da solicitudine fi alligado de ligami di subiection diabolica, e sempre involto in li peccadi."

13. ASV, SSGE 41, ch. II: "Onde inspiradi nui dalla Divina gratia pensassemo, e trattessemo como per dilection de Fraternitade, et de adiutorio de Oration a salude dele nostre aneme possamo acquistar, recordandose quel della Biade San Jacomo Apostolo, lo qual dise: 'Ore l'un per l'altroazo, che vui sie salvi, perché molto val la continua preghiera del zusto.' " The words of St. James are found in James 5:16.

14. ASV, SSM 216, prologue: "Nui dovemo per quella Carità de servir al prossimo con tutta nostra intentione . . . con opere perfette che sia a laude de lui, e salvamenta delle nostre aneme."

15. ASV, SSMC 233bis, prologue: "la caritate covre la multetudene deli pecadi." The passage in 1 Peter 4:7–9 is "And above all things have fervent charity among yourselves: for charity shall cover the multitude of sins." The similar passage in James 5:19–21, which caused the confusion, is "Let him know, that he which converteth the sinner from the error of his way shall save a soul from death, and shall hide a multitude of sins." Another

factor in creating the confusion might have been the recognition that other confraternities cited the passage from James discussed earlier.

16. ASV, SSM 216, prologue: "non cercava altra gloria, se non la Crose del nostro Signor Gesù Christo, e al suo exemplo dovemo humiliare l'anime nostre, e li corpi in disciplina carnale, e spirituale."

17. ASV, SSMC 233bis, prologue: "zascadun cum paxe e quieto si atenda, e no diga parole ociose e vane, e no se leve in superbia l'un contra l'autro, e no se contenda in ira, ma solamente parle e diga cose che pertegna ala salude dele aneme."

18. ASV, SSGE 41, ch. III: "volemo che tutto quello che da mo avanti se farà se debbia far all'honor, e stado de Misser lo Doxe, e del Comun de Venexia e de tutta la Patria."

19. ASV, SSGE 41, ch. I: "All'honor del magnifico Signor Messer Jesù Christo, e de la gloriosissima Vergene Mare Madona Sancta Maria, e del Beatissimo, e preciosissimo Apostolo, et Evangelista Misser San Zane Cavo, e Confalonier de questa benedetta Scuolla."

20. ASV, SSGE 41, ch. III: "Conciosia che sempre nostra intention sia a far cose le qual sia . . . ad'honor de Dio, e della soa dolze mare Madona Sancta Maria, e del pietosissimo Misser San Zane Apostolo, et Evangelista Cavo e Governador de questa nostra fraternitade de disciplina. E ad honor del precioso Evangelista Misser San Marco Padron, e Governador, e defensor de questa benedetta Cittade, e volemo che tutto quello che da mo avanti se farà se debbia far all'honor, e stado de Misser lo Doxe, e del Comun de Venexia e de tutta la Patria, e de zascadun bon Christian."

21. ASV, SSM 216, prologue: "reverentia de tutta la Corte Celestial et a honore, e reverentia de Misser lo Papa, e delli suoi Frari, e de tutta la Giexia de Roma, zoè li fedeli Christiani, e a honore, e reverentia de Misser lo Doxe, e de tutta lo so bon Consegio, e a honor, e stado del Comun de Venexia."

22. Quoted in Watson, *Shakespeare*, 24. Watson's first chapter is a good survey of the changing concept of honor from the Greeks to the Renaissance.

23. Augustine, *The City of God*, 5:14. Quoted in Watson, *Shakespeare*, 30.

24. Ashley, *Of Honor*, 28.

25. Erasmus, *Colloquies*, 254, quoted in Shalvi, *Relationship of Renaissance Concepts of Honour*, 41.

26. Caravia, *Il sogno di Caravia* (Venice, 1541); translation by Richard Mackenney from Chambers and Pullan, *Venice*, 213–16.

27. On the role of the friars in Florentine confraternities see Weissman, *Ritual Brotherhood;* Henderson, "Confraternities and the Church"; and Wilson, *Music and Merchants*, 13–36. On Bologna, see Terpstra, "Confraternities and Mendicant Orders." On the role of preaching, see Weissman, "Sacred Eloquence."

28. For a general survey of the histories of the Venetian scuole, and of their art and architecture, see Pignatti and Wiel, *Scuole di Venezia*.

29. The major architects of the scuole and their projects are as follows: Pietro Lombardo (San Giovanni Evangelista, 1478–81, and San Marco, c.1485), Mauro Coducci (San Giovanni Evangelista, 1498 and 1512, and San Marco [rebuilding after a fire], 1490–95), Bartolomeo Bon (San Marco, 1480s, and San Rocco, 1516–24), Scarpagnino (San Rocco, 1527–49), Jacopo Sansovino (San Marco, 1532–34, and Santa Maria della Misericordia, from 1534), Longhena (San Teodoro, 1668–71), and Giacomo Massari (an enlargement of San Giovanni Evangelista, 1727, and a new façade for Santa Maria della Carità, 1756–65). See Pignatti and Wiel, *Scuole di Venezia*, and Fortini Brown, "Honor and Necessity." Of the more detailed studies of the architecture of individual scuole, the most important is Sohm, *Scuola grande di San Marco*.

30. Major painting commissions include: Jacopo Bellini (San Marco from 1421 and 1444 [both destroyed]), Gentile Bellini (San Giovanni Evangelista, 1460s [destroyed] and San Marco from 1494 [some still in place, others in the Accademia Gallery in Venice and the Brera Museum in Milan), Giovanni Bellini (San Giovanni Evangelista, before 1485 [destroyed] and San Marco, from 1504), Palma Vecchio (San Marco, 1504–34), Titian (Santa Maria della Carità, 1538; the Presentation of the Virgin is still in place), Veronese (Santa Maria della Misericordia), and Tintoretto (San Marco, 1547–86 [in the Accademia Gallery] and San Rocco, 1564–87). The cycles painted up through the early sixteenth century are discussed in Fortini Brown, *Venetian Narrative Painting*.

31. Unless otherwise specified, the information in the following sections is derived from the mariegole listed in n. 11.

32. ASV, SSGE 41, ch. V: "Ancora volemo et ordenemo, che zaschaduno, che vorrà entrar in questa nostra Fraternitade de disciplina de Comunal Conseio de tutti li nostri fradelli possa esser recevudo . . . se non solamente persone cinquecento, e cinquanta . . . nessuno possa esser recevudo el qual non possa far la disciplina, et observar li detti nostri ordeni, et anco sia di minor età d'anni vinti. E se segondo el debito de natura algun delli nostri fradelli morirà, volemo che delli primi che vorrà intrar sia recevudi quelli che parerà più sufficienti."

33. See p. xiii.

34. See Queller, *Venetian Patriciate*.

35. On the *cittadino* class, see Zannini, *Burocrazia e burocrati*.

36. See Pullan, *Rich and Poor*.

37. ASV, SSMC 233bis.

38. See Henderson, "Confraternities and Politics."

39. The *tollela* was a wooden plaque bearing the name of the brother which was inserted into a slot in a board kept in the scuola (much like hymn indicators in many churches today) to indicate the presence of that brother at required events. The term was also used to refer to the board itself, and therefore to those brothers whose names appeared there.

40. ASV, SSMC 233.

41. ASV, SSGE 41, ch. VII: "governador, e correzedor de tutti nui."

42. Ibid.: "scriver le raxon della scuola et dell'intrada, como delle spese."

43. ASV, SSM 216, ch. IV: "lo qual debbia fezer e governar la scuola quando el Vardian non vi fosse."

44. ASV, SSGE 41, ch. X: "Che per ben e utilitade delle aneme delli nostri fradelli, li quali per soa devotion se deletta de andar da mattin per questa cittade battandose per lo muodo che se va in li dì ordenadi."

45. ASV, SSGE 16. See Glixon, "Music and Ceremony."

46. ASV, SSM 82, 228, and 229.

47. ASV, SSGE 41, ch. VII: "E degani dodese, zoè do per zascadun sestiere, li quali zaschadun debba haver un ruodolo del so colomello, suso lo qual debbia esser scripti tutti li nomi delli nostri fradelli de quello colomello. E volemo, che li dicti degani sia tegnudi de comandar li detti nostri fradelli ogni dì ordenado, et ogni fiada."

48. Ibid., ch. LXVI.

49. The parallel to the civic government was not unique to Venice. Little sees a similar relationship in the confraternities of Bergamo. See Little, *Liberty, Charity, Fraternity*.

50. The Venetian form of the Italian "aggiunta." This was the term regularly used in the Venetian government for supplementary bodies added to the traditional legislative and judicial organs.

51. ASV, SSGE, 41, ch. X: "far tutte quelli cose che per lo misser Vardian e per li suo compagni li sarà comandade per li fatti della scuola."

52. Lester Little (*Liberty, Charity, Fraternity*) describes similar sets of regulations at the confraternities of Bergamo. For Florence and Bologna see Weissman, *Ritual Brotherhood*, and Terpstra, *Lay Confraternities*.

53. ASV, SSGE 41, ch. IV: "In prima mente volemo et ordenemo, che nessun de nui fratelli osa ne pressuma in algun muodo over inzegno, persino per altri, prometter, consentir, over trattar alguna cosa la quall sia contro l'honor e stado de misser lo Doxe, e del Comun de Veniexia."

54. This idea emerged out of a discussion following a paper by Dr. Abigail Firey entitled "Sin, Crime, Penance, and Law in the Early Middle Ages," presented at the University of Kentucky, January 2001.

55. Terpstra, "Renaissance Congregationalism." The passages quoted are on p. 33. For similarly detailed activities in France see Barnes, "From Ritual to Meditative Piety."

56. See Wilson, *Music and Merchants*, 46 and Henderson "Confraternities and the Church," esp. 74–75.

57. The most important study of the central role of death to confraternities (focusing on those of San Sepolcro, in central Italy) is Banker, *Death in the Community*. See also the same author's "Death and Christian Charity."

58. In Florence, as Henderson explains, the confraternities only entered the scene after the family had performed this traditional task. See Henderson, *Piety and Charity*, 155 ff.

59. See Little, *Liberty, Charity, Fraternity*, 90–91.

60. ASV, SSMC 233bis, ch. XXX: "de ii cibi senza pese, salvo se'l no fose meso acoser in le erbe."

61. Ibid., ch. XXXI: "E dita la messa, zascun deli frari devia disnar cum paxe, charitade, senza algun murmuramento, digando zascadun veritade, e parole ke faza ad edificacion dele aneme nostre. . . . E disnado li frari nostri tuti in paciencia, lo residuo sia dadho ali poveri, e lo ke mester farà."

62. On the Florentine situation see Weissman, "Brothers and Strangers," 27–45.

63. See Fortini Brown, "Honor and Necessity." It is notable that the Scuola di Santa Maria della Carità, in its decline in the eighteenth century, somehow managed to find funds of its own to build a new façade to a design by Giacomo Massari (replacing one of the fourteenth century).

64. The pioneering, and still authoritative, study of the role of the scuole in poor relief in Venice is Pullan, *Rich and Poor*.

65. ASV, SSMM 303.

66. ASV, SSGE 435.

67. ASV, SSR I 310.

68. See Pullan, *Rich and Poor*, 143–56.

69. For a detailed discussion of the interaction between the scuole and the Council of Ten up through the end of the fifteenth century, see Wurthmann, "The Council of Ten." See also Sbriziolo, "Per la storia delle confraternite veneziane. . . . Le scole dei battuti."

70. There is a copy of this decree in ASV, Inquisitori e revisori sopra le scuole grandi, Reg. 1, Capitolare I (1312–1710), f. 3.

71. ASV, Inquisitori e revisori sopra le scuole grandi 1, f. 7: "est magno tedio vicinii qui infirmitate gravati sunt, et etiam est fastidio sanis."

72. Ibid., f. 49^v: "è accresciuta a tanto la spesa che superfluamente si fa nelle scole

grandi di questa nostra città, sì de apparati come di pasti, che è ormai ridotta in una abominatione di sorte che non se li provedendo, buona parte del dinnaro delle scole, che deve andar in elemosine a poveri, si consumeria in tali abusi, e nel restante spendendo li guardiani grandi et presidenti di esse scole etiam del suo proprio dinnaro a pompa, fra breve spatio di tempo non si ritroveria chi voglia entrarvi, per non poter o non voler concorrer di spender con li suoi processori, et però, Andarà parte che per auttorità di questo consiglio sia statuito, che da mo nell'avvenire in alcuna delle dette cinque scole non si possa far apparato over conciero o altro ornamento o manifattura, salvo le spaliere a longo i banchi con li suoi bancali sopra di quelli, et così non possano, nè del dinnaro della Scola nè del suo, far pasto nè collation, sì in scola come fuori di scuola, sotto pena di pagar ducati 50 da esser dispensati a poveri frattelli di essa scola."

73. See D'Angiolini and Pavone, *Guida generale*, 1080.

74. Ibid.

75. Ibid., 1085.

76. Primarily in the series of Cauzioni, ASV, SSR II.

77. See below, ch. 3.

78. These Faustini papers are in ASV, SSM 99–120 and 184–95. For a detailed treatment of the operatic activities documented here, see Glixon and Glixon, "Marco Faustini and Venetian Opera" and Glixon and Glixon, *Marco Faustini and Operatic Production*.

79. When I conducted my research, none of these *fondi* except for that of San Rocco had been indexed, although the project had been started several times. One of my major tasks, therefore, was compiling my own inventories of the archives, sometimes with the aid of helpful archivists, especially Dr. Francesca Cavazana Romanelli. Recently, the staff of the Archivio has completed an initial inventory of all of them, which will be useful until complete indexes are available.

80. The archive was reorganized in 1980 by Dottoressa Marina Magro, and again in 2002.

Chapter 2

1. The pioneering work on Venetian civic processions, their origins, development, and significance, is Muir, *Civic Ritual*. More recently, Casini has extended Muir's work, and also confronted the Venetian situation with that of Florence, in *I gesti del principe*. His observations on the scuole grandi are on pp. 15–63.

2. On the evolution of the official Venetian ritual calendar, see Muir, *Civic Ritual*, 57–72.

3. ASV, SGSMC 233bis, ch. X: "Ancora ordenemo, e fermamente statuimo, che tuti li frari de questa nostra fraternitade e scola, se li serà en questa patria, senza zusto inpedimento, in questi infrascriti dì, continuamente debia convegnir ensenbre, ala glesia e logo dela Biada Vergene Maria dela Caritade, cum ogna paxe, et humilitade, senza alguna murmuracion, se debia despuiar, e cum verberacion e cum paxe debia andar in procesion per la terra, cum la croxe, e cum li cirii grosi enpresi. En queste precesion se debia far, ogna prima domenega de zascadun mese de l'ano. Et in le quatro feste de Senta Maria, zoè la soa purification, la soa anunciacion, la soa asension, et in la soa nativitade. Et eciamdeo in la festa de la sension de Cristo. Et in la festa de miser Sen Marco evangelista da la procesion. Et in lo dì de venere sento. Et in lo dì deli morti po la festa d'ogni senti. Et in questo dì deli morti sia fata cantar una mesa devotamente per anema de tuti li nostri frari, che de questo segolo se pasadi. E volemo che specialmente, in questi dì infrascriti, zoè in le quatro feste de Senta Maria, et in la sension de Cristo, et in la festa de Sen Marco dala procesion,

et in lo dì de venere sento, et in lo dì de tuti li morti, caschadun deli nostri frari debia portar e tignir inpreso un cirio en man de fin che se fate le dite procesion."

4. See ASV, SGSMC 233bis, ch. VI. At the Scuola di San Marco, this was only once a year, at Easter. See also pp. 24–25, this volume.

5. ASV, SGSMM 3: "che lo dì de misser San Vido debia da mo avanti esser dì ordenado como se li oltri per bon stado e per mantegnimento dela nostra cità de Venesia."

6. The myth of Venice has been treated in many places. One of the best discussions is in Muir, *Civic Ritual*, ch. 1.

7. ASV, SGSMM, busta A, no. 1, 26 May 1359: "per puixor afari i qual a zascun nostro frar, si per forestieri como per i suo mestieri."

8. On the relic, its miracles, and the paintings depicting them, see Fortini Brown, *Venetian Narrative Painting*.

9. While the preaching of a sermon by the scuola's chaplain cannot be ruled out, there is no evidence of the hiring of outside preachers, nor of the selection of a chaplain based on his ability or fame as a preacher, nor are there extant sermons, manuscript or published, connected with the scuole. On the tradition of sermons in Florentine confraternities, see Weissman, "Sacred Eloquence." On *sacre rappresentazioni*, see Barr, "Music and Spectacle" and Newbigin, "The Word Made Flesh."

10. ASV, SSGE 16, section [8]: *Feste*: "El zorno de misser San Zuane a dì xxvii dexenbrio se fa solene festa et se die advertir de non far gran festa perche se fa de beni dela scuola."

11. ASV, SSM 216, ch. XX: "Ancora volemo che in la festa de misser San Marco del mese d'avril tutti li frari de questa nostra fraternitade debbia esser con le soe cape a procession con cirii impresi in le sue man e debbia far cantar una messa sotto confession in quella giesia. E zascaduna fiada che se va in procession ad'honor, e reverentia de misser San Marco diebbiase inzenochiar davanti la porta della detta giesia, e zascadun debba dir tre Pater Nostri, et tre Ave Marie, azo, che la cittade de Venetia e tutti quelli, che habita, habbia e haverà bon stado."

12. ASV, SSGE 46, f. 57ᵛ: "Item de far convochar tuti i prevedi de la schuola lo dì de Sen Stefano che vien ad esser la vizilia de misser Sen Ziane chonfalonier de questa benedeta fraternitade, i qual prevedi, tuti chon suo pluviali honorevel e magnifichamente sonando li organi debia chantar la vesporo a reverencia del biado evangelista nostro governador, li qual prevedi sempre tignando impresa una chandela grossa in man per homo se chonzam muodo de chuoro l'un per l'altro zioè la mitade da l'un di ladi e l'altra mitade da l'altro davanti l'altar de la schuola de misser Sen Ziane. El qual vesporo dito misser lo vardian e compagni die far una piatanza ai prevedi sovra scriti. Item se die far convochar per lo simele tuti li diti prevedi e i fradelli de la nostra schuola l'altro dì, zioè in lo dì de misser Sen Ziane. I qual tuti prevedi regoladi chomo è dito de sovra, diebia chantar la messa solenne. La qual messa dita i fradelli si die despoiar e andar in procession in questo muodo, zioè che i diti prevedi die andar avanti chon le relige de la schuola soto una ombrella de panno d'oro over de seda. E in lo dito dì se die portar la croxie de cristalo. E fate le dite chose se die dar a ziaschadun di prevedi avanti che se parta el so pan e la so chandella."

13. ASR, *Libro di ordeni 1521*: "El zorno dela Madona de marzo sia la festa principal dela Schuola dela Charità; la nostra Schuola è obligada andar a honorarla per che loro vien da nui ala nostra solemne festa. Et portasse el christo, 4 cirii doro, et xii dopieri doro, tutti afestadi, et li cantadori de canto et li sonadori, et vasse da matina a hora consueta."

14. ASR, *Libro di ordeni 1521*: "poi andar ala Schuola de San Marco a honorarli, et cantando cum li vostri cantadori de canto in sala, poi cantate nel suo albergo, salutandovi

Vardian cum Vardian alegrandose insieme. Et alhora miser lo vardian de San Marco vi da uno mazo ligado de candele."

15. ASV, SSMM 4, f. 64.

16. ASV, SSMM 166, f. 382^{r-v}.

17. In, for example, the 1365 choirbook of the Scuola della Carità, BNM, Lat. II, 199 (2426). The opening illumination, with several brothers in their capes, is reproduced as plate 1 in Glixon, "Late Medieval Chant," 201.

18. Sanudo, *Diarii*, 13:132–36. A translation of the section of this description dealing with the scuole grandi was published in Glixon, *"Far una bella procession."*

19. ASV, SSGE 16, section 7.

20. ASV, SSGE 46.

21. ASR, *Libro de ordeni 1521*.

22. ASV, SSGE 16. One additional document, of 1666, describes the basic route the Scuola di San Giovanni Evangelista used to get to the Piazza on all of these occasions, with a change that was to be made at that time: the brothers were to go past San Stin, Sant'Agostin, San Polo (approaching through the sottoportico), to the Rialto, over the bridge, and to San Marco via the Marzaria, eliminating the earlier practice of also passing by San Lorenzo and San Zaccaria. The older route was considerably longer than the newer, direct route, and the extra time spent in procession meant significantly greater expense in wax for candles, which was to be avoided.

23. See also Glixon, *"Far una bella procession"* and Glixon, "Music and Ceremony."

24. ASR, *Libro de ordeni 1521*: "El zorno de San Marco Evangelista se va a offerir ala Illustrissima Signoria in Giesia de San Marco. Se porta doi soleruoli d'oro, et adornasi de tabernaculi, et metesse el dedo de San Rocho et altro ornadi de candele et perfumegi, et portasse doi ombrele doro fornide de arme dele cinque schuole grande et arme del papa et ambassadori de potentati. Item al partirse dela Schuola se manda avanti xxiiii dopieri d'oro cum le tre zoie per dopier et le so verdure. Item driedo a ditti dopieri se mette li sonadori de arpe, viole, et lauti numero iiii. Poi driedo el nostro glorioso confalon, cioè el crucifixo adornado cum la sua zoia primaria e bella de vari ornamenti e perfumegi de oxeleti. Item dananti al ditto Christo doi ciri grandi et doi altri ciri d'oro adredo tutti con zoie et verdure. Item se puol anche portare el cirio grosso qual se porta anche la note del Venere Sancto . . . Item se porta i dopieri picoli indoradi, et portasse in mano, sono in tutto dopieri numero xx, partidi a questo modo, et metesse dopieri dentro de cera de pexo de lire 3 l'uno con le sue verdure. Dinanti al primo soleruol se porta di soprascritti dopieri numero vi. Dredo al ditto soleruol se ne porta altri dopieri numero vi che vien a esser dinanti al segondo soleruol. Dredo al segondo soleruol se ne porta de ditti dopieri numero viii, che son in tutto dopieri d'oro pizoli numero xx. Item dapoi questo sono li nostri cantadori de canto che cantano al usato. Dapoi loro sono el nostro Capelan dela nostra Giesia con uno Zago con una candela per uno in mano. Dapoi el Vardian Grando con tutta la sua bancha portando una candela in mano consueta, con tutto el resto di fradelli."

25. Ibid.: "Se aferma a mezo el coro de San Marco con la Santissima Croxe, zoè si mete el soler in tera et quela se toca per el nostro Capelan con le macete d'arzento, et portase al Serenissimo Principe per segnarse, et similiter ali Signori Ambasadori, et di mano in mano a tuta la Signoria, ancora se porta le sotoschrite candele le qual se distribuise . . ."

26. The various types of musicians called for in these documents will be discussed in the following chapters.

27. ASR, *Libro de ordeni 1521*: "Item se veste anzoli de nostre vestimente numero xxiiii, i quali portano in mano diversi arzenti cum fiori dentro et ruoxe. Item li nostri fradelli portano in mano arzenti de diversi sorte, le qual tutte arzentarie se manda avanti el Vardian et compagni, et poi li cantadori de canto vanno avanti dela Bancha cantando.

Li sonadori vanno dananti al Christo. Poi tutti li fradeli cum so candele in mano seguitano driedo la bancha."

28. ASV, SSGE 16: "Dopieri d'oro fornidi con verdure zogie consuete—no. 24."

29. Ibid.: "Fase qualce volte qualce representation de figure antique segondo sacra scritura, come apar a misser lo guardian et compagni."

30. ASR, *Libro de ordeni 1521*: "Nui fessemo uno belletissimo aparato de solerii et andanti a piedi: signification del Testamento vechio fatto tutto ale spexe de miser lo Vardian et de i governanti dela Bancha, per che cusì sempre se ha observato."

31. Sanudo, *Diarii*, 20:274–75: "San Rocho, di la qual è guardian sier Zuan Calbo drapier grando, fo benissimo in hordene con anzoli, arzenti et molti soleri et demostration a piedi dil Testamento vechio, et tra li altri soleri uno mondo con uno putin, et in uno altro una nave con uno piava pesse in mar, et su uno altro alcuni putini nudi. Et eravi *etiam* li 4 doctori di la Chiexia a cavalo: San Hironimo, Santo Agustin, Sancto Ambrosio, Sancto Gregorio. *Conclusive* fu bel veder . . ."

32. Sanudo, *Diarii*.

33. See above, n. 18.

34. Sansovino, *Venetia città nobilissima*. The 1585 procession is described on pp. 457–66, and that of 1598 on pp. 432–38. These descriptions first appeared in the 1608 edition, enlarged by Giovanni Stringa, a canon at San Marco, and were retained in the 1663 version, edited, with further additions, by Giustiniano Martinoni.

35. Ibid., p. 463: "David, vestito regalmente, con arpa in mano, con la quale soavissimamente suonava."

36. Ibid.: "i Pastori sopra un palco, che nella loro capanna per allegrezza suonavano, & un'Angelo gli soprastava cantando, *Gloria in excelsis Deo.*"

37. Ibid., p. 464: "il Giudicio universale, dove era nostro Signore in loco eminente, & che come dalla parte diritta haveva fiori, & rose, così dalla sinistra haveva una pungentissima spada; con quelli promettendo a gli eletti ogni contento, & felicità, & con questa a dannati ogni penna, & angoscia: al basso si vedevano i morti uscir dalle sepolture, & si sentiva (senza veder però) strepito grandissimo di trombe, & tamburi, che pose ne' circonsttanti grandissimo terrore. Seguiva un Regale suonato perfettamente da un fanciullo."

38. Ibid, p. 433: "una bellissima donna, figurata per la Pace, accompagnata sopra il solaro istesso da un maraviglioso, & nobilissimo concerto di liuti, che eccellentissimamente suonavano, & davano a tutti contento."

39. Ibid., p. 434: "Iddio Padre Eterno, & stava sopra la palla del Mondo, & à i piedi di quella erano cinque valenti Musici, che cantavano con somma melodia, ringratiando sua Divina Maestà della Pace, data à questi due Rè." One of the officers of the Scuola di San Teodoro, Giovanni Luigi Collini, published a booklet in 1598 describing the floats carried by the brothers on this occasion: *ESPLICATIONE DEI CARRI TRIONFALE FATTI NELLA PROCESSIONE PER LA PACE Tra Franza, e Spagna, Dalla Scuola di S. Teodoro, il di 26. Luglio 1598.* (Venice: Marc'Antonio Zaltieri, 1598) [BNM Misc. 180.10]. Collini explains the *carro* described in the Sansovino guide as follows: "The ninth and last triumphal cart was full of divine grandeur, on which was seated Eternity, adored by the ancients as a god, and called by us Time . . . and below were seated five musicians in white robes, who, with beautiful sounds sang of the joy of the said Secolo, and for the many joys [he provided] they called him happy and blessed, so that he could well thank Heaven for such a happy and tranquil state." ("Il nono, & ultimo carro Trionfale era piena di divina grandezza, sedendovi sopra il Secolo, da gli antichi adorato per Dio, e da noi dimandato il Tempo . . . & a basso gli stavano sedendo cinque musici in habito bianco, che con vaghissimi accenti cantavano l'allegrezza del sudetto Secolo, e per tanti gaudii lo chiamavan felice, e beato, onde ben potea ringratiar il Cielo d'un si felice e si tranquillo stato.") Collini

describes music on one other *carro*, not referred to in the 1663 publication: "The third was filled with joys, contentments, and infinite happiness, in other words, there was that very Happiness . . . and to demonstrate how much this happiness delighted the hearts of men, there were four musicians seated at her feet, who, among joyous greenery, with sweet and gentle music sang her praises, showing that to everybody, happiness always has pleased, pleases, and will please greatly." ("Il terzo era colmo di gaudii, contenti, & alegrezze infinite, anzi che ivi era l'allegrezza istessa . . . e per dimostrare quanto nel cuor de gli huomini sia giocondo questa allegrezza, le stavano quattro musici sedendo ai piedi, che tra gioiose verdure, con soavi, e dolci accenti cantavan le sue lodi, mostrando che ad ognun'uno sommamente è piacciuta, piace, e piacerà sempre l'allegrezza.") The descriptions of the remaining *carri* (St. Theodore, Peace, Venice, liberality, religion, the world, and "conservatione") make no mention of music.

40. Sansovino, *Venetia città nobilissima*, 435: "un giovane bellissimo, che haveva un pie sopra il Mondo, & l'altro, come in aria, & non cadeva, riccamente vestito, & suonava una tromba squarciata da guerra eccellentissimamente, intitolato per la Fama, che andava per tutto il Mondo."

41. Ibid., p. 437: "con quattro figliuoli, che cantavano musicalmente in lode della pace."

42. ASV, SSR II 45, f. 21ᵛ: "Reverendissimo monsignor Patriarcha holim al presente par che fa qualche ano anno persuaso et pregato tute le Schuole che voleseno andar la Domenega Lazara dapoi manzar a una prozesion che sua Reverendissima Signoria fazevano per tuti li piovani de la tera, et questa anche fazevano per molte reliquie ano trovato in ditta giexia, et maxime uno pezo del legno dela Chroxe del nostro Signor Idio, siche per tute queste cause sua Reverendissima Signoria fano tal prozesion a laude e gloria de misser Domene Dio . . ."

43. ASV, SSGE 16, section "Feste": "se comenza andar la note a Castelo, se parte da caxa a cercha ore niove et se va con visitation." For the calculation of time in this period see Talbot, "*Ore italiane.*" The timing may have been planned so that the procession ended with a mass at dawn.

44. ASV, SSGE 16, section "Feste": "Se fa le infraschrite visitation, et prima: a San Salvador si canta una laude; a Santo Sepulcro, et si canta una laude; a Santo Ixepo, et se canta una laude; al'Ospedal de misser Jesù Cristo, cioè in la giesia, et se canta una laude; a Santo Antonio, et se canta una laude; a Santa Ana, et se canta una laude; a San Piero de Castelo, et li soto confesion se canta una laude dapoi al'altar nostro consueto, et el penelo a la banda destra, et al dito altar se alde mesa dal nostro Capelan . . . ; Se porta per l'altar quatro pezi de candele zale et xii per meter sopra li feri dela capela et al retorno se va ala Madona dele Verzene, et li se canta una laude; a San Daniel, et se canta una laude; ala Madona del'Arsenal se canta una laude; al'Ospedal de San Martin, et li se canta una laude; a Santa Maria dela Celestia, et li se canta una laude; a San Lorenzo, et li se canta una laude; a San Zacharia, et li se canta una laude; a San Marco, et a lo altar delo Santissimo Sachramento se canta una laude, et poi si vano a caxa."

45. For a discussion of this issue for some Bolognese confraternities, see Terpstra, "Confraternities and Local Cults."

46. ASV, SSGE 16, section "Feste": "La quarte domenega de Quaresima se va la note a Castelo con li modi et visitation dite di sopra, et se dimanda ali monasteri dele done monace nostre sorele se ne sono morte quel'ano algune et quante, et esendone morte se fa per li nostri cantadori vechi le cirimonie sopra le arce se fano ala sepoltura deli nostri fradeli, arecordando a tuti che loro sono obligati a dir li Pater noster come ali frateli come se disa a luogo de morti, non se li dize de farli dir mese perché questo non si fa per monache. Se va insieme el guardian da Matin vechio et el novo; el vechio de sopra et il

novo de soto et dita la mesa a Castelo et venuti in giesia de Madona Santa Maria dele Vergine et cantada per li nostri cantori soleni una laude." On the identification of "cantadori vechi" as funeral singers, see chapter 4.

47. ASR, *Libro de ordeni 1521*.

48. ASV, SSGE 16, section "Feste": "scontrandosi se tocha la man et dase l'osculo della paxe del nostro Signor Dio, dicendo 'La pace del nostro Signor Dio sia senpre con vui,' et seli da la palma che se porta in man et lui fa simelmente."

49. ASR, *Libro de ordeni 1521*: "La ditta domenega del olivo se canta uno bello passio nela nostra Giesia, et se fano do pergoletti uno per banda dela capella granda, cioè zoxo di schalini coverti de tela negra. E in uno stano quatro cantaori, ne l'altro pergoletto sta uno sacerdote el qual biscanta el testo. Questi cinque hanno lire 3 per uno. Poi sie preti che rispondeno la messa hanno soldi x per uno . . ."

50. ASV, SSGE 16, section "Feste:" "Batudo queli che per sua devotione vegnerano."

51. Perhaps the best evidence for the earlier date of the text is the placement of the procession for the feast of San Lio, which takes place in April, near the beginning of the Venetian year, at the end of the chronological list as if it were a late addition, although it is copied by the same hand as an integral part of the book. This feast was instituted in the fifteenth century in commemoration of a miracle that occurred at the bridge of San Lio. While in 1570 the procession had been observed for more than a century, it occurs out of place and with the notation that this is so because it has only been done "in recent times" ("da pocho tenpo in qua"). The document therefore preserves, at least in part, a text that dates from the middle of the fifteenth century with an addition from that date. See also Glixon, "Music and Ceremony."

52. ASR, *Libro de ordeni 1521*: "La Zuoba Santa se porta la nostra Spina miraculoxa sopra de uno bello soler con la ombrela fatto tutto da novo questo anno. A questo modo la vien portada, et prima: El tabernaculo con la Spina in cima el soler con otto candelerii de arzento, con otto candele de onze 4 l'una, et fra uno candelier et altro sia uno oxeleto impiado overo altri perfumegi, et sia el tabernaculo coverto de uno velo negro . . . Item quatro di nostri fradelli che porta l'ombrella. Item 8 sacerdoti vestidi de piviali negri con uno dopier per homo in mano, sono dopieri 8, quatro denanti e 4 drio el soler. Item quatro sacerdoti vestidi de tonexela negra che portano el soler dela ditta spina, sono in tutto sacerdotti xii, e hanno per suo premio soldi x per uno. Item doi zagi con doi turiboli che vadi dagando l'incenso avente el ditto soler. Item doi altri zagi che porti doi nanxele nele qual siano dentro storas belzui. La dita Zuoba Sancta se porta el nostro Christo vestido de negro, et 4 ciri vestidi de negro. Item se porta dopieri 60 in astadi per che cusì e sta termenado questo anno da tutte le Schuole d'acordo, per che anche è un bel portar; poi se porta ferali doradi quanti piace, ma li 60 dopieri basta; poi se porta a mano quanto piace ali fradeli." I would like to thank Bonnie Blackburn for the identification of the Venetian 'nanxele' as a form of 'navicelle'.

53. Ibid.: "Et in Giesia fano la sua devotion e poi cantano, et poi despoliano el nostro glorioxo confalon despoiado el Christo, allora el nostro Vardian Grando misser Bernardo de Marin baxa i piedi del nostro Christo chiamando misericordia."

54. Ibid.: "Arecordene che la Zuoba Sancta se manda i masseri a portar el nostro frontespizo dove è depento suxo el Crucifixo cum li batudi in zenochioni in Giesia de San Marco, el qual se apicha sopra la porta del Choro cum le sue candele."

55. It may be that the practice was changing, since by the eighteenth century, and perhaps earlier, the procession was limited to the Piazza and Basilica San Marco.

56. ASV, SSGE 16, section "Feste." The document indicates two visits to the Hospital of Sant'Antonio, but the second is probably an error, since the usual visit to the Hospital of Gesù Christo is omitted. For the visit to San Lio see below.

57. On such activities in Assisi, see Barr, "From Devozione to Rappresentazione."

58. See ASV, SSGE 148, f. 73^v.

59. See Fortini Brown, "An Incunabulum."

60. See Fortini Brown, *Venetian Narrative Painting*.

61. ASV, SSGE 16, section "Feste": "de borsa de queli dela banca."

62. San Giovanni's explanation of this general reciprocal agreement, contained in the prescriptions for the feast of San Rocco (ibid.), is delightfully circular: "we go there because they are doing their procession, and this because we go in procession with them because also on our feasts they come in procession with us" ("se va alora che loro fano la sua procesion et questo percé andemo in procesion con loro perché ance andemo con loro perce ance dale nostre feste loro vien in procesion in nostra conpagnia.")

63. There is some evidence, however, that the ceremony was suspended at some point, and not held regularly again until after 1552 (SSGE 141, f. 293).

64. ASV, SSGE 16, section "Feste": "con la Croce Miracolosa sopra el soler grando et la onbrela granda."

65. Ibid.: "et si toca le macete d'argento et si segnia el Reverendo Piovan et li altri sacerdoti et li altri circostanti."

66. ASV, SSGE, busta 146, f. 19.

67. ASR, *Libro de ordeni 1521*.

68. Ibid: "li cantadori di canto davanti al Christo cum li sonadori nostri."

69. Ibid.: "da matina a hora consueta a far compagnia a la sua procession."

70. ASV, SSGE 16, section "Feste": "la causa de questa cirimonia altramente non si sano, ne non si trova nele nostre schriture, salvo quanto è dito di supra."

71. ASV, SSGE 16: "una puarela de legno in fasuola in forma de primo vaser che significa la Nostra Dona." This image is described in an earlier document as "una verzene in faxinola in similitudene de la nostra dona che naxie in tal dì" (ASV, SSGE 46, f. 40).

72. ASR, *Libro de ordeni 1521*: "Poi la notte se va con la scuola ale Giesie per la terra segondo la usanza nostra, pregando lo eterno et magno Iddio per le anime de li nostri fradeli defuncti."

73. ASV, SSGE 16, section "Feste": "dove se fa uno exequio soto el portego dela giesia dove el nostro guardian da Matin, dove è 'l nostro monimento, debesi commemorar a tutti li fratelli."

74. ASV, SSMC 258, f. 157: "Il dì de morti debba andar la scuola fino a San Basegio, et venir zoso per la fondamenta fino alla Trinità, et in Chiesia della Carità, dove finir si debba le essequie et oration per li nostri fratelli defunti senza andar vagando altrove per la terra."

75. ASV, SSGE 16, section "Feste": "in significacion e memoria di nostri fradelli morti."

76. ASR, *Libro de ordeni 1521*: "se fa baldachin nela nostra Giesia de San Rocho, e metese el cadeleto con el pano da morti rechamado, et se fa in ditto cadeleto uno vestido che par che sia morto, et se mete le candele atorno ditto baldachin ma ditte candele non se impizano."

77. ASV, SSGE 16, section "Feste": "E dita la mesa mortor se die far la procession e circhondar lo campo sento chon verberacion e disiplina per anema di nostri fradelli passadi di questa vita al altra."

78. ASV, SSM 17, f. 62^v: "et dapoi se vien sopra le arche dove sono sepulti li nostri fratelli, et li se dite l'offitio de i morti abundanter prexente el vardian e compagni e tutta la fraterna, dela qual devotion sono etiam obligati specifice venir tutti i nostri fradelli preti, et cum le sue cotte et stole cantar et orar pro animabus fratrum nostrorum defunctorum."

79. ASV, SSMC 268, f. 49: "Il che como a reccato la venerazione, rispetto, e concorso

de divoti, et applauso della Città, così merita d'esser maggiormente sostenuta et infervor-ata."

80. ASV, SSR II 39, 13 August 1741.

81. ASV, SSGE 154, f. 390: "inni di lode al Signore con il suono dell'organo, e poxia il salmo Miserere con la Benedizione accompagnandola processionalmente in Scola per esser riposta nel conservatorio al suo altare." On the mansionari di coro and coriste as musicians, see below ch. 7.

82. ASV, SSGE 16, section "Feste": "nostre cere et dopieri et spaliere."

83. ASV, SSGE 46, f. 55: "in chanto e chon organi."

84. See Wilson, *Music and Merchants*, 60–61.

85. ASV, SSR I 41, ff. nn.; 19 June 1539.

86. ASV, SSMC 257, ff. 2–3: "per satisfazion di li nobeli nostri fradeli et altri fradeli divotti di la Schuolla nostra . . . far cantar uno bela et solene messa grande."

87. Ibid., f. 14.

88. ASV, SSGE 144, ff. 74–76: "diligentia a cantar la messa anco nella Chiesa tanto per tempo anticipatto che possino servire de su nella Scola."

89. ASV, SSGE 16, section "Feste."

90. ASV, SSM 17, f. 60: "sì per salute dele anime di fratelli, come per honorificentia dela scuola, la qual de raxon se die exaltar sopra tutte le altre per esser la piui bella et sotto al titulo de misser San Marco."

91. ASV, SSR II 39, ff. nn.; 13 July 1741: "soliti ad officiarsi ad ora incommoda, e senz'alcuna assistenza de devoti."

92. ASV, SSGE 16, section "Feste": "va almen fino a San Rocho."

93. ASV, SSMC 233bis, ch. XI: "Sempre ogno dì de luni de tuto l'ano, e lo sia dita et cantada una mesa per anema de tuti li nostri frari che de questo segolo se pasadi, e paserà."

94. ASV, SSR II 45, f. 93: "una mesa in chantto all'altar del Christto."

95. ASR 14, ff. 294ᵛ–295.

96. On funerals at confraternities primarily in Bologna, see Terpstra, "Death and Dying." On parallel practices in Florence, see Henderson, *Piety and Charity*, 159–63.

97. ASV, SSGE 16, section "Funerali."

98. ASV, SSGE 16: "Jexu cristo misericordia." The mariegola of San Marco (ASV, SSM 216) indicates the singing of nearly identical words ("Jesus misericordia").

99. ASV, SSMC 233bis, ch. 18: "Madona Senta Maria, receve sto peccatore, fa vui prego a Ieso Christo ke la debia perdonare."

100. For example, the mariegola of the Carità (ibid.) specifies that the brothers should go in this procession "with peace and quiet, with the discipline and beating" ("E vadha cum paxe et paciencia in procession, cum disciplina e verberation." This was also the practice among the Florentine flagellant confraternities. See Henderson, *Piety and Charity*, 159.

101. ASV, SSGE 16: "el canto suo."

102. Ibid.: "Frateli cari, si vi la paso al Nostro Signor Dio de tirar a se l'anima de questo nostro fratelo, et vi aricordo che semo obligati a dir cinquanta Pater Nostri et cinquanta Ave Marie, e nui faremo dir le cinquanta mese, aciò che l'eterno Dio conducha l'anima sua ali beni de vita eterna."

103. ASV, SSM 216, ch. 27: "tutti li frari di questa fraternitade debbia vegnir la prima domenega da puo che elli lo saverà con le sue cape e far dir messa alla giesia de San Zane Polo, e dobbiate batter, come el corpo fosse presente. Et similmente se debbia far tutte le altre cose in le messe, et in le oration, si como si fa a quelli li qual è al presente . . ."

104. ASV, SSMM 261, no. 108.

105. ASV, SSM 12, insert between ff. 101ᵛ and 102.

106. ASV, SSM 229.

107. ASV, SSGE 16.

108. See Henderson, *Piety and Charity*, 163–68 on commemorative services in Florence and elsewhere.

109. On the Northern polyphonic commemorations see Forney, "The Role of Secular Guilds"; ead., "Music, Ritual and Patronage"; Haggh, "The Meeting of Sacred Ritual and Secular Piety"; Schreurs, "Muziek voor de Onze-Lieve-Vrouwebroederschap in Tongeren"; and Strohm, *Music in Late Medieval Bruges*, esp. ch. 4. The Florentine lauda services are discussed in Wilson, *Music and Merchants*, ch. 2.

Chapter 3

1. ASV, SSMC 233bis, chs. XI and XXI.

2. Ibid., ch. XXI: "che'l vardian, e li soi compagnoni debia eser soliciti, e procurar che sempre ogno dì de luni de tuto l'ano, e lo sia dita et cantada una mesa per anema de tuti li nostri frari che de questo segolo se pasadi, e paserà."

3. Ibid., ch. XI.

4. ASV, SSMM A, no. 1, ch. 16.

5. IRE, PATR 1 O 12, f. 48ᵛ–55ᵛ [210–24]: "a cantar in coro alla messa."

6. ASV, SSGE 46, f. 57ᵛ.

7. Ibid., f. 51ᵛ.

8. Ibid., f. 72: "Prima se die far benedir la chandele lo dì de madona Senta Maria che vien a dì ii de febrer, e benedide le dite candele, el prevede a l'altar chantando *Lumen ad revelationem gencium* de dar una dele candele grosse che tien i oficiali ale messe . . ."

9. The words *Lumen ad revelationem gencium* occur in several places in the liturgy for the Purification of the Virgin: as a responsory verse in the second nocturne of Matins, as a verse of the Tract *Nunc dimittis*, and as the fifth antiphon for Lauds.

10. A more detailed version of the following material was previously published as Glixon, "Late Medieval Chant."

11. BNM MS Lat. II, 119 (2426) [henceforth GC].

12. This type of book was probably typical of the scuole grandi, although it is the only one extant. The earliest surviving inventory of the possessions of the Scuola di San Giovanni Evangelista, for example, dated 21 March 1400 (ASV, SSGE 71, f. 4), includes the following entry: "one large and beautiful missal, bound in velvet with gilded nails" ("1 mesal grando e belo choverto de veludo con chioldi indoradi").

13. GC, f. [1ᵛ]: "Questo antefanario fo fato far deli propri beni dela scuola e fraternitade dela preciosa vergene mare madona Sancta Maria dela Charitade. In ben e salvation dele aneme nostre, e de tuti li nostri frari vivi e morti. Azo che de tuti beni che per questo serà cantadi e diti, nuy siemo participeveli in ben e salvation dele nostre aneme."

14. See Levi d'Ancona, "Giustino del fu Gherardino da Forlì."

15. GC, f. I: "In hoc Libro continentur Introytus, Graduale, Alleluia, Offertorium, et . . . , In misis Beate virginis Marie per totum anni circulum cum Kyrie, Gloria in excelsis, et Credo in unum deum, et omnibus necesariis in eisdem cum nota." The scribe has written, where the word "communio" should be, the letters "pt" with a sign of abbreviation that would together usually be resolved as "post." It is possible that he began to write "postcommunio" instead of "communio," and when he realized his error, simply stopped where he was and continued with the remainder of the sentence. The book contains communions, but not postcommunions.

16. ASV, SSMC 253, f. 19; 23 June 1493.

17. See Cattin, *Musica e liturgia.*

18. See ibid., 1:38–40.

19. On this history, see ibid., 32–33.

20. Treviso, Biblioteca comunale, MS 252.

21. Ibid., f. 1: "Questo messal fo conprado et adornado como apar dele proprie borse et beni deli valevele homeni dela scuola et fraternitade de la precioxa vergene mare madona santa maria dela caritade, in ben e salvation dele aneme nostre et de tuti li nostri frari vivi e morti."

22. I have not made a comparison between the other propers in the missal and the corresponding ones in the Marciana and Roman traditions, so it is not possible to exclude Venetian influences entirely.

23. Levi d'Ancona, "Giustino del fu Gherardino da Forlì."

24. Note that this is based on observation, not on a scientific study, and the varying quality and color of the vellum creates some problems of evaluation.

25. This observation is based on a comparison of the only two melodies Cattin published that are found here also.

26. It does not appear among the 702 melodies listed in Miazga, *Die Melodien des einstimmigen Credo.* The same melody or a similar one (it is apparently nearly illegible) can be found on f. 90 of BNM MS Lat. III, 111 (2116), a damaged (and not presently consultable) St. Mark's missal from the middle of the fourteenth century. See Cattin, *Musica e liturgia,* 2:410.

27. On the organs and organists of San Marco, see Caffi, *Storia della musica sacra,* 1: 55–62 and 2:7–22, and Fano, *Profilo di una storia,* 22–31.

28. IRE, PATR 1 O 12, f. 18ᵛ. All the following accounts regarding the organ are from the same volume, which consists of extracts from the old account books made in the eighteenth century as part of a lawsuit involving the land on which the monastery of the Misericordia was constructed. I would like to thank Dr. Giuseppe Ellero, director of the IRE archive, for directing me to this document.

29. See Lunelli, *Studi e documenti,* 195.

30. IRE, PATR 1 O 12, f. 52: "a cantar in coro alla messa e che sona l'organo."

31. The secular clerics were pre Andrea de San Silvestro (1372–77), pre Daniel de Benedetto (1405–6), and pre Zuan de Sen Bernaba (served around 1419). The monastics were fra Anzolo (1378–79), fra Antonio di Crosechieri (around 1380), one or more unnamed friars, some from the Servi (1381–1404), fra Zuane dei Servi (1407–9), and fra Gasparin Fosso (1411–19).

32. See Lunelli, *Studi e documenti,* 195–96.

33. ASV, Miscellanea carte non appartenenti ad alcun archivio, B.1, no. 1. This document was originally published in Cecchetti, "Un organo nella Scuola."

34. ASV, SSGE 71, f. 4: "1 organo grando in gliessia sul pergolo."

35. ASV, SSGE 72, f. 100ᵛ.

36. Ibid., f. 104.

37. Ibid., inventories: "1 horgano nuovo".

38. Ibid., f. 104: "non esser a quella bonttà e perfezion che'l dovea esser . . . de honor di la nostra Schuolla."

39. Ibid., inventories: "uno organo nuovo non chonpido."

40. Ibid., f. 190; maistro Marcho's receipt, dated 8 January 1443, is on f. 181ᵛ.

41. The scuola's inventory of 1421 (in Biblioteca del Museo Civico Correr, Mariegola 19) lists "a large organ in the church with its accessories" ("uno organo grando in glexia con li soi fornimenti").

42. ASV, SSM 243.

43. ASV, SSM 16, ff. 4–5: "facere pulsari suam organum soleniter."

44. ASV, SSM 121, fasc. B, f. 14.

45. ASV, SSM 243, f. 45: "e per un horgano £6 da picolo, e per chonzar algune chane del dito organo che fo vaste £5 s.8 . . ."

46. ASV, SSGE 3, f. 6: "et tuti li frari debia andar cum quel corpo ad sepelirlo, cum verberation et disciplina como va in procession, cantando per la sua anema, in fin ad luogo lave se die sepelir."

47. ASV, SSMC 233bis, ch. XVIII: "che zascadun frar de questa fraternitade sia tegnudho de andar a sepelir li frari nostri, ke de questo segolo paserà, e vadha cum paxe et paciencia in procession, cum disciplina e verberation, cantando questo verso: 'Madona senta maria, receve sto pecatore, fa vui prego a Ieson Christo ke li debia perdonare.' "

48. See Wilson, *Music and Merchants*, and Barr, *The Monophonic Lauda*.

49. No musical sources containing laude that might be connected with any of the Venetian confraternities survive. It is not unlikely that the music used in the early fifteenth century was similar to that preserved in the manuscript BNM Lat. IX, 145, which probably originated in a Venetian monastic environment in the first half of the century. See Cattin, "Il manoscritto Venet. Marc. Ital. IX, 145." The collection is edited by Cattin as *Laudi quattrocentesche*.

50. ASV, SSGE 47, November: "andar sora le nostre arche el la star in zignochioni con verberation e disiplina fazando cantar i nostri chantadori como se farà siando morto un de i nostri fradeli."

51. Ibid., f. 5.

52. Ibid., f. 49: "nostro cantador."

53. ASV, SSM 243.

54. Ibid., f. 157: "per non esser in ordine la cholazion."

55. ASV, SSM 243, f. 171: "A dì [31] ditto [August 1438] per resto di spese per 2 tronbeti et barche." It is important to note that there is a clear distinction, in Venetian practice, between the professions of *trombador* and *trombetta*. The former, almost always associated with piffari as a member of an ensemble, is a musician, while the latter is a herald, whose musical abilities, if any, were probably limited to the playing of fanfares and signals. This distinction also holds true in other cities. See, for example, D'Accone, *The Civic Muse*.

56. ASV, SSM 243, f. 45: "4 sonaori d'arpa e un de lauto."

Chapter 4

1. ASV, SSGE 140, f. 157[v]: "Inclitto et eccelentissimo Consilio Magnifici Domini Consilio Dieci. Humilmente suplica el Vardian e compagni, officiali della Scuola de missier San Zuane Vanzelista, che conciosia la ditta scuola habbia de grandissima necesitade de cantadori, i quali acompagna quella cantar in procession di corpi et altre sue solenitade uzade, como è chiaro e notto alle Signorie Vostre, e sì per puochi cantadori alla ditta scuola come ancor per la vechieza de quelli che al presente sonno; alla qual cosa se el non se provede de cantadori che se rezeva sotto quelli che son al presente, da i qualli imparà il suo costume e modo uzado de cantar, de breve mancherà per muodo che la ditta scuola non haverà cantadori alle ditte procession, corpi, e dì ordenadi e altre solenitade fa la ditta scuola. Et azò che non segua tal inconvenienti ala honor de Dio e del Glorioso Apostolo Evangelista missier San Zuane, degniasse la prefatta inclitta Signoria Vostra concieder alla ditta scuola che el Vardian della ditta Scola, che è all presente e che per l'avegnir sarà, possa lasar spoiar alla ditta Scola fina homeni sie, che non sia della ditta scuola, i qual acompagna accompagna [*sic*] la ditta scuola per cantadori quotiesqunque la ditta scuola se spoierà,

azoche de i ditti a tempo debbitto se possa recever che la ditta scuola non mancha di cantadori."

2. ASV, CD, registro 13, f. 37v.

3. See Gambassi, *"Pueri cantores"* and Cattin, "Church Patronage," 23. For the founding of the San Marco singing school, see Gallo, *Antonii Romani Opera,* xiii.

4. ASV, CD, registro 13, f. 49ᵛ.

5. Ibid., f. 83ᵛ: "quoniam propter pestem non habeat cantatores."

6. Ibid., f. 90.

7. Ibid., ff. 90ᵛ and 95.

8. Ibid., registro 14, f. 113ᵛ.

9. Ibid., f. 117: "Ut ad laudem dei et gloriose crucis domini nostri Iesu christi, Quandocumque in processionibus et aliter portatur per civitatem cantetur amene et dulcetur in cantu glorificetur nomen domini, et magnificetur exaltatio sancte crucis."

10. Ibid., registro 16, f. 2: "Devotissime supplicatur pro parte guardiani et sociorum scole verbatorum Sancti Marci, quod cum cantores diu sint effecti ita senes, ut cum magna difficultate haberi possint ad corpora sepelienda, ad processiones et ad devotiones per civitatem, quoniam infirmi sunt, et non sit conveniens, quod illi homines in illo habitu vadant per Civitatem tacendo velut mortui sed vadant canendo laudes deo, iuxta consuetum." The request from the Carità follows on f. 89.

11. Quaranta, *Oltre San Marco,* 133–37.

12. ASV, CD, reg. 13, f. 26ᵛ. Cited in Quaranta, *Oltre San Marco,* 134 and Sbriziolo, "Per la storia delle confraternite veneziane. . . . Le scole dei battuti," 748.

13. ASV, CD, reg. 12, ff. 11–16; the final decree dated 28 May 1438. Cited in Quaranta, *Oltre San Marco,* 134 and Sbriziolo, "Per la storia delle confraternite veneziane. . . . Le scole dei battuti," 752.

14. ASV, SSM 228 and 229.

15. ASV, SSM 228, Libro Antico di Contabilità, 1452, ff. nn.

16. Both in ASV, SSM 228.

17. Ibid., Libro Antico di Contabilità, 1478, ff. nn.: "Questi sono i cantori che canta i corpi e per la via" and "Questi sono i cantadori che se adopera zoè de laude e de prezission."

18. ASV, SSM 16bis, pt. 2, f. 47: "Esendo nezesario per la nostra Schuolla aver chantadori da laude, per honor di le prezision ed altra solenità se fano per la Schuolla nostra . . . Batista de Felipo . . . per amastrar i nostri garzoni chantadori." The reference to *garzoni chantadori* probably refers not to their age—that is, they were not children—but to their experience; "garzoni" is the standard term used by the Venetian guilds to refer to apprentices.

19. Ibid., f. 52: "El se intende per tuti quanta deligentia habia sempre habudo Andrea da Monte nostro cantador a dover vegnir a la Schuola e chantar ai corpi, in modo che'l se puol dir che quasi non sia altri cantadori che lui che canti a corpi al presente. Per la qual cossa sono sta admonidi i altri cantadori che debia imparar a cantar."

20. ASV, SSM 229, Libro Antico di Contabilità, 1482, f. 24ᵛ and 1484, ff. nn.

21. ASV, SSM 16bis, pt. 1, f. 5ᵛ: "El se denota per honor de questa nostra benedeta Schuola che el se abia a proveder a le chose nezessarie le qual hochore a la zornada, le qual hè de nezesetà averlo ai bixogni, et maxime de i chantadori de laude, i quali el ne son gran manchamento ala nostra benedeta Schuola, e però . . . Ser Batista die aver apresso de lui, e per sua compagnia a chantar, tre altri garzoni, al quali el dito Ser Batista ideo a maistrar et insegnar."

22. ASV, SSM 229, Libro Antico di Contabilità, 1484, ff. nn.

23. ASV, SSM 4, f. 168ᵛ.

24. See Ongaro, "Chapel of Saint Mark's," 40.

25. ASV, SSM 16bis, pt. 2, f. 62: "Consit che la Schuola nostra soleva aver 8 chantadori de chanto figurado per onorar le messe et vespori de feste et altri solenità de questa nostra Schuola, dal qual 8 al presente se ne trova solum 4. Et perchè tra altri ornamenti molto è da comendar a simile solenità simel chantadori, et avendose oferto maestro Piero da Fosis, messer pre Marco Bussati, messer pre Antonio Schatoler, et messer pre Nicolò Balanzer de esser a suplimento dei diti 8."

26. See Ongaro, "Chapel of Saint Mark's," 47 ff.

27. ASV, SSM 16bis, pt. 1, f. 26: "Per che fra le altre chose che son nezesarisime a questa nostra Schuolla sono i chantadori de laude, senza i quali mal se puol far l'onor dela Schuolla nostra, ed eziam nezesario a provedere de aver persone che in ogni ochorensia, si dele feste chome prezision ed ogni altra solenità e festività, se posi et debi adoprar, et si tenori chomo sorani et chontra."

28. Ibid., f. 29.

29. ASV, SSM 82, Giornale de Vicarii, 1494–95.

30. ASV, SSM 229, Libro Antico di Contabilità, 1497.

31. ASV, SSMC 236, f. 23^{r-v} (= 29^{r-v}): "ogni fiada che el Confalon dela Santa Croxe andar con i nostri fradelli fuori dela scuola, si a prezision et altri luogi, de cantar laude et altre devozion."

32. Ibid.: "al sepelir de nostri fradelli de cantar servado el suo consueto."

33. Ibid.: "Et essendone in la Scuolla di nostri fradelli che sapi far tal offizio ne sia tolti altratanti in suo luogo . . ."

34. ASV, SSMC 253, f. 18^v: "li ditti, over la mazor partte de loro, ano deliberato non observar alchuna chosa per loro promesa, anzi ttottalmente ano intterotto ttal ordene ett promision per loro fatta, in modo che quando el vien el vien [*sic*] i tenori el mancha i sovrani, e quando ne son quelli duo el mancha i conttra, per modo che mai sono in ordene a ttal suo chantti, grandissima confuxion, ett inchargo de questta benedetta Schuola."

35. Ibid., f. 19: "quattro alttre voxe bone e sufizienttes, zoè do sovrani e do ttenori e un conttra."

36. Ibid., f. 27. Chamelin cannot be specifically identified as one of the singers of San Marco named Niccolò, but his northern origin makes such a connection with the cappella likely.

37. ASV, SSR II 44, f. 1.

38. The solicitousness of the Scuola di San Marco is amusingly evident in one entry in the account book for 1484 (ASV, SSM 229, Libro Antico di Contabilità, 1484, ff. nn.). One of the cantadori de laude, Marco Rosso, was given 12 soldi to buy a chicken, because he was ill; even in fifteenth-century Venice, chicken soup was a preferred remedy!

39. ASV, SSMM 166, f. 7: "dimentigandose el temor et amor de Dio e de la sua madre glorioxa Verzene Maria . . . tene muodo che quelo non solivase per sopelir se prima non ebi quel pagamento che a lor parese."

40. Ibid., f. 25: "per osservar el titollo de questa glorioxa scuola che si ditta Madre de Mixerichordia."

41. ASV, SSM 16bis, pt. 1, f. 9: "non avendo quelo mener la Schuolla da quelli talli chossa alguna in quella fiada, li detti chantadori abiano pazenzia."

42. ASV, SSMM 166, f. 7: "Poi finse che lui fese sangue del naxo e montò in barcha ochultamente, la qual era apariada ala riva de Palazo, et andosene a solazo a Mazorbo . . . e lasò la Schuola andar con inchargo e vergogna per Piaza."

43. ASV, SSMC 253, f. 5^v: "el qual proxonttuoxementte, porttando pocha riverenzia

a misser lo Vardian, e volttandoge le spalle, e con meno timor de Dio nè dei hordeni della Schuolla nostra, e con moltte parolle iroxe e inzurioxe, dimostrando pi[ù] presto iniquittà che charittà."

44. Ibid., f. 24ᵛ: "ha usato parole iniurioxa et non conveniente contra tuti li offitiali de l'Albergo."

45. Ibid., pt. 1, ff. nn.; 21 January 1447: "Al presente non essendo devotion, ne virtù, ma solum deshonestà, questi cantar e vegnir alla Scola per praticar cose dishoneste et abominevoli che i hanno fatto e fanno alla zornada, con grandissimo incargo e vitupero di tuta questa benedetta fraternita, e contro l'essercitio spiritual e virtuoso dovemo observar e far osservar a tutti quelli son in questa scuola."

46. Ibid., ff. nn.; 9 December 1464: "i quali cantadori stetteno in ditta tanferuzo fina al doppo disnar . . . quelli cantadori comenzò con parole inzuriose e dishoneste condur i nostri masseri, inzuriando e manazando; quelli non habbiando in reverenza el Vardian e compagni per modo che li fu una desonesta cosa."

47. See Fenlon, "St. Mark's before Willaert."

48. Luisi, *Laudario giustinianeo.*

49. Cattin, "Il manoscritto Venet. Marc. Ital. IX, 145." The collection is edited by Cattin as *Laudi quattrocentesche.*

50. Cattin, "Nuova fonte italiana." Much of the music was edited by Cattin in *Italian Laude and Latin Unica.*

51. ASR, Mariegola, f. 88. For more on the trombe e piffari of the doge, see Muir, *Civic Ritual,* 209–13.

52. ASV, SSM 228, Libro Antico di Contabilità, 1475, ff. nn. and 1478, ff. nn.

53. ASV, SSM 2.

54. ASV, SSM 229, Libro Antico di Contabilità, 1482.

55. ASV, SSGE 10, f. 11.

56. The two pictorial representations of this ensemble, in paintings for San Giovanni Evangelista (see below), depict an instrument that most closely resembles a rebec.

57. ASV, SSM 16bis, pt. 1, f. 9; 6 May 1486: "ttutti nostri prezission e solenittade le qual achade."

58. ASV, SSM 82, Giornale de Vicarii, 1494–95, ff. 2 and 13.

59. ASV, SSM 229, Libro Antico di Contabilità, 1497, f. 3: "Sonadori ai bixogni."

60. ASV, SSMM 166, f. 34.

61. For more on the paintings in this cycle, and other cycles for the scuole, see Fortini Brown, *Venetian Narrative Painting.*

62. This was discussed earlier in Brown, "On Gentile Bellini's Processione," and Glixon, "Lutenists in Renaissance Venice." Luisi ("Per una identificazione") argues that these musicians belong not to San Giovanni Evangelista, but to the Scuola di San Marco. His evidence is that they are not wearing the cappa of San Giovanni Evangelista (nor are they wearing that of any other scuola), and that there is no documentation for singers at San Giovanni Evangelista for that time (which, of course, is not evidence at all). He suggests that these musicians represent, in fact, the tail end of the preceding scuola in the procession, San Marco, and identifies them on that basis. There are several clear arguments against this hypothesis. First, it seems unreasonable that the artist would so prominently feature employees and brothers of San Marco in a painting meant to honor San Giovanni Evangelista. Second, these musicians are in the proper place to belong to San Giovanni Evangelista, near the relic and the officers; the tail end of any scuola's portion of a procession was always made up of ordinary brothers. Finally, the lutenist depicted by Bellini in this painting (identified by Luisi as Bastian da lauto of San Marco) is also portrayed in another painting

for San Giovanni Evangelista, ignored by Luisi, Lazzaro Bastiani's *Donation of the Relic of the Holy Cross* (see Glixon, "Lutenists in Renaissance Venice," 17 and plates 2 and 3); there is no reasonable explanation for the appearance of a musician from San Marco at this event.

63. That changing strings was generally recognized as a frequent occurrence even by non-musicians is evident in another painting for the Scuola di San Giovanni Evangelista. In the painting by Lazzaro Bastiani discussed above, the lutenist is in the process of preparing a new string, apparently just removed from a box he carried with him, to be installed on his lute. See Glixon, "Lutenists in Renaissance Venice,", 17; the painting and the relevant detail are reproduced there as plates 2 and 3.

64. ASV, SSM 229, Libro Antico di Contabilità, 1497, ff. 43ᵛ and 46ᵛ.

65. ASV, SSM 17, f. 10: "per zentileza et non per obligo."

66. ASV, SSGE 72, ff. nn., membership list.

67. Ibid., ff. 204ᵛ–254.

68. IRE, PATR 1 O 12, ff. 57ᵛ–58ᵛ [228–30].

69. Ibid., f. 58ᵛ [230] and ASV, SSMM 302.

70. IRE, PATR 1 O 12, f. 58ᵛ: "1477 8 luglio accordo con un Mistro fecce il nostro organo in la Gesia della Misericordia."

71. ASV, Monastero di Santa Maria della Carità, Busta 28 pergamene, no. 1404. Twenty years earlier, the scuola had contributed 70 ducats toward the construction of an organ loft, but the documents do not indicate whether a new instrument was also built at that time (ASV, SSMC 236, f. 2 (= 8).

Chapter 5

1. ASR 15, f. 20: "Ressultando in non poco honor di la Scola nostra de misser San Rocho l'haver musici eccelentissimi et dilligenti, quali nelle feste principali venghino et siano pronti a cantar li divini officii."

2. The musical activities of the scuole grandi during this period were first explored by Denis Arnold in two articles: "Music at the Scuola di San Rocco" and "Music at a Venetian Confraternity."

3. ASV, SSGE 16, section [8], "Feste."

4. Rodolfo Baroncini has reached the same conclusion. See Baroncini, "Voci e strumenti."

5. ASR, *Libro di ordeni 1521.*

6. See Bryant and Pozzobon, *Musica devozione città.* See also my review in *Early Music History* 16 (1997): 310–17.

7. A rare exception occurs in the works of Innocentius Dammonis, published as Petrucci's *Laude libro primo* in 1508. This book contains one true five-voice lauda, "Amor, Iesù, divino," and opens with two Latin fragments that, with their canons realized, are for six voices. See Glixon, "Polyphonic Laude."

8. ASV, SSM 19, f. 125ᵛ: "cantar . . . la messa granda."

9. ASV, SSGE 144, f. 186ᵛ: "dir mese grande et risponder mesa."

10. ASV, SSM 20, f. 105: "chanttando l'esequio di mortti sopra le arche de la scuola nostra."

11. For example, ASV, SSMM 168, ff. 48ᵛ–49.

12. ASV, SSR II 45, f. 13.

13. ASV, SSR II 720, f. 11ᵛ.

14. ASV, SSGE 145, f. 201ᵛ.

15. ASV, SSGE 140, f. 156ᵛ: "ala honor de Dio e del Glorioso Apostolo Evangelista missier San Zuane."

16. ASV, SSM 19, f. 82ᵛ: "a honor del signor Idio."

17. ASV, SSR II 45, ff. 40ᵛ–41: "non posendosse far di mancho per timor de el glorioxo Idio et di misser San Rocho che la scuola nostra abi quatro cantori."

18. ASV, SSGE 144, f. 186ᵛ: "a onor della Santissima Croce."

19. ASV, SSM 17, f. 108ʳ⁻ᵛ: "per honorar il culto divino."

20. ASV, SSMM 166, f. 154ᵛ: "nezesario." ASV, SSGE 146, ff. 37ᵛ–41ᵛ: "necessario." ASV, SST 14, f. 1ᵛ: "le cose necessarii."

21. ASV, SSMC 255, f. 23ʳ⁻ᵛ: "chosa importantissima."

22. ASV, SSM 18, f. 120ᵛ: "Chossa laudabile, onorevole, et necessaria."

23. ASV, SSGE 141, f. 306: "per honor de questo città."

24. ASV, SSMM 167, f. 340: "honorevolezza delle processioni."

25. Ibid.: "honorevolezza della schuolla nostra."

26. ASV, SSGE 144, f. 186ᵛ: "per onor della scola nostra."

27. ASR 15, f. 20: "per la honorevolezza et decoro di essa nostra scuola."

28. ASR 17, f. 81ᵛ: "in honore et grandezza della schola nostra."

29. Ibid., ff. 151ᵛ–152: "la richiede . . . la nobilità di questa dignissima scuola."

30. ASV, SSMM 168, f. 397: "acciò non perdi per l'avvenire appresso alle sudette scole grande, et a tutta la città che quella reputazione nelle quale sempre s'è conservata."

31. ASV, SSM 24, f. 35: "nelle processioni rispetto alle altre scuole grandi, le quali oltra detto ornamento antiquo et ordinario l'avanzavano di maniera, che era cosa miserabile il veder la scuola del prottettor nostro a passar in quella maniera."

32. ASV, SSM 17, f. 16: "honor et reputtation de questa bancha et fraternita."

33. Ibid., f. 46ᵛ: "vergogna."

34. ASV, SSR II 45, f. 32: "molte voltte siano abutto dela vergogna per non esser chantori ezelentte."

35. ASV, SSMM 166, f. 347: "Non è danaro dela schuola nostra che sia spexo con mancho fruto et con più vergogna et inchargo deli ministri quanto è il pagamento fato ali chantadori nuovi, quali per il suo mal modo di cantar, et senza alquna armonia et dolzeza di cantar, sono in contemptu et de suma desplizienzia in genere a tuti."

36. ASV, SSM 20, f. 167ᵛ: "Essendo honesta cosa il proveder alla honorevoleza della nostra fraterna, come hanno sempre fatto i nostri degni progienitori, i qualli cum ogni diligientia hanno da ogni tempo procurado che la scuola nostra sia in tute le cose dele più honorate de questa città, et perché il tenir cantori solenni, masimamente quelli che sonno soliti de servire la scuola nelli anni passati, che sono in efeto dei primarii de questa terra, è cosa di molta honoreveleza."

37. ASV, SST 14, f. 47ᵛ: "quatro cantori suficientti et a paragoni delle altre schuolle."

38. ASV, SSM 17, f. 111ᵛ.

39. ASV, SSMM 166, f. 353: "avendo auto optima informazion et fato esperienzia dela sufizienzia deli infrascritti."

40. ASV, SST 14, f. 1ᵛ: "Visto et aldido molti musici . . . boni et suficienti a tal virtù."

41. ASV, SSGE 145, f. 207ᵛ: "D'ordine del magnifico signor guardian grande della Scuolla de misser San Zuane Evangelista de Battudi di Venetia si fa saper a cadaun cantor che prettende mettterse alla prova di cantor sollene della detta scuola, debbi comparer alli 3 april prossimo doppo' disnar, che sua magnificentia vuol venir alla elletion."

42. ASV, SSM 19, f. 134ᵛ: "sua magnificentia fece intender per avanti a tuti i cantori nel ditto Monestero de San Zuanne Polo che chi prettende vengano a darse in nota per hozi."

43. SSR II 45, f. 32: "esser chosa di qualche importanzia, è stato questi zorni pasate chantar in la giexia nostra piui compagni de chantori muxizi, et alditto inseme con la bancha una e piui volte."

44. ASV, SSM 17, f. 108^{r-v}: "Et perché hauto qualche bona voze e qualche persone verttuoxa, le alttre schuole, non observando lo amor che se rezercha ad haver una con l'alttra, con promision de magior salario a fato levar quelle dal servizio nostro ett andar al suo. "

45. On musicians at Santi Giovanni e Paolo, see Blackburn, "Petrucci's Venetian Editor" and Quaranta, *Oltre San Marco*, 69–77. On music at Santo Stefano, see Miller, "The Composers of San Marco and Santo Stefano" and Quaranta, 77–83.

46. ASV, SSGE 141, f. 66. The hiring in 1536 of five "cantadori zoveni" at D. 2 each for the year to sing in processions may have been some sort of experiment (ASV, SSGE 141, f. 57^v). The specific term used does not appear elsewhere in the documents, the names are not those that appear in the decree of the following year, and the salary is lower than that usually paid to the cantadori nuovi.

47. Ibid.: "non voler più questa spesa de cantadori."

48. ASV, SSGE 142, f. 38^v: "Havendo per esperientia conosciuto li incomodi che si patiscono nell'aspettar li cantori soleni obligati alla chiesa de misser San Marco," and "vicini alla nostra scuola, et commodi, et che commodamente possano, et si offriscono servirla."

49. Ibid., f. 60^v.

50. Ibid., f. 203.

51. Ibid., ff. 273–274^v.

52. ASV, SSGE 403.

53. ASV, SSGE 144, f. 155^{r-v}: "Che de cetero non si possa sotto alcun protesto, via, et modo et forma che immaginar si posso far ellettione overo tenir cantori sollenni." The amount of the galley tax levied on the scuole varied, not only over time, but based on what the government thought each could afford at the moment.

54. Ibid., f. 186^v.

55. ASV, SSGE 145, f. 201^v.

56. ASV, SSGE 146, ff. 37^v–41^v.

57. Ibid., f. 221.

58. Ibid., f. 268.

59. ASV, SSGE 330, 1632–33.

60. ASV, SSGE 147, ff. 130^v–132^v.

61. Ibid., ff. 134^v–135.

62. Ibid., f. 184^v.

63. ASV, SSMC 255, f. 22.

64. Ibid., f. 23^{r-v}.

65. ASV, SSMC 236, ff. 65^v–66: "conobbe per la verità esser meglio, et appresso il Signor Iddio, et appresso li catholici et pii, spender questi 70 over 80 ducati in subvenir tanti poveri nostri o in maridar tante povere donzelle che spender danari in essi cantori, a pompa et boria del mondo."

66. ASV, SSMC 258, f. 22: "solicitamente et sufficientissimemente, con satisfattion et honorevolezza della scuola nostra et de tutta la città, che altramente da simil homeni non si poteva aspettar . . . assompsi, approbati, et confermati . . . in ogni tempo."

67. Ibid., f. 121: "voce a proposito" and "essendo sta conduto in Capella di San Marco doi voce, uno Joseph Bressan che canta il contralto, et l'altro un Antonio de Ribera Spagnuolo che canta il soprano, che sonno voci ellette."

68. Ibid., f. 245^{r-v}.

69. ASV, SSMC 259, f. 92.

70. ASV, SSMC 320.

71. ASV, SSMC 262, f. 367^v.

72. Ibid., f. 377^v.

73. ASV, SSMC 320.

74. ASV, SSMM 166, f. 75.

75. Ibid., f. 123^v: " boni et perfeti cantadori."

76. Ibid., f. 154^v.

77. Ibid., f. 201^v.

78. ASV, SSMM 303, p. 349R.

79. ASV, SSMM 166, f. 347: "senza alquna armonia et dolzeza di cantar."

80. Ibid., f. 353.

81. Ibid., f. 377^v.

82. See p. 115.

83. ASV, SSMM 167, f. 103^v.

84. Ibid., ff. 198^v and 199.

85. Ibid., f. 291.

86. Ibid., ff. 340 and 359^v.

87. Ibid., f. 366^v.

88. ASV, SSMM 168, f. 49.

89. Ibid., f. 307^v (both).

90. Ibid., f. 397.

91. Ibid., f. 453.

92. ASV, SSMM 169, f. 11^v.

93. ASV, SSMM 312.

94. Ibid.

95. ASV, SSMM 170, f. 97^v.

96. ASV, SST 14, f. 1^v.

97. Ibid., f. 2.

98. Ibid., f. 16: "siamo serviti come siamo et come ben sano tutte Vostre Signorie," and f. 16^v.

99. Ibid., f. 44.

100. Ibid., f. 47^v.

101. ASV, SST 1, ff. nn.; 1563–86 and ASV, SST 2, ff. nn.; 1587–1616.

102. ASV, SST 15, f. 20.

103. Ibid., f. 25^{r-v}.

104. ASV, SST Miscellanea, Registro Cassa Scuola e Commissarie, 1628, f. 3L.

105. ASV, SSM 17, f. 16.

106. Ibid., ff. 24^v and 45^v.

107. Ibid., f. 46^v.

108. Ibid., f. 55.

109. Ibid., ff. 74 and 83.

110. ASV, SSM 19, f. 77.

111. Ibid., f. 82^v.

112. Ibid., f. 134^v. Ciera later published two books of madrigals and some sacred music. See *NG*, s.v. Ciera, Ippolito.

113. Ibid., f. 108^{r-v}.

114. ASV, SSM 18, f. 4.

115. Ibid., f. 92.

116. Ibid., f. 94^v.

117. ASV, SSM 19, f. 125^v.

118. ASV, SSM 73.

119. ASV, SSM 19, f. 166ᵛ, SSM 20, ff. 29ᵛ and 91ʳ⁻ᵛ.
120. ASV, SSM 20, f. 142ᵛ. For more on Londariti, see Panayotakis, *Franghiskos Leontaritis*.
121. ASV, SSM 21, f. 55ᵛ.
122. ASV, SSM 22, f. 40.
123. Ibid., f. 266ᵛ; SSM 23, ff. 113ᵛ and 179.
124. ASV, SSM 23, f. 246ʳ⁻ᵛ.
125. ASV, SSM 24, f. 35.
126. Ibid., f. 184ᵛ and SSM 230.
127. ASV, SSM 25, ff. 59ᵛ and 186.
128. ASV, SSM 27, f. 20.
129. Ibid., f. 27ᵛ.
130. ASV, SSR II 44, f. 57ʳ⁻ᵛ.
131. ASV, SSR II 45, f. 12ᵛ.
132. Ibid., f. 13: "potteremo aver di primi chanttadori dila ttera."
133. Ibid., f. 32.
134. Ibid., ff. 39ᵛ–40.
135. Ibid., ff. 40ᵛ–41.
136. Ibid., ff. 43ᵛ and 87ᵛ.
137. ASV, SSR II 46, f. 28ᵛ.
138. ASV, SSR II 720, f. 11ᵛ.
139. ASR 14, ff. 311ᵛ and 340ᵛ.
140. Ibid., f. 379.
141. ASR 15, f. 6ᵛ.
142. Ibid.
143. Ibid., f. 20.
144. Ibid., ff. 18ᵛ–19.
145. Ibid., f. 22ᵛ.
146. Ibid., ff. 101ᵛ–102 and ASV, SSR II 423, f. 101.
147. ASR 16, f. 77.
148. ASR 17, f. 76ᵛ.
149. Ibid., f. 81ᵛ: "in honore et grandezza della schola nostra."
150. Ibid., ff. 135ᵛ–136ᵛ.
151. Ibid., ff. 151ᵛ–152: "la richiede . . . la nobiltà di questa dignissima schola."
152. Ibid., ff. 297ᵛ–298.
153. ASV, SSMC 253, f. 97 (35).
154. ASV, SSM 73.
155. ASV, SST 14, f. 3ᵛ; ASV, SSMC 253, f. 97 (35); and ASV, SSMM 253, pt. 1, ff. nn.; 10 April 1565.
156. ASV, SSMC 253, f. 97 (35) and ASV, SST 14, f. 3ᵛ.
157. ASV, SSGE 16, Funerali.
158. ASV, SSMM 253, pt. 1, ff. nn.; 23 August 1556.
159. ASV, SSMM 167, f. 32ᵛ.
160. For example, ASV, SSM 17, ff. 21ᵛ and 74ᵛ.
161. ASV, SSM 17, f. 25: "che alquni d'esi vengono et alquni non, et tamen dividono tal lor regalia tra loro chusì venuti chomo non venuti."
162. ASV, SSGE 141, ff. 82ᵛ–83: "una pessima et vergognosa corruttella, che quando è accetado qualche persona all'altar della Santissima Croce per nostro fradello, avanti che quel tal possi metter gli piedi fuora della scuola, li è tanta turba' de tali mali nostri fratelli

atorno che, o per bontà, o per vergogna, li è forza' distrazar molti soldi con loro, non senza tumulto et a grande vituperio nostro."

163. ASV, SSR II 47, ff. 25ᵛ–26: "cantar alla elevation del nostro Signor misser Jesù Christo et così dapoi la messa le laude et oration in similibus."

164. ASV, SSMC 256, f. 16ʳ⁻ᵛ.

165. Ibid., f. 16ᵛ.

166. ASV, SSMC 255, f. 156ᵛ: "dar al ditto Ser Francesco li tenori et li sorani, aciò che'l dito Ser Francesco posino inparar quelo el non sa." It is also possible that Alvixe Varoter was supposed to give Francesco Brisighella written music, rather than teach him, but, since Brisighella was unable to write (he had somebody else sign his name to the agreement since he did not know how), that seems less likely.

167. See Cattin, "Il manoscritto Venet. Marc. Ital. IX, 145."

168. ASV, SST 14, f. 2.

169. Ibid., ff. 1ᵛ and 16.

170. Ibid., f. 16.

171. Ibid., f. 70.

172. ASV, SSM 25, f. 21 and ASV, SSMC 260, ff. 170ᵛ–171ᵛ.

173. ASR 16, f. 222: "che non arecano comodo né ornamento alcuno, come è quello delli cantori da corpo, che più tosto al giorno de hoggi è fatto il loro canto ridicolo."

174. ASV, SST 5, f. 11.

175. ASV, SSM 17, f. 20.

176. Ibid., f. 60: "una devotissima usanza et a Dio gratissima, pariformiterque honorificha ala città nostra, necnon ala scuola nostra particulariter."

177. Ibid.: "moltiplicar le preditte devotion, sì per salute dele anime di fratelli, come per honorificentia dela scuola, la qual de raxon se die exaltar sopra tutte le altre per esser la piui bella et sotto al titulo de misser San Marco."

178. Ibid.: "a tutta la messa debano sonar."

179. ASV, SSM 18, f. 4.

180. ASR, *Libro di ordeni 1521*, ff. nn.

181. ASV, SSR II 47, f. 4.

182. Ibid., f. 16ᵛ.

183. Ibid., f. 4: "sonar con tutte le sorte di instrumenti che si sonano."

184. ASV, SSM 17, f. 60: "sì de trombe e piffari, come de fiauti et corneti."

185. ASV, SSR I 347, ff. nn.

186. Baroncini, "Contributo alla storia del violino." Many of the documents cited below are transcribed in Baroncini's appendix.

187. ASV, SSMM 4, f. 63: "I sonadori nuovi che sonono de lironi over violoni."

188. ASV, SSMM 166, f. 230.

189. ASV, SSM 4, f. 168ᵛ.

190. ASV, SSMM 166, f. 271ᵛ.

191. ASV, SSR II 46, f. 10: "sonadori vechii . . . sonadori de violoni."

192. ASV, SSR II 45, f. 92: "li nostri sonadori di arpa ett lautto ett viola." See Baroncini, "Contributo alla storia del violino," 93.

193. ASV, SSGE 141, f. 65ʳ⁻ᵛ.

194. ASV, SSMC 255, f. 146ᵛ.

195. ASV, SSM 21, f. 156ᵛ and ASV, SSM 73, ff. 97ᵛ–98.

196. ASV, SSM 73, ff. 149ᵛ–150ᵛ, 169ᵛ–170, and 185ᵛ–186.

197. ASV, SSMM 169, f. 92.

198. I have hypothesized elsewhere that a collaboration between the two is supported

by the evidence of the published laude of Innocentius Dammonis. While this unique survival of Venetian laude for this period does include music most suitable for performance by three instruments (perhaps lute, harp, and fiddle) and solo voice, there is nothing to connect it with any of the scuole grandi, though it might well have been used at some scuole piccole housed in San Salvatore, where Dammonis was a friar. Evidence for performance of instruments and voice together in non-processional liturgical settings in the sixteenth century is also rare, being limited to instructions for the instrumentalists to play "throughout the mass."

199. ASR, *Libro di ordeni 1521*, ff. nn.

200. ASV, SSGE 16.

201. ASV, SSR II 47, f. 102: "sonando moltte canzon ett alttri soni più presto lassivi che devotti . . . sonar mottetti et laude ad onor del nostro Signor Dio et prottetor nostro San Rocho . . . sonar canzon autt cosse amoroxe."

202. ASV, SSGE 141, f. 65ʳ⁻ᵛ: "E tutte le altre feste che la scuola andasse."

203. ASV, SSMC 258, ff. 162ᵛ–163.

204. ASR 15, f. 7ʳ⁻ᵛ: "non fanno la mittà delle procession che femo nui, perché nui femo il dopio procession di quello che fanno loro."

205. ASV, SSMC 253, ff. 203ᵛ–204 (44ᵛ–45) and ASV, SSGE 141, f. 103ᵛ.

206. On music at feste, see Quaranta, *Oltre San Marco*, ch. 6.

207. ASV, SSR II 47, f. 69ᵛ.

208. Ibid.: "esendo hobligatti quando acompagnaranno la Schuola nostra sì nelle nostre prozesion la prima domenega del mexe, come nelle alttre prozesion ett zorni di solemnità quando ditta nostra Schuolla andarano fuor di caxa con solemnittà, porttar li suoi instrumenti con li quali vanno a sonnar ale feste ett nozze per la tterra et non alttramentte."

209. Ibid.: "ett eziam debino sonar a ttutte le nostre messe hordinade, non avendo da sonar a nozze alchunna." Baroncini (p. 118) argues that this phrase means, instead, that the players were banned from playing in weddings, but that seems to me inconsistent with the context (note in particular that the previous phrase in the document refers to their playing at such events) and what we understand about the employment situation of musicians such as these. An annual salary of 4 ducats would have been considered only a guaranteed supplement to the considerably greater income they relied on from secular events. In addition, the language of the document, while not entirely unambiguous, does not support Baroncini's interpretation. The standard wording in parallel situations would employ a form of the verb *dovere*.

210. ASV, SSR II 47, f. 112ᵛ and ASR 14, f. 235. There is some confusion over the amounts in these documents. The 1551 decision refers to a salary of 8 ducats, one from 1552 refers to an unspecified raise, and another from 1561 indicates a raise of 3 ducats, but documents of 1566 and 1577 make it clear that the salary had not gone above 10. It seems likely that either some of the raises never took effect, or that they were rescinded (or treated as temporary).

211. ASV, SST 14, f. 42.

212. On the Paganini, see Baronicini, p. 90.

213. ASV, SST 14, f. 43ᵛ.

214. Ibid., f. 43ᵛ.

215. ASV, SSMC 258, ff. 162ᵛ–163.

216. Ibid., f. 204: "persone atte et assai a proposito . . . valor et fama."

217. ASR 15, ff. 40ᵛ–41.

218. ASV, SSM 23, f. 67ᵛ: "sianno lasato intender di non voler più servir ad esa scuolla se non li vien dato salario a ragion di anno come fanno le altre scuolle."

219. Ibid.

220. ASV, SSGE 143, f. 160.

221. ASV, SSMC 259, f. 34^{r-v}: "haver al suo servitio di migliori sonadori che si trova."

222. Ibid.: "che prima l'animo nostro era di voler ducatti vinti al'anno per ziascuno, se in un'altra nostra scritura si risolvessimo al meno in ducatti disdotto, ma per mostrare che desideriamo servirgli, e anco l'amorevolezza delle magnificentie vostre resti maggiore verso di noi, si rissolviamo di servirgli a raggione de ducatti sedici all'anno per ciascuno."

223. ASV, SSMM 167, f. 340: "per esser necessitadi di far quello che tutte le altre scholle costumano di far . . . et pagarli a modo loro."

224. ASV, SSMM 168, f. 20^v.

225. ASV, SSM 23, f. 246^{r-v}; ASV, SSMC 259, f. 92; ASV, SSMM 167, f. 291; and ASV, SSGE 144, f. 155^{r-v}.

226. ASV, SSM 24, f. 35: "ha fatto effetto tutto contrario all'intentione . . . spender molto più di quello che s'haveria fatto a proportione in così fatte occasioni."

227. ASR 14, f. 288^{r-v}.

228. ASR 15, ff. 181^v–182: "mi son affatica' a trovar compagni di migliori della terra per honor et servicio di questa religiosissima scola."

229. Ibid., f. 232; ASR 16, ff. 61^v–62; ASR 16, f. 172^v.

230. ASV, SST 14, ff. 40^v–42: "Tu menti sì li per la gola, tristo che pensi con tal mezi tuorne il nostro," and "Quando si troveremo fuori delo albergo si daremo dele feride, mariol tristo che sei."

231. ASV, SSMC 262, f. 102^v.

232. ASR 17, ff. 76^v and 135^v–136^v.

233. ASV, Monastero di Santa Maria della Carità, Busta 28 pergamene, no. 1404.

234. ASV, SSMC 253, f. 229^v (71^v): "bona summa di danari in reparation de dicto organo senza haver habudo sufragio algun dala dicta schuola nostra."

235. ASV, SSMC 258, f. 3^{r-v}: "il migliore et il più perfeto che se atrova in questa ciptà."

236. Ibid.: "in modo che per molti et molti anni la scuola sarà liberada da tal spesa."

237. Ibid., f. 76^v.

238. ASV, Monastero di Santa Maria della Carità 5, no. 1908.

239. ASV, SSMC 257, f. 15 and ASV, SST 97, ff. nn. (The 1565/66 account book from the Scuola della Carità has been misfiled in this busta of the Scuola di San Teodoro.)

240. ASV, SSMM 166, f. 205.

241. IRE, PATR 1 O 12, f. 8 [p. 133]. This is probably the Massimiliano da Udene who collaborated in the building of an organ in Capo d'Istria in 1564. See Lunelli, *Studi e documenti*, 202.

242. Many of the references are preserved only in later copies (in IRE, PATR 1 O 12) of documents of which the originals are no longer extant. The list includes a Zuan Prudenti in 1567 followed, in 1569, by Gerolemo de Prudenti, perhaps the same individual, with the name miscopied by the later scribe. Zuan Prudenti reappears in 1573, the year after Andrea Romanin, who served until 1580, is first listed. It is possible that Romanin served for one year, left, and then returned, or also that, once again, there was a copying error of some sort (perhaps Prudenti was simply paid back wages after he stopped serving).

243. ASV, Monastero di Santo Stefano 4, Proposizioni del Convento 1578–1615, f. 48^v.

244. ASV, SSR II 720, f. 33: "in total ruina . . . che sia belo e bon."

245. ASR 14, f. 291^v.

246. Ibid., ff. 294^v–295.

247. Ibid., ff. 307 and 331. For more on Colombo, see Lunelli, *Studi e documenti*, 171–72.

248. ASR 16, f. 135.

249. Ibid., f. 273^v.

250. ASR 17, f. 183^v: "in malissimo stato, né si può più adoperarlo in divina fontione per esser rotto e tutto mal al'ordine per la vechiezza di esso, non essendolo stato fatto cosa alcuna che è più di anni 40 incirca . . . l'urgentissimo bisogno in che si atrova, hanno fato veder da pratici et peritti . . ."

251. ASV, SSGE 141, f. 239^v: "essendo cosa justa et honesta di proveder a laude del Signor Dio."

252. ASV, SSGE 142, ff. 7^v–8: "in termene tal che non vi è ordine di poterlo aconciar che stii bene, e che quello possi adoperar nelle occorentie. Et essendo neccessario proveder per honor della maestà de Dio, se de detta nostra scola."

253. Ibid.: "uno novo che sia perfetto . . ."

254. ASV, SSGE 142, f. 156^v; ASV, SSGE 143, f. 88; ASV, SSGE 403, ff. nn., 1580; and ASV, SSGE 143, f. 155^v. On Colonna, who worked also in Padua and Treviso, and as tuner at the Basilica di San Marco, see Lunelli, *Studi e documenti*, 173–74.

255. ASV, SSGE 144, f. 157^v: "le cane del qual vengono consumate dalla ruggine, et con notabilissima vergogna et danno nostro."

256. Ibid., f. 165. Fra Iseppo was attached to the Carmelite order. See Lunelli, 193.

257. ASV, SSGE 144, ff. 168 and 171.

258. Ibid., f. 260^v.

259. ASV, SSGE 147, f. 176^{r-v}.

260. ASV, SSGE 144, f. 185.

261. ASV, SSGE 145, f. 237^v.

262. ASV, SSGE 141, f. 2^v.

263. Ibid., f. 4^v.

264. Ibid., f. 31.

265. Ibid., f. 47^v.

266. ASV, SSGE 144, f. 185.

267. Sponga had been a student of Andrea Gabrieli, and also published, in 1595, a book of ricercars and other organ works, dedicated to Lodovico Usper, a brother in the scuola. He would later publish several books of sacred and secular vocal music.

268. ASV, SSGE 144, f. 185.

269. Ibid., ff. 204^v and 213.

270. He did, at least temporarily, return to organ playing, serving as organist at the church of San Salvatore in 1614 (Dalla Libera, *L'arte degli organi,* 74) and as deputy at the Basilica of San Marco in 1622 and 1623, using the name he adopted in his later life, Usper (or Susper), after his patron.

271. ASV, SSGE 145, f. 125

272. Ibid., f. 126

273. Ibid., ff. 168 and 182^v.

274. Ibid., f. 191. Both Francesco Sponga and Gabriel Sponza (this sort of variation in names is not unusual in these documents) also went by the name of Usper or Susper. He published *Madrigali concertati* (Venice, 1623) and several works in his uncle's collections. On Rizzo, see below, and n. 284.

275. ASV, SSGE 145, f. 207^v.

276. ASV, SSGE 404.

277. ASV, SSGE 147, f. 137^v.

278. ASV, SSR II 46, f. 65^v.

279. Ibid., ff. 82^v and 87^v.

280. ASV, SSR II 47, f. 13^v.

281. Ibid., f. 98.

282. ASV, SSR II 423, f. 22ᵛ.

283. ASR 14, ff. 294ᵛ–295.

284. Bell'haver (whose name is also spelled Bellavere and several other ways), was a well-known composer. Extant works include a book of madrigals and other vocal and instrumental works in anthologies.

285. ASR 15, ff. 11 and 11ᵛ: "sacerdotti, violini, cantori, et altri."

286. Ibid., ff. 91ᵛ–92.

287. ASR 16, f. 192ᵛ. Picchi was also a composer, and published two books of keyboard music: *Intavolatura di balli* (Venice, 1621) and *Canzoni da sonar* (Venice, 1625). Grillo published a volume of sacred music in 1618 (*Sacri concentus ac symphoniae* (Venice, 1618), and several other works of his appear in anthologies. Rizzo published three books of sacred works for voices and instruments in 1612, 1614, and 1620/21.

288. ASV, SSR II 414, f. 5.

289. ASR 16, f. 201. On Picchi, see below and n. 284.

290. Ibid., f. 209.

291. ASR 17, f. 1ᵛ: "Essendo vachatto il locho de organista per la morte del quondam Giovanni Battista Grillo, et essendosi fatti far li soliti proclami conforme a l'ordinario, né essendo comparsi altri, che Don Zuanne Priuli organista, però, L'anderà parte . . . che sii eletto detto Don Zuanne Pichi per organista nostro."

292. ASV, SSR II 172, ff. nn.; 21 October 1635 and SSR II 175, ff. nn.; 1642.

293. ASR 17, ff. 164ᵛ–165.

294. Ibid., f. 218.

295. ASV, SSM 16, ff. 4–5.

296. ASV, SSM 22, f. 210.

297. ASV, Monastero di Santa Maria della Carità 18, f. 1ᵛ.

298. ASV, Monastero di Santa Maria della Carità 43, no. 70, ff. 34ᵛ–120ᵛ.

299. ASV, SSMC 257, ff. 2–3: "per honor et dicoro di la squola nostra . . . cantar uno bela et solene messa grande in sala di la squola nostra."

300. Ibid., f. 14.

301. ASV, SSGE 144, ff. 74–76.

302. ASV, SSGE 145, ff. 203–204: "si debbano cantar, et non leggerli, et siino detti con devotione et edificatione."

303. ASV, SSGE 141, ff. 489ᵛ–490: "Acciò che la nostra chiesa sia fornitta de sacerdotti virtuosi, e che le feste si possi cantar in canto figuratto."

304. ASV, SSR II 47, ff. 15–16.

305. ASR 14, f. 380: "Havendo bisogno la chiesia nostra per le solennità di divini officii che di continuo si dieno far in riverentia del Signor Dio et del glorioso misser San Rocho protetor nostro, et per la dignità et honorevolezza di quel sacrosanto tempio, di cinque mansonarii, quali insieme con il nostro capellano attendino al coro, et senza di quali non si puol far."

Chapter 6

1. As allowed by church practice, such vigils were often celebrated even when not in the official church calendar.

2. ASV, SSR II 114, no. 7 includes a listing of the objects brought for display at one occasion in the eighteenth century, including 108 carpets, 102 embroidered cushions, 46 embroidered chairs, 85 paintings (not listed individually), and 684 silver objects (including 318 vases of various sizes).

3. ASV, SSM 17, f. 74: "Perché senpre a tenpi dela festa nostra de misser San Marcho la schuola nostra a diferenzie con li chantadori che se tuol per la dita festa, et ogni volta el bixognia inovar pati."

4. Ibid.: "hogni anno la vezilia de misser San Marcho vegnir ala schola nostra et in la sala nostra chantar el vespero con le solenità consuete, e poi el zorno dela festa la matina vegnir a chantar la mesa et da poi dixnar el vesporo."

5. ASV, SSM 17, f. 100: "per spragnar el denar de la scuola."

6. ASV, SSM 18, f. 57: "capo di canttadori per do vespori e la mesa di mortti."

7. ASV, SSMM 303, p. 208L.

8. This company has been discussed in greater detail in Glixon, "A Musicians' Union."

9. ASV, Consiglio dei Dieci, Parti Comuni, filza 59, no. 68, Allegato III, f. 1: "Essendosi gli infrascritti cantori in nome della Santissima Trinità, per conservatione della pace, et accressimento della utilità, uniti et colligati per dover fare amorevolmente tutte le feste che a loro saranno comesse, et mettere insieme tutti li guadagni che da quelle si caveranno, da dovere essere tra tutti partiti con equal portione, da boni fratelli, sì per ovviare alli contrarii che potriano facilmente nascere, et causare tra loro dissensione et discordia, sì anche per stabilire di tutti loro una compagnia in modo tale che habbia a durare quanto dureranno le vite delli compagni."

10. ASV, SSMC 236, ff. 65$^\mathrm{v}$–66: "Non satii nè contenti ancora, questi tal cantori, di haver reduto questa nostra schuola a tal passo, anzi con l'anima colmo di avidità, hano creato una obrobriosa conventicula et secta, et quella capitulata per man di nodaro publico, con alquanti capituli abominosi et neffandi, li quali tutti redondano a maleficio grandissimo da tutte chiesie et loci catholici et pii, et specialmente a maeleficio extremo delle schuole grande de batudi, et delli sui poveri. " There are copies of this document also in ASV, SSGE 8, ff. 65–66$^\mathrm{v}$ and ASV, Consiglio dei Dieci, Parti Comuni, Filza 59, No. 68, Allegato III, ff. 2$^\mathrm{v}$–3$^\mathrm{v}$.

11. ASV, Consiglio dei Dieci, Parti Comuni, Reg. 21, f. 7.

12. Ibid., Parti Comuni, filza 59, no. 68, Allegato II.

13. Ibid., Allegato I: "Havendo, con summa prudentia et optima consideration, li nostri sancti padri introducti li soni et musica nela Giesia Sancta, iuxta il precepto del Profeta David, che neli salmi canta 'Psallite Domino in cithara, et voce psalmi, in tubis ductilibus et voce tube cornee,' et 'Laudate Domino in tympano et choro, in cordis et organo'; perché, in vero, non possiamo laudar il nostro Signor Idio di tante manere di lode, che più non siamo tenuti. E poi se invitano con questo meggio li populi a frequentar le chiesie sancte et altri lochi pii, ove si excitano a devotione, et non dano loco ad otio, che sol esser causa di ogni male. Et essendo la musica per li optimi effeci che sempre ha partorito continuata fin a questo tempo in tutte le cità di fideli, et in questa sua, come quella che sempre è stata osservantissima del culto divino sopra tutte le altre; si rendemo certi, nui guardiani delle schole di batuti . . . , che non sia stata mente di questo Illustrissimo Conseio di prohibir totalmente l'uso della musica ale schole, sì anchor per honor di questa felicissima cità, ove tutto il mondo concorre, et poi per utile dele schole, le facultà di quali sono accresute per il concorso dele persone che quelle frequentano mediante le musiche et altre cerimonie exterior." The biblical citations are variants of Ps. 97:5–6 and Ps. 150: 4.

14. ASV, CD, Parti Comuni, Reg. 21, ff. 12$^\mathrm{v}$ and 36$^\mathrm{v}$.

15. Ibid., f. 12$^\mathrm{v}$.

16. ASV, CD, Parti Comuni, Filza 60, no. 73, Allegato.

17. Ibid., no. 73: "parne che la grandezza che porta con se esse scole habbia da esser accompagnata con essi cantadori, sì come sempre si è consuetado fare, havendo ben modo

esse scole di poter sparagnar li sui danari, scansando molte altre spese che superfluamente fanno."

18. ASV, CD, Parti Comuni, Reg. 21, f. 38ᵛ.

19. ASV, SSMM 167, ff. 26–27ᵛ.

20. ASV, SSGE 142, ff. 242ᵛ–243 and 273–274ᵛ.

21. The account book, a giornale for 1565 and 1566, has been misfiled in ASV, SST 97.

22. ASV, Procuratori de supra, busta 91, processo 208, fascicolo 2, f. 56ʳ⁻ᵛ: "omnibus et singulis predicti ecclesie cantoribus huiusmodi ecclesie . . . ex duobus una solum modo societas fiat."

23. ASV, SST 14, f. 107ᵛ: "per termina le cosse della festa."

24. ASV, SST 5, ff. nn., 7 November 1587: "possano esser elletti quelli che più piacerà."

25. ASV, Capi del Consiglio dei Dieci, Reg. 29, ff. 102ᵛ–103: "intendendo con quanta difficultà, et interesse loro li guardiani grandi, vicarii, et guardiani da mattino delle scuole grandi si possono servir nelle solennità di esse scuole delli musici cantori et sonatori di questa città, sì per le concorrentie che sono fra essi musici, come per la qualità delle mercedi che sono da loro ricercate, da che nasce in cadauna occasione molti rumori et disordini . . . Sue Signorie Eccelentissime . . . terminano et statuiscono: che Baldissera Donato colla sua compagnia debba servir nelle solennità delle scuole della Misericordia, di San Marco, et di San Zuanne, et che pre Zuanne detto il Chiozoto servir debba pur colla sua compagnia alle scuole della Carità, di San Rocho, et di San Todero."

26. Ibid., ff. 104ᵛ–105: "che quella di Girolamo da Udene debba servire alle scuole di San Marco et della Carità, quella delli Favretti alle scuole di San Zuanne et di San Todero, et quella di Bassani alle scuole della Misericordia et di San Rocho."

27. Ibid., f. 24.

28. Ibid.

29. ASV, SSGE 16, section "Feste": "de non far gran festa."

30. ASV, SSGE 142, ff. 242ᵛ–243.

31. Ibid., ff. 273–274ᵛ.

32. ASV, SSGE 144, f. 155ʳ⁻ᵛ: "l'eccesso delle domande ingorde delli musici et le molte molestie di tuor più d'una compagnia et multiplicità d'organi."

33. Ibid., f. 222ʳ⁻ᵛ: "per proprio apetito."

34. ASV, SSGE 146, f. 163.

35. Ibid., f. 255ʳ⁻ᵛ: "È introdotto pernicioso abuso nella scola nostra da certi anni in qua, che viene tralasciato di riverire nel giorno della Santissima Croce questa santa reliquia con quell'honore di musica, che pur per avanti sempre è stato solito di fare senza interruttione, acciochè dalla città fosse reduco in quanta veneratione è stata sempre tenuta. Et questo per tralasciarsi de fare il rodolo ordinario dalli quattro capi insieme con li degani, col scosso del qual rodolo si faceva tal sollenità, nè dovendosi in modo alcuno permettere che tal disordine vadi più avanti, così per dimostrare la religione devotissima, et grandezza della scola nostra, come per sodisfare a queli che con non poco scandalo mormorano, che non si facci tal fontione . . . che de cetero sia obligato il guardian grande, il giorno che farà l'accettatione del suo carico, fare un rodolo . . ."

36. ASV, SSMC 259, ff. 212ᵛ–213: "per compiacer a cantori et sonatori hanno tolto due, tre, et 4 compagnie con spesa grande della scola . . ."

37. ASV, SSMC 260, f. 59ʳ⁻ᵛ: "spender gran quantità di danaro della sua borsa . . . perché molte fiate diversi sogetti che sarano attissimi al governo della scola aboniscono l'occasione d'esser elletti per fugir l'incomodo della spesa . . . perché succederebbe con molta mormoratione de tutta la nobilità et civiltà che concore in tal giorno."

38. ASV, SSMC 261, ff. 82ᵛ–88: "sperando che a laude di Dio e della Maddona Santissima si contenterà spender del suo."

39. ASV, SSMC 261, f. 100ʳ⁻ᵛ: "ad honor della Beata Vergine nostra protetrice et per reputatione della scola nostra."

40. The listing for 1595 is in ASV, SSR II 418, that for 1598 in ASV, SSR II 703, and those from 1598 onward in the chronological series of cauzioni beginning in ASV, SSR II 155. Within these buste the loose sheets are arranged approximately chronologically. Unless otherwise mentioned, all the information in this section derives from these buste. Some of this material has been discussed previously in Arnold, "Music at the Scuola di San Rocco," and id., *Giovanni Gabrieli*, ch. 8.

41. Coryat, *Coryat's Crudities*, 1:390–91.

42. In some years the name is missing or the person is not identifiable.

43. *Canzoni et sonate del Signor Giovanni Gabrieli* . . . (Venice: Gardano, 1615).

44. *Symbolae diversorum musicorum* . . . (Venice: Vincenti, 1620) [RISM 1620²].

45. There have been a number of recreations of the 1608 festa, most notably recorded versions directed by Roland Wilson (*The Feast of San Rocco, Venice 1608*. New York: Sony Classical [S2K 66 254], 1995) and Paul McCreesh (*Music for San Rocco*. Hamburg: Deutsche Grammophon GmbH [Archiv 449 180–2], 1996). Neither conductor claims that the music recorded was actually part of the 1608 event, but (reasonably) that it might have been, and that all of the works (by Giovanni Gabrieli and Bartolomeo Barbarino in the McCreesh version, by Gabrieli, Alessandro Grandi, Giovanni Battista Cima, Barbarino, Monteverdi, and Bellerofonte Castaldi in the Wilson version) could have been performed by the forces described by Coryat and documented in the pay slip. While their chief aim is to reproduce the splendor of the occasion, both include, as a work almost certainly performed there, the Gabrieli Sonata for three violins referred to above. Wilson also suggests that it is "almost certain," because of its unusual instrumentation of four cornetti and ten trombones, that Gabrieli's Sonata XVIII (from the 1615 *Canzoni e sonate*) was performed at this occasion. Finally, both conductors make claims for the Magnificat for thirty-three parts in seven choirs (an incompletely preserved larger version of the seventeen-voice Magnificat from the 1615 *Symphoniae sacrae*). They suggest that such a work would have been the most likely reason for the presence of seven organs at San Rocco (though they suggest no evidence that each choir in a multi-choir work required a separate organ).

Chapter 7

1. ASV, SSMM 170, f. 150: "Le scuole grandi di questa città comparsano tutte a gara a venerare la religione e decorare quella città; tra tutte non è mai stato inferiore per gratia d'Iddio questa nostra, solo pure che ne' tempi presenti si farà credere con qualche descapito di reputatione in risguardo che esse fuori senza sonatori, che pure si vedono et odono in tutte li altri."

2. ASV, SSMC 263, f. 264: "con qual lustre et pompa magiore che n'è stimata posibile."

3. ASV, SST 16, ff. 42ᵛ–43ᵛ.

4. Ibid., ff. 72ᵛ–76.

5. ASV, SST 101 and SST 94.

6. ASV, SSMM 257, pt. 1, no. 47: "un servigio reso necessarii da tanti secoli."

7. ASV, SSMM 262, n. 81.

8. ASV, SSMM 208, pt. 2.

9. ASV, SSMM 249, ff. nn., 10 February 1799.

10. ASV, SSGE 148, f. 120.

11. ASV, SSGE 331, ff. nn., 20 March 1670.

12. The extant membership lists of the Venetian instrumentalists' guild are published in Selfridge-Field, "Annotated Membership Lists."

13. ASV, SSGE 148, ff. 421ᵛ–433 and SSGE 149, f. 165.

14. ASV, SSGE 149, f. 165.

15. Ibid., f. 187ᵛ: "essendo cosa di tanta premura, necessità, et bisogno."

16. ASV, SSGE 156, ff. 13–14: "di maggior abilità e pratica nel sonare gli instrumenti."

17. ASV, SSGE 436, f. 267L.

18. ASV, SSR II 41, ff. nn.; c.25 November 1754: "essendo huomo d'abilittà e cognitione per ben esseguire le sue parti."

19. ASV, SSR II 60, p.12.

20. ASR 18, f. 127: "non solo mai si vedono tutti, anzi comparano pochi, e molte volte nessuno."

21. ASV, SSR II 34, ff. nn., 17 July 1677.

22. ASR 18, ff. 154ᵛ and 162.

23. ASR 18, f. 162.

24. ASV, SSR II 51, ff. 69ᵛ–70: "il grave sconcerto . . . scandalo appresso la gente, e lamentazione di quei reverendi capitolari."

25. ASV, SSR II 51, f. 70.

26. ASR 9, f. 250 (1732); ASV, SSR II 39, ff. nn., 20 March 1740; ASV, SSR II 40, ff. nn., 13 March 1746; and ibid., 28 April 1748.

27. ASR 17, ff. 297ᵛ–298.

28. ASR 18, f. 83.

29. See above, n. 12.

30. ASV, SSMM 207 and 208.

31. ASV, SSMM 324, p. 49.

32. ASV, SSMM 95, 23 September 1773.

33. ASV, SSMM 261, no. 108.

34. ASV, SSMM 249, ff. nn., 10 February 1799.

35. ASV, SSMM 207 and 208.

36. ASV, SST 16, ff. 44ᵛ–46ᵛ: "preti cantori."

37. Ibid., ff. 72ᵛ–76.

38. ASV, SST 101, ff. nn., 2 March 1727.

39. ASV, SST 94, ff. nn., 20 January 1787.

40. ASV, SST 77, no. 63.

41. ASV, SSMM 257, pt. 1, no. 7.

42. ASV, SSMM 97, pp. 91–92 and ASV, SSMM 249, ff. nn., 10 February 1799 [m.v.].

43. ASV, SSM 251.

44. ASV, SSM 231, no. 16.

45. ASV, SSM 254, f. 230L.

46. ASV, SSMC 271, ff. 205ᵛ–206.

47. ASV, SSMC 272, f. 97.

48. ASV, SSMC 230.

49. ASV, SSMC 274, ff. 31ᵛ–32.

50. ASV, SSMC 220, ff. nn., 8 August 1698.

51. ASV, SSMC 268, f. 49: "inutile et inoperoso . . . elletti e pagati . . . le di loro fontioni."

52. ASV, SSMC 268, f. 202ʳ⁻ᵛ: "trasportate ad altre più loro geniale funzioni in altre chiese."

53. ASV, SSMC 270, f. 140ᵛ.

54. ASV, SSMC 272, f. 97.

55. ASV, SSMC 230.

56. ASV, SSMC 198, ff. nn., 20 September 1795.

57. Ibid., ff. nn., 27 September 1795: "dedicato essendosi ad assistere alla direzione delle pubbliche azioni teatrali . . . ma singolarmente in quella parte che riguarda la giusta pronunciazione, l'esatto gesto pantomimico, ed i retti movimenti degli attori . . ."

58. Ibid.: "ma meglio ancora e con maggiore decenza e puntualità."

59. ASV, SSMC 198, ff. nn.

60. ASV, SSGE 24, ff. nn.; 2 March 1760: "della natural tutta la maggiore abilità per il canto."

61. ASV, SSGE 154, ff. 389ᵛ–392 (the motion to institute new rules) and SSGE 69 (the printed booklet).

62. ASV, SSGE 24, no. 16.

63. ASV, SSGE 154, f. 426ʳ⁻ᵛ: "tutti capaci et idonei per il canto fermo e figurato."

64. ASV, SSGE 155, f. 247ᵛ.

65. ASV, SSGE 436.

66. ASV, SSGE 155, ff. 272ᵛ–273.

67. ASV, SSGE 362, ff. nn.

68. ASR 17, f. 255 and ASR 18, ff. 72ᵛ–73.

69. Ibid.

70. ASR 19, f. 221.

71. ASR 20, f. 86ʳ⁻ᵛ.

72. Don Steffano Filipponi, after thirty years' service, in 1695 (ASR 19, ff. 181ᵛ–182ᵛ), and padre Giovanni Maggioni, after thirty-five, about 1790 (ASV, SSR II 455).

73. ASV, SSR II 39, ff. nn., 13 August 1741.

74. Ibid., 13 July 1741: "officiata col vero ordine proprio della santità del luoco, et atto ad accrescere la devozione e concorso de' fedeli. Scoprendosi perciò con senso interno di dolore, che la chiesa nostra . . . resta oggi mai quasi del tutto abbandonata."

75. ASV, SSR II 91, ff. nn., 3 March 1754, capitolo sesto, and ibid., a list of the days on which polyphony was required: Christmas, fourth Sunday of Lent (for the end of the officers' terms), Easter, Purification, Ascension, Pentecost, last Sunday of May, first Sunday of August, Assumption, last Sunday of September, and Saint Andrew.

76. ASV, SSR II 38, ff. nn., 21 August 1729: "vengono decentemente cantate in esso le divine lodi."

77. In, for example, the confirmation of the choir on 1 May 1732 (ASR 21, f. 250).

78. ASV, SSR II 38, ff. nn., 16 July 1738.

79. ASV, SSR II 39, ff. nn., 13 August 1741: "di maggior abilità."

80. ASV, SSR II 40, ff. nn.; 8 March 1744: "che dovendo il vice corista restar prescielto dal numero dei mansionarii di chiesa non si dà forse mai il caso che possa farsi scielta né d'una buona voce, né di religioso che sia istrutto nel canto con indecoro delle sacre fonzioni."

81. ASV, SSR II 40, ff. nn.; 7 February 1744.

82. ASV, SSR II 51, f. 25ᵛ.

83. ASV, SSR II 41, ff.nn., 7 March 1751.

84. ASV, SSGE 41, ff. nn., 17 March 1717.

85. ASV, SSR II 91, ff. nn., 3 March 1754: "nessuna essendo l'abilità del canto."

86. Ibid., capitolo quarto.

87. ASV, SSR II 31, ff. nn., 11 December 1766.

88. ASV, SSR II 60, p. 103.

89. ASV, SSR II 285, no. 489: "un antifonnario, che corrispondesse al bisogno."

90. ASR, LIBER MISSARUM AD USUM ECCLESIAE SANCTI ROCCHI VE-
NETIIS ANNO DNI M.DCCLIV.

91. ASV, SSR II 329, no. 422: "Indispensabile fu riconosciuta la neccessità di provedere questa nostra chiesa de nuovi libri corali per servizio delle messe e vesperi, che
sogliono con frequenza solennizarsi nella medesima. Riformato il vecchio libro, d'un tal
genere fu allo stesso aggionto un secondo tomo continente dodeci nuove messe, tutte scritte
con caratteri stampatelli in partidura, il che rende a sufficienza fornito quel coro per la
riccorrenza delle varie fonzioni occorrenti fra l'anno, oltre tutte le feste nelle quali solen-
nizzasi la messa cantata . . ."

92. ASR, LIBER SECUNDUS MISSARUM AD USUM ECCLESIAE SANCTI
ROCCHI. VENETIIS ANNO DOMINI MDCCLXXV.

93. ASV, SSR II 191, ff. nn., 2 April 1676.

94. ASV, SSR II 421, ff. nn.

95. ASV, SSR I 89, no. 85.

96. In the series of cauzioni, ASV, SSR II 262–85.

97. ASV, SSR II 273, no. 326.

98. ASV, SSR II 277, no. 328.

99. ASV, SSR II 452, no. 81.

100. ASV, SSR II 66, no. 64.

101. ASV, SSR II 51, f. 25^v.

102. Ibid.: "totalmente all'oscuro."

103. ASV, SSR II 455, ff. nn.; October [December?] 1763.

104. ASV, SSR II 32, ff. nn.; 6 August 1769.

105. ASV, SSR II 461, ff. nn.

106. Ibid.

107. There is no record of the actual decision to reduce payments, but the action is
referred to in a document of 1691, ASV, SSMC 265, ff. 228^v–230^v.

108. Ibid.

109. ASV, SSGE 24, no. 22.

110. In the sixty previous years, eight different organists held the post. Levis was a
priest and organist at the church of Santa Maria Mater Domini (ASV, PC 73, 1785) and
also served as organist at the Scuola del Santissimo Sacramento in San Cassiano in 1775–
76 (Archivio Parocchiale di San Cassiano, Capitoli della Scuola 1738–1843, p. 118) and at
the Scuola del Santissimo Sacramento in San Silvestro from 1782 to 1784 (Archivio Parocchiale di San Silvestro, Libro di Capitoli 1737–1812). According to the diarist Pietro
Gradenigo, Levis also directed the music for feste at San Cassiano in 1754 (BC, Gradenigo
2, f. 108) and at San Giacomo di Rialto in 1772 (ibid., Gradenigo 35, f. 57^v). Some of
Levis's compositions are preserved in BNM MS Ital. IV 1205 (10921).

111. ASV, SSGE 69.

112. ASV, SSGE 333, ff. nn., 9 May 1681: "L'honore de Dio et il culto della santa
chiesa." For more on Beni, see Lunelli, *Studi e documenti*, 159–60.

113. ASV, SSGE 149, f. 142^v: "Ritrovandosi da qualche tempo in qua rotto l'organo
della chiesa nostra."

114. ASV, SSGE 151, ff. 135 and 352^v–353, and ASV, SSGE 434, f. 275.

115. ASV, SSGE 151, f. 255^v and SSGE 424, ff. nn., 5 June 1729. Beni was still in
the post as late as 1757, when the organ became unusable, and was about to be replaced.

116. ASV, SSGE 461, f. 410L. On Piaggia, see Lunelli, *Studi e documenti*, 215–16.

117. The hiring of Piaggia, his death, and Merlini's hiring are all recorded in a document of 1771: ASV, SSGE 369, ff. nn., 26 August 1771. For more on Merlini, see Lunelli,
Studi e documenti, 203.

118. ASR 17, f. 292^v.

119. ASV, SSR II 48, f. 43. Sartorio died on 17 October 1680. For more on Fuga, see Vio, "Un maestro di musica."

120. ASR 19, ff. 128–29.

121. ASR 20, f. 274^{r-v}.

122. ASV, SSR II 37, ff. nn., 16 March 1727.

123. ASV, SSR II 39, ff. nn., 28 December 1743.

124. Ibid., 12 January 1743 [m.v.].

125. Ibid.: "il ditto organo per conto dell'artefice che l'ha costrutto era perfetto, ma che da chi lo suonò era stato scordata con pericolo di pregiudicii maggiori quando continuasse a suonarlo, non potendo un organo di recente costrutto e rare volte suonato esser scordatto se non quando s'impieghi in suonarlo chi almeno non abbia una mediocre abilità."

126. Ibid., 29 January 1743, ASR, Registro delle Parti 10, f. 173^v, and ASV, SSR II 266, no. 416.

127. ASV, SSR II 267, no. 289. Pasinetto's election is recorded in ASV, SSR II 40, ff. nn., 5 and 8 March 1744.

128. ASV, SSR II 41, ff. nn., about 1 March 1755 and 2 March 1755.

129. ASV, SSR II 415, ff. nn., 1776.

130. SSR II 43, ff. nn.; 23–24 February 1784: "Ho sentito prima il reverendo Don Giacomo Segato, il quale abilissimo riuscì alla mia cognizione, e nella giustezza del suo tastaggio, e nella graziosità delle sue suonate; ho sentito ancora il reverendo Antonio Nitor, soggetto in vero di grande abilità, e il suonar suo mi parve assai franco e spiritoso, ma più pronto che non vorebbe l'orecchio avido di gustar quella nota, che il di lui tasteggio bene spesso divora."

131. ASV, SSR II 59, p. 136 and ASV, SSR II 376, ff. nn., 1 September 1797.

132. ASV, SSR II 65, ff. nn., 1798.

133. ASR 18, f. 226^v and ASV, SSR II 197, no. 246. On Giorgio, see Lunelli, *Studi e documenti*, 191.

134. ASR 19, f. 98^{r-v}.

135. ASV, SSR II 408, ff. nn., 31 January 1726.

136. ASV, SSR II 50, f. 113. Several drawings for the case are preserved in ASV, SSR II 416. One of these is reproduced in Glixon, " 'Ad honor de misser San Rocco,' " pl. 7.

137. ASV, SSR II 449, ff. nn., June 1742. On Nacchini, see Lunelli, *Studi e documenti*, 205–11.

138. ASV, SSR I 506, f. 250L.

139. ASV, SSR II 288, no. 101. On Dacii, see Lunelli, *Studi e documenti*, 175–76.

140. ASV, SSR II 382, Fabrica della Chiesa, no. 62. He also, in 1758, rebuilt the pedalboard and tracker mechanism of the small organ the scuola kept in the hall of the scuola itself (ASV, SSR II 295, no. 406). For more on Callido, see Lunelli, *Studi e documenti*, 165–67.

141. ASV, SSR II 303, no. 417.

142. ASV, SSR I 507, f. 187L.

143. ASV, SSR II 315, no. 395.

144. ASV, SSR II 33, ff. nn., 18 September 1774.

145. ASV, SSR II 43, ff. nn., 24 May 1789. On Merlini, see Lunelli, *Studi e documenti*, 203.

146. ASV, SSR II 184 and 185.

147. See Roche, *North Italian Church Music*, ch. 5.

148. ASV, SSMC 287, ff. nn., 19 March 1752 and identically in account books for the following years.

149. ASV, SSMC 271, ff. 205ᵛ–206.

150. BC, Gradenigo 13, f. 11ᵛ: "Nella Scuola Grande della Carità si espone la Porpora di Nostro Signore con messa in musica, e con indulgenza plenaria procurata dal famoso Bessarione Cardinale Niceno." An announcement of this event further describes the "sacra porpora" as bearing many stains of the blood of Christ (ASV, SSMC 199, ff. nn.; 8 April 1797).

151. ASV, SSMM 172, f. 388ᵛ: "Non si può negare, che la principal solennità della nostra Scola, solita celebrarsi nel giorno della Santissima Concettione della Beata Vergine . . . sia praticata con qualche minor lustro di quello si osserva nella maggior parte delle scole grandi, il che accade in riguardo della grave spesa che occorre nell'addobbar l'albergo e li due gran saloni di sopra e di sotto, da'che procede, che alle volte si tralascia di far cantar la messa in musica, com'è stato sempre solito de' nostri precessori."

152. The 1646 decision is referred to in a document of 1739: ASV, SSGE 152, f. 181ᵛ.

153. Ibid.

154. ASV, SSGE 154, ff. 389ᵛ–392.

155. ASV, SSR II 182, ff. nn., 16 August 1658 and ASV, SSR II 191, ff. nn., 14 August 1676.

156. ASV, SSR II 421, ff. nn.

157. ASV, SSR II 38, ff. nn. 16 August 1736 and ASV, SSR II 456, ff. nn., 1738.

158. ASV, SSR II 40, ff. nn., 14 July 1748.

159. ASV, SSR II 40, ff. nn.; 22 February 1749: "ma si crede ben improprio assai et indecente, che un giorno di tanta solennità nella mattina coll'ordine stesso non si canti la santa messa, quando in ogn'altro giorno festivo è solita questa chiesa di sempre cantarli in terzo, e quando non v'ha scola, né chiesa, né scola, né suffraggio, né fraglia per miserabile che sia, che non solennizi il giorno del santo suo titolare con messa cantata nella chiesa o scola in cui sia erretto altare del santo titolare medesimo."

160. ASV, SSR II 891, ff. 3–4.

161. BC, Gradenigo 37, ff. 120–21: "In questa mattina sua Serenità con numerosa comitiva di senatori passò alla Chiesa di San *Rocco* . . . et ivi ascolta messa privata, ma peraltro accompagnata da musicali *motteti*, et armoniche sinfonie . . . si da principio . . . alla gran messa e sopra magnifico *palco* si viddero li primari musici, e suonatori sotto la virtuosa direzione dell'oltrascritto Sig. Maestro *Bertoni*, già applaudito da numerosissimo concorso di Popolo" [emphases in the original]. The other references are in Gradenigo 5, f. 67ᵛ (1759), Gradenigo 33, f. 20 (1771), and Gradenigo 34, f. 26ʳ⁻ᵛ (1772).

162. BC, Gradenigo 33, f. 20. This scene is depicted in Canaletto's *The Doge Visiting the Church and Scuola di San Rocco* (c.1735) in the National Gallery, London.

163. See Valder-Knechtges, *Die Kirchenmusik Andrea Luchesis*, 36.

164. Archivio musicale della Cappella Marciana, A.129/1–36. See Passadore and Rossi, *San Marco*, 2:286–87.

165. Archivio musicale della Cappella Marciana, B.591/1–54. See Passadore and Rossi, 2:670.

166. ASV, SSR II 51, f. 3ᵛ: "che convenirano di farsi in chiesa per l'effetto della musica."

167. ASV, SSGE 371, no. 110.

168. ASV, SSMC 309, ff. nn., 12 March 1767.

169. ASV, SSMC 273, f. 55.

170. Ibid., f. 55ʳ⁻ᵛ.

171. ASV, SSR II 69, April–January 1789: "Riflesso imparzialmente quanto più decorosa nella festività del glorioso San Rocco, per occasione della musica che con tanta

pompa solenizasi nella di lui chiesa a gloria di esso santo, e a riverente significazione del specioso onore ch'ella riceve nella visita in detto giorno del Serenissimo Principe, fosse per essere la stabile costruzione d'una cantoria di buona forma e vaga architettura, con intagli e dorature, qual l'armonico del luoco ricerca, piutosto che vanamente dispendiare nella di lui annuo facittura per mano di conzador."

172. It was rediscovered in 1995, disassembled, in a Venetian warehouse. See Cesco, "Note integrative." A photograph of the cantoria installed in the church in the 1920s is reproduced there as pl. 10.

173. For an important new study of this institution, see Traverso, *La Scuola di San Fantin*.

174. ASV, Scuola Grande di Santa Maria della Consolazione e San Girolamo 44.

175. ASV, Scuola Grande di Santa Maria della Consolazione e San Girolamo 4, p. 130.

176. Ibid., pp. 132–35.

177. Ibid., p. 135.

178. ASV, Scuola Grande di Santa Maria del Rosario 2, ff. 31–32ᵛ.

179. ASV, Scuola Grande di Santa Maria del Rosario, Notatorio 2, ff. 45–46ᵛ.

180. ASV, Scuola Grande di Santa Maria del Carmine 16, ff. nn., 24 September 1728 (a reconfirmation of the old statutes).

181. ASV, Scuola Grande di Santa Maria del Carmine 14.

182. BC, Gradenigo 67, tomo 14, f. 18ᵛ: "fu impegno del signor mercadante Francesco Piccardi guardiano della ricca scuola esborsare con generosità dinaro, acciò, e il palco, e la musica, e la comparsa, fosse superlativa, all'innumerabile edificazione del concorso."

183. BC, Gradenigo 67, tomo 33, ff. 108ᵛ–110ᵛ: "Vennero eretti nella capella maggiore *due* palchi, *uno* dirimpetto all'altro, assai elegantemente architettati, sopra li quali diresse la musica il Reverendo *Don Francesco Polazzo*, il tutto a spese del ricco guardiano Bianchi, uno tra li appaltatori del dazio del tabacco" [emphases in the original]. The platforms probably faced each other across the nave of the church in front of the high altar.

184. ASV, SSR II 295, no. 409.

185. ASV, SSR II 417, no. 34 and BC, Gradenigo 10, f. 27ᵛ.

186. ASV, SSR II 305, no. 388.

187. ASV, SSR II 335, no. 502 and SSR II 417, January–February 1778.

188. ASV, SSR II 342, no. 507.

189. ASV, SSM 254, f. 95L and 239L.

190. Ibid., f. 92L.

191. ASV, SSGE 350, ff. nn. 25 January 1798.

Chapter 8

1. On this problem, see Mackenney, "The Scuole Piccole of Venice." On those foundations that appear in the records of the Council of Ten, see Sbriziolo, "Per la storia delle confraternite veneziane: Dalle deliberazioni miste." An important new study of the scuole piccole in the Middle Ages is Ortalli, *Per salute delle anime*.

2. The scuole piccole were, in fact, among the most important patrons, along with patrician families and trade guilds, of altars in Venetian churches. See Humfrey, "Competitive Devotions."

3. The most comprehensive treatment of this subject is Banker, *Death in the Community*. On Venice in particular, see Cadel, "Il sentimento della morte."

4. On the problem of determining the size of a scuola piccola, which arises because of inconsistent records and the changing nature of individual scuole, see Mackenney, "Con-

tinuity and Change," in particular 389–90. See also Mackenney, "Devotional Confraternities."

5. This scuola was the patron for the famous set of paintings by Carpaccio now in the Accademia Gallery in Venice. See Fortini Brown, *Venetian Narrative Painting*.

6. ASV, PC, reg. Z.

7. See Mackenney, "Continuity and Change," 392–94. On the role of women in the scuole piccole, see Ortalli, *per salute delle anime*, ch. 4

8. Many of the trade guilds also established confraternities to assist the members in the spiritual realm, complementing the worldly role of the guild itself, but these will not be considered in this book. Unlike all the scuole piccole, who were under the jurisdiction of the Provveditori di Comun, the *scuole delle arti*, as the guild-linked confraternities were called, were supervised by the same body that oversaw the guilds themselves, the Giustizia Vecchia. This separation has been maintained in the modern structure of the Archivio di Stato, in which the extant archives of the scuole piccole have been gathered in the *fondo* "Scuole piccole e suffraggi," and the documents of the trade guild scuole are kept with those of the guilds themselves, in the *fondo* "Arti." On the guilds and their attached scuole see Mackenney, *Trademen and Traders*.

9. On the origins and characteristics of confraternities devoted to the Holy Sacrament, see Barbiero, *Le confraternite del Santissimo Sacramento*. The earliest in Venice were founded in 1502 or 1503, more in 1506 and 1507, and in almost all parishes by 1550. On a possible origin for the movement in Venice see Mackenney, "Continuity and Change," 395 ff.

10. On the altars of these scuole see Cope, *The Venetian Chapel of the Sacrament* and Hills, "Piety and Patronage."

11. On the developing relationship between scuole such as these and the parish ecclesiastical authorities, see Black, "Confraternities and the Parish."

12. See Mackenney, "Continuity and Change," 394–95.

13. The rituals of similar institutions in some central Italian cities are discussed in Falvey, "Early Italian Dramatic Traditions."

14. A similar institution in Florence is discussed in Trexler, "Charity and the Defense of Urban Elites."

15. The records of the scuole piccole were scattered at the time of their suppression after the fall of Venice, and much was lost. The largest collection of mariegole is now in Venice in the library of the Museo Correr, which owns over 100. As these manuscripts were often beautifully illuminated, they quickly found their way to auction houses and private collectors when Venice collapsed. They can now be found in libraries throughout Europe and America. Fortunately, the Provveditori di Comun, the government body with responsibility for the scuole piccole, copied the mariegole into twelve large volumes during the eighteenth century, and these still survive in the Archivio di Stato di Venezia in the fondo Provveditori di Comun as Registri n-bb. The Archivio di Stato also retains a large collection of other documents of the scuole piccole in the fondo Scuole Piccole e Suffraggi. Other documents are preserved in the Archivio di Stato in the archives of monasteries that housed scuole. Finally, some records have remained in the archives of the parish churches. Many of those archives are still *in situ* (that is, in the consolidated parishes of the Napoleonic era), and are difficult to consult, but some have been brought to the Archivio Storico del Patriarcato di Venezia; the plans are ultimately for all the parish archives to be housed there.

16. Some of the material in this chapter was published previously in Glixon, "*Con canti et organo*."

17. Elena Quaranta, in her survey of the mariegola copies in ASV, PC and some other documents, records fifteen scuole using instruments at their festa before 1500. Six of these make only a generic reference to sonadori, with most of the rest calling for *trombe e piffari*

or one of the two. Quaranta, *Oltre San Marco*, 107–10. Quaranta devotes chapter 5 of her study to the scuole piccole, and chapter 7 to the issue of music at religious feste in general.

18. ASV, PC, reg. R, f. 105: "siando insembre adunati, et congregati tutti per dovere fare la festa de Santa Maria de Gratia in la glexia de Sant'Eustachio, la qual festa viene a mezzo agosto, e per dovere accrescere et multiplicare la scola si mettemo soldi diese per borsa ciascaduno de noi, e di questi dinari femo principio, e si toglieno due trombe, due pifferi, e uno naccharino per honorare la detta festa, e del resto de denari principio de fare uno pasto."

19. ASV, PC, reg. R, ff. 337ᵛ–338: "sonar secondo l'usanza della scuola."

20. Ibid.

21. BC, Mariegola 137, f. 13ᵛ.

22. ASV, SP 24, no. 1: "die sonar ale feste di Sancta Anna."

23. ASV, SSMM 7 (this document was placed in the *fondo* of the Scuola Grande della Misericordia in error, and is being recatalogued as part of ASV, SP). On the trombe and piffari of the doge, see p. 87.

24. ASV, SP 726.

25. ASV, Monastero di Santi Giovanni e Paolo, b. VII, a printed summary of a legal dispute between monastery and scuola, pp. 3 and 5.

26. ASV, PC, reg. AA, f. 323.

27. ASV, Monastero di Santa Maria Gloriosa dei Frari 97, no. 2, ch. 26, 1442: "al vesporo, et ala messa."

28. ASV, PC, reg. BB, f. 74ᵛ: "sia tolto trombe e piferi per el primo e segondo vespero e la messa."

29. ASV, PC, reg. U, f. 28ᵛ: "per honorare Iddio come fano le altre scuole nelli giorni delle sue feste . . . debbano sonar la vigilia di San Gallo, et quella di San Mauritio a vespero, et la matina seguente all'aurora, et quando si leverano il gastaldo et compagni per andar a offerire, et così quando si leverà il corpo e sangue di Christo." This document is quoted and discussed in Quaranta, *Oltre San Marco*, 150–51.

30. ASV, Monastero di Santa Maria Gloriosa dei Frari 100, no. 1: "con quatro trombe e trombete e nacharini, con do ziaramelle." It is likely that "trombe" here refers to trombones, as in "trombe e piffari," while "trombete" would be more the sort of instruments used primarily in fanfares, that is straight trumpets. This is the only reference in any of the documents of the scuole to "ziaramelle," which though sometimes taken to mean a kind of recorder, here probably indicates what Venetians (these are Milanese) refer to as piffari, that is shawms. In other words, though the order is a bit confused, these were two standard ensembles, one of two shawms and four trombones, and the other of trumpets and drums.

31. The "fontego" was probably the government grain warehouse at the Rialto; it seems that wind players were employed there, perhaps to announce sales of flour. The famous player Silvestro Ganassi, also known as Silvestro dal Fontego, and author of the wind-instrument treatise *La fontegara* (Venice, 1535), was presumably a member of this ensemble. Zuane is identified two years later as Zuan Maria del Cornetto, who was a piffaro of the doge from 1502 until his death in 1557. He was renowned for his skill, and was sent to Rome for the year 1520 at the personal request of Pope Leo X. He was also cited by Andrea Calmo and Ortensio Lando (Ongaro, personal communication).

32. ASV, PC, reg. BB, f. 63–63v: "Item che la Vezilia de Misser Santo Antonio mandar se dieba uno solareto adornado et con uno puto vestito da anzolo a trombe e pifari a San Marco et a Rialto."

33. ASV, SP 209, Reg. Cassa 1612–1764.

34. ASV, PC, reg. N, f. 2ʳ⁻ᵛ: "procession, vesperi, canti, et organo."

35. ASV, SP 599.

36. ASV, SP 420/1, Notatorio 1532–57, f. 29.

37. Ibid.: "far . . . da liber serva."

38. ASV, PC, reg. AA, f. 76: "non possino spender per far la nostra festa della Visitation della Madonna del mese di luglio in cantori, sonadori, concieri, et altre spese delli beni della scola si non lire sei di pizzoli." Quaranta lists more than twenty of this type; see *Oltre San Marco*, 107–10.

39. ASV, SP 420/1, f. 67: "È introdutta una dannoxa, et obbrobriosa coruttella nella schuola nostra zircha la spexa che si fa nel celebrar et solenizar la festa nostra il giorno dela Natività dela Madona, ala qual se non si provede con presto rimedio se andarebe de anno in anno peggiorando, tal che in progresso di tenpo se atroverà facilmente delli guardiani, che senza timor de Idio, ma più tosto pieni di ponpa mondana, se farano licito di spender ducati 100, il che seria chon dano di la schuola, et poveri nostri fratelli." It was Quartari who, in 1553, as guardian grande of the Scuola Grande di Santa Maria della Misericordia, reacted so strongly to the new singers' company. See p. 152. See also Luisi, *Laudario giustinianeo*, 1:416.

40. ASP, Parrocchia di San Marco, San Giuliano, Scuola del Santissimo Sacramento, Libro di Cassa 1502–1688.

41. Ibid., f. 3.

42. Ibid., f. 14: "chantadori che salmizò."

43. Ibid., f. 18.

44. Ibid., f. 16.

45. Ibid., f. 34: "queli che sonò drio con arpa ett lautto ett violeta."

46. Ibid., f. 60.

47. Ibid., f. 61.

48. Ibid., f. 63.

49. Ibid., f. 102.

50. ASV, SP 599.

51. ASV, SP 602/4, f. 10. Pre Ettor served as organist for the Scuola Grande di San Giovanni Evangelista from before 1526 to after 1527 (see p. 142.)

52. "Fra Battista" is probably fra Battista de Coradi, who served at the Cappella di San Marco from at least 1515 until his dismissal in 1532 (Ongaro, personal communication). Fra Battista joined the Scuola Grande di San Giovanni Evangelista in 1517. On Zuan Maria, see above, n. 31.

53. In addition to the usual payments in that year was one of 2 soldi for "a porter who carried the singers' books." Such a payment occurs nowhere else in the archives of either the scuole piccole or the scuole grandi. Otherwise, it appears that the music was the responsibility of the hired musicians.

54. ASV, SP 602/4, f. 71ᵛ.

55. ASV, PC 11, f. 93ᵛ.

56. ASV, SP 706/1, f. 154ᵛ.

57. ASV, SP 711, Cassa 1577–1713, ff. nn.

58. Ibid.: "quali vanno a mio danno."

59. It is likely that "Soardi" is actually a misspelling of the name of Piero Savoldi, who was cassier of the company of singers c.1615–16 (Ongaro, personal communication).

60. Archivio della Parrocchia di San Salvatore, Scuola di San Mattia in San Bartolomeo, Atti b. 2, Registro spese, 1571.

61. ASV, Monastero di Santa Maria Gloriosa dei Frari, 104/1, ff. 53–54.

62. ASV, PC, reg. T, f. 444ᵛ.

63. Archivio della Parrocchia di San Giacomo dall'Orio, Scuola del Santissimo Sacramento in San Giacomo, Registro cassa 1568–79.

64. Ibid., f. 20.

65. ASV, SP 380/4.

66. See above, ch. 3, for a discussion of a book owned by the Scuola Grande di Santa Maria della Carità.

67. ASV, SP 669, Capitoli 1492–1699, f. 2ᵛ [new series]: "Ancora volemo et ordenemo chel se debbia far uno antefonario in carta bona a Don Desiderio monecho a San Gregorio, cum questi patti: ch'il ditto Don Desiderio se obliga de non spender più de ducati 2 in la carta de cavretto che sia bona, et s'el spenderà più spenda del suo, et s'el suo scriver et aminiar de azuro et de zenabrio ducati 3, resalvando li principii che se die miniar de penello. Intendando ch'el ditto debbia far tanta opera in ditto libro quando è de necessità per ditta nostra scuola."

68. ASV, PC, reg. U, f. 582: "messe dei dì ordenadi . . . e far sonar l'organo a suo spese, in caso che'l no fese sonar che nui posemo tuor un maistro che'l sona, dagando i soldi sedese, e se l'organo fosse vasto per muodo che'l no se podesse sonar, che nui possemo tuor un maistro con el suo organo, dagando i soldi vinti, desfalcando i ditti soldi sedese, o vinti che se pagasse della soprevesion."

69. ASV, PC, reg. Z, ff. 34ᵛ–35ᵛ.

70. Ibid.: "a gloria di Sua Divina Maestà, e della Beatissima Vergine Maria, et de Madonna Santa Marta, et de missier San Nicolò nostro protettor."

71. ASV, SP 296, Riduzioni e parti, no. 12.

72. ASV, SP 296, Giornale 1541–80, folios unnumbered. On Colonna, who was also the salaried organ tuner for the Basilica of San Marco, see Lunelli, *Studi e documenti*, 173–74.

73. ASV, SP 296, Giornale 1580–1615.

74. ASV, SP 296, Riduzioni e Parti, no. 23 and Giornale 1580–1615.

75. ASV, SP 67/6, f. 47.

76. Ibid., f. 52ᵛ. The priest is also referred to as Gherardin or Guardini.

77. ASV, SP 71/1, f. 41.

78. Ibid., f. 52.

79. ASV, SP 67/6, f. 57: "per esser la cassa granda et l'organo pizzolo."

80. ASV, SP 71/1, f. 32. This is undoubtedly the builder Leandro who worked in Venice and elsewhere in the Veneto from the 1560s to the 1580s. See Lunelli, *Studi e documenti*, 196–97.

81. ASV, SP 67/6, ff. nn.

82. ASV, PC, reg. AA, f. 205: "che esendo l'organo così buono et bello nella detta chiesa è anco necessario trovare un valente homo che'l sona, et non uno zavataro che il guasti."

83. Ibid.: "un valent'homo, che'l sonar."

84. The corresponding decisions by the other scuole at San Nicolò survive as follows: Scuola di Santa Croce in ASV, PC, reg. AA, f. 246; Scuola di San Nicolò in reg. Z, f. 151ʳ⁻ᵛ; and Scuola della Visitazione della Beata Vergine in reg. Z, f. 51ᵛ.

85. ASP, Parrocchia di San Nicolò dei Mendicoli, Registro Scuole e Oratorio, p. 83.

86. See ch. 3, note 48.

87. BC, Mariegola 71, ch. 20: "dar ordine di chi imponga l'ufficio, di chi dica le lezioni, l'antiphone, gli hynni, i versetti, e tutte le altre cose occorrenti secondo i tempi . . . ; habbia l'occhio a imporre il sermone, le stanze di passione, il capitolo, le preci, la lauda, e in somma tutto quello che fusse giudicato a proposito per consolatio de' fratelli, a huomini perciò sufficienti . . . ; Sia lor' cura nel salmeggiare de l'ufficio, di far sedere quella parte del choro che debbe, e far' star' in piede quella a chi tocca."

88. Ibid., ch. 25.

89. Ibid.: "Quivi senza strepito ne mormorio seguiti l'ordine del'ufficio, non alto né basso, ma concordandosi con il tuon' degli altri . . ."

90. Ibid.: "Possan' solo, volendo, proveder per lor' consolazione di musica forestiera."

Chapter 9

1. Some of the material in this chapter was published earlier in Glixon, "*Far il buon concerto.*"

2. ASV, PC, reg. N, ff. 377ᵛ–378ᵛ.

3. Ibid., f. 374ᵛ.

4. Arzignan was a singer at San Marco from 1600 until at least 1620 (Ongaro, personal communication) and also served at the Scuola Grande di San Rocco around 1641.

5. Ibid.: "Che fra il numero de Suonatori essendo da tutti giudicato superfluo il trombone . . ."

6. ASV, PC, reg. BB, f. 638: "il giorno primo maggio dell'anno predetto solennizare la sua fondazione, et principiò con apparati decorosi nella chiesa, et sopra il predetto altare, accompagnati ancora da celebre musica concertata dalla virtù dell'Eccelente e Reverendo Don Natal Monferrati, uno delli primi arrollati e descritti nella confraternita medesima, così nella messa, come nel vespero."

7. ASV, Monastero di Santa Maria Gloriosa dei Frari, b. 100, no. 1, f. 93: "L'illustrissimi Signori . . . Proveditori di Comun, havendo dall'esposittione fatta per parte della Corte Patriarcale de questa città conosciuto quanto con zelo proprio di Christiana religione si procurir di ridur le musiche solite farsi nelle solenità festive a quella regola decorata e devota che ben corisponda alla Pietà publica, mentre massime sono passati per gli abusi a tal segno che non sono ne gl'habiti de musici medemi ma etiamdio negl'instrumenti musicali et nelle parole che si cantano si vede anzi riguardasi il dileto de gli ascoltanti che la divotione, alla quale è ordinato l'instituto pio di simili solenità. Hanno li Signori Illustrissimi, confirmandosi con la religiosa applicattione della corte medema patriarcale, ordinato che in avenire siano tenuti li guardiani, gastaldi, e ogni altra sorte di capi delle dette scole al nostro maggistrato soggiete, nelle solenità di musiche non permettere che siano usati instrumenti se non gli ordinarii usitati nelle chiese, astenendosi particolarmente dal uso d'instrumenti bellici, come sono trombe, tamburi, et simili più acomodati ad usarsi ne gli esserciti che nella casa di Dio, similmente obligandosi medesememente a fare che li musici tutti, così ecclesiastici come secolari, vadano vestiti con le cotte, habito proprio da usarsi nelle chiese, et finalmente a non permettere che in esse musiche sia fatta traspossittione di parole, overo cantate parole inventate da nuovo e non descritte sopra libri sacre, salvo che all'Offertorio, all'Ellevattione, et doppo l'Agnus Dei, et così alli vesperi tra li salmi, si possano cantar motteti di parole pie et devote, et che siano cavate da libri sacri, o auttori ecclesiastici sopra il qual particolare potrano et dovrano quelli che non havessero cognittione bastevole ricever l'instruttione da Reverendi Parochi, et sacerdoti delle chiese, o altre persone inteligenti, sotto pena per cadauna volta contravenendo di ducati 25." This transcription is from the copy in the mariegola of the Scuola dei Milanesi at the church of the Frari, but identical copies can be found in nearly every surviving mariegola, and in the nearly 200 copies of mariegole in the registers of the provveditori themselves. The document is also transcribed, from another source, as document 124 in Moore, *Vespers at St. Mark's*, 1:278–79.

8. ASPV, Parrocchia di Santa Maria del Giglio, Scuola di Santa Caterina, Libro di Amministrazione 1620–91, folios unnumbered.

9. Ibid., Capitoli 1642–1703, Copia deli Rodoli, ff. nn.

10. Archivio Parrocchiale di San Nicolò dei Mendicoli, Registro Scuole e Oratorio, p. 14.

11. Ibid., f. 15.

12. Ibid.

13. ASV, Monastero dello Spirito Santo 16: "Et una volta già pocchi anni volevanno far cantar la messa granda . . . ma con sì poca solennità et musica, che causò più tosto derisione che devotione, se bene havevano incaparati, et apparechiati, e pronti li migliori musici della città, sì da voce, come da instrumenti, come è antico costume, et per disprecio non volse il guardian di quel anno lasciar far la musica solita et ordinaria, ma li fece tacee, se ben poi li dui dì seguenti, havendo egli dormito su quella sua opinione, si fece in chiesia la musica consueta delli altri anni . . ."

14. Ibid., no. 9, f. 6.

15. Ibid., b. 17, no. 1.

16. ASV, Monastero dello Spirito Santo 16, no. 9, f. 11ᵛ. Cavalli's autograph receipt, dated 10 June 1637, is on f. 13. This latter document and some of those below are cited in Niero and Vio, *La Chiesa dello Spirito Santo*.

17. ASV, Monastero dello Spirito Santo 16, no. 9, f. 17: "Notta de spese fatte della reverenda madre sor Faustina Dolfin, abbadesa del monasterio del Spirito Santo, per occasione de far far le feste et solenità dele Pentecoste, che tocava far la Scola del Spirito Santo. Per la Musicha—D.100 d.–."

18. Ibid., f. 20. This is Rovetta's signed receipt. Rovetta was at this time serving in San Marco as vice maestro di cappella, a post he assumed in 1627. In 1644 he was promoted to maestro di cappella, a post he held until 1668.

19. ASV, SPS 670, Notatorio 1679–1701, f. 36. It is not clear how serving in this expensive post could assist him in alleviating his financial burdens. Most likely, as rector he would be able to claim reimbursements, although this was not usually done for expenditures that were not supposed to be the responsibility of the scuola.

20. Ibid., f. 95.

21. Ibid., f. 107ᵛ.

22. On their service in the cappella, see Emans, "Die Musiker des Markusdoms." The information on Giovanni da Pesaro and Facin is on pp. 76 and 69, respectively.

23. Ibid., ff. 110ᵛ–111: "delli sudetti musici parte otto, et sonatori il terzo di meno del primo giorno."

24. Ibid., ff. 147ᵛ–148ᵛ.

25. Ibid., f. 153ʳ⁻ᵛ: "havendo oservata la distributione delle vocci, et instrumenti, è necesario, che il primo giorno per far il buon concerto acresca il numero degli instrumenti, et regalli per li due giorni suseguenti le vocci in suplimento di detto primo giorno per non ecceder alla decretatta spesa."

26. I have here interpreted "viole" as viole da gamba and "violette" as violas. Though terminology in archival documents is always uncertain, the unusual precision and apparent musical knowledge of the author of this particular document suggest that precise meanings can be determined.

27. For example, a *Laudate pueri* for three voices and orchestra. See *New Grove II*, s.v. "Lotti, Antonio."

28. Ibid., ff. 193ᵛ–194: "sola spesa di ducatti ottanta D.80:– al'anno con l'impiego di quelle voci et instrumenti che proportionalmente potranno entrarvi a misura della spesa da esserne praticatti."

29. ASV, PC, reg. BB, ff. 141ᵛ–142.

30. Ibid., f. 142ᵛ.

31. ASV, Monastero di Santa Maria Gloriosa dei Frari 103.

32. ASV, PC, reg. BB, f. 68ᵛ.

33. ASV, Monastero di Santa Maria Gloriosa dei Frari 98/1 and 98/2.

34. ASV, PC, reg. S, f. 191: "con canti et suoni in musica secondo che potremo."

35. ASV, SP 71/2.

36. Ibid., f. 47: "l'officiatura delle compiette e sabati."

37. The payments also include £48 for music for the feast of Sant'Antonio "according to the usual practice" ("secondo il costume ordenario").

38. ASV, SP 248/2: "volendo noi far musicha dobiamo trovar noi, et pagarli musichi del nostro."

39. ASV, SP 248/1, f. 74: "anco di cantar le Lettanie della Beata Vergine tutti li Sabbati dell'anno."

40. Ibid.: "quattro voci delle migliori e due istromenti."

41. Ibid.: "intonar le littanie con una voce tutti li Sabbati dell'anno."

42. ASV, SP 24/2, Libro di parti 1621–1716.

43. ASV, SP 596/2, ff. 9ᵛ–10: "Vada parte, che nell'espositioni che si fanno gli quarta dominica de mese annualmente, si faccia un concerto di musica, con mottetti et sinfonia, et in fine dappo' il sermone cantino le litanie, col Tantum ergo; da doversi spendere nella sudetta musica duccati trenta in circha, da esser fatta scritura con un maestro di musica cossì della spesa come delle persone che doverano intervenire a canttare et suonare, accioche resti edificato magiormente il popolo, et infervorato alla devotione."

44. Ibid., ff. 6ᵛ–7: "una messa con l'organo in canto fermo."

45. Ibid., f. 14: "et condure anco secco cinque parti, cioè un organista, due vocci, due violini, overo una viola in loco d'uno delli violino, da dover suonare et cantare mottetti dal principio dell'esposizione sinno al fine con terminare con le litanie, et Tantum ergo."

46. Archivio Parrocchiale di San Canciano, no. 24, Cassa, Scuola del Santissimo Sacramento in San Canciano, 1616–1710, f. 12.

47. Archivio Parrocchiale di San Geremia, Scuola del Santissimo Sacramento in San Geremia, Riceveri, 1613–1751, ff. 75, 79, and 82ᵛ.

48. Archivio Parrocchiale di San Luca, Registro Cassa della Scuola del Santissimo Sacramento in San Luca, 1675– , Guida per li Signori guardiani.

49. Archivio Parrocchiale di San Felice, Registro Cassa Scuola del Santissimo Sacramento in San Felice, 1596–1630, ff. nn.

50. Ibid., Cassa della Scuola del Santissimo Sacramento in San Felise, 1632–1699, ff. nn.

51. Archivio Parrocchiale di San Giacomo dal'Orio, Scuola del Santissimo Sacramento in San Giacomo, Registro Cassa 1620–89, f. 200.

52. Ibid., Registro Cassa 1689–1757, ff. 50 and 53.

53. On this practice at Florentine laudesi companies, see Wilson, *Music and Merchants*, 49–53.

54. ASP, Parrocchia di San Moisè, Scuola del Santissimo Sacramento, Commissaria Bonci, 1, Catastico, p. 6: "cantato in musica con instrumenti sopra l'organo."

55. No documents dating from after the sixteenth century survive for the confraternity of the Florentines, discussed in chapter 8.

56. ASV, Fraterna Grande Sant'Antonino 1, f. 259ʳ⁻ᵛ: "Quando vi serà congregato buon numero di frattelli, il Reverendo Padre, se sarà presente, pur il custode, comincierà il mattutino e si reciterà in due cori, ma chiaramente, distintamente, et divotamente, et con voce più tosto bassa che alta, et così si dirano anco le laudi."

57. Ibid.: "Nell'Altare dell'Oratorio si potrà cellebrar la Santa Messa ogni prima Do-

menica del mese et nell'Assunzione et Annunciazione della Gloriosa Vergine, ma si dica una messa solamente da sacerdote aprovato, et in alcun tempo non si admetta nell'oratorio concerto, canto, o musica, ma sì li divini uficii come la messa si cellebrino a voce bassa."

58. Ibid., f. 381: "per non distraere l'affetto della divozione."

59. Ibid., f. 327ᵛ: "e subito s'ingenochieranno tutti cantandosi Benedicta."

60. Ibid.: "per intermedio, et per levar il tedio."

61. Ibid.: "seguirando tutti li figliuoli a doi a doi processionalmente cantando qualche lode spirituale della dottrina. Finita la lode anderanno con la pace del signore modestamente a casa."

62. Ibid., f. 373ᵛ.

63. ASV, PC, reg. S, f. 393.

64. ASV, PC, reg. T, f. 468. This is probably Vincenzo Colonna. See ch. 8, n. 72.

65. ASV, PC, reg. R, f. 383: "per una volta tanto."

66. Ibid., ff. 383ᵛ–389ᵛ.

67. On Sandrioli, see Lunelli, *Studi e documenti*, 220.

68. Archivio Parrocchiale di San Trovaso, Scuola del Santissimo Sacramento in San Trovaso, Capitoli, 1585–1673, f. 41: "essendo questa opera così honorevole, et bisognosa fatta per honorar et dar laude al Nostro Signor iddio, et alla Suo Gloriosa Vergine Madre Maria Advocata Nostra."

69. Ibid., f. 44.

70. ASV, PC, reg. P, f. 69ʳ⁻ᵛ: "essendo in esterminio et estremissimo bisogno . . . che non si può sonare."

71. ASV, Santa Maria Gloriosa dei Frari 97, no. 23, ff. 24ᵛ–25: "quale si trova in tanta e in tantta destrucione che non si potra più suonare . . . faciano la limosina allegramente et abondante."

72. Probably the son of the Istrian organ builder Simone Lupini. See Lunelli, *Studi e documenti*, 199.

73. ASP, Parrocchia di Santa Maria del Carmelo, Fabbriceria, Chiesa Succursale di San Barnaba, Atti Generali 12, fasc. 24, Mariegola, 1563– , f. 21ʳ⁻ᵛ and ASP, Parrocchia di Santa Maria del Carmelo, Scuola del Santissimo Sacramento in San Barnaba, Capitoli 1, 1643–1789, f. 2ᵛ: "in cattivo stato et a bisgono di esser governato."

74. ASP, Parrocchia di Santa Maria del Carmelo, Scuola del Santissimo Sacramento in San Barnaba, Capitoli 1, 1643–1789, f. 7.

75. Ibid., Registri Cassa 2, 1642–1763, ff. nn.

76. ASV, Archivio Notarili 3506, Atti Paulini, ff. 1283ᵛ–1285 (copy in ASV, PC, reg. AA, ff. 408ᵛ–409).

77. ASV, Archivio Notarili 3767, Atti Paulini, f. 107.

78. ASV, PC, reg. AA, ff. 246ᵛ–247: "non sappiamo chi el sona, ne meno concorriamo alla elletione di detto sonador."

79. ASV, PC, reg. S, f. 122ᵛ and ASV, Capi del Consilio dei Dieci, Notatorio, reg. 44, ff. 58ᵛ–59ᵛ.

80. ASV, PC, reg. R, ff. 310–11.

81. Ibid.

82. ASP, Parrocchia del Angelo Raffaele 16, fascicolo "Organo sua Fabbrica," p. 6: "non debba ingerirsi in alcuna cosa spettante alla Veneranda Scola del Santissimo Sacramento in detta chiesa."

83. Ibid.: "la qual debba servire per sempre in avenire senza, che mai più nè il guardiano presente, nè a venturi, nè alcun altro di bancha, o altro di detta scola habbino obligo di addimandarli cosa alcuna circa quanto di sopra è stato dichiarito."

84. Ibid, pp. 12 and 20. On Beni, see n. 112, chapter 8.

85. Ibid., p. 25.

86. ASV, Monastero di Santa Croce 10, processo no. 28: "Scriture per l'organo."

87. ASP, Parrocchia del Angelo Raffaele 16, fascicolo "Organo sua Fabbrica," pp. 10–11. Interestingly, despite the order of the Provveditori sopra Monasteri of several decades earlier (see above), among those churches in this listing is Santa Croce.

88. Ibid., p. 26.

89. Ibid., pp. 23–24.

90. ASV, PC, reg. Q, ff. 98–110: "*Come, e quando si debba solennizare la Festa di Santa Cecilia*: Vada parte che la solennità di Santa Cecilia debba essere santificata da tutti li confrateli cantando la messa et il vespero li 22 novembre all'hora solita in chiesa di San Martino, e doveranno tutti impiegati secondo l'abilità sua, et in conformità del bisogno, che haverà il signor maestro o il signor vice maestro; uno de' quali doverà far la musica, cioè il signor maestro quando possi, e non potendo lui il signor vice maestro."

Chapter 10

1. See Glixon, "Images of Paradise."

2. At the Scuola di Santa Maria dei Mascoli; ASV, SP 146, Registro Cassa, 1772–1806.

3. ASV, SP 137, Libro cassa 1719–1804.

4. At the Beata Vergine del Rosario in San Domenico (ASV, SP 220/1), Santa Croce in San Pietro di Castello (ASV, SP 317, Registro Cassa 1782–1805), San Giuseppe in San Giuseppe (ASV, SP 388, Cassa 1706–1806), and Beata Vergine della Cintura in San Giuseppe (ASV, SP 123, Riceveri 1766–1804). Also ASV, Monastero di San Daniele 42.

5. ASV, SP 137, Libro cassa 1719–1804; and ASP, Parrocchia San Moisè, Scuola del Santissimo Sacramento, Commissaria Bonci, Cassa 1718/19–73.

6. ASV, Monastero di Sant'Andrea della Zirada 56.

7. Beata Vergine Assunta in Santa Maria in Broglio, Beata Vergine delle Grazie in Santa Marina, Beata Vergine del Rosario in Santa Maria Zobenigo, Beata Vergine del Rosario in San Paternian, Spirito Santo in Spirito Santo, Beata Vergine del Gonfalon in San Bernardo di Murano, Santissimo Sacramento in San Severo, Sant'Anna in San Paternian, San Giuliano in San Giuliano, San Giuseppe in San Giuseppe, San Vincenzo Ferrer in Sant'Agostin, San Vincenzo Ferrer in Santa Maria Zobenigo, and Santissimo Sacramento in San Moisè. Menegatti also served at numerous nunneries.

8. ASV, SP 137, Libro Cassa 1/19–1804.

9. ASV, SP 123, Riceveri, 1766–1804, 31 August 1766: "la mattina messa cantata con mottetto, et il doppo pranso esposizione con salmi e sonate, reposizione con letanie."

10. ASV, SP 137, Libro cassa 1719–1804, p. 4.

11. Ibid., p. 2.

12. Ibid., p. 74.

13. ASV, SP 220/1.

14. ASV, SP 682/3.

15. ASV, SP 388, Cassa 1766–1806.

16. ASV, SP 311/2, no. 1 (second series). The coro of St. Mark's was the choir of priests responsible for singing chant, as opposed to the cappella, with both lay and clerical musicians, responsible for polyphony.

17. Ibid., 2 May 1768.

18. ASV, SP 311/2, no. 58.

19. Ibid., no. 47, insert.

20. ASP, Parrocchia di San Marco, Parrocchia di San Giuliano, Scuola di San Giuli-

ano, Libro Secondo della Compagnia di San Giuliano, 1749–63, Atti, f. 1: "ad onore di Dio, e maggior decoro della chiesa di San Giuliano, fare nel giorno di detto santo una musica, solenne messa, e vespero."

21. Ibid.

22. Ibid., 1751: "per compire con perfezione l'orchestra musicale nel giorno della nostra solennità."

23. Ibid., 1753.

24. Ibid., 1756.

25. Ibid., 1763.

26. ASV, SP 69/5, ff. nn.

27. ASV, SP 91, f. 19ᵛ–20.

28. ASV, SP 239/1, ff. nn.

29. ASV, SP 224bis, Quaderno Cassa, 1735–82.

30. Ibid. and ASV, SP 225, Libro Colti 1783–1805.

31. ASV, SP 9, Riceveri, 1767–1801, ff. nn.

32. ASV, SP 627/2, Registro Cassa, 1782–1806, insert.

33. Ibid., 30 July 1783.

34. Ibid., an inserted printed tariffa of 1805.

35. The singing of the *Tantum* is recorded only at the Suffragio di Morti at San Salvatore. ASV, SP 479, ff. 63–64.

36. Ibid., ff. 118–19.

37. ASV, SP 9, Riceveri, 1767–1801.

38. ASV, SP 467/1.

39. ASV, SP 479, ff. 118–19.

40. ASV, SP 316 and ASV, SP 367.

41. ASV, SP 463, Cassa, 1725–72.

42. It is unclear whether the processions described as being on Good Friday at most of the scuole piccole, and those on Maundy Thursday evening at the scuole grandi were really at the same time. The Venetian day is often reckoned as beginning with sundown, so a procession in the evening at the end of Maundy Thursday could also be construed as Good Friday.

43. ASV, SP 584/1, insert.

44. ASV, SP10/1, f. 42.

45. ASV, SP 486, Atti Diversi 1760–1801, ff. nn., 1 April 1774; and ASP, San Fantin 34: Tomo XXXV: San Gaetano, f. 26.

46. ASV, SP 467/2.

47. ASV, SP 627/2, inserted tariffe of 1781 and 1805.

48. ASV, SP 69/5.

49. ASP, Parrocchia San Moisè, Scuola del Santissimo Sacramento, Commissaria Bonci 3, Cassa 1705–18 and Commissaria Bonci, Cassa 1718/19–73. On Vinacesi, see Talbot, *Benedetto Vinaccesi*.

50. ASV, SP 389, Cassa 1750– .

51. ASV, SP 460/2, ff. nn., 20 August 1730.

52. BC, Mariegola 79, f. 1: "sacerdotes cantum ad usum pontifice capelle colentes." Translations from the Latin courteously provided by Dr. Jennifer Tunberg, of the University of Kentucky.

53. Ibid., f. 1: "studemus voces nostras ad censuram artis, et regulam formare, ut eam efficiant harmoniam, que fideles in ecclesia suaviter retineat, et ad audiendo officia divina prolictet."

54. Ibid., f. 3ᵛ: "esse debeant experimentum faciat num ad usum capelle plenam teneat cantandi cognitionem."

55. ASV, SP 460/2.

56. ASV, SP 479, Congregationi e Regolationi 1728–65, f. 10ᵛ.

57. Ibid., 3 January 1733/34.

58. ASV, SP 479, ff. 118–19.

59. Giorda served at the Scuola dello Spirito Santo at the Spirito Santo, and Moro at both the Spirito Santo and San Gaetano in San Fantin.

60. ASV, SP 479/2, p. 213.

61. Ibid., f. 108.

62. Ibid., f. 109ʳ⁻ᵛ.

63. ASV, SP 672/1.

64. Ibid., 26 May 1748.

65. Ibid., 18 February 1752 and 26 December 1755.

66. The increase was four "zecchini." The value of the zecchino had been set, in 1749, at £22. See Papadopoli Aldobrandini, *Le Monete di Venezia*, 3:1004.

67. ASV, SP 672/1, 8 October 1758.

68. ASV, SP 668, Registro Cassa 1778–1805 (new capo at Spirito Santo) and ASV, SP 479/3, pp. 34–35 (renunciation at Suffragio di Morti).

69. ASV, SP 91, Parti della Scuola, no. 10.

70. Ibid., no. 12.

71. ASV, SP 481, Viaggio di Roma, 1700, pt. 1, Lettere. I have not been able to determine Rota's specific connection with the suffragio.

72. All the records for this trip are in ASV, SP 364/1.

73. All the records for the 1750 trip are in ASV, SP 364/3 and 364/4.

74. The reasons for this change are unclear, since 1 paolo usually traded at a value of slightly less than 1 Venetian lira. Perhaps the singers wished to avoid the complications of such exchanges.

75. ASV, SP 364/3, 7 April 1750: "persone delle più abili e delle più distinte."

76. ASV, SP 294, Notatorio secondo, 1693–1763, f. 15.

77. Ibid., f. 124. Capelli was possibly a member of a family of organ builders from Vicenza who also worked in Venice in the early eighteenth century. See Lunelli, *Studi e documenti*, 204.

78. ASV, SP 294, Notatorio secondo, 1693–1763, f. 160.

79. Moscatelli was a student of Nacchini. See Lunelli, *Studi e documenti*, 204.

80. ASV, SP 294, Notatorio secondo, 1693–1763, f. 165: "armonioso e perfetto."

81. ASV, SP 295, Notatorio 1764–1807, f. 4ᵛ.

82. Beginning, at the latest, in 1766. Ibid., f. 14ᵛ.

83. Ibid., ff. nn., 23 February 1787 and 27 March 1789: "a stato di perfezione come ora si trova." Amadio is not recorded elsewhere as an organ builder.

84. ASV, Scuola Grande di Santa Maria del Rosario, reg., f. 96.

85. ASV, SP 372/1, 6 April 1788.

86. ASV, SP 460/2, 26 August 1725.

87. Ibid., 23 August 1735.

88. Ibid., 1 February 1791/92. This includes a copy of Merlini's repair invoice.

89. ASP, Parrocchia Santa Maria del Carmelo, Fabbriceria, Chiesa Succursale di San Barnaba, Atti Generali 12, fasc. 24, Mariegola, 1563– , f. 35: "indecoroso alla chiesa, et alla scola stessa."

90. The specifications of the completed organ are at ibid., f. 36ʳ⁻ᵛ, and the list of donors on f. 37ʳ⁻ᵛ.

91. ASV, SP 380/2, no. 38.

92. ASP, Parrocchia Santa Maria del Carmelo, Scuola del Santissimo Sacramento in San Barnaba, Capitoli 1, f. 195.

93. Ibid., f. 377ᵛ.

94. Ibid., f. 208.

95. Ibid., ff., 356ᵛ–357. This includes detailed specifications for the completed instrument.

96. ASP, Curia Patriarcale, Sezione Antica, Actorum Generalium 13, f. 494: "un opera tanto necessaria, e possino esser decorati le sacre funzioni al maggior culto di Dio Signore onde chiesa . . . esclami con voci di giubilo Laudate eum in cori, et organo."

97. Ibid., ff. 46ᵛ (San Cassiano), 164ᵛ (Santa Maria Maddalena), and 522 (San Polo); ASV, PC 77 (San Simeon Profeta).

98. ASV, Procuratori de supra, reg. 102, Scuola del Santissimo Sacramento, f. 39: "Come però l'organo fu fabricato da distinto Artefice colla unione di molti registri, così esige anche un suonatore distinto, che lo sappia ben maneggiare, come anche è riuscito di trovare distinto maestro che lo fa sempre più spicare con aggradimento della parochia, e della città tutta, così merita anche esso un competente onorario, che non sia lontano dal merito del maestro."

99. ASP, Parrocchia Santa Maria del Carmelo, Scuola del Santissimo Sacramento in San Barnaba, Capitoli 1, f. 290ʳ⁻ᵛ.

100. Ibid., f. 362ᵛ.

101. Ibid., ff. 410 and 413.

102. Ibid., ff. nn.

103. For an annual exposition of the Sacrament, from the guild of the fustagneri (makers of fustian, a coarse cotton cloth) for their three feasts, from the Scuola della Beata Vergine for their festa, from the shoemaker's guild for the feasts of St. Louis and St. Ariano, for the feast of St. Gaetano, probably from the Suffragio di Morti, and for the ottavario di Morte, again probably from the suffragio.

104. BC, Mariegola 41, 1531– , appended at the end of the volume.

Chapter 11

1. Stevens, *Letters of Claudio Monteverdi*, 191.

2. This idea has also been explored, besides in my own earlier publications, in Quaranta, *Oltre San Marco*, and in a 1999 conference at the Fondazione Levi in Venice entitled "Produzione, circolazione e consumo. Per una mappa della musica sacra nel tardo Medioevo al primo Seicento," organized by David Bryant and Elena Quaranta. It is planned for the proceedings of this conference to be published. On Quaranta's methodology, see above, n. 1 to the preface.

Appendix 1

1. For more detailed discussions of Venetian ceremonies see Muir, *Civic Ritual;* Casini, *I gesti del principe;* Casini, "Ceremoniali"; Ambrosini, "Cerimonie, feste, lusso"; Renier Michiel, *Origine delle feste veneziane;* Urban Padoan, "Feste ufficiali e trattenimenti privati"; Urban Padoan, "Les fêtes de la République Sérènissime"; and Niero, "Spiritualità popolare e dotta."

Appendix 2

1. ASP, Curia patriarcale, Sezione antica, Actorum generalium 9, 1688–1706, ff. 211ᵛ–213 and 214–15.

2. B.V. = Beata Vergine; B.V.M. = Beata Vergine Maria.

3. It is probable that in most cases the scuole went in procession beginning at their church, and proceeding to Piazza San Marco; where the choir sang is not clear.

4. The feast of Corpus Christi was the intended feast of every one of the seventy parrochial Scuole del Santissimo Sacramento. However, because of the official procession in Piazza San Marco (and a second one in the afternoon to the church of Corpus Domini), in practice many of the Scuole del Santissimo Sacramento moved their celebrations to the following Sunday or to another date. Listed here are those scuole for which the documents indicate either that this was to be their feast, or that they were to move it to some un-specified date. If the documents make no mention of the feast at all, then that scuola has been omitted, though it probably celebrated on or near the date of Corpus Christi.

5. It is not clear which of the numerous St. Alexanders was the patron of this scuola, but this seems most likely, as the annual election of officers, usually held shortly before a scuola's festa, was the third Sunday of August.

GLOSSARY

albergo	the room in a scuola, usually on the second floor, where the officers conducted their business and held their meetings
andata	one of the annual occasions on which the doge leaves the Palazzo Ducale ceremonially, and visits another location, usually a church, in the city
Avogadori di Comun	one of the state judicial bodies; adjudicated some disputes involving the scuole
bagnadori	those fadighenti whose task was to wash the body of a deceased brother in preparation for burial
banca	the highest council of a scuola, composed of the guardian grande, guardian da mattin, vicario, and the twelve degani
battudi, battuti	flagellants
benintrada	the fee assessed a new member of a scuola
busta	a folder or box of loose archival documents
campo	the main square of each Venetian parish
cancelliere, cancelleria	an employee of a scuola grande who conducted the day-to-day business in lieu of the guardian grande; the room, usually on the ground floor, where the cancelliere worked
cantadori nuovi, cantadori di laude	semi-professional processional singers of the scuole grandi; in some scuole the term was applied to the professional singers
cantadori vecchi, cantadori di corpi, cantadori di morti	fadighenti of the scuole grandi assigned to sing at funerals
cantadori solenni, cantori solenni	the professional singers of a scuola grande
capitolo, chapter	the assembly of all present and past officers of a scuola grande, along with others of the office-holding class

341

cappa	the ceremonial robe of a scuola, bearing the scuola's insignia; worn by all members in processions
cassa	the cash box of a scuola
cassier	the hired cashier of a scuola
cauzioni	the loose pay slips and receipts of the Scuola di San Rocco
chapter general	the assembly of all voting brothers of a scuola grande, convened twice a year to elect officers and consider especially important issues
cittadino	citizens; the class of professionals and civil servants
commissaria, commissario	the estate of a deceased brother or benefactor managed by a scuola; the official elected to manage that estate
coretto	a small choir, perhaps an ensemble of soloists, often employed alongside a full choir (the *coro*)
corista	a member of the priestly choir of a scuola; also referred to as mansionario di coro
Council of Ten, Capi of the Council of Ten	one of the chief magistracies of Venice, charged with overseeing state security, and with ultimate authority over the scuole grandi; the Capi were three members of the council, serving in rotation, who could take actions without convening the entire council
deffensori	elected officers who represented a scuola in legal matters
degano	the twelve junior members of the banca, ten elected at the same time as the guardian grande (*degani di tutt'anno*), and two six months later (*degani di mezz'anno*)
denaro	a Venetian monetary unit; see p. xiii
disciplinati	flagellants; those who practice the "discipline"
doge	the elected head of state of Venice; served for life
ducat, *ducato*	a Venetian monetary unit; see p. xiii
fadighenti	poor brothers of a scuola grande admitted free of charge in exchange for carrying out duties in processions and elsewhere
falsobordone	chordal recitation formula for the singing of psalms and canticles
festa	a celebration, usually that for the patron saint of a scuola of church
filza	a packet of loose papers, originally spindled and tied with string
fondamenta	a street alongside a canal
fondo	a collection within an archive
gastaldo	the chief officer of a scuola piccola (sometimes called guardian or rector)
giornale, giornale cassier	a daily account book, recording income and expenditures as they were made

guardian da mattin	the officer of a scuola grande in charge of processions
guardian grande	the chief officer of a scuola grande
Inquisitori e revisori sopra le scuole grandi	the government magistracy, originally appointed by the Council of Ten, and then later elected by the Senate, to supervise the activities of the scuole grandi
lauda	a non-liturgical, religious song, usually in Italian
lira	a Venetian monetary unit; see p. xiii
luminaria	the annual fee for a member of a scuola grande, designated to pay for candles for processions
mansionaria, mansionario	an endowment for the celebration of regular commemorative masses; the priest selected to celebrate the masses
mansionario di coro	a member of the priestly choir of a scuola; also referred to as corista
mariegola	the statute book of a scuola
masseri	poor brothers of a scuola elected to carry out tasks assigned them by the guardian grande
monte	an accumulation of funds or other assets to be drawn upon when needed
nonzoli	see *masseri*
notatorio	the volume in which were recorded all official acts and elections of a scuola
ottavario	a popular religious commemoration, parallel to the liturgical octave, during the eight days following a feast
parte	a motion presented to the banca or chapter
partidor	the division of expenses among officials of a scuola
Piazza San Marco	the main square of Venice, in front of the ducal basilica of San Marco; there is only one square in Venice called piazza (see also *campo*)
piffari	players of wind instruments
piovano	chief priest of a parish
popolano	any Venetian (other than a member of the clergy) not a patrician or cittadino
Procuratori di San Marco	high Venetian officials, elected for life; one group of Procuratori (the Procuratori *de supra*), administered the basilica of San Marco
Provveditori di Comun	a Venetian magistracy that, among other matters, supervised the scuole piccole
quaderno, quadernier	the official account book of a scuola, organized by type of expenditure; the hired bookkeeper of a scuola
registro	a bound archival volume
rispetto	substitute (as in *cantadore di rispetto*, a substitute singer)
rodolo	a list recording voluntary contributions for a specific purpose

scrivano	originally, the elected bookkeeper of a scuola; later an officer without specific duties other than serving on the banca
scuola	a confraternity
scuola grande	originally, one of the four flagellant confraternities of Venice; later, one of a group of six (ultimately eight) large confraternities
scuola piccola	one of many smaller confraternities in Venice; any confraternity other than a scuola grande
Senate	the most important legislative body of Venice
sessanta	the group of sixty poor brothers of a scuola; from the fifteenth century composed primarily of fadighenti
sestiere	one of the six districts of Venice: San Marco, Cannaregio, and Castello on the east and north of the Grand Canal; San Polo, Santa Croce, and Dorsoduro on the west and south
sindici, sinici	officers of a scuola, usually three in number, charged with verifying that actions conform to existing regulations and precedent
soldo	a Venetian monetary unit; see p. xiii
sonadori	instrumentalists
suffragio	a confraternity whose concern is with souls of the dead or dying
tariffa	a list of prescribed expenditures
tollela	a wooden slat placed into a board to indicate that a brother, especially a fadighente, is present; also used to refer to the list of such brothers
triduo	a popular religious commemoration, three days long, in connection with an important feast
vicario	an officer of a scuola grande designated to substitute for the guardian grande should the need arise; a member of the banca; sometimes assigned responsibility for certain processions
zonta	a group of former officers, usually twelve in number, elected as a supplement (Italian *aggiunta*) to the banca

BIBLIOGRAPHY

Archival Sources

Listed below are the principal series of archival documents used for this study and other individual volumes that provided information (not listed are the numerous documents of the scuole and government authorities that did not produce relevant information). In some fondi, registri and buste are numbered separately, and are so indicated; for others, such as the scuole grandi, there is one comprehensive numbering system, so the format is not listed. For descriptions of the various classes of documents, see chapter 1. Unless otherwise indicated, all of the collections are located in Venice. A project is currently under way to make all of the documents available on the internet.

ARCHIVIO DI STATO DI VENEZIA

Archivio notarili, Atti, Notaio Paulini, buste 3506, 3547, 3767
Consiglio dei dieci
    Parti, registri 13, 14, 16, 18, 19, 25
    Parti communi, registri 11, 21; filza 59
    Capi del Consiglio dei dieci, registro 29
Fraterna grande di Sant'Antonino 1
Fraterna prigioni 2, 3
Inquisitori e revisori sopra le scuole grandi
    capitolari: 1–2 (1312–1778)
    decreti e scritture: 4–7 (1694–1797)
    terminazioni e sentenze: 9–13 (1667–1805)
    scuole piccole: 60
Miscellanea di carte non appartenenti ad alcun archivio 1
Monastero di Sant'Alvise 1
Monastero di Santa Caterina di Venezia 20
Monastero di San Domenico, Libro di resti
Monastero di San Giacomo della Giudecca 18
Monastero di Santi Giovanni e Paolo, buste O, VII, XIII

Monastero di Santa Maria della Carità 5, 18, 43
Monastero di Santa Maria Gloriosa dei Frari 97–105
Monastero di San Salvatore 50
Monastero dello Spirito Santo 1, 16, 17
Provveditori di Commun
    capitolare: buste 1–3 (1272–1716)
    atti: buste 9–37 (1518–1797)
    terminazioni: buste 61–77 (1690–1797)
    matricole scuole e sovvegni: registri n–bb
Scuola grande di San Giovanni Evangelista
    mariegole: 3 (1307, Italian), 7 (1261, Latin), 41 (a late 14th-c. copy of the 1307 Italian
        mariegola)
    "libri pergamene" and other collections before the beginning of the series of notatori:
        41, 43, 46–47, 71, 72 (14th–15th c.; the latter two also include cerimonials, lists
        of officers, inventories, and membership records)
    notatori: 140–57 (late 15th c., with copies of some earlier documents, through 1788)
    indexes and summaries: 15, 27–33, 35, 38–40, 42, 44–45, 48–49, 135–39
    atti diversi dei cancellieri: 330–50 (1586–1800; but complete only from about 1630)
    approvazioni: 50–67 (1685–1801)
    membership lists:
        mariegole: 4–6, 8–14 (14th–16th c.)
        mari fratelli: 17–18 (17th c.)
        registri banche: 9, 73
        other lists: 20
    giornali cassier (and scontro): 464–75 (18th c.)
    quaderni cassa: 435 (1601–4), 436–42 (late 18th c.), 461 (1757–71), 462 (1738–48)
    receipts: 403 (1574–90), 404 (1605–36)
    cerimonial: 16 (1570)
    employee and service records: 24–26 (18th c.)
    inventories: 76–78
    other: 34, 36, 37, 69, 75, 85, 92, 388, 423–24, 427, 471
Scuola grande di San Marco
    mariegole: 216 (a 17th-c. copy of a 14th-c. Italian version)
    notatori: 16, 16bis, 17–38 (1428–1806)
    indexes and summaries: 8–9, 214–219
    atti diversi dei cancellieri: 54–70 (1593–1806, but complete only from 1693)
    atti diversi: 202–13 (late 17th c., with copies of some earlier documents, through 1806)
    approvazioni: 221–25 (1680–1796)
    membership lists:
        mariegole: 4–6 (15th–17th c.)
        luminarie: 73
        officers: 6, 39–40
        other lists: 7, 41–42
    giornali cassier (and scontro): 244–50 (1696–1753)
    quaderni cassa: 230 (1597–1615), 243 (1430–38), 251–54 and 260–63 (18th c.)
    accounts of the vicario: 82, 228–29 (15th–16th c.; these also include lists of fadighenti
        and service records for processions)
    inventories: 46–47
    other: 12, 13, 53, 74, 76, 78, 80, 85, 121–22, 124, 135–36, 220, 231–33
Scuola grande di Santa Maria della Carità

atti diversi: 452–63 (17th–18th c.)
approvazioni: 348–63 (1712–97)
quaderni cassa: 505–12, 601 (1726–1806)
other: 4, 5, 41, 73, 88–91, 93, 435, 440, 643, 502

Scuola grande di San Rocco, seconda consegna
    notatori: 44–47, 720 (1488–1558)
    notatori of the cancellaria: 49, 50–51, 59–60 (1596–1797)
    indexes and summaries: 1–6, 48, 581
    atti diversi dei cancellieri: 34–43 (1671–1792),
    atti diversi: 452–63, 63–69 (17th–18th c.)
    cauzioni (filze of the guardian grande): 155–379 (1599–1806)
    membership lists: 72–77 (17th and 18th c.)
    giornali cassier (and scontro): 110 (1659), 391 (1758), 626 (1799)
    receipts: 423–34 (1487–1748; complete only from mid-17th c.)
    employee and service records: 91–92 (libri di coristi, 18th c.)
    other: 58, 81, 114, 380–82, 385, 389, 394, 408–09, 413–15, 417–21, 449, 601, 625,
        637, 645, 670, 703, 715, 808, 824, 891

Scuola grande di San Teodoro
    notatori (capitolari, parti): 13–19 (1552–1806)
    indexes and summaries: 5–7, 79
    atti diversi dei cancellieri (filza parti): 67–79 (1635–1796)
    atti diversi: 98–104 (1506–1804; complete only for the 18th c.)
    approvazioni: 80–83 (1682–1796)
    membership lists:
       mariegole: 1–4 (1561–1636)
       other lists: 21–23, 114
    giornali cassier (and scontro): 65, 93, 113, 114 (all 18th c.)
    quaderni cassa: 106–11 (1715–1800)
    accounts of the guardian da mattin: 97 (1554)
    inventari: 28
    other: 24, 59, [115]

Scuole piccole e suffraggi 1–4, 6–10, 12, 14, 21, 23–27, 38–43, 48, 50–51, 55, 57, 57bis,
    66–67, 69, 71, 79, 86, 89, 91, 93–95, 101–2, 108–9, 112, 115–16, 118, 123–25,
    132, 135, 137, 141, 143, 146, 155, 157, 180–81, 206, 209, 220–21, 223, 224bis,
    225, 233, 235, 238–39, 248, 251–52, 254, 257, 274, 294–96, 302–3, 305, 307–9,
    311–12, 314, 316–17, 322, 341–42, 344, 350–52, 354, 364, 366–67, 369–73,
    380, 383, 385, 388–89, 391, 393, 403, 406, 412, 420–21, 436, 436bis, 437bis, 443,
    448–49, 451–52, 460, 463–65, 467, 469–71, 473, 479, 481, 486–87, 489, 492,
    495, 568–69, 576, 582, 584–85, 589, 591–93, 596–99, 602, 605–06, 618, 627–28,
    632, 639, 646–47, 666, 668–70, 672, 681–84, 702–3, 706–7, 711–15, 719, 721–
    22, 726

OTHER ARCHIVES AND LIBRARIES

Archivio della scuola grande arciconfraternita di San Rocco
    mariegola (1478)
    notatori (registri delle parti; 1488–1822)
    notatorio del cancelliere (1798–1805)
    membership lists:
       lists of officers: 1480–1896
       other: 1737–20th c.

cerimonial: "Libro di ordini, 1521", rituale (18th c.)
choirbooks: Liber missarum 1754, Liber secundus missarum 1775
Archivio storico del patriarcato di Venezia
 Curia Patriarcale, Sezione Antica, Actorum Generalium, buste 9, 13, 14, 22 (1688–1706
  and 1767–95)
 Parrocchia di San Fantin
  registro 34: Scuola di San Gaetano
  Scuola del Santissimo Sacramento (cassa 1689–1775)
 Parrocchia di San Lio
  Scuola del Santissimo (serie cronologica)
 Parrocchia di San Marco, Parrocchia di San Giuliano
  Scuola dei Devoti della Beata Vergine (atti 1749–89)
  Scuola di San Giuliano (libri della compagnia 1749–79)
  Scuola di San Rocco (parti 1611–1752, cassa 1595–1724, riceveri 1617–1709 and
   1709–1802)
  Scuola del Santissimo Sacramento (parti 1605–1716, cassa 1502–1688, riceveri 1621–
   1783)
 Parrocchia di Santa Maria del Carmelo, Fabbriceria
  Chiesa succursale di San Barnaba
   atti generali, busta 22: Scuola di Sant'Appolonia
   atti generali, busta 12: Scuola del Santissimo Sacramento
   Scuola del Santissimo Sacramento (capitoli 1643–1808, cassa 1642–1763)
  Chiesa succursale di Santa Margherita
   Scuola del Santissimo Sacramento (cassa 1576–1679)
 Parrocchia di Santa Maria del Giglio
  Scuola del Rosario (scitture diverse 1780–1803)
  Scuola di Santa Catterina di Siena (capitoli 1642–1703, libri di amministrazione 1620–
   91)
  Scuola del Santissimo Sacramento (cassa 1685–1729)
 Parrocchia di San Martino
  busta D1: Agonizzanti in San Martino
 Parrocchia di San Moisè
  Scuola del Santissimo Sacramento (catastico, riceveri 1709–1800, commissaria Bonci
   catastico, commissaria Bonci cassa 1686–1773, commissaria Bonci riceveri 1705–34
   and 1784–96)
Archivio IRE (Istituzioni per ricovero e di educazione), Archivio patrimoniale, PATR 1
 O 12 (documents concerning Scuola grande di Santa Maria della Misericordia)
Archivio parrocchiale di San Canciano (transferred in 2001 to Archivio storico del patriar-
 cato)
 Sacro Cuor di Gesù (ricevute 1738–1811, parti 1738–)
 Scuola del Santissimo Sacramento e San Massimo (capitoli 1625–1737 and 1738–1843,
  cassa 1616–1710, riceveri 1611–1704)
Archivio parrocchiale di San Cassiano
 Scuola del Santissimo Sacramento (mariegola 1739, capitoli 1775–1823)
Archivio parrocchiale di San Felice (transferred in 2001 to Archivio storico del patriarcato)
 Chiesa di San Felice (sommmario instrumenti)
 Compagnia di San Giuseppe (cassa 1740–66)
 Compagnia di San Francesco di Paola (cassa 1756–66)
 Scuola di San Felice (cassa 1630–1700)
 Scuola del Santissimo Sacramento (mariegola, capitoli 1699–1750, libri di cassa 1596–
  1749, comparto di spese 1773–1830, riceveri 1748–79)

Scuola del Santissimo Sacramento in Santa Sofia (capitoli 1721–71, cassa 1748–66)
Archivio parrocchiale di San Geremia
    Scuola del Santissimo Sacramento (riceveri 1613–1751, comparti 1735–1841)
    Suffragio de' Morti (memorie, 1777)
    Scuola del Santissimo Sacramento in Santa Lucia (cassa 1763–1807)
Archivio parrocchiale di San Giovanni in Bragora
    busta 74: Scuola della Santissima Annunziata, detto dal Zio
    busta 75: Scuola di San Giovanni Elemosinario
    busta 98: Sovvegno della Beata Vergine Addolorata in Sant'Antonin
    busta 99: Scuola della Beata Vergine del Carmine, San Giuseppe, e San Luigi Gonzaga
        in Sant'Antonin
    buste 115, 118: Scuola del Santissimo Sacramento
Archivio parrocchiale di Santa Maria del Rosario (I Gesuati)
    Chiesa di Sant'Agnese (capitoli 1745–89; documents regarding Scuola del Santissimo
        Sacramento in Sant'Agnese)
Archivio parrocchiale di San Giacomo dall'Orio
    Chiesa di San Giacomo dal'Orio (varia, catastico della chiesa; documents concerning the
        Scuola del Santissimo Sacramento)
    Scuola del Santissimo Sacramento (capitoli 1794, libri di cassa 1568–79 and 1620–1757,
        riceveri 1731–82 and 1783–86)
    Scuola del Santissimo Sacramento in San Boldo (cassa 1717–1807)
    Scuola del Santissimo Sacramento in San Stae (mariegola)
Archivio parrocchiale di San Luca
    Scuola del Santissimo Sacramento (capitoli 1728–1814, libri di cassa 1675–1807)
Archivio parrocchiale di San Marcuola
    Scuola del Santissimo Sacramento (capitoli 1756–1833, cassa 1704–89)
Archivio parrocchiale di San Pantalon
    Scuola del Santissimo Sacramento (mariegola)
Archivio parrocchiale di San Salvatore
    Scuola di San Mattia in San Bartolomeo (registro spese 1571)
    Scuola del Santissimo Sacramento in San Bartolomeo (capitoli 1759–1805)
Archivio parrocchiale di San Silvestro
    Scuola del Santissimo Sacramento (catastico, capitoli 1737–1822)
    Scuola del Santissimo Sacramento in Sant'Appolinare (catastico delle scritture)
    Scuola del Santissimo Sacramento in San Giovanni Elemosinario (cassa 1796–1807)
Archivio parrocchiale di San Simeon Profeta (San Simeon Grande)
    Chiesa di San Simeon Profeta (memorie di chiesa; documents concerning Scuola del
        Santissimo Sacramento)
    Compagnia di San Pietro Appostolo (costituzione 1782, atti 1766–1839, piano econ-
        omico 1772 and 1805, regolamento 1797)
Archivio parrocchiale di San Trovaso
    Scuola del Santissimo Sacramento (mariegola, capitoli 1585–1673, cassa 1762–1807)
Biblioteca del Museo Correr
    mariegole: 10 (San Giuseppe in San Silvestro), 16 (Santissimo Sacramento in San Sa-
        muele), 19 (Scuola Grande di San Marco), 21 (San Teodoro in San Salvatore), 41
        (Santissimo Sacramento in San Tomà), 45 (Santa Croce e San Giacomo in San
        Fantin), 58 (Santa Maria della Concezione at the Gesuiti), 64 (Sovvegno di Preti
        Secolari in San Giovanni Elemosinario), 71 (Scuola dei Fiorentini in Santa Maria
        Gloriosa dei Frari), 79 (San Gregorio in Santi Filippo e Giacomo), 86 (Beata Vergine
        del Carmine in Santa Maria del Carmine), 113 (San Girolamo in San Girolamo),
        118 (Santa Catterina dei Sacchi in Santa Catterina), 131 (Santissimo Sacramento in

Santa Sofia), 137 (San Martino in San Martino), 138 (Beata Vergine di Pietà in San Giovanni Elemosinario), 178 (Sant'Antonio di Padova in Santa Maria Maddalena), 183 (Santa Croce in San Moisè), 201 (San Moisè e San Vettor in San Moisè), 221 (Oratorio della Dottrina Cristiana in San Bartolomeo)

Codici Cicogna 3063 (Suffraggio di San Bernardino in San Giobbe)

Codici Gradenigo 67 (diary of Pietro Gradenigo)

Biblioteca Nazionale Marciana, MS Lat. II, 119 (2426) (chant book for Scuola Grande di Santa Maria della Carità, 1365)

New York, Pierpont Morgan Library, Mariegola of the Scuola di Santa Maria Nuova in San Salvatore

Princeton, New Jersey, Princeton University Art Museum, Mariegola of the Scuola del Santissimo Sacramento in San Geremia

Printed Sources

Ambrosini, Federica. "Cerimonie, feste, lusso." In *Storia di Venezia*, vol. 5, ed. Alberto Tenenti and Ugo Tucci, 441–520. Rome: Istituto della Enciclopedia Italiana, 1996.

Angelozzi, Giancarlo. *Le confraternite laicali: Un'esperienza cristiana tra medioevo e età moderna.* Brescia: Queriniana, 1978.

Arnold, Denis. *Giovanni Gabrieli.* London: Oxford University Press, 1979.

———. "Music at a Venetian Confraternity in the Renaissance." *Acta Musicologica* 37 (1965): 62–72.

———. "Music at the Scuola di San Rocco." *Music & Letters* 40 (1959): 229–41.

Ashley, Robert. *Of Honor.* Edited with introduction and commentary by Virgil B. Heltzel. San Marino, Calif.: The Huntington Library, 1947.

Banker, James R. "Death and Christian Charity in the Confraternities of the Upper Tiber Valley." In *Christianity and the Renaissance*, ed. Verdon and Henderson, 302–27.

———. *Death in the Community: Memorialization and Confraternities in an Italian Commune in the Late Middle Ages.* Athens, Ga. and London. University of Georgia Press, 1988.

Barbiero, Giuseppe. *Le confraternite del Santissimo Sacramento prima del 1539.* Treviso: Tipografia Acr Vedelago, 1941.

Barnes, Andrew E. "From Ritual to Meditative Piety: Devotional Change in French Penitential Confraternities from the 16th to the 18th Century." *Journal of Ritual Studies* 1:2 (1987): 1–26.

———. "Poor Relief and Brotherhood." *Journal of Social History* 24:3 (1991): 603–11.

Baroncini, Rodolfo. "Contributo alla storia del violino nel sedicesimo secolo: I 'sonadori di violini' della Scuola Grande di San Rocco a Venezia." *Recercare* 6 (1994): 61–190.

———. "Voci e strumenti nella 'processione in piazza San Marco': considerazioni metodologiche in margine a un celebre dipinto di Gentile Bellini." *Fonti musicali italiane* 5 (2000): 77–88.

Barr, Cyrilla. "From Devozione to Rappresentazione: Dramatic Elements in Holy Week Laude of Assisi." In *Crossing the Boundaries*, ed. Eisenbichler, 11–32.

———. *The Monophonic Lauda and the Lay Religious Confraternities of Tuscany and Umbria in the Late Middle Ages.* Kalamazoo, Mich., 1988.

———. "Music and Spectacle in Confraternity Drama of Fifteenth-Century Florence." In *Christianity and the Renaissance* ed. Verdon and Henderson, 376–404.

Bertoldi Lenoci, Liana, ed. *Confraternite, chiesa e società.* Fasano: Schena Editore, 1994.

———. *L'istituzione confraternale: Aspetti e problemi.* Biblioteca della Ricerca, Puglia Storica 9. Fasano (BR): Schena Editore, 1996.

Black, Christopher F. "Confraternities and the Parish in the Context of Italian Catholic

Reform." In *Confraternities and Catholic Reform in Italy, France, and Spain*, ed. Donnelly and Maher, 1–26.

Blackburn, Bonnie J. "Petrucci's Venetian Editor: Petrus Castellanus and his Musical Garden." *Musica Disciplina* 49 (1995): 15–45.

Bornstein, Daniel E. *The Bianchi of 1399: Popular Devotion in Late Medieval Italy*. Ithaca and London: Cornell University Press, 1993.

Brown, Howard Mayer. "On Gentile Bellini's Processione in San Marco (1496)." In *IMS Report, Berkeley 1977*, 649–58. Kassel: Bärenreiter, 1981.

Bryant, David, and Michele Pozzobon. *Musica devozione città: La Scuola di Santa Maria dei Battuti (e un suo manoscritto musicale) nella Treviso del Rinascimento*. Treviso: Fondazione Benetton Studi Ricerche/Editrice Canova, 1995.

Cadel, Anna Maria. "Il sentimento della morte nelle scuole piccole veneziane." *Ateneo veneto* 34 (N.S.= CLXXXIII; 1996): 113–28.

Caffi, Francesco. *Storia della musica sacra nella già cappella ducale di San Marco in Venezia dal 1318 al 1797*. Venice: Antonelli, 1854–55.

Caravia, Alessandro. *Il sogno di Caravia*. Venice, 1541.

Casini, Matteo. "Ceremoniali." In *Storia di Venezia*, ed. Gino Benzoni and Gaetano Cozzi, 7 (*La Venezia Barocca*), 107–60. Rome: Istituto della Enciclopedia Italiana, 1997.

———. *I gesti del principe: La festa politica a Firenze e Venezia in età rinascimentale*. Venice: Marsilio, 1996.

Cattin, Giulio. "Church Patronage of Music in Fifteenth-Century Italy." In *Music in Medieval and Early Modern Europe*, ed. Iain Fenlon, 21–36. Cambridge: Cambridge University Press, 1981.

———. "Il manoscritto Venet. Marc. Ital. IX, 145." *Quadrivium*, 4 (1960): 1–60.

———. *Musica e liturgia a San Marco*. 4 vols. Venice: Edizioni Fondazione Levi, 1990–92.

———. "Nuova fonte italiana della polifonia intorno al 1500 (MS Cape Town, Grey 3.b.12)." *Acta Musicologica*, 45 (1973): 165–221.

———, ed. *Italian Laude and Latin Unica in Ms. Capetown, Grey 3. b.12*. Corpus mensurabilis musicae, 76. American Institute of Musicology, 1977.

———. *Laudi quattrocentesche del cod. veneto Marc. Ital. IX 145*. Bologna: Italgraf, 1958.

Cecchetti, Bartolomeo. "Un organo nella Scuola di S. Maria della Valverde Madre di Misericordia in Venezia." *Archivio Veneto* 29 (1885): 413.

Cesco, Lorenzo. "Note integrative." In *La Scuola Grande di San Rocco nella musica e nelle feste veneziane*. Quaderni della Scuola Grande Arciconfraternita di San Rocco 2 (1996): 33–39.

Chambers, David, and Brian Pullan. *Venice: A Documentary History*. Oxford: Blackwell, 1992.

Collini, Giovanni Luigi. *ESPLICATIONE DEI CARRI TRIONFALE FATTI NELLA PROCESSIONE PER LA PACE Tra Franza, e Spagna, Dalla Scuola di S. Teodoro, il di 26. Luglio 1598*. Venice: Marc'Antonio Zaltieri, 1598.

Confraternitas. Bulletin of the Society for Cofraternity Studies. Toronto: Centre for Reformation and Renaissance Studies, 1990– .

Cope, Maurice. *The Venetian Chapel of the Sacrament in the Sixteenth Century*. New York: Garland, 1979.

Coryat, Thomas. *Coryat's Crudities*. Glasgow: James MacLehose and Sons, 1905.

D'Accone, Frank A. *The Civic Muse: Music and Musicians in Siena during the Middle Ages and the Renaissance*. Chicago: University of Chicago Press, 1997.

———. "Le compagnie dei laudesi in Firenze durante l'Ars nova." In *L'Ars nova italiana del Trecento*, 253–80. Certaldo: Edizioni Centro di Studi sull'Ars Nova Italiana del Trecento, 1969.

Dalla Libera, Sandro. *L'arte degli organi a Venezia.* Venice: Istituto per la collaborazione culturale, 1962.

D'Angiolini, Piero, and Claudio Pavone. *Guida generale degli archivi di Stato italiani.* Rome: Ministero per i Beni Culturali e Ambientali, Ufficio Centrale per i Beni Archivistici, 1981–94.

Daniel, E. Randolph. "Joachim of Flora and the Joachite Tradition of Apocalyptic Conversion in the Later Middle Ages." Ph.D. diss., University of Virginia, 1966.

De Sandre Gasparini, Giuseppina. "Il movimento delle confraternite nell'area veneta." In *Le Mouvement confraternel au Moyen Age. France, Italie, Suisse,* 361–94. Rome: Ecole Française de Rome, 1987.

———. "La pietà laicale." In *Storia di Venezia II: L'Età del Comune,* ed. Giorgio Cracco and Gherardo Ortalli, 929–61. Rome: Istituto della Enciclopedia Italiana, 1995.

Donnelly, John Patrick, and Michael W. Maher, eds. *Confraternities and Catholic Reform in Italy, France, and Spain.* Sixteenth Century Essays and Studies 44. Kirksville, Mo.: Thomas Jefferson University Press, 1999.

Eisenbichler, Konrad. *The Boys of the Archangel Raphael: A Youth Confraternity in Florence, 1411–1785.* Toronto: University of Toronto Press, 1998.

———, ed. *Crossing the Boundaries: Christian Piety and the Arts in Italian Medieval and Renaissance Confraternities.* Early Drama, Art, and Music Monograph Series 15. Kalamazoo, Mich.: Medieval Institute Publications, Western Michigan University, 1991.

Elizari Huarte, Juan Francesco. "Gremios, cofradias y solidaridades en la Europa medieval: aproximación bibliográfica a dos decadas de investigaciones históricas (1971–1991)." In *Cofradias, gremios y solidaridades en la Europa medieval,* XIX Semana de Estudios Medievales, Estella, 20 a 24 de julio de 1992, 319–416. Pamplona: Fondo de Publicaciones del Gobierno de Navarra, 1993.

Emans, Reinmar. "Die Musiker des Markusdoms in Venedig 1650–1708." *Kirchenmusikalisches Jahrbuch* 65 (1981): 45–81.

Falvey, Kathleen, "Early Italian Dramatic Traditions and Comforting Rituals: Some Initial Considerations." In *Crossing the Boundaries,* ed. Konrad Eisenbichler, 33–55.

Fano, Fabio. *Profilo di una storia della vita musicale in Venezia dalle origini alla vigilia della fioritura rinascimentale.* Biblioteca di Quadrivium 1. Bologna: Antiquae Musicae Italicae Studiosi, 1975.

Fenlon, Iain. "St. Mark's before Willaert." *Early Music* 21 (1993): 547–63.

Flynn, Maureen. *Sacred Charity: Confraternities and Social Welfare in Spain, 1400–1700.* Ithaca, NY: Cornell University Press, 1989.

Forney, Kristine K. "Music, Ritual and Patronage at the Church of Our Lady, Antwerp." *Early Music History* 7 (1987): 1–57.

———. "The Role of Secular Guilds in the Musical Life of Renaissance Antwerp." In *Musicology and Archival Research/Musicologie et recherches en archives/Musicologie en archiefonderzoek,* 441–61. Brussels: Bibliotheca Regia Belgica, 1994.

Fortini Brown, Patricia. "Honor and Necessity: The Dynamics of Patronage in the Confraternities of Renaissance Venice." *Studi veneziani,* N.S. 14 (1987): 179–212.

———. "An Incunabulum of the Miracles of the True Cross of the Scuola Grande di San Giovanni Evangelista." *Bolletino dei Civici Musei Veneziani d'arte e di storia,* N.S. 27:1–4 (1982): 5–8.

———. *Venetian Narrative Painting in the Age of Carpaccio.* New Haven: Yale University Press, 1988.

Gallo, F. Alberto, ed. *Antonii Romani Opera.* Antiquae musicae italicae monumenta veneta sacra 1. Bologna: Università degli Studi di Bologna, Istituto di Studi Musicali e Teatrali, Sezione Musicologica, 1965.

Gambassi, Osvaldo. *"Pueri cantores" nelle cattedrali d'Italia tra medioevo e età moderna: le scuole eugeniane, scuole di canto annesse alle cappelle musicali.* Historiae musicae cultores biblioteca 80. Florence: Leo S. Olschki, 1997.

Glixon, Beth, and Jonathan Glixon. *Marco Faustini and Operatic Production in Seventeenth-Century Venice.* American Musicological Society Studies in Music. New York: Oxford University Press (forthcoming).

————. "Marco Faustini and Venetian Opera Production in the 1650s." *Journal of Musicology* 10 (1992): 48–73.

Glixon, Jonathan. " 'Ad honor de misser San Rocco': la musica nella scuola grande, 1478–1806." In *La Scuola Grande di San Rocco nella musica e nelle feste veneziane.* Quaderni della Scuola Grande Arciconfraternita di San Rocco 2 (1996): 7–32.

————. *"Con canti et organo*: Music at the Venetian *Scuole Piccole* in the Renaissance." In *Music in Renaissance Cities and Courts: Studies in Honor of Lewis Lockwood,* ed. Jessie Ann Owens and Anthony Cummings, 123–40. Warren, Mich.: Harmonie Park Press, 1997.

————. *"Far il buon concerto*: Music at the Venetian Scuole Piccole in the Seventeenth Century." *Journal of Seventeenth-Century Music* 1:1 (1995). Online. Available: www.sscm.harvard.edu/jscm/v1/no1.

————. *"Far una bella procession*: Music and Public Ceremony at the Venetian *scuole grandi*." In *Altro Polo: Essays on Italian Music of the Cinquecento,* ed. Richard Charteris, 148–75. Sydney: The University of Sydney Press, 1989.

————. "Images of Paradise or Worldly Theaters?: Towards a Taxonomy of Musical Performances at Venetian Convents." In *Essays on Music and Culture in Honor of Herbert Kellman,* ed. Barbara Haggh Huglo. Epitome Musicale. Paris: Editions Minerve, 2001.

————. "Late Medieval Chant for a Venetian Confraternity: Venice, Biblioteca nazionale marciana, Ms Lat.II, 119 (2426)." *Musica Disciplina* 49 (1995): 7–43.

————. "Lutenists in Renaissance Venice: Some Notes from the Archives." *Journal of the Lute Society of America* 16 (1983): 15–26.

————. "Music and Ceremony at the Scuola Grande di San Giovanni Evangelista: A New Document from the Venetian State Archives." In *Crossing the Boundaries,* ed. Eisenbichler, 56–89.

————. "Music at the Venetian 'Scuole Grandi,' 1440–1540." Ph.D. diss., Princeton University, 1979.

————. "A Musicians' Union in Sixteenth-Century Venice." *Journal of the American Musicological Society* 36 (1983): 392–421.

————. "The Polyphonic Laude of Innocentius Dammonis." *Journal of Musicology* 8 (1990): 19–53.

Greci, Roberto. "Economia, religiosità, politica. Le solidarietà delle corporazioni medievali nell'Italia del Nord." In *Cofradias, gremios y solidaridades en la Europa medieval,* XIX Semana de Estudios Medievales, Estella, 20 a 24 de julio de 1992, 75–99. Pamplona: Fondo de Publicaciones del Gobierno de Navarra, 1993.

Haggh, Barbara. "The Meeting of Sacred Ritual and Secular Piety: Endowments for Music." In *Companion to Medieval and Renaissance Music,* 60–68. London: Schirmer, 1992.

Henderson, John. "Confraternities and Politics in Fifteenth-Century Florence." *Collegium medievale* 2:1 (1989): 53–72.

————. "Confraternities and the Church in Late Medieval Florence." In *Voluntary Religion,* ed. W. J. Sheils and Diana Wood, 69–83. Studies in Church History 23. London: Blackwell, 1986.

————. "The Flagellant Movement and Flagellant Confraternities in Central Italy, 1260–1400." In *Religious Motivation: Biographical and Sociological Problems for the Church Historian*, ed. Derek Baker, 147–60. Special issue of Studies in Church History 15 (1978).

————. "Penitence and the Laity in Fifteenth-Century Florence." In *Christianity and the Renaissance*, ed. Verdon and Henderson, 229–49.

————. *Piety and Charity in Later Medieval Florence*. Chicago: University of Chicago Press, 1997.

Hills, Paul. "Piety and Patronage in Cinquecento Venice: Tintoretto and the Scuole del Sacramento." *Art History* 6:1 (1983): 30–43.

Humfrey, Peter. "Competitive Devotions: The Venetian *Scuole Piccole* as Donors of Altarpieces in the Years around 1500." *Art Bulletin* 70 (1988): 401–23.

Levi d'Ancona, Mirella. "Giustino del fu Gherardino da Forlì e gli affreschi perduti del Guariento nel Palazzo Ducale di Venezia." *Arte Veneta* 21 (1967): 34–44.

Little, Lester K. *Liberty, Charity, Fraternity: Lay Religious Confraternities at Bergamo in the Age of the Commune*. Bergamo: Pierluigi Lubrina Editore; Northampton, Mass.: Smith College, 1988.

Luisi, Francesco. *Laudario giustinianeo*. 2 vols. Venice: Fondazione Ugo e Olga Levi, 1983.

————. "Per una identificazione dei musici raffigurati nella Processione in Piazza San Marco di Gentile Bellini." *Notizie da Palazzo Albani* 20 (1991): 73–79.

Lunelli, Renato. *Studi e documenti di storia organaria veneta*. Florence: Leo S. Olschki, 1973.

Mackenney, Richard. "Continuity and Change in the Scuole Piccole of Venice, c.1250–1600." *Renaissance Studies* 8 (1994): 388–403.

————. "Devotional Confraternities in Renaissance Venice." In *Voluntary Religion*, ed. W. J. Sheils and Diana Wood, 85–96. Studies in Church History 23. London: Blackwell, 1986.

————. "The Scuole Piccole of Venice: Formations and Transformations." In *The Politics of Ritual Kinship: Confraternities and Social Order in Early Modern Italy*, ed. Nicholas Terpstra, 172–89. Cambridge: Cambridge University Press, 1999.

————. *Trademen and Traders: The World of the Guilds in Venice and Europe, c.1250–c.1650*. Totowa, NJ: Barnes and Noble, 1987.

Matricola del sovvegno de' signori musici sotto l'invocazione di S. Cecilia vergine & martire nella chiesa di S. Martino. Venice: Antonio Bosio, 1691. [copy in BC, Opuscoli Cicogna 1132.1]

Meersseman, Gilles-Gerard. *Ordo fraternitatis: Confraternite e pietà dei laici nel mondo medioevo*. 3 vols. Italia Sacra: Studi e Documenti di Storia Ecclesiastica 24–26. Rome: Herder Editrice, 1977.

Miazga, Tadeusz. *Die Melodien des einstimmigen Credo der römisch-katholischen lateinische Kirche*. Graz: Akademische Druck- und Verlagsanstalt, 1976.

Miller, Roark. "The Composers of San Marco and Santo Stefano and the Development of Venetian Monody (to 1630)." Ph.D. diss., University of Michigan, 1993.

Monti, Gennaro Maria. *Le confraternite medievali dell'alta e media Italia*. 2 vols. Venice: La Nuova Italia, 1927.

Moore, James Harold. *Vespers at St. Mark's: Music of Alessandro Grandi, Giovanni Rovetta, and Francesco Cavalli*. 2 vols. Ann Arbor, Mich.: UMI Research Press, 1981.

Moryson, Fynes. *An Itinerary Containing His Ten Yeeres Travell through the Twelve Dominions of Germany, Bohmerland, Sweitzerland, Netherland, Denmarke, Poland, Italy, Turky, France, England, Scotland & Ireland*. Glasgow: James MacLehose and Sons, 1907.

Il movimento dei disciplinati nel settimo centenario dal suo inizio (Perugia – 1260), Convegno internazionale: Perugia, 25–28 settembre 1960. Perugia: Deputazione di Storia Patria per l'Umbria, 1960.

Muir, Edward. *Civic Ritual in Renaissance Venice.* Princeton: Princeton University Press, 1981.

———. *Ritual in Early Modern Europe.* Cambridge: Cambridge University Press, 1997.

Newbigin, Nerida. "The Word Made Flesh. The Rappresentazioni of Mysteries and Miracles in Fifteenth-Century Florence." In *Christianity and the Renaissance,* ed. Verdon and Henderson, 361–75.

Niero, Antonio, and Gastone Vio. *La chiesa dello Spirito Santo in Venezia.* Venice: Collana Venezia Sacra, 1981.

Niero, Antonio. "Spiritualità popolare e dotta." In *La chiesa di Venezia nel Seicento,* ed. Bruno Bertoli, 253–90. Venice: Edizioni Studium Cattolico Veneziano, 1992.

Ongaro, Giulio. "The Chapel of Saint Mark's at the Time of Adrian Willaert (1527–1562): A Documentary Study." Ph.D. diss., University of North Carolina at Chapel Hill, 1986.

Ortalli, Francesca. *"Per salute delle anime e delli corpi": Scuole piccole a Venezia nel tardo medioevo.* Presente storico. Venice: Marsilio, 2001.

Panayotakis, Nikolaos M. *Franghiskos Leontaritis (Londariti): Musicista cretese del Cinquecento— Testimonianze sulla sua vita e la sua opera.* Venice: Istituto Ellenico di Studi Bizantini e Postbizantini di Venezia, 1990.

Papadopoli Aldobrandini, Nicolò. *Le monete di Venezia.* 3 vols. Venice: Ongania, 1893. Repr. Bologna: Forni, 1997.

Passadore, Francesco, and Franco Rossi. *San Marco: Vitalità di una tradizione, il fondo musicale e la Cappella dal Settecento ad oggi.* Venice: Edizioni Fondazione Levi, 1994.

Pignatti, Terisio, and M. Agnese Chiari Moretto Wiel. *Le scuole di Venezia.* Milan: Electa, 1981.

Prosperi, Adriano, "Il sangue e l'anima: Ricerche sulle compagnie di Giustizia in Italia." *Quaderni storici* 17 (1982): 959–99.

Pullan, Brian. *Rich and Poor in Renaissance Venice.* Cambridge, Mass.: Harvard University Press, 1971.

———. "The Scuole Grandi of Venice: Some Further Thoughts." In *Christianity and the Renaissance,* ed. Verdon and Henderson, 272–301.

Quaranta, Elena. *Oltre San Marco: organizzazione e prassi della musica nelle chiese di Venezia nel Rinascimento.* Florence: Leo S. Olschki, 1998.

Queller, Donald E. *The Venetian Patriciate: Reality Versus Myth.* Urbana: University of Illinois Press, 1986.

Reeves, Marjorie. *The Influence of Prophecy in the Later Middle Ages: A Study in Joachimism.* Oxford: Clarendon Press, 1969.

Renier Michiel, Giustina. *Origine delle feste veneziane.* Venezia: Scarabellin, 1916.

Risultati e prospettive della ricerca sul movimento dei disciplinati: Convegno Internazionale di Studio, Perugia, 5–7 dicembre 1969. Perugia: Deputazione di Storia Patria per l'Umbria, 1972.

Roche, Jerome. *North Italian Church Music in the Age of Monteverdi.* Oxford: Clarendon Press, 1984.

Rusconi, Roberto. "Pratica culturale e istruzione religiosa nelle confraternite italiane del tardo Medio Evo: Libri da compagnia e libri di pietà." in *Le mouvement confraternel au Moyen Age: France, Italie, Suisse. Actes de la table ronde . . . Lausanne 9–11 mai 1985.* Collection de l'Ecole Française de Rome 97, 134–53. Rome: Ecole Française, 1987.

Sansovino, Francesco. *Venetia città nobilissima et singolare descritta in XIIII. libri . . . Con aggiunta . . . da D. Giustiniano Martinoni . . .* Venice: Curti, 1663. Repr. Farnborough: Gregg, 1968.

Sanudo, Marin. *I diarii di Marino Sanuto (MCCCCXCVI–MDXXXIII) dall'autografo Marciano ital. cl. VII codd. CDXIX–CDLXXVII*, ed. Rinaldo Fulin et al. 59 vols. Venice: F. Visentini, 1879–1903.

Sbriziolo, Lia. *Le confraternite veneziane di devozione: Saggio bibliografico e premesse storiografiche (dal particolare esame dello statuto della scuola mestrina di San Rocco)*. Quaderni della Rivista di Storia della Chiesa in Italia 1. Rome: Herder Editrice, 1968.

———. "Per la storia delle confraternite veneziane: Dalle deliberazioni miste (1310–1476) del Consiglio dei Dieci. Le scole dei battuti." In *Miscellanea Gilles Gerard Meersseman*, 715–64. Italia Sacra: Studi e Documenti di Storia Ecclesiastica 15. Padua: Antenore, 1970.

———. "Per la storia delle confraternite veneziane: Dalle deliberazioni miste (1310–1476) del Consiglio dei Dieci. *Scolae comunes*, artigiane e nazionali." *Atti dell'Istituto Veneto di Scienze, Lettere ed arti. Classe di scienze morali, lettere ed arti* 126 (1967–68): 405–42.

Schreurs, Eugen. "Muziek voor de Onze-Lieve-Vrouwebroederschap in Tongeren in de 15e en de 16e eeuw: De uitbouw van een professioneel muziekensemble." *Revue belge de musicologie* 47 (1993): 49–79.

Selfridge-Field, Eleanor. "Annotated Membership Lists of the Venetian Instrumentalists' Guild, 1627–1727." *Royal Musical Association Research Chronicle* 9 (1971).

———. *Venetian Instrumental Music from Gabrieli to Vivaldi*. New York: Praeger, 1975.

Shalvi, Alice. *The Relationship of Renaissance Concepts of Honour to Shakespeare's Problem Plays*. Salzburg Studies in English Literature. Salzburg: Institut für Englische Sprache und Literatur, Universität Salzburg, 1972.

Sherr, Richard. "The Performance of Chant in the Renaissance and its Interactions with Polyphony." In *Plainsong in the Age of Polyphony*, ed. Thomas Forrest Kelly, 178–208. Cambridge: Cambridge University Press, 1992.

Sohm, Philip L. *The Scuola Grande di San Marco, 1437–1550: The Architecture of a Venetian Lay Confraternity*. New York: Garland Publishers, 1982.

Sperling, Jutta Gisela. *Convents and the Body Politic in Late Renaissance Venice*. Chicago: University of Chicago Press, 1999.

Stevens, Denis. *The Letters of Claudio Monteverdi*. Rev. ed. Oxford: Clarendon Press, 1995.

Strohm, Reinhard. *Music in Late Medieval Bruges*. Oxford: Clarendon Press, 1985.

Talbot, Michael. *Benedetto Vinaccesi: A Musician in Brescia and Venice in the Age of Corelli*. Oxford: Clarendon Press, 1994.

———. "*Ore italiane*: The Reckoning of the Time of Day in Pre-Napoleonic Italy." *Italian Studies* 40 (1985): 51–62.

Terpstra, Nicholas. "Confraternities and Local Cults: Civic Religion between Class and Politics in Renaissance Bologna." In *Civic Ritual and Drama*, ed. Alexandra F. Johnston and Wim Hüsken, 143–74. Ludus: Studies in Medieval and Early Renaissance Theatre and Drama 2. Amsterdam: Rodopi, 1997.

———. "Confraternities and Mendicant Orders: The Dynamics of Lay and Clerical Brotherhood in Renaissance Bologna." *Catholic Historical Review* 82:1 (1996): 1–22.

———. "Confraternities and Public Charity: Modes of Civic Welfare in Early Modern Italy." In *Confraternities and Catholic Reform in Italy, France, and Spain*, ed. Donnelly and Maher, 97–121.

———. "Death and Dying in Renaissance Confraternities." In *Crossing the Boundaries*, ed. Eisenbichler, 179–200.

———. *Lay Confraternities and Civic Religion in Renaissance Bologna*. Cambridge: Cambridge University Press, 1995.

———. "Renaissance Congregationalism: Organizing Lay Piety in Renaissance Italy." *Fides et Historia* 20:3 (1988): 31–40.

————, ed. *The Politics of Ritual Kinship: Confraternities and Social Order in Early Modern Italy.* Cambridge: Cambridge University Press, 1999.

Toesca, Piero. *Italienische Miniaturen der Fondazione Giorgio Cini.* Vicenza: Neri Pozza, 1977.

Traverso, Chiara. *La scuola di San Fanti o dei Picai.* Venice: Marsilio, 2000.

Trexler, Richard C. "Charity and the Defense of Urban Elites in the Italian Communes." In *The Rich, the Well Born, and the Powerful: Elites and Upper Classes in History,* ed. Frederic Cople Jaher, 64–109. Urbana: University of Illinois Press, 1973.

Urban Padoan, Lina. "Feste ufficiali e trattenimenti privati." In *Storia della cultura veneta,* vol. 4/I (*Il Seicento*), 575–600. Vicenza: Neri Pozza, 1983.

————. "Les fêtes de la République Sérènissime." In *Venise en fête,* ed. Fiora Gandolfi, Giandomenico Romanelli, and Lina Urban Padoan, 11–140. Paris, 1993.

Valder-Knechtges, Claudia. *Die Kirchenmusik Andrea Luchesis (1741–1801): Studien zu Leben und Werk des letzten kurkölnischen Hofkapellmeisters.* Beiträge zur rheinischen Musikgeschichte 134. Berlin: Merseburger, 1983.

Verdon, Timothy, and John Henderson, eds. *Christianity and the Renaissance: Image and Religious Imagination in the Quattrocento.* Syracuse, NY: Syracuse University Press, 1990.

Vio, Gastone. "Giovanni Legrenzi ed il Sovvegno di Santa Cecilia." In *Giovanni Legrenzi e la cappella ducale di San Marco,* Quaderni della *Rivista italiana di musicologia* 29, pp. 115–132. Florence: Olschki, 1994.

————. "Un maestro di musica a Venezia: Lodovico Fuga (1643–1722)." In *Antonio Vivaldi: Teatro musicale, cultura e società,* ed. Lorenzo Bianconi and Giovanni Morelli, 547–78. Quaderni vivaldiani 2. Florence: Olschki, 1982.

Watson, Curtis Brown. *Shakespeare and the Renaissance Concept of Honor.* Princeton: Princeton University Press, 1960.

Weissman, Ronald F. E. "Brothers and Strangers: Confraternal Charity in Renaissance Florence." *Historical Reflections/Réflexions historiques 15 (1988): 27–45.*

————. "Cults and Contexts: In Search of the Renaissance Confraternity." In *Crossing the Boundaries,* ed. Eisenbichler, 201–20.

————. *Ritual Brotherhood in Renaissance Florence.* New York: Academic Press, 1982.

————. "Sacred Eloquence: Humanist Preaching and Lay Piety in Renaissance Florence." In *Christianity and the Renaissance,* ed. Verdon and Henderson, 250–71.

Wilson, Blake. *Music and Merchants: The Laudesi Companies of Republican Florence.* Oxford: Clarendon Press, 1992.

Wurthmann, William B. "The Council of Ten and the *Scuole Grandi* in Early Renaissance Venice." *Studi Veneziani* NS 18 (1989): 15–66.

Zannini, Andrea. *Burocrazia e burocrati a Venezia in età moderna: i cittadini originari (sec. xvi–xviii).* Istituto Veneto di scienze lettere ed arti. Memorie. Classe di scienze morali, lettere ed arti 47. Venezia: Istituto Veneto di scienze lettere ed arti, 1993.

INDEX